Multiwavelength Optical Networks

Multiwavelength Optical Networks
A Layered Approach

Thomas E. Stern
Krishna Bala

ADDISON-WESLEY

An imprint of Addison Wesley Longman, Inc.

Reading, Massachusetts   Harlow, England   Menlo Park, California
Berkeley, California   Don Mills, Ontario   Sydney
Bonn   Amsterdam   Tokyo   Mexico City

The publisher offers discounts on this book when ordered in quantity for special sales. For more information, please contact:

Corporate, Government, and Special Sales Group
Addison Wesley Longman, Inc.
One Jacob Way
Reading, Massachusetts 01867

Library of Congress Cataloging-in-Publication Data
Stern, Thomas E.
    Multiwavelength optical networks : a layered approach / Thomas E.
  Stern, Krishna Bala.
       p.   cm.
  Includes bibliographical references.
  ISBN 0-201-30967-X
    1. Optical communications.   2. Computer network architectures.
  3. Multiplexing. 4. Light—Wavelength.   I. Bala, Krishna.
  II. Title.
  TK5103.59S74   1999
  621,382'7--dc21   99-18432
                                    CIP

ISBN 0-201-30967-X
Text printed on recycled and acid-free paper.

1 2 3 4 5 6 7 8 9 10 – CRW – 03 02 01 00 99

First printing, May 1999

To Monique for so many years
of love and devotion

T.E.S.

CONTENTS

9 CURRENT TRENDS IN MULTIWAVELENGTH OPTICAL NETWORKING   661

APPENDICES
A GRAPH THEORY   679

LIST OF FIGURES

LIST OF TABLES

At the present time, the telecommunications industry is undergoing unprecedented change, brought on largely by the shift from a voice-centric to a data-centric world—a consequence of the rapid growth of the Internet together with other data networking applications.

In the past, telecommunications network design and economics were dictated by voice traffic considerations. With the change to data-dominated traffic, a new generation of networks is taking shape—one that requires a fundamental modification in the principles of network design, control, and management. At the core of the next generation is the multiwavelength (wavelength–division multiplexed) optical network—the subject of this book.

As opposed to many other books on optical fiber communications, our emphasis is on methodologies for network analysis, design, control, and fault management rather than on optical transmission technology. The book is intended as a text for students specializing in telecommunications and as a reference for practicing engineers and researchers. Here we provide a discussion of enabling technology at a level necessary to understand the devices on which multiwavelength networks are built. However, for the reader seeking a deeper treatment of the underlying photonic principles and technology, we recommend one of the many excellent texts devoted to these subjects (for example, see Agrawal97[1] and Saleh+91[2]).

This book focuses on four classes of optical networks, presented within the framework of a multiwavelength network architecture. The classes, presented in increasing order of complexity are: static networks, wavelength-routed networks, linear lightwave (waveband-routed) networks, and logically routed networks. The latter class consists of networks composed of an electronic overlay on an optical infrastructure.

Different parts of the book will be appropriate to different audiences. Chapters 1, 2, 3, and 9 would be suitable for a short (12- to 15-hour) course on optical networks for electrical engineering or computer science majors. These chapters give a basic, *qualitative* description of multiwavelength networks without going into the fundamental aspects of the enabling technology and without treating networking methodologies

---

[1] G. P. Agrawal. *Fiber-Optic Communication Systems, Second Edition* (Wiley Series in Microwave and Optical Engineering). New York: John Wiley & Sons, 1997.

[2] B.E.A. Saleh and M. C. Teich. *Fundamentals of Photonics*. New York: John Wiley & Sons, 1991.

in depth. This material explains the place of optical networks in the world of communications (Chapter 1), describes the multiwavelength network architecture and its basic network building blocks (Chapter 2), shows how connectivity is achieved both optically and electronically (Chapter 3), and gives a glimpse of optical networking trends as of early 1999 (Chapter 9).

A comprehensive quantitative graduate course would want to include the remaining chapters. Technological foundations are covered in Chapter 4, followed by a presentation of static networks in Chapter 5, wavelength routed and linear lightwave networks in Chapter 6, and logically routed networks in Chapter 7. Survivability and fault recovery are presented in Chapter 8.

Exercises are provided for Chapters 2 through 8. Many of them are open ended and some are closer to projects (for example, simulation studies). This is in keeping with the fact that we are dealing with a rapidly moving field.

Six appendices are included. Three of them provide necessary background for those unfamiliar with various areas: Appendix A deals with graph theory, Appendix C summarizes the pertinent aspects of Markov chains and queues, and Appendix F presents an overview of the SONET standard. The remaining appendices contain algorithms for solving certain problems that arise in Chapters 5 and 6: a fixed-scheduling algorithm for shared media (Appendix B), an algorithm for finding limiting cuts (i.e., bottlenecks) in a network (Appendix D), and an algorithm for minimum interference routing in linear lightwave networks (Appendix E).

Certain sections will be of special interest to designers of current and near-term networks because they deal with contemporary architectures. Others are more forward-looking and will be of more interest to researchers. A road map for the book indicating various possible itineraries appears in Section 1.7.

ACKNOWLEDGMENTS

The origins of this book date back to 1990 when we organized a small group, within the Center for Telecommunications Research (CTR) at Columbia, to investigate lightwave networks. The book would not have been possible without the CTR and without the inspiration of its founder, Mischa Schwartz. Thomas Stern would like to express his thanks to Mischa, his friend and colleague for more than two decades, for introducing him to networking and for many years of close interaction. It was Mischa's boundless energy, enthusiasm, and understanding of the broad scope of telecommunications that sustained and motivated all of us working in the field at Columbia.

We have had the privilege of working with an excellent group of students and colleagues while the material in this book was germinating. Many of the new concepts included here originated with doctoral students in the Lightwave Networks Research Group. We particularly wish to acknowledge the work of Neophytos Antoniades on wavelength domain simulation, Eric Bouillet on routing and wavelength assignment, George Ellinas on fault recovery, Song Jiang on multicast networks (hypernets), and Jacob Sharony on optical switch architectures.

We also benefited from interaction with many more colleagues, including Tony Acampora, Emmanuel Desurvire, Milan Kovacevic, Rick Osgood, and Mal Teich at Columbia; and G. K. Chang, Kwok Cheung, Evan Goldstein, Ioannis Roudas, and Rich Wagner at Bellcore. Much of the book was class tested and debugged in a graduate course on multiwavelength networks at Columbia, and we are indebted to the students in that course as well as to many others who contributed in various ways. Worthy of special mention are Aklilu Hailemariam, Irene Katzela, Gang Liu, Tomohiro Otani, K. Petropoulos, Amy Wang, and W. S. Yoon.

We are indebted to Matt Goodman, Ioannis Roudas, Mischa Schwartz, and Ben Yoo for their careful reading of the manuscript and their many useful comments. Dr. Roudas also contributed exercises for Chapter 4. The reviews and suggestions of John Midwinter and Allan Willner are also greatly appreciated.

The authors gratefully acknowledge the National Science Foundation and the industrial participants of the Center for Telecommunications Research for their sponsorship of the CTR as an Engineering Research Center during the period that the research for this book was taking place.

We also wish to express our thanks to Marilyn Rash, our production coordinator at Addison Wesley Longman, for her patience and good humor while dealing with our considerable last-minute tinkering.

Finally, Thomas Stern expresses his profound gratitude to his wife, Monique, for being there with her support through trying times, and Krishna Bala is greatly indebted to his wife Simrat and son Tegh for putting up with his long hours at the keyboard as he wrote the book.

CHAPTER ONE

The Big Picture

At the time this is being written, optical (lightwave) networks, as opposed to optical fiber transmission links, are just beginning to appear on the scene. Although it is certain that these networks will play a key role in the future worldwide telecommunications infrastructure, developments in optical technology are moving so fast that the exact form the networks will take is still not clear. The purpose of this book is to lay out a general framework for thinking about, designing, and analyzing lightwave networks in general, and wide area multiwavelength optical networks in particular. Our objective is to make this framework broad enough so that it is useful no matter how these networks evolve in the future, yet specific enough so that it guides current workers in the field.

1.1 Why Optical Networks?

We are now at the threshold of important new developments in networking. Therefore, it is worthwhile to address two questions right at the start: Why are lightwave networks needed, and what are the larger issues that are promoting and/or hindering their development and deployment?

First the question of "need." Whenever a new technological development comes on the scene, there is a technology push toward deploying new systems that make use of it. This has been the case with vacuum tube, semiconductor, and now fiber optic and photonic technology. Ever since the fabrication of the first low-loss optical fiber by Corning Glass in 1970, a vision of an all-optical information highway has intrigued researchers, service providers, and the general public. Despite the deployment of enormous quantities of optical fiber throughout the world, we are very far from exploiting its capacity. For example, large metropolitan areas now have aggregate quantities of fibers in the ground numbering in the thousands. Yet the traffic carried over those areas is many orders of magnitude below the usable capacity of those fibers. In fact, the typical aggregate telephone traffic during a peak period in the United States is less than the channel capacity of a single fiber!

This wide mismatch between aggregate fiber capacity and aggregate carried traffic might be attributed to the fact that the need, or the *demand pull*, is not there. There is some truth in this, but it is not the whole story. Communications applications abound that require the high bandwidths available only with fibers. Services that depend crucially on a lightwave network infrastructure include Internet browsing; video on demand; video phone and video teleconferencing; high-resolution medical image archiving and retrieval (and other "telemedicine" applications); text, image, video, and multimedia document distribution; remote supercomputer visualization; and many more to come. Most of these involve masses of visual information and/or very fast response times. A telecommunications infrastructure that can support these applications on a worldwide basis, while providing high-quality service, requires truly ubiquitous wide area lightwave networks, and will indeed push the currently installed fiber capacity to (and beyond) its limits.

If there is so much fiber capacity already deployed, why isn't it being used? One reason is that the "last mile" (that is, the distribution network that is the bridge between the high-speed fiber backbone and the end users) is still in a relatively primitive state at this time. Another reason is that the fibers in the ground are not organized into an architecture that makes their huge capacity available for new broadband services.

In addition to these technological impediments there are many others: economic, legal, administrative, organizational, and political. Thus, the information superhighway is still a dirt road; more accurately, it is a set of isolated multilane highways with cow paths for entrance and exit ramps. However, the main obstacle to networking progress at present is probably the well-known chicken-and-egg effect. The demand for the services that could be supported by a new optical network infrastructure awaits the realization of that infrastructure, but the massive investment required to realize it will not materialize until the potential investors see some sign of a market for these new services. FM radio, color television, and many other communications innovations were all temporary victims of this effect until something triggered the simultaneous growth of markets and investments.

The time is now ripe for the deployment of wide area multiwavelength optical networks. First, the technology to support them is advancing inexorably, the most important recent development being the commercialization of erbium-doped fiber amplifiers (EDFAs). Second, a fast-growing market for wavelength division multiplexing (WDM) transmission systems has emerged among network operators who need to increase their capacity to respond to an increased demand for broadband services. This increase in demand has created a market-driven competitive environment that has already produced impressive results. New high-performance, reliable, and cost-effective technology is now available, which will in turn drive additional increases in demand. Third, many large multiwavelength broadband network demonstration projects are currently in progress worldwide [IEEE96]. And, last but not least, the recent explosion in interest in the Internet and the proliferation of Internet service providers are creating a demand (and a source of funding) for a vast increase in the capacity and quality of the international communications infrastructure on which it and other wide area network (WAN) services depend.

1.2 Wide Area Optical Networks: A Wish List

Networks are necessary to facilitate the sharing of communications and other resources (e.g., computing power) among a geographically distributed community of users. The traditional telephone networks (circuit switched) and data networks (packet switched) are specially engineered to provide this resource-sharing service to voice and data users respectively. Networks of asynchronous transfer mode (ATM) switches and Internet protocol (IP) routers provide similar resource-sharing facilities for a wide variety of broadband and multimedia services. Most of the telecommunication networks in use today (including many specialized networks such as cable TV systems) have optical fiber in them somewhere; however, this does *not* make them optical networks. In practically all cases in which fiber is used today, it is deployed in transmission links as a direct substitute for copper. This is because of its many superior properties: extraordinary bandwidth, low loss, low cost, light weight and compactness, strength and flexibility, immunity to noise and electromagnetic interference, security and privacy (it is difficult to tap them), and corrosion resistance.

Although all of these qualities make the fiber a technological marvel, fibers do not become networks until they are interconnected in a properly structured architecture. For our purposes, an *optical* (or *lightwave*) *network* is a telecommunications network with transmission links that are optical fibers, and with an architecture that is designed to exploit the unique features of fibers. As we shall see, suitable architectures for high-performance lightwave networks involve complex combinations of both optical and electronic devices. Thus, as used here, the term *optical* or *lightwave network* does not necessarily imply a *purely* optical network, but it does imply something more than a set of fibers terminated by electronic switches.

Figure 1.1 gives a multilayered view of the networks to be discussed. It shows an underlying optical infrastructure in the *physical layer*, providing basic communication services to a number of independent logical networks (LNs), each one specialized in providing a particular service to a group of users. The services shown in the figure are Internet connections, a video-on-demand distribution system, plain old telephone service (POTS), and demand-assigned purely optical connections (or *clear channels*). Note that the ATM LN is itself an infrastructure for a higher *virtual connection layer*, which can support a variety of services. (An example of Internet access is shown in the figure.)

For reasons to be explained in Section 1.3, the optical infrastructures in the networks with which we deal are called *transparent* or *purely optical networks*. The "glue" that holds the transparent optical network together fits roughly into two basic classes: the optical network nodes (ONNs), which connect the fibers within the network, and the network access stations (NASs), which interface user terminals and other nonoptical end systems to the network. This infrastructure is illustrated in Figure 1.2. Shown as rectangles in the figure, the NASs (or *stations* for short) provide the terminating points (sources and destinations) for the optical signal paths within the physical layer.

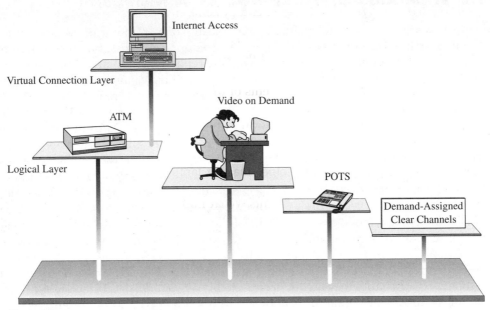

FIGURE 1.1 Multilayered network.

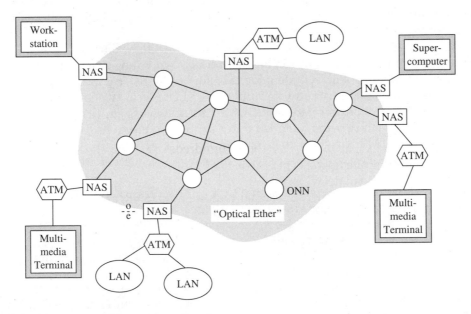

FIGURE 1.2 Physical picture of the network.

The communication paths continue outside the purely optical part of the network in electrical form, either terminating at end systems (for example, user terminals) or traversing electronic switching equipment (e.g., ATM switches).

The ONNs (or *nodes* for short), shown as circles in Figure 1.2, provide the switching and routing functions that control the optical signal paths, configuring them to create desired source–destination connections. The stations and nodes contain the optoelectronic and photonic components of the network: lasers, detectors, couplers, filters, optical switches, amplifiers, and so on. These components work together with the fibers to produce the required optical signal connectivity. The underlying optoelectronic and photonic technologies are not nearly as well developed and as inexpensive as their electronic counterparts. It is in this area that much development is now in progress, with the objective of making large lightwave networks economically viable. Architectures for the next generation of lightwave networks depend in a crucial way on these developments. What makes this dependence particularly challenging is that we are on the beginning of the learning curve for much of the enabling technology, so that the constraints it imposes are changing rapidly. Our discussion of network architectures and performance is thus tied closely to the characteristics of the underlying technology, with the caveat that it is a fast-moving target.

Although a bottom-up look at lightwave networks shows that their architectures and performance are tied closely to technological constraints, it is just as important to take a top-down look, in which the requirements of the users and service providers (i.e., the objectives) come first. Wide area lightwave networks will necessarily serve large, heterogeneous, geographically dispersed user populations, and they should be designed with the following objectives in mind:

- Connectivity
  - Support a very large number of stations and end systems
  - Support a very large number of concurrent connections including multiple connections per station
  - Support multicast connections efficiently

- Performance
  - High aggregate network throughput (hundreds of terabits per second)
  - High user bitrate (gigabits per second)
  - Small end-to-end delay
  - Low error rate (digital)/high signal-to-noise ratio (SNR; analog)
  - Low processing load in nodes and stations
  - Adaptability to changing and unbalanced loads
  - Efficient and rapid means of fault identification and recovery

- Structural features
  - Scalability
  - Modularity
  - Survivability (fault tolerance)

- Technology/cost issues
  - Access stations: small number of optical transceivers per station and limited complexity of optical transceivers
  - Network: Limited complexity of the optical network nodes, limited number and length of cables and fibers, and efficient use (and reuse) of the optical spectrum

As we look at existing and proposed network architectures, it is important that we keep this wish list in mind.

1.3 Optics versus Electronics: The Case for Transparent Multiwavelength Networks

There are certain functions that come naturally to each technology. As shown in Figure 1.2, the NASs represent the optoelectronic interface between the electronic domain (the equipment outside the purely optical portion of the network) and the optical domain, sometimes called the *optical ether*. The stations provide the basic functions of getting the light into the fibers (with lasers) and getting it out (with photodetectors). When the signals are in optical form, photonic technology is well suited to certain simple signal-routing and switching functions within the nodes. With static photonic devices, it is fairly easy to perform functions such as optical power combining, splitting, filtering, and wavelength multiplexing, demultiplexing, and routing. By adding suitable control, the static devices can be controlled dynamically (switched) at slow to fast speeds (milliseconds in the case of mechanical or thermal control and microseconds in the case of electronic control).

The enormous usable bandwidth of a single fiber (tens of tera-Hertz) is at the same time a great asset and a great challenge. It is technologically impossible to exploit all of that bandwidth using a single high-capacity channel. Thus, to make efficient use of the fiber it is essential to *channelize* its bandwidth. This is most easily accomplished by superimposing many concurrent signals on a single fiber, each on a different wavelength; that is, by using WDM. Thus this book focuses on *multiwavelength* or WDM network architectures. The relative ease of signal manipulation in the wavelength (or optical frequency) domain, as opposed to the time domain, suggests that current optical technology is particularly suited to multiwavelength techniques. In WDM networks each optical transmitter (receiver) is tuned to transmit (receive) on a specific wavelength, and many signals operating on distinct wavelengths share each fiber.

It should be observed that all photonic routing and switching functions within the optical domain in these networks are *linear* operations. Thus, at the optical level the network consists of only linear devices, either fixed or controllable. To distinguish these linear networks from other types of optical networks, we shall refer to them frequently as *transparent optical networks*. Typical *nonlinear* operations performed in networks include signal detection, regeneration, buffering, and logic functions (e.g., reading and writing packet headers). These are very difficult to perform in the optical domain with present-day technology.[1] Furthermore, nonlinearities make the signal path opaque rather than transparent. Some of the advantages of keeping nonlinear operations out of the signal path are (1) the end-to-end optical path behaves as a literally transparent[2] "clear channel" so that there is nothing in the signal path to limit the throughput of the fibers (a transparent channel behaves very much like an ideal communication channel with almost no noise and a very large bandwidth) and (2) the architecture of the optical network nodes can be very simple because they have essentially no signal processing to do. (Optical node simplicity also means simplicity of network control.)

There are also downsides to transparency. First, problems caused by equipment failures tend to propagate throughout the network, making fault management a more complex issue than in nontransparent networks. Similarly, impairments such as switch cross-talk, noise, fiber dispersion, and nonlinear effects accumulate over long paths, limiting the geographic "reach" of an optical connection. Second, by definition, *inband* information (e.g., control information carried in packet headers in data networks) such as source and destination address, sequence number, channel number, parity check bits, and so forth, cannot be used while the signal is in optical form. Because of this, transparent optical networks cannot perform the various processing functions required in traditional packet-switched data networks.

It is important to note that the inband control information carried with the data in IP (packet-based) or ATM (cell-based) networks is the key to achieving a high degree of virtual connectivity in these networks. Typically, many virtual connections are multiplexed on each physical connection and sorted (switched) on a packet/cell basis at each network node using information contained in the packet or cell headers. Maintaining transparency in the physical layer eliminates the intelligence necessary to process this information, and therefore tends to produce an optical "connectivity bottleneck" in transparent networks. Thus, there is a case to be made for opaque optical networks [Bala+95].

The properties of electronics are complementary to those of optics. Electronic processing is ideal for complex nonlinear operations, but the limited speed of electronic and optoelectronic devices (e.g., electronic switches, memory devices, processing units, and so on), and the high processing load imposed on electronics in broadband networks, causes the well-known "electronic bottleneck" in optical transmission systems. Putting an electronic termination on an optical fiber reduces the potential multiterabit-per-second throughput of the fiber to a multigigabit-per-second

---

[1] Some nonlinear processing functions have been implemented purely photonically in the laboratory, including purely optical packet buffering and switching. However, the current state-of-the-art for nonlinear devices is not nearly as advanced as it is for linear components. For these reasons we use the terms *transparent optical network* and *purely optical network* interchangeably in this book.

[2] Transparency implies that signals with any type of modulation schemes (analog or digital), any bitrate, and any type of format can be superimposed and transmitted without interfering with one another, and without their information being modified within the network. Opaque networks do not have these properties.

trickle: the maximum throughput that can be expected of the electronics. This is the origin of the highway/cow path analogy we used in Section 1.1. More succinctly, optics is fast but dumb, whereas electronics is slow but smart, and this state of affairs is expected to persist at least into the foreseeable future.

1.4 Optics and Electronics: The Case for Multilayered Networks

Because of the size and complexity of the networks we are considering, and because of the fact that lightwave technology alone cannot satisfy our wish list, we turn to the multilayered model of Figure 1.1. Elaborating on the discussion of Section 1.2, this layered network has as its physical foundation a multiwavelength purely optical network. Superimposed on the physical layer are one or more LNs, each of which is designed to serve some subset of user requirements and is implemented as an *electronic overlay* superimposed on the physical layer.

The physical layer makes a large pool of bandwidth available to the LNs in the form of transparent end-to-end connections. These high-bandwidth optical channels may be used to provide a dedicated communications backbone for an LN (e.g., an ATM network), or they may be demand assigned for temporary activities such as remote access to supercomputers. Each LN might be customized for a specific purpose, and may be managed independently of the others. For example, the LN could be an ATM network that provides services such as local area network (LAN) interconnection, multimedia teleconferencing, and Internet connections.[3] Because ATM networks have their own layered architecture, another virtual connection layer is shown on top of the ATM logical layer in Figure 1.1. The virtual connections are supported by an electronic network of ATM switches.

Many virtual connections are typically multiplexed onto each logical link in the ATM network, and that network in turn relies on the pool of bandwidth offered by the underlying (optical) physical layer to provide the capacity necessary for its logical links. Another LN might be comprised of telephone carrier equipment (circuit switches, digital cross-connects, and so forth) organized to provide ordinary and enhanced telephone service, including integrated services digital network (ISDN) connections. Still another might be devoted to providers of video-on-demand services. Electronic switching equipment in the logical layer acts as a "middleman," taking the high-bandwidth transparent channels provided by the physical layer and organizing them into a form acceptable and cost-effective for the users. In addition, sophisticated users requiring high bandwidth have direct access to demand-assigned optical connections without the intervention of an electronic middleman.

Figure 1.2 illustrates in more detail how the physical layer, shown as a set of fibers connected by ONNs, is interfaced at its edges to various types of electronic switching

---

[3] To support the Internet connections, another sublayer of IP routers would be carried on top of the ATM layer.

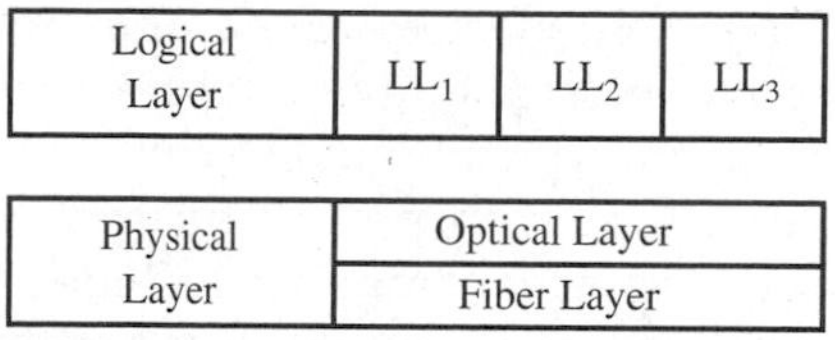

Logical Layer	LL$_1$	LL$_2$	LL$_3$

Physical Layer	Optical Layer
	Fiber Layer

FIGURE 1.3 Layered view of an optical network.

equipment and end systems through the NASs. LANs and other equipment (multi-media terminals in this case) are interconnected through an LN composed of ATM switches, whereas high-end workstations and supercomputers have direct access to demand-assigned optical channels through their own stations.

In Figure 1.3, the architecture of the overall network is shown reduced to its constituent layers, each one providing support for the layer above it, and using the services of the layer below it—a natural extension of the idea of layered architectures to optical networks. The layering formalism is introduced here to partition a complex set of interactions among network components into a small number of more manageable pieces. The characteristics of the logical layers depend on the architectures of the various LN overlays (if any). In Figure 1.3 we show three parallel and independent logical layers—LL_1, LL_2, and LL_3—all supported by the physical layer. The physical layer, representing the purely optical network, is now shown divided into an optical layer and a fiber layer. The former contains the optical connections supported by the fibers, and the latter embodies the layout of the physical infrastructure itself: the fibers, switches, and optical transceivers. In Chapter 2, the layered view of optical networks is expanded into a complete multiwavelength network architecture.

Why is a hybrid approach required for WANs? Although some early optical networks proposed for LANs and metropolitan area networks (MANs) were purely optical, the current state-of-the-art suggests that neither optics nor electronics alone can provide all the features listed in Section 1.2. Using today's technology, purely optical wavelength-selective switches are capable of interconnecting tens of fibers operating in a WDM mode, switching and routing each wavelength independently, and yielding aggregate throughputs in the range of many terabits per second while supporting hundreds of optical connections. On the other hand, electronic packet/cell switches are currently limited in throughput to approximately 100 Gbps. However, they can support a very large number of relatively low-bitrate virtual connections.

The difference in the two approaches is *granularity*. Optical switches are operated most easily in a *circuit-switched mode*, in which the information-bearing units (optical clear channels) being switched are few but large (in bandwidth), and the holding times for a given switch configuration are typically long (seconds or more). Circuit-switched operation of the optical nodes is perfectly suitable for the physical layer shown in Figures 1.1 and 1.3. Dedicated connections supporting the various LNs are normally held in static configurations for durations of hours, days, or more. Demand-assigned connections are held typically for minutes or hours. Thus the number of circuits being set up and taken down per unit time is relatively small. This type of operation requires little processing, and provides a high aggregate throughput.

Conversely, electronics is employed in situations in which there are many information units (e.g., individual packets or cells) being switched per unit time. Because the units are typically small (in bits) and because each unit is processed individually, this leads to a heavy processing load, with a relatively low throughput limited by the processing power of the switch. Wide area networks must handle both large and small information units: hence the need for marrying both electronic and optical switching technologies. The hybrid approach, described in the next section, exploits the unique capabilities of each while circumventing their limitations.

1.5 LAN Interconnection: A Killer Application

Broadband WANs must be capable of supporting high connectivity, high throughput, and heterogeneous traffic mixes. Applications that place high demands on a network in these categories are good tests of network performance; that is, they are *killer applications*. Two such applications come to mind: Internet access and LAN interconnection. In the discussion that follows we focus on the latter, but the basic characteristics of the problem apply equally well to the former.

Consider a future WAN serving as a backbone that interconnects a large number of high-speed LANs (say, 10,000), accessing the WAN through LAN gateways. Each LAN might serve hundreds of active users. Some of the equipment on the LANs could be servers that require virtual connections to many clients distributed among the other LANs, so that the aggregate traffic in and out of each LAN (perhaps several gigabits per second) could require virtual connectivity to most of the other LANs on the network. The aggregate traffic among all the LAN gateways carried on the backbone network would be tens of terabits per second. (This example corresponds in size, but not in throughput, to the present-day situation on the Internet. Currently there are tens of thousands of LANs interconnected on the Internet, but their traffic volume is much less than we postulate here.)

Let us examine the optical, electronic, and hybrid alternatives. Consider first a purely optical network supporting LAN interconnection. It would resemble a modified version of Figure 1.2, with the LANs attached directly to NASs without the intervening (electronic) ATM switches, as shown in Figure 1.4. There may be considerably fewer optical nodes than NASs (i.e., each node may serve many stations). In the purely optical case, each NAS interfaces one or more LAN gateways to the backbone, so that the NAS connects its gateways to the other gateways on the network through individual optical connections. This could require millions of connections (99,990,000 for full connectivity among 10,000 LANs). It is the high-connectivity requirement that makes this application a killer. To implement full connectivity, each station must maintain 9,999 connections, one to each other gateway (assuming one LAN gateway per NAS). This means either equipping each station with that many optical transceivers, or providing extremely rapid optical connection switching. No matter how it is realized, this degree of connectivity is well beyond the reach of current optical technology.

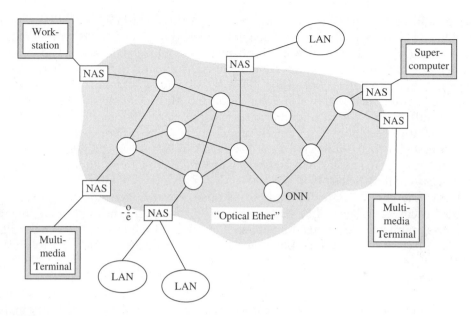

FIGURE 1.4 Purely optical network.

On the other hand, a purely electronic version of Figure 1.2 has its own problems. This would be implemented with electronic rather than optical switches at the network nodes. Electronics could easily support the required connectivity via virtual connections. However, the electronic processing bottleneck at the switches would make it impossible to sustain the required multiterabit throughput on the backbone.

Now return to the hybrid ATM/optical configuration shown in Figure 1.2. Here, both objectives are achieved. An LN composed of ATM switches provides the necessary connectivity through suitable virtual channels (VCs) that are demultiplexed, switched, and remultiplexed at each ATM switch, and the physical layer supports the required throughput over dedicated, high-bandwidth (optical) backbone connections carrying the aggregated VCs on logical links between the ATM switch ports. This example illustrates the fact that the test of a good lightwave network is whether it can achieve both high throughput and high connectivity at a reasonable cost.

1.6 A Little History

The idea of a high-speed optical transmission system (in free space) was considered as early as 1958, when the laser was conceived [Schawlow+58], and guided wave optical transmission was exhibited in the laboratory in the mid 1960s [Kao+66]. However, practical optical transmission systems did not become possible until the production of the first low-loss fibers and the invention of the semiconductor laser diode, both around 1970. By refining the optical tranceivers and reducing fiber loss, the effectiveness of optical transmission systems (measured in bitrate–distance product) grew roughly at an exponential rate from the early 1970s to the late 1980s, with bitrates as high as 8 Gbps over distances of 100 km achieved in the mid 1980s [Miller+88]. The first optical fiber trans-Atlantic cable (using electronic repeaters) was laid in 1988. The distance limitations due to fiber attenuation disappeared in the late 1980s, almost overnight with the emergence of the EDFA [Desurvire+87, Mears+87, Mears+86]. Over the ensuing years interest in long-distance optical transmission using EDFAs grew rapidly [Saito+90]. In laboratory experiments, in which long distances are simulated using closed loops with amplification, and in which fiber dispersion effects are eliminated using solitons, transmission distances have been extended essentially without limit. For example, [Nakazawa+93] reported a 10-Gbps soliton system operating over a total distance of 10^6 km.

During the late 1970s to the middle 1990s, fiber transmission capacity roughly doubled each year (Figure 1.5). Note particularly the significant jump in aggregate transmission bitrates to the terabits-per-second range in the late 1990s using multiwavelength (WDM) techniques. But more recent results are off the chart! For example, 360 Tbps was achieved over 9,000 km in 1997 [Otani+97].

Standards for the exploitation of optical fibers for high-speed digital transmission were developed in the late 1980s, culminating in the synchronous optical network (SONET) standard with its synchronous transport signal (STS) hierarchy in the United States, and the more-or-less parallel synchronous digital hierarchy (SDH) international standard promulgated by the International Telecommunications Union–Telecommunication Standardization Sector (ITU-T) [Ballart+89, Boehm90]. Both of these standards pertain to optical transmission links carrying synchronous bitstreams terminated by electronic switches. Soon after SONET and SDH were introduced, the concept of a broadband integrated services digital network (B-ISDN) became widely accepted as a means of supporting all sorts of multimedia services on a common network [CCITT92].

For a number of reasons, a packet-switched transport service is the most appropriate for many integrated services applications. Therefore, in the 1990s, much activity has been devoted to developing ATM as the preferred transport service for B-ISDN. The cell-based transport technique in ATM (essentially a fixed-length, fast packet-switching system) lends itself well to a wide variety of multimedia applications, and at the same time is well adapted to high-speed switching techniques [de Prycker91]. In parallel with ATM, the Internet protocol suite, which was one of the earliest packet-switching protocols, continues to be refined to keep pace with the burgeoning growth of Internet applications. Although these activities do not bear directly on the subject of this book, it is likely that SONET, SDH, ATM, and IP LNs will be the principal users of optical network capacity in the future.

Interest in lightwave networks began in the mid 1980s [Henry89], but the technological barriers to the deployment of large-scale networks remained formidable until the advent of the fiber amplifier. Systems efforts during the pre-EDFA era were focused on a simple architecture, appropriate for LANs or MANs: the broadcast-and-select network [Mukherjee92a]. In a typical network of this type, each access station is equipped with a single laser transmitter capable of generating light at a fixed

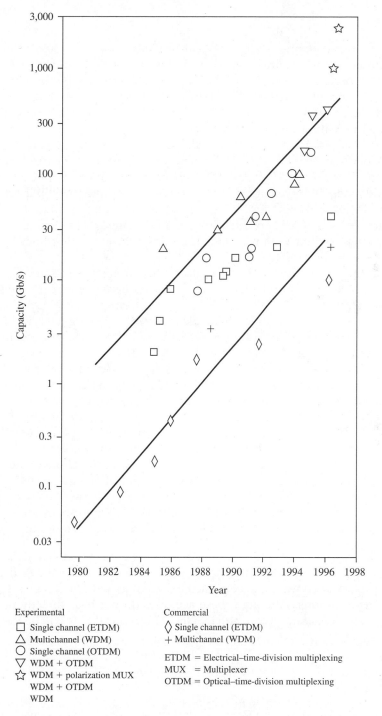

FIGURE 1.5 Evolution of optical fiber transmission capacity. (After (Netravali97). Copyright ©1997, *The Bell Labs Technical Journal*. All rights reserved. Reprinted with permission.)

wavelength, and contains a single optical receiver capable of being tuned to the wavelength of any transmitter. Signals from all transmitting stations are combined in a centrally located optical star coupler, a passive device that broadcasts an attenuated version of the combined signals back to each receiver. By selecting the appropriate wavelength, each receiver can accept the signal injected by the corresponding transmitter, thereby creating a transparent connection from the transmitter to that receiver.

Probably the earliest prototype of a broadcast-and-select network was LAMBDANET [Goodman+87, Goodman+86]. Broadcast-and-select networks do not scale well to large sizes primarily because they rely on rapid tuning of optical transceivers over a wide range of wavelengths, waste optical power, and, most important, make poor use of the optical spectrum. More general mesh topologies were soon proposed to eliminate the constraints of broadcast-and-select networks. In these networks, alternate paths together with wavelength routing produce possibilities for reuse of the optical spectrum [Hill88].

At about the same time that wavelength routing was proposed, the *multihop concept* was suggested to obtain high connectivity without requiring expensive, tunable optical transceivers. Multihop networks were early examples of the hybrid approach described in Section 1.4 [Acampora87, Mukherjee92b], relieving the connectivity bottleneck at the optical level by adding packet or cell switches in an electronic LN overlay.

In the late 1980s to mid 1990s, activity intensified in optoelectronic and photonic technology, as well as in the demonstration and deployment of new network architectures. While multiwavelength technology matured, experimental work continued in more speculative areas entailing nonlinear optical devices. Units, such as all-optical switches, optical logic devices, and optical storage elements are of interest to move the nonlinear operations now executed in electronics down to the optical level. Potential applications are in optical packet switching and optical computing.

Ambitious optical network testbeds were deployed in the United States, Europe, and Japan, involving the maturing multiwavelength technology as well as incorporating the management and control equipment necessary for making these networks operational and reliable. [IEEE93, IEEE96, IEEE98]. These testbeds showed for the first time that optical technology could be taken out of the laboratory to produce cost-effective operational networks.

The testbed activity was a precursor for a sudden upsurge of interest in the commercial deployment of multiwavelength technology. At this writing, the demand pull for optical networking that appeared to be nonexistent just a year ago is accelerating rapidly. Many new ventures have been initiated to supply multiwavelength transmission products, and these will be followed undoubtedly by related switching products. As the new networks evolve, network management concepts adapted to optical networks are also evolving. A new look at survivability and fault management is a special priority because a single cable cut can (and has) disrupted a huge volume of traffic.

This recent activity provides the context for this book: a rapidly advancing and maturing technology base, together with a recognition among the users and providers of telecommunications services that optical networks are here to stay.

1.7 Overview and Road Map

Lightwave networks can be characterized broadly in terms of three basic features:

1. Physical (fiber) topology
2. Functionality in the links, the optical network nodes, and the access stations
3. Control algorithms for assigning, routing, and multiplexing connections

A rich physical topology provides many alternate paths among access stations, increasing the aggregate capacity of the network as well as its potential survivability and adaptability to changing load patterns. But the properties of the physical topology cannot be exploited without sufficient functionality in the links and the network nodes and access stations.

By link functionality we mean good transmission properties (large bandwidth–distance product). Useful functional properties of nodes and stations include controllable switching and multiplexing features. Without controllability in the nodes and stations, optical channel assignments and signal paths must remain fixed at all times so that connections are frozen, and the network has no flexibility in responding to changing conditions. Conversely, a high degree of node and station controllability under the supervision of a network management system improves the efficiency of resource utilization, allows the network to maintain satisfactory performance in the face of fluctuating demand, and enables it to reconfigure itself in case of component failures. Of course, controllability implies the existence of suitable control algorithms to coordinate the functions of the various network entities. Three basic features—topology, functionality, and control—interact closely to influence overall network performance (Figure 1.6).

As might be expected, there are many opportunities for cost–performance trade-offs. Thus, high functionality in the nodes and access stations improves performance, but this comes at a price. The same can be said of the richness of the physical topology. Also, to compensate for the limitations of the network resources, one can attempt to optimize performance through sophisticated control algorithms. However, optimality generally comes at the price of controller complexity. Thus, the cost–performance trade-offs involve complex interactions among all the basic features.

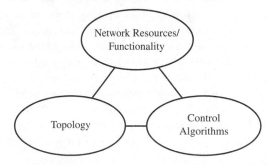

FIGURE 1.6 The performance triangle.

In a field of engineering where the technology is mature (e.g., in digital electronics), systems can be understood, analyzed, and designed with only a limited understanding of the physical principles involved. (A designer of a personal computer is not particularly concerned with electromagnetic theory.) On the other hand, when the enabling technology is rapidly evolving, as in the case of optical networks, a more thorough understanding of technology and its relation to system performance is required. Thus, a good grasp of optical networks requires an understanding of the interrelations between two bodies of knowledge that traditionally have been treated separately: the physics of the underlying devices and the mathematical methodology required to analyze, design, and control systems incorporating these devices.

The emphasis of this book is clearly on methodology rather than devices. However, we weave the physical and mathematical sides of networking into an integrated whole by linking physical constraints with performance analysis and design concepts whenever possible. In addition, we integrate current practice, generic models, and futuristic concepts. By emphasizing linkages across traditional lines, our intention is to break down the compartmentalization that tends to hinder progress.

We recognize that integration across a broad range of material presents a challenge to the reader. The interconnections make it difficult to isolate sets of topics matched to the background and interests of each reader, and some readers may feel caught in a tangled web. To help the disoriented traveler, we provide a simple road map in Figure 1.7 as a guide through the labyrinth.

As shown in the figure, the first three chapters are required for an understanding of the rest of the subject matter. These are accessible to readers with only a limited background in networking and physical principles. After the broad view of Chapter 1, Chapter 2 introduces the multiwavelength network architecture, describing the layers of connectivity in a wavelength division multiplexed network. The chapter focuses on the functionality of optical network elements—links, nodes, and access stations—and their relation to network performance. Chapter 3 gives an overview of the various layers of network connections. Purely optical networks are discussed first, starting from the simplest (static) networks and then considering the two controllable classes: wavelength routed networks and linear lightwave networks.

The former class supports point-to-point connections, while the latter supports multipoint connections, representing a more general view of transparent optical networks and their functionality. Because the physical layer alone is not sufficient to serve the most demanding needs of network users, as illustrated by the killer application of Section 1.5, the chapter concludes with a discussion of logically routed networks—hybrid networks consisting of an electronic overlay on an optical infrastructure. Chapters 2 and 3 are largely qualitative and serve as introductions and "pointers" to material explored quantitatively in later chapters.

The rest of the book may be read more selectively. It is linked to the earlier material, as shown in Figure 1.7. For those with only a limited understanding of the physical side of networking, Chapter 4 provides a concise treatment of physical principles and device technology. It is not intended to be all-encompassing, because other

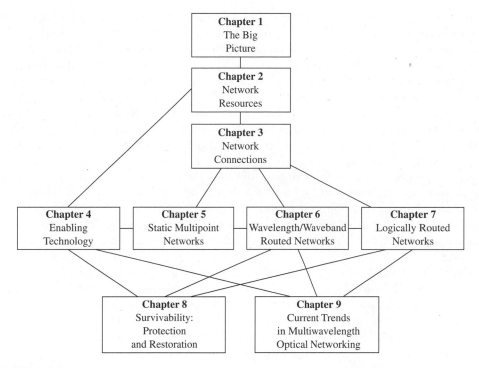

FIGURE 1.7 Road map.

works are solely devoted to these topics—for example, see references [Agrawal97] and [Saleh+91]. Some of the material involves fundamentals and generic concepts (e.g., Sections 4.1 through 4.3), whereas other portions are largely devoted to current technology (e.g., Sections 4.9 through 4.12). The focus is on physical and technological constraints that limit network performance. These include limits on WDM channel-packing density, optical receiver performance, geographic reach of optical connections, and technological limitations imposed on optical switches.

The remaining chapters are more specialized. Chapters 5 through 7 present a thorough treatment of the generic multiwavelength optical network.[4] Static networks based on shared optical media are covered in Chapter 5. The chapter discusses multiplexing and multiple-access techniques, traffic flow constraints, capacity

---

[4] The necessary background in graph theory, Markov chains, and queueing theory is included in Appendices A and C, and some algorithms for special aspects of network provisioning and control appear in Appendices B, D, and E.

assignment, and optical packet-switching. Wavelength routed and linear lightwave networks are examined in Chapter 6, with discussions of routing and channel assignment, as well as the relationship between optical-switch functionality and network performance. Some case studies about current network design economics appear in Section 6.7.[5] Chapter 7 deals with logically routed networks. It is here that the overall network design problem appears for the first time. We present methodologies for designing a logically routed network to satisfy a prescribed traffic requirement, while observing the constraints imposed by a given fiber topology, the limitations of the network components, and the limited capacity of the available optical spectrum.

The very important issue of optical network survivability and fault recovery is introduced in Chapter 8, with an emphasis on self-healing using automatic protection switching. Finally, in Chapter 9, we tie the generic concepts of earlier chapters to recent trends in network deployment. An infinite variety of additional issues arise when operating networks in the real world that are often missed in an abstract view of things.

Parts of Chapter 4, the beginning part of Chapter 8, all of Chapter 9, and Section 6.7 provide examples of the current state-of-the-art in technology, network design, and network operation, as well as the trade-offs between optical and nonoptical networking solutions. These will be of particular interest to those involved in near-term network deployment. However, this is the most "perishable" material in the book. Let the reader beware!

Some of the more advanced and speculative sections in the book may be skipped initially by readers learning about optical networks for the first time. In Chapter 5, Section 5.2.3, Code Division Multiple Access, and parts of Sections 5.5 and 5.6, which deal with demand-assigned connections and packet switching in the optical layer, can be bypassed by those new to the field. The same is true for parts of Chapter 6, including the material on ring decomposition in Section 6.3.5, optimization in Section 6.3.7, and some of the more specialized topics on LLNs in the latter part of the chapter. In Chapter 7, most of the material on point-to-point logically routed networks will be of interest to all readers, whereas Sections 7.3 and 7.4 on hypernets are more futuristic in nature than the rest of the chapter. The latter sections of Chapter 8, on optical layer protection in mesh topologies, are currently open research areas.

Readers involved in research on next-generation networks would normally focus on the complement of the subject matter of interest to the novice. Thus, for example, rings, which are "old hat" to the researcher, could be skimmed in favor of more

---

[5] A brief overview of the SONET standard is given in Appendix F. It provides background for this section as well as parts of Chapter 8.

advanced topics—optimization and LLNs, in Chapter 6. Researchers might also focus on hypernets in Chapter 7 and general optical layer protection in Chapter 8.

In summary, it should be possible to customize an itinerary suitable for anyone interested in exploring the fascinating world of optical networking. Bon voyage!

1.8 Bibliography

[Acampora87] A. S. Acampora. A multichannel multihop local lightwave network. In *Proc. IEEE Globecom.*, pp. 1459–1467, Tokyo, Japan, November 1987.

[Agrawal97] G. P. Agrawal. *Fiber-Optic Communication Systems, Second Edition* (Wiley Series in Microwave and Optical Engineering). New York: John Wiley & Sons, 1997.

[Bala+95] K. Bala, R. R. Cordell, and E. L. Goldstein. The case for opaque multiwavelength optical networks. In *Proc. LEOS Summer Topical Meeting*, Keystone, CO, August 1995.

[Ballart+89] R. Ballart and Y-C. Ching. SONET: Now it's the standard optical network. *IEEE Communications Mag.*, March:8–15, 1989.

[Boehm90] R. J. Boehm. Progress in standardization of SONET. *IEEE Lightwave Communication Systems*, 1(2):8–16, 1990.

[CCITT92] CCITT. *Recommendation i.121, Broadband Aspects of ISDN.* Geneva: CCITT, 1992.

[de Prycker91] M. de Prycker. *Asynchronous Transfer Mode: Solution for Broadband ISDN.* Chichester, England: Ellis Horwood, 1991.

[Desurvire+87] E. Desurvire, J. R. Simpson, and P. C. Becker. High-gain erbium-doped traveling-wave fibre amplifier. *Optics Lett.*, 12(11):888, 1987.

[Goodman+87] M. S. Goodman, C. A. Brackett, R. M. Bulley, et al. Design and demonstration of the LAMBDANET system: A multi-wavelength optical network. In *Proc. IEEE Globecom.*, pp. 1455–1458, Tokyo, November 1987.

[Goodman+86] M. S. Goodman, H. Kobrinski, and K. W. Lo. Application of wavelength division multiplexing to communication network architectures. In *Proc. IEEE Int'l Conf. Commun.*, pp. 931–934, Toronto, 1986.

[Henry89] P. S. Henry. High-capacity lightwave local area networks. *IEEE Communications Mag.*, 27(10):20–26, 1989.

[Hill88] G. R. Hill. A wavelength routing approach to optical communications networks. In *Proc. IEEE Infocom.*, pp. 354–362, New Orleans, March 1988.

[IEEE98] IEEE. High-capacity optical transport networks. *IEEE J. Select. Areas Commun.*, 16(7), 1998.

[IEEE96] IEEE. Special issue on multiwavelength optical technology and networks. *IEEE/OSA J. Lightwave Technology*, 14(6), 1996.

[IEEE93] IEEE. Special issue on broad-band optical networks. *IEEE/OSA J. Lightwave Technology*, 11(5/6), 1993.

[Kao+66] C. K. Kao and G. A. Hockham. Dielectric-fiber surface waveguides for optical frequencies. *Proc. IEEE*, 113(7):1151–1158, 1966.

[Mears+86] R. J. Mears, L. Reekie, S. B. Poole, and D. N. Payne. Low-threshold, tunable CW and Q-switched fibre laser operating at 1.55 μm. *Electron. Letters*, 22(3):159, 1986.

[Mears+87] R. J. Mears, L. Reekie, I. M. Jauncey, and D. N. Payne. Low-noise erbium-doped fibre amplifier operating at 1.54 μm. *Electron. Letters*, 23(19):1026, 1987.

[Miller+88] S. E. Miller and I. P. Kaminow. *Optical Fiber Telecommunications II.* New York: Academic Press, 1988.

[Mukherjee92a] B. Mukherjee. WDM-based local lightwave networks—Part I: Single-hop systems. *IEEE Network Mag.*, 6(3):12–27, 1992.

[Mukherjee92b] B. Mukherjee. WDM-based local lightwave networks—Part II: Multihop systems. *IEEE Network Mag.*, 6(4):20–32, 1992.

[Nakazawa+93] M. Nakazawa, K. Suzuki, E. Yamada, et al. Experimental demonstration of soliton data transmission over unlimited distances with soliton control in time and frequency domains. In *Proc. IEEE/OSA Optical Fiber Commun. Conf.*, Paper PD7, Washington, DC, 1993.

[Netravali97] A. N. Netravali. The impact of solid-state electronics on computing and communications. *Bell Labs Technical Journal*, Autumn 1997.

[Otani+97] T. Otani, T. Kawazawa, K. Goto, et al. 16-channel 2.5 Gbit/s WDM transmission experiment over 9,000 km by using gain equalised amplifier repeaters. *Electron. Letters*, 33(4): 309–310, 1997.

[Saito+90] S. Saito, T. Imai, T. Sugie, et al. An over 2,200 km coherent transmission experiment at 2.5 Gbps using erbium-doped fiber amplifiers. In *Proc. IEEE/OSA Optical Fiber Commun. Conf.*, Paper PD2, Dallas, 1990.

[Saleh+91] B.E.A. Saleh and M. C. Teich. *Fundamentals of Photonics.* New York: John Wiley & Sons, 1991.

[Schawlow+58] A. L. Schawlow and C. H. Townes. Infrared and optical lasers. *Phys. Rev.*, 112(6):1940, 1958.

CHAPTER TWO

Network Resources

Ultimately, the performance of a network is limited by the quantity and functionality of its physical resources. In this chapter we examine the various functions performed in a multiwavelength network, emphasizing the role of the optical resources (located in the physical layer of Figure 1.3) in providing connectivity and throughput. (Henceforth we use the terms *transparent optical*, *purely optical*, and just *optical* interchangeably to refer to entities in the physical layer.) To provide a proper framework for the discussion that follows we start in Section 2.1 with a description of layers and sublayers of the multiwavelength network architecture.

The functional characteristics of the optical resources—the network links, the optical network nodes (ONNs), and the network access stations (NASs)—are discussed in Sections 2.2, 2.3, and 2.4 respectively. As pointed out in Section 1.5, the additional functionality provided by an electronic overlay is often required to satisfy network requirements. Thus, in Sections 2.5 and 2.6 we consider hybrid networks that contain a purely optical network infrastructure complemented by an electronic overlay. Section 2.5 deals with special-purpose overlay processors (OLPs) for enhancing the performance of the optical network without adding electronic switching.

Going beyond an enhanced physical layer, Section 2.6 describes the essential features of logically routed networks (LRNs) relying on the resources of the physical layer to provide high throughput, and the processing power and routing capabilities in the logical switching nodes (LSNs) to provide high connectivity.

2.1 Layers and Sublayers

In Figure 2.1(a) the layered view of the optical network, first introduced in Figure 1.3, is expanded into the sublayers of the multiwavelength network architecture. To fix ideas, the structure of the higher layers is shown to represent a packet/cell-switched logical network (LN), including a virtual connection layer, which might correspond to the ATM logical network, shown in Figure 1.1. The functionality to be described is representative of a WAN operating with dedicated and/or demand-assigned (circuit-switched) optical connections. In smaller networks (e.g., optical LANs) some of the functions described may be nonexistent.

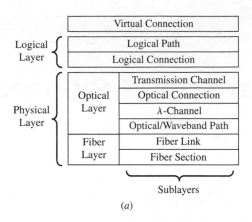

(a)

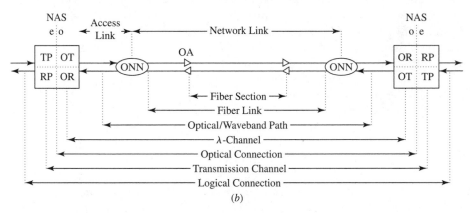

(b)

FIGURE 2.1 Layered view of optical network connections.

In describing the architecture we start in the optical layer of Figure 2.1(a), and work down from the interface between the logical and physical layers to the fiber layer. In terms of hardware, the logical–physical layer interface is located at the external (electronic) ports of the NASs. A detailed look at a typical point-to-point connection is presented in Figure 2.1(b). As indicated, the access stations terminate the optical connections, and serve to interface electronic end systems (user equipment) or switches (communications carrier equipment) to the optical network. (As mentioned earlier, the access station acts as the boundary between the electronic and optical domain, moving information between its external ports on one side of the electro-optic interface and optical ports on the other.) On its optical side, each NAS connects to an ONN through an *access link*, which consists of one or more pairs of access fibers.[1] Optical

---

[1] For survivability, a station might connect to two (or more) network nodes, a configuration analogous to *dual homing* in current telecommunication networks. In dual homing a facility, such as a telephone central office, is connected to two hubs (nodes) of a backbone network.

signals are exchanged between the station and the network by optical transceivers in the station. Each node is connected to neighboring nodes by pairs of fibers, which constitute *internodal network links*. We call the graph that describes the interconnections of the network links and network nodes the *physical topology* of the network. A long link may contain one or more optical amplifiers to compensate for attenuation in the fiber, so that the link becomes a series connection of several fiber sections between amplifiers. For simplicity we usually assume that fibers are used in unidirectional pairs to support bidirectional transmission. (In practice, single fibers are sometimes used for bidirectional transmission to reduce cost.)

The sublayers of the optical layer are a function of the way in which the optical spectrum is partitioned. The smallest entities in the partition are λ-*channels*, each of which is assigned a distinct wavelength (or optical frequency). These are the basic information carriers in the physical layer. At this point, the λ-channels are assumed to be routed (switched) independently by the ONNs. (This is the way most multiwavelength networks are configured at present.) A more elaborate two-tiered partitioning involving wavebands is introduced in Section 2.2.

Each point-to-point optical connection (OC) is carried on a λ-channel and is created by (1) assigning a λ-channel to the source transmitter and destination receiver on a selected wavelength, and (2) by establishing an optical path (OP) through a sequence of network nodes to carry that wavelength from source to destination. These actions are normally under the control of a network manager, the details of which we leave for later.

We call a unidirectional connection between external ports on a pair of source and destination NASs a *logical connection* (LC). This connection carries a logical signal in some agreed-on electronic format (e.g., ATM cells, IP packets, SONET digital bitstreams, or analog video). Each logical signal format is tailored to the needs of a particular LN or end system. All LCs draw on the resources of the physical layer, as shown in Figure 1.1. Each LC is carried on an optical connection through the intermediary of a *transmission channel*. The transmission channel performs a conversion of the logical signal to a *transmission signal*. This conversion (as well as certain multiplexing functions in the case of multipoint connections) takes place in the *transmission processor* (TP), with the reverse operations implemented in the *reception processor* (RP). Just as the logical signal format must be adapted to the LN that it serves, the transmission signal format must be matched to the requirements of the optical equipment that carries it. For example, the transmission signal must be limited to a bandwidth constrained by the characteristics of the optical transmitter (OT), the optical receiver (OR), and the permissible spectrum occupancy of the optical channel carrying it.

It is important to note how the optical connections are established through the coordinated actions of the nodes and stations. It is the function of the terminating NASs to tune their transceivers to the assigned wavelength of the λ-channel, thereby establishing the optical *connection*. Similarly, it is the role of the nodes to create an optical *path* on that wavelength, thereby establishing the support for a *potential* connection. Activation of a connection on the OP only occurs when the transceivers are properly tuned.

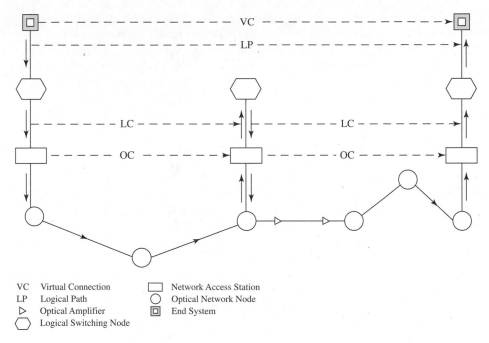

FIGURE 2.2 A typical connection.

The main consideration in breaking down the optical layer into sublayers is to account for multiplexing, multiple access (at several layers), and switching. Using multiplexing, several logical channels may be combined on a λ-channel originating from one station; using multiple access, λ-channels originating from several stations may carry multiple LCs to the same destination; and through switching, many distinct optical paths may be created on different fibers in the network, using (and reusing) λ-channels on the same wavelength.[2]

In the fiber layer the optical path is carried by a succession of *fiber links* that connect the network nodes. (The fiber layer is subdivided further into the fiber link sublayer supported by the fiber section sublayer.) Each of the internodal connections along an optical path constitutes an *optical hop*.

A typical connection illustrating these concepts is shown in Figure 2.2. A virtual connection between a pair of end systems is carried on a logical path (LP) that consists of two LCs terminated by logical switching nodes. The first and second LCs are carried on two- and three-hop OCs, respectively. (The access links are not counted as hops.)

Although this discussion has been limited to point-to-point connections to simplify the exposition, the terminology also applies to multipoint connections. As a matter

---

[2] Optical spectrum reuse is a recurring theme throughout the book because it is the key to scalability of optical networks to large sizes.

of fact, optical multipoint connections play a unique and important role in the multi-wavelength network architectures to be discussed later. Now let us examine each of the key components in more detail.

2.2 Network Links: Spectrum Partitioning

A large number of concurrent connections can be supported on each network link through successive levels of multiplexing as discussed earlier. A schematic view of the fiber resources illustrating this concept appears in Figure 2.3.

A typical network link consists of a cable containing several (sometimes more than 100) fibers, which are used as bidirectional pairs. (Given the cost of the right-of-way and labor in laying a cable, it would be very inefficient to deploy a cable that consists of only a single fiber pair.) This bundling of fibers into one cable is an example of *space–division multiplexing* in the fiber layer. The usable optical spectrum on a single fiber is wide enough to carry many high-speed optical connections through several additional levels of multiplexing. In our discussions, wavelength division is the basic multiplexing technique, with each fiber carrying connections on many distinct wavelengths (λ-channels). This is indicated by a coarse and fine division of the optical fiber spectrum within the wavelength dimension in Figure 2.3. (An explanation of the coarse/fine spectrum division is given later.) First, the spectrum is divided into wavebands, and these are divided further into λ-channels. The assigned wavelengths of the λ-channels must be spaced sufficiently far apart to keep neighboring signal spectra from overlapping. (Overlapping signal spectra cause interchannel cross-talk; in other words, interference among the signals at the optical receiver.) Figure 2.4(a)

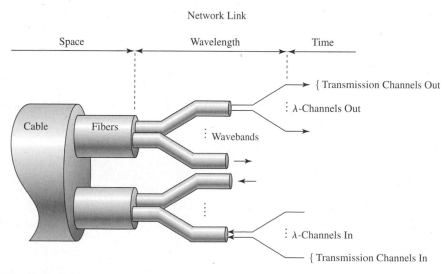

FIGURE 2.3 Fiber resources.

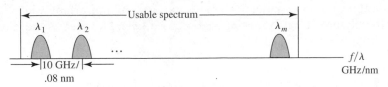

(a) λ-channel Spacing for Separability at Receivers

(b) λ-channel Spacing for Separability at Network Nodes

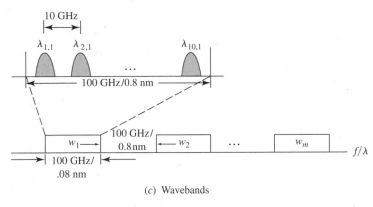

(c) Wavebands

FIGURE 2.4 Wavelength and waveband partitioning of the optical spectrum.

shows an example of a WDM wavelength assignment, in which the λ-channels are spaced 10 GHz apart in optical frequency.

Note that an optical wavelength scale is also shown, because wavelength is often used in specifying optical components. Because wavelength λ and frequency f are related by $f\lambda = c$, where c is the velocity of light in the medium, we have the relation

$$\Delta f \approx -\frac{(c\Delta\lambda)}{\lambda^2} \tag{2.1}$$

between small changes in frequency Δf and wavelength $\Delta\lambda$. This gives a correspondence between wavelength and frequency intervals of 100 GHz ≈ 0.8 nm in the range of 1,550 nm, where most modern lightwave networks operate.[3]

The total bandwidth of each channel (i.e., the optical bandwidth occupied by the modulated laser signal) is shown (see Figure 2.4, shaded areas) to be somewhat less

---

[3] This is the region of minimum attenuation in an optical fiber.

than the frequency spacing in order to leave sufficient "guard bands" to allow for imprecision and drift in laser transmitter tuning and to make it possible to separate adjacent signals at the receivers with reasonably simple receiving equipment (see Chapter 4). The 10-GHz channel spacing shown in this example is sufficient to accommodate λ-channels carrying aggregate digital bitrates on the order of 1 Gbps, or occupying analog bandwidths on the order of 1 GHz.[4] Efficient use of channels with this much capacity frequently requires sharing one λ-channel among several lower rate transmission channels. A common way of doing this is by time–division multiplexing/multiple access techniques, indicated by the time dimension in Figure 2.3 (see Section 3.2.1).

The 10-GHz channel spacing shown in Figure 2.4(a) is very dense by current standards, but it would be feasible for accommodating many high-capacity λ-channels on a single network link, given the characteristics of typical optical transceivers. However, we must also anticipate the limitations of the ONNs because they have the job of routing each optical connection on a specified path through the network. Recall that in networks containing optical switching nodes, several λ-channels may be multiplexed on each fiber, with each routed selectively on a different path based on its wavelength. To accomplish this the nodes must have the capability to "recognize" each λ-channel on an incoming fiber independently and to direct it to a specified output fiber. This is referred to as *wavelength-selective routing* or simply *wavelength routing*.

Now the characteristics of current optical node technology (see Chapter 4) suggest that the relatively close channel spacings that can be resolved by optical receivers (e.g., 10 GHz) are much too close to permit independent wavelength routing of each channel at the network nodes.[5] In fact, in today's switched multiwavelength networks the λ-channel spacings are typically more than 100 GHz. Thus there is an order of magnitude mismatch between the spacings required in the λ-channel layer and the optical path layer. A wider spacing of the λ-channels to 100 GHz, permitting individual wavelengths to be routed independently, is shown in Figure 2.4(b). Note that this reduces the channel density and hence the fiber throughput by a factor of ten.

Such a loss of throughput is certainly to be avoided if possible. A brute force (and costly) way of solving this problem would be to refine the switching node technology to produce an order of magnitude improvement in its resolution. A less costly approach, and one that partially circumvents the problem, is shown in the two-tiered spectrum partition in Figure 2.4(c). Here we define a waveband as the smallest segment of the spectrum that is resolvable in the node (i.e., in the optical path), in contrast to the λ-channel, which is the smallest unit resolvable in the access station by a

---

[4] In the digital case this represents a modulation efficiency of 0.1 bps/Hz, which is poor for electronic systems, but state-of-the-art for optical systems.

[5] One reason for this is that many nodes may be traversed on a long optical path. At each node the imperfections in signal resolution (optical filtering) for closely spaced channels result in signal attenuation, distortion, and switch cross-talk, which accumulate along the path.

tunable receiver.[6] Below the plot of λ-channels in Figure 2.4(c) is another plot showing a coarser partition of the spectrum into wavebands.

In this example we show wavebands with a width of 100 GHz placed at intervals of 200 GHz (i.e., separated by guard bands of 100 GHz). Wavebands with this width and separation are resolvable by waveband-selective optical nodes without pushing the current state-of-the-art; that is, each waveband can be recognized and switched (routed) independently at each network node without introducing excessive signal impairment. Each of these wavebands has enough capacity to support many individual λ-channels. (Ten are shown in the figure.) This second partition of the spectrum requires positioning of wavebands in the optical layer as shown in Figure 2.1(a). Now the waveband carries an optical path and the optical/waveband path may carry several λ-channels. Several wavebands may now be multiplexed on each fiber (waveband multiplexing) and several λ-channels may be multiplexed on each waveband (wavelength multiplexing). The resultant space–waveband–wavelength multiplexing is indicated schematically in Figure 2.3.

In subsequent chapters we discuss both the one-tiered and two-tiered approach to spectrum partitioning. Clearly, the partitions of Figure 2.4(a) and (b) can be considered special cases of Figure 2.4(c). If the sparse spacing of Figure 2.4(b) is used to allow each λ-channel to be switched individually, this corresponds to an *m*-waveband system with one λ-channel per waveband. If the dense spacing of Figure 2.4(a) is used to achieve higher throughput, with channels spaced so close that they cannot be switched individually, then we have a single-waveband network. (Of course, the distinction between the two cases depends on the characteristics of the network nodes. If the nodes have *no* waveband selectivity then *any* spectrum spacing is equivalent to a single-waveband partition.) To simplify the terminology, from now on we refer to networks using the spacing of Figure 2.4(b) as *wavelength-routed networks*, and those using the spacing of Figure 2.4(c) as *waveband-routed networks*. A more graphic depiction of the three alternatives in spectrum partitioning and their influence on network operation is shown in Figure 2.5.

A multiwavelength network with λ-channels on m wavelengths, $\lambda_1, \lambda_2, \ldots \lambda_m$, spaced far enough apart to be switched independently (a wavelength-routed network), can be envisioned as m copies of one network, each with the same physical topology, as shown in Figure 2.5(b). An optical connection between a pair of stations runs on an optical path laid out on the copy of the network corresponding to the connection's assigned λ-channel. The layers of the figure illustrate nicely the concept of *wavelength continuity:* A signal generated at a given wavelength must remain on that wavelength (i.e., on the corresponding copy of the network) from source to destination.[7] If the wavelength spacing is so close that wavelength-selective switching is impossible (the single-waveband case), all λ-channels are forced to share a single

---

[6] We assume a simple, direct detection receiver; in other words, a photodetector possibly preceded by a tunable optical filter, which can select and detect the instantaneous power in any desired λ-channel (see Section 2.4.2).

[7] An exception to this occurs in networks containing wavelength interchangers (see Section 2.3.3).

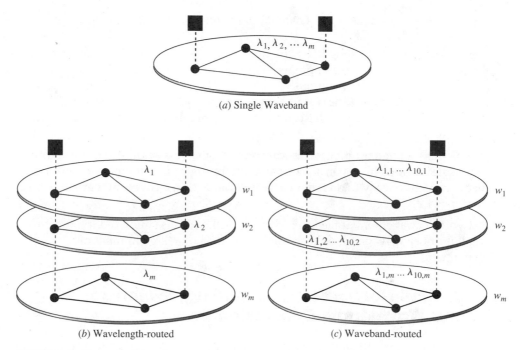

(*a*) Single Waveband

(*b*) Wavelength-routed   (*c*) Waveband-routed

FIGURE 2.5 Network picture based on spectrum partitioning.

copy of the network—see Figure 2.5(a). Finally, if a two-tiered partitioning is used, then we have a waveband-routed network, in which there are as many copies of the network as there are wavebands, and several (in this case ten) λ-channels share each copy of the network, as in Figure 2.5(c).

How do these approaches compare? Using the numbers in the example of Figure 2.4, we find that the *wavelength*-routed case has a fiber throughput reduced by a factor of ten compared with the single-waveband case. This is the price paid for being able to route each λ-channel independently. The *waveband*-routed case is a compromise between the two extremes of complete wavelength routing and none at all. The example of Figure 2.4(c) uses ten λ-channels in each waveband for an aggregate capacity five times that of the wavelength-routed case and one half of the single-waveband case. (The same effect would be achieved if the ten λ-channels were replaced by a single very high speed λ-channel operating in the range of 10 Gbps.) As shown in Section 3.4, waveband routing imposes some special routing constraints not present in wavelength-routed networks. The constraints are due to the fact that all λ-channels sharing a common waveband are forced to "stick together" on the same optical path.[8] These partially offset the throughput gains produced by waveband routing.

---

[8] The constraints on waveband routing of groups of λ-channels within the same waveband are identical to those affecting wavelength routing of groups of time–division multiplexed channels carried on the same wavelength.

The coarse/fine (waveband/λ-channel) partition has the following advantages:

1. Regardless of the wavelength density on the fiber, it is less costly to switch/route the optical signals as a small number of aggregated groups of channels, with each group contained in a continuous waveband, rather than as a large number of individual λ-channels. (The cost of a wavelength-selective switch typically increases at least linearly with the number of segments of the spectrum it switches independently.)

2. In many cases (e.g., multipoint optical connections), it is actually desired to route a "bundle" of λ-channels on a common path through the network—something that is especially easy to do if these channels lie within a common waveband (see Section 3.4.2).

3. Network management at the level of the optical nodes is simplified if there are a small number wavebands to keep track of instead of a large number of λ-channels.[9]

2.3 Optical Network Nodes: Routing, Switching, and Wavelength Conversion

The functions of the optical path layer (establishing paths for the optical signals) are implemented in the ONNs. Therefore, the more functionality these nodes have, the more flexible is the network in reacting to fluctuating user demand, changing loads, and equipment problems, and the better it will perform under all types of conditions. One way of viewing functionality is in terms of the way various degrees of freedom (or *dimensions*) are exploited. Most networks make use of the space dimension by assigning different signals to different fibers. Through multiplexing, multiwavelength networks make use of the wavelength dimension and perhaps the time dimension if time–division multiplexing is used. However, the amount of "mileage" obtained from the various dimensions depends on what happens to the multiplexed signals as they pass through the network nodes. In this section we examine the basic types of node functionality, classified in increasing order of complexity as follows:

- Static nodes
    - Directional couplers (including signal combiners, splitters, and star couplers)
    - Static routers (including waveband multiplexers and demultiplexers)
- Dynamic (switching) nodes
    - Permutation switches

---

[9] This is analogous to the management advantages in traditional telephone networks, accruing from the use of digital cross-connect systems (DCSs) for provisioning a high-bandwidth digital infrastructure. In this case the DCS switches bitstreams in highly aggregated units (e.g., 45 Mbps or higher) rather than switching each telephone trunk individually.

– Generalized switches
– Linear divider–combiners (LDCs)
– Waveband–space switches
– Waveband–space–time switches
– Wavelength interchanging switches

2.3.1 Static Nodes

Figure 2.6 illustrates three simple optical network topologies with nodes (shown as circles) that are comprised solely of static devices. (These structures are suitable mainly for LANs and MANs.) In each, the physical topology is in the form of a tree. This means

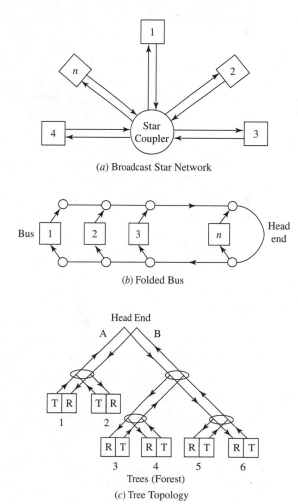

(a) Broadcast Star Network

(b) Folded Bus

(c) Tree Topology

FIGURE 2.6 Tree physical topologies.

that no alternate paths are available for optical path routing, so that the role of the nodes is relatively limited. In each case we assume that the node serves to combine and/or divide (split) signal power without any wavelength selectivity, so that signals propagate through the network in the direction of the arrows. (In the figure each unidirectional fiber is shown individually with an arrow that indicates its direction of propagation.) Thus in the *broadcast star network* of Figure 2.6(a), n access stations are joined by access links to a single node, which is an $n \times n$ *star coupler*, combining all n inbound signals and broadcasting them on each outbound access fiber.

In the *folded bus* shown in Figure 2.6(b), optical power from each station is coupled onto the upper bus through a 2×1 combiner. The transmitted signals from the n access stations propagate to the right, so that a combination of all signals appears at the head end and is then distributed from the lower end of the bus, through 1×2 dividers (optical taps) to the receivers in the stations. The network of Figure 2.6(c) contains six stations joined in a tree topology. Signals from the set $\{1, 2\}$ are combined and then multicast to the set $\{3, 4, 5, 6\}$ and those from the set $\{3, 4, 5, 6\}$ are combined and multicast to the set $\{1, 2\}$. Because there are two fiber–disjoint trees here carrying signals in opposite directions, it is possible to run signals in both directions reusing the same wavelengths without causing any interference between them. This is a rudimentary illustration of how the fiber topology can help or hinder the reuse of the optical spectrum. (Spectrum reuse is not possible in the star and bus topologies of Figures 2.6[a] and [b].) The star and bus will be of special interest to us later. Note that if there is no wavelength selectivity in the nodes, the two networks are functionally the same. Each is a broadcast network that can potentially support $n(n-1)$ unidirectional point-to-point connections among the n stations (not counting connections from a station back to itself). (However, the star is more efficient than the bus in conserving signal power—see Problem 4.)

2.3.1.1 Directional Couplers

Each of the nodes in the previous examples can be built using one or more 2×2 *directional couplers*. A 2×2 directional coupler, is an optical four-port, which we represent as shown in Figure 2.7, with ports 1 and 2 designated as input ports and $1'$ and $2'$ designated as output ports.[10] Optical power enters the coupler through fibers attached to the input ports, is combined and divided linearly, and leaves via fibers attached to the two output ports. Provided that the signals entering each input port originate at *distinct optical sources*,[11] the action of the coupler can be expressed in terms

---

[10] By designating certain ports as inputs and others as outputs we imply that the power propagates in the indicated directions only, a condition that depends on the internal characteristics of the coupler as well as the external network to which it is connected. (See Section 4.9.2 for a more complete description of multiport devices in terms of incident and reflected waves.)

[11] This ensures that the optical fields of signals interacting with each other in the coupler are not coherently related, so their relative phases and polarizations can be ignored. In this case, the operation of the device can be expressed as an input/output power relation, which does not depend on the specific relations among the fields.

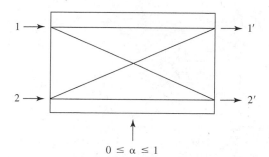

FIGURE 2.7 Directional coupler.

$0 \leq \alpha \leq 1$

of input signal powers P_1 and P_2, and output powers $P_{1'}$ and $P_{2'}$. The power relations are given by

$$P_{1'} = a_{11} P_1 + a_{12} P_2$$
$$P_{2'} = a_{21} P_1 + a_{22} P_2$$

(2.2)

For ideal symmetric couplers, the *power transfer matrix* $A = [a_{ij}]$ is of the form

$$A = \begin{bmatrix} (1-\alpha) & \alpha \\ \alpha & (1-\alpha) \end{bmatrix}$$

(2.3)

where the parameter α may take on any value between 0 and 1. As defined in Equation 2.3, this is a *passive and lossless device,* meaning that power is conserved for the signals passing through it. If the parameter α is fixed, we call it a *static device.* If α can be varied through some external control (for example, electronic or mechanical), then the device is *dynamic* or *controllable.* Now suppose, for example, that $\alpha = 1/2$ (fixed). If signals are present at both inputs, the device acts as a 2 × 2 star coupler—see the $n = 2$ case of Figure 2.6(a).

If we set $P_2 = 0$, it acts as a power divider—as used on the lower bus in Figure 2.6(b), and if we use only output port 1', terminating port 2' with an (absorbing) dummy load, it acts as a combiner—as used on the upper bus in Figure 2.6(b). In the latter case it is important to observe that even if the coupler is lossless, there is an inevitable *combining loss* (dissipated in the dummy load).

In reality, all physical devices are lossy. In a lossy 2 × 2 directional coupler, for example, $a_{11} + a_{21} < 1$ and $a_{12} + a_{22} < 1$, indicating the presence of excess losses due to device imperfections. Excess losses are to be distinguished from combining losses, which are inevitable, even in ideal devices.

Other more elaborate types of static nodes can be constructed by interconnecting 2 × 2 couplers. For example, Figure 2.8 shows a 16 × 16 star coupler built using an array of 32 2 × 2 star couplers arranged in a Banyan structure [Hui90, p. 99]. A setting of $\alpha = 1/2$ is used for each coupler. (If each 2 × 2 is lossless then the complete 16 × 16 system will be lossless.)

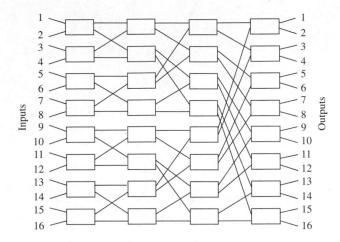

FIGURE 2.8 A 16 × 16 star coupler.

In the dynamic case, an ideal directional coupler would be fully controllable through the range $\alpha = 0$ (the *bar state*) to $\alpha = 1$ (the *cross state*). Controllable directional couplers are used commonly as building blocks for optical switches, using only the bar and cross states, and thus acting as binary switching devices [Hinton93] (see Section 2.3.2.1). If both input/output ports are used, they act to permute the two inputs between the two output ports. If only a single input/output port is used, the device acts as a simple on–off switch. But the directional coupler is also useful as a building block for more complex network nodes, in which α is used as a continuously variable parameter. For example, using only ports 1 and 1', the device becomes a variable attenuator.

The power transfer relations introduced in Equation 2.2 generalize naturally to larger numbers of ports and to waveband selective configurations. For an $r \times n$ multiport device operating on m wavebands, they can be written in the form

$$P'(w_k) = A(w_k)P(w_k), \quad k = 1, 2, \ldots, m \tag{2.4}$$

where A is an $n \times r$ power transfer matrix, $P(w_k)$ is a column vector of r input powers, and $P'(w_k)$ is a column vector of n output powers. The waveband argument indicates that power is specified as a function of waveband. The element, $a_{ij}(w_k)$, of $A(w_k)$ represents the power-transfer ratio from input port j to output port i valid for waveband w_k.[12] As in the 2 × 2 case, the elements of a general power-transfer matrix may be either static or controllable. In the latter case, the matrix represents a waveband-selective switch (see Section 2.3.2.4).

---

[12] By using a discrete set of wavebands, it is implied that the multiport operates uniformly on all signal frequencies within each waveband.

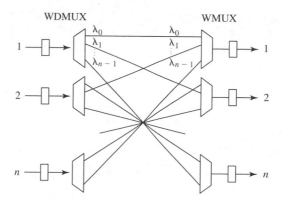

FIGURE 2.9 Static routing node.

2.3.1.2 Static Routers

A serious defect of the broadcast star in Figure 2.6(a) is that without waveband or wavelength selectivity, all signals entering the star coupler are combined on all outbound fibers. This limits the total throughput to the usable capacity of a single fiber, thereby reducing the capacity available to any one station by a factor of $1/n$. One way of improving the throughput of this network is by replacing the star coupler with a static routing node.

Figure 2.9 shows a static router with n input and n output fibers, each carrying up to n distinct λ-channels, with wavelengths chosen from a set $\Lambda = \{\lambda_0, \lambda_1, \ldots, \lambda_{n-1}\}$. (For simplicity we discuss this device in the context of wave*length* routing, but the discussion can be transposed to the wave*band* routing domain by replacing wavelength with waveband throughout. In spectral partitions with one λ-channel per waveband the two terms are equivalent.) Each input fiber is connected to a $1 \times n$ wavelength demultiplexer (WDMUX), which spatially separates the wavelengths on the fiber. Similarly, each output fiber is connected to an $n \times 1$ wavelength multiplexer (WMUX), which is identical to the demultiplexer but is used in the opposite direction of signal flow, that combines the different wavelengths onto that fiber. We assume that a fiber has a capacity of n λ-channels. The wavelengths are assumed to be individually recognizable by the demultiplexer, so that this is a wave*length*-routed network. (We consider the whole "fabric" of WDMUXs, WMUXs, and their interconnecting fibers as contained in a single "black box"; that is, they act as a single node.)

There are n^2 fibers between the input and output stages, connected in a way that prevents identical wavelengths from different input ports from being combined on the same output port, thus avoiding interference among the different channels. The physical path that a signal takes through the node is determined uniquely by its wavelength and port, with the routing rule as follows: A signal on input port j, carried on wavelength λ_k, is routed to output port i, where $k = (i - j) \bmod n$. For example in a 4×4 network, a signal entering on port 2, to be routed to output port 1,

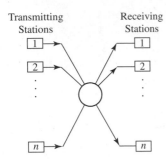

Transmitting
Stations

Receiving
Stations

FIGURE 2.10 Directed star.

would use λ_3.[13] Using the matrix notation of Equation 2.4, the power-transfer ratios for the $n \times n$ system using the preceding "arithmetic" routing rule are: $a_{ij}(w_k) = 1$ when $k = (i - j) \bmod n$, and $a_{ij}(w_k) = 0$ otherwise. Note that if input and output ports with the same label correspond to fiber pairs carrying signals in opposite directions in the same link, then the wavelength λ_0 produces loopback connections. Thus, if loopback connections are excluded, only $n - 1$ wavelengths are required for routing.

Multiports with similar but more general wavelength permutation connectivity have been termed Latin routers [Barry+93], after the *Latin square*, an $n \times n$ array where each entry contains one of n numbers with no number appearing in a row or column more than once. The Latin square is equivalent to a power-transfer matrix, A, for a Latin router, where all entries for some number, k, correspond to the 1s in $a_{ij}(w_k)$. The reference [Barry+93] describes some multistage fabrics for general Latin routers.

If it is used in conjunction with tunable transceivers, the static wavelength router functions as a permutation switch (see Section 2.3.2.1). For example, consider the router of Figure 2.9 placed at the center of the *directed star network* of Figure 2.10, replacing the star coupler. (The directed star is similar to the undirected case in Figure 2.6(a) except that the transmitters and receivers have been separated to reflect the fact that they may belong to different access stations.) A connection is established between any transmitter–receiver pair by tuning both transmitter and receiver to the unique wavelength that is routed on a path between the desired input/output ports.[14]

More generally, up to n signals, each at a distinct wavelength in the set Λ, can be routed from each input fiber to each output fiber in this manner. Thus, suppose each transmitting station is equipped with an array of n transmitters each tuned to one of the n wavelengths in Λ, with a similar arrangement of tuned receiver arrays in the receiving stations. Using all transmitters and receivers simultaneously would create full connectivity among all transmitting and receiving stations at maximum

---

[13] Although Figure 2.9 shows a node constructed with bulk components, integrated optic static routers have also been fabricated in the form of arrayed waveguide gratings (see Section 4.9.5).

[14] Another way of making the router function as a permutation switch is by placing wavelength interchangers in the input/output ports, as indicated by the rectangles in Figure 2.9 (see Section 2.3.3).

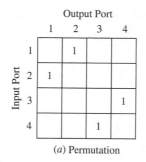
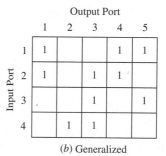

FIGURE 2.11 Space switch connection matrices.

throughput (n^2 fully utilized channels). In this arrangement, the use of the more complex (but static) node architecture together with the transceiver structures that can exploit it allows for an n-fold reuse of the optical spectrum. Compare this with the broadcast star, in which the throughput is limited to n fully utilized channels—the available capacity of a single fiber.

2.3.2 Dynamic Nodes

The simplest dynamic optical node is a space–division switch without any waveband selectivity. This is commonly called an *optical cross-connect* (OXC). It routes the signals on each input port to one or more selected output ports. Space–division switches come in two flavors: *permutation* and *generalized*. In an $n \times n$ permutation space switch, connections between input and output ports are point to point; neither one-to-many nor many-to-one connections are allowed. Thus, the admissible connection patterns are in the form of permutations, as illustrated by the connection matrix in Figure 2.11(a).[15] (A permutation switch is square, and its connection matrix has exactly one, 1, in each row and each column.) The specific connection pattern is selected under external control (i.e., switches are active devices in the sense that an external control agent is present).[16] An $n \times n$ nonblocking permutation switch can create any one-to-one connection pattern, so that it has $n!$ possible input/output patterns or *connection states*. This seems like a lot, but relatively speaking it is not.

A generalized space switch can create any input/output pattern, including one-to-many and many-to-one connections. A connection pattern for a generalized 4×5 switch is illustrated in Figure 2.11(b). (Connections are shown by 1s.) Counting all the possibilities in the case of an $r \times n$ generalized switch, we find 2^{nr} connection

---

[15] Note that the connection matrices in the figure are *transposes* of the corresponding power transfer matrices.

[16] The terms *active* and *passive* are tricky. Unless amplification is present in the signal path, an optical node, or any other device in the network for that matter, is "seen" by the optical signals flowing through it as a *passive* device because no energy is supplied to the signal as it traverses the device. We generally use the term *passive* in that sense. Nevertheless, energy is required for control, so a power source must be present for controllable devices. Hence, controllable (dynamic) devices are often termed *active* in the literature, and static devices are called *passive*.

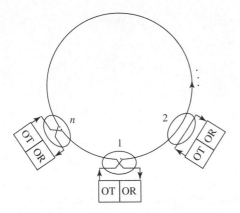

FIGURE 2.12 Unidirectional ring.

states. Because they are capable of creating multipoint as well as point-to-point connections, two additional control possibilities exist in generalized switches. For each one-to-many connection, it is possible to specify how the input power splits among the various outputs, and for each many-to-one connection, the combining ratios among the various input powers can be specified. We call generalized switches that control these power-dividing and -combining ratios linear divider-combiners. Because combining and dividing ratios can take on a continuum of values, LDCs have an infinite number of connection states.

It is important to note that generalized switches have the ability to terminate a connection, thus "dumping" its signal internally (by setting all elements of a row of the power transfer matrix equal to zero), whereas permutation switches do not. Similarly, they have the ability to set the power to zero on any output port (by setting all elements of a column equal to zero), whereas permutation switches do not. The connection termination property has important practical implications, because in a network built around permutation switches, unwanted closed paths may be created inadvertently, causing degradation in network operation.

To illustrate, consider the network in Figure 2.12, which consists of n access stations each containing a pair of OTs and ORs connected to a unidirectional ring via a network node comprised of a 2×2 coupler operating as an add–drop switch. With its coupler in the cross state (the add–drop state), a station is coupled into the ring so that it transmits to the next station on its right, which is in the add–drop state, and it receives from the station to its left, which is also in the add–drop state. With its coupler in the bar state the station is bypassed. Figure 2.12 shows a condition in which station 1 transmits to station n, and n transmits to 1. A problem arises if all couplers are in the bar state. In this case a closed loop exists.

At first glance this would not appear to create a problem. However, in a network with long fiber spans, there would normally be amplifiers in the links. Assuming that the gains are adjusted to compensate for the losses over the links and nodes, we have a ring with a loop gain of unity. Because each amplifier generates some spontaneous emission noise, the gain in the ring will cause the noise power to grow

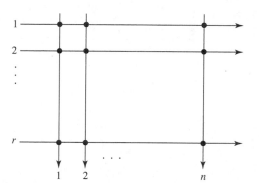

FIGURE 2.13 Cross-bar switch.

without bound (or at least until the amplifiers saturate). Problems of this type have been observed in WDM ring networks, in which closed paths may exist for certain wavelengths, with the amplified noise robbing power from and interfering with signals at other wavelengths. Permutation switches therefore must be interconnected with care!

2.3.2.1 Permutation Switches: Characterization and Complexity

There is a vast amount of literature on switches dating from the early days of telephony.[17] Although technology has progressed from electromechanical to electronic to photonic (optical), the basic structure of the switch "fabric" has remained largely unchanged. One of the simplest structures that is adapted to both permutation and generalized switch operation is the *crossbar*. As shown in Figure 2.13, an $r \times n$ crossbar switch consists of r input lines, n output lines, and rn *cross-points* located at the intersections of the lines. The implementation of the cross-points has progressed from electromechanical relays through electronic gates to controllable optical couplers.

In an $n \times n$ crossbar switch, a permutation connection is made by closing one cross-point in each row and each column. (Multicast connections can be made by closing more than one cross-point in a row.) The main problem with the crossbar, used as an $n \times n$ permutation switch, is that the number of cross-points grows as n^2, which is far more than necessary to create all possible permutation connections. Because optical switching devices are costly, switch fabric realizations with a minimum of these devices are desirable.

A common method of constructing large switch fabrics that are more economical regarding cross-points is through a multistage fabric. A popular configuration is a three-stage arrangement, which can be configured to produce many different types of switches. As we shall see, multistage configurations usually can be realized with far fewer cross-points than the crossbar, especially for large-size switches. Figure 2.14

---

[17] For a good view of developments from classical theory to photonic switching, see [Benes65, Hui90, Hinton93].

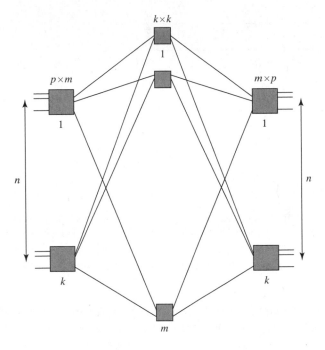

$k \times k$

$p \times m$

$m \times p$

n

n

k

k

m

FIGURE 2.14 Clos switch.

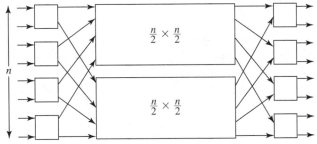

$\frac{n}{2} \times \frac{n}{2}$

$\frac{n}{2} \times \frac{n}{2}$

n

FIGURE 2.15 Recursion for Benes switch.

shows an $n \times n$ symmetric three-stage *Clos network* (see [Hinton93, p. 93]) composed of k $p \times m$ switches in the first stage, m $k \times k$ switches in the middle stage, and k $m \times p$ switches in the third stage, where $n = kp$. One possible way of realizing each of the smaller switches is as a crossbar.

For $n \times n$ permutation switches with n a power of 2, the general Clos structure of Figure 2.14 can be "factored" recursively to produce a *Benes switch fabric*, which is one of the most economical permutation switches in terms of cross-points. The idea is shown in Figure 2.15. In the first factorization we take $p = m = 2$ so that there are two $(n/2) \times (n/2)$ switches in the middle stage, and all first and third stage switches are 2×2. Now, each middle-stage switch can be factored in the same way, and the process repeated until the middle-stage switches are 2×2. The result is an array of 2×2 switches. The Benes switch for the case $n = 8$ is shown in Figure 2.16. It is left as

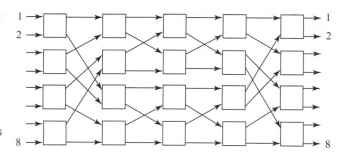

FIGURE 2.16 An 8 × 8 Benes switch.

an exercise for the reader to show that a general $n \times n$ Benes switch can be built using $(n \log_2 n - n/2)$ 2×2 elements.

Multistage switch fabrics such as the Benes, composed of 2×2 elements, are particularly attractive in the optical domain. The reason is that each element (a 2×2 permutation switch) is operated in only two states: the bar and cross states defined in Section 2.3.1.1. Therefore, it can be implemented optically using a controllable directional coupler, with a power transfer matrix of the form of Equation 2.3. Systems composed of arrays of 2×2 directional couplers, operated in various modes, appear frequently in this book. We have already seen an example in the Banyan network of Figure 2.8, in which each element was operated as a (static) star coupler.

The minimum number of binary switching elements required for a permutation switch can be deduced by equating *connection states* to *switch states*. A switch having S connection states requires at least $\log_2 S$ binary switching elements (giving S switch states). Because a permutation switch has $S = n!$ connection states, we find that the minimum number of switching elements for *any* realization using any type of binary devices is $\log_2(n!)$, which (using Sterling's formula) is approximately $(n \log_2 n - 1.44n)$ for large n. Comparing this number with the number of elements required in the Benes switch, we find that the Benes fabric is very close to optimal in its use of hardware.

Characterization of Blocking Permutation switches are classified in terms of their blocking characteristics. In discussing blocking performance, it is assumed that we are considering sequences of demand-assigned connections between input and output ports on the switch, with requests for connection establishment and termination occurring at random points in time. An $n \times n$ switch is "*rearrangeable*" or *rearrangeably nonblocking* if there exists a set of paths through the switch fabric (i.e., a set of switch states) that realizes each of the $n!$ connection states. The term *rearrangeable* comes from the fact that it may be necessary to rearrange currently active connections to support a request for a new connection between a pair of idle input and output ports. Rearrangeable switches have two problems:

1. For any given set of desired connections (any given permutation of inputs to outputs), the required device settings to route connections through the switch are not determined easily.

2. Connections in progress may have to be interrupted momentarily while rerouting is taking place to accommodate new connections.

The good news about rearrangeable switches (of which the Benes is one) is that they can be realized with a minimum amount of device hardware. The price of hardware simplicity is control complexity.[18]

Wide-sense nonblocking networks are those that can realize any connection pattern without rearranging active connections *provided* that the correct rule is used for routing each new connection through the switch fabric. These require more hardware than rearrangeable networks, and still need intelligent routing algorithms, but have the advantage that active connections need not be interrupted.

Strict-sense nonblocking networks require no rearrangement and no complex routing algorithm. New connection requests are allowed to use any free path in the switch. As might be expected, these networks require still more hardware than the wide-sense nonblocking fabrics—this cost being traded for the lack of connection disruption and simplicity of routing.

The Clos network of Figure 2.14 can be constructed to be either wide sense or strictly nonblocking. A necessary condition on the number of middle-stage switches to make the network wide-sense nonblocking is $m = \lfloor 2p - p/k \rfloor$, where $\lfloor x \rfloor$ denotes the largest integer equal to or less than x [Smith+76]. If $k = 2$ then a necessary and sufficient condition to make it wide-sense nonblocking is $m = \lfloor 3n/2 \rfloor$ [Benes65]. A necessary and sufficient condition to make the Clos network strict-sense nonblocking is $m = 2p - 1$. For our purposes, strict-sense nonblocking switches are the simplest and most practical, but not always cost-effective. If the sizes of the switches in its three stages are optimized, it can be shown that a strict-sense nonblocking Clos switch can be realized with approximately $4\sqrt{2}n^{3/2}$ cross-points.

Another way of realizing a strictly nonblocking switch is through *space dilation* of the original Benes fabric. An m-fold space dilation of an $n \times n$ Benes switch is created in the general three-stage form of Figure 2.14. The dilated switch is built using n $1 \times m$ switches in the input stage, n $m \times 1$ switches at the output, and m Benes networks in the middle stage. With $m = \log_2 n$, it turns out that this system, called a *Cantor network*, is strictly nonblocking because a free path through the fabric can always be found for any pair of idle input/output ports via one of the m middle switches. This switch has $O(n[\log_2 n]^2)$ cross-points, which is an improvement over the strictly nonblocking version of the Clos switch for sufficiently large n.

In terms of the number of cross-points required for strictly nonblocking switches, multistage fabrics do not start to become worthwhile until the switch size is fairly large ($n > 32$). However, for rearrangeable or wide-sense nonblocking switches, multiple stages are definitely more economical.

At this point it is worth noting the contrasting features of the traditional and optical network switching requirements. In traditional networks switches often have very

---

[18] See [Hui90, p. 77] for a control algorithm, known as the *looping algorithm*, for the Benes switch.

large numbers of ports, and cross-points (realized electronically) are very inexpensive. Conversely, optical switches are orders of magnitude smaller and their cross-points are orders of magnitude more expensive. Now, in large switches it is possible to take advantage of laws of large numbers to reduce dramatically the hardware complexity of the switch in return for accepting some small blocking probability (meaning that not all possible connection patterns can be realized). Typical telephone switches with n on the order of 10^5 operate with blocking probabilities on the order of 10^{-3} or less. This is not particularly relevant to optical switches however, because their size is more likely to be on the order of ten.

On the other hand in traditional networks, rearrangeable and wide-sense non-blocking switches are rarely used because the computational complexity involved in finding and executing an appropriate routing algorithm is overwhelming for large-size switches and is not worth the savings in switch hardware. In the optical domain, however, switches are small, so that routing complexity for rearrangeable and wide-sense nonblocking switches is reduced. Furthermore, in WDM networks the routing algorithm is used only in the space dimension, so that algorithmic complexity is that required for a single waveband only, whereas the hardware savings are roughly proportional to the number of wavebands being switched. Also, computational speed can be increased by doing computations for all wavebands in parallel. These considerations suggest that it is worth taking a second look at the rearrangeable and wide-sense nonblocking category for optical applications.

Another issue that is important in optical switches is cross-talk. In electromechanical or electronic switches, the cross-points are close to ideal; a switch is either definitely open or closed. In optical switches, the binary elements (controllable couplers) typically used as cross-points may have as much as a 5% cross-state "leakage" when they are set to the bar state, and vice versa. This necessitates using switch fabrics with special designs involving extra binary elements to reduce cross-talk (see Section 4.11.1). Thus, a minimum cross-point realization is not always the best.

An Example of a Wide-Sense Nonblocking 3 × 3 Switch   Figure 2.17 shows an example of a 3 × 3 wide-sense nonblocking permutation switch built using four controllable directional couplers, operating as binary switching devices [Ellinas+97]. A rearrangeably nonblocking switch requires at least three binary elements so that this is an economical realization. The switch has six possible connection states, and 16 switch states. Table 2.1 lists the correspondence between connection states and switch states for the fabric of Figure 2.17, where 0 and 1 are used to designate the bar and cross states respectively. For example, the connection from input 1 to output

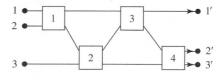

FIGURE 2.17   A 3 × 3 wide-sense nonblocking switch.

TABLE 2.1 Wide-Sense Nonblocking Switch States

Connection state	Switch state	Switch state	Forbidden state
a (11 22 33)	A (0101)	A' (1010)	A'' (0000)
b (11 23 32)	B (1011)	B' (0100)	B'' (0001)
c (13 22 31)	C (1110)	C' (0111)	—
d (12 21 33)	D (1101)	D' (0010)	D'' (1000)
e (12 23 31)	E (1111)	E' (0110)	—
f (13 32 21)	F (1100)	F' (0011)	F'' (1001)

$1'$, 2 to $2'$, and 3 to output $3'$ is denoted as connection state $a = \{(11), (22), (33)\}$. The switch state with switches 1 and 3 in the bar state, and 2 and 4 in the cross state is denoted as (0101). Thus, connection state a corresponds to three possible switch states: $A = (0101)$, $A' = (1010)$ and $A'' = (0000)$.

With all three connections active, a state transition cannot occur unless at least two of the connections are terminated. Thus there are only three possible ways for a connection transition to occur while one connection remains active and unchanged. Because connection state transitions must be made without disturbing active connections, the 2×2 switches carrying any unchanged connection are not allowed to change state during a transition. This means that certain switch states are forbidden. For example, Table 2.1 lists A'' as forbidden because it is impossible to make a transition from this state to another state while connection (22) remains unchanged without disturbing that connection. (The existence of forbidden states is proof that this switch is not strictly nonblocking.) Figure 2.18 shows a state transition diagram for this switch comprising the 12 usable states. Note that there are two switch states corresponding to each connection state, with one or the other being used depending on the way in which the system reached that state. Thus, for example, if the current switch state is A and the next connection state is b, then the next switch state is B', which is reached from A by changing switch 4 from cross to bar.

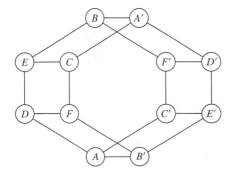

FIGURE 2.18 State transition diagram for a 3×3 switch.

2.3.2.2 Generalized Switches

Because the number of connection states of a generalized $r \times n$ switch is 2^{nr}, it is clear that we need at least nr binary elements to realize it. This is the number of cross-points used in the traditional crossbar switch, and one way of realizing generalized optical switches is through an optical version of the crossbar.

Figure 2.19 shows one possible realization [Sharony94]. It consists of three stages, the first and third of which are static and the middle stage is controllable. Stage 1 consists of an array of r $1 \times n$ signal dividers (splitters), and stage 3 is a similar array of n $r \times 1$ signal combiners (which could be realized with the same type of hardware, used in the opposite direction of signal flow). The middle stage consists of rn binary on–off switches, which could be realized, for example, using the 2×2 coupler of Figure 2.7. Any generalized connection pattern of the type shown in Figure 2.11(b) can be created by turning on a middle-stage switch for each 1 entry in the connection matrix. Assuming that the splitting (combining) stages produce equal splitting (combining) ratios for each signal, this switch will produce an input/output power relation in the form

$$P' = AP \tag{2.5}$$

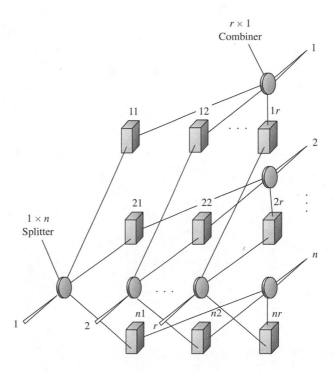

FIGURE 2.19 Generalized optical switch.

where P and P' are vectors of input and output powers respectively, and the elements of the $n \times r$ power transfer matrix A are

$$a_{ij} = \begin{cases} 1/nr & \text{if switch } ij \text{ is on} \\ 0 & \text{otherwise} \end{cases} \tag{2.6}$$

2.3.2.3 Linear Divider–Combiners

Although the crossbar is an extremely simple configuration, it has the disadvantage that the two passive stages produce a combined signal attenuation (splitting loss followed by combining loss) of $1/rn$. A different approach, which has less inherent loss, and at the same time offers complete generality in setting combining and dividing ratios is shown in Figure 2.20. We call this a δ–σ LDC. It consists of a power dividing stage followed by a power combining stage, both of which are controllable.

A 4×4 example is shown in Figure 2.20(a). It has a two-stage power dividing network fed by four input fibers followed by a combining network (the reverse of the dividing network), connected to four output fibers. Each box in the figure represents a 2×2 controllable coupler operated as a continuously adjustable power divider or combiner. This structure generalizes in a straightforward way to an $r \times n$ LDC—as shown schematically in Figure 2.20(b)—that requires a total of $[r(n-1) + n(r-1)]$ couplers. If we denote by δ_{ij} the fraction of power from input port j directed by its divider to the combiner for output port i', and denote by σ_{ij} the fraction of power received from the divider serving input port j and combined onto output port i', then the elements of the power transfer matrix for this LDC are given by

$$a_{ij} = \delta_{ij}\sigma_{ij} \tag{2.7}$$

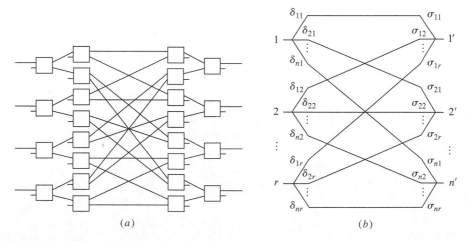

FIGURE 2.20 δ–σ Linear divider–combiner.

The dividing and combining ratios are varied by setting the coupler states appropriately. In the ideal case of lossless couplers, the ratios are subject to the physical constraints

$$\sum_i \delta_{ij} = 1 \tag{2.8}$$

and

$$\sum_i \sigma_{ij} = 1 \tag{2.9}$$

Within these constraints, arbitrary combinations of inbound signals at the node can be directed to each outbound fiber. For example, if the coupling state for each 2×2 coupler in Figure 2.20(a) is set at 0.5, the LDC operates as a 4×4 star coupler, with $a_{ij} = 1/16$ for all i and j. If each 2×2 coupler is used only in a binary (bar/cross) state, the system operates as a permutation switch. Note that any input signal can be "dumped" (i.e., absorbed in the switch) by directing it to an ouput port with a combining ratio that is set to zero. For example, a signal at input port i can be terminated by setting $\delta_{ik} = 1$ and $\sigma_{ik} = 0$. Similarly, the power at output port j' can be set to zero by letting $\delta_{kj} = 0$ and $\sigma_{kj} = 1$.

Note that the crossbar of Figure 2.19 can be converted to an LDC by making the dividing and combining ratios in Equation 2.6 more general. If the on–off switches are replaced by continuously variable attenuators, the elements of the power transfer matrix become $a_{ij} = \alpha_{ij}/nr$, where α_{ij} is the transmission constant for the ijth attenuator in the crossbar. The only functional difference between this and the δ–σ configuration is that the constraints on a_{ij} given in Equations 2.7, 2.8, and 2.9 are replaced by

$$0 \leq a_{ij} \leq 1/nr \tag{2.10}$$

These switch fabrics are representative of a very large class of configurations. Many variants are possible for adapting to special situations or for reducing cost. For example, less hardware is needed if full connectivity is not required. Figure 2.21 illustrates a case of a switching node of degree three (connected to three bidirectional links), where loopback connections along the same link are not required. A δ–σ LDC for this node can be realized with six (instead of 12) 2×2 couplers as shown.

As another example, the large controllable component count in the LDC of Figure 2.20 can be reduced, at the cost of additional splitting (combining) loss, by replacing the controllable dividing (combining) stage with a fixed dividing (combining) stage, as is used in the crossbar of Figure 2.19. The elements of the power transfer matrix of an $r \times n$ LDC are then given by

$$a_{ij} = \delta_{ij}/r \tag{2.11}$$

for a fixed combining stage, and

$$a_{ij} = \sigma_{ij}/n \tag{2.12}$$

for a fixed dividing stage.

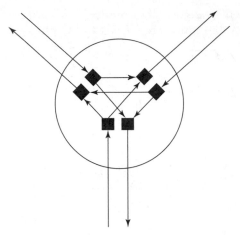

FIGURE 2.21 A node without loopback connections.

Different switch architectures and switch configurations produce different effects on signal power levels at the output ports. For example, considering square switches built from ideal lossless couplers, the Benes switch and the $\delta-\sigma$ LDC are lossless when used as permutation switches, whereas the optical crossbar incurs a loss of $1/n^2$ for any switch configuration. When configured as a broadcast star, however, both the crossbar and the $\delta-\sigma$ LDC produce a $1/n^2$ combining/splitting loss, whereas the Banyan realization (Figure 2.8) produces the minimum possible loss of $1/n$. (The Banyan structure does not, however, contain enough couplers to be used as a nonblocking switch.)

2.3.2.4 Waveband-Space Switches

By adding waveband selectivity in various ways, the basic switch fabrics described earlier can be converted to waveband-selective switches (WSSs). (Recall that any spectral selectivity in our optical switches is assumed to be limited to wave*bands*—the "coarse" subdivisions of the optical spectrum defined in Section 2.2.) In an m-waveband WSS, signals carried on m wavebands drawn from a set $\mathcal{W} = \{w_1, w_2, \ldots, w_m\}$ are multiplexed on each input fiber. An $r \times n$ WSS directs these signals in a waveband-selective manner to the n output ports. Thus, the switch operates on mr inputs. (Although there may be several λ-channels grouped on each waveband, as far as the switch is concerned the waveband is the smallest recognizable entity.) The switching pattern is independently controllable for each waveband.

Figure 2.22 shows one way of realizing a WSS using a three-stage configuration, with the middle stage composed of m switching layers, each one operating on signals in one waveband. The m wavebands on each input fiber are separated spatially into m layers by WDMUXs in the first stage. Each layer is a waveband-independent $n \times n$ space switch, which operates on all signals in one waveband. The space switching can be of any type, from permutation to LDC. The switched signals are recombined on the output fibers by WMUXs in the third stage.

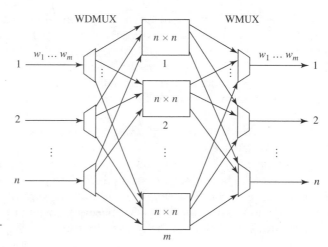

FIGURE 2.22 Three-stage realization of a waveband–space switch.

This realization of a WSS used a combination of fixed (passive) waveband-selective devices (WMUXs and WDMUXs) and dynamic but waveband-insensitive switching devices. A more compact way of realizing the system would be to use waveband-selective or *multiwaveband* switches (MWSs). Waveband-selective directional couplers (i.e., 2×2 MWSs), have been constructed using a variety of technologies, with a capability of independently and simultaneously switching several wavebands under external control. Typical waveband widths and spacings are on the order of a nanometer (see Section 4.9.6). The power transfer matrix for a lossless symmetric 2×2 MWS is of the form of Equation 2.3, where the parameter α is now a function of waveband w. Figure 2.23 shows a 2×2 MWS operating on m wavebands. The switch is set in the cross state for w_i and w_j, and in the bar state for all other wavebands. Each of the space-switching fabrics of Figures 2.16, 2.19, and 2.20 can be converted to an m-waveband WSS simply by replacing each switching device by an MWS operating on m wavebands.

Using the power transfer matrix of Equation 2.4 to represent a permutation switch, $A(w_k)$ is a permutation matrix for each w_k in the set $\mathcal{W}$ whereas in a waveband-selective

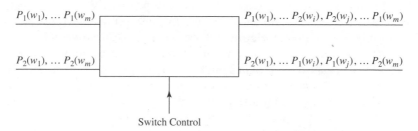

FIGURE 2.23 Multiwaveband directional coupler.

LDC, each element of A may take on a continuum of values. The elements of A will, of course, change in response to external control. Thus, each switch configuration is defined by m independently controllable matrices $A(w_1), A(w_2), \ldots, A(w_m)$—one for each waveband. For example, in the realization of Figure 2.22, the setting of the kth layer of the switch would be identified with $A(w_k)$.

The most commonly used WSSs operate as wavelength-selective permutation switches, which are called *wavelength-selective cross-connects* (WSXCs). For $n \times n$ m-waveband WSSs, there are $(n!)^m$ connection states for the permutation case and $2^{n^2 m}$ connection states in the generalized case. Because mn entities are being switched when the fibers carry m wavebands, one might first think that the permutation or generalized switch should have $(nm)!$ and $2^{(nm)^2}$ connection states respectively. This is not so because of the wavelength continuity constraint: Wavelengths of signals do not change in passing through a WSS, so less switching alternatives exist in the wavelength dimension than in the space dimension.

2.3.2.5 Wavelength–Space–Time Switches

When used as a node in a large circuit-switched network, the WSS described earlier would normally be reconfigured on a relatively slow time scale. For example, dedicated connections used to provision one of the specialized LNs shown in Figure 1.1 might be held for very long periods of time, much like connections through digital cross-connects in traditional networks. For demand-assigned connections, the time scale would be faster—on the order of minutes or hours. For efficient operation in a circuit-switched mode, the time required to establish and terminate each connection (including routing computations, signaling, and switch reconfiguration) should be small compared with the holding time (for example, on the order of seconds for demand-assigned connections). This is no problem using the WSS structures discussed earlier. However, there are other cases when much faster switch reconfiguration time scales are required. For example, consider a wavelength routed network (one λ-channel per waveband), in which each λ-channel entering a switch is carrying several logical channels time–division multiplexed into slots (of microsecond duration) in a fixed periodic time frame (see Section 3.2.1). In this case each time slot is equivalent to a subchannel of the λ-channel.

Now suppose we want to switch the subchannels independently among different space ports on a time slot-by-time slot basis. This requires rapid switching (on a microsecond time scale) to route each time slot independently to a different output port. With proper time slot synchronization among all the entering signals, the switch could be reconfigured to create a different space connection pattern for each wavelength in each time slot, producing switching in three dimensions: a wavelength–space–time switch. Assuming a frame with l time slots, the total number of connection states for an m-wavelength $n \times n$ (permutation) switch would be $(n!)^{lm}$. In a wavelength–space–time switch, the time dimension behaves much like the wavelength dimension: The number of connection states does not grow as rapidly with l (or m) as it does with n. This reflects *time slot continuity* through the switch; in other words, information entering in a particular time slot leaves in the same time slot. As the central node in a star network, this kind of switch is an interesting alternative to the passive star. Using time and wavelength, a set of lm logical connections (one for each time–division subchannel and each λ-channel) can occupy each input port, resulting in a total of lmn independently switched connections using m wavelengths.

Because of time slot continuity, the optical wavelength–space–time switch is not as versatile as its electronic counterpart. In the electronic domain, space–time switches normally use *time slot interchange* (TSI) in addition to space switching. With TSI, the order of the time slots in the frame is permuted as they pass through the switch. This produces more connection states but requires buffering. Photonic implementations of TSI have been proposed, with optical buffering realized using switched-fiber delay lines [Hinton93, p. 117]. However, buffering is an operation that requires complex (read *expensive*) photonic technology, and one that violates signal format transparency. Therefore it is excluded from our discussion of transparent optical networks.

Extending wavelength–space–time switching to a WAN is extraordinarily difficult due to the synchronization problem. In large networks most optical paths have multiple optical hops, so that different propagation delays exist on each path between switches. This requires resynchronization at each node, which (like TSI) requires optical buffering. Thus, while wavelength–space–time switching is an interesting alternative in centralized networks, it will not be explored further here.

2.3.2.6 Cross-talk

The cost–performance trade-offs in each of the switching devices described earlier should not be forgotten. One important performance consideration in a switch is *cross-talk*, which results when some of the power from an input signal leaks through to an unintended output port. (This was one of the transmission impairments listed in Section 1.3 as a downside to transparency.) For example, the directional coupler defined in Equation 2.3 is in the bar state when its control parameter $\alpha = 0$. However, for any real device α can be made close to but not exactly equal to zero. If $\alpha = \epsilon > 0$ when the switch is meant to be in the bar state, we have on port $1'$

$$P_1' = (1 - \epsilon)P_1 + \epsilon P_2 \tag{2.13}$$

where the presence of P_2 (at the same nominal wavelength as P_1) represents undesired leakage of the signal entering on input port 2 to output port $1'$. This leakage constitutes *co-channel heterodyne cross-talk* between the signals entering on the two input ports (see Section 4.8). When a switch is composed of a multistage fabric, as in Figure 2.16, there are many sources of cross-talk on a signal path within one ONN, compounding this problem. Furthermore, when an optical path consists of several hops, the cross-talk accumulates from each optical node along the path. The accumulated cross-talk causes interference at the optical receiver, with a consequent deterioration of the bit error rate (BER) or SNR.

In addition to co-channel heterodyne cross-talk, leakage paths can also cause *co-channel multipath cross-talk*, which occurs when a portion of the signal power leaks through an unintended path within a switch fabric and recombines with the original signal. The recombination may be "downstream" on a parallel path or "upstream" on a feedback path. Multipath cross-talk is more troublesome than heterodyne cross-talk because the recombining optical fields originate from the same source so that phase and polarization relations influence the magnitude of the resultant interference. In waveband–space switches *inter-channel cross-talk* may also be present, either due to imperfect waveband demultiplexing or imperfect operation of multi-waveband switches. These phenomena and means of combatting them are explored in more detail in Chapter 4.

The main point to be observed here is that cross-talk effects increase with the size of a switch, the number and packing density of the wavebands, and the imperfections in the basic building blocks. As shown in Chapter 4, it is possible to offset some of the cross-talk effects due to imperfect components by using more complex switch architectures. However these require a higher component count, and therefore an increased cost. Herein lies a basic three-way cost–performance trade-off: Large-size switches that handle many densely packed wavebands are desirable for increasing optical network connectivity and throughput, but require high-quality (and hence expensive) component technology and/or a high component count for satisfactory performance.

Another cost–performance issue stems from the relation between component count and switch functionality (closely related to switch states). The component count is $O(n \log n)$ for $n \times n$ rearrangeable switches, and increases as we go to wide-sense nonblocking, strictly nonblocking, and generalized switches, and LDCs. The more switch states, the larger the required component count and/or the more complex the components (i.e., the higher the cost). But, as mentioned at the beginning of this section, switches with a large number of states offer better network performance in terms of throughput, connectivity, flexibility and survivability. These trade-offs between network performance and switch functionality are discussed in more detail in later chapters.

2.3.3 Wavelength Converters

The basic optical transmission channel considered here has been a λ-channel, which was assumed to remain on a fixed wavelength from end to end—a condition called *wavelength continuity*. Here for the first time we introduce the operation of *wavelength conversion*, which violates the wavelength continuity condition.

An ideal wavelength converter is a single input/output device that converts the wavelength of a λ-channel appearing on its input port to a different value at its output port, but otherwise leaves the optical signal unchanged. It is useful to separate wavelength converters into two categories: those based on optical-gating effects and those using wavelength mixing, called *coherent converters*.[19] Optically gated converters typically operate on a single input signal and are not transparent to bitrate and modulation format, whereas the wavelength mixing converters operate transparently on multiple signals within a broad band of wavelengths (see Section 4.10). Because

[19] A third category involves electronic signal processing to achieve the equivalent of wavelength conversion. It is discussed in Section 2.5.

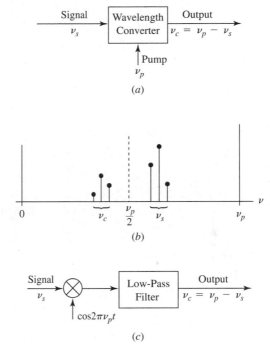

FIGURE 2.24 Wavelength conversion as a linear operation.

of our emphasis on transparency, we only consider the latter category here. Within this category, devices based on four-wave mixing and difference frequency generation (also called *three-wave mixing*) have been demonstrated. Our discussion is confined to difference frequency generation.

An illustration of the operation of a difference frequency generating parametric wavelength converter or *difference frequency converter,* DFC for short [Yoo+95], is shown in Figure 2.24(a). A signal at optical frequency ν_s is applied to the input port and mixed with a pump signal at frequency ν_p. The DFC contains an optical medium that possesses a second-order (square-law) nonlinearity, so that various sum and difference frequencies may be present at the output. If the proper phase-matching conditions are satisfied within the converter, only the difference frequency $\nu_c = \nu_p - \nu_s$ is present. Expressing this in terms of wavelengths, we have $1/\lambda_c = 1/\lambda_p - 1/\lambda_s$. Typical spectral relations are shown in Figure 2.24(b). Here, three input signals are shown in a band at nominal frequency ν_s, and the pump frequency is chosen at slightly less than double the signal frequency. For these frequency relations, the output spectrum is an attenuated mirror image of the input spectrum, reflected about the "mirror frequency" $\nu_p/2$.[20]

---

[20] This means that the spectrum of each input signal is inverted. The inversion is removed by an even number of passes through DFCs. Spectrum inversion can be used to an advantage in compensating for fiber dispersion (see Section 4.3.2.3).

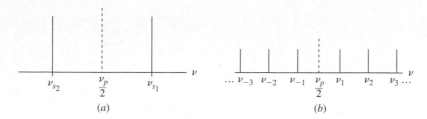

FIGURE 2.25 Wavelength interchanger.

Although the DFC depends on nonlinearity to produce frequency conversion, it can actually be modeled mathematically as a (time-varying) linear device, as shown in Figure 2.24(c). In the model, the input signal is multiplied (modulated) by a sinusoid at the pump frequency, and the product is low-pass filtered to retain only the difference frequency terms. Thus, for all practical purposes, it produces wavelength conversion while exhibiting the transparency we expect of any linear device. The conversion is controllable by varying the pump frequency. If only two input signals are present, and it is desired to interchange their optical frequencies, this can be done by placing the mirror frequency midway between the signal frequencies, producing a *wavelength interchanger* as shown in Figure 2.25(a).

Because the DFC acts as a linear device, it obeys the same conversion rules for superimposed signals as for individual ones; that is, it is a "bulk" conversion device. For example, suppose a set of signals at equally spaced optical frequencies is present at the input of a DFC. Then, by placing the mirror frequency midway between two of the signal frequencies, as shown in Figure 2.25(b), the DFC interchanges signal frequencies in pairs: $\nu_1 \rightarrow \nu_{-1}$, $\nu_{-1} \rightarrow \nu_1$, $\nu_2 \rightarrow \nu_{-2}$, $\nu_{-2} \rightarrow \nu_2$, and so on. It is also possible to use two pump frequencies to produce a more elaborate interchange pattern. (More than two pump frequencies make the device impractical, introducing unwanted converted frequencies that cannot be filtered out.) Two proposed uses of wavelength converters are (1) to be used as components of a wavelength-interchanging switch and (2) to reduce the complexity of photonic switch fabrics.

Wavelength-Interchanging Switches   Wavelength-interchanging switches, also known as wavelength-interchanging cross-connects (WIXCs), do both space switching and wavelength conversion. An example of a 2×2 WIXC is shown in Figure 2.26. Three optical signals are active on the input ports. $S_1(\lambda_1)$ and $S_2(\lambda_2)$ appear on port 1 at the indicated wavelengths, and $S_3(\lambda_1)$ enters on port 2. The switch is shown in the bar state for S_2 and S_3, and in the cross state for S_1. In addition, the wavelength of S_1 has been changed to prevent a wavelength conflict at output port 2′. This example generalizes in a natural way to switches of higher dimension.

An $n \times n$ wavelength-interchanging (permutation) switch operating with m wavelengths carries up to m signals on distinct wavelengths on each input port, and switches them independently and interchanges their wavelengths in any pattern,

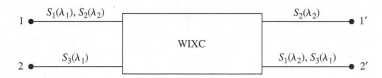

FIGURE 2.26 Wavelength-interchanging switch.

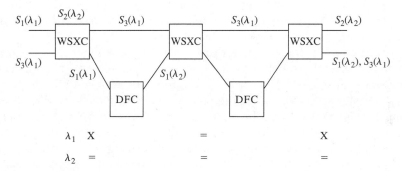

FIGURE 2.27 WIXC implementation.

subject to the constraint that the wavelengths of all signals appearing at a common output port are distinct. This is exactly analogous to an $n \times n$ electronic space–time switch equipped with time slot interchangers, and operating in an m-time slot frame. The number of connection states is $(nm)!$ instead of $(n!)^m$ in the case of a waveband–space switch. The extra states exist because the wavelength converters violate wavelength continuity. This offers an additional degree of freedom to the network node, which may improve network performance (see Chapter 6).

As in other types of optical switches, it is important to find switch architectures for WIXCs, which use costly components sparingly. An architecture that uses a combination of 2×2 WSXCs and difference frequency wavelength interchangers to realize a general WIXC is proposed in [Antoniades+96]. It is based conceptually on a modified Benes structure called a *twisted Benes switch fabric*, with DFCs placed between the stages. Figure 2.27 shows a realization of the 2×2 two-wavelength WIXC in the example of Figure 2.26, implemented using this approach. It requires three WSXCs and two DFCs used as single-wavelength interchangers. The settings of the WSXCs (bar or cross for each wavelength) to produce the signal configuration shown in Figure 2.26 are indicated in Figure 2.27.

The realization procedure yields a general structure for any $n \times n$ m-wavelength WIXC, provided that n and m are powers of 2. For example, a 2×2 four-wavelength WIXC can be built with five 2×2 wavelength selective switches and four four-wavelength interchangers. The general structure, based on the twisted Benes fabric, requires $2\log_2(nm) - 1$ multiwavelength switching stages and $2\log_2(nm) - 2$

wavelength interchanger stages. Because of their relation to the Benes switch, these structures are rearrangeably nonblocking. To add another connection on an idle pair of ports and wavelengths, it may be necessary to rearrange active connections.

One application of WIXCs is to circumvent connection blocking problems associated with the wavelength continuity constraint. Recall that all optical signals multiplexed on the same fiber in a multiwavelength network must be assigned distinct wavelengths so that they can be distinguished at the receivers without interchannel interference. But the wavelength continuity condition sometimes makes it impossible to satisfy the distinct wavelength requirement, resulting in blocked connections. In these cases a WIXC can be used to resolve the conflict.

To illustrate, consider the wavelength-routed network of Figure 2.28(a), operating with two independently routed wavelengths λ_1 and λ_2. Two optical connections are active, with optical signal $S_2(\lambda_2)$ carrying a connection from station 2 to 4 on wavelength λ_2, and signal $S_3(\lambda_1)$ connecting station 3 to 6 on wavelength λ_1. Suppose a new connection is required from 1 to 5. If a wavelength-continuous λ-channel is used for the new connection, neither of the two wavelengths can be assigned to it without causing a conflict. A solution to the problem is shown in Figure 2.28(b). Here, the new connection is carried on signal S_1, with its wavelength changed from λ_1 on the first part of its path to λ_2 on the last part. The central node of the network is the 2×2 WIXC, which was shown previously in isolation in Figure 2.26. The port labels in that figure match the corresponding points in Figure 2.28(b). The applications of WIXCs in more general network settings are discussed in Chapter 6.

Photonic Switch Applications   Two applications of wavelength converters to photonic switches are described next. In each case, the converter, acting as a tunable transmitter, enhances the functionality of a static or dynamic node configuration.

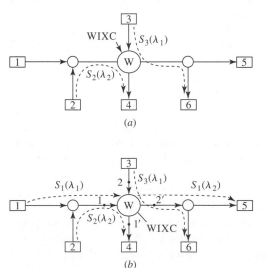

(a)

(b)

FIGURE 2.28 Wavelength-routed network.

Consider the static router shown in Figure 2.9. As described in Section 2.3.1.2, when the router is used as the central node of a star network, it directs source signals to desired destinations based on their wavelengths. If the source stations have tunable transmitters, the combination of transmitter tuning in the stations and wavelength routing in the node produces the effect of a space switch. In this way the wavelength dimension is used to make the static router act like a dynamic device. It is more difficult to achieve this result in topologies more complex than the star because a signal may traverse several routing nodes along its source-to-destination path, with each successive node requiring a different wavelength to route the signal correctly. Because a λ-channel maintains wavelength continuity along its path, it would be impossible to use this technique to route the signal properly through cascaded nodes. The problem can be solved by adding controllable wavelength interchangers to the system. The static router becomes a permutation switch if controllable wavelength interchangers are inserted in its input fibers (see [Alexander+93, p. 729]).

Imagine that the small rectangles preceding the WDMUXs in Figure 2.9 are controllable wavelength interchangers. If each input fiber carries a single λ-channel, the interchanger changes its wavelength λ_i to some other value λ_j, chosen to route the signal to the desired output port. The resultant combination of controllable interchangers and static router thus has the functionality of a space switch. Now suppose that n different λ-channels are present on each input fiber, with their wavelengths chosen from a set of n, recognized and routed by the wavelength router. Then an array of n interchangers is required on each input port, whose function is to permute the wavelengths of the λ-channels to new wavelengths chosen to route each channel to the desired output port. The resultant combination of wavelength interchangers and the wavelength router now acts as a wavelength–space switch. If it is required that the λ-channels leaving the node continue on some arbitrarily specified wavelengths, then a second stage of wavelength conversion may be added on the output fibers, as indicated by the second set of rectangles in Figure 2.9. In that case the overall system functions as a WIXC.

Another application of wavelength interchangers uses the wavelength dimension to improve the functionality of space switches without increasing the amount of optical switching hardware [Sharony94]. As an example, consider the Cantor network described in Section 2.3.2.1. This changes an $n \times n$ Benes network from rearrangeably nonblocking to strictly nonblocking. But the performance improvement is achieved at the expense of a considerable increase in hardware, because $\log_2 n$ identical space layers plus their interconnecting networks are now required instead of one. The same improvement in functionality can be obtained without replicating hardware by exploiting the wavelength dimension. In this case a single Benes switching network is used, with each 2×2 coupler replaced by a 2×2 MWS capable of switching independently each of $m = \log_2 n$ wavelengths in a set Λ. The effect is to create a wavelength–space switch with m wavelength layers. If the source of each input signal is a tunable transmitter, then its signal is tuned to a wavelength in Λ on which a free path exists between the desired source/destination ports. If the input signals have arbitrary wavelengths not under the control of the switching node, then the effect of a tunable transmitter is achieved by including wavelength interchangers at each input port to convert the incoming signal wavelengths to values that correspond to free paths.

What has been done here is to improve the functionality of a system operating originally only in the space dimension (no wavelength multiplexing is used *external* to the switch), by using the wavelength dimension *internal* to the switching node. Wavelengths of signals outside the node are assumed to be arbitrary. This approach to extending well-known space-switching configurations to the wavelength dimension can be applied in a wide variety of switch architectures [Sharony94]. Whether it is advantageous in any particular situation depends on the feasibility and relative cost of replacing one type of hardware with another.

In the context of transparent optical networks, wavelength conversion is currently a controversial issue for at least the following three reasons:

1. Transparent wavelength converters are considerably more difficult and costly to implement than the simple combiners, splitters, switches, and filters we have considered thus far.

2. Nontransparent converters introduce nonlinear effects into the signal path, making it opaque to signal formats.

3. It is not clear whether the performance gains that can be achieved with wavelength conversion are worth the cost.

For these reasons the wavelength converter is considered a last-ditch measure in subsequent chapters, to be used when all else fails.

2.4 Network Access Stations

The functions in the logical connection transmission channel, and λ-channel layers of our network architecture, shown in Figure 2.1, are implemented in the NASs. The NAS uses the services of the optical path layer to provide LC services to end systems or electronic switching equipment attached to its external ports. Thus, the access station is involved in two functions. First, it interfaces the external LC ports to the optical transceivers. Second, it implements (in the transceivers) the functions necessary to move signals between the electronic and optical domains. These functions can become quite complex, especially when the connections are multipoint. In this section we discuss the structure of the NAS, focusing on the functionality required for supporting point-to-point LCs and optical layer signals. Section 3.2.1 deals with the functions specific to multipoint connections: multiplexing, multicast, multiple access, and demultiplexing.

A typical access station is presented in Figure 2.29. The transmitting side consists of a transmission processor (TP) with a number of LC input ports and transmission channel output ports. The output ports of the TP are connected to optical transmitters (OTs), and each transmitter is in turn connected to an outbound access fiber (using a signal combiner or WMUX if there are several transmitters multiplexed on one fiber).

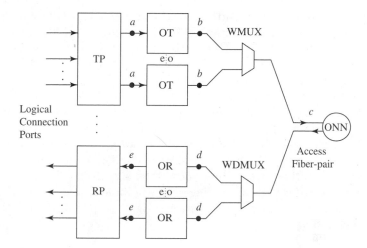

FIGURE 2.29 Network access station.

The function of the TP is to convert each logical signal to a transmission signal in a form suitable for modulating a laser in the OT. In some cases, for example, on-off keying (OOK), where a binary digital signal turns the laser on and off, there is little or no processing. In other cases, the conversion may itself involve a modulation process at a subcarrier level—for example, phase shift keying (PSK) and frequency shift keying (FSK) for digital signals, and AM or FM for analog signals (see Section 5.2.2). These represent a second level of modulation preceding the laser modulation operation. Transmission signals are present at points a in Figure 2.29, and optical signals are generated at points b, with the multiplexed optical signals appearing at c. The TP may also perform a multiplexing function if the data streams from several LCs are to be combined onto a common λ-channel for distribution via an optical multicast connection to several destinations.

Assuming that it is tunable, each OT transmits an optical signal on a wavelength assigned by the network manager. The OTs may be fabricated in the form of an integrated array of fixed tuned lasers multiplexed onto the access fiber. If only one laser in the array is active at a time, this combination acts as a single transmitter, tunable over the set of wavelengths generated by the array. Alternatively, assuming that all wavelengths are distinct, the system might transmit simultaneously on several fixed wavelengths, each carrying its own LC.

On the receiving side, the optical signal arriving on an inbound access fiber is split or wavelength demultiplexed and the resultant signals are passed on to the optical receivers (ORs). They convert the optical power to electrical transmission signals, which are corrupted versions of the original transmitted signals. Additional electronic operations are required in the reception processor (RP) to convert the corrupted transmission signal to a logical signal. For example, digital signals may be regenerated to produce a "clean" logical signal (possibly with some bit errors), and analog signals may be filtered to remove noise, distortion, and interference accumulated in the transmission process. In addition, when several incoming signals are multiplexed on the same access fiber (as in many-to-one connections), the RPs and ORs may implement the receiving side of a multiple access protocol (see Section 3.2.1).

An example of the functions performed by a pair of NASs, A and B, in creating a point-to-point LC is shown in Figure 2.30. An LC, denoted $[A, B]$ in the figure, originates at one of the external input ports of station A. It may be multiplexed in the TP with other LCs entering at other input ports. The LC is carried on a transmission channel (point a), which modulates a laser in the OT, producing an optical signal carried on a λ-channel at wavelength λ_1, appearing at point b. The OT is the point of origin of the optical connection, denoted $(A, B)_{\lambda_1}$, which carries LC $[A, B]$ to station B. If there are other OTs in the station, their signals may be multiplexed together, with the combined signals appearing on the outbound access fiber at point c. This point is the origin of an optical path, denoted $\langle A, B \rangle_{w_1}$ to indicate that the path is carried on waveband w_1.

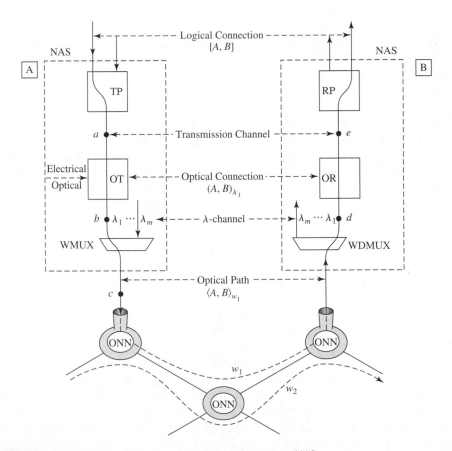

FIGURE 2.30 Example of a logical connection between two NASs.

As shown in Figure 2.30, the optical path traverses three ONNs and terminates on the inbound access fiber of station B. (Another optical path on waveband w_2, with a different source and destination, is shown traversing the same network nodes.) At the entrance to the station, optical connection $(A, B)_{\lambda_1}$ is demultiplexed from any other optical connections that might have entered the station on the same access fiber. The resultant demultiplexed signal (point d) is converted to a transmission channel in the OR, and finally undergoes any required additional electronic operations (e.g., regeneration, demultiplexing) in the RP. The logical connection terminates at one of the output ports of station B.

In the previous example, a single bidirectional pair of access fibers served to connect the access station to a port on an ONN. (Only the transmitting side of station A and the receiving side of station B were shown.) Other configurations might use multiple pairs of access fibers, each one connecting a transmitter–receiver pair to a separate port on a network node, or to separate network nodes. Many variants are possible. An example is provided in Figure 2.31, which shows a wavelength add–drop multiplexer (WADM) attached to an NAS through several fiber pairs. (This is a natural arrangement when the NAS and WADM are co-located.) We have already seen an add–drop switch, in the form of a 2×2 coupler, in Figure 2.12.

The WADM is a direct generalization of that to the multiwavelength case, in which the WADM, operating as a wavelength-selective switch, independently adds and drops each wavelength on a pair of inbound and outbound unidirectional internodal links. The WADM shown in Figure 2.31 has the general three-stage structure of Figure 2.22, modified so that the connections to the NAS are made *inside* the WDMUX and the WMUX. Thus, a separate pair of access fibers is required for each wavelength. One advantage of this configuration is that there is no need for receiver tuning or demultiplexing because only one wavelength reaches each receiver. Other access arrangements adapted to special network applications appear in Section 3.3.2.

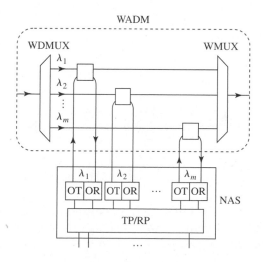

FIGURE 2.31 WADM–NAS combination.

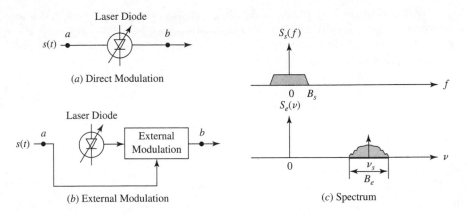

FIGURE 2.32 Optical transmitter.

2.4.1 Transmitting Side

Figure 2.32 shows the details of the modulation process. (The points a and b correspond to similarly labeled points in Figure 2.29.) Two possible OT configurations are shown. In a directly modulated laser diode (see Figure 2.32[a]), the laser drive current is modulated by the transmission signal $s(t)$ appearing at point a, whereas in an externally modulated transmitter, an electro-optic modulator is driven by the modulating waveform $s(t)$ to vary the optical signal emitted by the laser diode. (The mechanisms, advantages, and disadvantages of direct and external modulation are discussed in Section 4.5.2.) The optical field $\mathcal{E}(t)$ of a laser tuned to an optical frequency ν_s can be represented as the real part of a complex signal:

$$\mathcal{E}(t) = Re\left[E(t)e^{j2\pi\nu_s t}\right] \tag{2.14}$$

The *complex envelope* $E(t)$ can be written in the form

$$E(t) = \sqrt{2I(t)}e^{j\varphi(t)} \tag{2.15}$$

where $I(t) = |E(t)|^2/2$ is the instantaneous optical signal intensity (proportional to power P), and $\varphi(t)$ is the instantaneous phase. If the laser is *intensity modulated* by $s(t)$, we have

$$I(t) = I_0[1 + ms(t)] \quad 0 < m \le 1, |s| < 1 \tag{2.16}$$

where I_0 is the intensity of the unmodulated signal and m is the modulation index. The phase φ contains components due to the complexities of the modulation process (pure intensity modulation is not achievable in practice) as well as random phase fluctuations due to the laser itself.[21] If the modulating signal $s(t)$ is restricted to a bandwidth B_s, then s and $\mathcal{E}$ have power spectral densities $S_s(f)$ and $S_e(\nu)$ respectively, as shown in Figure 2.32(c). Note that only the positive frequencies of $S_e(\nu)$ are shown.

Recall that in amplitude modulation (as opposed to intensity modulation), the bandwidth of the modulated signal is just twice that of the baseband modulating signal. However, in intensity modulation of a laser, the bandwidth B_e of the optical field is considerably more than this because of the square root in Equation 2.15 as well as the extraneous phase and frequency modulation represented by $\varphi(t)$.

2.4.2 Receiving Side

There are several common OR structures. The simplest is the direct detection receiver shown in Figure 2.33. In the tunable version shown in Figure 2.33(a), the optical signal is first passed through an optical filter, and is then detected by a photodetector (PD) to produce a photocurrent $i(t)$ at point e. (Points d and e in Figure 2.33 correspond to the same points in Figure 2.29.) The spectrum $S_e(\nu)$ of the input optical field $\mathcal{E}(t)$ and the spectrum $S_i(f)$ of the output photocurrent are shown in Figure 2.33(b). Note that two λ-channels are shown on the access fiber, at optical frequencies ν_1 and ν_2.[22] The receiver is tuned to select the former by appropriately positioning its optical filter transfer function H_{OF}. (Of course, this selection is only possible if the two optical signal spectra do not overlap.)

Ideally the photodetector, acting as a photon counter, produces a photocurrent that is an exact replica of the instantaneous optical intensity impinging on it; in other words, it acts as a square-law detector of the optical field. More precisely,

$$i(t) = RI(t) = \frac{R}{2}|E(t)|^2 \qquad (2.17)$$

where R is the responsivity of the photodetector. Thus, if intensity modulation is used to generate the optical signal $\mathcal{E}(t)$, as in Equation 2.16, this receiver will recover the transmission signal $s(t)$. It is important to note, however, that a direct detection receiver does not recover any phase information, so it cannot be used to recover optical phase- or frequency-modulated signals.[23]

---

[21] The randomness in the lasing process also produces fluctuations in intensity, called *relative intensity noise* (RIN; see Section 4.6.4). The effect of RIN is omitted here.

[22] The set of optical frequencies that reaches the input of a particular receiver depends on the selectivity (if any) of the splitting/WDMUX device in front of it, as well as the waveband selectivity and setting of the network node. Recall that a waveband-selective switching node directs all signal power in a selected waveband to each desired output port. The waveband may contain a set of several closely spaced λ-channels, from which the desired channels must be selected by the receiver.

[23] By appropriately shaping the optical filter transfer function H_{OF}, it is possible to introduce frequency discrimination in front of the photodetector, thereby making it possible to detect frequency-modulated signals. See [Kaminow+87] for an application to frequency shift keying.

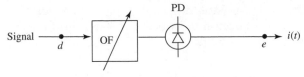

(*a*) Tunable Direct Detection Receiver

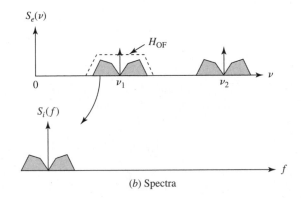

(*b*) Spectra

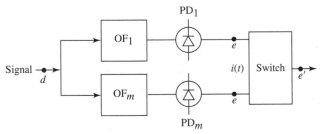

(*c*) Arrayed Receiver

FIGURE 2.33 Optical receivers.

Precision tunable filters (especially widely and rapidly tunable filters) are difficult to fabricate, and hence are costly. Another way of producing the equivalent of receiver tunability is to use an array of m photodetectors, each preceded by a fixed optical filter tuned to a different frequency, as in Figure 2.33(c). Using an $m \times 1$ (electronic) switch, an equivalent receiver tunable over the m filter frequencies is obtained (point e'). Without the switch, the resultant system receives m simultaneous signals (point e).

As indicated, the direct detection receiver normally cannot recover frequency and phase information. Furthermore, it has less than ideal noise discrimination properties. These problems are essentially absent in the coherent heterodyne receiver. In principle, heterodyne detection gives the best possible reception, and is the most versatile. Modeled after the ubiquitous heterodyne radio receiver, the heterodyne approach is

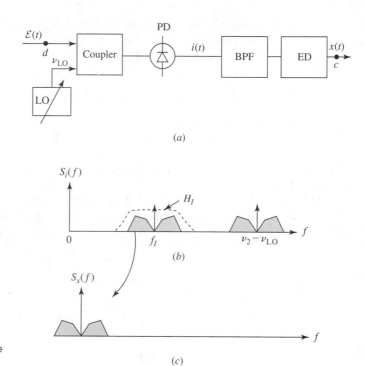

FIGURE 2.34 Heterodyne receiver and spectra.

shown in Figure 2.34. The incoming optical signal $\mathcal{E}(t)$ at frequency ν_s is first combined in a passive coupler with a signal at optical frequency ν_{LO}, generated by a local oscillator, LO (a tunable laser). The combined signal is detected by the photodetector. Because the photodetector behaves as a square-law device, the photocurrent $i(t)$ contains a component at *intermediate frequency* $f_I = \nu_s - \nu_{LO}$, where the local oscillator frequency ν_{LO} is chosen very close to the signal frequency, giving an f_I at a point in the radio frequency spectrum that is chosen for convenience in subsequent electronic signal processing. The signal $i(t)$ is passed through a bandpass filter (BPF) with transfer function H_I centered at f_I, and the resultant filtered signal is detected again by an electrical detector to produce the desired output signal $x(t)$.

Next we show that the heterodyne receiver eliminates the need for a tunable optical filter. Consider the case when the λ-channel at optical frequency ν_1 is to be selected from the pair of incoming optical signals at neighboring frequencies ν_1 and ν_2. Let the combined optical field be

$$\mathcal{E}(t) = Re\left[E_1 e^{j2\pi \nu_1 t} + E_2 e^{j2\pi \nu_2 t} + E_L e^{j2\pi \nu_{LO} t}\right] \tag{2.18}$$

where

$$E_i(t) = |E_i(t)| e^{j\varphi_i(t)} \tag{2.19}$$

and

$$I_i(t) = |E_i(t)|^2/2 \tag{2.20}$$

Now, assuming that the local oscillator is tuned to frequency $\nu_{LO} = \nu_1 - f_I$ and its power is much greater than the incoming signal power, the photocurrent at the output of the detector is approximately

$$i(t) \sim I_L + \sqrt{I_1 I_L}\cos(2\pi f_I t + \varphi_1 - \varphi_L) + \sqrt{I_2 I_L}\cos(2\pi[\nu_2 - \nu_{LO}]t + \varphi_2 - \varphi_L) \qquad (2.21)$$

where low-power terms have been neglected.[24]

The positive frequency spectrum $S_i(f)$ of the photocurrent is shown in Figure 2.34(b). Note that the phase of the desired signal φ_1 is present in the photocurrent of Equation 2.21, so that phase- and frequency-modulated information can be recovered at the receiver.

The bandpass filter selects the signal centered at frequency f_I and rejects the other signal. The final electrical direct detection stage recovers the desired signal $x(t) \sim E_1(t)$ at point e, with the spectrum $S_x(f)$, as shown in Figure 2.34(c).

The heterodyne receiver has three advantages over the direct detection receiver:

1. It has inherently better noise reduction properties producing better SNRs or, equivalently, BERs.

2. It can demodulate all types of optical signals, including those using frequency and phase modulation.

3. It is tunable without requiring a tunable optical filter.

The primary (and significant) disadvantage of this receiver is that it is complex and expensive to build.

2.5 Overlay Processors

As indicated in previous sections, an optical WAN eventually "runs out of steam" if all connections are required to be optically transparent end to end. One reason is that the "reach" of an optical connection is limited by transmission impairments such as noise, dispersion, nonlinear distortion, and optical node cross-talk, all of which accumulate along a transparent path. Even when reach is not the issue, there are many cases when some additional functionality at the optical layer serves to enhance its performance. In all of these situations, it is useful to insert some additional (nonlinear) functionality at the upper edge of the physical layer (in the transmission channel sublayer of Figure 2.1).

In this section we focus on *overlay processors* (OLPs), which we define as network entities that process transmission channel signals electronically,[25] interfacing to the

---

[24] Equation 2.21 is an idealized expression that ignores the effects of inexact polarization alignment, local oscillator phase noise, and other problems in physical realization.

[25] In principle, nonlinear operations on signals can be performed in the optical domain as well, as mentioned in Section 1.3. However, in keeping with the current state-of-the-art, we associate nonlinear signal processing with electronic implementation.

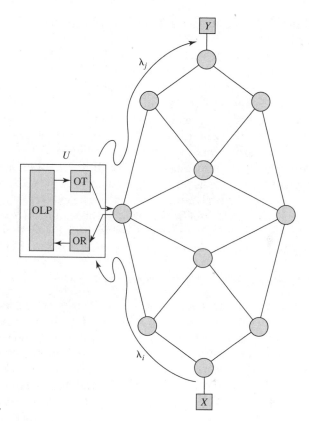

FIGURE 2.35 Overlay processor.

optical transceivers but not to the logical layers. Overlay processing is generally for-mat dependent, so transparency is lost when signals traverse OLPs. A typical station containing an OLP is shown as station U in Figure 2.35. Note that the OLP replaces the TPs and RPs, and has no interface with the outside world. Its purpose is merely to process signals in electronic form at the outputs of the optical receivers, and reinsert the processed signals into the network via the optical transmitters. There are many possible functions for such devices. We provide two examples.

2.5.1 Regeneration

Consider establishing a logical connection between stations X and Y in Figure 2.35, in which the stations are beyond each others' reach in the sense that the quality of the signal would be unacceptable if it were transmitted purely optically from X to Y. A solution to the problem is to relay the signal through station U, which contains an OLP whose function is to *regenerate* the signal so that a clean version of it is reinserted into the network and retransmitted from U to Y. The resultant LC from X to Y is thus carried on two concatenated optical connections. Of course, this is only possible if the transmission channel carrying the signal operates with a well-defined format, say a 1-Gbps digital bitstream carried as a binary intensity-modulated signal.

Assuming that this is the case, the OLP accepts the signal from the OR, detects (reshapes) the bitstream, retimes it, and passes the regenerated version of the signal on to the OT. These are the functions typically performed by a 3R regenerative repeater.[26] Network elements of this type, which combine an optical receiver, some degree of regeneration and an optical transmitter, are called *transponders*. If a transponder transmits on a different wavelength than that of the received signal, it is also performing a wavelength interchange operation as a byproduct of regeneration.

Although there may be some finite BER accompanying this process, the degradation due to bit errors is far less than what would be experienced by trying to extend the purely optical path beyond its reach. The example shown in Figure 2.35 is a unidirectional case. (A bidirectional regenerator requires two transceivers.) More elaborate variants of the regenerator might include processors that support format conversion, error correction, and other signal transformations at the transmission channel level.

2.5.2 Wavelength Interchange

In routing optical connections through a transparent optical layer containing no wavelength interchangers, wavelength continuity is required end to end. Thus, even if two stations are within reach of each other optically, it may be impossible to make a connection between them if no wavelength-continuous optical path is free to support it without interfering with other connections. (An example of this problem was shown in Figure 2.28, for which optical wavelength interchange was presented as a possible solution.) The equivalent result may be obtained by using a wavelength-interchanging OLP.

Referring again to Figure 2.35, suppose a connection is required from station X to Y, but no wavelength-continuous path exists. If paths can be found from X to U and from U to Y, say on wavelengths λ_i and λ_j respectively, then an end-to-end path can be relayed through U using the appropriate wavelengths. First, an optical connection is established from X to U using λ_i and from U to Y using λ_j. This carries an optical signal from X to U, which is converted to electronic form in the receiver of station U, and is passed through the OLP to the OT in the station. The transmitter, tuned to λ_j, places the resultant signal on the optical path to station Y. The function being performed in the station is equivalent to wavelength conversion, but it is accomplished in the electronic domain. Although the operation of the OLP in this case is minimal[27]—simply connecting the receiver and transmitter back to back—the effect on network operation may be substantial.

---

[26] A repeater executing optical reception/retransmission together with the two other operations of reshaping and retiming is called a 3R regenerative repeater. Eliminating retiming results in a 2R repeater, and further eliminating reshaping results in a 1R repeater. The 1R repeater acts as a format-independent OLP.

[27] The OLP may also perform some linear filtering in the case of analog signals, or regenerating in the case of digital signals.

As is shown in Section 6.4, significant enhancement of network performance through reduced connection blocking is sometimes achieved by using wavelength interchange in the optical network. This is a cost-effective way of realizing that function. As in the case of regenerative repeaters, wavelength-interchanging overlays are format dependent, but in return for this dependence they can provide signal regeneration functions as a by-product of the conversion function. (We have already seen that signal regenerators can perform a wavelength-interchange function as a by-product of regeneration.)

In large, geographically dispersed networks, enhancement of optical layer performance can be realized by placing a number of NASs equipped with versatile OLPs at strategic points throughout the network. If these stations contain multiple transceivers, they can act as optical layer "servers" available to provide regeneration, wavelength conversion, and possibly other optical layer enhancement functions to several simultaneous connections. These functions are especially important in cases when two or more isolated and independently managed optical networks are to be concatenated by extending connections from one network to the other. In this case the OLP performing network concatenation would have separate access links to the different networks, and would be controlled jointly by them both.

2.6 Logical Network Overlays

Moving up to the logical layer in the multiwavelength network architecture, there is a wide variety of electronic LN overlays that can be used for implementing various, specialized user services over an optical network. These overlays will themselves have layered architectures. Without entering into the details of the logical network structure, a generic arrangement for a *logically routed network* (LRN) is shown in Figure 2.36. (The rationale for LRNs was explained in some detail in Section 1.5.) The hexagons in the figure are *logical switching nodes* (LSNs), which communicate with each other through logical links, forming a logical topology superimposed on the physical layer. By showing the logical topology as a collection of nodes and links in the logical layer, we simplify the representation of the logical network, concealing unnecessary detail in the supporting optical network.

A blown-up view of a typical LSN appears in Figure 2.36, which shows an electronic logical switch (LS) interfaced to the optical network through an NAS. The LSN may also be interfaced to end systems through ports external to the network. Each logical link is realized as a unidirectional or bidirectional logical connection (see Figure 2.1) between a pair of source and destination access stations, and each LC is in turn carried on an optical connection, routed through the fibers on an optical path. (Typically, the optical path may involve several optical hops.) The logical and physical topologies are independent of each other, with each logical link being embedded in a dedicated path in the physical topology. The logical topology is reconfigurable by changing the optical connections among the supporting NASs. Reconfigurability is possible because the optical infrastructure is *controllable*.

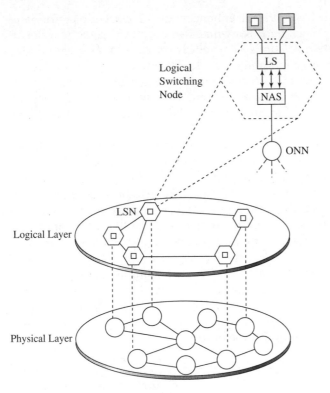

FIGURE 2.36 Logically routed network.

The generic LRN shown in Figure 2.36 may take many specific forms, depending on the structure of the LS. Consistent with current and evolving standards, three important types of LRNs are SONET networks, ATM networks, and IP networks.

2.6.1 SONET Networks

SONET networks are based on transmission links carrying digital synchronous transport signals (STS) at standard rates that range from STS-1 (51.48 Mbps) to STS-48 (2.48832 Gbps) and higher.[28] These signals are supported by corresponding optical carriers, OC-1 to OC-48, which are constructed by scrambling the STS-n signal and converting it to optical form. The basic STS-1 is carried in a 125-μs frame containing transport overhead plus the information payload. Higher rate STS-n signals are

---

[28] In Europe and Asia the North American SONET standard is replaced by a more or less equivalent SDH (synchronous digital hierarchy) standard.

formed by byte-interleaving STS-1s. The frame structure is fairly complex, incorporating overhead for both communications and maintenance functions.[29]

The logical switch in a SONET network is a SONET Digital Cross Connect System (DCS) or add–drop multiplexer (ADM). The DCS and ADM play the same roles in the logical layer that a WSXC and WADM play in the physical layer. In current SONET networks the DCSs are interconnected through internodal point-to-point fiber links carrying OC-n signals, and are connected to local equipment through electronic add–drop ports. The function of a DCS is to demultiplex, switch (route), and remultiplex the signals with which it interfaces. An ADM performs operations similar to a DCS except that the ADM has only two internodal ports, like the WADM of Figure 2.31.

The inter-DCS connections (corresponding to the logical links in Figure 2.36) are operated as dedicated connections, and the signals carried on the internodal links range from STS-1 to STS-48 rates, with higher rates to come. At its external local equipment interface, the DCS or ADM exchanges digital signals with end systems at DS-1 (1.544 Mbps) or DS-3 (44.736 Mbps) rates. The end systems using these signals may be located in telecommunications carrier central offices or on the premises of large users. A DCS or ADM demultiplexes signals on its inbound internodal links down to a low rate (e.g., STS-1 or STS-3), sorts and cross-connects these signals (dropping some signals to end systems), and remultiplexes the cross-connected signals (including signals added from end systems) onto the outbound internodal links. Thus each internodal logical link operating at a high bitrate typically carries many time-division multiplexed lower rate signals. An end-to-end connection terminating at externally attached end systems will typically traverse several SONET DCSs, resulting in a multiple-hop source–destination path. The SONET network typically "provisions" and holds these connections over long time periods.

In currently operational telecommunication networks the SONET network uses point-to-point optical fiber transmission links for its inter-DCS connections, without the intervention of a reconfigurable physical layer. This is shown in Figure 2.37(a), in which the fibers are interfaced directly to the DCS through its own optical transceivers. Until recently, these transmission links were single wavelength, carrying only one bidirectional logical link. They were therefore grossly underutilized. However, with the trend toward WDM transmission, the transmission links are now being operated on multiple wavelengths, so that they can carry several parallel logical connections either from the same or different electronic equipment. In this case, the link terminating equipment, which interfaces the DCS (or similar equipment) to the fiber transmission link, is called a *WDM terminal, Wavelength terminal multiplexer*, or *WDM transport system*. Typically, the interconnections between the link terminating equipment and the electronic switching equipment are optical. For example, a SONET DCS might

---

[29] One of the most important features of the SONET standard is a comprehensive set of maintenance and protection switching functions implemented using the transport overhead—see Chapter 8, Appendix F, and [Wu92, p. 38].

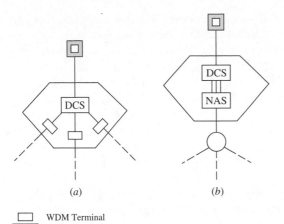

☐ WDM Terminal
DCS SONET DCS

FIGURE 2.37 SONET DCS.

transmit and receive OC-n optical signals in the 1,300-nm band on its input/output ports. The output signals from the DCS are connected to WDM terminals via short lengths of fiber. Each terminal then converts these signals to electrical form and remodulates them onto another optical carrier at a wavelength (normally in the 1,550-nm range) suitable for long-distance WDM transmission. The reverse operations are carried out at the receiving end of the link transmission link.[30]

One difficulty with this arrangement is that there is no possibility for optically reconfiguring the SONET network, either for load redistribution or for fault recovery. Furthermore, if the equipment interfaced to the WDM terminal does not generate a throughput comparable with the capacity of the transmission link, much of the fiber capacity will be wasted. Finally, each WDM terminal can only connect the DCS to one other switching node. A more flexible and efficient arrangement is shown in Figure 2.37(b). An NAS, together with an ONN (e.g., a wavelength selective cross-connect), replaces the WDM terminals on the three links in Figure 2.37(a). Now, the logical connections from the DCS can be routed to different destinations under the control of the optical node. By superimposing the DCS on a purely optical network, additional flexibility is introduced, with optical multiplexing and logical network reconfiguration made possible by control in the optical layer.

It is interesting to view the functions of the SONET switch in terms of granularity. The signals it exchanges with the optical network are highly aggregated and well adapted to the capacity of the optical transmission channels. Those exchanged with the end systems are typically of a much finer granularity, adapted to the needs of the attached telecommunications equipment. In the DCS, information channels of

---

[30] Two WDM terminals connected back to back can serve as an OLP for purposes of electronic wavelength interchange and/or regeneration.

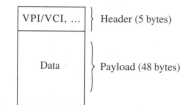

FIGURE 2.38   ATM cell format.

relatively fine granularity are sorted individually and then reaggregrated for transport on the logical links. This illustrates the use of electronics (in the DCS) to provide the fine-granularity sorting needed for high connectivity, while using optics to carry coarse-granularity traffic at high throughputs.

2.6.2 ATM Networks

An ATM logical network is very similar to a SONET network except that the basic entities processed by the LSNs are cells rather than synchronous bitstreams. The logical switch in these networks is an ATM (cell) switch. ATM was developed to support broadband services that require a wide range of bandwidths and quality of service. It uses the ATM cell as the basic information unit: a fixed-length structure that contains 53 bytes, of which five constitute the header and the rest are data (Figure 2.38). The header contains a virtual channel identifier (VCI) and virtual path identifier (VPI), as well as header error control, flow control, and priority and other information.

Typically an ATM network is configured in the form of a virtual topology that consists of dedicated *virtual paths* (VPs), acting as virtual internodal links joining pairs of ATM switches. (Each VP may traverse several ATM switches between its end points.) End users request demand-assigned *virtual channels* (VCs) to support each application, with the bandwidth and other characteristics of the VC designed to provide the required quality of service for that application. The VPs are sized to carry many asynchronously multiplexed VCs. As indicated by the virtual connection layer in Figure 1.1, the VC is the entity carrying cells end to end in an ATM network. Because the cells are multiplexed asynchronously on the internodal links, the VC and VP information is necessary for sorting and routing individual cells within the ATM switches. Each cell header is read by the switch, and the cell is directed to the output port specified by the VCI, the VPI, and the routing table stored in the switch.

As shown in Figure 2.39, the ATM switches are joined together through inter-nodal logical links and are interfaced to end systems through external ports. An end system could be a workstation, a LAN gateway, a supercomputer, or any other device equipped with an ATM interface. As in the SONET case, a typical connection between end systems (carried on a VC) will traverse several switches between source and destination, resulting in a multihop logical path. The internodal links connecting the ATM switches can be realized in various ways. Figure 2.39 shows three possibilities.

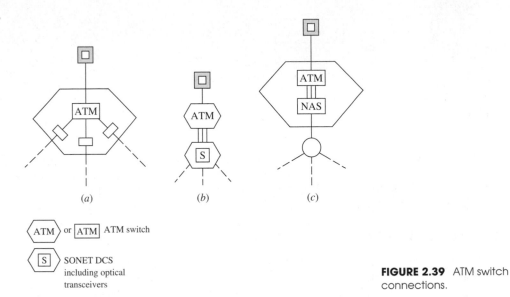

FIGURE 2.39 ATM switch connections.

In Figure 2.39(a), the internodal ports on the switch are connected directly to point-to-point digital transmission links, which might be fiber links terminated with the necessary optical transceivers. These links form a logical topology, that cannot be reconfigured without physically changing the connections. (This is analogous to the SONET DCS network connection of Figure 2.37[a].)

An alternative is to use a hybrid ATM-over-SONET structure as shown in Figure 2.39(b). Now the ATM switch acts as an end system attached to the external ports of a SONET DCS, and each ATM internodal logical connection is carried on a SONET STS routed through the DCS to another ATM switch. (The network of ATM switches may represent just one of many applications served by the SONET infrastructure, and the SONET network may in turn be one LN supported by a larger optical network infrastructure.) In this case reconfiguration is possible at the SONET level by changing the routing within the DCS.

Figure 2.39(c) shows a third alternative, in which the ATM switch accesses an optical network directly through its own NAS. This is analogous to the SONET DCS configuration shown in Figure 2.37(b). As in the SONET case, a logical topology for the ATM network is constructed by creating the desired logical connections among the NASs, and reconfiguration is possible through control in the optical layer.

2.6.3 IP Networks

An IP logical network is a packet-switched LN with information units that are Internet packets. It is similar in structure to an ATM network. However, the LSNs are IP routers (packet switches) rather than ATM switches. Internet packets are of variable length and are generally much longer than an ATM cell. The function of an internet router is to examine incoming packets, determine destination addresses, compare them with the contents of a routing table stored in the router, and then forward the packets to the appropriate output interface.

The Internet is a highly dynamic structure with switching nodes that are IP routers, and it is composed of many interconnected, individual networks with frequently changing topologies. Thus, one of the fundamental capabilities of IP routers is the creation of routing tables that adjust themselves automatically to changes in network topologies caused by link and equipment failures, and by addition or deletion of fibers or wavelengths between routers.

Networks of IP routers can be configured over optical infrastructures using the various options suggested previously for SONET and ATM networks, with the additional option of running the IP routers on top of ATM switches and/or SONET DCSs.

We shall explore logically routed network (LRN) structures in considerable detail in Chapter 7. ATM or IP networks serve as useful specific examples of generic cell- or packet-switched LRNs.

As will be shown, LRNs can be constructed with logical connectivity that is more general than a collection of point-to-point logical connections. Through the use of optical multicast connections in the underlying physical layer, logical *hypernets*, can be built with logical topologies that consist of *multipoint* logical connections. Hypernets are ideal structures for supporting multicast virtual connections, which are becoming increasingly important in many Internet and multimedia applications.

2.7 Summary

Having presented the essential resources of the networks being explored in this book we can now summarize their relationship to network functionality. Figure 2.40 shows a taxonomy of multiwavelength networks, classified according to

- Physical topology
- Optical connectivity
- Optical node functionality
- Station and overlay functionality
- Network architecture

The physical topologies break down into trees (no alternate paths exist) or a general topology (providing alternate paths and hence better response to changing loads and faults). The optical connectivity may be static or controllable, depending on the functionality of the ONNs. In the simplest case, the nodes are static coupling devices with no spectral selectivity. Better performance, including wavelength reuse, is achieved with static wavelength/waveband-selective nodes, and the most versatile networks contain controllable nodes, ranging from space switches, through waveband–space–time switches to WIXCs. Switches may operate in a simple

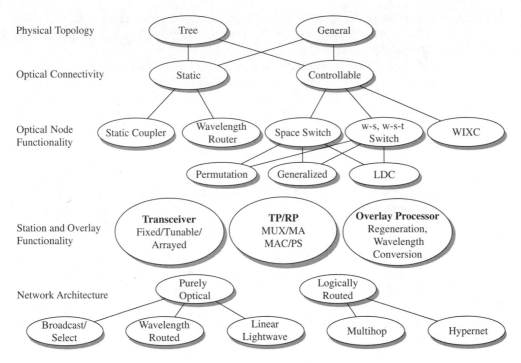

FIGURE 2.40 *Taxonomy of multiwavelength networks.*

permutation mode or may provide generalized switching functions to support multipoint optical connectivity.

The functionality of the NASs and electronic overlays complements the capabilities of the resources in the network nodes. Station equipment at the optical level ranges from a single fixed-tuned optical transceiver to multiwavelength transceiver arrays, with the latter configuration providing multiple simultaneous optical connections. In addition, the electronic TPs and RPs in a station may be equipped to execute multiplexing/multiaccess functions to increase connectivity via multipoint connections. A particularly flexible means of operating multipoint connections is through packet switching in the optical layer, implemented through a media access control (MAC) protocol executed within the TPs and RPs. The stations might also support OLPs executing signal regeneration to extend optical reach, and electronic wavelength interchange to improve network performance.

Network architectures built on these components may be purely optical, containing only the physical layer in Figure 2.1(a), or may be hybrid (logically routed), containing one or more logical network overlays. The purely optical networks range from the simple broadcast star, with a tree topology and containing no control in the ONNs, to wavelength-routed linear lightwave networks, with general topologies and possessing substantial controllability. In wavelength routed networks, each optical connec-

tion is point to point and is routed independently through the network on its own
λ-channel. In the linear lightwave network, multicast optical connections that provide
the necessary optical infrastructure for hypernet LRNs are supported. Logical switching in the LRNs provides additional switching and processing capabilities, greatly
increasing the potential connectivity of the network. These networks may be based
on point-to-point logical connection topologies, in which case they are called *multihop
networks*, or they may have hypernet structures, which achieve greater connectivity
by combining logical switching with multipoint optical connections.

Subsequent chapters explore each of these major classes of networks in detail.

2.8 Problems

1. List and discuss the factors that limit channel spacing in wavelength-routed networks and
   waveband-routed networks.

2. What are the factors limiting throughput in the following types of networks:
   (a) A star coupler-based LAN
   (b) A purely optical wavelength-routed WAN
   (c) A WAN consisting of electronic switches joined by point-to-point WDM links

3. For the 8 × 8 Benes switch:
   (a) If all 2 × 2 switching elements are in the bar state, determine the connection state of the
       switch.
   (b) Find a switch setting (a set of device states) to produce the following connection state:

Input	Output
1	7
2	5
3	4
4	8
5	1
6	2
7	6
8	3

4. Compare the power distribution rule for the star coupler with that of the folded bus.
   (Assume in both cases that there are no *excess* losses in the devices or attenuation in the
   fibers.)
   (a) Show that in the 16 × 16 star coupler of Figure 2.8 each output port receives the sum of
       the powers entering at all input ports attenuated by a factor of 16.
   (b) Show that in a folded bus with sixteen stations, configured to act as a star coupler,
       the best one can achieve is an attenuation factor of 256. (*Hint:* See Sections 4.9.2 and
       6.5.7.)
   (c) Generalize this to the $n \times n$ case.

5. Prove that an $n \times n$ Benes switch uses $n \log_2 n - n/2$ binary elements.

6. Compare the number of cross-points (binary switching elements) for the $n \times n$ crossbar and Benes switches with $\log_2(n!)$ for $n = 4, 8, 16$.

7. Compare the number of cross-points in a 16×16 strictly nonblocking Clos switch to those in the same size Benes switch. Assume that the parameters in the Clos switch are $p = k = 4$, and that each smaller switch is realized as a crossbar.

8. This problem concerns cost trade-offs in WSS realization using either the three-stage architecture of Figure 2.22 or using MWSs as the elementary switching devices. Assume that the device costs are C_{cc} for a 2×2 controllable coupler (or on–off device), mC_{mux} for an m-wavelength MUX or DMUX, nC_p for an n-fold passive splitter or combiner, and mC_{mws} for an m-wavelength 2×2 MWS.

   (a) For a four-waveband 8×8 permutation switch using a Benes fabric, find the range of values of C_{mws} over which the MWS realization is more economical than the three-stage realization. Express your answer in terms of the other cost parameters.

   (b) Repeat the previous part for a generalized switch fabric of the type shown in Figure 2.19.

   (c) Generalize the previous results to m-waveband $n \times n$ switches.

9. Consider a 48×48 permutation switch connecting three cables, each containing 16 bidirectional fiber pairs.

   (a) Indicate how many connection states are required, propose a possible strictly nonblocking switch design based on binary switching elements, and indicate how many binary elements it uses.

   (b) Now, suppose that the switch connections are only required to be made on a fiber-to-cable basis without loopback connections. That is, each inbound fiber in one cable must be connected to an outbound fiber in a prescribed (different) cable, but it doesn't matter which outbound fiber is used. Again, indicate how many connection states are required, propose a possible strictly nonblocking switch design, and indicate how many binary elements it uses (hopefully fewer than in the previous case). In counting connection states *do not* distinguish between different fibers in the output cables.

10. Show how the physical constraints of the various switch fabrics lead to Equations 2.8, 2.9, 2.10, 2.11, and 2.12.

11. In the WIXC of Figure 2.27, assume that the inputs are as shown in the figure. Find the device states (i.e., the settings of the three WSXCs) to send $S_2(\lambda_1)$ and $S_3(\lambda_2)$ to the upper output port, and $S_1(\lambda_1)$ to the lower output port.

12. Show a design for a 2×2 four-wavelength WIXC using five 2×2 WSSs and four wavelength interchangers.

13. List as many functions as you can for OLPs, and suggest realizations.

14. Invent some new forms of LRN overlays on optical networks.

15. Discuss some of the problems of managing and controlling a network that is independently reconfigurable at several different layers: virtual, logical, and physical. For example, how should fault recovery be managed? How should reconfiguration be managed in the face of congestion?

2.9 Bibliography

[Alexander+93] S. B. Alexander, R. S. Bondurant, D. Byrne, et al. A precompetitive consortium on wide-band all optical networks. *IEEE/OSA J. Lightwave Technology*, 11(5/6):714–735, 1993.

[Antoniades+96] N. Antoniades, K. Bala, S.J.B. Yoo, and G. Ellinas. A parametric wavelength interchanging cross-connect (WIXC) architecture. *IEEE Photonics Technology Letters*, 8(10): 1382–1384, 1996.

[Barry+93] R. A. Barry and P. A. Humblet. Latin routers: Design and implementation. *IEEE/OSA J. Lightwave Technology*, 11(5/6):891–899, 1993.

[Benes65] V. E. Benes. *Mathematical Theory of Connecting Networks and Telephone Traffic*. Academic Press, New York, 1965.

[Ellinas+97] G. Ellinas, G. K. Chang, M. Z. Iqbal, J. Gamelin, and M. R. Khandker. Wavelength selective cross-connect architecture interconnecting multiwavelength self-healing rings. In *Proc. IEEE/OSA Optical Fiber Commun. Conf.*, Dallas, February 1997.

[Hinton93] H. S. Hinton. *An Introduction to Photonic Switching Fabrics*. New York: Plenum Press, 1993.

[Hui90] J. Y. Hui. *Switching and Traffic Theory for Integrated Broadband Networks*. Norwell, MA: Kluwer Academic Publishers, 1990.

[Kaminow+87] I. P. Kaminow, P. P. Iannone, J. Stone, and L. W. Stulz. FDMA-FSK star network with a tunable optical filter demultiplexer. *Electron. Letters*, 23:1102–1103, 1987.

[Sharony94] J. Sharony. *Architectures of Dynamically Reconfigurable Wavelength Routing/Switching Networks*. PhD thesis. Department of Electrical Engineering, Columbia University, New York, 1994.

[Smith+76] D. G. Smith and M. M. Rahmnekhan. Wide-sense nonblocking networks, and some packing algorithms. In *Int. Teletraffic Cong.*, pp. 542-1–542-4, Melbourne,1976.

[Wu92] T-H. Wu. *Fiber Network Service Survivability*. Norwood, MA: Artech House, 1992.

[Yoo+95] S. J. B. Yoo, C. Caneau, R. Bhat, and M. A. Koza. Wavelength conversion by quasi-phase-matched difference frequency generation in AlGaAs waveguides. In *Proc. IEEE/OSA Optical Fiber Commun. Conf.* (paper PD14-2), San Diego, February 1995.

CHAPTER THREE

Network Connections

The multiwavelength network architecture described in Section 2.1 contained several layers of connections. By exploiting the various alternatives in each layer, it is possible to produce a rich set of transport network configurations. This chapter explores how a desired connectivity pattern can be established using the combined functionality contained in the various layers. The approach is to examine the properties of different classes of networks through a sequence of simple illustrative examples. The design objective in each example is to provide a prescribed connectivity to a set of end systems.

Our first example is shown in Figure 3.1. Five geographically dispersed end systems are to be interconnected by a transport network, which is to be specified. Suppose that a dedicated set of connections is desired (shown as dashed lines in the figure), providing full connectivity. This might correspond to a LAN interconnection application, wherein the end systems are gateways providing internetworking capability among five LANs. Figure 3.2(a) shows one possible transport network, whose

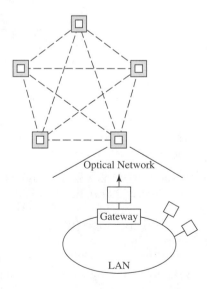

FIGURE 3.1 End systems: LAN interconnection.

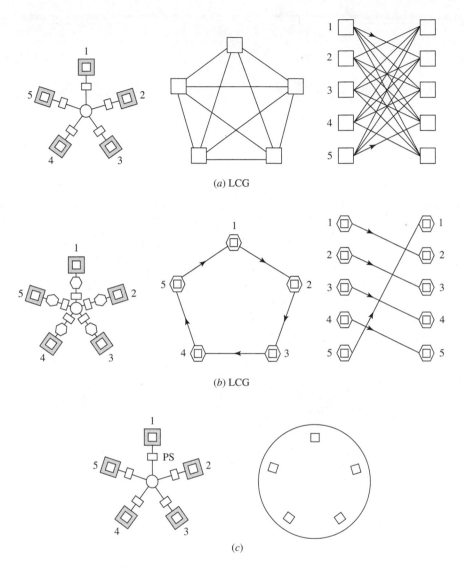

(*a*) LCG

(*b*) LCG

(*c*)

FIGURE 3.2 Star physical topology.

physical topology (PT) is a star, in which the central node is a star coupler of the type shown in Figure 2.6(a). Each end system is connected to the star through its own network access station. Full connectivity requires 20 unidirectional *logical connections* (LCs). The logical topology (LT) for the network is shown in the *logical connection graph* (LCG) in Figure 3.2, where each bidirectional link represents two unidirectional logical connections. A bipartite representation of the LCG is also shown, in which transmitting and receiving stations are separated, so that an arc from vertex *i* to *j*

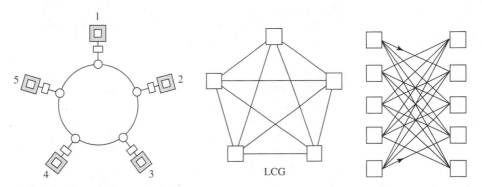

FIGURE 3.3 Bidirectional ring physical topology.

represents an LC originating at station i (the left vertex) and terminating at station j (the right vertex).

Each network access station (NAS) interfaces four pairs of logical connections to its attached end system to produce the fully connected logical topology shown in the figure. The LT shows the connectivity realized in the transport network as "seen" by the end systems, but suppresses the details of the underlying physical layer. When a set of LCs is realized over a given transparent optical infrastructure, the logical topology is said to be *embedded* in the supporting PT. In the case at hand the LT is a set of links that connects directly all pairs of end systems. The burden of supporting full logical connectivity is borne completely by the optical network, which requires multiplexing of many optical connections on each fiber, together with replication of optical and/or electronic equipment within the NASs to support multiple connections. If WDM is used on the star, each LC requires a distinct wavelength and its own transmitter–receiver pair. (No spectrum reuse is possible; see Section 3.2.) Thus a fully connected LT requires four optical transceivers in each station, with each transmitter operating on a different wavelength, for a total of 20 wavelengths.

Another possible realization, in the form of a transparent optical bidirectional ring containing wavelength-routing optical network nodes, is shown in Figure 3.3. Each end system is connected through its own NAS to an ONN. This time if we use WDM it turns out that only three or four wavelengths are needed to support the 20 logical connections,[1] indicating that a substantial degree of spectrum reuse is possible if wavelength routing is employed.

As a third option, returning to the simpler star network, we can reduce the connectivity burden on the physical layer by inserting a logical switching node (LSN) between each end system and its NAS as shown in Figure 3.2(b). This provides a switching function at the electronic level, which will share the task of providing full

[1] The exact number of required wavelengths depends on the stations' access connections (see Section 3.3).

connectivity. (Another alternative for reducing the connectivity burden uses packet switching in the optical layer, as illustrated in Figure 3.2(c). It will be discussed in Section 3.2.2.)

In our LAN interconnection example, the LSNs might be ATM switches whose function is to receive data packets (converted to the form of ATM cells) from their attached LAN gateways, and to route the cells through a sequence of LSNs and then to the destination LANs. (In an alternative configuration, the ATM switches could be replaced by IP routers.)

A possible LCG and its bipartite representation for this case is shown in Figure 3.2(b). Only five LCs are present now, requiring a total of five wavelengths and one optical transceiver per station, and producing a logical topology in the form of a unidirectional ring connecting the five LSNs. It is now the LSNs and their interconnecting logical links that are seen by the end systems as their transport network, in contrast to the cases of Figure 3.2(a) or Figure 3.3, in which the transport network was purely optical. So far we do not have complete connectivity among the end systems. This is provided by moving up to the virtual connection layer of Figure 2.1(a) and superimposing a set of 20 virtual paths (VPs) on the logical topology of Figure 3.2(b) to form a fully connected virtual topology that corresponds to the dashed lines in Figure 3.1.

Note that the VPs must be supported by *logical paths* (LPs) consisting, in most cases, of more than one *logical hop*. The network of LSNs realizes the VPs by sorting and forwarding the cells according to their destinations. In the case when the LSNs are ATM switches, these operations are executed by reading the VPIs in the cell headers (see Section 2.6). This is a simple example of a transparent optical network with a *logically routed* or *multihop electronic overlay*. In this case the physical layer is required to support only five logical links, with the remaining connectivity supplied electronically in the overlay. In comparison with the purely optical star, the wavelength requirement has been reduced by a factor of four. However, many VPs must be now multiplexed on each logical link. This logical layer multiplexing (and switching) is possible because of the functionality in the LSNs. Each logical connection is now shared by ten multiplexed VPs (why?), so that the total capacity of the network is reduced to 10% of the capacity available in the case of the bidirectional ring (see Section 3.5).

It is important to note that in each of these examples, the logical topology is *independent* of the physical topology into which it is embedded. Furthermore, it is generally reconfigurable and therefore adaptable to changing conditions. For comparison, consider traditional networks made up of point-to-point transmission links (optical or otherwise) that interconnect LSNs. The logical topologies of these networks are identical with their physical topologies. A commonly used physical configuration is a bidirectional ring, which resembles the transparent optical ring of Figure 3.3.[2]

---

[2] Bidirectional rings based on point-to-point optical fiber links are used commonly in SONET networks as well as in the fiber distributed data interface (FDDI) LAN/MAN standard [Ross89].

The nodes in the traditional ring are logical switches, so that the logical topology resembles that of Figure 3.2(b) (except that the logical ring is generally bidirectional) and the topology is frozen once the transmission links are in place. In contrast, the transparent optical ring of Figure 3.3 is configured to produce a fully connected LT, a topology that could be reconfigured by changing settings in the ONNs and NASs without reconnecting fiber links.

It should now be clear that there are many possibilities for realizing connectivity in multiwavelength optical networks. The resultant logical and virtual topologies are generally reconfigurable, and offer many cost–performance trade-offs. The remainder of this chapter illustrates how connectivity is created in each layer, focusing on relations among physical constraints, device functionality, connectivity, and throughput. To avoid unnecessary complications, the exposition proceeds from simple to complex classes of networks based on the level of controllability in the network nodes:

- Static (broadcast-and-select) networks
- Wavelength routed networks
- Linear lightwave networks (LLNs)
- Logically routed (hybrid) networks (LRNs)

These four categories correspond to the network classes shown from left to right in the taxonomy of Figure 2.40. The static category comprises transparent optical networks based on static network nodes with no wavelength selectivity (in other words, single-waveband networks). Any signal introduced into such a network propagates along all possible paths, tending to "flood" the network, and eliminates possibilities for reusing the optical spectrum on different fibers. For all practical purposes, this limits the PT to a tree (or a collection of separate trees), and eliminates the function of the optical path sublayer in Figure 2.1(a). Hence the size, throughput, and flexibility of static networks are limited. (They are typically used as LANs or MANs.)

The only way to support many simultaneous connections in these networks is through optical multiplexing, multicast, and multiaccess techniques. The basic features of this approach are discussed in Section 3.2. By adding either static or dynamic wavelength selectivity to the network nodes, we obtain wavelength routed networks (WRNs), wherein spectrum reuse and hence improved performance becomes possible through the use of appropriate connection control algorithms. These networks normally have more general physical topologies.

Wavelength routed networks are discussed in Section 3.3. Consistent with the way in which typical WRNs are operated, the discussion there is limited to point-to-point optical connections, which can be realized in networks equipped with wavelength-selective cross-connects (permutation switches; see Section 2.3.2).

In Section 3.4 the discussion is extended to LLNs, which are a generalization of wavelength routed networks, characterized by the fact that their optical nodes are waveband-selective linear divider combiners (LDCs) rather than permutation switches. The properties of LLNs are more general than those of wavelength routed networks, in two respects:

1. They are *waveband* rather than *wavelength* routed. In other words, their spectrum partitioning can be visualized as shown in Figure 2.4(c), rather than Figure 2.4(b).
2. They support multipoint optical connections in addition to point-to-point connections.

The multipoint optical switching capability of an LLN offers a wealth of connection alternatives. Among them is the possibility of tying subsets of NASs together into fully connected *multipoint subnets* (MPSs). This is a particularly effective way of creating high connectivity in large networks, as well as providing a transparent optical support adapted naturally to logical multicast connections.

Section 3.5 introduces LRNs, constructed using electronically switched overlays supported by a transparent optical substructure. Networks with two types of logical topologies are described: those in which the basic logical link is (fixed capacity) point to point, and those with multipoint logical links. We call the latter category *hypernets*. Although point-to-point logical topologies (multihop networks) can be implemented over wavelength routed optical networks, hypernets require an LLN physical layer to support their multipoint links. The shared-capacity multicast connections in the logical layer are supported by MPSs in the physical layer. The chapter concludes with a summary and comparison of the different approaches to realizing network connectivity.

To set the stage for the discussion of these different network structures, we must have at least a rudimentary idea of how connections can be managed. Management and control issues in large networks encompass an enormous range of critical functions, some of the most important being

- Fault management (including fault detection and service restoration)
- Performance management (monitoring the performance of the various network elements and connections)
- Configuration management (provisioning and reconfiguration of network connections)

Associated with these are signaling and many other operations, administration, and maintenance functions. These topics are still in their embryonic form for optical networks, and must evolve as the networks themselves evolve (see [Wei+98] and [Maeda98]). In the next section we address the issue of *connection management and control*, which encompasses both long-term provisioning (configuration management) and short-term connection control. The objective is to provide some understanding of what operations must take place to establish connections in an optical network, and how these operations might be implemented.

3.1 Connection Management and Control

In any large network connections do not remain static. In the case of *demand-assigned* connections, users become active, request specific connections, and then disconnect. In the case of *dedicated* or *provisioned* connections, changes in traffic conditions or network faults dictate changes in routing, wavelength assignment, and bitrates. Our repeated use of the term *connection* implies that information flow is normally *connection oriented* in the networks we are discussing.

Any connection-oriented network requires a system for connection management. Our layered view of the network allows us to look at optical, logical, and virtual connection management as three (almost) separate issues. At each layer the protocols for connection management consist of three phases: connection establishment, information transfer, and connection release. In the most elaborate case, exemplified by the virtual, logical, and physical layers in the network of Figure 3.2(b), these phases must occur within each layer. Typically, the higher the layer, the more frequent are the connection changes. Thus, the optical connections would normally be provisioned on a dedicated basis, with changes made only for fault restoration. The logical connections might also be fixed perhaps with some modifications to support changing load distributions. On the other hand, most of the virtual layer connections would be demand assigned.

Looking at the connectivity from the top down, suppose Figure 3.2(b) represents an ATM network in which some of the end systems are individual users of data services (e.g., workstations and terminals) and others are various types of servers. A typical application requires a user to connect to a server. To establish this connection the user requests a connection through the transport network, which is realized on a virtual channel (VC), carried on a specified VP.

To support its expected traffic demand, the ATM network must be configured on a dedicated LT (in this case a unidirectional ring) capable of carrying the antici-pated load. This is accomplished when the ATM network is initialized, at which time the appropriate LCs are created using the available resources in the physical layer. Dedicated VPs are then established between the switches in a topology designed to support the expected offered traffic. (In larger networks, additional NASs providing services to other users might access the optical infrastructure using both dedicated and demand-assigned optical connections.)

Using traditional point-to-point transmission links, the logical and physical topolo-gies of the ATM network are identical, so that initialization is straightforward. Once the logical topology has been chosen, ports on the LSNs are interconnected accord-ingly using point-to-point links that are either owned by the network operator or leased from another carrier. However, creation of a target LT over a transparent optical network is a more complex operation—an inevitable consequence of the many connection alternatives available in the physical layer.[3]

Now let us focus on connections within the physical layer of a WRN. Optical connection establishment consists of setting up a path through a sequence of optical network nodes for an assigned wavelength and then tuning source transmitter and destination receiver(s) to the chosen wavelength.[4] These are the operations occuring in the optical path and λ-channel sublayers respectively. Thus, connectivity at this level is realized through the combined action of the optical transceivers and the network nodes. For demand-assigned connections, connection establishment and release involves signaling between the party initiating the action and a network manager, followed by issuance of routing and wavelength assignment commands from the network manager to the network elements (stations and network nodes) involved in the connection. These commands are normally determined either through table look-up or by the execution of an appropriate routing and wavelength assignment algorithm. (In the case of dedicated connections, the various connection management operations would normally be executed manually off-line.)

The exact form of the network manager (e.g., either centralized or distributed) is not important at this point, nor are the details of the signaling system (e.g., either multiplexed onto the information-bearing fibers or realized as a separate low-speed data network). To fix ideas, Figure 3.4 shows one way the connection management system might operate. Each optical network node contains an optical switch together with an optical node controller (ONC). An optical network manager (ONM) is attached through an access link to node C of the optical network. It is simply an NAS supporting a network management processor. In addition to the connection control functions described here, in a large network the ONM would normally execute various other operations, administration, and maintenance functions, such as monitoring, fault diagnosis and restoration, statistics gathering, and so forth. In this example we assume that the ONM, the various ONCs, and all NASs intercommunicate via an optical signaling network multiplexed onto the information-bearing fibers.[5] For simplicity we assume here that a single dedicated wavelength shared among all network elements is used for signaling.

As shown in Figure 3.4, the ONC is composed of an access station connected optically to a port on its switch through an access fiber pair, and a control processor

---

[3] When transmission links are leased from another carrier, there are similar connection alternatives in the physical layer, but they are handled by the carrier providing the links. The operator of the logical network is shielded from this part of the problem, in effect isolating management of the logical layer from that of the physical layer. Although we use layering in this book to simplify the description of complex networks, the logical and physical layers of the network are still treated as an integrated whole.

[4] At this point it is assumed that transceiver tuning remains fixed for the duration of a connection. In later sections we consider multipoint connections involving rapid retuning of transceivers during the information transfer phase of the connection.

[5] If there are optical amplifiers along the fiber links, the signaling network would normally include connections to the amplifiers for surveillance purposes.

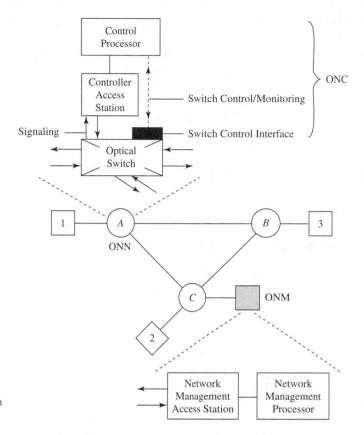

FIGURE 3.4 Connection
management system.

connected electrically to the switch control interface as indicated by the dashed connection in the figure. Commands received from the ONM are interpreted in the control
processor of the ONC, which issues electrical commands to configure the switch as
required. (The ONC might also send information back to the ONM regarding switch
status, power levels of signals transiting the switch, faults on the links, and so on.)

3.1.1   Optical Connections

Suppose station 1 in Figure 3.4 wishes to set up an optical connection to station 3. Using
the signaling network it sends a connection establishment request to the ONM, which
determines an optical path, say the one-hop path from node A to B, and selects an
available wavelength. The ONM then signals nodes A and B to set up the correct path
for the assigned wavelength, and signals stations 1 and 3 to tune to that wavelength.
The information transfer phase can then begin. Connection release would normally
be initiated by a signal from one of the communicating stations to the ONM, which
would then signal all participating network entities to release the connection. Note
that if the network nodes contain generalized switches, then *optical multicast paths*

can be set up in the form of trees, wherein the optical signal power is split, with a portion reaching each destination station. For example, station 1 can multicast to 2 and 3 through a tree rooted at the source node (*A* in this case). Furthermore, many-to-one optical paths such as a path from 1 and 2 to 3 can be set up in a similar fashion using a tree rooted at node *B*, which combines the signals from the transmitting nodes.

The total time required for establishing and releasing an optical connection includes signaling time (including propagation delays), routing and wavelength assignment computation time, optical node switching time, and transmitter–receiver tuning time. Because this total can be substantial (possibly on the order of 100 ms for propagation times alone), optical connections should generally be held for much longer periods of time (seconds or more) for efficient operation.

3.1.2 Logical Connections

Once an optical connection exists, one or more logical connections can be carried on it through the assignment of suitable transmission channels, which serve to adapt each LC to its supporting optical connection. Referring to Figure 2.30, a point-to-point LC originates at an external port on the transmission processor (TP) of the source station, which converts the logical signal to a suitable transmission signal, appearing at point *a* in the figure. This is in turn converted to an optical signal, appearing at point *b*, which may be multiplexed with other optical signals before it leaves the NAS. The process is reversed at points *d* and *e* in the receiving side of the destination station. Because all operations concerning LCs and their associated transmission channels take place within NASs, *logical connection management does not require the intervention of the ONCs once the supporting optical paths are in place.*

As a result, connection reconfiguration within a logical network can often take place through distributed connection management protocols executed cooperatively among the participating NASs without calling on the functions of lower layer (optical path layer and below) network entities. (Examples of this appear in subsequent sections.) This can greatly simplify the various network management and control functions, and provides further justification for viewing the multiwavelength network in terms of independent logical and physical layers and sublayers.

3.1.2.1 Stream and Packet Traffic

During the information transfer phase, it is useful to distinguish between two types of data flow on a logical connection: *stream type* and *asynchronous* (packet or cell) *traffic*. Stream traffic, exemplified by SONET STSs described in Section 2.6, typically supports voice, fixed bitrate video, and similar applications. In the case of stream traffic, the information entering and exiting a logical port on an NAS is in the form of a continuous, synchronous bitstream. To support this type of traffic, the transmission channel carrying the LC must act as a dedicated, fixed-capacity "pipe." In the asynchronous case, typically used in computer, variable bitrate video, and multimedia applications, the information flow is in the form of random bursts carried in data packets or cells. In this case each packet or cell carries explicit addressing information in a header, processed by various network entities involved in routing the data along a path to its destination.

The distinction between stream type and asynchronous traffic is not always obvious. Thus, in packet-based systems, a random sequence of packets is typically embedded into a synchronous bitstream by encapsulating the packets into data frames separated by "idle" characters. Similarly, when a sequence of ATM cells is carried on a SONET connection, the data cells are carried within an STS bitstream interspersed with idle cells. In this case, the useful information is "bursty" or asynchronous, but the bitstream carried by the optical network is steady or synchronous. For our purposes, the traffic type is characterized by the way in which the NASs operate on the bitstream. If the bits are processed transparently, without distinguishing the individual information-bearing packets/cells from the idle bits, it is considered to be stream type. If the individual packets/cells are extracted from the bitstream when it enters the transmission processor, and headers are read for the purposes of multiplexing, scheduling, routing, and so forth, the traffic is considered to be asynchronous. The latter mode of operation corresponds to packet or cell switching within the optical layer. Typically this requires that transmission and reception processors execute a media access control (MAC) protocol designed for sharing one or more λ-channels dynamically among many logical connections. Although synchronous traffic is always connection-oriented, asynchronous traffic may be either connection-oriented or connectionless. For example, traffic in IP networks is normally connectionless: Packets are launched into the network as individual entities without establishing a virtual connection.

3.1.2.2 Multipoint Logical Connections

The efficient realization of one-to-many and many-to-one logical connectivity among stations is an important issue in optical networks. A station maintains *one-to-many* logical connectivity if it is the source of more than one simultaneous logical connection. Similarly it maintains *many-to-one* logical connectivity if it is the destination for more than one LC. For a station accessing a network node through a single pair of fibers, one-to-many logical connectivity requires multiplexing several transmission channels on the outbound access fiber, and many-to-one connectivity requires that transmission channels from several source stations share the inbound access fiber using some multiple access procedure. These multipoint connections are crucial for achieving high connectivity in optical networks.

When multiplexing and multiple access are used for multipoint connections, the issue of *addressing* arises. Addressing methods are linked to the particular multiplexing techniques being used. For example, with synchronous time–division multiplexing (TDM), addressing is implicit in the position of a data segment in a periodic time frame, and thus very little processing is required for the multiplexing/multiaccess operations in the NASs (see Section 3.2). However, in the asynchronous case, each packet/cell header must be processed individually in the station's transmission processor (reception processor, RP) to execute the multiplexing (demultiplexing) function on an outbound (inbound) transmission channel. Thus, packet switching in the optical layer typically carries with it considerable computational overhead within the NASs.

3.2 Static Networks

As we have seen, in static networks the physical layer is stripped down to its bare essentials: passive splitting/combining nodes interconnected by fibers to provide static fiber connectivity among some or all pairs of optical transmitters and receivers (OTs and ORs). This was illustrated in the examples of Figure 2.6, which show full potential connectivity from each transmitting to each receiving station in the case of a star or bus, and partial connectivity in the case of a tree. Because the OPs cannot be modified, connection control in static networks is confined to the λ-channel and transmission channel sublayers. This means that if the NASs have a means of signaling among themselves, connection management can be executed in the NASs without the intervention of a separate ONM. Consider the broadcast star example of Figure 3.5,

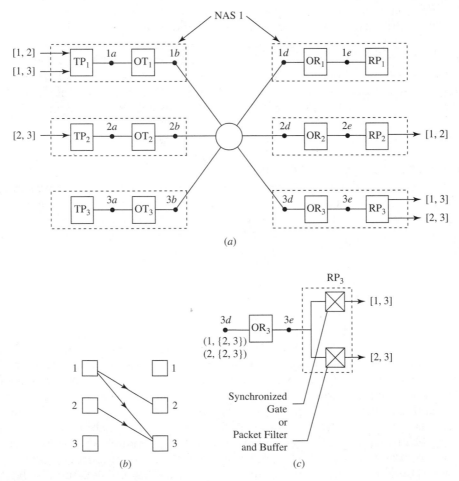

FIGURE 3.5 Star coupler example.

which consists of a star coupler connecting transceivers in three stations. This is an example of a *static shared medium network*.

As described in Section 2.3.1, the star coupler combines signals from all transmitting stations and broadcasts them to all receiving stations.[6] Thus a receiver can make a logical connection with any transmitting station by selecting the information destined for it and discarding the rest. This is the essence of the *broadcast-and-select method* of operating shared-medium optical networks. Its most attractive feature is that the broadcast function permits complete optical connectivity among all pairs of transmitting and receiving stations because every receiver "sees" every transmitter. This has a downside, however. Two transmitters emitting optical signals at the same time must transmit on distinct wavelengths. If they use the same wavelength, they will interfere with each other at all receivers, destroying any useful information flow.

This *distinct channel assignment* (DCA) *constraint* prevents any reuse of the optical spectrum in broadcast networks. It should be noted that broadcast-and-select is not limited to networks based on star couplers. For example, any of the tree networks in Figure 2.6 can be operated in a broadcast-and-select mode. Each of them combines signals from a set of transmitters and broadcasts them to a set of receivers. (In the case of Figure 2.6[b], all transmitted signals are combined at the head end of the bus and broadcast to all receivers, and in the case of 2.6[c], each of the two unidirectional trees provides signal combining and broadcasting for the subsets of transmitters and receivers which it interconnects.) We now examine the operation of static networks using the broadcast star as an illustrative example.

3.2.1 Point-to-Point and Multipoint Connections

Although the discussion thus far has focused on point-to-point connections, the broadcast star is a natural medium for creating multipoint connections for enhanced connectivity, and these play an important role in the discussion that follows. To keep track of what is happening we use different notation for connections in each layer:

1. A unidirectional point-to-point *optical path* from station a to station b is denoted as $\langle a, b \rangle$, and a multicast path from station a to the receiving set $\{b, c, \ldots\}$ is denoted as $\langle a, \{b, c, \ldots\} \rangle$.

2. A unidirectional point-to-point *optical connection* from station a to station b is denoted as (a, b). To show the wavelength of a λ-channel carrying the connection, say λ_k, we use the notation $(a, b)_k$. A multicast optical connection from station a to the receiving set $\{b, c, \ldots\}$ is denoted as $(a, \{b, c, \ldots\})$.[7]

---

[6] If transmitter–receiver pairs are shown with corresponding numbers, as in this case, they are assumed to belong to the same station, and the network is called an *undirected star;* otherwise, it is referred to as a *directed star.*

[7] An optical path from a station a to a receiving set B can carry any optical connection from a to a receiving set $C \subseteq B$.

3. A unidirectional point-to-point *logical connection* from an external port on station a to one on station b is denoted as $[a, b]$, and a multicast LC from a to a set $\{b, c, \ldots\}$ is denoted as $[a, \{b, c, \ldots\}]$. In a multicast LC, the transmitting station sends the *same* information to all receiving stations. (If station a transmits *different* information streams to a set of destination stations, the connections would be designated $[a, b]$, $[a, c], \ldots$.)

As we shall see, there is a significant difference between the realization of a set of *one-to-many* LCs comprised of several point-to-point connections (say, $[a, b]$ and $[a, c]$) and the related *multicast* connection $[a, \{b, c\}]$. The former requires multiplexing of two distinct information streams at the transmitting station, whereas the latter does not. This means, for example, that a multicast LC can be supported by creating a multicast optical path in the form of a directed tree that delivers the same signal to several destinations.[8]

Summing up the possibilities at the logical level, there are three possible types of logical connectivity on the transmitting side:

1. *One-to-one*: A source station maintains a *point-to-point* logical connection with a single destination.

2. *Multicast*: A source station maintains a *multicast* logical connection with several destinations.

3. *One-to-many*: A source station maintains several *point-to-point* logical connections to different destinations.

Note that an n-fold multicast connection can always be realized as a set of n point-to-point connections, but it is generally wasteful of communication resources to do so. On the receiving side the possibilities are one-to-one, in which a destination station maintains a logical connection with a single source, and many-to-one, in which a destination station maintains several point-to-point logical connections from different sources. The term *multipoint* is used generically to designate an arrangement including one-to-many, many-to-one, and/or multicast logical connections.

Now let us illustrate the layers of connectivity using the example of Figure 3.5. The star coupler provides a permanent broadcast optical path of the form $\langle i, \{1, 2, 3\} \rangle$ from each transmitting station to the set of all receiving stations (including loopback paths from each station to itself) independent of the wavelength being used. Thus, suppose station 1 transmits on wavelength λ_1. Then a point-to-point optical connection $(1, 2)_1$ is set up by tuning a receiver in station 2 to λ_1, and a multicast optical connection,

---

[8] Multicast logical connections can also be created by forming a directed tree in the electrical domain. For example, the *drop-and-continue* function in an add–drop multiplexer (ADM) on a SONET ring executes this type of operation by electrically "bridging" a signal to drop it at a station and at the same time continue it to the next station on the ring.

say $(1, \{2, 3\})_1$, is created by tuning receivers 2 and 3 to λ_1. Because the signal power originating from station 1 is split among all receiving stations, exactly the same information reaches both stations 2 and 3. It is important to note that the optical path produced by the broadcast star offers the potential for various types of point-to-point and multicast optical connections, but the actual connections are realized through the actions of the access stations (transmitter–receiver tuning). Furthermore, the optical power from all transmitters is always delivered to all receivers whether they use it or not.

Moving up to the logical layer, suppose the point-to-point LCs [1, 2], [1, 3], and [2, 3] are to be realized, as shown in the bipartite LCG in Figure 3.5(b). Both one-to-many and many-to-one LCs are present. Depending on the throughput requirements and available network resources, these connections can be realized in various ways. The simplest approach is by "brute force," using WDM and wavelength–division multiple access (WDMA). If three wavelengths—λ_1, λ_2, and λ_3—are available, then three optical connections—$(1, 2)_1$, $(1, 3)_2$, and $(2, 3)_3$—are set up, which in turn carry the corresponding LCs. Note that this requires two optical transmitters in station 1 and two receivers in station 3, and provides the full capacity of a λ-channel to each LC. (The NASs in Figure 3.5(a) are assumed to contain the necessary number of transceivers, even though they are not shown explicitly.) One-to-two logical connectivity from station 1 is realized by multiplexing the two wavelengths λ_1 and λ_2 onto its outbound fiber (WDM), and two-to-one connectivity at station 3 is realized by accessing the station with λ-channels on wavelengths λ_2 and λ_3 superimposed on its inbound fiber (WDMA).

Now suppose the two point-to-point connections [1, 2] and [1, 3] are carrying the same information. They can be replaced by a multicast LC [1, {2, 3}]. The multicast connection could be supported by the same optical connections as used for the point-to-point case simply by modulating the two optical transmitters in station 1 by the same transmission signal. However, a more economical way of achieving the same result is to use a single multicast optical connection $(1, \{2, 3\})_1$, eliminating one transmitter in station 1, and using only two wavelengths instead of three, while achieving the same throughput. Because the multicast connection [1, {2, 3}] is still just one connection, it can be realized without multiplexing. This simple example shows that there are often several alternatives for realizing connections at the logical and optical levels, so judicious choices are important to obtain cost-effective results.

For larger networks a high degree of multipoint connectivity is often required, as suggested in the LAN interconnection example of Section 1.5. However, the WDM/WDMA approach of dedicating a λ-channel to each LC becomes prohibitively expensive and quickly exhausts the available optical spectrum as the number of connections increases. Thus, other methods of achieving high logical connectivity while using less network resources (wavelengths and transceivers) must be employed. These typically involve combinations of wavelength–division and other multiplexing and multiple access techniques. Two additional cases: time–division and time–wavelength–division will suffice for illustration.

FIGURE 3.6 Time-shared medium.

3.2.1.1 Time–Division Techniques

TDM and time–division multiple access (TDMA) are methods of realizing multipoint connectivity which is particularly cost-effective in terms of optical resources. At any one time, a large network will be carrying many optical connections, some dedicated and some demand assigned. All of these are sharing the network resources subject to certain admission control rules, executed by the ONM to ensure satisfactory operation of the network. With demand-assigned (circuit-switched) traffic, the connection pattern evolves with time as active connections are released and new ones are established. These events generally occur on long time scales (seconds or more) for reasons explained at the beginning of this chapter. In addition to this "slow" time sharing of network resources, when TDM/TDMA is used sharing also occurs on a much faster (microsecond) time scale by interleaving concurrent connections in time.

To illustrate the different time scales, Figure 3.6 shows the signals appearing at one of the receivers when the LCs in the example of Figure 3.5 are realized, with one transmitter or receiver per station and only one wavelength λ_1, by time sharing the optical medium. Is this a sequence of circuit-switched connections or a set of simultaneous time-multiplexed multipoint connections? It all depends! If the time scale is on the order of seconds or more, then the figure shows circuit-switched connections, with the idle times between the information flows used for connection establishment and release. On the other hand, if the time scale is microseconds, there is no time for connection changes between information flows, and the picture must represent TDM/TDMA. In this case, the two LCs [1, 2] and [1, 3] are time–division multiplexed onto a transmission channel in station 1, and the optical transmissions from stations 1 and 2 each access the same λ-channel during different time intervals—an example of TDMA. The time interleaving might be on a packet, cell, byte, or bit basis.

The essential differences between the circuit-switched and multiplexed cases concern how the connections are managed. In the circuit-switched case, each connection is released before the next is established; in the multiplexed case, both connections are established before the information transfer phase, and are maintained simultaneously in time. (Because the optical path is static in this example, all connection management can occur via signaling among the access stations.) Note that in either case the total amount of time required to transmit a given number of bits (the throughput in bits per second, neglecting idle periods), is the same and is limited by the capacity of the shared λ-channel. (In the WDM/WDMA case, in which three λ-channels were used, the maximum throughput was three times as much as in TDM/TDMA, illustrating the fact that there is no free lunch. If less optical resources are used, less transmission capacity is available.)

Now let us examine the multipoint case in more detail. Observe that because all information is transmitted on wavelength λ_1, all transmitters and receivers remain tuned to λ_1 at all times, creating the multicast optical connections $(1, \{2, 3\})_1$ and

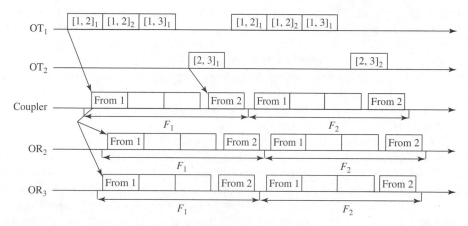

FIGURE 3.7 A TDM/TDMA schedule.

$(2, \{2, 3\})_1$.[9] Using TDM at the transmission channel level, the information streams for connections [1, 2] and [1, 3] arriving at the two input ports on station 1 in Figure 3.5 are multiplexed onto a single transmission signal (point $1a$) that modulates the transmitter OT_1. The TP contains buffers and synchronization equipment for interleaving the two information streams. The transmission channel supporting these multiplexed LCs is carried on the optical connection $(1, \{2, 3\})$. The LC [2, 3] is carried on optical connection $(2, \{2, 3\})$ without any multiplexing.

Because both optical connections are carried on the same wavelength, an *optical multiple access scheme* is necessary to keep the two signals from interfering with each other at the receivers, and to distinguish the different information streams. In this example we use TDMA, in which the two optical signals are transmitted in nonoverlapping "bursts" by switching the transmitters on and off intermittently. The overall connection arrangement is therefore a combination of TDM at the logical (transmission channel) level and TDMA at the optical (λ-channel) level. At each receiver the optical signal is first converted to electronic form (at points $2e$ and $3e$ in Figure 3.5) and then demultiplexed to extract the information destined for it, and the rest is discarded. Demultiplexing requires synchronized gates or "packet filters" in the RP, as shown in Figure 3.5(c) for station 3. The packet filters are required if bitstream interleaving is done on a packet/cell basis (see Section 3.2.2).

A typical schedule of transmissions for this example is shown in Figure 3.7. In the figure, transmissions occur in synchronized time slots of equal length, where the notation $[a, b]_n$ in a slot means that it is used for the LC $[a, b]$, with n indicating that this is the nth segment of the data stream transmitted on that connection. The first two time traces in the figure show the information streams as they appear at the

---

[9] Note that the loopback connection from 2 to itself is not needed but is an unavoidable result of the broadcast topology.

transmitters OT_1 and OT_2, and the third shows the streams interleaved as they appear at the coupler. Note that the different propagation delays between the stations and the coupler indicate that station 1 is farther away from the coupler than station 2. The last two traces represent the streams as they appear at receivers OR_2 and OR_3, showing that station 3 is closer to the coupler than station 2. Multiple access synchronization is required at the transmitters to produce nonoverlapping optical signals at the coupler (and hence at each receiver), taking into account different propagation delays from each transmitter to the star coupler.

Although the multiplexed stream from one transmitter can be contiguous in time, small *guard times* are required between signals from different transmitters to provide tolerance for small errors in synchronization. The schedule shown has a fixed periodic frame pattern, with F_1 and F_2 being two successive frames containing four slots per frame. In this case, the destination address of each data segment is implicit in its position in the frame, so no explicit addressing need be carried with the information itself to indicate to which logical channel it belongs. This is typical of a *fixed* (as opposed to a *dynamic*) capacity allocation. (The fraction of the frame time allocated to each logical channel is proportional to its allocated capacity.)

Several operations that require exchange of control information are involved in initializing the connections. A frame schedule must be determined by a connection manager and must be made known to all participating stations. Also, each station must acquire frame, slot, and bit synchronization. These functions take place during the connection establishment phase. The only control information needed during the information transfer phase is that required for maintaining timing synchronization. This is generally an operation that requires very little overhead.[10] To keep latency times and buffer sizes small, the slot and frame sizes should be small. However, for efficient operation the slot size should be much larger than the guard time. These two considerations dictate schedules with a small number of slots per frame, with slot and frame sizes typically on the order of microseconds for transmission channel bitrates on the order of gigabits per second. These aspects of connection control and synchronization are typical of all TDM/TDMA systems regardless of the underlying technology.

The previous TDM/TDMA example illustrated how time–division techniques can be used to create multipoint logical connectivity with a minimum of optical transmitting and receiving hardware, and minimal use of the optical spectrum. In realizing multipoint connections, four successive operations were involved:

1. Logical channel multiplexing in the transmitting stations
2. Optical multicast, enabling each transmitter to reach several receivers

---

[10] In systems based on undirected stars or their equivalent, as in the current example, all stations see all transmissions, including their own. This makes it relatively easy to execute mutual synchronization. The RP in each station can observe the arrival times of all signals, and the station's TP can use this information to adjust the transmitted bursts to fall correctly into their allocated time slots. In cases in which all stations do not see all transmissions (for example, directed stars), some feedback for synchronization purposes must be provided from the receiving stations to the transmitting stations via a separate control channel.

3. Optical multiple access, enabling several transmitters to access each receiver

4. Logical channel demultiplexing in the receiving stations

All multipoint connections in optical networks generally rely on the same fundamental operations, as we see in subsequent chapters.

3.2.1.2 Time–Wavelength-Division Techniques

The previous illustrations showed how either TDM/TDMA or WDM/WDMA could be used to achieve multipoint connectivity. The former was economical in the usage of optical hardware and the optical spectrum, but had limited throughput due to the fact that transceivers were idle part of the time and only one λ-channel was used. The latter had high throughput, but required more optical transceivers and more spectrum. Is there a way of obtaining the best features of both? Figure 3.8 shows another example using the broadcast star network of Figure 3.5. This time, suppose full logical connectivity is required (without loopback connections) as shown in the LCG of Figure 3.8(a). The logical channels are now created using multiple wavelengths as well as multiple time slots. In contrast to the WDM/WDMA case, each station contains only a single transceiver. However, to achieve the necessary multipoint connectivity, some tunability of the transceivers during the information transfer phase of the connections is needed. Because optical connectivity between a given transmitter–receiver pair is created by tuning both to a common λ-channel, a number of tuning options are available: Use fixed transmitters with tunable receivers (FT-TR), tunable transmitters with fixed receivers (TT-FR), or tunable transmitters with tunable receivers (TT-TR). In this simple example we use the FT-TR option, in which case each transmitter is tuned permanently to a distinct wavelength (that is, a unique λ-channel is "owned" by each

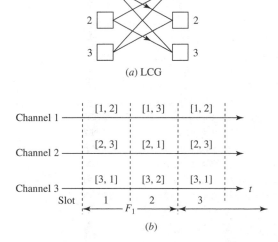

(a) LCG

(b)

FIGURE 3.8 TDM/T-WDMA.

transmitter). Each transmitted signal fans out through the star coupler, reaching all three receivers (including its own).

If only one-to-one logical connectivity were desired, then all connections could be realized by equipping each destination station with a single receiver that remains tuned to the desired transmitter's wavelength for the duration of a connection. To rearrange the connections on a circuit-switched basis, the receivers would be retuned, but because receiver tuning occurs as part of connection establishment, low tuning speeds (milliseconds) would be acceptable. Here we are seeking multipoint logical connectivity, which can be achieved by using a single, *rapidly* tunable OR at each station and using TDM in the transmitters. This arrangement potentially provides full, simultaneous logical connectivity among all sources and destinations. Any receiver wishing to select information from a given transmitter tunes to that transmitter's wavelength whenever the transmission signal contains information for it, resulting in a time–wavelength–division multiple access (T-WDMA) scheme.

To create a prescribed set of source–destination LCs, appropriate TDM schedules must be set up for each transmitter so that the desired information can be extracted by each receiver from the various transmitted information streams using a suitable tuning rule. This creates a TDM/T-WDMA system. In contrast to the TDM/TDMA case, in which transmitters operated in nonoverlapping bursts to avoid interference, the TDM/T-WDMA system can operate with all transceivers active at all times, providing more efficient usage of the optical equipment. A possible time–wavelength schedule using a periodic frame with two equal size time slots is shown in Figure 3.8(b), which displays the interleaved transmissions on each channel (wavelength) as seen at the star coupler.

Each transmitter multiplexes the logical channels destined to the other two receivers into a fixed TDM frame, with all stations transmitting simultaneously on different wavelengths. The transmitters must be synchronized with each other at the star coupler, as shown in Figure 3.8(b), so that the TDM frames for each wavelength are aligned to allow *conflict-free* receiver tuning schedules.[11] A receiver conflict occurs if information from two different transmitters, destined for the same receiver, is transmitted during overlapping time intervals, making it impossible for the receiver to pick up both transmissions. In a conflict-free schedule, no destination station may appear more than once in each time slot because this would require the station's receiver to tune to two different wavelengths at the same time. Note that the conflict-free condition is satisfied in Figure 3.8(b). In the first slot stations 1, 2, and 3 tune to wavelengths 3, 1, and 2 respectively, and in the second slot they tune to 2, 3, and 1 respectively. Because all channels and all transceivers are active at all times, the network resources are utilized to maximum efficiency.

---

[11] As in the TDM/TDMA case of Figure 3.7, this may require accounting for unequal propagation delays to the coupler. In certain extreme cases involving long distances and/or large fiber dispersion, synchronization at the coupler is insufficient to avoid conflicts in TDM/T-WDMA. These occur when the differences in propagation times for different wavelengths may be great enough so that different λ-channels are aligned at the coupler but are misaligned by the time they reach the receivers.

Note that the four ingredients of multipoint connectivity are present in the TDM/T-WDMA case:

1. Logical channel multiplexing at the transmitters using TDM

2. Optical multicast via the star coupler

3. Optical multiple access using T-WDMA

4. Logical channel demultiplexing by tuning the receivers to the right wavelength at the right time

Multipoint connections can be realized using many types and combinations of multiplexing and multiple access. These are discussed in more depth in Chapter 5.

3.2.2 Packet Switching in the Optical Layer: The MAC Sublayer

The fixed capacity allocation produced by the periodic frame structure in the previous examples is well adapted to stream-type traffic. However, in the case of asynchronous packet traffic[12] this approach may produce very poor performance. To see why, consider two basic characteristics of applications typically carried using packet switching:

1. *Burstiness:* The "bursty" nature of the information flow tends to produce poor transmission efficiency if fixed capacity allocation is used.

2. *Need for high logical connectivity:* In typical packet-switched applications it is common for a station to require simultaneous logical connections with a large number of other stations. (This is one of the primary advantages of packet-switched transport.) Although the aggregate traffic may be large, each logical connection between a pair of stations typically carries only a very small fraction of the total.

These considerations suggest that dedicating a fixed capacity to each LC is difficult, inefficient, and offers poor quality of service. For example, imagine extending the broadcast star example of Figure 3.5 to 100 stations, each supporting an end system operating as a LAN gateway and requiring an LC to each of the 99 other gateways. Full connectivity using TDM/TDMA would require 9,900 time slots—one for each LC—which would lead to poor optical transceiver utilization and high delays.

The poor transceiver utilization results from the fact that each transmitter or receiver is idle 99% of the time. The delay is due to the fact that when a LAN has traffic ready to be transmitted to another LAN (say, a file to be transferred), it needs a large capacity allocation immediately. Instead, it only has one slot available out of 9,900 in

---

[12] Henceforth we usually employ the term *packet* generically to refer either to fixed-length cell-based or variable-length packet-based data flow.

a long frame. For example, with a 1-Gbps channel bitrate, the effective capacity allocated to one connection is only 101 Kbps. The inferior performance is a consequence of the fact that we are treating packet traffic exactly as if it were stream traffic, and assigning a fixed-capacity pipe to each LC.

On the other hand, by implementing a packet-switching function that reaches down into the optical layer it is possible to maintain a very large number of LCs simultaneously using *dynamic capacity allocation*. This is accomplished by exploiting the essential advantage of the packet approach: packet-by-packet addressing and control. In packet traffic the identity of the LC to which a packet belongs (that is, addressing information), together with other control information, is carried in each packet's header. Traditional packet-switched transport networks process the packet headers in their logical switching nodes (packet switches), where they perform packet sorting and routing and other control functions. They typically have a sparsely connected logical topology.

For example, without looking below the logical link layer, the network of Figure 3.2(b) appears to be an ordinary packet-switched network with a logical topology in the form of a unidirectional ring. Packets delivered to the ring by the end systems are forwarded to the next LSN until they reach the destination node, at which point they exit to the end system. The binary decision forward/exit is made by reading the packet header. Now if the packets are processed in the transmission/reception processors of the NASs instead of in the LSNs, the packet-switching functions can be executed in the optical layer.[13] This is especially advantageous in the case of broadcast networks for three reasons:

1. Full logical connectivity for packet streams is supported easily by the fully connected optical infrastructure already in place.

2. Optical broadcast together with packet processing in the NASs amounts to parallel packet processing using the resources of all stations simultaneously, instead of sequential processing of all packets in each LSN they traverse.

3. An optical broadcast path is the most efficient support for logical multicast connections.

A schematic representation of a network executing packet switching in the optical layer is shown in Figure 3.2(c). On the left we show an underlying structure in the form of our ubiquitous broadcast star, the same physical topology that supported the fully connected logical topology in Figure 3.2(a) and the logical ring in Figure 3.2(b). Now the NASs are labeled *PS* to indicate the presence of an optical layer packet-switching function replacing the electronic switching executed in the LSNs of Figure 3.2(b).

---

[13] The reader should note the difference between *packet switching in the optical layer*, described here, and *optical packet switching*. The latter term, as it is used normally in the literature, refers to systems in which packet headers are processed *optically*, whereas the processing described here takes place in the transmission channel layer and is electronic.

The logical topology is now shown as a "cloud" containing the five NASs. This is meant to symbolize the fact that all stations share a common broadcast medium, as opposed to the case of Figure 3.2(a), in which five stations are joined by 20 individual point-to-point LCs.

Now to achieve full connectivity on the broadcast star without resorting to logical switching, we use the broadcast-and-select property of the star, in which information in the form of packets is broadcast to all receivers. Each one selects those destined for it and discards the others. Although broadcast-and-select with fixed capacity assignments for stream traffic was described in Section 3.2.1, we now have the potential for dynamic capacity assignment. The TPs can schedule packets based on instantaneous demand, priorities, and quality of service requirements for different traffic classes.

Comparing the logical topologies in Figures 3.3, 3.2(a), and 3.2(c), they all show full connectivity among the stations over a single logical hop. Their difference lies in how capacity is assigned. In the case of Figure 3.2(c), the capacity of the broadcast star is shared dynamically among the five stations, whereas in the other cases, a fixed capacity is assigned to each logical link. In all cases, the actual physical topology—a ring or star—is hidden from view and is largely irrelevant.

To delve further into implementation of packet switching in the optical layer, it is useful to recall its antecedents. Packet switching over a shared medium existed well before the deployment of optical fibers. Examples of conventional shared media are terrestrial radio and satellite, in which the medium is free space (the "ether"), and wired buses and rings, in which the medium is a copper cable. When these were introduced into data networks, special MAC protocols were developed to adapt the higher layers of the network architecture to the unique features of the shared medium. The role of the MAC protocol is to replace the standard data link control (DLC) protocols designed for a point-to-point link by procedures for efficient utilization of a medium accessed simultaneously by many users. Most MAC protocols are designed for LANs and MANs, and the basic problem they must address is contention resolution; that is, how to control the scheduling of packet transmissions among many contending stations so that the system performs as efficiently as possible.

The most commonly used shared *optical* medium is the broadcast star. Control of optical media requires a MAC protocol that has many of the same features as the earlier MAC protocols, yet is adapted to the unique properties of optical networks. A good way to understand how an optical MAC protocol should operate is to examine a LAN protocol designed for a wired bus—carrier-sense multiple access with collision detection (CSMA/CD). Employed in Ethernet, this is probably the most widely used MAC protocol today. To illustrate, consider the system of Figure 3.9(a). Four stations are shown connected to the bus, which propagates signals in both directions. The station access arrangement appears in Figure 3.9(b), indicating that the end system (for example, a data terminal, personal computer, or workstation) is interfaced to a transceiver coupled into the cable. (Typically the interface is located in the end system, and the transceiver is located at the cable tap.) A packet to be transmitted from the end system is passed to the interface, which encapsulates it into a format suitable for transmission on the cable, and buffers it to await transmission.

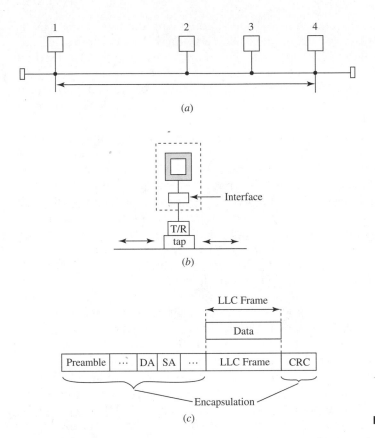

(a)

(b)

(c)

FIGURE 3.9 CSMA/CD.

A simplified picture of the encapsulated format is shown in Figure 3.9(c). The information from the end system is first enveloped in a variable-length logical link control (LLC) frame, to which is added a *preamble* to allow the receiver to synchronize and recognize the beginning of the frame. A header including destination address and source address[14] also precedes the LLC frame, which is followed by a group of cyclic redundancy check bits (CRC) used for error detection.

The procedure for transmitting the frames is as follows: On receipt of a data frame from the end system, the interface sends the encapsulated frame to the transceiver for transmission on the cable as soon as the transceiver senses the cable to be idle (the "carrier sense" part of the protocol). If, during transmission of a frame, the transceiver detects another frame on the cable (in other words, a *collision*—the "collision detection" part), it aborts its transmission and schedules the frame for retransmission at a later time.

---

[14] If the LAN is part of a larger network (for example, a subnet of an internet), then the LAN addresses are *local* addresses, which differ from *global* internet addresses. In some of our subsequent discussions of packet switching in subnets of large optical networks, this local/global distinction is needed.

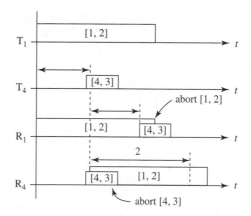

FIGURE 3.10 CSMA/CD collision.

A characteristic of this and many other MAC protocols is the possibility that a frame will be lost, thereby requiring retransmission. The CSMA/CD protocol is a refined version of the random access protocol known as ALOHA, first used on a terrestrial radio medium at the University of Hawaii [Abramson73]. Random access uses neither carrier sense nor collision detection. However, the two protocols share the following three properties:

1. There is no coordination among transmissions from different stations.
2. Collisions can occur.
3. If collisions occur, retransmissions are used to recover lost packets.

The refinements in CSMA/CD over random access simply reduce the probability of collisions and mitigate their effects when they occur.

Figure 3.10 shows the events associated with a collision, for which it is assumed that packet transmission times are long compared with τ—the end-to-end propagation time on the bus. A worst case is shown in which stations 1 and 4, at opposite ends of the bus in Figure 3.9(a), are transmitting to stations 2 and 3 respectively. Time traces as seen at transmitters T_1 and T_4 and receivers R_1 and R_4 are shown. Observe that T_1 begins transmission of a frame [1, 2] first, and it takes a time τ to propagate to station 4. Just before it reaches the other station, T_4, thinking the cable is idle, begins to transmit a frame [4, 3], which propagates to the left, toward station 1.

Both of these transmissions begin to overlap on the bus, garbling the information received at stations 2 and 3. But shortly after beginning its transmission, R_4 detects the collision with [1, 2], which has now reached station 4. This causes T_4 to abort its transmission as shown. None of this is known to station 1 until approximately τ seconds later, when the inital portion of [4, 3] reaches the other end of the cable, at which time R_1 detects the collision and aborts its transmission [1, 2]. The total time occupied on the cable by this event is slightly more than 2τ. This represents time lost for useful transmissions and limits the maximum throughput of the system. Furthermore, each collision and retransmission causes an additional delay until the frame is finally transmitted successfully. It should be clear from the figure that the smaller the end-to-end propagation time τ, the less time is lost in collisions.

In fact, it turns out that the throughput efficiency of CSMA/CD under high loads is approximately $1/(1 + 5a)$, where $a = \tau/m$, and m is the frame transmission time. Thus, perfect efficiency (no time wasted in collisions) is approached as propagation time gets small (i.e., a short cable) and/or frame transmission times get large (i.e, many bits per packet and/or low transmission bitrates). For example, typical parameters for Ethernet might be a cable of length 2.5 km, a transmission rate of 10 Mbps, and a frame length of 1,000 bits. Taking the speed of light in the cable as 1.5×10^8 m/sec, this gives an end-to-end propagation time of approximately 10.9 μs, $a = 0.109$, and a throughput efficiency of approximately 0.65. The short propagation time means that the overall delay for successful packet transmission, even after several retries, is quite small.

Unfortunately, all of this changes radically in the context of optical networks. First, we are generally interested in networks (MANs and WANs) of far wider geographic extent than Ethernets. Second, the bitrates on a single λ-channel are typically in the gigabit-per-second range. As a consequence we have $a \gg 1$, which makes CSMA/CD impossible! What are the alternatives? To suggest some approaches, think of implementing optical layer packet switching on the star of Figure 3.5 operating in a broadcast-and-select mode.

To fix ideas, let us extend the TDM/TDMA and TDM/T-WDMA examples of Figures 3.7 and 3.8 to packet switching. In these two cases we created three and six *fixed-capacity* LCs respectively by using a periodic slot assignment. Now, one of our objectives is to achieve *dynamic* capacity allocation; that is, to implement complete and instantaneous sharing of the broadcast medium on demand. The role of the MAC protocol is indicated schematically in Figure 3.11, which shows an NAS with packet-switching functionality. We assume now that the data belonging to LCs [1, 2] and [1, 3]

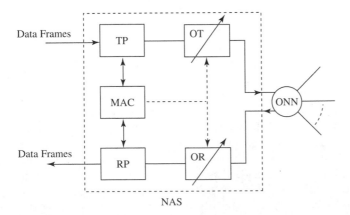

FIGURE 3.11 NAS equipped for packet switching.

flow from the end system to the NAS over either two separate external ports or over a single port in the form of randomly interleaved packets. It is then up to the TP to recognize the individual packets and process them accordingly, encapsulating them into a properly addressed format (similar to the CSMA/CD format of Figure 3.9). The encapsulated packets must then be scheduled and transmitted under the supervision of a suitable MAC protocol (indicated by the MAC block in the station).

How should this protocol operate? It all depends on the objectives to be achieved and the information and resources available to the participating stations. For simplicity let us begin with the assumption of a single, shared channel using only time–division techniques. Suppose the packets are of fixed length, so they can be inserted into slots of equal length. Now the time traces in Figure 3.7 can be reinterpreted in a packet-switched context. The time slots are no longer grouped into a periodic frame schedule; instead, packets are transmitted on a slot-by-slot basis. Ignoring the fixed periodic schedule in Figure 3.7, the data segments can now be interpreted as packets, where, for example, the notation $[1, 2]_2$ represents a packet with source and destination addresses 1 and 2 respectively, and with sequence number 2.

The reception processors in the stations must now contain suitable packet filters, which have the functions of stripping the encapsulation, reading local destination addresses, capturing all packets destined for the station, routing them to the correct external ports, dropping the unwanted packets, and performing error checking. Thus, in this example the reception processor in NAS 2 must filter out all packets belonging to LCs $[1, 3]$ and $[2, 3]$, retaining only those on $[1, 2]$. Note that dynamic scheduling allows for the capacity to be allocated based on instantaneous demand: When a station has a packet to transmit, it schedules it in the next available slot. It is this feature of packet switching that allows us to treat the broadcast star as a *shared-capacity* rather than *fixed-capacity* medium.

The difficult part of dynamic scheduling is that, in the absence of a periodic frame structure, some sort of coordination and synchronization among the transmitters is needed to resolve contention among the stations for the available channel capacity. It is the function of the MAC protocol to arbitrate contention, attempting to keep collisions to a minimum and rescheduling transmissions in cases of lost packets. The simplest protocols (e.g., random access) have no coordination and minimize collisions by keeping traffic levels low. More complex protocols rely on one or more separate "control channels" to supply coordination and scheduling information, thereby reducing collision probabilities or avoiding them altogether. (The example in Figure 3.7 shows perfect scheduling with no collisions, which is not generally achieved in commonly used MAC protocols.)

Although the contention problem is the bad news in multiwavelength broadcast networks, the good news is that multiple wavelengths are available to use for concurrent transmissions. To illustrate, consider a packet-switched generalization of the TDM/T-WDMA case of Figure 3.8, as shown in Figure 3.12. We continue with the assumption of a slotted system with six active logical channels. Figure 3.12(a) shows four slots in a possible sequence of packet transmissions using three λ-channels and FT-TR. Note that the schedule is now assigned dynamically according to the demand

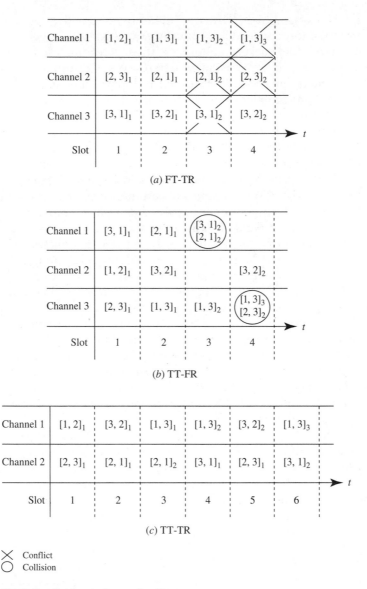

FIGURE 3.12 Packet switching in the optical layer.

of each station, with connection [1, 3] carrying more traffic than the others. Note also that there is a receiver conflict in the third and fourth slots, with receiver 1 required to tune to two different channels in slot 3 and receiver 3 required to tune to two different channels in slot 4. In these cases each receiver must make a choice, picking up one transmission and losing the other.

Figure 3.12(b) shows a variation of the previous case, using three channels and TT-FR. The same sequence of packet transmissions appears, but in this case they are carried on different channels because the channel assignment is determined by the destination address rather than the source address. As a result, the conflicts that appeared in the third and fourth time slots in the previous example are now replaced by *collisions* in those slots. This is a more serious problem because a collision mutilates both packets, resulting in double the loss of the FT-TR case.

Figure 3.12(c) shows another version of the same example, using only two channels and requiring tuning of both transmitters and receivers. Now a properly coordinated *channel–slot schedule* is shown, in which all of the packets are transmitted in six time slots (the minimum possible number with two channels) without losses. Note that the channel–slot assignment is done on a packet-by-packet basis, and results in a different interleaving of packets than in the previous cases. However, it can be seen from the sequence numbers that the packets are delivered in the proper order.

Although the previous examples focused on point-to-point LCs, multicast connections come "free" simply by including the multicast destination addresses in the packet headers. (Of course, packet scheduling must be arranged to accommodate the multicast addresses without conflicts.)

In comparing the previous examples it can be seen that each is characterized by different constraints on capacity sharing. In TDM/TDMA, the medium (one λ-channel) is fully shared among all logical channels. In FT-TR, TT-FR, and TT-TR, partial sharing takes place in which all logical channels originating at a given station may share a capacity not exceeding one λ-channel, with the same type of sharing occurring for all channels terminating at a given station.[15]

The conflicts and collisions (and concomitant packet loss) in the FT-TR and TT-FR cases resulted from a lack of coordination among the stations. To avoid losses, two conditions must exist:

1. The transmitting stations must agree among themselves on a conflict- and collision-free set of channel–slot assignments.

2. The receiving stations must know these assignments so that they can tune properly to pick up the packets destined for them.

Both of these conditions require the following actions:

1. Each station must request permission to transmit to a specified destination.

2. A control algorithm must be executed (either centralized or distributed among all stations).

3. A scheduling decision must be communicated to the concerned parties.

---

[15] All remarks here on conflicts and collisions in shared channel systems are predicated on the assumption of a single transceiver per station. In cases where stations may have arrays of transmitters and/or receivers, the rules governing conflicts and collisions are more complex (see Section 5.4).

Depending on the network configuration, these actions require exchanges of vary-ing amounts of control information among the stations. This might be done on one or more wavelengths or time slots reserved for that purpose, and in some cases it might require additional optical transceivers. Control information for scheduling sub-sequent packets can also be piggybacked on information packets. In the FT-TR and TT-TR cases, both transmitting and receiving stations must exchange control infor-mation, but in TT-FR it is only the transmitters that need to agree on a schedule to avoid collisions because no conflicts are possible.

In typical packet-switched broadcast-and-select systems there is usually a compro-mise between ideal lossless communication (requiring extensive exchange of control information together with possibly complex scheduling computations) and uncoor-dinated lossy transmissions. The compromise involves a trade-off between cost (in terms of NAS complexity and spectrum utilization) and performance (in terms of throughput, loss, and delay). The performance-to-cost ratio for most MAC protocols diminishes as the number of stations increases.

The procedures governing exchange of control information, conflict resolution, and recovery from losses are the distinguishing features of MAC protocols. Fig-ure 3.11 indicates as dashed lines the various control paths associated with media access control. In the most general case the MAC protocol coordinates many activi-ties executed in the other components of the NAS, including scheduling, transceiver tuning, and signaling to and from other stations. Because the specifics of these ex-changes vary from one protocol to another, we defer further remarks to Section 5.6, where a more detailed treatment of packet switching in the optical layer is presented.

It is instructive to place the optical layer MAC protocols in the context of the multiwavelength network architecture. The relations among the layers are most eas-ily understood by comparing them with MAC protocols in a conventional layered network architecture: the Open Systems Interconnection (OSI) Reference Model (see [Schwartz87], p. 15). The second layer of the OSI model is the DLC layer, whose func-tion is to ensure reliable and ordered delivery of data frames over a point-to-point link (see Figure 3.13). The DLC layer uses the services of the physical layer, which provides for transmission of the underlying bitstream on a point-to-point physical medium such as a wire or fiber.

As shown in Figure 3.13, in the case of shared media these two layers are replaced by three: the LLC and MAC sublayers, and a new physical layer adapted to multiaccess on the shared medium. For example in CSMA/CD, the higher level features specific to this protocol, including encapsulation and decapsulation, scheduling transmissions and retransmissions, and error detection, are performed in the MAC sublayer. Lower level functions associated with the physical medium, including sensing the idle chan-nel and detecting collisions, as well as bit transmission and reception, are performed in the physical layer. The remaining high-level functions associated with error-free delivery of frames in the correct sequence take place in the LLC sublayer. Comparing this layered view with the hardware implementation of CSMA/CD shown in Fig-ure 3.9(b), the physical layer would normally be implemented in the transceiver, the

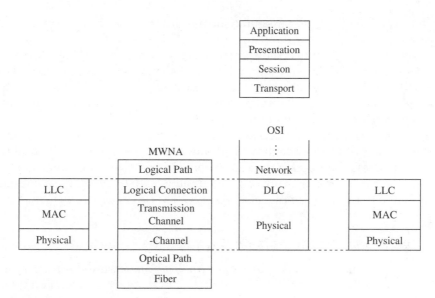

FIGURE 3.13 MAC protocol in the layered architecture.

MAC sublayer in the interface, and the LLC sublayer in the interface and/or the end system.

Now let us turn to the optical network case. The position of optical layer packet-switching functions in the multiwavelength network architecture is shown in Figure 3.13 for comparison with the OSI protocol stack. In this case, similar LLC, MAC, and physical layers can be defined, which take the place of the logical connection, transmission channel, and λ-channel sublayers as shown. The location of the MAC and physical layers at a level corresponding to the transmission channel and λ-channel layers reflects the fact that medium access generally requires special operations on the bitstream (frame encapsulation and decapsulation, packet filtering, parity check computation, and so forth) and may require control of the optical transceivers (rapid tuning for WDMA operation and/or on–off switching for TDMA operation).

As in the case of conventional packet-switched networks, an LLC frame enveloping the useful data is prepared in the LLC sublayer and is passed down to the MAC sublayer together with the local address (i.e., the identity of the NAS) to which it is destined. The MAC sublayer encapsulates it for transmission on the optical medium in a format similar to Figure 3.9(c). Included in the encapsulation is the source address (the address of the transmitting NAS) and the destination address (the destination NAS specified by the LLC sublayer). The encapsulated frame is then passed to the physical layer, which does the actual transmission on the optical medium, executing the necessary slot synchronization and transmitter tuning. Encapsulated frames received by an NAS are passed up from the physical layer to the MAC sublayer, which performs error detection and packet filtering (i.e., address checking), strips away the encapsulation, and passes the successfully received frames up to the LLC sublayer.

In the case of a purely optical transport network (e.g., end systems attached directly to NASs, as in Figure 3.2[a], the logical link layer would normally reside in the end system, with the MAC and physical layers in the NAS. On the other hand, the transport network may consist of several packet-switched optical subnets joined together through an overlay that consists of logical switching nodes (e.g., ATM switches). In this case we have two layers of packet switching. Now the LLC sublayer would be located in the LSNs, where a routing table would determine the next (optical layer) destination address. In this case the destination address may be the local subnet address of an intermediate station on a logical multihop path to the ultimate destination (see the shuffle hypernet example in Section 3.5.2.1).

3.2.3 Additional Comments on Broadcast-and-Select

We have seen that static networks can be operated in a broadcast-and-select mode with either fixed-capacity or dynamically scheduled (packet-switched) LCs. Fundamental to broadcast-and-select is the fact that LCs can be created and reconfigured solely by the actions of the access stations, with logical connectivity ranging from a few point-to-point connections to complete multipoint connectivity. The multiplexing and multiple access procedures necessary for realizing high connectivity rely in important ways on resource sharing: in the stations and on the fibers. This is a recurring theme throughout the book.

The broadcast-and-select principle based on a star, bus, or tree physical topology cannot be scaled to large networks for three reasons:

1. *Spectrum use:* Because all transmissions share the same fibers, there is no possibility of optical spectrum reuse, so the required spectrum typically grows at least proportionately to the number of transmitting stations.
2. *Protocol complexity:* Synchronization problems, signaling overhead, time delays, and processing complexity all increase rapidly with the number of stations and the number of LCs.
3. *Survivability:* There are no alternate routes in case of a failure. Furthermore, a failure at a critical point (either the star coupler or the head end of a folded bus) can bring the whole network down.

For these reasons, a practical limit on the number of stations in a broadcast star is approximately 100. Nevertheless, we show in Section 3.4.2 how larger networks can be constructed using broadcast-and-select subnets as basic building blocks. Using this technique, it is possible to construct networks that circumvent the limits of geographical reach imposed by the optical technology, as well as the limits of connectivity and throughput imposed by economics.

3.3 Wavelength Routed Networks

In the previous section we limited consideration to connections over networks with fixed optical paths and no wavelength selectivity in the nodes. Much more flexibility is achieved when wavelength selectivity and/or controllability is introduced in the optical path sublayer. In this section the networks being considered are wavelength routed, in the sense that each λ-channel can be recognized in the ONNs and routed individually. This provides the maximum control of signals within the optical path sublayer. We assume throughout that the stations contain transceivers tunable over the full range of usable wavelengths, and the network nodes are either static wavelength routers or wavelength-selective optical permutation switches (WSXCs). This implies that all optical paths are point-to-point, so the only way multipoint logical connectivity can be achieved is by using several point-to-point optical connections (WDM/WDMA). This normally requires one optical transceiver for each connection.[16] (Multipoint connections supported by multipoint optical paths are discussed in the context of linear lightwave networks in Section 3.4 and in Chapter 6.) To keep things simple, we also assume in this chapter that *there is no wavelength conversion in the network*. (Wavelength conversion in WRNs is considered in Chapter 6.) As indicated in Figure 2.5(b), a wavelength routed network with m λ-channels can be viewed as m independently controlled copies of the original network.

Because all connections are point-to-point, the distinctions between connectivity at the optical path, optical connection, and LC levels disappear, so it is sufficient to deal with optical connections only, with the understanding that an optical connection $(a, b)_i$ supports a corresponding LC $[a, b]$ and is supported by a corresponding optical path $\langle a, b \rangle$. In moving from the static networks of Section 3.2 to the WRNs in this section, we shift our focus from *logical connections* created by the actions of the NASs alone to *optical connections* created by the coordinated actions of the NASs and the optical network nodes.

Wavelength selectivity in the ONNs offers considerable advantages in terms of spectrum reuse, even without control of the optical paths. Consider, for example, full interconnection of five end systems (without loopback) using a star network with a central node that is now a static wavelength router of the type shown in Figure 2.9.

Figure 3.14 shows the resultant network, in which each NAS contains four transceivers tuned to route optical connections to the other four NASs and to receive signals from the others. Using the wavelength assignment rule described in

---

[16] In theory, a multipoint connection can be set up in a wavelength routed network using time– and wavelength–division techniques. Thus, if a single transmitting station is connected to several receiving stations, with each connection realized on a point-to-point optical path using a distinct wavelength, then a one-to-many connection can be realized by tuning the transmitter rapidly over all wavelengths in the set. A similar arrangement can be constructed for many-to-one connectivity using receiver tuning. In principle, many-to-many connectivity can also be achieved by tuning both transmitters and receivers rapidly. However, this approach becomes exceedingly complicated due to the fact that each path has a different propagation delay. Therefore, we do not pursue it further here.

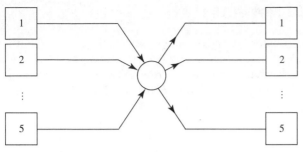

(*a*) Wavelength Router

Destination

Source	1	2	3	4	5
1		1	2	3	4
2	4		1	2	3
3	3	4		1	2
4	2	3	4		1
5	1	2	3	4	

(*b*) Wavelength Assignments

FIGURE 3.14 Wavelength routed star network.

Section 2.3.1.2, these connections can be realized using four wavelengths for a fivefold reuse of the optical spectrum. The wavelength assignments for the optical connections are shown in Figure 3.14.

Comparing the static router with the broadcast star of Figure 3.2(a), we find that five times as many wavelengths are necessary to support full connectivity in the broadcast star, reflecting the lack of wavelength reuse in the broadcast network.

3.3.1 Routing and Channel Assignment

Except for special cases of relatively small networks, in which optical paths may remain fixed indefinitely, WRNs need some sort of control in their ONNs. Thus we now move on to networks containing wavelength-selective optical switches. In establishing an optical connection we must deal with both channel assignment and routing. Channel assignment (executed in the λ-channel sublayer) involves allocating an available wavelength to the connection and tuning the transmitting and receiving station to the assigned wavelength. Routing (executed in the optical path sublayer) involves determining a suitable optical path for the assigned λ-channel and setting switches in the network nodes to establish that path. It should be noted that an optical path in a WRN is associated with a particular wavelength, so a path cannot be set up until a wavelength is allocated.

3.3.1.1 Dedicated and Switched Connections: Rearrangeability

Implementation of routing and channel assignment (RCA) is a quite different problem depending on whether the optical connections are dedicated or switched. Dedicated connections are assumed to be held for a relatively long period of time. This would be the case, for example, for connections provisioned to support a logical network overlay riding on top of the optical infrastructure. These connections would be chosen at the design stage of the LN and perhaps modified occasionally in response to changing load conditions or equipment failure. Switched (demand-assigned) connections, on the other hand, are established and released on demand, with holding times that might be as short as a minute or less.

For our purposes the characteristic that distinguishes dedicated from switched connections is that requests for the former occur in the form of a *prescribed set*, whereas switched connection requests occur as a *random sequence.* Thus, the complete set of dedicated connections for an LN is established when that network is initialized. However, requests for switched connections are signaled to an optical network manager as they occur, and the ONM has the responsibility of deciding whether to accept or to block the request. This admission control decision is based on various considerations, including the current network load, fairness, priorities, and so forth. For simplicity we assume here that the only factors that govern acceptance of a connection are the physical constraints on RCA that either permit or block the connection. It should be clear that the ability of a network to accept a switched connection request depends on its current state; that is, the pattern of connections that are currently active in the network. As we shall see, *rearrangement* of active connections can sometimes create free paths for new requests that would otherwise be blocked.

3.3.1.2 Channel Assignment Constraints

We illustrate the constraints on channel assignment in WRNs using the example of Figure 3.15. The figure shows a network containing seven access stations and three ONNs. Each internodal link consists of a single pair of unidirectional fibers. Because the physical topology is a tree, there is only one possible optical path between any pair of stations, so there are no routing decisions to be made. Because there is no wave-

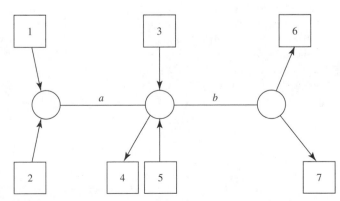

FIGURE 3.15 Channel assignment example.

length conversion in this network, each optical connection must obey the wavelength continuity condition already invoked in Section 2.2. Suppose that the available optical spectrum contains two λ-channels on wavelengths λ_1 and λ_2. The unidirectional optical connections $(2, 4)$, $(1, 6)$, and $(5, 7)$ are to be established. Assume first that they are *dedicated* connections. By inspecting the complete set, it is clear that the wavelength assignment $(2, 4)_1$, $(1, 6)_2$, and $(5, 7)_1$ is a feasible choice because connections superimposed on common fibers are always assigned distinct λ-channels. As indicated earlier, this DCA *condition* is one of the basic optical network routing constraints. It ensures that the optical signals sharing a fiber do not interfere with each other at the receivers.

Now suppose the same set occurs as part of a sequence of *switched* connections as follows. The first request is for connection $(2, 4)$, which is assigned λ_1. This is followed by $(3, 6)$ and $(5, 7)$, which are assigned λ_1 and λ_2 respectively. Then $(3, 6)$ is terminated and a request for $(1, 6)$ is received. Because λ_1 is now in use on link a and λ_2 on link b, the current state of the network makes it impossible to add the new connection without a DCA violation, and it is blocked. Note that blocking was caused by an unfortunate evolution of the state of activity in the network. However, if it were possible to *rearrange* the active wavelength assignments to $(2, 4)_1$ and $(5, 7)_1$, then the new request could be accepted using λ_2.[17] We have encountered an analogous rearrangeability problem before in the context of permutation switches (see Section 2.3.2.1). In the switch, however, the entity being rearranged is a path rather than a wavelength assignment. In a larger WRN, connection rearrangement might involve changing both optical paths (rerouting) and channel assignments.

This is generally impractical for two reasons:

1. It requires momentary interruption of active connections, which may be unacceptable to users.

2. Finding a rearrangement that "opens up" the network to the new connection request typically requires solving an extremely complex combinatorial problem.

We therefore rule out the possibility of rearranging switched connections. Note, however, that given a prescribed set of dedicated connections, knowledge of all connections on the list can often be used to accommodate them without conflicts. Thus we see that blocking is more likely to occur when assigning a sequence of switched connections rather than a set of dedicated ones, and it is more likely to occur without wavelength converters than with them.

As one more variant of this example, suppose we change things by using only a single wavelength, but putting two fiber pairs in each internodal link; that is, we trade a twofold reduction in spectrum usage for a twofold increase in fibers. How does network performance change? In all the cases cited earlier there were never more than

---

[17] If wavelength conversion was allowed, the new connection could be accommodated without rearrangement by assigning it λ_2 on link a and λ_1 on link b.

two connections active on an internodal fiber (and only one connection active on each access fiber). This implies that all connections can be accommodated on the modified network while using (and reusing) only one wavelength.

There is an important observation here: Networks with multifiber links perform better than those with multiple wavelengths. The rule is that a network operating on F wavelengths with one fiber pair per link can never perform better (and generally will perform worse) than the same network with its links increased to F fiber pairs and its spectrum decreased to a single wavelength. However, a network operating on F wavelengths with one fiber pair per link and all of its nodes equipped with wavelength converters is *equivalent* to the same network with its links increased to F fiber pairs and its spectrum decreased to a single wavelength.[18]

The reason for these relations is that multiwavelength networks without wavelength converters operate under the constraint of wavelength continuity, but there is no equivalent constraint in multifiber networks, nor in networks using wavelength conversion.

To summarize the previous discussion as it applies to wavelength routed networks without wavelength converters, we see that routing and channel assignments are subject to the following two constraints:

1. *Wavelength continuity:* The wavelength of each optical connection remains the same on all links it traverses from source to destination.

2. *Distinct channel assignment:* All connections sharing a common fiber must be assigned distinct channels. (This applies to access links as well as internodal links.)

Note that the first is a constraint imposed by the laws of physics, whereas the second is a design constraint required for proper network operation. At this point it is important to clarify the meaning of the phrase *distinct channel*. In the context of this section, channel means λ-*channel*, so that distinct channel assignment means distinct *wavelength* assignment. However, we have already seen a case, in Figure 3.7, in which signals on the same wavelength were superimposed on the same fibers (the outbound fibers on a star) without interfering. This was possible because they were nonoverlapping in time. In that example, the noninterfering channels corresponded to optical signals sharing a common wavelength but confined to different time slots using TDMA. More generally, we shall define channels to be distinct if they can be distinguished at a receiver when superimposed on its access fiber. Distinct channels are normally *orthogonal*, typically nonoverlapping in either optical frequency or time. As we consider more complex multiplexing and multiple access schemes in later chapters, the meaning of distinct channels is reexamined.

Although the DCA condition is necessary to ensure distinguishability of signals on the same fiber, it is possible (and generally advantageous) to *reuse* the same wavelength

---

[18] This assumes that each ONN is capable of permuting connections among all fibers on a link.

on fiber–disjoint paths. This includes paths that may be carried on different fibers contained in the same (multifiber) link. Channel assignment constraints equivalent to the DCA condition exist in all types of communication networks. However, the wavelength continuity condition is unique to transparent optical networks, making routing and wavelength assignment a more challenging task than the related problem in conventional networks.

As suggested in Figure 1.6, the performance of a network depends not only on its physical resources, but also on how it is controlled. Routing and channel assignment is the fundamental control problem in large optical networks. Generally, the RCA problem for dedicated connections can be treated off-line, so that computationally intensive optimization techniques are appropriate. On the other hand, routing and channel assignment decisions for switched traffic must be made rapidly, and hence suboptimal heuristics must normally be used. The objective of an RCA algorithm is to achieve the best possible network performance within the limits of the physical constraints.

The RCA problem can be cast in numerous forms. For example, in the case of dedicated connections we may wish to accommodate a prescribed set of optical connections using a minimum number of wavelengths or using the shortest optical paths for each connection consistent with a limit on the number of available wavelengths. In the case of switched connections, the objective might be to maximize the offered traffic given a fixed number of wavelengths and a specified limit on blocking probability. The next section includes a few simple examples, confined to dedicated connections only. A more comprehensive look at RCA for both dedicated and switched connections appears in Chapter 6.

3.3.2 Routing and Channel Assignment Examples

Several examples of RCA are presented to illustrate various possible trade-offs among network resources and performance. All examples deal with finding optical connections that provide full logical connectivity among five stations; that is, embedding a fully connected five-station logical topology on the given physical topology while observing the constraints of the network. An RCA solution that satisfies the constraints is given in each case. Although this is presented as a *dedicated* connection problem, its solution gives an RCA rule for demand-assigned connections as well. If the five stations make point-to-point connection establishment/release requests in a random sequence, the requests can always be accepted without blocking as long as the RCA rule found for dedicated full connectivity is used.

In these and other examples to follow in later sections, the wavelength assignments are dependent on the manner in which the NASs are connected to their ONNs. A typical arrangement, in which a single-fiber-pair access link connects an NAS to an ONN, appears in Figure 2.29. In the case at hand, the ONN contains a wavelength-selective cross-connect, and the two access fibers connect to an input and output port on the WSXC. In the NAS, several optical transmitters are multiplexed onto the outbound access fiber, and several optical receivers are fed by the signals demultiplexed from the inbound access fiber. The transmission/reception processors interface the transceivers to the external ports, and may include electronic multiplexing/demultiplexing and switching equipment for connecting specified data streams from the transceivers to designated logical input/output ports. Although all transmitters and receivers may be tunable, the DCA condition requires that *all inbound (outbound) channels must be distinct*, in this case, because they share common fibers.

Figure 3.16 shows a different version of the NAS–ONN connection. Now n, the number of fiber pairs in the access link, is the same as the number of internodal links incident on the node. In the most general case, each access fiber directed outbound from the NAS may multiplex signals from several fixed or tunable optical transmitters, and each access fiber directed inbound to the NAS may feed signals to several fixed or tunable optical receivers. Thus, the contents of each of the n boxes labeled OTs/ORs in Figure 3.16 corresponds to the optical portion of the NAS in Figure 2.29. Again, the transceivers are interfaced to external input/output ports through TPs/RPs that may be used for cross-connecting data streams in an arbitrary fashion between the transceivers and end system equipment. In this case there are *no limitations* on channel assignment due to the access fibers, because the access fibers can accommodate as many channels as the internodal fibers incident on the network node.

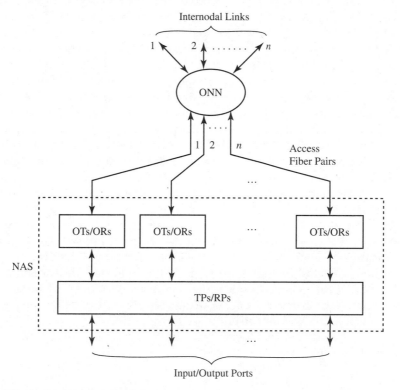

FIGURE 3.16 Nonblocking access link.

We shall refer to these multifiber-pair access connections as *nonblocking access links*. Carrying the nonblocking idea one step further, suppose that the usable optical spectrum contains Λ λ-channels, and that each OTs/ORs box contains an array of Λ fixed tuned transceivers covering the complete set of channels. Now the NAS (and its access fibers) can support as many optical connections as the internodal links incident on its ONN can carry. We shall refer to this arrangement as a *nonblocking NAS,* meaning that no potential optical connection terminating on that NAS will be blocked due to limitations in the station or its access link.[19]

3.3.2.1 The Bidirectional Ring

Our first example is that shown in Figure 3.3, wherein a fully connected logical topology containing five NASs is to be embedded on a ring. Because each LC requires a point-to-point optical connection in this case, four optical transceivers are needed in each NAS. The objective now is to specify RCAs using a minimum number of wavelengths. As mentioned earlier, the feasible wavelength assignments depend on how each NAS is connected to the network. The simplest approach is the configuration of Figure 3.17(a), which uses the single-fiber-pair access connection of Figure 2.29.

In the ring of Figure 3.17(a), the network nodes are WSXCs with three input and output ports, routing each wavelength around a ring or between a ring and an NAS. The rings are labeled *L(R)* for left (right) propagation past the NASs. Each NAS has four tunable optical transmitters multiplexed onto its outbound access fiber and four receivers fed from its inbound access fiber. Because this is a two access fiber connection, the optical connections are subject to the DCA condition on the access links; each inbound (outbound) connection to an NAS must be on a distinct wavelength.

A bipartite *optical connection graph* (OCG) for this example is shown in Figure 3.17(b). The DCA requirements on the access links translate into a classic edge–coloring problem on the OCG. Selecting distinct wavelengths is equivalent to coloring the edges of the OCG so that all edges incident on the same vertex have different colors. It is well known that this problem can always be solved in bipartite graphs using a number of colors equal to the maximum degree of the vertices, which in this case is four. This is only a necessary condition, however, because DCA must also be observed on each internodal fiber in the ring.

A solution to the RCA problem, in this case using *shortest path routing*, is shown in an RCA table in Figure 3.17(c), which indicates the path and wavelength assigned to each optical connection. (An entry in the table of the form (nL) means that the corresponding connection is routed on ring L using wavelength λ_n.) Shortest path routing means that each connection is routed on the ring (L or R) yielding the least number of optical hops: in this case, no more than two. Note that the problem is solved using four wavelengths, for a spectrum reuse factor of five.

Another approach uses a nonblocking two-fiber pair access link following the interconnection structure depicted in Figure 3.16.

---

[19] The nonblocking condition does *not* apply to connections from other NASs attached to the same ONN.

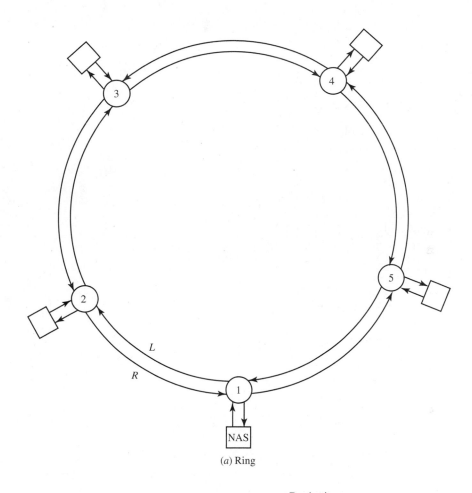

(a) Ring

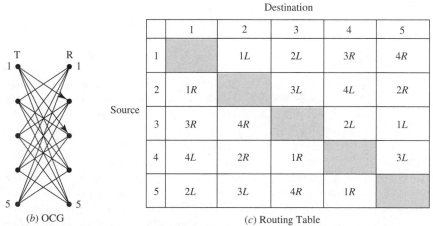

(b) OCG

Destination

	1	2	3	4	5
1		1L	2L	3R	4R
2	1R		3L	4L	2R
3	3R	4R		2L	1L
4	4L	2R	1R		3L
5	2L	3L	4R	1R	

Source

(c) Routing Table

FIGURE 3.17   Bidirectional ring: single access fiber pair.

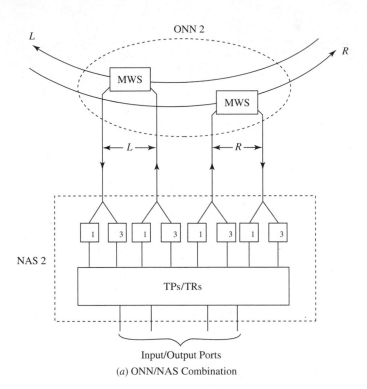

ONN 2

L

R

MWS

MWS

← *L* →   ← *R* →

NAS 2

| 1 | 3 | 1 | 3 | 1 | 3 | 1 | 3 |

TPs/TRs

Input/Output Ports

(a) ONN/NAS Combination

Destination

		1	2	3	4	5
	1		1*L*	2*L*	2*R*	1*R*
	2	1*R*		1*L*	3*L*	3*R*
Source	3	2*R*	1*R*		2*L*	1*L*
	4	2*L*	3*R*	2*R*		3*L*
	5	1*L*	3*L*	1*R*	3*R*	

(b) Routing Table

FIGURE 3.18 Bidirectional ring: two-access fiber pairs.

In this case, the ONN–NAS combination can be realized as shown in Figure 3.18(a). Now the NAS consists of two separate pairs of transceivers, with each pair multiplexed onto a separate access link *L* or *R*, connected to one of the rings. Using two access fiber pairs instead of one removes the DCA constraint on the access links, so fewer wavelengths are required. Because the allowable interconnections are limited, the WSXC can be realized using two 2×2 multiwavelength switches, one for each ring, operating as *wavelength add–drop multiplexers* (WADMs). Each WADM can be in the bar (=) or cross (**X**) state for each wavelength independently. When in the bar state for a wavelength λ_i, it passes that wavelength along the ring; when in the cross state, it drops the wavelength from the ring, routing it to a receiver in the NAS, and simultaneously adds a signal at the same wavelength to the ring, originating at a transmitter paired with the receiver. In effect there are two separate ring–ONN–NAS combinations grouped together at each node. The external input/output ports are connected to the transceivers through the TPs/RPs.

A possible set of wavelength assignments using shortest path routing is shown in the RCA table in Figure 3.18(b). For example, the assignments for NAS 2 correspond to the transceiver tuning for that NAS, as shown in Figure 3.18(a). This RCA requires only three wavelengths instead of four for full connectivity, due to the fact that wavelengths can be reused on the same access link (but not on the same access *fiber*). It is optimal in the sense that three is the minimum number of wavelengths required for full connectivity irrespective of how the NAS–ONN connection is realized. (A more general treatment of RCA on rings appears in Section 6.3.4.2.)

3.3.2.2 A Mesh Network

Now consider the five stations connected to ONNs in the mesh network of Figure 3.19. Our objective is the same as it was in the case of the ring: Find an RCA using a minimum number of wavelengths to realize the fully connected OCG shown in Figure 3.17(b). Again, each NAS must have a total of four transceivers. In this case a lower bound on the number of required wavelengths is two, no matter what routing is used and no matter what access connections are used. (Why?) Now let us first assume single fiber pair access connections, which means that the lower bound is raised

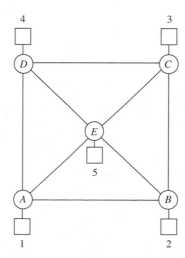

FIGURE 3.19 A mesh network.

to four because four connections must share each access fiber. It is left as an exercise for the reader to show that four wavelengths are sufficient using shortest path routing.

Unfortunately, this result does not provide any improvement in spectrum utilization over the bidirectional ring, despite the richer physical topology of the mesh. This is because the access fibers are the bottleneck. To remove this bottleneck, suppose a nonblocking multifiber-pair access link is used for each station. (No increase in the number of transceivers is required.) In this case all connections can be realized using two wavelengths, representing a tenfold reuse of the spectrum.[20] The exact wavelength assignment is left as an exercise for the reader.

These RCA examples illustrate some key issues in the design and control of wavelength routed networks. In particular, they show a trade-off between the extent of the fiber topology and the optical spectrum requirement: The more fibers there are and the more "densely" they are interconnected, the less wavelengths are needed. In this trade-off the functionality of the network node is a limiting parameter because the WSXC permits only point-to-point connections. The networks described in the next section broaden our view to include multipoint optical connectivity, thereby expanding greatly the options in implementing desired connectivity patterns.

3.4 Linear Lightwave Networks: Waveband Routing

The three classes of purely optical networks discussed in this chapter all have the same basic structure: NASs and optical nodes interconnected by fiber links. Their differences reside in the functionality of the nodes. The static networks described in Section 3.2 and the wavelength routed networks of Section 3.3 represent two extremes of ONN functionality: the former having no wavelength selectivity and no control, and the latter having independent control of each wavelength. The static case comprises *static single-waveband networks,* whereas the wavelength routed case corresponds to *dynamic single-wavelength-per-waveband networks.*

The LLNs described in this section subsume both of the other two classes as special cases. We use the term *LLN* to designate any network with nodes that perform strictly *linear* operations on optical signals. The most general type of LLN has nodes that function as waveband-selective linear divider combiners (LDCs) (that is, generalized optical switches). Recall from Section 2.3.2.3 that an LDC performs controllable optical signal routing, combining, and splitting. The combining function allows for the multiplexing of channels from several inbound fibers onto a single outbound fiber, and the splitting function provides for multicasting of optical power from a single inbound fiber to several outbound fibers. These functions are required to support *multipoint* optical connectivity.

---

[20] The minimal required number of access fibers varies from station to station, depending on the routing and wavelength assignments.

As was the case for WRNs, we exclude wavelength conversion from the LLNs and assume that switching within an optical network node occurs on a slow time scale, with switches changing their settings only during optical path establishment and release. Waveband selectivity in the nodes means that the optical path layer routes signals as bundles that contain all λ-channels within one waveband.

One can conceive of many special cases of LLNs. First, there are the "limiting" cases mentioned before. The static networks treated in Section 3.2 are examples of networks having no wavelength selectivity within their ONNs (single waveband networks), in which the nodes are fixed but still have combining and splitting functionality. At the other extreme, the wavelength routed case of Section 3.3 has no combining and splitting functions, but spectral resolution is refined to the point where the bundles recognized by the nodes consist of only one λ-channel.

Another important category is a single-wavelength-per-waveband network possessing combining and splitting properties (i.e., an "enhanced" WRN, containing LDCs in its nodes rather than permutation switches). Such a network is capable of establishing optical multicast connections as well as optical many-to-one connections on a wavelength-by-wavelength basis. A simple application of optical multicast is a "drop-and-continue" function at the optical level, providing an efficient way of distributing information on a common λ-channel to multiple destinations. Optical many-to-one connections are useful for time–division multiplexing of LCs originating at different access stations onto a common λ-channel. Neither one of these functions can be realized using an ordinary WRN operating with permutation switches.

Because ordinary wavelength routed networks are limited to point-to-point optical paths, there is no need to distinguish between a logical connection, an optical connection, and an optical path in those networks. However, with the potential for multipoint paths in LLNs, all layers of connectivity and their interrelations must be examined more carefully. We already saw an example of this in the broadcast star. For example, in Figure 3.5, using WDM/WDMA the LCs [1, 2] and [1, 3] are carried on individual optical connections $(1, 2)_1$ and $(1, 3)_2$, which are in turn carried by the multicast optical path $\langle 1, \{1, 2, 3\} \rangle$.

On the other hand, in the TDM/TDMA case the same LCs are time–division multiplexed on a single multicast optical connection $(1, \{2, 3\})$ carried by the OP $\langle 1, \{1, 2, 3\} \rangle$. In each case the optical path reaches all destinations, intended or not, because there is no controllability or selectivity in the star node. How are the LCs sorted out in the receiving stations? In the WDM/WDMA case the optical connections (and the LCs they carry) reach only their intended destinations because the ORs are assumed to tune *selectively* to the assigned wavelengths. On the other hand, in the TDM/TDMA case all optical connections are carried on the same wavelength, so selecting the proper LC at the receiving stations must be accomplished at the transmission channel level through time–division demultiplexing. Lastly, in the TDM/T-WDMA case, LCs must be sorted out by combined actions at the λ-channel level (receiver tuning) and at the transmission channel level (time–division demultiplexing).

These connectivity alternatives reappear, coupled with the added possibilities of switching optical paths, as we examine the properties of LLNs.

3.4.1 Routing, Channel Assignment, and Power Distribution

The two constraints on optical connections applicable to wavelength routed networks (wavelength continuity and distinct channel assignment) also apply to LLNs. But when each waveband contains multiple channels (a condition unique to LLNs), additional constraints apply within each waveband. Furthermore, the fact that LDCs are used in the nodes means that rules must be defined for distributing power on multipoint optical paths. We examine these issues now.

3.4.1.1 Routing Constraints

The following additional routing constraints apply to LLNs.

- *Inseparability:* Channels combined on a single fiber and situated *within the same waveband* cannot be separated within the network.

- *Distinct source combining (DSC):* Only signals from distinct sources are allowed to be combined on the same fiber.

Inseparability is a consequence of the fact that the LDCs operate on the *aggregate* power carried within each waveband without distinguishing between signals on different channels within the band; that is, inseparability is a condition imposed by the architecture of the optical switch, combined with the choice of channel spacing.

Figure 3.20(a) illustrates inseparability. It shows two point-to-point optical connections $(1, 1^*)$ and $(2, 2^*)$ assumed to be within the same waveband. Connection $(1, 1^*)$ is routed via the minimum-hop path $\langle 1, 1^* \rangle$ comprising the nodes A–B–C–F–G, and connection $(2, 2^*)$ is routed along its own minimum-hop path via the nodes A–B–D–E. The label S_i on a link in Figure 3.20 denotes a signal generated at a source station i. Observe that power from both sources is combined on fiber a. Thus the DCA condition requires them to be on distinct channels. For example, they might be carried on different wavelengths within the same waveband (WDMA) or on the same wavelengths but in different time slots (TDMA). Because the two signals are in the same waveband, they cannot be separated at node B. Thus, to route them both to their destinations, node B must *multicast* both signals to nodes C and D, expanding the intended point-to-point paths to multicast optical paths $\langle 1, \{1^*, \underline{2^*}\} \rangle$ and $\langle 2, \{\underline{1^*}, 2^*\} \rangle$—an unavoidable result of inseparability. Note the appearance of unintended destinations (underlined). We call these unintended destinations *fortuitous destinations*, and refer to the unintended paths as *fortuitous paths*.

In Figure 3.20, intended paths are shown as solid lines and fortuitous paths are indicated with dashed lines. These extra paths may *potentially* cause interference at the receivers. However, as long as the DCA condition is observed, interference among superimposed channels can be avoided by tuning in the desired channel and tuning out the undesired one. For example, in the case of WDMA this would mean tuning the optical receiver to select the correct wavelength and reject any others, implying that the selectivity is implemented in the λ-channel layer. On the other hand, if

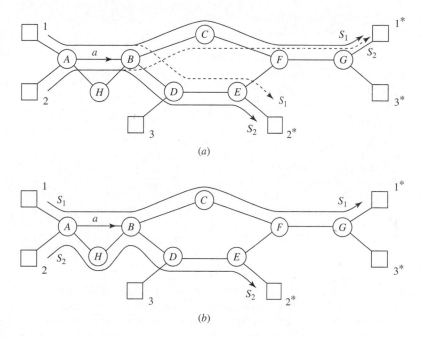

FIGURE 3.20 Inseparability.

TDMA is used to distinguish the superimposed channels, the receiving station would select the intended channel in its RP by capturing information in the proper time slots. In this case, selectivity is implemented in the transmission channel layer.[21]

Inseparability causes connections that share a common fiber on a common waveband to branch out of their original paths, fanning out onto an optical path in the form of a directed tree, with new, fortuitous destinations added to the tree as new paths are activated within the same waveband. The set of destinations (both intended and fortuitous) for each source consists of all destinations downstream on the tree from that source. Fortuitous destinations tend to waste fiber resources and power, and are therefore to be avoided if possible. In this case, the fortuitous destinations could have been avoided by rerouting $(2, 2^*)$ on a longer path, via node H, as shown in Figure 3.20(b). Inseparability does *not* apply to connections in different wavebands, which are routed independently of one another. Thus, fortuitous paths associated with inseparability do not exist in wavelength routed networks. In WRNs all optical paths are point to point so that connections from different source stations on the same wavelength are never combined on the same fiber.

---

[21] Fortuitous paths occurred in the broadcast star example of Figure 3.2 without referring to them as such. For example, using WDM/WDMA, all signals reach all three destination stations, but each signal is only intended for one of them.

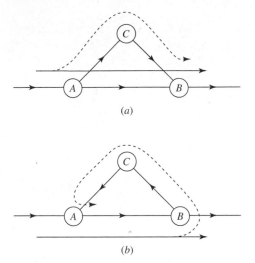

(a)

(b)

FIGURE 3.21 Two violations of DSC.

Now let us examine the distinct source combining constraint.[22] The DSC condition forbids a signal from splitting, taking multiple paths in the network, and then recombining with itself. Figure 3.21 shows two ways a source may combine with itself. In Figure 3.21(a), the signal power is split into two parallel paths and then later recombined downstream, whereas in Figure 3.21(b), a portion of the signal is fed back onto the upstream portion of its path. In both cases, the combined signals interfere with each other, garbling their information.[23] Even if routing decisions are made correctly to avoid DSC violations, some low-level DSC violations may still occur because of imperfections in hardware. For example, DSC violations in Figure 3.21 could be created due to small leakage paths through the optical switches in nodes A and B. These effects, which are unavoidable in any purely optical network (either wavelength or waveband routed), produce cross-talk, which is tolerable as long as it is kept sufficiently small (see Section 4.11.1). From now on, when we speak of DSC violations, effects due to nonideal hardware are ignored.

Figure 3.22 illustrates how a correct but poor routing decision may produce an inadvertent violation of the DSC condition. With connections $(1, 1^*)$ and $(2, 2^*)$ in progress, as shown in Figure 3.20(a), a new connection $(3, 3^*)$ is routed via path $D–E–F–G$. All three connections are assumed to be in the same waveband but on distinct channels. The signals as they appear with the new connection in place are

---

[22] Without calling it by that name, the DSC requirement was invoked in Section 2.3 in discussing power relations in directional couplers.

[23] Garbling is due to the fact that the signal is combined with a delayed replica of itself, creating interference at the receiver. Long delays cause interference in the demodulated signal, which translates into noise and distortion for analog signals and bit errors for digital signals. Short delays (on the order of the optical signal's coherence time) produce interference at the level of the optical fields, analogous to multipath effects in radio transmission.

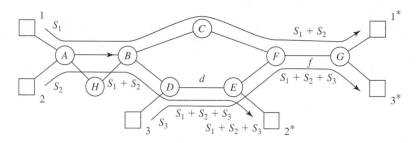

FIGURE 3.22 Inadvertent violation of DSC.

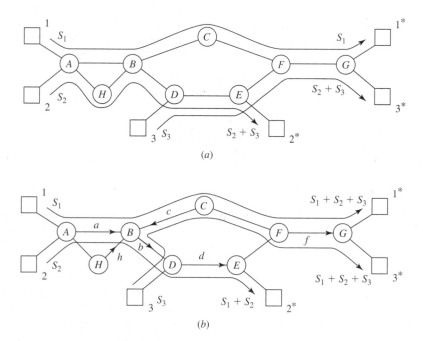

FIGURE 3.23 Avoidance of DSC violations.

shown in Figure 3.22. Due to inseparability, signal S_3 carries with it (fortuitously) portions of signals S_1 and S_2 after combining with them on fiber d. This causes S_1 (which split at node B) to recombine with itself on fiber f, violating the DSC condition. (The same holds true for S_2.) The new connection therefore must not be routed along the path shown. It could, however, use that path if it was assigned to a different waveband, because inseparability would not apply in that case. Two other solutions to this problem are shown in Figure 3.23. Figure 3.23(a) solves the problem by rerouting connection $(2, 2^*)$ via node H, and in Figure 3.23(b) the problem is solved by routing $(3, 3^*)$ via the path D–B–C–F–G.

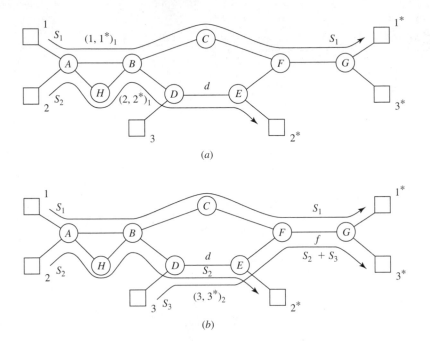

$$(a)$$

$$(b)$$

FIGURE 3.24 Color clash.

Inseparability can also indirectly cause violations of the DCA condition. We call these *color clashes*. This may occur when activation of a new connection results in combining onto the same fiber two or more connections (on the same waveband) that were already in progress on previously disjoint paths. If these connections use the same channel, a color clash occurs. To illustrate, consider the example in Figure 3.24. In Figure 3.24(a) two connections $(1, 1^*)$ and $(2, 2^*)$ are shown occupying disjoint paths. Wavelength λ_1 is assigned to both of them. Now a new connection $(3, 3^*)$ is assigned to path D–E–F–G using the same waveband. Because S_3 shares link d with S_2, it is assigned a different wavelength, λ_2. The effect of adding connection $(3, 3^*)$ is shown in Figure 3.24(b). Note that, due to inseparability, all three signals are now carried on fiber f. Because S_1 and S_2 are now on the same fiber, using the same λ-channel, they produce a color clash. This violation could have been avoided if all three connections had been assigned distinct wavelengths.

Among the four constraints discussed earlier, wavelength continuity and inseparability are both consequences of physical laws and technological constraints; the others—DCA and DSC—are routing requirements imposed to ensure satisfactory operation of the network. When we discuss routing and channel assignment later, the role of the DCA and DSC constraints is of paramount importance. The examples used to illustrate the constraints bring out once again the difficulties associated with demand-assigned as opposed to dedicated connections. If the state of the network happens to evolve in a way that tends to "clog up" the fibers as connections are assigned in sequence (dynamically), then it may be difficult or impossible to assign new connections without violating the routing and channel assignment constraints. With rearrangeability, however, the original routing and channel allocations are not irrevocable.

Thus, changing the path of $(2, 2^*)$ to pass through node H, as in Figure 3.20(b), would have avoided violation of the DSC condition. Similarly, changing the wavelength assignment of $(1, 1^*)$ to λ_3 in Figure 3.24(b) would have avoided a color clash. Because we have decided that rearrangeability (resulting in service disruption) is not a reasonable option, it is especially important that the algorithms used for dynamic routing and channel assignment in these networks have a certain amount of foresight built into them. Even though future connection requests may not be predictable, it is still possible to make optical path and channel allocations in a way that tends to reduce the probability of blocking for new connections. For example, the color clash example of Figure 3.24 suggests that λ-channel assignments within a common waveband should be made in a way that *minimizes* the reuse of each wavelength; an idea that is counterintuitive because wavelength reuse is desirable for conserving the optical spectrum. We study these questions in more detail in Chapter 6.

3.4.1.2 Power Distribution

As pointed out in Section 2.3.2.3, there is an extra degree of freedom in an LDC (a generalized optical switch) compared with a permutation switch. In the LDC it is possible to specify combining and dividing ratios, which ultimately determine how power from the sources in the network is distributed to the destinations. Recall that the LLN can be viewed as a set of independently controllable layers, one for each waveband, as in Figure 2.5(c). Thus combining and dividing ratios in each waveband-selective LDC can be set differently for each waveband. We illustrate power distribution within a waveband using the example of Figure 3.23(b). Consider the three connections $(1, 1^*)$, $(2, 2^*)$, and $(3, 3^*)$, with corresponding source signals S_1, S_2, and S_3. They are assumed to use the same waveband on distinct channels. These are each point-to-point optical connections, and if their supporting optical paths were also point to point, no combining or splitting would be involved. However, because of inseparability, their optical paths are $\langle 1, \{1^*, \underline{2^*, 3^*}\} \rangle$, $\langle 2, \{2^*, \underline{1^*, 3^*}\} \rangle$, and $\langle 3, \{3^*, \underline{1^*}\} \rangle$ respectively, where the underlining represents fortuitous destinations. We now have a set of superimposed multicast optical paths that form a directed tree in which signal powers are combined and split at various points.

How should the signal combining and dividing ratios be chosen? This question cannot be answered without knowing something about the LDC architecture, as well as the operating objectives. To fix ideas, suppose that the ONNs consist of ideal (lossless) δ–σ LDCs of the general form shown in Figure 2.20, and the fibers are lossless as well.[24] Suppose further that the objective here is to split each source's power equally

---

[24] Practically speaking, this means that all *excess* losses in switching components and all fiber losses are exactly compensated by amplification (not explicitly shown) in the ONNs and along the links.

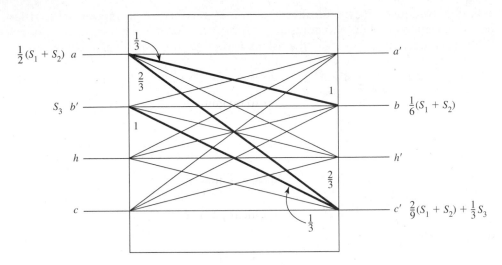

FIGURE 3.25 Illustration of power distribution.

among all destinations it reaches, and to combine equally all sources arriving at the same destination. The details of combining and dividing are illustrated in Figure 3.25, which shows the LDC at node B of the network in Figure 3.23(b). In this and subsequent discussions we adopt a standard notation for labeling fibers in bidirectional links. Each link is shown with a reference arrow and a label, where the label designates the fiber carrying signals in the direction of the reference arrow, and a corresponding primed label denotes the fiber carrying signals in the opposite direction. For example, in Figure 3.23(b), fiber a carries signals from node A to B, and a' carries signals in the reverse direction.

The LDC in Figure 3.25 shows the four fiber pairs connected to its input/output ports together with the signal powers entering and leaving on each fiber. For example, the value S_3 on fiber b' indicates that the full power from NAS 3 is carried on that fiber, whereas $\frac{1}{6}(S_1 + S_2)$ on fiber b indicates that powers from stations 1 and 2 are combined equally on b, and are attenuated by a factor of six. The active paths through the LDC are shown as heavy lines, with values of the combining and dividing ratios (σ and δ) indicated at the combining and dividing stages. The rules used to compute the combining and dividing ratios in this example are defined in Section 6.5.7. The resultant power distribution throughout the network works as follows. First, power from sources 1 and 2 is combined equally at node A, yielding a power of $\frac{1}{2}(S_1 + S_2)$ on fiber a, which reflects a combining loss of 0.5. The indicated combining and splitting operations at node B produce the powers shown on fibers b and c' in Figure 3.25, which are delivered eventually to the three destinations after an equal split at node G. It is left to the reader to verify that by using these combining and splitting ratios each source's power is split and combined equally as required. (The general formula for the resultant power distribution is given in Equation 6.71.)

3.4.2 Multipoint Subnets in LLNs

In the previous examples, attempts to set up several point-to-point optical connections within a common waveband led to the unintentional creation of multipoint optical paths, and consequent extra complications in routing and channel assignment and power distribution. In view of these additional complications in waveband routed networks (LLNs), one might ask what is to be gained by adding this extra complexity? One answer is that waveband routing leads to more efficient use of the optical spectrum, given the technological constraints of the ONNs (see Section 2.2). Another answer is that the multipoint optical path capability, which showed up accidentally earlier, can be turned to our advantage in creating *intentional* multipoint optical connections. Because of this property, LLNs can deliver a high degree of logical connectivity with minimal optical hardware in the access stations. This is done by creating controllable multicast and multiaccess optical paths that support both one-to-many and many-to-one optical connections. This multipoint optical connectivity property is one of the fundamental advantages of LLNs over point-to-point wavelength routed networks. We illustrate its power through a few examples in Section 3.4.3, which compares the WRN and LLN approaches.

Figure 3.26(a) shows a network containing seven stations interconnected on an LLN with a mesh physical topology. As is seen in subsequent examples, it is often useful to

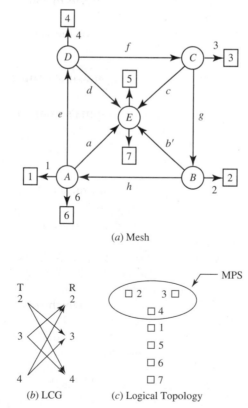

(*a*) Mesh

(*b*) LCG

(*c*) Logical Topology

FIGURE 3.26 Seven stations on a mesh.

create full logical connectivity among specified "clusters" of stations within a larger network. We call such clusters *multipoint subnets* (MPSs). Suppose, for example, that the set of stations {2, 3, 4} is to be interconnected in this way. The LCG defining full connectivity in this subset (without loopback connections) is shown in Figure 3.26(b), together with the resultant logical topology (Figure 3.26[c]). Note that the unconnected stations are shown isolated from each other, and the stations contained in the MPS are shown enclosed in a "cloud," indicating that there is full logical connectivity among all of them. Recall that this type of representation was used earlier in Figure 3.2(c) to symbolize stations sharing a common broadcast medium. We shall see that these two interpretations are closely related.

How is full logical connectivity realized on the MPS? One possibility is to create an optical path on a single waveband in the form of a tree joining the stations, where the path is "carved out of" (embedded in) the larger network by setting the LDCs appropriately. Figure 3.27(a) shows a shortest path tree connecting the three stations. The actual signal paths on the tree can be chosen in various ways. One convenient approach is to define a "root node" as the basis for an embedded broadcast star; that is, we route all signals from the stations to the root (now playing the role of a star coupler), combine them there, and broadcast the combined signals back to all stations.

Figure 3.27(b) illustrates the equivalence between the tree, rooted arbitrarily at node C, and a broadcast star. The fibers and nodes along paths taken by the signals to and from the root are indicated in Figure 3.27(b), using the labeling convention defined earlier. (Fibers sharing the same link are now shown separately, and nodes traversed twice are duplicated.) If a δ-σ LDC is used in node C, then it would be set as shown in Figure 3.27(c). The solid lines indicate the combining and dividing paths if the node is operated as a star coupler without loopback paths (a nonreflecting star), and the dotted lines indicate added paths for loopback operation (a reflecting star). In each case the combining/dividing ratios are equal for all ports: $\frac{1}{2}$ for the case without loopback and $\frac{1}{3}$ with loopback. (Although the specified LCG does not include loopback connections in this case, they are useful for control purposes—for example, synchronization in a TDMA system—and for determining propagation delays to the root, knowledge of which may be required in a MAC protocol.)

Once an optical path is established to emulate a broadcast star, that is exactly what is "seen" by the stations. In other words, the desired MPS has been created by embedding its LCG into the the physical topology of a mesh network in the form of a broadcast star. The embedded star can now be operated exactly like any other shared broadcast medium. Any multiplexing and multiple-access channel-sharing methods applicable to broadcast stars can be used, including fixed capacity allocation, dynamic capacity allocation, TDM/TDMA, and TDM/T-WDMA. For example, a single λ-channel might be allocated to the MPS, in which case all stations would share the channel in a TDM/TDMA mode. If several λ-channels are available within the waveband supporting the MPS, then a TDM/T-WDMA implementation might be used. In each case, the full capacity of all allocated λ-channels would be available for sharing among all LCs. It is for this reason that we represent the MPS as a multipoint link that contains a set of stations sharing a common capacity.

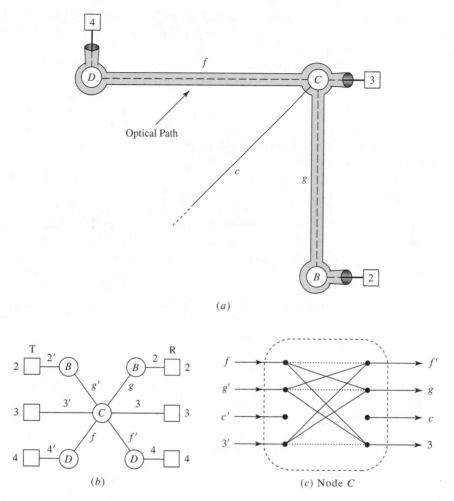

FIGURE 3.27 Tree embedded in mesh.

After the optical path supporting the MPS has been created by fixing the settings of the participating ONNs, there are no further control functions required within the optical path layer. Thus, control of the MPS, once it is configured, is completely in the hands of the NASs. The choice of multiplexing and multiple access techniques, establishment and release of logical connections, apportionment of shared capacity, and so forth, can all be implemented through suitable signaling among the stations in the MPS without any interaction with the ONNs.

The concept of the MPS is very general. From a top-down point of view, the stations contained in an MPS (e.g., the stations in the "cloud" in Figure 3.26[a]) appear at the logical level as a fully connected subset allocated some total capacity, which is shared among all LCs. Logical connections within an MPS may be multicast as well as point to point. As conditions evolve, the logical aspects of the MPS might be reconfigured by adding or deleting stations or by modifying capacity allotments. The details of how the connections are implemented in the physical layer are concealed and are unimportant from a logical layer point of view.

On the other hand, from a bottom-up physical layer view, there are many possible ways of implementing a given MPS, including the choice of waveband, channel, and optical path; the use of single or multiple transceivers in the stations; single- or multiple-fiber pairs in the access links; different multiplexing and multiple access schemes; fixed or dynamic capacity assignment (packet switching); and so forth. Furthermore, it is possible to reconfigure these physical layer aspects of an MPS in response to changes in load (e.g., add or subtract channel allocations) or in response to network faults (e.g., route the supporting optical path around failed links or nodes). Lastly, many variants of the fully connected MPS are possible. For example, if we remove the transmitting connections from stations 3 and 4 in Figure 3.27(b), the result is a multicast optical path from station 2 to stations 3 and 4. Similarly, removing the receiving connections from stations 2 and 3 results in a multiaccess path from transmitting stations 2 and 3 to receiving station 4.

The MPS reappears in the next section as a basic building block of a hypernet.

3.4.3 A Seven-Station Example

Now let us test the LLN concept against the wavelength routed network approach. The test case will be the implementation of full logical connectivity among a set of seven end systems. We assume throughout that each end system is connected to an NAS and then to a network node through a nonblocking access link. The optical transceivers in the stations are assumed to be tunable over the full spectrum needed to support the connections, where each transmitter runs at a bitrate of R_0 bits per second, which may be taken to be the full capacity of a λ-channel. Implementation on three physical topologies—(1) the bidirectional ring, (2) mesh, and (3) multistar—is compared.

Implementation on a bidirectional ring is considered a point of reference. We then compare approaches using the mesh of Figure 3.26 and the multistar configuration of Figure 3.28(a). The topology of the mesh was chosen arbitrarily and has no relation to the logical topology being implemented. In contrast to the mesh, the multistar structure was custom designed to support the seven-station example. The different physical topologies were chosen to illustrate their effect on station and optical spectrum resource utilization. This is the first (but not the last) time we encounter a multistar topology. Until now, the underlying fiber placements were assumed to be given; that is, *the network implementer was assumed to have no control over the physical topology*, which is not necessarily adapted to the needs of the end systems. When using a multistar arrangement, the assumption is exactly the opposite. The fiber topology is now put in place expressly to serve the network being implemented; that is, the design of the physical topology is part of the overall network design.

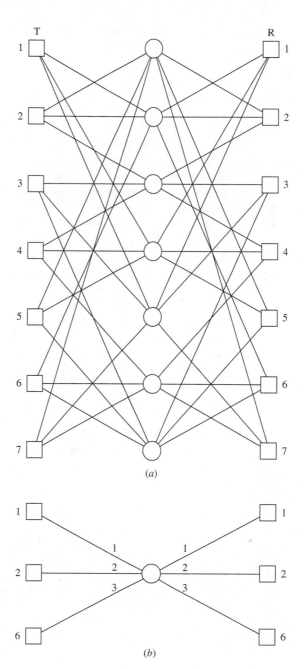

FIGURE 3.28 Multistar network.

At the logical level, three logical topologies are considered: point-to-point (42 unidirectional LCs), fully shared multipoint, and hypernet (partial sharing). The first is realized using wavelength routing, and the others are realized using multicast optical connections in an LLN.

3.4.3.1 Wavelength Routing

In the case of wavelength routing, the nodes in all physical topologies considered are wavelength-selective permutation switches. Because individual point-to-point optical connections are required for each LC in this case, six transceivers are needed in each station. For the bidirectional ring, it can be shown[25] that full interconnection of seven stations requires six wavelengths, which results in a wavelength reuse factor of seven for the 42 LCs. For the mesh, it is left as an exercise for the reader to show that the connections can be realized with four wavelengths (a wavelength reuse factor of 10.5), which is the minimum possible number.

In the multistar topology, each station accesses three stars, using two transceivers on each star. The two transceivers accessing one star are multiplexed onto a single access fiber pair. The central node of each star, a WSXC, is set to operate as a permutation wavelength router of the type shown in Figure 2.9, where the routing rule is as follows: A signal on input fiber i, carried on wavelength λ_k, is routed to output fiber j, where $k = j - i \bmod 3$. For example, the star joining stations $\{1, 2, 6\}$ is shown in Figure 3.28(b). With the fibers numbered as in the figure, the wavelength assignments for the six optical connections on the star are: $(1, 2)_1$, $(1, 6)_2$, $(2, 1)_2$, $(2, 6)_1$, $(6, 1)_1$, and $(6, 2)_2$. Because two wavelengths are used on each star, and these can be reused on all stars, the reuse factor for the 42 connections is 21. For all three physical topologies the network has a total capacity of $42R_0$ bps, and each LC has a fixed-capacity allotment of R_0 bits per second.

3.4.3.2 LLN Realization: Fully Shared Logical Topology

In each wavelength routed network realization, full connectivity was realized necessarily using point-to-point LCs, with a fixed capacity assigned to each. However, in an LLN realization we have the option of replacing point-to-point logical connections with MPSs; that is, we may group stations together into fully connected subsets, in which the LCs joining the stations in the subsets share a common capacity.

Extending the idea of the MPS to its ultimate limit in this example we may include all seven stations in a single subnet. Irrespective of the underlying physical topology, this can always be accomplished by choosing any convenient tree that links all seven stations to form an optical path that supports all optical connections among the stations. Following Section 3.4.2, the tree can be used to emulate a broadcast star. In the case of the bidirectional ring of Figure 3.29(a), any node can be chosen as the root node for the star, with its LDC set to do full combining and broadcasting for all λ-channels on a specified waveband. All other nodes serve to complete the tree configuration,

---

[25] See Section 6.3.4.2.

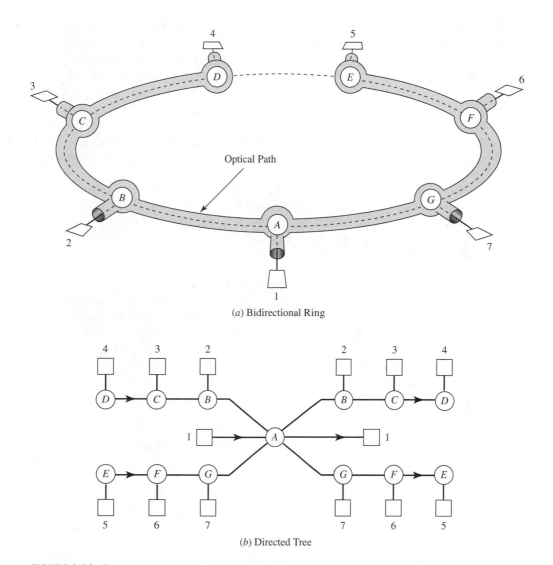

FIGURE 3.29 Embedded star on a bidirectional ring.

joining the NASs to the root node. In this case node *A* has been chosen as the root node so that the optical paths can be redrawn in the form of a directed tree as shown in Figure 3.29(b). Depending on the selectivity of the LDCs, the waveband allocated to the star may be "thin," holding only a single λ-channel, or "thick," containing the full usable optical spectrum. (The latter case would hold if the LDCs had no waveband selectivity.)

In either case, the combined capacity of all allocated λ-channels is available for sharing among the seven stations. (A negative feature of the embedded star is that there is no spectrum reuse, so the total throughput can never be more than the combined capacity of all allocated channels.) If only one λ-channel is used, all stations can share the channel using TDM/TDMA, and this requires only a single transceiver per station. This is the most economical realization in terms of station cost. In this case, the total network capacity is R_0. If more than one λ-channel is used, full utilization of the channels requires either multiple transceivers or rapidly tunable transceivers in the stations. For example, if seven λ-channels are available, then the TDM/T-WDMA approach of Section 3.2 could be employed in an FT-TR arrangement with one fixed transmitter and one tunable receiver in each station. This would yield a total network capacity of $7R_0$ bps.

The same approach can be applied to the mesh of Figure 3.26. For example, node E in the figure can be taken as the root of an embedded star. Except for the different physical topology, all aspects of the discussion of the bidirectional ring apply here as well. (In fact, the seven stations accessing the embedded star have no way of knowing in what physical topology their MPS is embedded.)

3.4.3.3 LLN Realization: Hypernet Logical Topology

The point-to-point and fully shared logical topologies represent two extremes for realizing full connectivity among seven stations. Compromise solutions are also possible. Figure 3.30(a) shows a seven-node hypernet logical topology in the form of a hypergraph[26] with seven hyperedges. Each hyperedge represents an MPS that contains three stations. Note that all stations in a common hyperedge can communicate with each other because they are members of the same MPS. Because there is full logical connectivity among all stations (vertices) within an MPS (hyperedge), and all LCs share a common capacity, there are in effect six LCs "hidden" in each hyperedge, all sharing the same capacity. In this example the logical topology is arranged so that each station can reach any other station via one of the three hyperedges to which it is connected. This is a way of providing full logical connectivity among *all* stations without placing them in the same MPS.

Just as the point-to-point links comprising an LCG are represented conveniently as a bipartite graph linking source and destination stations, the MPSs (multivertex hyperedges) comprising a *logical connection hypergraph* (LCH) can be represented by a tripartite graph, as shown in Figure 3.30(b). Here each hyperedge of the LCH is represented as a central vertex connecting a transmitting set on the left to a receiving set on the right. For example, hyperedge E_1 connects the transmitting set $\{2, 5, 7\}$ to itself. When each hyperedge's transmitting and receiving sets are identical, the hypergraph is called *undirected*, which is analogous to an undirected graph.

So far we have a top-down view of the network. Now, suppose this logical topology is to be realized in the mesh network of Figure 3.26 as a set of embedded multicast stars. A routing tree must be chosen for each of the seven MPSs, and wavebands must be assigned to the trees so that the routing constraints are satisfied. A solution to this

---

[26] See Appendix A for the definition of a hypergraph.

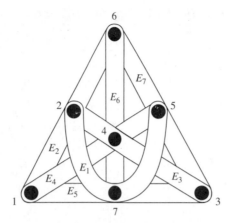

(a) Hypergraph Logical Topology

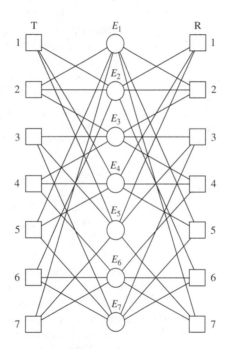

FIGURE 3.30 Seven-node hypernet.   (b) LCH Tripartite Graph

problem is shown in Table 3.1. The tree for each hyperedge is given, together with its waveband assignment. (The details of tree realization were discussed in Section 3.4.2. The tree for hyperedge E_3 is displayed as an illustration in Figure 3.27.)

Note that the assignments are made so that no waveband is used more than once on a link, ensuring that the DCA condition holds on all links. The routing and

TABLE 3.1 Tree Routing on Mesh

Hyperedge	Stations	Tree	Waveband
1	2, 5, 7	b	1
2	1, 2, 6	h	1
3	2, 3, 4	f, g	1
4	1, 4, 5	a, d	1
5	1, 3, 7	a, c	2
6	4, 6, 7	d, e	2
7	3, 5, 6	b, g, h	2

waveband assignments have been accomplished with a total of two wavebands, which is the minimum number possible. As can be seen, it was possible to achieve a minimum waveband assignment using shortest path routing of all trees except that supporting E_7, which required three links. As in the previous example, this realization can be implemented with various numbers of λ-channels per waveband and various numbers of transceivers per station. Suppose, for example, that we allocate three λ-channels per waveband with the channels accessed using TDM/T-WDMA operating in FT-TR mode. This could be implemented using a single transceiver in each station to access each MPS, requiring three transceivers per station, one for each MPS to which it is connected. The total network capacity is then $21R_0$, with a capacity of $3R_0$ shared among six logical connections in each MPS.

3.4.3.4 Multistar Realization

In the previous example we chose a logical topology (a seven-hyperedge hypergraph) and embedded it on a given physical topology, in this case a mesh. There was no relation between the chosen LT and the prescribed PT. However, as mentioned earlier, one is sometimes free to *design* the PT to suit the chosen LT. In the case of hypernets, a *multistar realization* is a natural design approach, in which the tripartite graph representation of the LCH can be viewed as defining a multistar physical topology. For example in the LCH of Figure 3.30(b), suppose each hyperedge corresponds to a broadcast star, in which the central vertex represents the star coupler, directing signals from the transmitting set to the receiving set. In this example, each station is connected to three stars, allowing it to reach all other stations.

As seen from the stations, this multistar realization has the same characteristics as the case of multiple broadcast stars embedded on the mesh physical topology of Figure 3.26. The only difference is that all stars are realized on separate fibers, so we no longer need two wavebands to support the MPSs. To conform to the previous example, a single waveband containing three λ-channels can be reused on each star, with TDM/T-WDMA operation on the star using FT-TR. This would require three transceivers per station, and would give a total network capacity of $21R_0$.

TABLE 3.2 Seven-Station Comparisons

Type of Network	Physical Topology	Logical Topology	Reuse Factor	No. of Transceivers per Station	Spectrum	Network Capacity
WRN	Ring	Pt.-Pt.	7	6	1,200	$42R_0$
WRN	Mesh	Pt.-Pt.	10.5	6	800	$42R_0$
WRN	Multistar	Pt.-Pt.	21	6	400	$42R_0$
LLN	Any	Fully shared	1	1	200	$5R_0$
LLN	Mesh	Hypernet	3.5	3	400	$21R_0$
LLN	Multistar	Hypernet	7	3	200	$21R_0$

WRN = wavelength routed network; LLN = linear lightwave network; Pt.-Pt. = point to point.

By this time the reader should have realized that the multistar topology used in the earlier WRN example was derived from the hypergraph development presented here. The only difference is that the nodes in the WRN case perform wavelength permutation instead of simple combining and broadcasting.

3.4.3.5 Comparisons

Table 3.2 summarizes the main features of the various seven station realizations presented earlier. It compares them based on spectrum utilization, reuse factor, transceivers per station, and total network capacity. Because there are so many variables in these examples, we must be careful not to compare apples with oranges! For the purpose of comparing spectrum usage, some assumptions must be made about wavelength and waveband spacing. Figure 3.31 shows the assumed values. For the wavelength routed case, Figure 3.31(a) shows a 200-GHz spacing between centers of wavebands, with a guard band of 75 GHz between wavebands and a single λ-channel in each waveband. Figure 3.31(b) shows the case of the LLN, in which the 125-GHz usable bandwidth of a waveband supports up to five λ-channels on 25-GHz spacings. This λ-channel spacing could accommodate optical signals running at bitrates as high as OC-48 (2.5 Gbps) on each channel. Thus, for example, the hypernet realization on a mesh requires two wavebands and uses three λ-channels in each waveband. Assuming that a full waveband is dedicated to the hypernet regardless of whether all of its channels are used, we assign a spectrum allocation of 400 GHz to this case.

How does the spectrum utilization compare? In going from the ring to the mesh to the multistar, spectrum utilization tends to decrease and the reuse factor increases, as is to be expected with the improved physical topologies. The LLN realizations are more economical of spectrum and transceiver usage than the WRN case, with the fully shared LLN realization requiring the least resources. (Reuse factors in WRNs and LLNs are difficult to compare because WRNs use point-to-point optical connections whereas LLNs use multicast connections.) Because network capacity is directly

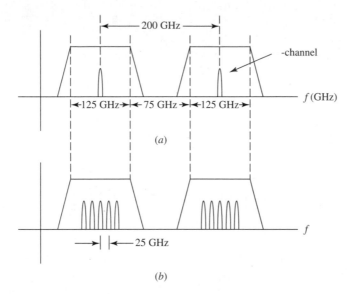

FIGURE 3.31 Assumed channel spacings.

proportional to the number of transceivers, the WRN realizations have the most capacity. Of course, there are other factors to take into account, such as rapid tuning requirements in multichannel LLN realizations and lack of channel sharing in WRNs.

Channel sharing has some significant advantages that are not immediately apparent. When a pooled capacity is shared among many logical connections, that capacity can be allocated to match unbalanced traffic distributions and can be reapportioned as traffic demand changes. Furthermore, in a shared medium it is possible to provide dynamic capacity allocation by implementing packet switching in the optical layer (see Section 3.2.2). For example, in the case of a fully shared logical topology, all 42 LCs could be operated in a packet-switched mode so that each connection receives the capacity it needs just when it needs it. In the WRN case, the fixed capacity allocations make it impossible to adapt to unbalanced traffic. Consequently, traffic imbalances result in reduced network throughput. Finally, as mentioned earlier in this chapter, shared-medium multipoint optical connections act as a natural support for multicast logical connections.

3.5 Logically Routed Networks

The examples in the previous sections illustrate various alternatives for implementing high logical connectivity in transparent optical networks while keeping resource utilization under control, limiting station complexity to a few optical transceivers, and using a few hundred giga-Hertz of optical bandwidth. This was possible because the networks were small, containing at most seven stations. When we move to larger networks, the transparent optical approach soon reaches its limit. For example, we found that six wavelengths and six optical transceivers per station were necessary and sufficient to achieve full logical connectivity among seven stations on a bidirectional ring using wavelength routed point-to-point optical connections. But suppose we increase the number of stations to 22. Then the number of wavelengths increases more than tenfold to 61, requiring many tera-Hertz of optical bandwidth, and the number of transceivers per station increases to 21 (see Section 6.3.4.2). Economically and technologically, this is well beyond current capabilities. When the limits of optics are exceeded we must turn to electronics (i.e., *logically routed networks*).

In Section 2.6 the concept of a logical network overlay was presented, wherein logical switching nodes interconnect a set of logical links, forming an electronically switched logical topology (i.e., an LRN). The example of Figure 3.2(b), which consists of a unidirectional ring logical topology embedded in a star physical topology, was a very simple illustration of how switching in the logical layer can remove some of the connectivity burden from the purely optical portion of the network. We shall now extend that approach to larger networks. To fix ideas, in the discussion that follows it is useful to focus on connection-oriented asynchronous traffic, using ATM switches as the LSNs. In this case the connections between end systems are virtual and are carried by VCs supported by VPs. However, the development applies equally well to stream traffic, in which the LSNs might be SONET digital cross-connect systems or similar devices, and the end-to-end connections would consist of synchronous bitstreams in the form of dedicated circuits running at DS1 or DS3 bitrates (1.544 or 44.736 Mbps respectively), or higher. These would typically be used as supports for higher layers of connections, which might be made through either telephone central offices (for POTS), IP routers (for computer data), or ATM switches (for multimedia services).

The essential feature of the LSN is that it performs a sorting and routing function; that is, the traffic arriving on the input ports is demultiplexed into small units (for example, ATM cells or DS1 circuits) routed to the appropriate output ports and re-multiplexed onto the outbound links. This is illustrated in Figure 3.32, which shows an ATM switch acting as an LSN interposed between an NAS (accessing an underlying optical network) and two LAN gateways (the end systems). Note the difference between this configuration and that of Figure 3.1, which shows a similar connection *without* an LSN.

The difference between logical connections in a purely optical network and an LRN is illustrated nicely by Figure 3.2. In a purely optical network, the end systems connect directly to the external ports of the NASs, as exemplified by Figure 3.2(a), so transport between a pair of end systems is supported by the logical connections originating and terminating at the corresponding NAS ports. Assuming that all logical connections are point to point, this means that the transport network seen by the end systems can be described by a logical connection graph as shown in Figure 3.2(a), in which the vertices represent the NASs terminating those connections. In the case of an LRN, however, the LSNs create an extra layer of connectivity between the end systems and the NASs. Thus the end systems access the logical network through the LSNs, the LSNs access the transparent optical network through the NASs, and the NASs are interconnected through optical network nodes. The vertices of the connection graph

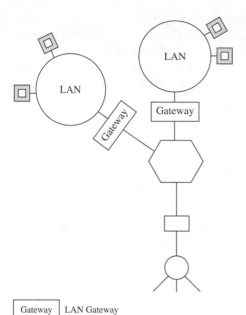

| Gateway | LAN Gateway |

FIGURE 3.32 Logical switching node used for LAN interconnection.

describing an LRN—for example, that of Figure 3.2(b)—are the LSNs instead of the NASs. If the underlying optical infrastructure is a wavelength routed network, each link in the logical topology is supported by its own point-to-point optical connection. But each optical connection requires one optical transceiver, so the number of logical connections incident on each LSN (a vertex of the logical connection graph), called its *degree*, is limited by the number of optical transceivers in the NASs serving the corresponding LSN. Because this number is generally small for reasons of cost, the connectivity among the LSNs is sparse.

Thus most paths between pairs of end systems require multiple logical hops, traversing several LSNs. At each LSN the traffic is sorted and routed on the next logical link toward its destination. A key performance measure for any LRN is the average number of logical hops experienced by its traffic. Because each unit of traffic uses a network link on each hop, the same unit of traffic *reuses* the network a number of times equal to its hop count. Therefore, the average link load is proportional to the injected traffic multiplied by the average hop count. Because links have limited capacities, *the maximum possible injected traffic, or network capacity, is inversely proportional to the average hop count.* Besides improving network capacity, lower hop counts improve many other measures of network performance. In the case of packet/cell traffic, fewer hops means less processing in the switches, less delay, less probability of cell loss, and better survivability, because each connection is less likely to encounter a link or node fault. Similar remarks apply to demand-assigned stream traffic except that delay and cell loss are replaced by call-blocking probability.

In this section we explore some of the properties of LRNs embedded on transparent optical infrastructures. Point-to-point logical topologies are considered first, followed by hypernets. This is followed by an example of a virtual topology supported by an LRN. The issue of the *design* of the logical topology is not considered here. However, this is an important factor in achieving high performance. The logical topology must be "matched" to the expected traffic distribution to keep the average hop count low, and at the same time it must be matched to the underlying optical infrastructure so that cost-effective embedding is possible. The design problem for LRNs is discussed in more detail in Chapter 7.

3.5.1   Point-to-Point Logical Topologies

As mentioned earlier, one of the objectives of using logical switching on top of a transparent optical network is to reduce the cost of the station equipment (particularly by reducing the complexity of the optics) while maintaining high network performance. Thus, we are interested in logical topologies that achieve a small average number of logical hops at a low cost (meaning, small node degree and simple optical components). An interesting class of regular logical topologies called *multihop networks* was proposed with this objective in mind. An example is *ShuffleNet*. The idea of the ShuffleNet design was to use simple station equipment (a small number of transceivers requiring no rapid tuning) and yet achieve good performance in networks scalable to large sizes.

Figure 3.33(a) shows an eight-node ShuffleNet logical topology. It consists of two stages with four LSNs each, joined by unidirectional links. There are 16 links, compared with a requirement of 56 for full logical connectivity. To clarify the flow of traffic, the first stage is repeated in dashed lines indicating that the topology forms a cylinder. As in the LAN interconnection example at the beginning of this chapter, each LSN performs two functions: It exchanges traffic with externally connected end systems, and it sorts and routes traffic in transit through the network to the destination end systems. A connection between any pair of end systems can be established over a suitable LP, and it is easily seen that any node can communicate with any other node using a number of logical hops not exceeding three. It turns out that with uniform traffic and shortest path routing, the average number of hops in this network is two. Figure 3.33(b) presents the LCG in our standard bipartite form. These networks are scalable to large sizes by adding stages and/or by increasing the degree of the nodes (see Section 7.1.1).

Up to this point nothing has been said about the underlying optical network. As originally proposed, a suggested implementation of ShuffleNet was on a folded bus, as demonstrated in Figure 3.33(c). This PT is equivalent to a broadcast star in the sense that it allows no spectrum reuse, and therefore 16 wavelengths are required for

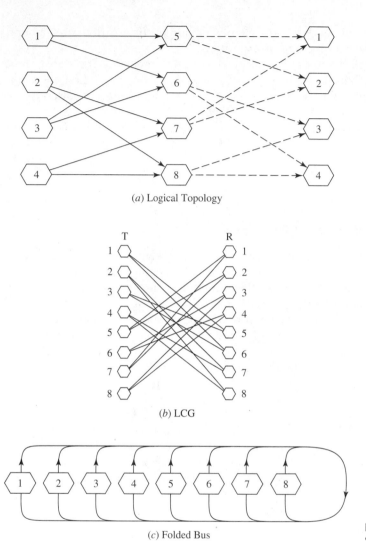

(a) Logical Topology

(b) LCG

(c) Folded Bus

FIGURE 3.33 Eight-node ShuffleNet.

the 16 point-to-point LCs. To improve spectrum utilization, let us now assume that the ShuffleNet is to be embedded in a wavelength routed bidirectional ring using single fiber pair access links and two transceivers in each station. Figure 3.34 shows the locations of nodes on the ring. (The arrows on each link simply define a reference direction for the fibers. Each link consists of a pair of bidirectional fibers.) Note that the node/station placements are *not* arranged in numerical order. They were, in fact, chosen to minimize the required number of wavelengths. A possible wavelength assignment is shown in Table 3.3, which indicates that the 16 LCs can be realized using only two wavelengths, for a reuse factor of eight. (Routing is always the shortest path on the ring.)

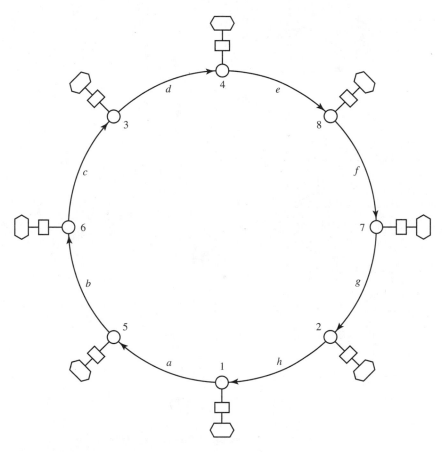

FIGURE 3.34 ShuffleNet embedding.

TABLE 3.3 Wavelength Assignments for ShuffleNet on a Ring

Source/ Destination	Node							
	1	2	3	4	5	6	7	8
1	-	-	-	-	1	2	-	-
2	-	-	-	-	-	-	1	2
3	-	-	-	-	2	1	-	-
4	-	-	-	-	-	-	2	1
5	1	2	-	-	-	-	-	-
6	-	-	1	2	-	-	-	-
7	2	1	-	-	-	-	-	-
8	-	-	2	1	-	-	-	-

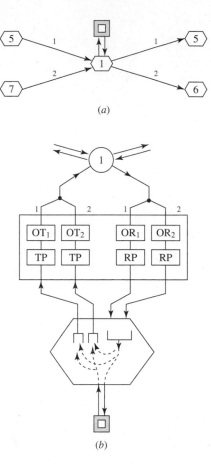

(a)

(b)   **FIGURE 3.35** Details of ShuffleNet node.

Figure 3.35 shows the details of node 1 in this realization. As shown in Figure 3.35(a), node 1 receives traffic from nodes 5 and 7 (in addition to injected traffic), and forwards nonexiting traffic to nodes 5 and 6. Packets from node 5 (7) are received on wavelength $\lambda_1(\lambda_2)$ and delivered to the LSN, where they are buffered and sorted as indicated in Figure 3.35(b). Those destined for the local end systems exit the network at this point, and the others are routed to the two transmitters. Packets whose next node is 5 (6) are delivered to OT_1 (OT_2). The total capacity of this network is $8R_0$ bps, where R_0 is the transmitter bitrate. This represents *one half* of the combined capacity of all transmitters, with the factor of $\frac{1}{2}$ appearing because the average hop count is two. For comparison, if full logical connectivity (56 LCs) was to be realized purely optically on the ring, this would require eight wavelengths with seven transceivers in each station, and would give a network capacity of $56R_0$.

3.5.2 Multipoint Logical Topologies: Hypernets

The seven-station example in Section 3.4.3 illustrated how high connectivity may be maintained in transparent optical networks while economizing on optical resource

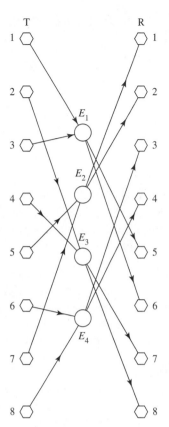

FIGURE 3.36 Shuffle hypernet.

utilization through the use of multipoint connections. These ideas are even more potent when combined with logical switching.

3.5.2.1 Shuffle Hypernet

As a simple example of the multipoint approach, suppose the eight-node ShuffleNet is modified to a *shuffle hypernet* by grouping subsets of four nodes into *hyperarcs*, as shown in Figure 3.36. The figure shows an LCH in the tripartite representation introduced earlier for a seven-node hypernet. Note that this is now a *directed* hypergraph, because the transmitting and receiving sets of each hyperarc (the directed version of a hyperedge) are not identical. (This reflects the fact that the LCG of the original ShuffleNet was directed.) Each hyperarc now represents a directed MPS that contains two transmitting and two receiving stations. How do we modify the bidirectional ring embedding to realize the hypernet?

First, to accommodate multipoint optical connectivity we replace the wavelength routing switches by LDCs. Then, following the general approach used in Section 3.4.2, we create an embedded *directed* broadcast star to support each MPS. For a directed star, a tree is found joining all stations in both the transmitting and receiving sets of the MPS. Any node on the tree can be chosen as the root. The LDCs on the tree are then set to create optical paths from all stations in the transmitting set to the root node,

TABLE 3.4 Tree Routing for Shuffle Hypernet

Hyperarc	Root Node	Tree
1	5	$a,\ b',\ c' : b$
2	2	$g,\ a',\ h' : h$
3	8	$e,\ f',\ g' : f$
4	4	$c,\ d,\ e' : d'$

and paths from the root to all receiving stations. All signals inbound to the root node are multicast to all stations on the outbound paths. The embedding follows the same pattern as that for the point-to-point ShuffleNet, except that sets of four point-to-point connections are replaced by trees. Table 3.4 shows a possible tree routing for this case, giving the root node and the fibers making up the tree supporting each hyperarc (MPS).

The tree entries in Table 3.4 refer to the internodal fiber labeling in Figure 3.34. Thus, for example, E_1 is realized as a star receiving signals from NASs attached to nodes 1 and 3 (using fibers a, b', c'), combining them at node 5, (the root node of the tree), and multicasting the combination to NASs attached to ONNs 5 and 6 (using fiber b). Referring to Table 3.4, we can see that all trees are embedded on fiber–disjoint paths, so that a single waveband is sufficient to realize all four MPSs. In the most economical implementation, a thin waveband containing a single λ-channel could be used with a TDM/TDMA access scheme to support all four LCs sharing the channel. This requires only one optical transceiver in each NAS compared with two transceivers for the point-to-point realization. (As usual, a thicker waveband, using TDM/T-WDMA, could provide more capacity without increasing the number of transceivers.) If packet switching is used in the optical layer, the capacity of the channel can be shared dynamically among all connections in each MPS.

The details of the operations taking place at node 1 are shown in Figure 3.37. Assuming that the traffic from nodes 5 and 7 in E_2 is in the form of a sequence of nonoverlapping packets interleaved arbitrarily in time as shown in Figure 3.37(a), the entire data sequence is picked up at the receiver in NAS 1 (and at NAS 2). The RP in NAS 1, acting as a packet filter, examines the destination addresses on the received packets and delivers all those intended for it (either transiting or exiting at its switching node) to the LSN for further processing. The other packets (intended for node 2) are dropped. The LSN checks the packet (final) destination addresses, delivering those destined for the local end system to the exit port and forwarding all others to the TP for further transmission into E_1. Addressing can be implemented in various ways.

In this example we assume that there are two levels of addressing. First there is a low-level address that may be contained in the "outer" encapsulation of the packets as they move through the MPSs. This is the local address shown in Figure 3.37, applying only to the nodes within one MPS. The outer encapsulation is stripped off in the LSN, revealing the final destination address, which is used to determine the remaining

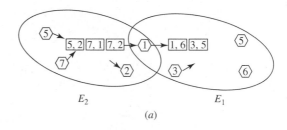

(a)

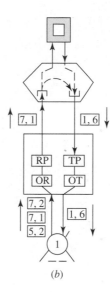

FIGURE 3.37   Details of node in shuffle hypernet.

(b)

routing. If the packet is to be forwarded into E_1, a new encapsulation is applied with new local source–destination addresses. For example, Figure 3.37(b) shows the three packets with source–destination addresses [5, 2], [7, 1], and [7, 2] arriving at the OR for station 1. Of these, only [7, 1] is passed on by the RP to the LSN. In this case, the LSN, after consulting its routing table, finds that the packet is to be forwarded to node 6. It is therefore reencapsulated with the new address [1, 6] and is sent to the OT for transmission into E_1. The switching functions in this network are exceedingly simple: Pick up the packets destined for the node and then either route them to the local end system or to the next MPS. No additional routing decisions are necessary.

3.5.2.2   Twenty-Two-Station Example

One more example is used to place the hypernet into a more general setting. The example also serves to outline a general approach for embedding logical topologies on prescribed physical topologies. Figure 3.38(a) shows a logical connection hypergraph that consists of 22 vertices (logical network nodes) and ten undirected hyperedges, with each hyperedge of size four (i.e., containing four vertices).

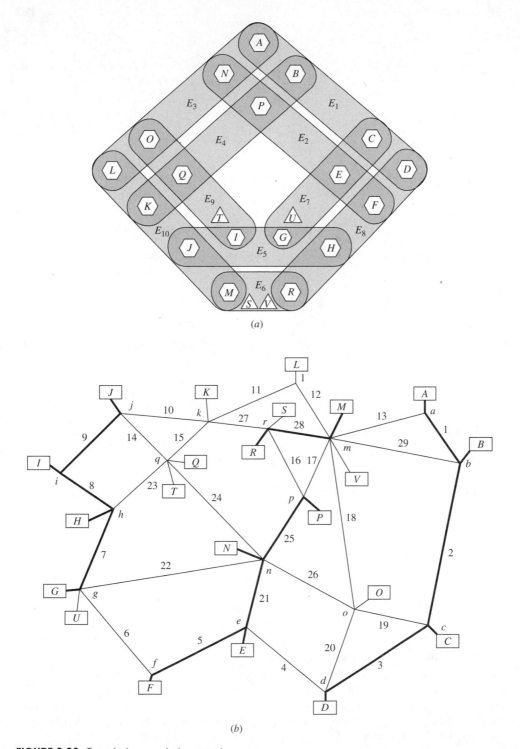

FIGURE 3.38 Twenty-two node hypernet.

To provide more generality to this example, two types of nodes are included: LSNs (shown as hexagons) and logical terminal nodes (LTNs) (shown as triangles). The terminal nodes have no logical switching function, and serve only as access points to interface end systems to the LRN. For example, in an ATM network the terminal nodes might execute ATM end node functions (such as call setup and admission control), and the LSNs would execute end node functions as well as call-routing functions (VP switching). The *degree* of a vertex in an undirected hypergraph is defined as the number of hyperedges to which it belongs.

In this example all LSN vertices are of degree two, whereas the terminal vertices are of degree one. Vertices within the same hyperedge can communicate over a single logical hop, whereas those in different hyperedges require several hops in tandem. For example, a packet moves between nodes U and C in one hop, but requires three hops between nodes U and K. The sorting and routing functions in the LSNs permit full connectivity among all pairs of nodes in this network, albeit over multiple logical hops in most cases. Using shortest path routing, the longest logical path between a pair of nodes is four hops (e.g., from U to S via G–J–M). This is called the *diameter* of the hypergraph. (The seven-node LCH in Figure 3.26 is an example of a hypergraph in which every vertex has degree three, every hyperedge is of size three, and any vertex can reach any other in a single logical hop. Thus the diameter is one, implying that no logical switching is required.)

We assume that the hypergraph has been chosen to match the traffic requirements of end systems attached to the nodes. On the other hand, it bears no relation to the physical topology that will support it. Figure 3.38(b) shows the location of the logical nodes on a prescribed physical topology to be called *Atlantis*. It is made up of 29 links and 18 optical nodes. The optical nodes contain LDCs; thus the optical infrastructure is an LLN. Each logical network node accesses the optical network through its own NAS, connected to an ONN by a single-fiber-pair access link. We wish to embed our hypergraph into Atlantis, making economical use of optical resources.

The general approach is shown in Figure 3.39(a), which shows several intersecting hyperedges of an arbitrary hypernet topology. They are to be embedded in the physical topology shown below them. As in our previous examples, each hyperedge represents a set of logical network nodes that are to be fully connected via an MPS realized in the purely optical network. For example, hyperedge E_1 contains four LSNs and a terminal node, all of which must be embedded as an MPS. The dashed vertical lines indicate access links connecting the logical nodes to ONNs, where, for example, the NAS supporting logical node A is connected via link a to optical node a.

Once more using the embedded broadcast star as a vehicle for realizing the MPS, we select a tree joining the logical nodes in the MPS (bold lines in Figure 3.39[a]), designating one ONN, say b, as its root. Because this is an *undirected* embedded star, the LDCs at the various nodes are set to route all optical signals from the transmitters in the five NASs to node b, and then multicast the combined signals back to the five NASs. In this way, all 20 logical connections within the MPS can be arranged to share the common multicast medium. (As usual, this can be done with or without loopback connections.) The resultant routing tree is shown in detail in Figure 3.39(b), indicating the fibers used for each connection.

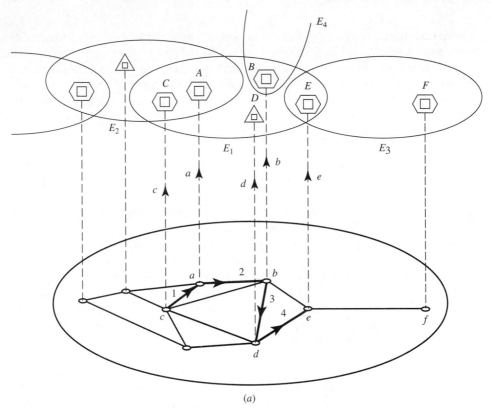

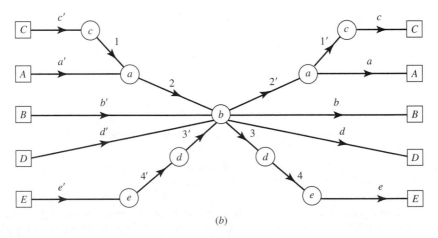

FIGURE 3.39 Hypernet embedding.

The general embedding procedure now consists of two parts:

1. Find a set of trees for the MPSs.
2. Assign wavebands to the trees to satisfy the DCA constraint.

The tree selection might be made to minimize tree size (shortest path routing), to avoid links loaded heavily with traffic from other users of the same infrastructure, and so forth. If minimization of optical spectrum utilization (i.e., assigned wavebands) is the priority, the trees should be routed to minimize their intersections. This may lead, at times, to using some circuitous routes. Because the degree of each LSN is two, there will always be a pair of trees that intersects on each access link. With single-fiber-pair access links, this means that a lower bound on the number of required wavebands is two.

It turns out that it is possible in this case to find trees and waveband assignments to support the ten hyperedges using a total of three distinct wavebands, for a reuse factor of 3.33. For example, a possible choice of trees for E_1, E_2, E_5, and E_6 is shown in Figure 3.38(b). Note that they are nonintersecting on all links, including their access links, and hence the same waveband can be reused on all of them. It is left as an exercise for the reader to find routing trees and waveband assignments for the remaining MPSs.

As in our other examples, either thin or thick wavebands can be used to implement the 12 required logical connections within each MPS. For example, if a single λ-channel is used in each waveband, the LCs can be realized using TDM/TDMA, with a single transceiver needed for an NAS to access one MPS. Because each LSN accesses two hyperedges, its supporting NAS needs two transceivers. The terminal node NASs only require one transceiver. On the other hand, if higher network capacity is desired, a TDM/T-WDMA system can be used over thick wavebands. Using four λ-channels in each waveband, for a total of 12 channels, and operating in FT-TR mode, each MPS now supports four times as much traffic as in the TDM/TDMA case, without increasing the number of optical transceivers. However, rapid receiver tuning is now required.

Again using the wavelength routed bidirectional ring as a baseline for comparison, we recall from the beginning of this section that 61 wavelengths are required for purely optical full connectivity among 22 stations, and 21 transceivers are required in each NAS. The improvement in spectrum usage in Atlantis compared with the ring is only partly attributable to a richer physical topology in this case. (Using a wavelength routed network with single-fiber-pair access links, the least possible number of wavelengths and transceivers for full connectivity with *any* physical topology is 21.) The key to optical resource conservation in this case is the hypernet logical topology. The number of transceivers is kept small by the combination of multipoint optical paths and logical switching, which means that each LSN's transmissions "fan out" to six other logical nodes using only two transmitters, with the same "fan in" advantage for the receivers. Spectrum usage is kept small by using a single routing tree to support 12 LCs in each MPS.

The hypernet model is not limited to LRNs realized on an optical infrastructure. Any large network characterized by highly connected clusters of nodes, with intercluster communication realized through specially equipped relay points, has the basic structure of a hypernet. For example, a cellular radio network is conveniently modeled as a hypergraph in which each hyperedge represents a cell, the LSNs correspond to base stations, and the terminal nodes correspond to mobile users. In another context, an internet can be modeled as a hypernet. In this case, the hyperedges represent constituent networks (subnets of the internet), the LSNs represent gateways between the subnets, and the terminal nodes represent hosts accessing the subnets. What these networks have in common is that each is made up of constituent parts wherein the capacity of each part (a wireless cell or a subnet) is shared among its included nodes.[27] End-to-end connectivity is maintained in any of these hypernets by finding a "good" logical path through the various relay points.

3.5.3 Virtual Connections: An ATM Example

It remains to move up to the virtual connection layer in the architecture of Figure 2.1(a). Because each application typically requires network connections with their own distinctive features, it is best to illustrate with a specific example. To this end we return to the problem of providing full connectivity among five locations. This time, suppose each location contains a number of end systems that access the network through an ATM switch. The interconnected switches form a transport network that provides B-ISDN services to the end systems. These might include LAN interconnection, multimedia conferencing, and so on. Our objective is to examine several alternative designs for the network and compare their merits. The focus is on how the required connectivity is distributed among the different network layers: virtual, logical, and optical. The following are the designs being compared:

1. A stand-alone ATM star

2. A stand-alone ATM ring

3. ATM over a network of SONET cross-connects

4. ATM over a WRN

5. ATM over an LLN

The two stand-alone cases are configured in the form of a set of ATM switches interconnected directly through dedicated point-to-point transmission links, each containing a single pair of fibers, as shown in Figure 3.40. The switches access the fibers through optical transceivers, creating a pair of LCs in opposite directions on each link. Case 1, the star, consists of five end nodes performing ATM end node functions,

---

[27] In the case of an internet, complete sharing within a subnet may not always be a good model of what is actually happening.

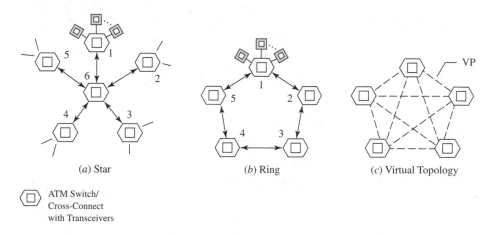

(a) Star   (b) Ring   (c) Virtual Topology

ATM Switch/
Cross-Connect
with Transceivers

FIGURE 3.40   ATM stand-alone networks.

and a sixth "transit" node performing ATM cross-connect functions only (see Figure 3.40[a]). The ring of case 2 (see Figure 3.40[b]) is bidirectional, with each of the five nodes performing end node and VP add–drop functions. The virtual topology for all cases is fully connected, as shown in Figure 3.40(c), in which an ATM VP exists for each pair of end nodes. The end systems communicate over virtual connections assigned on demand to the appropriate VPs. As can be seen, all VPs in the star require two logical hops, whereas in the ring they require either one or two hops using shortest path routing.

The remaining three cases are illustrated in Figure 3.41. Here we assume that our ATM network is just one of several logical networks using the services of a larger infrastructure. In Figure 3.41(a) (case 3) the nodes of the underlying network are SONET DCSs interconnected by point-to-point transmission links. (In this case there may be many fiber pairs per link because the infrastructure is assumed to be supporting much more traffic than the logical network under discussion.) Inasmuch as cases 1 through 3 are all based on electronic switching nodes interconnected by point-to-point links, they do not fall under our definition of optical *networks*. However, they represent competing architectures for solving the design problem we have posed, and thus it is important to compare their properties with the optical network approaches (cases 4 and 5).

The ATM network is shown *embedded* in the larger DCS network in Figure 3.41(a). There are five ATM switches, which are supported by what *they* see as a logical topology whose switching nodes are the DCSs. Again, a fully connected set of VPs must be established, in which each VP is routed over a shortest logical path through the DCS network. All shortest paths are assumed to pass through node 6, consisting of two logical hops and resulting in a star configuration supporting the ATM switches.

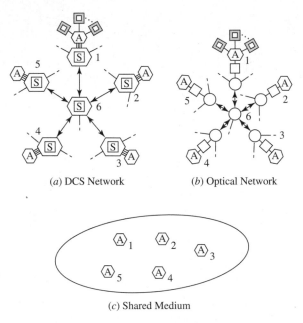

(*a*) DCS Network   (*b*) Optical Network

(*c*) Shared Medium

ⒶATM Switch
⑤SONET DCS
○ONN

FIGURE 3.41 Embedded ATM network.

In Figure 3.41(b), the infrastructure supporting the ATM network is purely optical. Its topology is the same as the previous case, but the DCSs are now replaced by optical network nodes. For case 4, the ONNs are assumed to be WSXCs, whereas for case 5 they are LDCs. In the former case, a logical connection supported by a λ-channel is dedicated to each VP, whereas in the latter case all VPs are supported by logical connections that share a common optical medium.

Further details of design and performance require some knowledge of traffic demand. To fix ideas, let us assume a uniform traffic distribution among the stations, with each VP requiring one unit of capacity to support the expected demand.[28] A unit is considered to be 600 Mbps (approximately the STS-12/OC-12 bitrate). In each case, the λ-channels and the transceivers are assumed to run at rates as high as 2.4 Gbps (approximately the STS-48 rate); thus a λ-channel carries up to four units of traffic. Now let us consider each design in turn, comparing them on the basis of (1) allocated optical spectrum, (2) total optical transceivers, (3) processing load in the nodes, and (4) other factors (reconfigurability, survivability, and so forth).

---

[28] The VPs are assumed to be "sized" to provide acceptable virtual connection blocking probability for the estimated offered traffic and to ensure satisfactory quality of service to all virtual connections admitted to each VP.

3.5.3.1 Case 1: Stand-Alone ATM Star

In this case, the fiber links are connected directly to ports on the ATM switches, as shown in Figure 3.40(a), creating a point-to-point optical connection for each fiber. Because each link carries four VPs in each direction, each optical connection must have a capacity of four units of traffic, which can be accommodated using a single λ-channel supporting a transmission channel running at the STS-48 bitrate. This means that one optical transceiver is required to terminate each end of a link, for a total of ten transceivers in the network. The end nodes process their own VPs, carrying an aggregate traffic of eight units, but node 6 must process all of the VPs, for a total of 20 units, which is 12 Gbps or an aggregate throughput of 28×10^6 cells/s. This represents a heavy processing load and is the bottleneck of the system.[29]

What is the allocated optical bandwidth in this system? Even though only one λ-channel is being used, the fact is that *the total bandwidth of each fiber is dedicated to this system*. In this case, as in all networks in which fibers are used as point-to-point transmission links terminated by optical transceivers, the *usable* capacity of the fibers corresponds to the capacity of the transceivers terminating them. In our example the system only uses the capacity of one λ-channel, which means that the rest of the fiber capacity is wasted! This is our old foe, the electronic (actually optoelectronic) bottleneck. Assigning more transceivers and λ-channels to the network would not help because the traffic does not require them. In addition to inefficient utilization of the fibers, another disadvantage of this system is that its survivability is poor. The network is cut in two if any single link is cut, and is completely destroyed if the ATM cross-connect in the central node goes down. Furthermore, there is no way to reconfigure the network either to recover from faults or to satisfy different traffic distributions.

3.5.3.2 Case 2: Stand-Alone ATM Ring

This case is similar to the previous one. Assuming shortest path routing, the average logical hop count for a VP is 1.5. Because each VP must be assigned one unit of capacity, this means that each fiber must have a capacity of three units. Assigning one λ-channel (and one transceiver) to each fiber as before, we can support the traffic requirement with 25% spare capacity in this case. (The difference between traffic flow on the fibers in cases 1 and 2 is due to the fact that the average hop count in the former case is 2, compared with 1.5 in the current case.) It is left to the reader to show that the processing load in each switch is ten units. Although this is worse than the processing in the end nodes of case 1, there is no processing bottleneck in this case because the network is completely symmetrical. We have the same problem with optical spectrum allocation as in case 1, but the network has better survivability. It can recover from any single link cut or node failure by rerouting the traffic from the failed link or node the "long way" around the ring. Also, there is some leeway for capacity reconfiguration

---

[29] However, the *granularity* of the connections processed by the central node (VPs) is coarser than that of the connections processed by the end nodes (VCs), which makes the central node's processing load *per cell* somewhat less.

due to the fact that there is some spare capacity. This means that some nonuniform traffic patterns can be accommodated.

3.5.3.3 Case 3: ATM Embedded in DCS Network

In this and the remaining two cases, the issue of resource allocation must be viewed differently because the underlying network resources are being shared between the ATM network under discussion and other network services. In the DCS network we assume that by making the appropriate cross-connections, the network of DCSs provides a dedicated, fixed bitrate connection between each pair of ATM switches, for a total of 20 unidirectional connections to support the 20 VPs. Each ATM switch accesses a DCS through four electronic ports in each direction, one for each VP, to which a capacity of one unit of traffic (STS-12) is assigned. Because four VPs are routed from each ATM switch through node 6, a capacity of four units is needed on each link joining an end node to the central node.

As shown in Figure 3.41(a), each DCS is connected to several fiber links (possibly containing several fiber pairs each). Each inbound (outbound) fiber connection normally carries several λ-channels, and hence the interface to each fiber must contain a WDMUX (WMUX) and an array of optical receivers (transmitters), one for each λ-channel. (We assume that each λ-channel carries an STS-48 signal; that is, four units of capacity.) As explained in Section 2.6, once the received signals are in electrical form, they are demultiplexed down to lower rates, cross-connected, and remultiplexed for transmission on outbound ports.[30] In the case of our ATM network, the DCS performs a sorting and routing function at a level of granularity equal to one unit of traffic. For example, consider the VP connecting node 1 to node 2. The DCS at node 1 receives an STS-12 signal for the logical connection carrying this VP from the attached ATM switch, multiplexes it with other signals, and transmits it via an OC-48 optical signal on a fiber connected to node 6. The DCS at that node again does a demultiplexing, routing, and remultiplexing operation, cross-connecting the STS-12 signal of interest to an outbound fiber directed to node 2, where it is again demultiplexed and delivered to the destination ATM switch. These cross-connect functions are required for all 20 VPs at node 6. However, it is much simpler to perform VP cross-connect functions at the STS-12 level than at the ATM cell level, which is what was done in case 1. (In both cases 1 and 3 we still need ATM cell switching at the end nodes.)

How does this configuration utilize resources? Here we must distinguish between resources used for the ATM network and those used for other services. As in case 1, a total of ten optical transceivers in the DCSs are allocated to the ATM network (although there may be many more allocated to other services). Similarly, one λ-channel is required on each fiber, with the rest of the optical spectrum used for other purposes. Thus the total bandwidth allocated to the ATM network is only that required for a single λ-channel. Survivability and reconfigurability are good because alternate paths

---

[30] All of this represents considerable electronic and optical complexity in each DCS. However, it must be recalled that the cost of the DCS is spread over many users sharing the same DCS network.

and additional bandwidth exist in the underlying DCS network. The main downside is that, as in case 1, each fiber is terminated at each node by optical transceivers. The electronic bottleneck reappears here in different guises, depending on how the DCSs are equipped. At one extreme they could be configured "minimally," with one OT or OR per fiber, to provide for a single OC-48 signal (one λ-channel) on each fiber. This would reduce the cost of the DCS, but would choke off the spectrum on the incident fibers, making them unavailable for other services. At the other extreme, at a much higher cost, a large array of transceivers could be used to terminate many λ-channels on each fiber. The resultant demodulated bitstreams transiting the node would then be electronically cross-connected, thereby "opening up" a larger portion of the fiber spectrum for use by other logical networks.

3.5.3.4 Case 4: ATM Embedded in a WRN

The electronic network nodes of the previous case are now replaced by optical network nodes containing WSXCs, as shown in Figure 3.41(b). This makes the network seen by the ATM switches purely optical. Each ATM end node switch is connected electronically to an NAS and then to its network node through an access link. Because this is a wavelength routed network, each VP in the virtual topology must be supported by a point-to-point logical connection terminating on a port of the ATM switch, which is in turn supported by a point-to-point optical connection occupying one λ-channel. This means that four transceivers are needed in each NAS at an ATM end node, but none are needed at node 6. The total complement of 20 transceivers is twice as many as in the previous cases, but up to four units of capacity are now available to each VP. This represents four times the required capacity, but because λ-channels cannot be shared in a wavelength routed network, it is the smallest possible capacity allocation.

Using the wavelength routing techniques described in Section 3.3.1, it is possible to find wavelength assignments and WSXC settings requiring a total of four wavelengths for all 20 VPs, and giving a spectrum reuse factor of five. This case, therefore, uses four times as many λ-channels as the DCS case. The remaining properties of the wavelength routed case are similar to the previous one, except that the complexity of the underlying network nodes is far simpler in the wavelength routed case than in the DCS case. In particular, transiting traffic on λ-channels used for other services can now be routed directly through the ONNs without doing optoelectronic conversion at each node. Of course, the optical switching capability for the additional channels must be built into the ONNs.

3.5.3.5 Case 5: ATM Embedded in an LLN

In this final case, the WSXCs in Figure 3.41(b) are replaced by LDCs, making multipoint connections and capacity sharing possible. A single waveband is assigned to the ATM network, and the LDCs are set to create an embedded tree on that waveband. Now 20 logical connections will be created on the tree to support the 20 VPs. The optical path for the tree is a star with its root at node 6. The LDC at the root is set to act as a star coupler on the allocated waveband so that all end nodes see a broadcast star with a total capacity of one waveband. The resultant logical topology is shown in Figure 3.41(c) as a single hyperedge containing all five ATM switches as vertices, implying that all 20 LCs are sharing the optical medium.

Because a total capacity of 20 units is needed for the network, we allocate five λ-channels (all in the same waveband) to the ATM network. The logical channels can be realized using many possible multiplexing and multiple access schemes. If a TDM/T-WDMA system with fixed transmitters and rapidly tunable receivers is used, only one transceiver per NAS is required as opposed to four in the wavelength routed case. Equal capacity can be assigned to each VP by allocating one channel–slot in each frame to its supporting logical channel. Furthermore, nonuniform capacity allocations can be accommodated easily simply by assigning different numbers of channel–slots to different logical channels (see Section 5.4). Thus reconfiguration to adapt to different traffic patterns is accomplished easily here.

Because all five λ-channels are confined to the same waveband, they require less optical bandwidth than the four channels used in case 4. Using the channel spacings in Figure 3.31, 200 GHz of optical bandwidth is needed in the LLN case compared with 800 GHz in the wavelength routed case. Finally, to exploit the shared medium fully, we may also use packet switching in the optical layer to achieve dynamic capacity allocation. As explained in Section 3.2.2, a significant by-product of optical layer packet switching is the fact that *multicast* LCs from one ATM switch to several others can be implemented in the optical layer simply by appending multicast addresses to the packets. This means that multicast does *not* require sending duplicate cells over multiple VPs.

Table 3.5 compares these five realizations. In terms of bandwidth utilization, the DCS network is the best. This assumes that many closely packed λ-channels are used on each fiber, exemplified by the channel spacing of Figure 2.4(a). (Because optical signals do not traverse any WSXCs, the wide guard bands between wavebands shown in Figure 3.31 are not needed on a single optical hop.) Among the embedded networks, cases 4 and 5 are transparent to transmission formats and therefore can accommodate heterogeneous traffic from other users, whereas case 3 is restricted to SONET services.

TABLE 3.5   Comparison of ATM Network Realizations

Case	Optical Spectrum Usage	No. of Optical Transceivers	Node Processing Load	Other
1	Very high	10	Very high	Poor survivability
2	Very high	10	High	—
3	Lowest	10	Medium	High DCS cost
4	Medium	20	Very low	—
5	Low	5	Very low	Rapid tunability required, optical multicast possible

Case 5 uses the fewest optical transceivers and has the potential for dynamic capacity assignment and optical multicast as well. Both cases 4 and 5 have the lowest processing loads. Of course, many other factors would influence the choice of realization, one of the most important being system cost. Per unit of throughput, the cost of an ATM switch is much higher than a SONET DCS, and both *should* be much more costly than a WSXC or an LDC once the enabling optical technology matures. Ease of control, management, and fault recovery are other important issues.

3.6 Summary

This chapter has given a largely *descriptive* picture of the four basic classes of multi-wavelength networks in order of increasing complexity: uncontrolled, wavelength routed, waveband routed, and logically routed. The objective was comparative analysis. In drawing comparisons, realistic, specific parameter values were used as much as possible so that quantitative comparisons could be made.

We found that the larger the network, the more complex the supporting architecture must be. The hardest part of scaling to large sizes is connectivity, because the number of possible end-to-end connections in a network grows as the square of the number of end systems. Connectivity in uncontrolled networks is limited by the inability to reuse the optical spectrum. Connectivity in wavelength routed networks is limited by the fact that an optical transceiver and a λ-channel are required for each logical connection. This limit is circumvented in waveband routed networks (LLNs) by using multipoint optical paths sharing the capacity of a common waveband. Multipoint paths are in turn limited by the fact that their combined throughput cannot exceed the capacity limit of the waveband they share. LRNs break the connectivity bottleneck, but do it by implementing high connectivity electronically, incurring concomitant high processing loads in electronic switching equipment.

The easiest aspect of scaling networks to large sizes is the throughput or network capacity requirement because optical fibers have so much capacity to start with and because each time we add an NAS to the network we add transceiver capacity. In moving from simpler to more complex architectures we find that the efficiency of optical resource utilization improves—more optical spectrum reuse and less optical transceivers required per station. At this point in time pronouncements on costs and technological limits are dangerous. The only certainty is that costs of optoelectronic and photonic components will decrease and performance will increase as technology matures. Another quasi certainty is that readers will see new enabling technology come on the scene that was unknown when this book was written. Thus, the cost–performance ratios for optical networks will surely improve with time.

The illustrative examples, even the 22-node case, were chosen intentionally as "toy" problems—small enough and simple enough to be solved by inspection, by trial and error, or by a small amount of hand calculation. They are to be considered as points of departure for a deeper exploration of the various issues introduced here: topological considerations at the physical and logical levels; routing, channel, and waveband assignment; methodologies for network design; and the relations between performance, control, and resource utilization. Each section points to a later chapter: The static networks discussed in Section 3.2 are studied in more depth in Chapter 5, wavelength/waveband routed networks discussed in Sections 3.3 and 3.4 are described again in Chapter 6, and LRNs (discussed in Section 3.5) are described in detail in Chapter 7.

The most important concept to retain from this chapter is the view of the overall network as many superimposed layers of connections. These connections can be configured to be one to one, one to many, many to one, and multicast. The end systems typically see a set of virtual connections that provide end-to-end transport on demand. The virtual connections are in turn supported by a network of logical connections matched to the needs of a community of end users. The links in the logical layer are realized as transparent optical connections, which are in turn supported by optical paths laid out on a fixed fiber topology. Except for the fibers, everything else in the network is reconfigurable, with each layer (to a large extent) independent of the others.

Virtual connections can be routed over many alternate logical paths, and logical topologies together with the optical connections/paths that support them can be reconfigured independently. We have seen that a large, purely optical network may serve as a common infrastructure for several independently managed logical networks, each one tailored to the needs of a different user community. Conversely, a logical network covering a geographic expanse extending beyond the reach of purely optical connections may be supported by several concatenated, independent optical networks, in which the end-to-end logical paths are formed as a sequence of separate parts joined together at logical gateways between networks. This extraordinary degree of flexibility produces opportunities and challenges that are explored in the rest of the book.

3.7 Problems

1. Show that if full virtual connectivity is required among the five stations in Figure 3.2(b), and if shortest path routing is used for the VPs, there will be ten VPs multiplexed on each LC. Generalize this result to the case of n stations.

2. The network of Figure 3.19 is operated as a WRN with each internodal link equipped with a single-fiber pair.

   (a) Explain why at least two wavelengths are required to support full optical connectivity among the five stations.

   (b) Assuming single fiber pair access links, find a possible RCA for the 20 optical connections using a minimum number of wavelengths.

   (c) Repeat part (b) using nonblocking access links and only two wavelengths.

3. The network of Figure 3.26 is operated as a WRN with each internodal link equipped with a single-fiber pair and each station having a nonblocking access link.

(a) Explain why at least four wavelengths are required to support full optical connectivity among the seven stations.

(b) Find a possible RCA for the optical connections required for full connectivity using a minimum number of wavelengths.

4. Consider power distribution in the network of Figure 3.23(b). With the power distribution rules described in Section 3.4.1.2 and in Figure 3.25, find the resultant power levels distributed to the three destination stations. Verify that they satisfy the objective of splitting each source's power equally among all destinations it reaches, and combining equally the powers from all sources arriving at the same destination.

5. Modify the seven-station example of Section 3.4.3 and Table 3.2 as follows. Let guard bands between wavebands be increased to 100 GHz, with the usable bandwidth maintained at 125 GHz. Assume that in the case of the WRN the optical signals can run at twice the bitrates of the LLN (e.g., 5 Gbps instead of 2.5 Gbps) because of their increased wavelength spacing. Recalculate the spectrum utilization and total network capacity in this case for each row in the table.

6. Complete the routing and waveband assignment for the hypernet of Figure 3.38. (Check your answer against Table 7.5.)

7. In case 2 of the ATM example of Section 3.5.3, verify that the processing load is ten units of traffic in each ATM switch.

3.8 Bibliography

[Abramson73] N. Abramson, The ALOHA system. In *Computer Networks*. Englewood Cliffs, NJ: Prentice-Hall, 1973.

[Maeda98] M. W. Maeda, Management and control of transparent optical networks. *IEEE J. Select. Areas Commun.*, 16(7):1008–1023, 1998.

[Ross89] F. E. Ross, An overview of FDDI: The fiber distributed data interface. *IEEE J. Select. Areas Commun.*, 7(7):1043–1051, 1989.

[Schwartz87] M. Schwartz, *Telecommunication Networks: Protocols, Modeling and Analysis*. Reading, MA: Addison-Wesley, 1987.

[Wei+98] J. Y. Wei, C.-C. Shen, B. J. Wilson, M. J. Post, and Y. Tsai. Connection management for multiwavelength optical networking. *IEEE J. Select. Areas Commun.*, 16(7):1097–1108, 1998.

CHAPTER FOUR

Enabling Technology

Throughout this book the approaches taken to system design and performance evaluation are based on the constraints of the enabling technology. Available fiber capacity is assumed to be limited by the constraints and imperfections of optical transceivers, amplifiers, and cross-connects. These constraints affect maximum available spectrum, wavelength/waveband spacing, and maximum bitrates per channel. Optical connections are assumed to have limited reach, both geographically and in terms of the number of optical cross-connects they may traverse. Sizes of switches as well as their speed, complexity, and functionality are also assumed to be limited by cost and performance constraints. Trade-offs between optical and electronic methods of implementing connectivity and routing are suggested, in which the optimal design point depends again on relative cost and performance of the enabling technologies.

Although emphasizing that these technological constraints are paramount, we purposely keep as much of a separation as possible between the architectures discussed in the book and the limitations of any *specific* technology. The reason is obvious: Today's technology is likely to be obsolete tomorrow. After perhaps a decade or more of gestation in the laboratory, photonic and optoelectronic technology is now undergoing an amazing transformation. Devices and systems that a year ago would have been too costly and too unreliable to use in the field are being deployed at an explosive rate, and a new industry is blossoming in response to the need for components for the new optical communications infrastructure.

Keeping this background in mind, we present in this chapter the essential features of representative devices and systems used in the implemention of multiwavelength optical networks. The objective is to convey an understanding of the principles that underlie the functioning of the basic components of these networks, together with some notion of the performance of typical current devices.

It is impossible in a few pages to give more than a glimpse of the state-of-the-art of current photonic and optoelectronic technology as it applies to optical networking. For a more complete treatment the reader is referred to books completely devoted to the subject (e.g., [Kaminow+97]).

4.1 Evolution of Transmission and Switching Technology

Advances in optical networking thus far have been largely in the area of point-to-point optical transmission. Transmission system performance is typically measured in terms of bitrate–distance products, where distance is measured from the source to the point at which a signal must be regenerated (i.e., "cleaned up").[1]

The evolution of telecommunications from the early days of the telephone to current optical fiber systems shows about three orders of magnitude of increase in bitrate–distance product each time a new technology is introduced—from megabits per second–kilometers for microwave relays to gigabits per second–kilometers for unamplified fibers to terabits per second–kilometers for amplified links. Developments in single-wavelength optical transmission through 1993 are shown in more detail in Figure 4.1, achieving bitrate–distance products in the tens of terabits-per-second–kilometers range. In multiwavelength transmission, recent "hero" experiments have gone still further. For example, a 360-Tbps–km experiment was performed in 1997 at KDD using 16 2.5-Gbps channels over 9,000 km with wavelength separations of 0.5 nm [Otani+97]. Results presented the following year by the same group increased the bitrate–distance product to approximately 530 Tbps–km using 60 channels at 5.3 Gbps over 1,650 km [Murashige+98]. The most recent soliton experiments both in the laboratory and in the field suggest that the reach of the optical fiber transmission link is for all practical purposes unlimited (see Section 4.3.3).

Advances in optical switching technology are following the scenario traced by earlier electronic networks. Developments in digital transmission (e.g., the T1 carrier system) made it cost-effective to move from analog to digital (i.e., time–division) switching, and therefore drove the development of digital switching technology. In a similar way, the current developments in multiwavelength transmission are already a driving force in the development of multiwavelength switching technology. Once that technology is in place on a large scale, wide area optical networks will become a reality.

As of this writing, transmission technology is much more mature than switching technology. Thus, this chapter focuses more heavily on the former than the latter. Sections 4.2 to 4.8 focus on the point-to-point transmission link. We begin with a brief overview of the components of the communication path, followed by a discussion of optical fiber transmission principles and transmission impairments. Amplifiers, transmitters, and receivers are then considered, to complete the picture. Sections 4.9 to 4.11 deal with the devices necessary to combine transmission links into networks: static coupling devices, switches, filters, multiplexers, and wavelength converters. Finally, an overall analysis of the end-to-end transmission path is undertaken, considering both transmission and switching impairments. We conclude with a case study, using wavelength-domain simulation to examine the cumulative effects of a large number of transmission path impairments on system performance (Section 4.12).

---

[1] Digital signal regeneration involves reshaping and retiming the pulses, operations that are almost always done electronically.

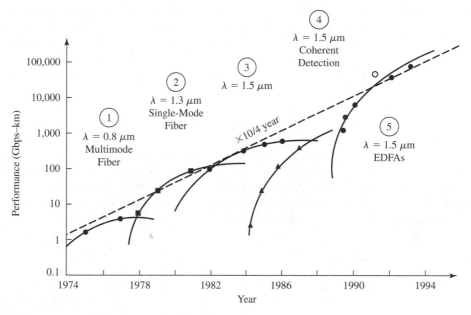

FIGURE 4.1 Recent advances in optical transmission.   (From (Desurvire94, Figure 7.1). Copyright © 1994. Reprinted by permission of John Wiley & Sons, Inc.)

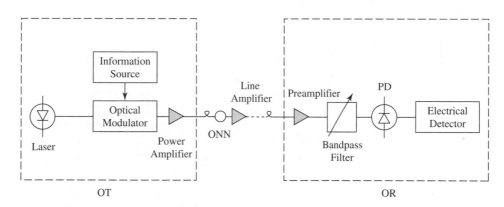

FIGURE 4.2 A point-to-point optical connection.

4.2 Overview of the Optical Connection

A point-to-point optical connection (OC) in a multiwavelength network consists of an optical transmitter (OT) and receiver (OR) joined by an optical path consisting of fiber links traversing one or more optical network (switching) nodes (ONN), as shown in Figure 4.2. In the example shown, a laser is modulated externally by an information source and is followed by a power amplifier that raises the power level launched on the fiber. Additional line amplifiers between fiber sections boost the power to compensate for attenuation along the line, and a preamplifier raises the power level at the input of the receiver to improve the signal-to-noise ratio (SNR) at the input to the electrical detector. A tunable optical bandpass filter is also shown, making this a tunable receiver. In digital systems, performance is measured in terms of bit error rates (BERs), whereas in analog systems the criterion is electrical SNR at the output of the receiver.

The performance is affected by imperfections in the optical transmitter (for example, laser drift and line width), transmission impairments in the fibers (attenuation, dispersion, and nonlinear effects such as four-wave mixing), amplifier characteristics (nonflat gain profile, amplified spontaneous emission noise), switch imperfections (cross-talk), and receiver imperfections (nonideal filtering and tuning, noise figure). Our discussion is limited for the most part to intensity-modulated direct-detection (IM/DD) systems. That is, the laser is intensity modulated either directly or externally, and the receiver uses direct detection of optical intensity.

4.3 Optical Fibers

This section begins with an exposition of how light propagates through optical fibers under ideal conditions. This is followed by a survey of the principal impairments in fiber propagation: attenuation, dispersion, and fiber nonlinearities. We conclude with a brief description of soliton propagation, which provides a promising approach to very long-distance optical transmission.

4.3.1 Principles of Guided Wave Propagation

The end-to-end optical path in a communication system consists of a series of guided wave structures: the fibers themselves, as well as the various components used for coupling signals in and out of the fibers and switching them from one fiber to another. Thus, we begin with a brief discussion of how light propagates through waveguides. In cases when geometries have large dimensions compared with a wavelength (for example, in multimode fibers or in free space), geometric optics is sufficient to explain the phenomena of interest. In other cases (for example, single-mode fibers), a wave picture is necessary.

4.3.1.1 Rays: Geometric Optics

The wave-guiding properties of an optical fiber are easily understood in the context of a multimode step-index fiber. (However, for reasons to be explained later, multimode fibers are rarely used in high-speed long-distance communications.) As shown in cross-section in Figure 4.3(a), a step-index fiber has a core of radius a with a constant refractive index n_1, and a surrounding glass cladding of outside radius b with a slightly lower index n_2.[2] The air surrounding the cladding has a refractive index n_0. Single-mode fibers typically have cores with diameters of 8 μm to 12 μm and a clad-

---

[2] The refractive index of a medium is the ratio of the speed of light in free space to the speed of light in the medium.

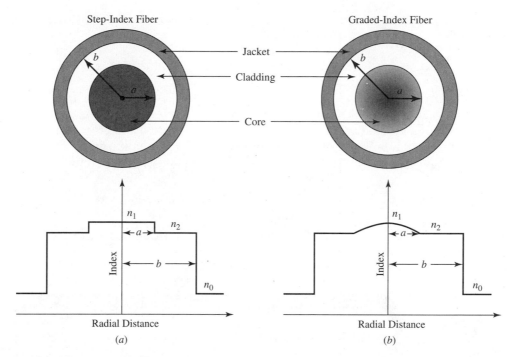

FIGURE 4.3 Refractive index profiles for fibers.   (From (Agrawal97, Figure 2.1). Copyright © 1997. Reprinted by permission of John Wiley & Sons, Inc.)

ding diameter of 125 μm, whereas multimode fibers have cores of approximately 50 μm in diameter.

Reflection and refraction at the boundary of two media are illustrated in Figure 4.4, which shows the case $n_1 > n_2$. The relations between the angle of incidence θ_i, the angle of reflection θ_r, and the angle of the transmitted ray (angle of refraction) θ_t are

$$\theta_r = \theta_i \tag{4.1}$$

and

$$n_1 \sin \theta_i = n_2 \sin \theta_t \tag{4.2}$$

where the latter is called *Snell's law*.

What makes fiber optics work is *total internal reflection*, which was first demonstrated by John Tyndall in 1854. Equation 4.2 shows that there is a *critical angle* $\theta_c = \sin^{-1} n_2/n_1$, where the transmitted ray lies right on the boundary. At angles of incidence greater than θ_c, all energy is totally reflected, resulting in a *guided ray*. It is these rays, guided within the core of the fiber, that carry our optical signals. Figure 4.5 illustrates guided and unguided rays. A ray entering the fiber at a sufficiently small angle of incidence (shown as the acceptance cone in the figure) is totally reflected, bouncing back and forth between the internal walls of the fiber as it propagates, whereas a ray incident outside the acceptance cone is partially refracted at each bounce. For rays

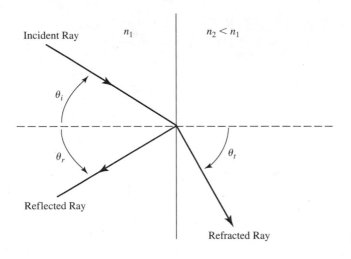

Incident Ray n_1 $n_2 < n_1$

θ_i

θ_r

θ_t

Reflected Ray

Refracted Ray

FIGURE 4.4 Snell's law.

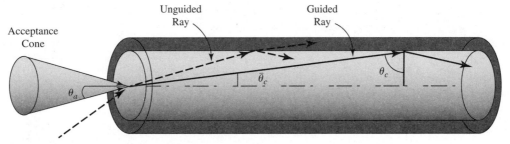

FIGURE 4.5 Ray propagation in a step-index fiber. (From (Saleh+91, Figure 8.1-3a). Copyright © 1991. Reprinted by permission of John Wiley & Sons, Inc.)

entering the fiber from air, the largest possible angle of incidence for guided rays is the *acceptance angle* θ_a, which equals

$$\sin^{-1}\sqrt{(n_1^2 - n_2^2)}.$$

The *numerical aperture* of the fiber is defined as

$$NA = \sin\theta_a = \sqrt{(n_1^2 - n_2^2)}.$$

Note that numerical aperture increases with the fractional refractive index change, $\Delta = \frac{n_1 - n_2}{n_1}$. In a typical cladded fiber, $\Delta \ll 1$; thus, only a narrow cone of light is accepted as a guided ray. However, in an uncladded fiber, both Δ and NA are large. (For an uncladded silica glass fiber, NA > 1, meaning that rays from all directions are accepted.)

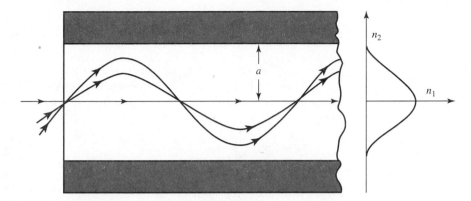

FIGURE 4.6 Ray propagation in a graded-index fiber.   (From (Agrawal97, Figure 2.3).
Copyright © 1997. Reprinted by permission of John Wiley & Sons, Inc.)

It is important to note that guided rays entering the fiber at slightly different angles
of incidence take shorter or longer paths from end to end. Thus, if a pulse of energy
incident on the fiber is spread throughout the acceptance cone, the arriving energy
is dispersed in time due to the different path lengths so that the pulse is "smeared
out" in time. This *multipath* or *intermodal dispersion* becomes worse for large numerical apertures. Thus, a high light-gathering ability does *not* make the fiber a good
communication medium.

To reduce the effects of intermodal dispersion, fibers are also manufactured with a
graded-index profile. The ideal graded index for reducing dispersion turns out to be one
in which *n* decreases parabolically from the center of the core to the cladding—see
Figure 4.3(b). With a graded index, the rays are bent as they approach the cladding,
as shown in Figure 4.6. This bending, together with the fact that rays farther from
the core travel faster (due to a lower *n*), can reduce intermodal dispersion by several
orders of magnitude.

4.3.1.2 Modes: The Wave Picture

Geometric optics fails to predict the behavior of light when the dimensions of the
confining medium are comparable with the wavelength, which is the case in single-
mode fibers and in most photonic devices. In this case the electromagnetic wave
picture is required. For this we must start with *Maxwell's equations*, the fundamental
equations governing all electromagnetic phenomena.

An electromagnetic wave is defined at any point in space and time by its electric
and magnetic field vectors $\mathcal{E}(\mathbf{r}, t)$ and $\mathcal{H}(\mathbf{r}, t)$ respectively, where $\mathbf{r}$ is a position vector
in some arbitrary coordinate system. These quantities are related by

$$\nabla \times \mathcal{H} = \frac{\partial \mathcal{D}}{\partial t} \tag{4.3}$$

$$\nabla \times \mathcal{E} = -\frac{\partial \mathcal{B}}{\partial t} \tag{4.4}$$

$$\nabla \cdot \mathcal{D} = 0 \tag{4.5}$$

$$\nabla \cdot \mathcal{B} = 0 \tag{4.6}$$

These are Maxwell's equations for a charge- and current-free medium, where the quantities $\mathcal{D}$ and $\mathcal{B}$ are the electric and magnetic flux densities respectively. In free space the flux densities are directly proportional to the corresponding fields. However, in general we have

$$\mathcal{D} = \epsilon_0 \mathcal{E} + \mathcal{P} \tag{4.7}$$

$$\mathcal{B} = \mu_0 \mathcal{H} + \mathcal{M} \tag{4.8}$$

where ϵ_0 and μ_0 are the electric permittivity and the magnetic permeability of free space respectively, and $\mathcal{P}$ and $\mathcal{M}$ are the polarization and magnetization densities respectively.

In almost all situations encountered in optical transmission, the medium is non-magnetic ($\mathcal{M} = 0$)—a condition that is assumed henceforth. The $\mathcal{P}$ vector can be related in complex ways to the corresponding $\mathcal{E}$ field, and it is this complex relationship in the glass medium that is responsible for most of the impairments in fiber transmission. Furthermore, by modifying this relationship in special ways through external control, it is possible to construct the many devices that are the building blocks of optical networks: switches, isolators, filters, and so forth.

A wave analysis of fiber propagation normally begins with an assumption of an "ideal" fiber, after which nonideal conditions are added as small perturbations on the ideal model. Let us assume the following ideal conditions. The medium is

- *Linear:* $\mathcal{P}$ is a linear function of $\mathcal{E}$.

- *Nondispersive:* The medium is nondispersive in time if $\mathcal{P}$ at any point in time is a function of $\mathcal{E}$ at the same point in time (in other words, the medium is memoryless). It is spatially nondispersive if $\mathcal{P}$ at any point in space is a function of $\mathcal{E}$ at the same point in space.

- *Homogeneous:* The relation $\mathcal{P}(\mathcal{E})$ is independent of **r**.

- *Isotropic:* The relation $\mathcal{P}(\mathcal{E})$ is independent of the direction of $\mathcal{E}$. In isotropic media, $\mathcal{P}$ and $\mathcal{E}$ are parallel.

Under these assumptions, Equation 4.7 can be written in the simpler form

$$\mathcal{D} = \epsilon \mathcal{E} \tag{4.9}$$

where the scalar constant ϵ is now the permittivity of the medium. Maxwell's equations can then be combined to yield the vector wave equation

$$\nabla^2 u - \frac{1}{c^2}\frac{\partial^2 u}{\partial^2 t} = 0 \tag{4.10}$$

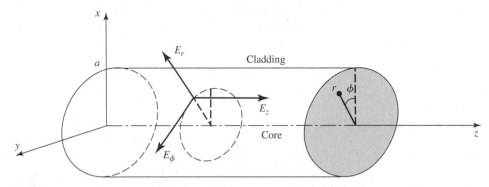

FIGURE 4.7 Cylindrical coordinates. (From (Saleh+91, Figure 8.1-4). Copyright © 1991. Reprinted by permission of John Wiley & Sons, Inc.)

where $c = 1/\sqrt{\epsilon \mu_0}$ is the speed of light in the medium. The wave equation is satisfied by each component of both $\mathcal{E}$ and $\mathcal{H}$.

Because of linearity, any solution of the wave equation can be represented as a linear combination of other solutions. This suggests representing the optical fields that satisfy that equation as sums of sinusoids; that is, moving from the time domain to the optical frequency domain. Let $\mathcal{E}(\mathbf{r}, t) = Re\{\mathbf{E}(\mathbf{r})e^{j\omega t}\}$ and $\mathcal{H}(\mathbf{r}, t) = Re\{\mathbf{H}(\mathbf{r})e^{j\omega t}\}$, where $\mathbf{E}$ and $\mathbf{H}$ are the complex envelopes of $\mathcal{E}$ and $\mathcal{H}$ respectively, and ω is the optical frequency in radians per second. Each of these functions represents a *monochromatic signal*. Substituting either of these into the wave equation, we obtain the *Helmholtz equation*

$$\nabla^2 U + k^2 U = 0 \tag{4.11}$$

where $k = \omega/c$ is called the *wavenumber*.

The story becomes much more involved from now on. Solutions of the Helmholtz equation must be found that match the boundary conditions of the fiber for the core and the cladding. Working in the cylindrical coordinate system of the fiber (Figure 4.7), the spatial variables are radius r, axial distance z, and angle ϕ. The classic approach uses separation of variables, in which case we seek solutions in the form

$$U(r, \phi, z) = u(r)e^{-jl\phi}e^{-j\beta z} \tag{4.12}$$

for an integer value of l.[3] These represent traveling waves along the axis z of the fiber, with *propagation constant β*.

Solutions of Equation 4.11 that satisfy the required boundary conditions exist only for certain permissible (characteristic) values of β. These values must satisfy the *characteristic equation* associated with Equation 4.11, which embodies the constraints of the fiber geometry. Each characteristic value of β yields a solution for $u(r)$—a Bessel

---

[3] Each component of the electric and magnetic fields is in this form.

function in the case of cylindrical geometry—and for each value of the index l in Equation 4.12, the characteristic equation has a discrete set of solutions: β_{lm}, for m, a positive integer. A solution of Equation 4.11 for each value of β_{lm} represents a *mode* in the fiber.

Note that there is a dependence on optical frequency (or wavelength) in Equation 4.11, through the wavenumber $k = \omega/c$, so that the propagating (guided) modes and the constants β_{lm} depend on the frequency of the optical signal. The function connecting each propagation constant β_{lm} to frequency ω is called a *dispersion relation*. It is this relation that determines the speed at which power in the mode propagates: its *group velocity* v_{lm}. The group velocity for a given mode is related to β by $v_{lm}^{-1} = d\beta_{lm}/d\omega$. When v_{lm} is frequency-dependent, monochromatic waves of different frequencies propagate at different speeds. This phenomenon is known as *waveguide dispersion*. Because a pulse of light contains energy distributed over a range of frequencies, each of these frequency components propagates at a different speed, resulting in a deformation (typically spreading) of the pulse as it propagates down the fiber (see Section 4.3.2.3).

There are only a finite number of guided modes in the fiber at any given frequency, corresponding to a finite number of values of β satisfying the boundary conditions. Each mode except the fundamental mode ($l = 0$, $m = 1$) has a cut-off frequency below which it cannot be sustained in the fiber. Thus, as the optical frequency is decreased (wavelength is increased), a point is eventually reached when only one guided mode exists. A fiber is single mode when it operates over the range of wavelengths sustaining only the fundamental mode.

These concepts have a more intuitive interpretation in the case $\Delta \ll 1$, which corresponds to typical fibers. In this case, the wave propagating down the fiber has only small field components in the z direction, so that it approximates a transverse electromagnetic (TEM) wave (i.e., a plane wave propagating along the axis of the fiber). The condition for single-mode operation of a fiber of radius a is given by this equation:[4]

$$2\pi(a/\lambda_0)NA < 2.405 \tag{4.13}$$

where λ_0 is the free space wavelength of the signal. Equation 4.13 indicates that for single-mode operation, a fiber must have a radius on the order of its wavelength of operation and/or a small numerical aperture.

Like plane waves, modes in waveguides have *polarization states*. For each mode (i.e., each value of β_{lm}), there are two linearly independent solutions of the wave equation, which correspond to two orthogonal polarization states. For example, linear polarization in the two Cartesian directions x and y represents two orthogonal states. The polarization states are actually two "degenerate" modes with the same propagation constant. In a fiber with a circular cross-section, the polarization state (i.e., the relative amplitudes of each polarization mode) tends to change randomly along the fiber due to minor defects in the fiber. This is because the symmetry of the fiber and the fact

---

[4] See [Saleh+91, p. 286].

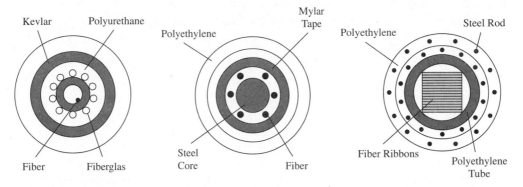

FIGURE 4.8 Commercial fiber cables.   (From (Agrawal97, Figure 2.20). Copyright © 1997. Reprinted by permission of John Wiley & Sons, Inc.)

that the two polarization modes propagate down the fiber at the same speed make it easy for power to be transferred from one mode to another. Sometimes it is desirable to eliminate this random drift in polarization, which can be done by forcing the two polarization states to have different propagation constants. In practice this is accomplished in *polarization-maintaining fibers* by making the cross-section of the fiber noncircular or by making the medium anisotropic.[5]

4.3.2 Optical Fiber Technology: Transmission Impairments

As demands for high performance increase, it becomes more and more important to minimize the effects of transmission impairments in fibers, either through improvement and redesign of the fiber itself or by compensating for deleterious effects. This section explores the limits imposed on transmission distance and bandwidth imposed by attenuation, dispersion, and certain nonlinear effects in fibers.

4.3.2.1 Fiber Geometry and Fiber Cables

Optical fibers for communications are normally made of silica, and are manufactured with a variety of geometries. Certain dopants (e.g., GeO_2 and P_2O_5) are used in the core to increase the refractive index, and others (e.g., B_2O_3) are used in the cladding to decrease the refractive index. The refractive index profile influences the waveguide dispersion and can be designed to manage the overall dispersion characteristics of the fiber (see Section 4.3.2.3).

The cables containing the fibers must be designed for mechanical and environmental protection as well as strength. Large cables may contain well over 100 individual fibers. Figure 4.8 shows some typical cable designs. One illustration depicts a ribbon cable, in which as many as 12 ribbons containing 12 fibers each are packed in one cable.

---

[5] Anisotropy can be induced by stressing the fiber in a particular direction.

4.3.2.2 Attenuation

Although the ideal fiber discussed earlier is a lossless medium, real fibers have losses due to a number of mechanisms. The simplest way to express these losses is through a relation of the form

$$dP/dz = -\alpha P \tag{4.14}$$

where P is the optical power propagating down the fiber at some point z, and α is a positive *attenuation coefficient*. Integrating Equation 4.14 gives

$$P_R = e^{-\alpha L} P_T \tag{4.15}$$

where P_T is the power launched into the fiber and P_R is the power received at the end of a fiber of length L. The attenuation coefficient is generally expressed in units of decibels per kilometer; that is,

$$\alpha_{\mathrm{dB}} = -\frac{10}{L} \log_{10} \frac{P_R}{P_T} \tag{4.16}$$

where L is in units of kilometers. In this case, the exponent in Equation 4.15 becomes $-0.23\alpha_{\mathrm{dB}}L$.

The coefficient α is a function of wavelength, as shown in Figure 4.9. As can be seen, the attenuation minimum occurs near 1,550 nm, and is approximately 0.2 dB/km in

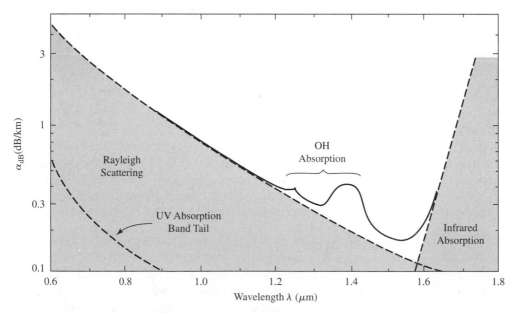

FIGURE 4.9 Attenuation as a function of wavelength.   (From (Saleh+91, Figure 8.3-2). Copyright © 1991. Reprinted by permission of John Wiley & Sons, Inc.)

currently used fibers. A secondary minimum of approximately 0.5 dB/km occurs near 1,300 nm. Most current systems operate near 1,550 nm.

As indicated in Figure 4.9, losses are due primarily to three effects: material absorption, Rayleigh scattering, and waveguide imperfections.

Material absorption occurs because of resonances of the silica molecules as well as the impurities in the fiber. Resonance absorption is indicated in the figure as ultraviolet (UV) absorption (due to electronic resonances at the short wavelengths) and infrared absorption (due to vibrational resonances at the longer wavelengths). The most serious impurity effect is due to OH ions (from traces of water in the fiber), which cause the major peak at 1,390 nm as well as several minor peaks.

Rayleigh scattering occurs because the medium is not absolutely uniform, which causes small fluctuations in the refractive index. This causes the light to be scattered, attenuating the propagating wave. Because the scattering is proportional to λ^{-4}, Rayleigh scattering is the dominant loss factor at the short wavelengths. This, together with infrared absorption at the long wavelengths, limits the usable optical spectrum to a range of approximately 800 to 1,700 nm (excluding the OH attenuation peaks), which represents approximately 20 THz of bandwidth.

Waveguide imperfections are caused by nonideal fiber geometries, which occur due to manufacturing imperfections and small bends and distortions in the fibers. Normally these add a relatively small additional component to the loss.

Although fiber loss was the major limiting factor in optical fiber transmission until the 1990s, this limitation was eliminated to a large degree, virtually overnight, with the introduction of the EDFA in 1989 (see Section 4.4).

4.3.2.3 Dispersion

With optical amplification greatly mitigating the effects of attenuation, the effects of fiber dispersion become more important. A narrow pulse launched on a fiber tends to smear out as it propagates along the fiber, with its width broadening as it progresses. When a pulse broadens to the extent that it overlaps neighboring pulses, the resultant *intersymbol interference* (ISI) sharply increases the BER. This *fiber dispersion* phenomenon imposes a limit on the bitrate that can be supported on a dispersive fiber of a given length. There are two basic dispersive effects in a fiber: *intermodal dispersion* and *chromatic dispersion*.

Intermodal Dispersion   The most serious form of dispersion, intermodal dispersion, occurs in multimode fibers because different modes have different group velocities. (This was illustrated in the geometric optics picture of propagation, in which different rays traveled different distances.) Because the pulse power is distributed (generally unequally) over different modes, replicas of a pulse, one for each mode, arrive at the destination with different propagation delays, spreading out the received energy. Figure 4.10 illustrates pulse-broadening effects in different types of fibers.

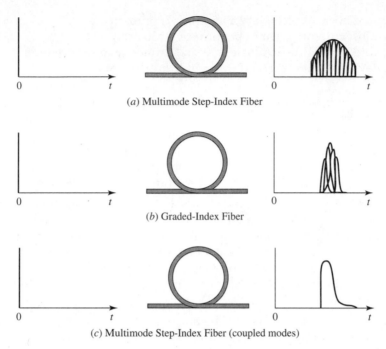

(a) Multimode Step-Index Fiber

(b) Graded-Index Fiber

(c) Multimode Step-Index Fiber (coupled modes)

FIGURE 4.10 Broadening of pulses due to dispersion.   (From (Saleh+91, Figure 8.3-8).
Copyright © 1991. Reprinted by permission of John Wiley & Sons, Inc.)

As shown in Figure 4.10(a), the pulse arrivals for different modes in a step-index
fiber are spread out in time, with different energy in each. Figure 4.10(b) depicts
how received pulses are bunched closer together in a graded-index fiber. In fibers
greater than a certain critical length, *mode coupling* due to material imperfections can
cause a reduction of the intermodal dispersion, as shown in Figure 4.10(c). Because
of intermodal dispersion, multimode fibers are limited to very low bitrate–distance
products (on the order of tens of megabits per second–kilometer for step-index fibers
and a few gigabits per second–kilometer for graded-index fibers).

Chromatic Dispersion   Although intermodal dispersion is absent in single-mode
fibers, there is another effect—*chromatic dispersion*—that occurs due to the frequency
dependence of the group velocity. There are two sources of chromatic dispersion,
(1) waveguide dispersion and (2) material dispersion.

A simple way of understanding chromatic dispersion without going into the exact
details of pulse shapes is to work in the frequency domain. Assuming that the transmitted pulse has a spectral width σ_ω in optical (radian) frequency, (or equivalently,
$\sigma_\lambda = \lambda^2 \sigma_\omega / 2\pi c$ in wavelength), each spectral component of the pulse arrives with delay $T = L/v_g$, where v_g is the group velocity for that component. The received pulse

width is then broadened by an amount

$$\sigma_T \approx L \left| \frac{d}{d\omega} v_g^{-1} \right| \sigma_\omega = |D| L \sigma_\lambda \tag{4.17}$$

where the *dispersion parameter* D (given in units of picoseconds per kilometer–nanometer) is defined as[6]

$$D = -\frac{2\pi c}{\lambda^2} \frac{d^2 \beta}{d\omega^2} \tag{4.18}$$

As indicated in Section 4.3.1.2, the propagation constant β in a single-mode fiber depends on frequency through the dispersion relations, which in turn depend on the geometry of the fiber. This is the source of waveguide dispersion. In addition, the material in fibers is time dispersive; that is, the polarization density $\mathcal{P}$ is not a memoryless function of $\mathcal{E}$ in the fiber medium. This time-dependent effect can be modeled as a frequency-dependent refractive index $n(\omega)$, which produces an additional, material-dependent frequency variation in β, so that

$$D = D_M + D_W \tag{4.19}$$

where D_M is the material dispersion and D_W is the waveguide dispersion. In general, both components are frequency dependent.

The material dispersion in standard silica fibers is negative at short wavelengths and positive at the longer wavelengths, passing through zero at approximately 1,300 nm. Because D_W is a function of fiber geometry, it is possible to produce fiber designs, called *dispersion-shifted fibers*, in which the contribution of D_W causes the zero-dispersion point to shift to the 1,550-nm range, thereby making minimum dispersion occur at the same wavelength as minimum loss. In *dispersion-flattened fibers*, the design produces a dispersion profile that is close to zero over a wide spectral range. These two cases are illustrated in Figure 4.11. A typical refractive index profile for a dispersion-shifted fiber is shown in Figure 4.11(a), together with the dispersion coefficient as a function of wavelength. The material dispersion is indicated by a dashed line and the combined material and waveguide dispersion is shown by a solid line. Figure 4.11(b) shows the same quantities for dispersion-flattened fibers.

Polarization Mode Dispersion   As mentioned earlier, the two polarization states of the fundamental mode may propagate at slightly different group velocities due to asymmetries in the fiber. This is known as *polarization mode dispersion* (PMD), which also produces pulse broadening.

The effects of PMD are considered to be negligible on a digital transmission link if the average time differential, $\Delta \tau_{PMD}$, between the two modes is less than one-tenth

---

[6] When operating at a zero-dispersion wavelength ($D = 0$), a more exact expression for pulse broadening, taking higher derivatives of β into account, is necessary.

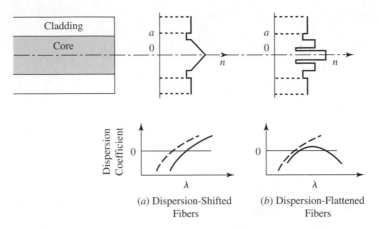

(a) Dispersion-Shifted
Fibers

(b) Dispersion-Flattened
Fibers

FIGURE 4.11 Dispersion coefficients as a function of frequency. (From (Saleh+91, Figure 8.3-6). Copyright © 1991. Reprinted by permission of John Wiley & Sons, Inc.)

of the bit period of the signal. For example, this gives an allowable value of average time differential of 40 ps for a 2.5 Gbps OC-48 signal or 10 ps for a 10 Gbps OC-192 signal.

The PMD effects accumulate in a "square root" fashion. Thus, for a link of length L km, we have

$$\Delta\tau_{\text{PMD}} = D_{\text{PMD}}\sqrt{L} \qquad (4.20)$$

where D_{PMD} is the PMD dispersion coefficient in ps/$\sqrt{\text{km}}$. In a normal (not polarization-maintaining) fiber, this effect is usually negligible compared to chromatic dispersion. Typical values of PMD are $D_{\text{PMD}} = 0.5$ ps/$\sqrt{\text{km}}$ for a standard single-mode fiber and $D_{\text{PMD}} = 2$ ps/$\sqrt{\text{km}}$ for a dispersion-shifted fiber, but can be as low as 0.15 ps/$\sqrt{\text{km}}$. However, PMD can be more serious in polarization-sensitive switching devices. For example, for a lithium niobate switch (see Section 4.9.1), a typical value of average time differential might be $\Delta\tau_{\text{PMD}} = 2$ ps. Thus, cascading of a large number of these can present dispersion problems at high bitrates.

Effects of Dispersion on Maximum Bitrates As stated earlier, it is the ISI due to pulse broadening that limits bitrates in dispersive fibers. A good estimate of the maximum permissible bitrate is obtained by assuming that the bitrate R_t cannot be allowed to exceed a value $R_{\text{max}} = k/\sigma_T = k/|D|L\sigma_\lambda$, where a reasonable value of k is 0.25, indicating a pulse overlap into the next bit interval of approximately 25%.

It remains to connect pulse spectral width σ_λ to other system parameters. Unfortunately, σ_λ depends in a complex way on the laser characteristics, the way in which it is modulated (direct or external), and the waveform of the modulating pulse. However, some simplified relations can be obtained in two limiting cases: (1) wide laser line width and (2) narrow laser line width.

In the first case, the laser line width (in optical frequency) is assumed to be much larger than the width of the Fourier transform of the pulse itself. The latter is on the order of T_p^{-1}, where T_p is the pulse width. This is typical of directly modulated or multimode lasers modulated at relatively low bitrates. In this case, $\sigma_\lambda \approx \sigma_l$, where σ_l is the laser line width (in wavelength units), so that

$$R_{max} \approx \frac{0.25}{|D|L\sigma_l} \qquad (4.21)$$

In the second case, the laser line width is assumed to be small compared with the pulse spectral width. This is called the *transform-limited case*. It applies, for example, to externally modulated single-mode lasers running at high bitrates (gigabits per second). We now have $\sigma_\lambda \approx \lambda^2/cT_p$. Assuming that $R_t \approx T_p^{-1}$, we have

$$R_{max} \approx \frac{1}{\lambda}\sqrt{\frac{0.25c}{|D|L}} \qquad (4.22)$$

Analog Modulation: Subcarriers   Effects of dispersion manifest themselves significantly but differently in analog-modulated systems. For example, consider an optical carrier, intensity modulated by a sinusoidal signal. This produces upper and lower sidebands with phases relative to the carrier that are modified by dispersion as the signal propagates down a fiber. This phase change can produce a situation in which the intensity modulation is almost completely converted to phase modulation. Using direct detection, the phase modulation will not be reproduced at the output of the photodetector, so that the modulating signal will be lost. These phase shifts due to dispersion limit the maximum possible modulation frequency. In an example of this effect, analyzed in [Meslener84], it is shown that a total dispersion of 2,000 ps/nm limits the modulation frequency to a maximum of approximately 5 GHz. (Dispersion of this magnitude might typically occur over 100 km to 200 km of standard single-mode fiber [SMF].) This is a serious limitation in subcarrier systems, in which the subcarrier frequencies can be in the 10-GHz range (see Section 5.2.2).

Dispersion Management   The history of fiber deployment throughout the world closely reflects the development of the related transmission system technology. Until the late 1990s most of the fiber in the ground in the United States and Europe was standard SMF, with properties that are consistent with the state of the transmission art in the mid 1980s. The dominant transmission systems at that time were "second-generation" systems (using the terminology in [Henry+88]). These systems, operating in the 1,300-nm band, became feasible when suitable laser and detector technology became available in that band. (At that time, the technology for the 1,550-nm band had not yet been developed.)

Dispersion was a particularly serious impairment in second-generation systems because single-mode lasers were not available at that time. Thus, the fact that 1,300 nm is close to the zero-dispersion point in an SMF made it a logical band in which to work even though attenuation is considerably higher than at 1,550 nm.

With the development of single-mode lasers (see Section 4.5.1)—the current "third-generation" systems—operating in the 1,550-nm band largely replaced the second generation. However, to deal with the nonzero dispersion in this band, the fiber deployed to optimize transmission performance was dispersion-shifted fiber (DSF). Because Japanese deployment followed that in the United States, DSF is the dominant fiber deployed in Japan today.

The advent of the EDFA, which operates in the 1,550-nm band, extended enormously the reach of these third-generation systems. And with that extension came the appearance of nonlinear transmission impairments; in particular, four-wave mixing. Nonlinear effects had been negligible before the EDFA because the maximum transmission distances between signal regenerators were on the order of hundreds of kilometers, compared with thousands of km for amplified systems. This was not long enough for nonlinear impairments to become significant.

It was quickly realized that minimization of dispersion in the fiber made the four-wave mixing problem worse. Thus, and fortuitously, the older SMF turned out to be better for combatting nonlinearities (see Section 4.3.2.4). It remained, however, to deal with dispersion.

It can be seen from Equation 4.22 that in the best possible case—the transform-limited regime—the dispersion-limited reach of a connection decreases with the square of the bitrate. Thus, to extend this limit, something must be done about the dispersion coefficient D. In attacking this problem, the most important observation is that it is a *linear* phenomenon. Thus its effects are reversible by cascading suitable, compensating linear components. One of the first approaches to dispersion management was to use lengths of dispersion-compensating fibers (DCFs) in cascade with a dispersive transmission link. The DCFs are designed to have a large negative dispersion in the 1,550-nm band to compensate for the 10 ps/nm–km to 20 ps/nm–km positive dispersion in SMFs.

Another approach uses a nonzero dispersion fiber (NDF) with small dispersion (positive or negative), tailored to reduce the effects of nonlinearities without significant pulse broadening. By using fiber spans with alternating positive and negative dispersion, the net dispersion coefficient can be made almost zero over a long span. At the same time, the nonzero dispersion over each span tends to reduce the effects of FWM [Chraplyvy+95]. In a recent experiment a 400-Tbps–km bitrate–distance product was achieved using combinations of positive-dispersion NDF and DCF [Srivastava+98].

Spectral inversion is still another approach to dispersion compensation [Gnauk+97]. In *midsystem spectral inversion*, the signal spectrum is inverted in the middle of a long span of dispersive fiber. In this way, the frequency dependence of the group velocity (which produces dispersion), experienced by the signal over the second segment of the span, is just the opposite of that experienced over the first half of the span. This is because the frequency components of the inverted signal spectrum "see" relative phase shifts that are just the opposite of those seen by the uninverted spectrum. The net effect is to cancel out the dispersion over the total span. Several processes have been used for implementing spectrum inversion, including four-wave mixing and difference-frequency conversion (see Sections 4.3.2.4 and 2.3.3).

Finally, in a fourth approach, chirped fiber Bragg gratings (FBGs) are used for dispersion compensation. In the work reported in [Garrett+98], six long (1-m) gratings were cascaded over 480 km of conventional fiber to achieve eight-channel transmission with a 38.4-Tbps–km bitrate–distance product. We leave the details of FBGs to Section 4.9.5.2.

As of this writing, dispersion compensation is a relatively new and rapidly developing activity. As indicated, there are several new and promising approaches. It is therefore likely that dispersion will soon be managed at will, and the dispersion problem will be largely vanquished as technology progresses.

4.3.2.4 Nonlinear Effects

Just as dispersion effects became significant when the attenuation problem was solved, nonlinear effects became dominant when dispersion was reduced. Although the nonlinear effects in fibers are very small, they can become important over long, amplified but unregenerated transmission spans. The following nonlinear effects are of concern in multiwavelength systems:

- Stimulated Raman scattering (SRS)

- Stimulated Brillouin scattering (SBS)

- Four-wave mixing (FWM)

- Self- and cross-phase modulation (SPM/XPM)

Stimulated Raman Scattering In each of the two scattering effects just listed, light interacts with the fiber medium producing inelastic collisions, during which the wavelength of the scattered photon is longer than that of the incident photon, meaning that energy is lost in the process. In each case, a signal present at the wavelength of the scattered photons can produce stimulated emission of another photon at the same wavelength, and hence amplification.

Stimulated Raman scattering involves energy loss to vibrational waves in the medium, with all waves interacting with each other as they propagate in the same direction in the fiber. In the case of a single-channel system, the threshold power at which SRS becomes important is very high: approximately 500 mW. Thus, as opposed to Rayleigh scattering, it is unimportant as a loss mechanism in communication systems. It does have important consequences in introducing cross-talk (intermodulation) in multiwavelength systems.

On the other hand, because SRS involves the transfer of power from the wave at the higher frequency to that at a lower frequency, it can be used to an advantage for optical amplification, in which the higher frequency light serves as a pump, amplifying the lower frequency wave carrying the signal to be amplified. This is a very broadband process (approximately 200 nm), which was proposed for fiber amplification as long ago as 1973 [Stolen+73]. Although it has been largely eclipsed by the EDFA, there has recently been renewed interest in Raman amplification in both the 1,300 nm and 1,550 nm bands.

Stimulated Brillouin Scattering   In SBS the power lost in the scattering process is transferred to an acoustic wave. In this case the scattered wave and the acoustic wave both propagate in the backward direction. As opposed to SRS, SBS is a very narrow-band process: The downshift in frequency for systems operating in the 1,550-nm band is approximately 11 GHz. For this reason there is no significant cross-talk effect, but the threshold for SBS is much lower than that for SRS—a few milliwatts for fibers longer than 20 km.

Four-Wave Mixing   FWM and phase modulation effects can be explained in terms of a nonlinear relation between $\mathcal{P}$ and $\mathcal{E}$, producing nonlinear refraction. In silica glass there is a small cubic term in this nonlinearity, related to a third-order nonlinear susceptibility $\chi^{(3)}$ (see [Agrawal95, p. 16]). The cubic relation between $\mathcal{P}$ and $\mathcal{E}$ can be expressed as a square-law nonlinearity in the refractive index:

$$n(\omega, |\mathcal{E}|^2) = n_0 + n_2|\mathcal{E}|^2 \tag{4.23}$$

where the first term represents the linear, frequency-dependent part of n, accounting for material dispersion, and the second term accounts for various nonlinear effects.

The relation in Equation 4.23 produces intensity-dependent and lossless[7] effects on the fiber, leading to pulse distortion when only a single signal is present, and cross-talk when several signals are present, as in multiwave systems. Although these effects are small, they can accumulate substantially on long, amplified fiber links. These effects are not always deleterious. They can sometimes be used to an advantage (see Sections 2.3.3 and 4.3.3).

Four-wave mixing can occur if three signals are present at neighboring optical frequencies ω_1, ω_2, and ω_3. The cubic nonlinearity then potentially produces additional signals at the sum and difference frequencies—for example, $\omega_4 = \omega_1 + \omega_2 - \omega_3$. (Another possibility exists with only two signals present at frequencies ω_1 and ω_2, giving $\omega_4 = 2\omega_1 - \omega_2$.) These signals occur only if certain "phase-matching" conditions are satisfied. Phase matching of two propagating waves occurs when their propagation constants are equal. In this case, approximate phase matching happens when the frequencies of all four signals are sufficiently close together. This condition occurs in the case of dense WDM systems running at moderate power levels. We then have $\omega_1 \approx \omega_2 \approx \omega_3 \approx \omega_4$, where $\omega_4 = \omega_1 + \omega_2 - \omega_3$. With phase matching, FWM accumulates along a long fiber line, imposing a severe distance limit on multiwave transmission. For example, a 32-channel system running at a power of 0.5 mW per channel with 50-GHz channel spacing on DSF is limited to approximately 100 km.

The problem of FWM on a DSF is exacerbated by the fact that the near absence of dispersion causes different frequency waves to propagate at nearly the same group velocity, producing approximate phase matching. A way to avoid FWM is to break the phase-matching condition by intentionally introducing dispersion. For example,

---

[7] Energy may be exchanged between propagating waves, but no energy is absorbed by the medium, as it is in SRS and SBS.

in an amplified SMF, the system described in the previous paragraph has negligible FWM for as long as 5,000 km! Thus it is possible to solve both the dispersion problem and the FWM problem simultaneously by introducing controlled alternating (positive and negative) dispersion throughout a long fiber link to disrupt phase matching while maintaining the net end-to-end dispersion near zero [Chraplyvy+95].

Self- and Cross-Phase Modulation   Refractive index nonlinearity can also produce small changes in the propagation constant as a function of intensity. Over a length of fiber, this produces accumulated phase shifts, which vary with intensity. The phase shifts represent SPM, producing a corresponding broadening of an optical pulse as it propagates down the fiber. To a first approximation this can be explained by the fact that the pulse is phase shifted by a different amount at each point in time, depending on its intensity at that time. When more than one signal is present, the nonlinear interactions between the signals can produce a related phenomenon—XPM—which depends on the aggregate power in all signals. This becomes more troublesome as more signals are superimposed on each other in multiwavelength systems.

Effective Interaction Length   Because the various nonlinear effects depend on intensity, they become less significant as the intensity of a wave decays. Thus, the nonlinear effects tend to disappear as the wave progresses down the fiber. This results in a limited effective length over which the fiber nonlinearity influences the wave. For a fiber with attenuation coefficient α, this *effective interaction length* is defined as

$$L_{\text{eff}} = \frac{1 - e^{-\alpha L}}{\alpha} \tag{4.24}$$

where L is the actual fiber length. For long fibers we have $L_{\text{eff}} \approx 1/\alpha$, which gives $L_{\text{eff}} \approx 20$ km in the 1,550-nm window.

It is important to note that the concept of effective interaction length applies to *unamplified systems*. In systems containing cascaded line amplifiers, each amplifier on the fiber typically restores the signal intensity to the value originally launched on the fiber, so that an additional length L_{eff} must be associated with each amplified span.

Nonlinear Effects in Multiwavelength Systems   As indicated, most of the nonlinear impairments in fibers increase with increasing numbers of simultaneous channels. Thus, it is of interest to study these effects in systems with many closely spaced channels. Figure 4.12 shows relations between maximum permissible power per channel and number of channels in a typical system, considering the various nonlinear effects individually. The case considered is a DSF of length 22 km operating in the 1,550-nm band with 10-GHz channel spacing. The criterion for determining upper limits is a 1-dB power penalty; that is, at the limiting power a typical channel will have its SNR degraded by 1 dB at the receiver due to the nonlinearity being examined.

In the case of SRS with many closely spaced channels, power is transferred from the higher frequency channels to the lower frequency ones; that is, the higher frequency channels act as pumps, amplifying the lower frequency channels. Because this pumping depends on the intensity at a particular point in time, the power transfer depends

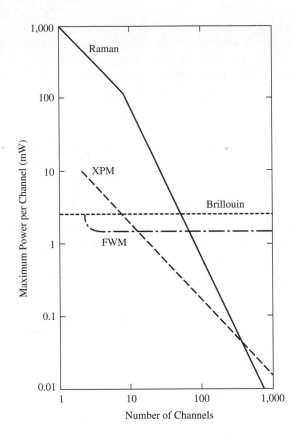

FIGURE 4.12 Limitations due to nonlinear effects in multiwavelength systems.   (From (Chraplyvy90, Figure 10). Copyright © 1990 IEEE. Used by permission of The Institute of Electrical and Electronics Engineers, Inc.)

on the bit patterns of the various waves, thus introducing a cross-talk effect. The Raman power limit in a multiwavelength system is illustrated in Figure 4.12. Another curve in the figure shows the power limit imposed by XPM, as a function of the number of channels.

In contrast to SRS and XPM, Figure 4.12 shows that the power limits imposed by FWM and SBS are independent of the number of channels. However, they are the critical ones for systems with a small number of channels.

Large Effective Area Fibers   Much recent effort has gone into the design of fibers with a large, "effective core area." The objective is to increase the area over which the optical signal power is distributed and yet keep the desired wave-guiding properties of the fiber.[8] The advantage of these fibers is that spreading the total optical power over a larger area reduces the optical field intensity in the core at any one point. This, in turn, reduces the various nonlinear effects discussed previously. Various designs

---

[8] A challenge in designing large, effective core area fibers is to keep the bending losses low. Larger core diameters tend to increase losses due to the bending of the fiber.

involving special (e.g., fluoride) doping, as well as special index profiles, produce effective core areas exceeding 100 μm^2, which is roughly twice the area of standard fibers, while maintaining the desired fiber properties [Kato+98].

4.3.3 Solitons

Well before the advent of fiber optic communications, it was known that a special type of solitary wave or *soliton* could exist in certain types of media that are both dispersive and nonlinear. Although each of these effects by itself tends to distort and broaden a propagating pulse, the right combination of dispersion and nonlinearity produces a narrow, stable pulse that propagates over long distances without any distortion whatsoever, with one effect compensating for the other. This, of course, is the ideal situation for long-distance communication.

The form of a soliton can be deduced by modifying the wave equation, Equation 4.10, to include a nonlinear and time-dispersive refractive index. For a wave propagating in the z direction we can write

$$\frac{\partial^2 E}{\partial z^2} - \frac{1}{c^2} \frac{\partial^2 (n^2 E)}{\partial^2 t} = 0 \qquad (4.25)$$

where n in Equation 4.25 is of the form of Equation 4.23.

By assuming a quadratic dependency of β on ω (corresponding to a linear dependence of group velocity on ω), assuming that the nonlinearities and dispersive effects are weak, and dropping "small" terms, it can be shown (e.g., see [Kazovsky+96]) that the complex envelope $u(z, t)$ of a soliton satisfies the *nonlinear Schrodinger equation*:

$$\frac{\partial u}{\partial z} = \frac{j}{2} \text{sgn}(\beta_2) \frac{\partial^2 u}{\partial t^2} - j|u|^2 u \qquad (4.26)$$

A solution of Equation 4.26, called the *fundamental soliton solution*, is[9]

$$u(z, t) = U_0 e^{jaz} \text{sech} \left(\frac{t - \beta_1 z}{T_0} \right) \qquad (4.27)$$

where $a = |\beta_2| / T_0^2$, T_0 is the pulse width, and β_1 and β_2 are, respectively, the first and second derivatives of β with respect to ω. Equation 4.27 represents a soliton with a shape shown in Figure 4.13.

The fundamental soliton is stable in the sense that if a pulse approximating a soliton in shape and amplitude is launched on a fiber it tends toward a soliton as it propagates, and thereafter retains the soliton form. Furthermore, solitons propagating in opposite directions pass through each other "transparently."

To maintain solitons over long distances, fiber amplification is required. Many soliton experiments using EDFAs and picosecond pulses were carried out in the 1990s.

---

[9] An infinite number of higher order solutions also exist.

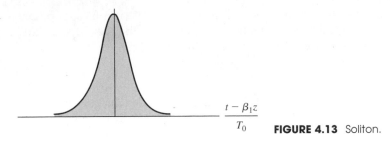

$$\frac{t - \beta_1 z}{T_0}$$

FIGURE 4.13 Soliton.

Typical experiments used a recirculating fiber loop containing several EDFAs to simulate long transmission links. An example is a demonstration of soliton transmission over a 15,000-km distance at 5 Gbps. The distance was simulated by a loop with 27-km EDFA spacing [Mollenauer+92].

4.4 Amplifiers

Because fiber attenuation limits the reach of a nonamplified fiber span to approximately 200 km for bitrates in the gigabit-per-second range, wide area purely optical networks cannot exist without optical amplifiers. Amplifiers are typically used in three different places in a fiber transmission link. As *power amplifiers* they serve to boost the power of the signal before it is launched on the line, extending the transmission distance before additional amplification is required. Amplifiers operating as *line amplifiers* are located at strategic points along a long transmission link to restore a signal to its initial power level, thereby compensating for fiber attenuation. Finally, as a *preamplifier*, the device raises the signal level at the input of an optical receiver, which serves to improve signal detection performance (i.e., the receiver sensitivity). In each case the desired properties are different. For power amplifiers the important feature is high gain; preamplifiers require a low noise figure, and line amplifiers require both. Optical amplifiers are also employed at various other points in a network (for example, within an optical switching node to compensate for losses in the switch fabric).

Semiconductor optical amplifiers (SOAs) were developed in the 1980s but they never had a serious impact on long-distance transmission because of a number of negative features discussed in Section 4.4.2. In the case of EDFAs, however, the situation was quite different. The first papers on EDFAs appeared in 1987 [Desurvire+87, Mears+87]. Within a few years of that time, 9,000-km unrepeatered transmission was demonstrated. Shortly thereafter, soliton experiments showed that transmission distances could be extended almost indefinitely. All of these experiments used EDFAs. It is not an exaggeration to say that these devices have revolutionized optical communications. We begin this section with a discussion of EDFAs, followed by a brief look at SOAs.

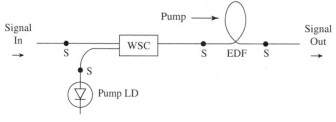

(*a*) Forward Pumping

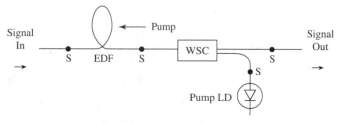

(*b*) Backward Pumping

FIGURE 4.14 Basic erbium-doped fiber amplifier structures. (From (Desurvire94, Figure 5.4). Copyright © 1994. Reprinted by permission of John Wiley & Sons, Inc.)

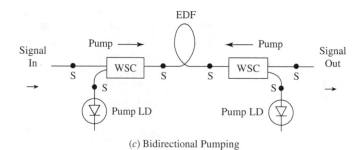

(*c*) Bidirectional Pumping

4.4.1 Erbium-Doped Fiber Amplifiers

The EDFA belongs to a family of rare-earth-doped fiber amplifiers, the class of other possible dopants including praseodymium (used for amplification in the 1,300-nm range), neodymium (originally used for very high-power lasers), and ytterbium (which has been used as a codopant with erbium). The important place of the EDFA in optical communications is due primarily to the fact that the properties of erbium produce amplification in a fairly wide band (approximately 35 nm) within the 1,550-nm low-attenuation window in fibers. Furthermore, the EDFA has many other desirable features that will become apparent as we proceed.

Three different EDFA structures are shown in Figure 4.14. In each case the amplifier is of the traveling wave type, consisting of a strand of single-mode fiber, typically on the order of tens of meters long, doped with erbium. (The points *S* in the figure represent fiber splices.) The EDFA is an optically pumped device, so energy is supplied

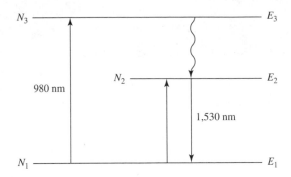

FIGURE 4.15 Energy levels in EDFA.

by an optical source (an LD), which injects power into the doped fiber at a wavelength matched to the characteristics of erbium (980 or 1,480 nm). Pumping can be either forward, backward, or bidirectional (see Figures 4.14(a) through (c) respectively). The pump is typically coupled into the transmission fiber via a wavelength-selective coupler (WSC). (EDFA modules used in the field typically include other components, such as optical isolators to eliminate reflected power, and various devices for signal power monitoring, stabilization, and control.) Amplification occurs by transfer of power from the pump wave to the signal wave as it propagates down the doped fiber.

Like many other forms of amplifiers of electromagnetic radiation, the EDFA operates via a three-energy level system. The model representing this process is shown in Figure 4.15. Levels E_1, E_2, and E_3 are the ground, metastable, and pump levels, respectively. The populations (fractional densities) of erbium ions in the three energy levels are denoted N_1, N_2, and N_3, where $N_1 > N_2 > N_3$ when the system is in thermal equilibrium (no pump or signal present). When pump and signal are present, these populations change as ions move back and forth between levels, accompanied by the emission or absorption of photons at frequencies determined by the energy-level difference. The wavelengths associated with the dominant transitions are indicated in Figure 4.15. The wavelength λ for each transition is given by the quantum relation $\lambda = hc/\Delta E$, where h is Planck's constant and ΔE is the difference in energy levels. In actuality, the three levels in the simplified diagram of Figure 4.15 are narrow bands, so each transition is actually associated with a band of wavelengths rather than a single line.

Two pump wavelengths are typically used for EDFAs: 980 nm and 1,480 nm. As shown in Figure 4.15, by absorbing energy from a 980-nm pump, Er^{3+} ions in the ground state are raised to state E_3. The rate at which these transitions occur is proportional to $N_1 P_p$, where P_p is the pump power. These excited ions decay spontaneously to the metastable state E_2, and this transition occurs at a rate much faster than the rate from level E_1 to level E_3.[10] This means that in equilibrium under the action of

---

[10] The transition is dominantly nonradiative, so energy is lost to the fiber medium rather than emitted in the form of radiation.

the pump, the ion population in the ground state is reduced and accumulates largely in state E_2. This process is referred to as *population inversion* because we now have $N_2 > N_1$, the reverse of the situation in thermal equilibrium. The transition rate from level E_2 to level E_1 is very slow compared with the other transitions, so that the lifetime τ, in the state E_2 (the reciprocal of its transition rate to E_1) is very long (approximately 10 ms). Similar pumping action can occur at 1,480 nm, in which case the ions are raised directly to the upper edge of the E_2 band. Reliable semiconductor laser pump sources have been developed for EDFAs at both the 980- and 1,480-nm pump wavelengths.

The wavelength band for transitions from state E_2 to the ground state is in the 1,530-nm range, making it ideal for amplification in the lowest attenuation window of fibers. The dominant transitions from E_2 to E_1 are radiative, which means that they are of two types: spontaneous emission and stimulated emission. In the former case, an ion drops spontaneously to the ground state, resulting in the emission of a photon in the 1,530-nm band, and this appears as additive noise. Spontaneous emission noise is an unavoidable by-product of the amplification process, predicted by quantum theory. It occurs with phase, direction, and polarization independent of the signal. In the case of stimulated emission, an incident photon in the 1,530-nm range stimulates the emission of another photon at the same wavelength in a coherent fashion (with the same direction, phase, and polarization). If the incident photon is from a signal, this produces the desired amplification of the optical field. However, the incident photon could also have originated as a spontaneous emission "upstream" on the fiber, in which case this is called *amplified spontaneous emission* (ASE), which represents the major source of noise in amplified fiber transmission systems.

4.4.1.1 Gain Profile

The fairly large amplification bandwidth of the EDFA is due to the finite width of the energy bands. The width of the energy bands is caused by a number of physical phenomena, including the *Stark effect* [Desurvire94, p. 8], which splits the main energy levels into many sublevels. Because the population is not distributed uniformly within the E_2 band, the gain is not flat. A typical plot of gain as a function of wavelength is shown in Figure 4.16. The uneven gain profile, with a peak at approximately 1,530 nm, produces significant problems in a multiwavelength system when many amplifiers are cascaded over a long transmission span. Not only does uneven gain amplify different wavelengths unequally, but it also causes a large accumulation of ASE at the peak of the gain profile, which can eventually saturate the amplifier. Because amplifier cascading on long links accentuates these effects seriously, gain flattening is an important consideration in EDFAs. Several solutions to this problem are currently in use. One approach is to modify the design of the amplifier itself by using different materials such as fluoride glass [Clesca+94]. Other approaches use gain equalization via controllable attenuators (as discussed later) or by inverse filtering. (See [Vengsarkar+96] for an example using fiber gratings.)

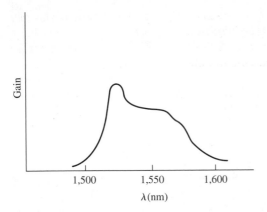

λ(nm)

Gain

FIGURE 4.16 EDFA gain profile.

4.4.1.2 Gain Saturation

The gain of an EDFA is approximately independent of the signal power as long as the pump power is made high enough so that the pumping rate is much larger than the stimulated emission rate. This is called the *unsaturated gain* or *small-signal regime*. The small-signal gain under these conditions is an increasing function of pump power. For a given fiber structure and doping, and a given pump power, there is an optimal fiber length that maximizes gain. For lengths smaller than the optimum, the pump power is not maximally utilized, and for larger lengths, pump power is exhausted somewhere along the fiber, and attenuation takes over. Typical optimal lengths are in the range of tens of meters. Maximum small-signal gains for EDFAs are typically 30 dB to 40 dB.

All amplifiers eventually exhibit gain saturation as the signal power is increased. In the saturated case, the signal extracts so much power from the pump as it propagates down the fiber that the stimulated emission rate becomes comparable with the pumping rate. The larger the input signal, and the higher the unsaturated gain, the sooner saturation is reached. As saturation increases, the gain decreases. The saturation output power P_{sat}^{out} is defined as the output power at which the gain is compressed by 3 dB. The values of P_{sat}^{out} for typical EDFAs are in the hundreds of milliwatts. It should be noted that ASE also contributes to saturation in an EDFA. When input signals are very small, it is the ASE that saturates the amplifier first. This is known as *amplifier self-saturation*.

Because saturation is a nonlinear effect, it produces a number of complications when multiple signals are being amplified. One problem is that the saturated gain for any one signal depends on the aggregate power of the other signals as well as its own power. Thus signals (as well as accumulated ASE) tend to "steal" power from each other. Useful analytical models for these effects appear in [Saleh+90] and [Jopson+91]. An advantageous effect of saturation is that a small amount of it in each amplifier in a cascade of several amplifiers tends to produce a self-regulating effect.

Several other nonlinear effects are a consequence of this power-stealing phenomenon, but on a shorter time scale. The amplifier gain at any instant in time is a function of the excited state population N_2, which is depleted momentarily by stimulated emission when a signal is present. One manifestation of this occurs when an intensity-modulated digital signal changes from a 0 to a 1. The resultant fluctuation in N_2 causes corresponding gain fluctuations, which are most pronounced in the saturated regime and in the presence of large signals. Another manifestation occurs when beats from two signals spaced closely in optical frequency cause gain fluctuations at the beat (difference) frequency.

The gain fluctuations affect all signals being amplified, and thus can potentially produce undesirable cross-talk, with one signal's intensity fluctuations changing the gain for the others. These effects are significant only when the gain dynamics are such that gain can vary on a time scale as fast as that of the signal fluctuations. A simplified interpretation of gain dynamics in an EDFA is based on the assumption that the maximum speed for gain fluctuations is on the order of the reciprocal of the lifetime in the excited state, which is approximately 10 ms. However, actual gain transients in EDFAs can occur on time scales of hundreds of microseconds, which cannot be predicted using the lifetime alone. (For a more detailed explanation see [Desurvire94, p. 417].)

In any case, these numbers indicate that signals fluctuating on time scales more rapid than, say, 100 μsec will not cause any significant cross-talk in EDFAs. This corresponds to a minimum bitrate of approximately 10 kbps to avoid cross-talk (or a WDM signal separation of approximately 10 kHz to avoid beat frequency effects). The lack of this cross-talk effect for bitrates higher than 10 kbps is one of the important advantages of the EDFA over the SOA (see Section 4.4.2).

4.4.1.3 Noise and Noise Figure

The ASE noise generated in an EDFA can be the limiting performance factor in an optical transmission link. It is therefore important to quantify this effect.

For an amplifier with gain G, the ASE noise power spectral density at the output at optical frequency v (in each polarization state) is [Agrawal97]

$$S_{\mathrm{sp}} = n_{\mathrm{sp}}(G - 1)hv \tag{4.28}$$

where n_{sp}, the spontaneous emission factor, is a function of the state population, and approaches its minimum value of 1 with full population inversion. The ASE noise spectrum for an EDFA is roughly the same shape as the gain profile.

The significance of the ASE noise is most clearly expressed in terms of SNRs and the *amplifier noise figure F_n*. These quantities are defined in terms of electrically detected signals in an ideal system, as illustrated in Figure 4.17. The noise figure is defined as

$$F_n = \frac{SNR_{\mathrm{in}}}{SNR_{\mathrm{out}}} \tag{4.29}$$

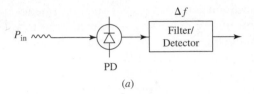

(a)

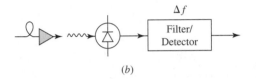

(b)

FIGURE 4.17 Illustration of noise figure.

where SNR_{in} is the electrical SNR seen when a signal of power P_{in} is converted to a photocurrent at the output of an ideal photodetector (PD)—see Figure 4.17(a). The noise in this case is *shot noise* due to the fact that the ideal detector is counting photons, which arrive randomly at the detector. (The detection process must be an integral part of any noise calculation, reflecting the quantum limits of lightwave transmission.) The numerator in Equation 4.29 is given by

$$SNR_{in} = \frac{(RP_{in})^2}{\sigma^2} = \frac{(RP_{in})^2}{2q\,RP_{in}\Delta f} = \frac{P_{in}}{2h\nu\Delta f} \tag{4.30}$$

where $(RP_{in})^2$ is the square of the average photocurrent, $\sigma^2 = 2q\,RP_{in}\Delta f$ is the shot noise power (the variance of the photocurrent), $R = q/h\nu$ is the responsivity of an ideal detector, q is the electron charge, and Δf is the bandwidth of the electrical detector.

The quantity SNR_{out} is the electrical SNR seen with the amplifier inserted before the photodetector—see Figure 4.17(b). To find SNR_{out} we compute the variance of the photocurrent after amplification with gain G. Because the detector acts as a square-law device, the photocurrent variance contains terms due to shot noise and ASE noise by themselves, as well as signal–spontaneous emission beat noise due to the mixing between the signal and the ASE in the photodetector. It turns out that the latter is the dominant term, provided that $G \gg 1$, and most of the ASE noise is filtered out at the input of the detector. This can be done by making Δf small enough to exclude extraneous noise but include the desired signal. Then we have

$$\sigma^2 \approx 4(RG\,P_{in})(RS_{sp})\Delta f \tag{4.31}$$

so that

$$SNR_{out} \approx \frac{G\,P_{in}}{4S_{sp}\Delta f} \tag{4.32}$$

Using Equations 4.28, 4.30, and 4.32, the noise figure is given by

$$F_n \approx 2n_{\text{sp}}(G-1)/G \tag{4.33}$$

which corresponds to at least a 3-dB SNR degradation in the high-gain case. (In real systems, F_n is typically at least 4 dB.)

4.4.1.4 Amplifier Chains

Over a long transmission link it is necessary to use several EDFAs interconnected by fiber sections to compensate for fiber attenuation.[11] The gain of each amplifier is normally adjusted so that it compensates for the attenuation on one section of fiber. The question of optimal amplifier spacing then arises. It turns out that this is a fairly complex issue that depends, among other things, on the way in which the amplifiers are pumped, effects of fiber nonlinearities, and practical issues such as amplifier accessibility, cost, and so forth.

We examine a fairly simple model here, in which a fiber of length L is divided into N sections of spacing $s = L/N$. An amplifier is placed after each section, with a saturated gain that just compensates for the fiber attenuation on one section: $G = e^{\alpha s}$.[12] The total accumulated noise power spectral density at the end of this chain (taking into account both polarization states) is then

$$S_n = 2NS_{\text{sp}} = 2n_{\text{sp}}(G-1)N = 2n_{\text{sp}}(e^{\alpha s}-1)N \tag{4.34}$$

Note from Equation 4.34 that for a fixed amplifier spacing, the effect of accumulated noise in the cascade grows linearly with the length of the link, but decreases as the amplifier spacing decreases (i.e., as the number of amplifiers increases). Thus, the optimal strategy in this case is to place a very large number of low-gain amplifiers very close together, with the limiting case being one long, distributed amplifier. Cost, however, dictates the opposite strategy! In current practice, a compromise is reached, with spacings ranging from 20 km to 100 km, typically giving an SNR at the receiver of at least 15 dB. The spacings are based on constraints such as maximum permissible power on a fiber,[13] effects of fiber nonlinearities, and receiver sensitivity.

---

[11] It is also possible to design the EDFAs as *distributed amplifiers* in which the doped fiber is long (on the order of kilometers) and the gain is distributed throughout its length [Desurvire94, p. 122].

[12] Exact compensation is not necessary. In a long chain, if the amplifiers are adjusted to have a small-signal gain slightly larger than the section attenuation, saturation tends to stabilize gains at a cascaded value that just compensates for the end-to-end fiber loss. This happens because if the signal amplification overcompensates for loss on the upstream stages, the resultant increased signal power drives the downstream amplifiers into saturation, thereby tending to stabilize the overall saturated gain.

[13] The maximum power is determined not only by the technological limitations—laser and amplifier output powers and fiber nonlinearities—but on *eye safety* as well. The latter consideration limits power to well under 100 mW, to limit risks to service personnel (see [ANSI88]).

4.4.2 Semiconductor Optical Amplifiers

The structure of an SOA is similar to that of a semiconductor laser (see Section 4.5.1). It consists of an active medium (a *p–n* junction) in the form of a waveguide, with a structure much like the stripe geometry laser described in Section 4.5.1. The mobile carriers (holes and electrons) now play the role of the Er^{3+} ions in the EDFA.

The energy levels of the electrons in a semiconductor are confined to two bands: the conduction band, containing those electrons acting as mobile carriers, and the valence band, containing the nonmobile electrons. A hole, representing the absence of an electron in the valence band, also acts as a mobile carrier. Mobile electrons and holes are abundant (i.e., are *majority carriers*) in *n*-type and *p*-type material, respectively.

The two energy bands in semiconductors play a role analogous to band E_2 and E_1 in the EDFA, but they are much broader than the EDFA bands. A *band gap*, E_g, separates the lower edge of the conduction band from the upper edge of the valence band so that the energy change involved in moving from one band to the other is at least E_g. Transfer of an electron from the valence band to the conduction band (with the absorption of energy) results in the creation of an electron-hole pair. One way in which this occurs is through the absorption of a photon, as in a photodetector (see Section 4.6.1). The reverse phenomenon, electron-hole recombination (with release of energy), occurs either nonradiatively (by transferring energy to the crystal lattice) or radiatively, with the emission of a photon.

The radiative case is of interest to us here for applications in light sources as well as amplifiers. Radiative electron-hole recombination occurs either spontaneously or through stimulated emission involving interaction with an identical photon. These two processes are analogous, respectively, to the spontaneous and stimulated emission processes in an EDFA. By proper choice of the semiconductor materials (e.g., InGaAs or InGaAsP) bandgaps that yield emission and/or absorption wavelengths in the ranges desired for optical communications (e.g., 1,300 or 1,550 nm) can be produced.

For photon emission to occur by electron-hole recombination at an optical frequency, ν, an electron-hole pair must be present with energy levels separated by an amount $\Delta E = h\nu$. Furthermore, if the recombination is by *stimulated* emission, a photon of the same frequency must be present to interact with the electron-hole pair. The conditions for these effects to occur depend on the various carrier concentrations and the photon flux in the *active region* (the layer around the *p–n* junction).

In an unbiased *p–n* junction, a "depletion layer" exists around the junction caused by diffusion of majority carriers across the junction, and subsequent recombination on the other side. This creates a net charge on each side of the junction and hence a retarding electric field, preventing further diffusion and draining carriers from the layer around the junction. The depletion layer can be broadened by reverse-biasing the junction, thereby augmenting the retarding field. This is the condition for operation of the *p–n* junction as a photodetector.

On the other hand, by forward-biasing, the retarding field is reduced, allowing more majority carriers to cross the junction, becoming minority carriers on the other side. This creates a condition favorable to recombination in the active region because once the mobile electrons from the n side cross over to the p side (at which point they become minority carriers), they encounter a large concentration of holes with which to recombine. A similar situation occurs for the mobile holes moving in the opposite direction. This effect, which increases the population of minority carriers in the active region on each side of the junction, is called *minority carrier injection.*

The current flow through the forward-biased junction acts as an electrical pump, supplying the energy necessary to produce an inversion of the carrier population in the active region. This is analogous to the Er^{3+} ion population inversion in the EDFA produced by optical pumping. The light-emitting diode (LED) is a simple application of radiative recombination. It is a forward-biased p–n junction producing its radiation by spontaneous emission. This effect is called *injection electroluminescence.*

Now suppose an optical signal is introduced into a waveguide embedded in a forward-biased p–n junction, which we now want to use as an amplifier. By applying sufficient injection current, conditions can be established in which stimulated emission dominates spontaneous emission and absorption in the guide. At this point, optical gain is produced, and the device becomes a semiconductor amplifier. Because the energy bands are broad in a semiconductor, the SOA amplifies over a much wider band than an EDFA.

Although its broadband gain characteristic is a positive feature, the SOA has a number of negative features. First, the carrier lifetime in the high-energy state is very short (on the order of nanoseconds). As indicated earlier, this means that signal fluctuations at gigabit-per-second rates cause gain fluctuations at those rates, producing cross-talk effects between simultaneously amplified signals. These effects do not occur in EDFAs until the bitrate drops into the 10-Kbps range. Second, because of its asymmetrical geometry, the SOA is polarization dependent. The EDFA, with its cylindrical geometry, is not. Third, the coupling losses between the fibers and the semiconductor chip reduce substantially the usable gain and output power. Nevertheless, SOAs lend themselves to applications in which they can be combined with other semiconductor components into optoelectronic integrated circuits (OEICs); for example, as a preamplifier in an OR or a power amplifier in a laser transmitter.

4.5 Optical Transmitters

The light sources for optical transmission systems have evolved from LEDs operating in the 850-nm range in the first-generation systems (in the 1970s) to semiconductor lasers, which are still evolving today. With some exceptions for short-distance and low-bitrate applications such as fiber-to-the-home,[14] virtually all optical transmission systems use semiconductor lasers as their light sources. This section is confined to that topic.

---

[14] See, for example, [Iannone+98].

4.5.1 Lasers

The *laser* (for "light amplification by stimulated emission of radiation") was invented by Schawlow and Townes in 1958, shortly after the *maser* (for "microwave amplification by stimulated emission of radiation"), which performed the same operation in the microwave domain. The first solid-state (ruby) laser was demonstrated by Maiman in 1960. Lasers exist in myriad forms, including gas lasers, dye (liquid) lasers, and fiber lasers. (One type of fiber laser consists of a ring of erbium-doped fiber (i.e., an EDFA closed on itself).[15])

A semiconductor laser, also called a *laser diode* or *injection laser*, is basically a device for converting electrical energy to monochromatic light. The conversion process requires two things: (1) an "active" medium with properties that facilitate conversion from electrical to optical energy and (2) a geometry suitable for generating and emitting a monochromatic light beam.

The principle of operation of a laser is the same as that for any other oscillator: gain plus feedback. In the case of a laser diode, the active medium is a forward-biased *p–n* junction. It has optical gain as a consequence of current injection, producing electrical-to-optical energy conversion. Furthermore, the active medium is enclosed in a geometry that provides optical feedback; in other words, a portion of the light that it amplifies is fed back to be reamplified, producing sustained oscillation when the net loop gain is greater than unity.

A basic laser structure, known as a *Fabry–Perot* (FP) *laser*, is shown in Figure 4.18. The active region is contained in an optical cavity of rectangular geometry, with partially reflecting mirrors on two sides. The cleaved surfaces (facets) in the figure act as mirrors, providing partial internal reflection because of the difference between the refractive index of the cavity material and air. With the exception of the partially reflecting mirrors this is very similar to the semiconductor optical amplifier described in Section 4.4.2. In an FP cavity, light is reflected back and forth between the mirrors, with certain wavelengths being reinforced by constructive interference when the successive reflections of the wave are in phase with each other. These resonances occur whenever the round-trip distance between the mirrors is a multiple of the wavelength in the material.

As in the case of SOAs (and LEDs), energy is converted from electrical to optical form through radiative recombination of holes and electrons in the active region. The necessary population inversion is achieved by current injection in the forward-biased junction. The longest wavelength of the photon-emission process is determined by the bandgap of the material, but the possible wavelengths of oscillation in the laser are limited to those reinforced by the geometry of the cavity.

Lasing is achieved by increasing the optical gain sufficiently to overcome losses (including the transmitted light) from the cavity. The minimum current required for lasing is called the *threshold current*. It should be noted that if the cleaved surfaces

---

[15] Recall that this type of configuration can arise in optical networks through the inadvertent creation of closed optical paths. See Figure 2.12.

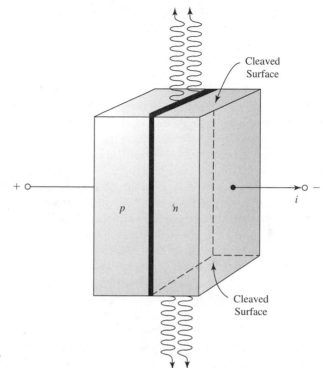

Cleaved
Surface

Cleaved
Surface

FIGURE 4.18 Fabry–Perot laser.
(From (Saleh+91, Figure 16.3-1).
Copyright © 1991. Reprinted by
permission of John Wiley & Sons,
Inc.)

in Figure 4.18 are given antireflection coatings, the device becomes a semiconductor amplifier. Light enters through one facet, is amplified, and leaves through the other.[16]

Practical laser structures use more complex geometries than that shown in Figure 4.18, and require special materials to produce light at the wavelengths needed for optical communication. To reduce the threshold current and to control the radiation pattern, either a *stripe geometry* or *buried heterostructure* (BH) is used. Each confines the light to a narrow region, which reduces the required threshold current and reduces the light-emitting area to a small spot instead of the broad beam shown in Figure 4.18. The optical properties of the material are "engineered" by choosing the materials (typically indium gallium arsenide phosphide [InGaAsP] for 1,300-nm and longer wavelengths), and adjusting the thickness of the active layer. Multiple quantum well (MQW) structures are designed with several very thin active layers stacked up, achieving high gain at high powers [Tsang87].

---

[16] In cases where the injection current is high enough to make stimulated emission dominate spontaneous emission, and yet the light loss through the facets is so high that the lasing threshold is not attained, the device emits light as a *superluminescent LED*.

4.5.1.1 Single-Frequency Operation

The early laser diodes were multimode, multifrequency devices. In the FP laser, for example, the cavity can support many modes (and frequencies) of oscillation. To obtain the monochromatic light that is necessary for high bitrate–distance products, the geometry must be modified to achieve single-frequency operation. By narrowing the active region, as in a BH laser, all cavity modes of an FP laser are suppressed except the longitudinal modes in the narrow, active strip. In this way it operates much like a single-mode waveguide, supporting longitudinal modes associated with different frequencies. To reduce operation to a single frequency, all but one of the longitudinal modes must be suppressed, resulting in *single longitudinal mode operation*. A number of approaches are used for this, including cleaved–coupled cavity (C^3) lasers, external cavity lasers, distributed Bragg reflector (DBR) lasers, and distributed–feedback (DFB) lasers. In each, a resonant element is introduced to single out the desired mode.

The most commonly used light sources for high-bitrate, long-distance transmission are the DBR and DFB lasers. Figure 4.19 shows their structure. The distributed Bragg gratings at the two ends of the DBR laser in Figure 4.19(a) replace the mirrors in an FP laser, reflecting light only at wavelengths related to the Bragg grating period (see Section 4.9.5.2). In this way the DBR laser operates in a single longitudinal mode (and frequency) defined by the Bragg grating. Similarly, in Figure 4.19(b), a periodic frequency-selective structure is introduced as a corrugation along the active layer in the DFB laser. The periodic structure produces distributed reflections (feedback) that reinforce each other only at wavelengths related to the periodicity of the corrugations. Although these devices are costly compared with multimode lasers, they are currently the workhorses of long-distance optical communications.

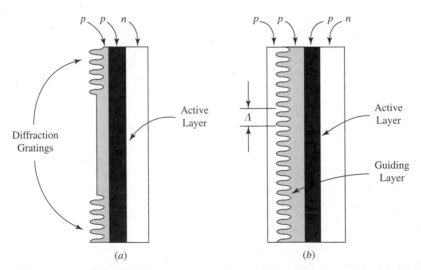

FIGURE 4.19 Single-frequency lasers.   (From (Saleh+91, Figure 16.3-10). Copyright © 1991. Reprinted by permission of John Wiley & Sons, Inc.)

4.5.1.2 Mode-Locked Lasers

In a multimode laser, the light that is produced has a wide spectrum, which typically manifests itself in the form of a wave with slowly and randomly varying amplitude and phase. However, light with a wide spectrum can also manifest itself in the time domain as a sequence of very narrow pulses. This happens if the relative amplitudes and phases associated with the different modes of a multimode laser are "locked" to values representing the Fourier coefficients for a periodic pulse train. This is the principle of the *mode-locked laser*. These devices are often used as sources of periodic picosecond pulses for soliton transmission. Pulse widths as short as 30 fs have been generated in this manner (for example, see [Saleh+91, p. 535]). Mode locking is usually implemented by modulating the laser gain periodically using a saturable absorber or a modulator inside the resonator.

4.5.1.3 Tunability

Laser tunability is important in many multiwavelength network applications. Slow transmitter tunability (on a millisecond time scale) is required for setting up connections in wavelength/waveband routed networks, and rapid tunability (on a micro- or nanosecond time scale) is required for time–wavelength–division multiple access applications. Furthermore, the local oscillator in a coherent receiver must also be tunable to track the transmitter frequency.

Slow tunability over a range on the order of 1 nm is effected easily via temperature control, which is used mainly for frequency stabilization (e.g., for locking a laser frequency to a frequency standard). Rapid tunability is achieved in DBR and DFB lasers by changing the refractive index, which can be done by changing the injected current in a local region around the grating. The design of the laser allows this to be done without disturbing the active region affecting the gain. This technique is used in multiple-electrode lasers to achieve tuning ranges as high as 51 nm [Amann94]. In these lasers, tuning may be either continuous or discrete. An example of the discrete case is a sampled-grating DBR laser, which can be tuned to one of 101 wavelengths spread over a 44-nm band [Delorme+98].

Another approach to rapid tunability is to use multiwavelength laser arrays with wavelengths that span the desired tuning range. One or more lasers in an array can be activated to produce simultaneous transmissions at selected wavelengths. An integrated array of 21 lasers with 3.72-nm wavelength spacing, combined and coupled into two optical amplifiers, is shown in Figure 4.20. The chip is 1×4 mm with the DFB laser array split into two groups of ten and eleven lasers, visible as horizontal stripes in the figure. The light from the lasers is fed to a star coupler (the dark area on the right), with two output waveguides fed to optical amplifiers on the far right of the chip.

Photonically integrated laser arrays are cost-effective in the sense that the per-wavelength cost of packaging, fiber pigtailing, and control circuitry is reduced. On the other hand, the manufacturing cost of an array is higher than that of an equivalent number of single lasers because of reduced yield with arrays.

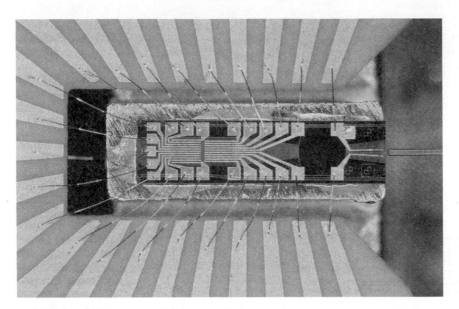

FIGURE 4.20 Laser array. (From (Soole+94, p. 59). Copyright © 1994 Bellcore. Reproduced with permission.)

4.5.2 Modulation

Lasers are modulated either directly, by varying the injected current, or externally, by passing the emitted light beam through a controllable device that changes the amplitude and/or the phase of the light. We consider each of these separately.

4.5.2.1 Direct Modulation

The behavior of the laser under small-signal and large-signal modulation is of interest in different contexts. When modulated with an analog signal, including subcarrier signals, the modulation index is likely to be small, to reduce nonlinear distortion, among other reasons. In that case, a small-signal model that assumes sinusoidal modulation is appropriate. The key performance parameter in this case is the *small-signal modulation bandwidth*, which is the modulation frequency at which the response drops by 3 dB. It can be shown that the modulation bandwidth is proportional to the frequency of relaxation oscillations in the laser, which increases with the square root of the bias current [Agrawal97, p. 114]. Lasers designed specifically for high-speed modulation have reached bandwidths of 24 GHz. This wideband response is particularly useful for multichannel subcarrier applications, in which the aggregate modulation bandwidths of all subcarrier channels is limited by the laser modulation bandwidth when direct modulation is used (see Section 5.2.2).

In digitally modulated systems, it is generally the large-signal modulation behavior that is of interest. For example, in an intensity-modulated system, the current may vary from near threshold for a 0 to twice threshold for a 1. But because changes in

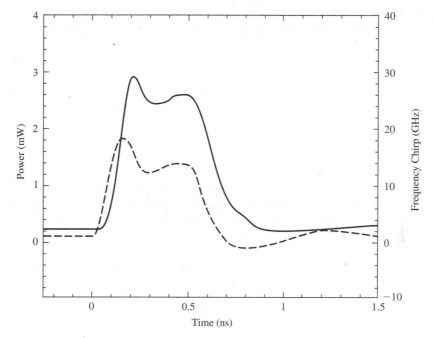

FIGURE 4.21 Pulse and accompanying chirp. (From (Agrawal97, Figure 3.23). Copyright © 1997. Reprinted by permission of John Wiley & Sons, Inc.)

current also produce changes in refractive index, they also create phase modulation (or equivalently, frequency modulation) along with the intended intensity modulation. This effect has been termed *chirp*, and it produces a significant broadening of the pulse spectrum. (The parameter involved in intensity–phase modulation coupling is called the *linewidth enhancement factor* because the phase modulation increases the effective spectral width of the emitted light.)

An example is shown in Figure 4.21, in which a laser is modulated with a rectangular pulse of width 500 ps, (the *solid* line) corresponding to a 2-Gbps bitrate. The optical frequency (the *dashed* line) increases on the leading edge of the pulse and decreases on the trailing edge, with a total excursion of approximately 20 GHz. (The limited modulation bandwidth produces the pulse distortion.) This spectral broadening can lead to serious dispersion problems on long fiber spans. Thus, direct modulation is generally avoided whenever possible on long- and/or high-bitrate transmission links.

The effects of chirp are also important in intensity-modulated analog systems when operated at sufficiently high modulation indices. A thorough analysis of the limits on analog transmission due to dispersion, using directly modulated lasers, appears in [Meslener84]. The effect of dispersion on a sinusoidally modulated optical carrier is examined, showing that frequency modulation effects due to direct modulation, combined with fiber dispersion, can produce serious harmonic distortion in systems that would be essentially distortion free if frequency modulation was absent.

4.5.2.2 External Modulation

External modulation, although requiring extra (and costly) components, avoids the chirp problems discussed earlier. It is, therefore, the technique of choice in high-performance long-distance systems. In external modulation, the laser output is constant, and it is modulated by inserting a controllable attenuator (or phase shifter) between the laser and the fiber link. A typical external modulator uses a Mach–Zehnder interferometer structure implemented on a LiNbO$_3$ substrate, as shown in Figure 4.22. In this device, the light is split equally between two parallel waveguides on the surface of the substrate and is then recombined at the output. A control voltage, V, applied to the electrodes shown in the figure creates a small change in the refractive index through an electro-optic effect. This causes a change in the propagation constant, and a relative phase shift at the point where the two waves combine. When no voltage is present, the relative phase shift is zero and the recombined signal exits the device without attenuation (except for the losses in the waveguides). When a voltage is applied that produces a phase shift of π between the two arms, the signal is extinguished. Thus, the device acts as a voltage-controlled switch. These devices operate at high speeds (e.g., 40 GHz) and can be fabricated using various materials.

External modulators can also be used for phase modulation in coherent systems using a single waveguide with an electro-optically modulated refractive index.

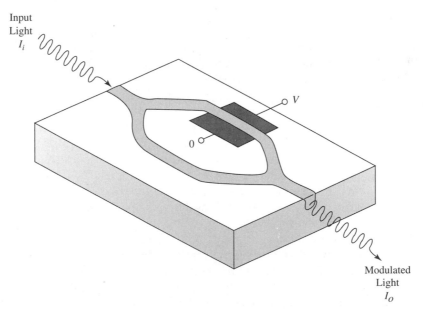

FIGURE 4.22 Mach–Zehnder interferometer.   (From (Saleh+91, Figure 18.1-5). Copyright © 1991. Reprinted by permission of John Wiley & Sons, Inc.)

4.6 Optical Receivers in Intensity-Modulated Direct-Detection Systems

The basic transmission link considered in this book involves an intensity modulated optical transmitter and a direct detection receiver as shown in Figure 4.2. In this section we focus on the receiver structure, consisting of the photodetector, a "front-end" amplifier (possibly incorporating equalization), and a detection circuit (in the case of digital transmission).

The photodetector converts the optical signal to a photocurrent, using direct detection, and the amplifier raises the power of the photocurrent to a level sufficient for further electronic processing. In the digital case, this processing is primarily clock recovery, sampling, and threshold detection to extract the digital bitstream from the received signal. We consider each of these components next.

4.6.1 Photodetectors

The photodetectors used in optical transmission systems are semiconductor photodiodes. In the simplest device, the $p-n$ junction, the operation is essentially the reverse of a semiconductor optical amplifier. As shown in Figure 4.23, the junction is reverse biased, enlarging its depletion layer, and in the absence of an optical signal only a small, minority carrier current, called the *dark current*, flows. A photon impinging on the surface of the device and entering the semiconductor can be absorbed by an electron in the valence band, transferring the electron to the conduction band. Each electron–hole pair produced this way in the depletion region contributes to the photocurrent $i(t)$. For this absorption to take place, the photon energy $h\nu$ must be at least as great as the bandgap energy of the material, E_g. Thus, photon absorption, and hence optoelectronic conversion, only occurs at wavelengths less than a *cutoff wavelength*, $\lambda_c = hc/E_g$. Typical materials with sufficiently large λ_c for optical fiber transmission systems are various forms of InGaAs and InGaAsP. These are wideband devices, in which the absorption and conversion process takes place over the entire spectrum of interest in optical fiber communications.

In a photodiode, the relation between the incident optical power P_{in} and the photocurrent I_p is given by $I_p = RP_{\text{in}}$, where the responsivity, R (in amperes per watt), is in turn given by

$$R = \eta q / h\nu \tag{4.35}$$

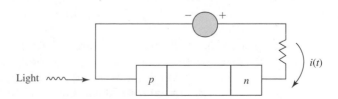

FIGURE 4.23 Photodiode.

In Equation 4.35, η is the *quantum efficiency* of the device, which depends on the fraction of incident photons absorbed. The absorption coefficient of the semiconductor materials currently in use is high enough so that a very thin slab of material (on the order of 10 μm) is sufficient to make $\eta \approx 1$.

4.6.1.1 PIN Photodiodes

Electrons (holes) are also produced by photon absorption in the p (n) regions, but the component of photocurrent due to these effects tends to distort the photodetector response. This is because the minority carriers in the p and n regions diffuse slowly into the depletion region, resulting in a delayed response compared with the dominant, depletion region drift response. (They may also be lost by recombination before reaching the depletion region.) The PIN photodiode (for p-type, intrinsic, n-type) solves these problems by increasing the width of the depletion region, thereby causing a larger fraction of the optical power to fall on the depletion region. With the PIN photodiode, an extra layer of intrinsic material (either undoped or lightly doped) is sandwiched between the p and n regions. Its effect is to improve the responsivity of the device by capturing most of the light in the depletion region. The PIN photodiodes in a more complex *double-heterostructure geometry*, which involves two extra layers of doped semiconductor, can be designed with close-to-ideal properties: near 100% quantum efficiency, absence of diffusion current, wide optical bandwidth, and large electrical bandwidths (in the tens of giga-Hertz).

4.6.1.2 Avalanche Photodiodes

The photocurrent generated by the photodiodes discussed thus far is limited by the fact that, at best, each photon produces one electron of photocurrent. This may not be sufficient when the incident optical power is very low. The circuitry following the photodiode, including the front-end amplifier, contains unavoidable sources of thermal noise. If the level of the photocurrent is too low, the photocurrent signal is lost in the thermal noise. This is where the avalanche photodiode (APD) comes in. The APD resembles a PIN photodiode with an extra gain layer inserted between the i and n layers. Its purpose is to provide a current gain.

If the photoelectrons produced in a photodiode are accelerated to sufficient speeds, they can produce additional electrons by colliding with the semiconductor material in a chain reaction, multiplying the number of electrons produced by each photon. This *impact–ionization* effect produces a current gain similar to that in a photomultiplier vacuum tube. The APD produces this result by using relatively large applied voltages to provide the necessary accelerating electric field (on the order of 10^5 V/cm) in the gain region of the APD.

The current gain in the APD produces a much larger responsivity than in conventional photodiodes, and thus is an effective means of overcoming thermal noise limitations in lower optical power systems. It does, however, introduce its own noise due to the unavoidable random nature of the electron multiplication process.

4.6.2 Front-End Amplifier: Signal-to-Noise Ratio

Two types of amplifiers are typically used following the photodetector: a high-input impedance voltage amplifier and a transimpedance amplifier, which is actually a current-to-voltage converter. (The transimpedance amplifier is most frequently used in current systems.) A circuit using the latter is shown in Figure 4.24(a). The photodiode is coupled to the input of a high-gain inverting operational amplifier as shown. A small-signal equivalent circuit model for this arrangement is shown in Figure 4.24(b). The current source I_{sig} represents the signal current, and R and C represent, respectively, the resistance and capacitance seen looking into the amplifier. The resistance is the parallel combination of R_{bias} and $R_a/(A+1)$, where $R_a/(A+1)$ is the equivalent input impedance of the amplifier. The bandwidth of the circuit is $B = 1/2\pi RC$. Because $A \gg 1$, the resistance R can be made small, so that the bandwidth B can be made large if desired.

The additional current sources, i_{sh} and i_d in Figure 4.24(b), represent the shot noise produced by the signal and the dark current respectively. Using these sources, we find that the SNR at the output of this circuit (assuming that amplifier noise is dominated by the thermal noise in the equivalent resistance R) is given by

$$SNR = \frac{I_{sig}^2}{\langle i_{sh}^2 \rangle + \langle i_d^2 \rangle + \langle i_{th}^2 \rangle} \tag{4.36}$$

In Equation 4.36 we have

$$\langle I_{sh}^2 \rangle = 2q\,I_{sig}\,B$$
$$\langle I_d^2 \rangle = 2q\,I_d\,B \tag{4.37}$$
$$\langle I_{th}^2 \rangle = 4KTB/R$$

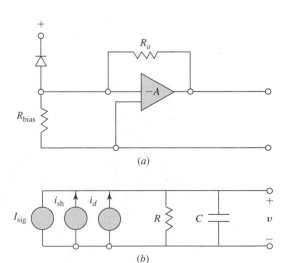

(a)

(b)

FIGURE 4.24 Transimpedance amplifier.

where K and T are Boltzmann's constant and absolute temperature respectively. The shot noise expression is given for a PIN photodiode. A modification, including an "excess noise factor" is necessary for APDs (for example, see [Agrawal97, p. 167]).

Because all of the noise terms here are proportional to the receiver bandwidth B, it is normally chosen as small as possible, to exclude noise, but large enough to pass the signal spectrum. Clearly, to improve the SNR it is desirable to make I_{sig} as large as possible, which can be done either by using an APD rather than a PIN photodiode, or by using an optical preamplifier before the photodetector. In both cases the SNR will be improved because of the gain of the APD or the amplifier, until the noise generated in the amplifying device (APD or optical amplifier), together with other noise and interference accumulated on the transmission link, dominate the receiver noise. In the case of the APD, there is an optimal value of the APD gain beyond which the SNR starts to deteriorate due to the excess noise factor (see Problem 7 at the end of this chapter).

The other noise and interference effects accumulated on a fiber link have not been included in Equation 4.36. They include accumulated ASE noise from amplifiers along the transmission link, distortion due to fiber dispersion, distortion and cross-talk effects due to fiber and amplifier nonlinearities, and various filter and switch cross-talk effects. They appear in Section 4.12, where we treat the complete end-to-end optical connection.

The shot noise terms in the previous SNR expressions are based on a Gaussian approximation of the shot noise probability density. This is an approximation that is valid (in digital systems) for optical power levels corresponding to a large number of photons transmitted in each bit interval. As the bitrate is increased and/or the optical power level is decreased, we eventually arrive at a point, called the *quantum limit*, where only a few photons are transmitted in each bit interval. In this case the Gaussian approximation is no longer valid, and the signal detection process must be viewed as a photon-counting process.

Suppose a digital signal is intensity modulated by on–off keying (OOK), at a bitrate R_b, with a 1 represented by an optical power $2P$, for an average power of P, assuming equiprobable 1s and 0s. This gives an *average* of $N_p = 2P/h\nu R_b$ photons for each 1 transmitted, and no photons when a 0 is transmitted, assuming no other sources of photons (noise). The optimal detector in this case would declare that a 0 was transmitted if no photons are counted in the bit interval, and declare that a 1 was transmitted otherwise. In this idealized model, there will never be a case when a 0 is mistaken for a 1. The opposite can happen, however. Because the counting statistics are Poisson, there is a finite probability, $P(0|1) = e^{-N_p}$, that a 0 is declared when a 1 was transmitted. The BER for the system in the quantum limit is, therefore, BER $= \frac{1}{2}e^{-N_p}$. For example, for a BER of 10^{-9} we need approximately 20 photons for each symbol 1, or an average of ten photons per bit. This results in approximately -60 dBm for a 1-Gbps signal in the 1,550-nm range. Powers in practical systems are typically well above -40 dBm, two orders of magnitude higher than the quantum limit. For an information-theoretic treatment of the quantum limit (for example, see [Stern60]).

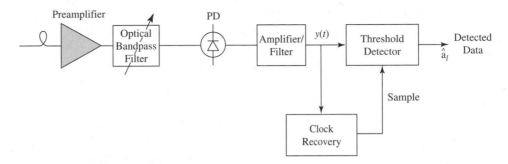

FIGURE 4.25   Binary receiver.

4.6.3 Digital Signal Detection: Noise, Interference, and Bit Error Rate

In a digital transmission link, the final step in the receiver is signal detection. We restrict ourselves here to the simplest (and most common) type of system: an IM/DD binary communication system using an OOK modulation format. As shown in Figure 4.25, the photocurrent is amplified and filtered, and the filter transfer function is chosen to preserve or enhance the signal waveform while suppressing noise. It typically has a bandwidth, B (in Hertz), somewhat less than the signal bitrate, R_b (in bits per second). A common choice is $B = 0.65 R_b$. The amplified and filtered signal is then sampled and threshold detected. Typical waveforms illustrating this process are shown in Figure 4.26.

The data signal that intensity modulates the laser transmitter is assumed to be an ideal train of rectangular pulses:

$$s(t) = \sum_{l=-\infty}^{\infty} a_l u(t - lT) \tag{4.38}$$

where

$$u(t) = \begin{cases} 1 & -T/2 < t \le T/2 \\ 0 & \text{otherwise} \end{cases} \tag{4.39}$$

and $\{a_l\}$ represents a sequence of data symbols (1s and 0s) with bit period T.

After traversing the transmission link, the receiver front end, and the filter, the transmitted data signal $s(t)$ (see Figure 4.26[a]) appears at the input of the sampling/threshold detection unit as a distorted and noisy waveform, $y(t)$—see Figure 4.26(b). The clock recovery unit, shown in Figure 4.25, processes $y(t)$ to determine at what points in time the signal should be sampled.[17]

---

[17] The clock recovery unit is essentially a variable frequency oscillator, phase locked to the data signal (i.e., a phase-locked loop). For it to work properly, there must be frequent transitions between 1s and 0s in the data signal, so that the circuit is able to discern the bit interval boundaries. This is generally ensured by "scrambling" the transmitted data stream to convert long strings of repeated symbols into interspersed 1s and 0s.

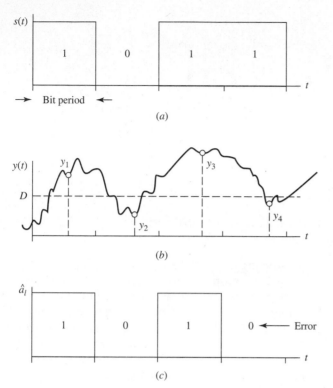

FIGURE 4.26 Typical waveforms in an IM/DD system.

Using this information, the received signal $y(t)$ is sampled periodically at a point t_0 within the bit period, chosen to provide a high probability of correct detection. The signal samples y_l are compared with a decision threshold D, shown as a *dashed* line in Figure 4.26(b), and a decision is made on the detected data symbol: $\hat{a}_l = 1$ if $y_l > D$, and 0 otherwise. Figure 4.26(c) shows the detected data symbols $\hat{a}_l$ corresponding to the transmitted data stream in Figure 4.26(a). Note the presence of a bit error in the fourth symbol.

The received waveform in Figure 4.26(b) is often represented in terms of an *eye diagram*, as shown in Figure 4.27. The eye diagram superimposes time traces corresponding to successive bit periods. This is what is seen on an oscilloscope synchronized to a sub-multiple of the bitrate of the transmitted signal. Figure 4.27(a) shows what a typical eye diagram would look like if all signal impairments were *deterministic* in nature. Each trace represents a distorted bit waveform (representing a 1 or a 0) over two bit periods, where the distortion is a result of dispersion, limited bandwidth, and deterministic nonlinearities, as well as the effects of square-law detection. All of these effects produce ISI, which is deterministically (but nonlinearly) related to the bit pattern. The ISI comes from the interfering effects of neighboring pulses that overlap in time due to dispersion.

Eye diagrams are used frequently for test purposes, during which the bitstream is generated as a periodic pseudorandom test pattern with a long but finite period. In

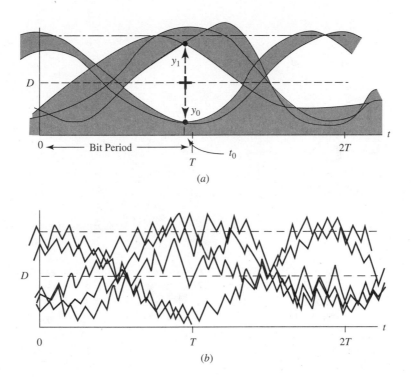

FIGURE 4.27 Eye diagram.

this case, individual traces contributing to the eye diagram repeat during each period of the test pattern. The cross within the "eye opening" in Figure 4.27(a) indicates a good point for sampling and setting the threshold. The traces below the cross are all due to 0s, and those above are due to 1s, which corresponds to an "open eye." The length y_1-y_0 indicates the size of the eye opening. The vertex of the cross is positioned at the chosen sampling time, t_0, and threshold setting, D. If sampling and thresholding are executed as shown, the BER will be zero. Notice, however, that as the eye opening (y_1-y_0) decreases, the allowable range of sampling and threshold settings diminishes. For small eye openings, a small amount of timing jitter in the transmitter or the receiver, or a slight misplacement of the threshold can produce a catastrophic BER even in the absence of any random noise.

Figure 4.27(b) shows the open eye with random noise added. Now, instead of a well-defined deterministic pattern, we have a "fuzzy" picture because the noise is not repetitive. Furthermore, the fuzziness produces occasional excursions of the waveform across the threshold, with corresponding bit errors. The more the eye closure, the more frequently an error occurs. Also, the wider the band of "fuzziness" (corresponding roughly to the random noise power), the higher the BER.

An exact determination of BER requires a detailed model of the processes along the transmission path. The relation between the waveform $y(t)$ and the original waveform $s(t)$ is extremely complex due to a succession of linear and nonlinear operations on the

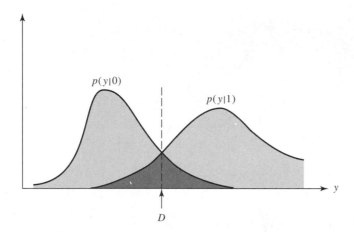

FIGURE 4.28 Ideal detection.

signal. The original data signal intensity modulates a laser that, if modulated directly, produces an optical field containing frequency modulation (chirp) as well as the desired intensity modulation. The optical field also includes intensity and phase noise, which are responsible for the finite line width of the unmodulated laser. The signal then experiences linear dispersion combined with the various nonlinear distortion and cross-talk effects, discussed in Section 4.3.2.4, and these effects accumulate with the length of the fiber. The signal also accumulates ASE noise from line amplifiers, and cross-talk from any optical cross-connects it traverses before reaching its destination. The resultant optical field presented to the photodetector undergoes another nonlinear operation (square-law detection), and is further contaminated by shot noise and amplifier noise before reaching the sampler and detector.

Imperfections in transmitter clocking and receiver clock recovery also introduce timing jitter, which degrades the detection process, as indicated earlier. It is clearly impossible to do an exact analysis of these effects. Fortunately, in any properly designed system all of these transmission and reception impairments must be *small*. For if they are not, the system will not be operating at the low BER required for digital optical transmission systems. This allows us to make many simplifying approximations and still come up with some useful results on BER.

We first reduce the mathematical model for the detection process to a pair of functions, $p(y|0)$ and $p(y|1)$, representing the probability density functions (PDFs) for the sampled amplitude at the input of the decision unit, conditioned on the transmission of a 0 or a 1 in the corresponding bit interval.[18] An illustration of typical PDFs appears in Figure 4.28, which shows an ideal detection process.

The basic assumption in this model is that the PDFs are conditioned *only* on one transmitted symbol, so the deterministic ISI effects represented by the eye diagram of

---

[18] The reception bit interval is delayed in time with respect to the transmission bit interval due to propagation delays.

Figure 4.27(a) can be ignored, as well as any statistical dependencies of the random noise effects on other symbols (or other signals).[19]

Assuming that 1s and 0s are equiprobable, it turns out that the setting of the decision threshold D that minimizes the probability of error (BER) is at the crossover of the two PDFs, as shown in Figure 4.28. This corresponds to *maximum likelihood* (ML) *detection* (see, for example, [Lee+94]). The ML detector declares that a 0 was transmitted when $p(y|0) > p(y|1)$ and that a 1 was transmitted when $p(y|1) > p(y|0)$. The total probability of error in this case corresponds to the dark area in Figure 4.28, where the probability of declaring a 1 when a 0 was sent (or the reverse) is shown as the dark area to the right (or the left) of D.

The picture becomes still simpler if we approximate the PDFs as Gaussian, so that

$$p(y|i) = \frac{1}{\sqrt{2\pi}\,\sigma_i} \exp\left[-\frac{(y - y_i)^2}{2\sigma_i^2}\right] \quad i = 0, 1 \tag{4.40}$$

where y_i is the mean value of y when symbol i is transmitted, and σ_i^2 is the noise variance. It can be shown that the probability of error P_e using the optimal threshold setting is then given by

$$P_e = \mathrm{erfc}(Q) = \frac{1}{\sqrt{2\pi}} \int_Q^{\infty} \exp(-\alpha^2/2)\, d\alpha \approx \frac{1}{Q\sqrt{2\pi}} \exp - \left(\frac{Q^2}{2}\right) \tag{4.41}$$

where

$$Q = \frac{y_1 - y_0}{\sigma_0 + \sigma_1} \tag{4.42}$$

and erfc is the complementary error function. Plots of the exact expression for P_e as a function of Q, and its exponential approximation, are shown in Figure 4.29. Note that the exponential approximation is excellent for small values of P_e, which is the range of interest to us here. The square of the argument Q in Equation 4.42 can be interpreted as an electrical SNR, as seen by the decision unit. Figure 4.29 illustrates the fact that the BER is a very sensitive function of Q so that very small improvements in SNR have very substantial effects on BER, with all of this being due to the fact that the noise is (approximately) Gaussian. For example, defining

$$Q_{dB}^2 = 20 \log_{10} Q \tag{4.43}$$

we find that $Q_{dB}^2 = 14.3$ dB for a BER of 10^{-7} while $Q_{dB}^2 = 15.4$ dB for a BER of 10^{-9}.

---

[19] Theoretically, it is possible to include ISI effects in the detection model by extending the conditioning over the set of all neighboring symbols in the bit sequence that contribute to ISI. However, this requires a detailed model for all of the transmission impairments producing the ISI, which is, in most cases, out of the question.

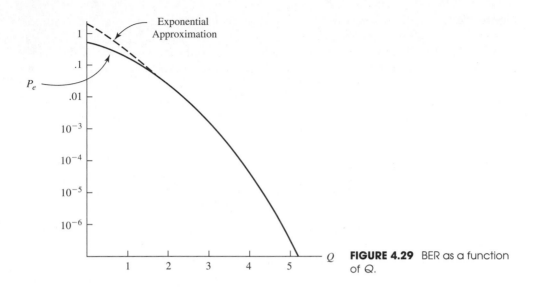

FIGURE 4.29 BER as a function of Q.

The Gaussian approximation is usually very good when there are many independent sources of random noise (although this is not always the case). Deterministic effects contributing to ISI can be lumped into the values of y_i. For example, a worst-case BER can be obtained by basing the argument $y_1 - y_0$ in Equation 4.42 on an eye diagram, obtained either by simulation or measurement. The eye opening $y_1 - y_0$ in Figure 4.27(a) corresponds to the worst case of ISI, and thus provides an upper bound on BER for any assumed noise variances.

The term *receiver sensitivity* is often used as a measure of receiver quality. We define it here to mean the average optical power required at the input to the receiver to achieve a given BER at a given bitrate R_b. Typical receiver sensitivities for $P_e = 10^{-9}$ and $R_b = 1$ Gbps are -26 dBm, -36 dBm, and -45 dBm for PIN, APD, and optical preamplifier receivers respectively. The best of these (-45 dBm) corresponds to more than 1,000 photons per bit—two orders of magnitude higher than the quantum limit.

4.6.4 Analog Systems: Carrier-to-Noise Ratio

There are several applications in which the laser transmitter is intensity modulated by an analog signal, which may be carrying any kind of information in either analog or digital form. The following are some examples:

- Cable television (CATV) distribution networks
- Distribution networks for microwave wireless systems
- Optical networks using microwave subcarriers (see Section 5.2.2)

In analog systems there is no decision mechanism, and the receiver performance is measured in terms of carrier-to-noise ratio (CNR). The CNR is defined as

$$CNR = \frac{I_{\text{sig}}^2}{\sigma_n^2} \tag{4.44}$$

where I_{sig} represents the signal component of the photocurrent and σ_n^2 is the total noise at the receiver. The latter is given by

$$\sigma_n^2 = \sigma_{\text{RIN}}^2 + \sigma_{\text{sh}}^2 + \sigma_{s-\text{ASE}}^2 + \sigma_{\text{ASE-ASE}}^2 + \sigma_{\text{th}}^2 \tag{4.45}$$

where the terms on the right side of Equation 4.45 are the laser *relative intensity noise* (RIN),[20] the shot noise, the two noise components caused by signal–ASE and ASE–ASE beating in the photodetector, and the receiver's thermal noise respectively. A quantitative treatment of these effects can be found in [Desurvire94].

The CNR for any particular system depends on a host of system parameters, which is beyond the scope of the current discussion. However, one consideration worthy of note is that when the information-bearing signal is in analog form (e.g., AM TV), it is often much more vulnerable to noise than when it is in digital form. For example, AM CATV systems require a 50 dB to 55 dB CNR, whereas the corresponding quantity, Q_{dB}^2, for an acceptable digital system is approximately 25 dB.

4.7 Coherent Optical Systems

The basic structure of the coherent (heterodyne) receiver is shown in Figure 2.34, and repeated in Figure 4.30 for convenience. The signal and local oscillator optical fields are combined in the coupler, and the resultant field is converted to a photocurrent, $i_{\text{ph}}(t)$, in the photodetector—see Figure 4.30(a). The photocurrent is then filtered in the bandpass filter (BPF), of bandwidth B_e, and is detected electrically in the electrical detector (ED). With signal and local oscillator powers of P_s and P_{LO} respectively, the photocurrent is given by

$$i_{\text{ph}}(t) = R\left[P_s + P_{\text{LO}} + 2\sqrt{P_s P_{\text{LO}}}\cos\left(2\pi f_I t + \varphi_s - \varphi_l\right)\right] \tag{4.46}$$

where R, f_I, φ_s, and φ_l are the photodetector responsivity, the intermediate frequency, the signal phase, and the local oscillator phase respectively. The effect of the bandpass filter and the electrical detector is to filter out any extraneous signals and noise, and to perform square-law detection of the remaining signal, giving a resultant signal power of $I_{\text{sig}}^2 = 2R^2 P_s P_{\text{LO}}$. The power spectral densities of i_{ph} and the output voltage, v, are shown in Figure 4.30(b). The unique property of the coherent receiver is that the signal power at the output of the detector is proportional to the local oscillator optical power

---

[20] The RIN is caused by random fluctuations in the optical field generated by the laser transmitter.

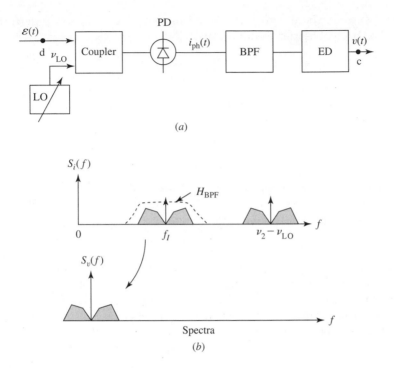

FIGURE 4.30 Heterodyne receiver.

P_{LO}, whereas the thermal receiver noise is independent of P_{LO}. The total noise power accompanying I_{sig}^2 is a sum of shot noise and thermal receiver noise, where the shot noise power $\sigma_{sh}^2 = 2RB_e P_{LO}$ is also proportional to P_{LO}. This means that by making the local oscillator power sufficiently large, the signal and shot noise terms can be made to dominate the thermal noise. In this *shot noise limit*, the electrical SNR is given by

$$SNR_e = \frac{RP_s}{qB_e} \tag{4.47}$$

With this SNR at the input to a decision circuit, the coherent receiver performs considerably better than a typical direct-detection receiver. However, this is an ideal model, which neglects possible polarization misalignment and laser phase noise in both the signal and the local oscillator waves.

4.8 Cross-talk

The discussion of receiver performance thus far has ignored an important, perhaps *the* most important, source of performance degradation: interference from unwanted signals (i.e., cross-talk). The effects of cross-talk on receiver performance are considered next. We focus on the digital transmission case.

Suppose a signal s with optical field $\mathcal{E}_s(t) = Re[\sqrt{2I_s}(t)e^{j2\pi v_s t + \phi_s}]$ is received at a direct-detection receiver equipped with a wideband photodetector followed by an electrical low-pass filter of bandwidth B_e, chosen according to the bitrate (bandwidth) of s. Accompanying the signal is an interferer x with an optical field $\mathcal{E}_x(t) = Re[\sqrt{2I_x}(t)e^{j2\pi v_x t + \phi_x}]$. The photocurrent at the output of the photodetector can then be written

$$i(t) = R\Big[I_s(t) + I_x(t) + 2Re\Big(\sqrt{I_s I_x}e^{j2\pi(v_s - v_x)t + \phi_s - \phi_x}\Big)\Big] \tag{4.48}$$

In Equation 4.48, I_s and I_x represent the signal and interferer intensities respectively, and $\sqrt{I_s I_x}$ represents a signal–interference "beat" term that appears because of the square-law detection process.[21]

There are three cases of interest, as shown in Figure 4.31(a), depending on the value of $|v_s - v_x|$:

- $v_s \neq v_x$: Interchannel cross-talk
- $v_s \approx v_x$: Co-channel heterodyne cross-talk
- $v_s = v_x$: Co-channel homodyne (multipath) cross-talk

In the first case, the *nominal* optical frequencies are different; in the second case, the nominal frequencies are the same but the absolute frequencies are slightly different; and in the third case, both frequencies are exactly the same (which only occurs if the two signals come from the same source).

These are illustrated in Figures 4.31(b) and (c). In Figure 4.31(b), two optical connections (S, S^*) and (X, X^*) are set up with a small amount of signal x "leaking" over to receiver S^*, as indicated by the dashed line. (This might be a result of switch cross-talk in optical node A.) The categorization of the interference in this case is based on the magnitude of the optical frequency difference. If the two connections are on different assigned wavelengths $\lambda_s \neq \lambda_x$, then $|v_s - v_x| > B_e$; that is, the beat interference term in Equation 4.48 lies outside the bandwidth of the receiver filter. In this case, it is only the interferer intensity I_x that affects signal detection and BER. This is *interchannel cross-talk*.[22]

If the two sources are transmitting on the same *nominal* wavelength (i.e., $\lambda_s \approx \lambda_x$, and $|v_s - v_x| < B_e$), then the beat interference term in Equation 4.48 lies within the bandwidth of the receiver filter. Now, both the interferer intensity and the beat frequency term affect signal detection, with the beat frequency term constituting *co-channel heterodyne cross-talk*.[23]

---

[21] This is the same effect that appears in a heterodyne receiver. As in that case, the magnitude of the beat term depends on the polarization alignment of the two contributing fields. We have chosen the "worst case" of perfect alignment.

[22] The interference at a receiver caused by interchannel cross-talk can be eliminated by placing a narrow-band optical filter in front of the photodetector.

[23] Cross-talk terminology varies considerably. Our co-channel heterodyne cross-talk is sometimes called *coherent common channel cross-talk*.

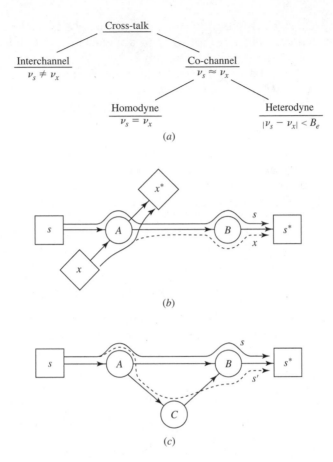

FIGURE 4.31 Types of cross-talk.

Lastly, Figure 4.31(c) shows a case in which a small portion, s', of the signal s leaks through a parallel path (dashed line), rejoining the desired signal at the receiver. Because s' arrives with a delay and phase shift, it acts as an interferer. We call this common-source interference *co-channel homodyne cross-talk*, *multipath cross-talk*, or *interferometric cross-talk* [Gimlett+89].[24] This case is the most difficult to deal with because the sign and magnitude of the cross-talk term depends on the relative phases (and polarizations) of the two signals.

Referring to Equation 4.48, the cross-product term at the output of the filter is $\sqrt{I_s I_{s'}} \cos[\phi_s(t) - \phi_{s'}(t)]$, where an argument t has been included in the phases to reflect the fact that s is not a constant-frequency optical signal but contains fluctuations in phase (and amplitude) due to laser linewidth as well as the modulation impressed on the laser. If the signals are exactly in phase at some point in time, the effect of

---

[24] Other sources of homodyne cross-talk are multiple reflections within a fiber, causing delayed replicas of the transmitted signal to be superimposed on it.

the beat term is to magnify the resultant signal (because the optical fields add, in this case), whereas the opposite is true if they are out of phase. When the time delay between s and s' is small (smaller than the signal's coherence time), then the phase fluctuations are correlated.[25] For longer delays, they are uncorrelated. In the correlated case, the interferer acts to produce a multipath fading effect, similar to that in radio transmission systems in which the interference varies slowly from constructive to destructive, depending on the instantaneous phase relations. In the uncorrelated case, the phase fluctuations due to laser linewidth, as well as intensity fluctuations due to modulation, produce a rapidly fluctuating noiselike cross-talk term.

In predicting performance when significant homodyne cross-talk is present, the best one can do in most cases is to assume a worst-case scenario, in which polarizations are aligned.

A convenient measure of cross-talk, or for that matter any type of signal impairment, is the impairment-induced *power penalty*. It indicates how much additional signal power is required to maintain a specified BER in the presence of the particular impairment. Expressed in decibels, it is defined as

$$\mathcal{P} = 10\log_{10}\left[\frac{\text{Power required with impairment}}{\text{Power required without impairment}}\right] \tag{4.49}$$

The power penalty incurred with homodyne interference illustrates the concept. Consider the following model. A large number, N, of interferers are present with random phases, each with an intensity $I_{s'} = \epsilon I_s$. Assuming aligned polarizations, it has been shown (see [Gimlett+89, Goldstein+94]) that the PDF for the resultant aggregate interference is approximately Gaussian, which leads to a power penalty given by

$$\mathcal{P} = -5\log_{10}[1 - 4Q^2 N\epsilon] \tag{4.50}$$

where Q is the Q-factor corresponding to the reference BER. For example, at a BER of 10^{-9}, $Q = 5.9$ ($Q_{dB}^2 = 15.4$).

Using Equation 4.50 the effect of the homodyne cross-talk power penalty can be plotted as shown in Figure 4.32(a). The solid and dashed curves show the BER without and with homodyne cross-talk respectively. The horizontal spacing between the two is the cross-talk power penalty. The dashed curve is plotted for $N\epsilon = 0.001$. Another curve for $N\epsilon = 0.009$ is plotted in Figure 4.32(b). Note that in this case there is an *error floor*, corresponding to the BER ($\approx 10^{-7}$), at which $4Q^2 N\epsilon = 1$, where the power penalty tends toward infinity. It is impossible to achieve BERs smaller than the error floor because of the nature of the cross-talk.

---

[25] The coherence time t_c for a laser is approximately equal to the reciprocal of its linewidth: $t_c = 1/\Delta\nu$. A related quantity, coherence length, $l_c = ct_c$, defines the distance between two observation points of the same signal required to decorrelate the two observed signals.

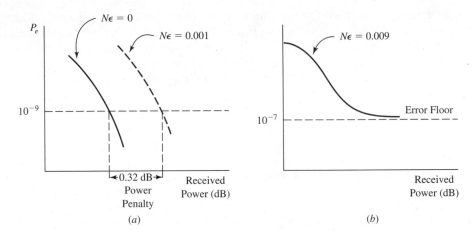

FIGURE 4.32   Power penalty with homodyne cross-talk.

4.9   Optical and Photonic Device Technology

The basic building blocks of optical network nodes are directional couplers (either static or dynamic) and wavelength-selective elements (filters). In typical optical node architectures, dynamic couplers (switches) together with static filters are combined to produce wavelength-selective cross-connects (WSXCs). In some cases wavelength selectivity is combined with controllability in the same device to produce multiwavelength switching elements.

Couplers, switches, and filters can be constructed using either bulk optical devices or integrated optics. The former category includes all-fiber devices such as fused-fiber directional couplers and fiber wavelength add–drop multiplexers (WADMs), as well as micro-optic components containing complete optical systems including lenses, mirrors, and so forth. Some, involving controllable geometries, are used as mechanically actuated switches. (The all-fiber devices are particularly attractive because they can be connected directly to transmission fibers with very small coupling losses.) The variety in this class is so great that we cannot do justice to it here. (See, for example, [Miller+88].)

Integrated optics is used to replace a set of bulk devices with fiber interconnections by one unit fabricated on a single substrate. One of the major advantages of integration is the cost savings involved in eliminating the interconnections, which are labor intensive and introduce coupling losses. The down side of integration is the higher manufacturing cost.

4.9.1   Couplers and Switches

We focus now on guided wave-controllable devices—that is, photonic switches. Good references on photonic switching principles and technology are found in [Hinton93;

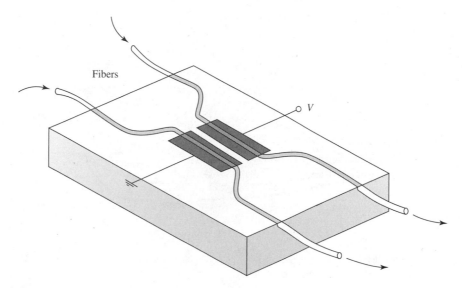

FIGURE 4.33 Directional coupler. (From (Saleh+91, Figure 21.1-7b). Copyright © 1991. Reprinted by permission of John Wiley & Sons, Inc.)

Midwinter93a,b]. Typical high-speed switches use LiNbO$_3$ devices, in which waveguides are fabricated on the surface of an LiNbO$_3$ substrate by various means. Controllable couplers are constructed in LiNbO$_3$, making use of an electro-optic effect wherein an applied electric field produces a change in the refractive index of the material. Because LiNbO$_3$ has a large electro-optic coefficient, it has been a preferred material for planar waveguide photonic switching devices. Another advantage is that switching times in LiNbO$_3$ devices are subnanosecond.

Two common geometries for controllable devices are shown in Figures 4.22 and 4.33. The first, the Mach–Zehnder interferometer, a single input/output device, was described in Section 4.5.2.2. The second, a controllable directional coupler, is based on the fact that when two waveguides are placed close together, coupling is possible between the two guides because of the overlap in their fields. (The light is not confined completely to the guides, with an evanescent field spreading out to the surrounding medium.) Provided that the propagation constants of the waves in the two guides are the same (the phase-matching condition), light entering one guide couples into the other, and vice versa. Depending on the length of the interaction region, the coupling may be partial or complete. In the configuration shown in Figure 4.33, a voltage applied to the electrodes increases the propagation constant in one of the guides and decreases it in the other. In this way the phase matching is controlled electrically, thereby controlling the coupling ratio between the ports. Referring to the conceptual model of Equation 2.3, varying the voltage varies the control parameter α, and places the coupler in the cross state, bar state, or any partial coupling state between the two. (The same basic principles are used for constructing 1×2 and 2×1 Y-branch switches.)

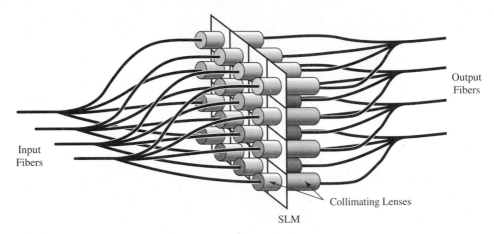

FIGURE 4.34 Crossbar switch based on SLMs.   (From (Dias+88, Figure 1). Copyright © 1988. Used by permission of *Optical Engineering.*)

Using the planar waveguide approach, switch fabrics composed of fairly large numbers of elementary switching elements can be integrated on a single substrate. For example, switches containing a total of 88 Y-branch elements have been fabricated on a single 8 × 80-mm substrate [Murphy+97].

4.9.1.1 Spatial Light Modulators

Another approach to switch fabric implementation is the *spatial light modulator* (SLM). An example of an optical crossbar of the type shown conceptually in Figure 2.19 appears in Figure 4.34. Fiber splitters, arranged vertically, direct light from the input ports to an array of SLMs. These are devices that can be made opaque or transparent under external control. Examples are liquid crystal devices (LCDs) and magneto-optic devices. Light impinging on each SLM is either transmitted or blocked, with the transmitted light destined for a given output port combined by the horizontally arranged combiners.

4.9.1.2 Typical Switch Characteristics

Characteristics of some typical, commercially available elementary switching elements follow. The key performance parameters are insertion loss (i.e., the excess loss incurred in transmitting a signal through the desired path) and cross-talk.

Lithium Niobate Interferometric Switch   This 2 × 2 electro-optic switch is based on the same interferometric principle as the Mach–Zehnder interferometer. However, it is a two-input/two-output device, as shown in Figure 4.35. In this case the control of the relative phases of the signals in the two arms separated by 3-dB couplers causes the device to be in either the bar or cross state.

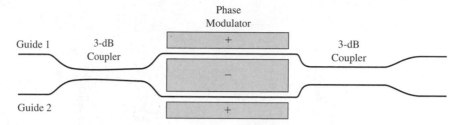

FIGURE 4.35 Mach–Zehnder switch.   (From (Korotky+88, Figure 11.4). Copyright © 1988. Used by permission of Academic Press.)

- Insertion loss, 5 dB
- Cross-talk, −18 dB

Thermo-optic Switch (Silica on Silica)   A 2×2 thermo-optic switch is based on the same principle as the $LiNbO_3$ Mach–Zehnder switch. Switch operation is initiated by changing the temperatures of the arms of the Mach–Zehnder relative to each other. Because this is a thermal effect, the switching speed is relatively slow (approximately 1 ms). A switch using silica waveguides on a silica substrate has the following characteristics:

- Insertion loss, 1.5 dB
- Cross-talk, −18 dB

Thermo-optic Switch (Polymer on Silicon)   The elementary switching element is a 1×2 Y-branch switch built with polymer waveguides on a silicon substrate. A 2×2 switch is constructed using four 1×2 elements. The switching operation is initiated by changing the refractive index of the material in the arms of the Y-branch by thermal control.

- Insertion loss, 2.5 dB
- Cross-talk, −20 dB

Optomechanical Switch   The simplest and most inexpensive technology is a fused-fiber 2×2 directional coupler, with a coupling ratio that is modified by bending (with a switching speed on the order of milliseconds). Other commercially available optomechanical devices use reconfigurable optics (lenses, mirrors, and so on). These devices are almost ideal, with very low insertion losses (for example, 0.5 dB) and very low cross-talk (−40 dB). Switching speeds are approximately 5 ms.

An approach still in the research stage uses "micromachined" mirrors to build integrated switch fabrics [Lin98] (see Figure 4.36). The mirrors are actuated electrostatically, and because of their size, switching speeds are in submilliseconds. Cross-talk is better than −60 dB, with insertion losses of approximately 3.5 dB for an 8×8 switch.

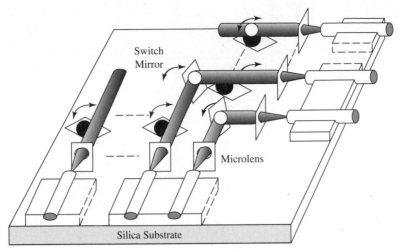

(a) Schematic Drawing of the Micromachined Free-Space Matrix Switch

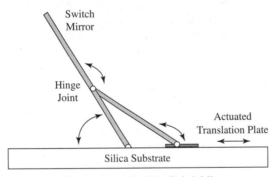

(b) Working Principle of the Switch Mirrors

FIGURE 4.36 Mechanical switch using micromachined mirrors. (From (Lin98, Figure 1). Copyright © 1998 IEEE. Used by permission of The Institute of Electrical and Electronics Engineers, Inc.)

4.9.2 Reciprocity

A fundamental property of Maxwell's equations in linear isotropic media is *reciprocity* [Ramo+94]. When applied to guided-wave optical systems, reciprocity has a simple informal interpretation: If a wave propagates from one point (an input) in a system to other points (outputs), then waves injected at those outputs will propagate backward to the input in exactly the same way.

A more quantitative definition of reciprocity is illustrated by the n port shown in Figure 4.37. Suppose it contains an arbitrary interconnection of linear components all built from isotropic materials. In Figure 4.37, the quantities a_k and b_k represent

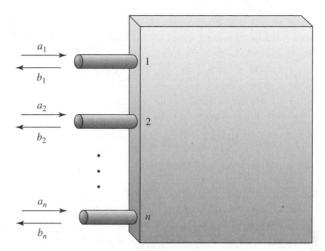

FIGURE 4.37 Illustration of reciprocity.

normalized complex amplitudes of incident and reflected waves respectively. The normalization is such that $\frac{1}{2}Re[a_k a_k^* - b_k b_k^*]$ is the net average power into port k. In the case of passive devices, the net power into the device, $\frac{1}{2}Re\sum_k[a_k a_k^* - b_k b_k^*]$, must be non-negative, and in lossless devices it must be 0.

If **a** and **b** represent the vectors of incident and reflected waves respectively, then their relationship is defined by

$$\mathbf{b} = \mathbf{Sa} \tag{4.51}$$

where **S** is called the *scattering matrix* for the n port. For reciprocal systems, **S** is symmetric. This implies that the individual responses (reflected waves) to single excitations (incident waves) are related by $b_i/a_j = s_{ij} = b_j/a_i$. Because these are relations among complex amplitudes, they are defined for each optical frequency and are generally frequency dependent. A frequency-dependent **S** represents any frequency-selective element such as a filter, WMUX or WDMUX. If the system is passive, we have $\mathbf{x}^{*t}[\mathbf{I} - \mathbf{S}^{*t}\mathbf{S}]\mathbf{x} \geq 0$ for all x, which means that the expression in brackets is a *Hermitian matrix*. If it is lossless, $\mathbf{S}^{*t} = \mathbf{S}^{-1}$; that is, **S** is a *unitary matrix*. If it is lossless and reciprocal, $\mathbf{S}^* = \mathbf{S}^{-1}$.

For example, the scattering matrix **S** for the 2×2 coupler in Figure 2.7 is a 4×4 matrix, which can be related to the power transfer matrix in Equation 2.3 as follows. Relabeling the output ports 1' and 2' as 3 and 4 respectively, we can partition **S** into four 2×2 submatrices S_{ij}, where S_{21} is the matrix relating the two incident waves at the input ports to the two reflected (outgoing) waves at the output ports. (For an ideal coupler, $S_{ii} = 0$.) It can be shown that

$$S_{21} = S_{12} = \begin{bmatrix} \sqrt{1-\alpha} & j\sqrt{\alpha} \\ j\sqrt{\alpha} & \sqrt{1-\alpha} \end{bmatrix} \tag{4.52}$$

The power transfer matrix of Equation 2.3 follows directly from Equation 4.52.

The most important consequence of reciprocity for our purposes is that if we know the optical field (and thus power) relationships for signals traversing a system in one direction, these relationships must also hold for signals traversing the same system in the opposite direction. The "system" may be a single device, a network element, or a whole network, as long as it is linear and reciprocal. It is for this reason that the standard building blocks of our systems can be used for pairs of similar operations simply by reversing inputs and outputs: Splitters become combiners,[26] and multiplexers become demultiplexers.

4.9.3 Nonreciprocal Devices

One reason for introducing the concept of reciprocity here was to point out that, in certain applications, *nonreciprocal devices* are needed. The simplest example is the fiber amplifier. If an EDFA is inserted in a fiber to amplify signals propagating from left to right, it will also amplify signals propagating in the opposite direction. Because there are often undesired signals moving in the wrong direction in a fiber (for example, due to small reflections at various points in a system), it is important to prevent this backward propagation. This requires a nonreciprocal device, called an *isolator.*

The principle of the isolator is shown in Figure 4.38. Incident light is vertically polarized by polarizer *A*, experiences a 45° clockwise rotation as it passes through the Faraday rotator, and continues on through polarizer *B*, which is oriented to allow it to pass unattenuated. A wave entering in the opposite direction through *B* starts off at the 45° polarization angle, is rotated *counterclockwise* another 45°, resulting in a horizontal polarization, and is therefore blocked by polarizer *A*. These opposite directions of polarization rotation can only occur in nonreciprocal devices. Faraday rotators are made of special materials that have nonisotropic dielectric properties in the presence of a constant applied magnetic field.

Another application of the Faraday rotator is in the *circulator* of Figure 4.41. The directions of circulation of the forward- and backward-propagating waves, as described in Section 4.9.5.2, can only be obtained in a nonreciprocal device.

4.9.4 Wavelength/Waveband-Selective Components

One of the factors determining how efficiently the fiber bandwidth can be exploited is the maximum packing density of wavelengths and wavebands.[27] This in turn is dependent on wavelength filtering and switching technology. The two critical areas of application of wavelength-selective devices in multiwavelength networks are in optical receivers (either fixed or tunable) and wavelength-selective switches (WSSs).

---

[26] The inevitability of combining losses is demonstrated easily using reciprocity. See Problem 9 at the end of this chapter.

[27] The distinction between wavelengths and wavebands was explained in Section 2.2. In this section the term *wavelength* is used inclusively and encompasses wavebands as well as wavelengths.

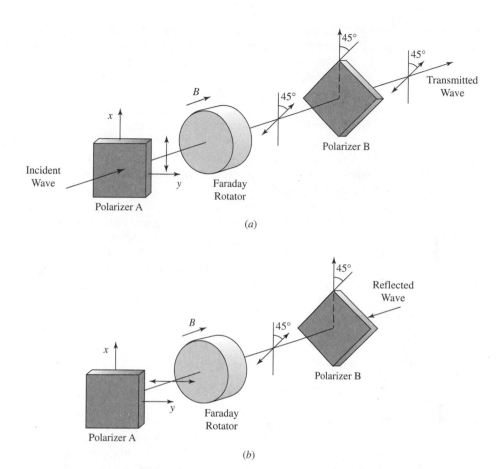

FIGURE 4.38 Optical isolator. (From (Saleh+91, Figure 6.6-5). Copyright © 1991. Reprinted by permission of John Wiley & Sons, Inc.)

Tuned (or tunable) optical receivers accessing a network node through a single fiber must select signals on a given wavelength and reject others on different wavelengths appearing on the same fiber. Undesired signals at different wavelengths that reach the photodetector constitute *interchannel cross-talk*, which degrades receiver performance just as co-channel cross-talk does. The ideal filtering devices for performing the selection should have flat passbands over the bandwidth of the λ-channel being selected, and high attenuation in the stop band. The steeper the "skirts" or side slopes of the filter transfer function, the less spacing (guardband) is needed between the wavelengths sharing a fiber to avoid interchannel cross-talk.

The passbands and the guard bands between them necessarily must be somewhat wider than minimum values calculated under ideal conditions to allow tolerance for laser and component misalignments, drifts, and imperfections. (See Section 4.12.2 for an example of the laser misalignment problem.)

Similar issues arise in the design of WSSs. In most cases, WSSs use the three-stage architecture of Figure 2.22, requiring wavelength demultiplexing, followed by space switching, followed by remultiplexing. The criteria concerning flatness and guard-bands that apply to receiver filters also apply to the demultiplexing/multiplexing transfer functions here, except that the numbers are likely to be different. Because an optical signal most likely traverses many demultiplexers and multiplexers on an end-to-end optical path, the overall transfer function seen by the signal is the result of cascading many elementary components. Each component has variable characteristics due to manufacturing imperfections, aging, and temperature, so that the bandwidth of the end-to-end transfer function seen by the signal can be much narrower than the bandwidth of an individual filtering element.

The problems caused by these imperfect filter characteristics are compounded by laser misalignment, with the overall effect translating into waveform distortion, ISI, and interchannel cross-talk.[28] If a system is not designed with appropriate tolerances, these effects eventually render purely optical paths traversing many WSSs unusable. To allow tolerances for imperfections, passbands and guardbands for independently routed wavelengths must be considerably larger than the spacings dictated by optical receiver requirements alone. It is for this reason that *waveband* routing, which wastes less bandwidth in guardbands, is more spectrally efficient than *wavelength* routing (see Section 2.2).

4.9.5 Wavelength-Selective Device Technology

Recently three technologies have emerged as especially promising for filtering and WDMUX/WMUX applications: multilayer interference (MI) filters, FBGs, and ar-rayed waveguide gratings (AWGs). It is a measure of the rapid advance of technology that none of these was mentioned in a comprehensive volume on optical fiber com-munications published eleven years ago [Miller+88]. The most important parameters for these devices are minimum wavelength spacing and insertion loss.

4.9.5.1 Multilayer Interference Filters

The principle of operation of the MI filter is illustrated in Figure 4.39(a). When operated as a WDMUX (or a drop filter), several input signals enter the device at point 1, with the signal to be dropped exiting at point 4. The filter consists of a glass substrate on which are deposited several layers of dielectric thin films (on the right side of the substrate in the figure). Their thicknesses and dielectric constants are arranged so that the interference caused by multiple reflections between the layers allows a selected wavelength to be transmitted to the right, and reflects the remaining wavelengths back through the glass and out the left side (point 2). In this case wavelengths λ_1 and λ_2 enter on the left, λ_1 is dropped on the right, and λ_2 exists on the left.

One of the attractive aspects of the MI filters is that the filter characteristics (center wavelength and passband) can be adjusted by the appropriate choice of layering

---

[28] An analytical study of this problem, based on realistic filter characteristics, appears in [Roudas+97].

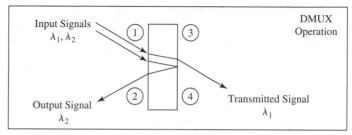

(*a*) Demultiplexing Mode

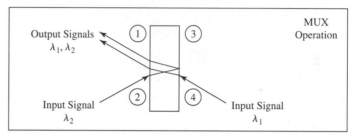

FIGURE 4.39 MI filter.

(*b*) Multiplexing Mode

geometry, producing a close-to-ideal optical frequency response: flat passband and steep side slopes. Because this is a reciprocal device, it acts as a WMUX if operated in the reverse direction, as shown in Figure 4.39(b). Now, channels on λ_1 and λ_2 enter at points 4 and 2 respectively and are multiplexed, exiting at point 1.

An integrated array of MI filters deposited on both sides of a substrate can be used as a multiwavelength WDMUX/WMUX as shown in Figure 4.40. The figure shows a schematic representation of the operation of the device as a WDMUX. Graded refractive index (GRIN) lenses are used to collimate the light before directing the signal at a slight angle to the MI filter. A first wavelength (channel 1) is dropped and collected by another collimating lens. All other wavelengths are reflected to the left. In this way, the remaining light is reflected from filter to filter with a single channel removed at each reflection. Typical parameters are

- Wavelength channel spacing, 100 GHz
- Insertion loss, 7 dB for 16 wavelengths

4.9.5.2 Fiber Bragg Gratings

Based on the Bragg effect, FBGs act as wavelength-selective mirrors. A grating reflects light with a wavelength corresponding to twice the grating period. In effect, the grating operates as a narrow-band reflecting filter. The FBGs are manufactured by "writing" the grating into a fiber containing photosensitive material. Exposing the

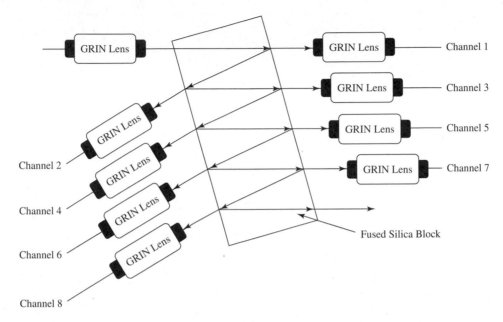

FIGURE 4.40 MI filter.   (From (Scobey+96, Figure 5). Copyright © 1996 IEEE. Used by permission of The Institute of Electrical and Electronics Engineers, Inc.)

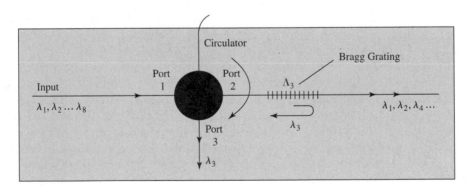

FIGURE 4.41 FBG used as a drop filter.

fiber to a periodic pattern of UV light produces a corresponding periodic variation of its refractive index.

The use of the FBG as a drop filter is shown in Figure 4.41. Multiple wavelengths propagate from left to right in the fiber, passing from port 1 to port 2 in the circulator. Wavelength 3 is reflected from the FBG, entering port 2, after which it exits at port 3. In typical applications, a WDMUX is built using a passive splitter, with each arm containing an FBG drop filter for one wavelength. This, however, incurs a splitting loss proportional to the number of wavelengths being demultiplexed. Typical characteristics for an FBG drop filter are

- Wavelength channel spacing, 100 GHz or 50 GHz
- Insertion loss, 2 dB to 3 dB (including circulator loss)

4.9.5.3 Arrayed Waveguide Gratings

The AWG or phased array (PHASAR) is an integrated form of the static wavelength router, shown conceptually in Figure 2.9. A signal entering a given input port on a given wavelength is routed to an output port determined by its wavelength. If only a single input port is used with n output ports, the device acts as a WDMUX, or if operated in the reverse direction, as a WMUX (reciprocity again). In an $m \times n$ system, it creates a static routing pattern determined by the geometry of the device.

Typically fabricated in silica on silicon technology, the AWG is a phased array of multiple waveguides with path length differences between neighboring guides arranged to create the desired phase relations at the output coupler c_o [Dragone+91] (Figure 4.42). The input signals pass through a combining coupler c_c, then through the waveguides, and exit selectively at the output coupler. The phase differences between signals routed through the different paths cause different wavelengths from the same input port to be routed to different output ports. Typical values for current commercial devices are

- Wavelength channel spacing, 100 GHz and 50 GHz
- Insertion loss, 7 dB for 16 wavelengths

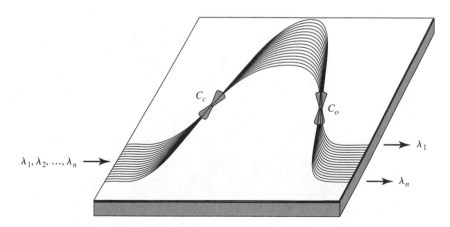

FIGURE 4.42 Arrayed waveguide grating.

4.9.6 Multiwavelength Switch Technology

Some devices designed as static filters, or WMUX/WDMUXs, can be converted to tunable or switched devices by controlling their parameters externally, thus converting them to switches selecting a single wavelength or waveband. For example, the reflection band of an FBG can be slightly displaced by stressing it to change its grating period. In this way, it can be switched under external (e.g., piezoelectric) control to either reflect or transmit a narrow band of wavelengths. (An optical cross-connect based on tunable FBGs is described in [Hjelme+98].)

Other devices are designed to switch several wavelengths independently; that is, they are multiwavelength switches (MWSs). We describe two of these in the next sections: the acousto-optic tunable filter (AOTF) and the liquid crystal multiwavelength switch.

4.9.6.1 Acousto-optic Tunable Filters

The AOTF has very versatile properties when used as an MWS [Smith+90]. As illustrated in Figure 4.43, the AOTF is a two-input/two-output device constructed on a LiNbO$_3$ substrate, which acts as a 2×2 controllable and wavelength-selective directional coupler. The basic AOTF implements a switching operation by "flipping" the polarization of the input wave, and hence is inherently polarization dependent. The device shown in the figure is a polarization-independent version of the elementary AOTF, implemented by polarization diversity techniques using polarization beam splitters (PBSs). An input is present on the upper left fiber, and it is split by the PBS into its two polarized components as shown. (The transverse magnetic [TM] and transverse electric [TE] polarizations correspond to the vertical and horizontal components

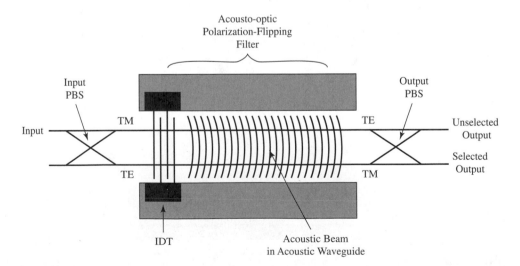

FIGURE 4.43 Acousto-optic tunable filter.

with respect to the substrate surface.) The TM component then traverses the upper waveguide and exits on the right. An electric interdigital transducer (IDT) formed by electrodes on the surface, driven by a radio frequency source, creates a surface acoustic wave that propagates in the same direction as the lightwaves. Through an acousto-optic effect in the material, this forms the equivalent of a moving grating, which can be phase matched to an optical wave at a selected wavelength by choosing the correct frequency of the electrical excitation. A signal that is phase matched (the *selected signal*) is "flipped" from the TM to the TE mode, so that the output PBS directs it to the lower output. The unselected signal exits on the upper output. A similar polarization-flipping and -selecting process takes place for the TE component. A signal entering on the lower port on the selected wavelength undergoes the same operations, exiting on the upper output port. Thus the device is in the cross state for the selected wavelength. By superimposing excitations of several frequencies, several wavelengths can be selected simultaneously, which makes this an MWS, as shown conceptually in Figure 2.23.

The switch states of AOTFs can be controlled independently for each wavelength over a continuum of values so that they can be configured to act as 2×2 wavelength-selective LDCs. They can be tuned over very wide ranges of wavelengths (up to 200 nm), and switching times are on the order of microseconds. Early versions had problems with insertion loss and side-lobe suppression. (Large side lobes in the selected wavelength transfer function produce high interchannel cross-talk.) However, recent versions have 30 dB side-lobe suppression and low loss [Jaggi+98]:

- Wavelength channel spacing, typically about 1 nm
- Insertion loss, 2 dB fiber-to-fiber

4.9.6.2 Liquid Crystal Multiwavelength Switch

Another realization of an MWS is the liquid crystal switch described in [Patel+95]. The simplest polarization-dependent form of a 2×2 liquid crystal switch is shown schematically in Figure 4.44. An input signal (indicated as input 1) is dispersed spatially (demultiplexed) using a grating device. Each wavelength component is directed through a polarization-selective deflective element (e.g., a calcite crystal). This is preceded by a liquid crystal element, whose function is to rotate the polarization of the beam traversing it when an electric field is applied, and to leave it unchanged otherwise. The controlled polarization rotation produces a controlled beam displacement, with the displaced beam remultiplexed onto output 2. If undisplaced, it is remultiplexed onto output 1. In the figure, one wavelength (the dark beam) is shown deflected to output 2. An array of beam deflectors under independent electrical control produces an MWS from input 1 to outputs 1 or 2. A similar operation is executed on a second signal entering on input 2 (not shown in the figure), so that the two operations result in a 2×2 MWS. These devices can be built with flat passbands and can accommodate a large number of channels. [Patel+95] describes an eight-wavelength device with 4-nm channel separation, -25-dB interchannel cross-talk, and less than 10 dB of

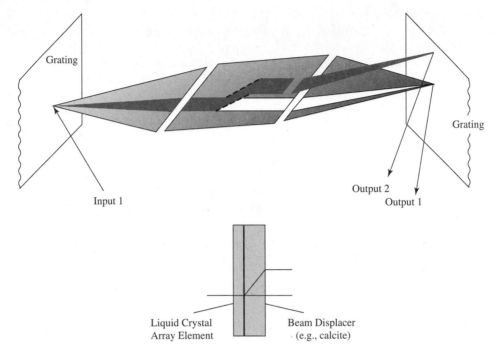

FIGURE 4.44 Liquid crystal MWS.   (From (Patel+95, Figure 1). Copyright © 1995 IEEE. Used by permission of The Institute of Electrical and Electronics Engineers, Inc.)

insertion loss. It can be made polarization insensitive by using polarization diversity techniques similar to those used for the AOTF in Figure 4.43.

4.9.7 Wavelength Dilation

The three-stage architecture for a WSS (refer to Figure 2.22) requires m space switches for a system operating on m wavelengths, together with a pair of WDMUX/WMUXs for each input/output port. The space switches can be of any form, either generalized or permutation. In the latter case, the WSS becomes a wavelength-selective cross-connect.

As pointed out in Section 2.3.2.4, any space-switch fabric can be converted to a WSS fabric by replacing each elementary switching device with an equivalent MWS. In this approach, no WDMUX/WMUXs are required. In the case at hand, the m-fold replication of space switches is replaced by a fabric of MWSs operating on m wavelengths.

Unfortunately, many types of elementary (2×2) MWSs are either costly or impossible to realize when m is large and/or the wavelength spacings are small. A compromise solution is a *wavelength-dilated* architecture, as shown in Figure 4.45 [Sharony+92]. At first glance, this appears to have the worst qualities of both the three-stage and the MWS approach. It is a three-stage architecture similar to Figure 2.22, but each space switching layer is replaced by an MWS fabric. The advantage is that there

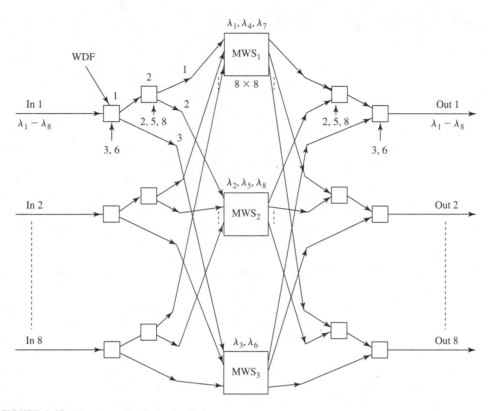

FIGURE 4.45 Wavelength-dilated switch.

are fewer MWS layers than space switches in the original three-stage configuration. Furthermore, each MWS fabric operates on fewer and more widely separated wavelengths than the single MWS fabric would process. This is accomplished by "combing out" subsets of wavelengths with spacings that are multiples of those in the original channel set.

In the example shown in Figure 4.45, an 8×8 switch operating on eight wavelengths is shown, with a factor of three wavelength dilation. It requires three 8×8 MWS fabrics, MWS_1, MWS_2, and MWS_3. The wavelengths on each input fiber are demultiplexed using a tree of wavelength-dropping filters (WDFs) and are remultiplexed using a similar tree operated in the reverse direction. The wavelengths dropped/added by each WDF are indicated with an arrow under the WDF. The set of wavelengths λ_1, λ_4, and λ_7 is directed from each input fiber to MWS_1; the set λ_2, λ_5, and λ_8 is directed to MWS_2; and λ_3 and λ_6 are directed to MWS_3. Note that each MWS must operate on two or three wavelengths with spacings that are three times as large as the original set. Thus, large guardbands are present between adjacent wavelengths, reducing interchannel cross-talk as well as the cost of the components. Because the WDFs are static devices (e.g., fiber Bragg gratings) their cost is considerably less than the switching devices, which have been reduced in number.

4.10 Wavelength Converters

Wavelength converters can be used as components of WIXCs, and (in combination with static wavelength routers) to implement WSXCs (see Section 2.3.3). The use of the WIXC as a switching option in wavelength routed networks is illustrated in Figure 2.28.

The principal devices for performing wavelength conversion can be roughly categorized as optoelectronic (optically gated) and coherent. (See [Yoo96] for a more complete account of wavelength conversion technology.) The optoelectronic wavelength converter is shown conceptually in Figure 4.46. An intensity-modulated signal at wavelength λ_1 is converted to electrical form in a photodetector, amplified, and used to modulate a laser operating at a different wavelength λ_2. This places it in the category of the transponders discussed in Section 2.5. Although these devices are good in terms of power output (gain), they are inherently nonlinear, and hence opaque. For example, two superimposed signals at different wavelengths cannot be converted simultaneously.

Another approach that is somewhat similar is *cross-gain compression*. In this case, both the signal to be converted (intensity modulated on wavelength λ_1) and a constant-intensity signal on the new wavelength λ_2 are applied to the input of an SOA. As explained in Section 4.4.2, the fluctuations of the input signal modulate the constant-intensity signal by stealing pump power from it. Thus, the cross-gain converter turns the normally deleterious cross-talk effect in the SOA to an advantage. Like the optoelectronic converter, this is a nontransparent device.

Among the coherent devices are those based on FWM and difference frequency conversion. The cross-talk problems produced by FWM on fibers were discussed in Section 4.3.2.4. In that case, it was indicated that when two signals at neighboring

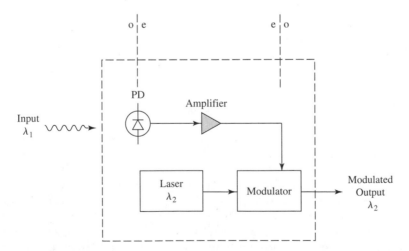

FIGURE 4.46 Optoelectronic wavelength converter.

optical frequencies ω_1 and ω_2 are impressed on a fiber with a cubic nonlinearity, an undesired cross-talk signal at a third frequency $2\omega_1 - \omega_2$ can appear. As in the case of SOA cross-talk, this effect can be turned to an advantage. If we let $\omega_1 = \omega_p$, a pump frequency, and $\omega_2 = \omega_s$, the signal frequency, and call $\omega_c = 2\omega_p - \omega_s$ the converted signal frequency, this becomes a frequency converter [Inoue+93]. Although this is a transparent conversion process, it is a very weak (inefficient) effect in fibers. It is also susceptible to additional undesired cross-mixing terms.

The difference frequency converter (DFC) was discussed in Section 2.3.3 [Yoo+96, 95]. This is based on a square law rather than cubic nonlinearity in the waveguide. The efficiency of the effect depends on how well phase matching is realized. It can be enhanced by special design of the waveguide in which the interaction occurs. Figure 4.47 shows the performance of a DFC based on a periodically domain-reversed aluminum

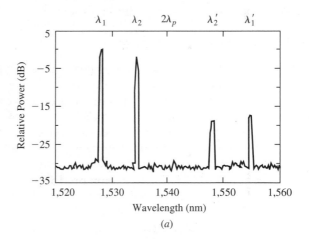

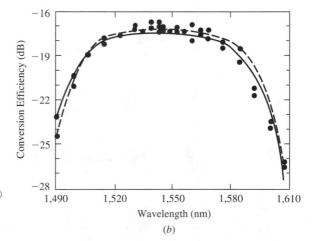

FIGURE 4.47 Performance of a difference frequency converter. (From (Yoo96, Figure 2). Copyright © 1996 IEEE. Used by permission of The Institute of Electrical and Electronics Engineers, Inc.)

gallium arsenide (AlGaAs) waveguide. Figure 4.47(a) illustrates the simultaneous conversion of two signals at 1,528 and 1,534 nm to 1,555 and 1,549 nm respectively. Note the spectrum "reflection" based on the pump wavelength (771 nm), as described in Figure 2.24. The various processes involved in fabrication render the device polarization independent, with a conversion efficiency of approximately -17 dB over a band of approximately 90 nm, as shown in Figure 4.47(b). (The *solid* and *dashed* curves in the figure represent points for two different polarization states.)

4.11 Space Switch Architectures

Some representative space switch architectures were described in Section 2.3.2, characterized as permutation switches, generalized switches, and linear divider combiners (LDCs). In this section we revisit the space switch, focusing on physical layer issues: losses, cross-talk, and fabrication complexity.

4.11.1 Crossbar Switches

Although Section 2.3.2 gave conceptual pictures of typical switch fabrics, understanding physical implementation requires a more concrete picture. Figures 4.34 and 4.48 show two alternate realizations of a 4×4 optical crossbar. An optical crossbar was first shown conceptually in Figure 2.19. In Figure 4.34, a version of the crossbar using passive splitters and combiners surrounding an SLM array is shown. It strongly resembles the switch in Figure 2.19, and can be used for permutation switching, generalized switching, or as an LDC. On the other hand, Figure 4.48 shows a different realization, suitable for integration on a single substrate. Let us call the former and the latter versions 1 and 2 respectively. In each of the two cases, n^2 elementary switching devices are used for an $n \times n$ switch. However, the devices are on–off switches in version 1 and 2×2 directional couplers in version 2.

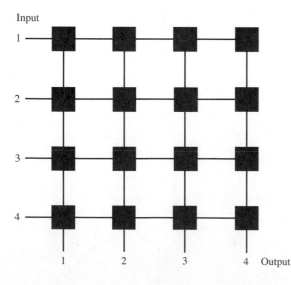

FIGURE 4.48 Optical crossbar switch.

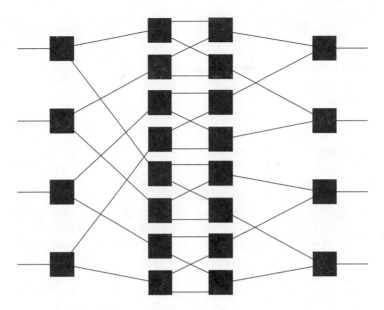

FIGURE 4.49   Router/selector.

Version 2 is not as flexible as version 1. For example, it cannot be used as a generalized switch, as defined in Section 2.3.2.2. If an attempt is made to create certain patterns of multipoint connectivity (e.g., inputs 1 and 2 to outputs 1 and 2), optical paths are created that violate the distinct source combining condition (see Section 3.4.1). Also, when version 2 is used as a permutation switch, some switch states block certain connections. Therefore, a special connection rule is required to avoid blocking states, and thus this is a wide-sense, rather than strict-sense, nonblocking switch. (In version 1 there is a unique switch state for each connection state, making it strict-sense nonblocking for permutation connections.)

Another problem with version 2 is that the various paths through the switch are not of uniform lengths, leading to unequal losses for different connections. However, a significant advantage of version 2 is that it can be integrated onto a single substrate without waveguide crossovers.

4.11.2 Routers/Selectors

Another switch fabric, shown in Figures 4.49 and 2.20(a), is known as a *router/selector*.[29] These figures show identical topologies, but the switching elements are grouped differently, with the former having fewer connection crossovers. For example, in Figure 4.49, all switches can be fabricated as an integrated component on a single substrate with only 12 waveguide crossovers. These structures are just as versatile as version

---

[29] The $\delta - \sigma$ architecture, shown in Figure 2.20(a) as a 4×4 LDC, is identical in form to the router/selector. The only difference is that the elementary switches in the LDC are allowed to run through a continuum of states, whereas those in the router/selector are used only in the cross and bar states.

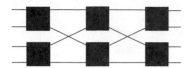

FIGURE 4.50 Benes switch.

1 crossbars. They can be implemented with both the splitting and combining stages, made up of controllable directional couplers, or with one or the other of the stages implemented with static devices, saving half of the controllable devices [Spanke87]. However, the latter case exhibits poorer cross-talk properties (see Section 4.11.3). Other combinations of static and controllable devices are also possible.

The $n \times n$ router/selector fabric implemented with all controllable devices uses $2n(n-1)$ controllable couplers compared with roughly half that many controllable devices in the version 1 crossbar. In return, the router/selector fabric has better performance than the crossbar when used as a permutation switch. In this application, all couplers are used only in the bar or cross states, so that there are no combining or splitting losses. In the version 1 crossbar there is always a splitting/combining loss of $1/n^2$. If the objective is to minimize the number of elementary switching elements, we must move to the rearrangeably nonblocking fabrics, exemplified by the Benes switches.

Figure 4.50 shows a 4×4 Benes fabric. The 8×8 version appears in Figure 2.16. As indicated in Section 2.3.2.1, the Benes fabrics can be converted to strictly nonblocking Cantor switches by using $\log_2 n$-fold space dilation. Space dilation is also useful for reducing cross-talk. For example, if only one of the two ports on each input element is used, and only one of the two output ports on each output element is used, the 8×8 Benes switch of Figure 2.16 becomes a two-fold dilated 4×4 switch with better cross-talk properties (see [Hinton93]). However, this improved performance requires more than three times as many switching elements as a 4×4 Benes switch.

One important performance measure for switches is the total attenuation from input to output. Most permutation switches are composed of multiple stages of 2×2 controllable couplers operated in the bar or cross states only. Most of our representative examples were of this form. If all these elements were ideal, and there were no losses in the interconnecting fibers or waveguides, the end-to-end paths through the switches would be lossless. However, each coupler has excess loss, which is usually the dominating loss in the fabric. Thus, the input-to-output loss is proportional to the number of stages the connection traverses, which is usually the same for all paths in multistage switches. (An exception is the version 2 crossbar, which is not in typical multistage form.) Comparing these examples, we find that the Benes switch is slightly better than the router/selector, with $2 \log_2 n - 1$ stages for the former and $2 \log_2 n$ for the latter.

4.11.3 Switch Cross-talk

More important than losses is the issue of cross-talk. As indicated in Section 4.8, cross-talk can occur when interfering signals travel on unintended "leakage" paths through

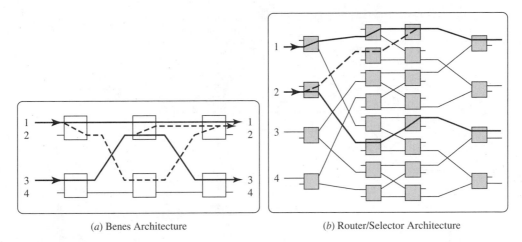

(a) Benes Architecture   (b) Router/Selector Architecture

FIGURE 4.51 Orders of cross-talk.

a network. But a switch fabric is itself a connection network, and because of the many paths in a typical switch, many cross-talk terms can be generated.

Switch cross-talk terms can be categorized by their *order*. As indicated in Equation 2.13, when any real 2×2 switching element is in the bar or cross state, a fraction ϵ of input signal power leaks into the wrong output port. The leakage parameter ϵ, usually expressed in decibels as $\epsilon_{dB} = 10 \log_{10} \epsilon$, is called the *cross-talk* of the switching element. A leakage path through a switching fabric that passes through k of these "wrong-way" hops attenuates the power of a signal traversing it by an amount $k\epsilon_{dB}$. This is called kth-order cross-talk. Clearly, the higher its order, the less troublesome the cross-talk.

Examples of cross-talk terms of various orders in three different realizations of 4×4 switches are shown in Figures 4.51 and 4.52. Intended paths are shown in bold and leakage paths are shown dashed. All connections are on the same nominal wavelength. In each case, a small portion of a signal applied to an input port leaks over to an undesired output port. In the Benes switch of Figure 4.51(a), a portion of the signal on input port 3 leaks to output port 1, passing through one wrong-way hop, which makes this a first-order heterodyne cross-talk. In addition, there is a second-order homodyne (multipath) cross-talk term due to the leakage path from input port 1 to output port 1. A second-order heterodyne cross-talk path is shown in the router/selector switch of Figure 4.51(b), and a third-order heterodyne path is shown in the enhanced performance switch of Figure 4.52. In each case the switch architecture is structured so that the orders shown in these illustrations are the lowest possible for the switch.

In general, increasing the order of cross-talk requires adding additional switching elements. For example, the 4×4 enhanced performance switch is constructed with 44 controllable, active switching elements, as well as four static splitters, to limit

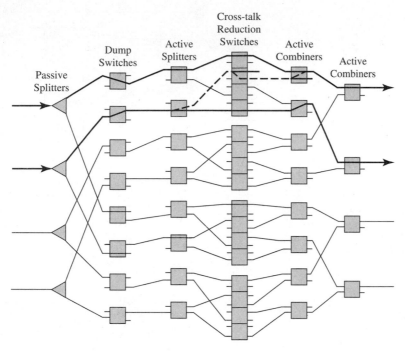

FIGURE 4.52 Enhanced performance switch.

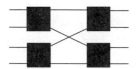

FIGURE 4.53 Space dilation.

cross-talk to third-order and above [Murphy+97]. For comparison, the Benes switch has first-order cross-talk but requires only six elements, whereas the router/selector switch has only second-order cross-talk and higher and requires 24 elements. It is also worth noting that the fabrics that are most economical in element usage generally produce multipath cross-talk due to DSC violations, whereas the switches designed with extra elements usually have no multipath cross-talk. For example, we have seen that the Benes switch, as shown in Figure 4.51(a), has a multipath cross-talk path in parallel with the desired path between input 1 and output 1. No such paths exist in the router/selector and enhanced performance switches.

One way of increasing systematically the order of cross-talk in any switch fabric is by space dilating each 2×2 switch. As shown in Figure 4.53, a set of four 2×2 switches can be configured to produce a space-dilated 2×2 switch with a second-order cross-talk. (Only one input is used on each switch on the left, and only one output is used on each switch on the right.) A complete fabric of these space-dilated switches would have the order of its cross-talk increased by a factor of two, but at a cost increased by a factor of four. For example, using space dilation for each elementary switch, the 4×4 Benes switch requires 24 elements, which is the same number as the 4×4 router/selector switch.

In addition to having less cross-talk, switch fabrics with extra elements are usually more versatile as well. Thus, for example, the router/selector configuration can be used for one-to-many (multicast) as well as many-to-one connections, provided that its elementary switches are allowed to assume intermediate states. (The crossbar of Figure 4.34 has this property using only two-state elementary switches.) Furthermore, cross-talk levels can often be reduced by appropriately setting unused switching elements.

4.12 The End-to-End Transmission Path: Reach

In our discussion of transmission impairments such as dispersion, noise, and fiber nonlinearities, each was treated in isolation so that some meaningful results on performance constraints could be obtained. Typically we found an approximate limit on transmission link length and/or bitrate due to each type of impairment.

In a wide area multiwavelength network, however, a purely optical connection traverses many different components: fibers, amplifiers, WMUXs, WDMUXs, and cross-connects, accumulating distortion, noise, and interference as it propagates. As noted earlier, the problem of accumulated transmission impairments on long, nonregenerated paths is one of the negative features of optically transparent networks. Thus the prediction of the combined effect of all these impairments is of crucial interest to the network designer. As we shall see, the complexity of the problem suggests that the best approach to performance evaluation in this case is simulation. However, a "brute force" approach to simulation is doomed to failure because of the sheer number of components involved and their complexity.

In the following sections we describe an efficient method of physical-layer simulation, and apply it to some case studies. The objective is twofold:

1. To suggest a way of improving the computational efficiency of physical-layer simulations

2. To illustrate how the reach of an optical path is constrained by combinations of technological limitations

4.12.1 Physical-Layer Simulation

The discussion of the many impairments affecting an optical transmission path should have made it clear that a purely analytical approach to predicting performance is not feasible. The development of efficient simulation tools for physical-layer performance analysis is therefore becoming an important issue. One of the problems with typical frequency-domain or time-domain simulators is that the computation time required for simulating long, transmitted digital sequences in a multiwavelength optical network environment makes these approaches impractical if not impossible with current computer power. The difficulty is due to the large time–bandwidth product of the signals being simulated.

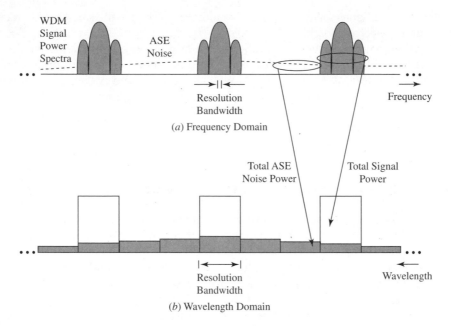

FIGURE 4.54 Wavelength-domain simulation.

In this section we describe one approach to the simulation of large systems, called *wavelength-domain simulation*, that reduces the computation time by using a coarse resolution in the frequency domain [Antoniades+98b]. The strategy of the overall simulation is to begin with a wavelength-domain simulation of a network to find pertinent signal, noise, and interference power levels only. This information is then used as a basis for a more refined time-domain simulation of specific signals of interest. This two-step approach enables handling systems with sizes that would render them intractable with other methods.

The wavelength-domain simulation is basically a low-resolution frequency-domain approach, and it is limited to linear systems. Figure 4.54 illustrates the general methodology. In a (high-resolution) frequency-domain simulation, shown in Figure 4.54(a), a multiwavelength signal is represented by sets of samples of the complex signal spectra, with a resolution bandwidth that is a small fraction of the bitrate in the case of digital signals.

However, in the (low-resolution) two-step process just described, the fine details of the frequency spectra are unimportant at the first stage of the simulation. Thus it is sufficient to use a much coarser resolution, as shown in Figure 4.54(b), which is the wavelength-domain representation.[30] In this case, the spectral components of the quantities of interest (WDM signal and ASE noise powers) are grouped into larger bins so that the fine structure of the frequency spectrum is lost. Typical effects studied

---

[30] Similar approaches exist under different names (for example, "power-budget simulation" [Rotolo+95]).

in the wavelength domain are evaluations of EDFA gain, ASE noise accumulation, and cross-talk in various network elements. The resolution bandwidth (or bin size) appropriate to multiwavelength networks is on the order of 0.1 nm to ensure that adjacent signals fall in different bins.

The rationale for using a coarse resolution is as follows. First, the frequency characteristics of typical optical components generally vary very slowly within an individual signal bandwidth, so that their action results in a simple scaling of each signal by a constant gain and a change of carrier phase. Second, noise spectra are also slowly varying functions of frequency. Third, insofar as the various interactions within the network are concerned, it is usually sufficient to characterize the signals themselves as constant, unmodulated carriers.[31]

The simulation process works as follows:

1. The network to be simulated is modeled as an interconnection of network elements, which are in turn constructed from components and elementary units such as isolators, filters, and controllable couplers. The wavelength-domain characteristics of these units are obtained either analytically or by empirical measurements.

2. The simulator evaluates a set of quantities at each elementary unit, including optical signal powers, ASE noise, cross-talk (interference) powers, and so on. When there are no closed loops in the optical paths, one iteration of the simulation is sufficient to compute all quantities, proceeding from the optical sources (lasers) to the destinations. Closed loops (feedback) can occur inadvertently (e.g., through cross-talk paths), in which case more than one iteration may be needed. (Because the feedback terms are normally small, not many iterations are needed for convergence.)

3. A conventional time-domain simulation is run to study the performance of selected optical paths. Having used the wavelength-domain simulation to determine the pertinent signal, noise, and interference power levels, the rest of the network is now suppressed, with each selected path viewed as an equivalent channel. Each equivalent channel is characterized by its dispersion and attenuation, together with the noise and interfering signals accumulated along the path. These are used to obtain information in the time domain, such as eye diagrams and BER. In some cases nonlinear impairments can be introduced at this stage.

Some case studies illustrating results that can be obtained with this approach are provided in the following two sections. Both cases pertain to the MONET testbed (see [Wagner+96]).

4.12.2 Study of a Wavelength Add–Drop Multiplexer Chain

In [Antoniades+97], the effects of filter imperfections and laser misalignments were studied in a system consisting of a chain of 50 WADMs. This might correspond, for

---

[31] This still allows for the study of effects such as the influence of aggregate signal power levels on EDFA gain and ASE noise because the signal variations due to modulation are much too rapid to affect these properties of the EDFA.

example, to a 50-node multiwavelength ring. The objective was to determine how many WADMs can be cascaded before the SNR drops below an acceptable level. The system that was simulated is shown in Figure 4.55. It is an eight-wavelength system, in which one channel is continued end-to-end, and the others are added and dropped periodically at various WADMs along the path.

Each WADM is constructed as shown in Figure 4.56. The actual structure is shown in Figure 4.56(a), where the WDMUXs and WMUXs consist of cascades of MI filters, with each signal passing through eight filters in each WADM. The variable attenuators are servo driven to equalize the signal levels, which are amplified nonuniformly by the EDFAs. Figure 4.56(b) is a block diagram that represents the modules and their interconnections used in simulating the WADM. The filter characteristics used in the simulation were based on measured transmittance and reflectance of actual components. In the simulation, the EDFA gains and ASE noise contributions are calculated based on aggregate signal power, using the models in [Saleh+90] and [Jopson+91].

Some typical results are shown in Figure 4.57, illustrating combined effects of laser misalignment and filter cascading. In Figure 4.57(a), the power spectral densities (PSDs) of the signal and ASE noise are shown after 24 WADMs, with a laser

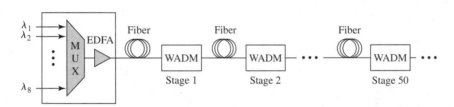

FIGURE 4.55   WADM chain.

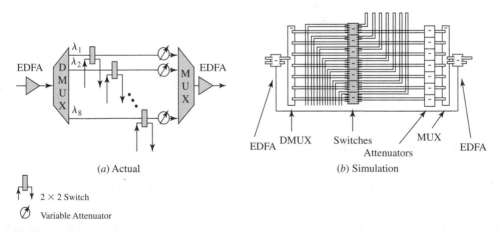

(*a*) Actual   (*b*) Simulation

2×2 Switch

Variable Attenuator

FIGURE 4.56   WADM structure and simulation model.

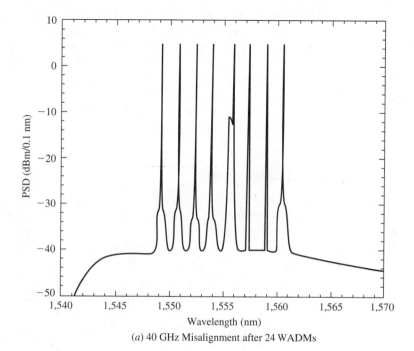

(*a*) 40 GHz Misalignment after 24 WADMs

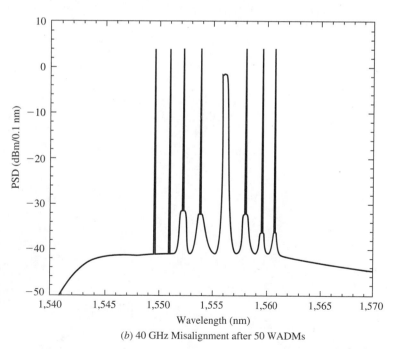

(*b*) 40 GHz Misalignment after 50 WADMs

FIGURE 4.57   Simulation results.

misalignment of 40 GHz in channel 5, which is the end-to-end channel being studied. (The powers shown are totals in a bandwidth of 0.1 nm, which is the bin size.) Despite the misalignment, which places it at the edge of the filter passbands, the variable attenuators are able to maintain uniform signal levels, but at the expense of increasing the noise level in channel 5. This reduces the SNR in that channel to approximately 20 dB, which is more than sufficient to sustain a BER of 10^{-9}. After 50 WADMs, it is impossible to equalize the signal level, and it drops below the noise level. (Similar results for laser misalignments of 30 GHz or less show satisfactory SNRs through the full chain of 50 WADMs.)

4.12.3 Study of WSXC Cross-talk

A more complex simulation is shown in Figure 4.58. Here, the objective is to evaluate the effects of cross-talk in WSXCs when embedded in a network with a mesh topology [Antoniades+98a]. Different WSXC architectures are compared to determine trade-offs between WSXC cost/complexity and cross-talk performance.

The network under study is composed of two wavelength terminal multiplexers (WTMs), three WSXCs, and four WADMs. In our generic terminology, the WTMs correspond to network access stations, the WSXCs to optical network nodes, and the WADMs are combinations of ONNs and NASs because they route connections as well as terminate them. It is an eight-wavelength system, in which one λ-channel (λ_8) is routed on a circuitous path throughout the network to observe the accumulated cross-talk effects in all network elements. The connection of interest passes through elements 9–4–5–6–7–3–4–7–1–2–3–8, in that order. (Note that the path traverses all WSXCs twice.) Three other connections on the same wavelength use portions of the

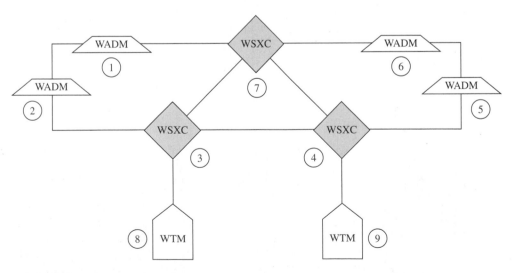

FIGURE 4.58 Network diagram.

same optical path in the reverse direction, being dropped and added at nodes 6 and 5. All eight wavelengths are present on each link.

The architecture of the 4×4 WSXCs is shown in Figure 4.59. It is a generalization of the WADM structure of Figure 4.56, with input and output EDFAs for compensating fiber and cross-connect losses, and variable attenuators for equalizing the eight-channel power levels. Signal power at the output of each input EDFA is maintained near 0 dBm. The architecture follows the generic three-stage structure of Figure 2.22. For performance comparisons, several different fabrics for the 4×4 space switches are tested. The WMUX/WDMUXs are cascades of interference filters, as in the WADMs.

The three alternative switch fabrics are those shown in Figures 4.51 and 4.52. They range from the Benes to the router/selector architecture to the enhanced performance architecture, with 6, 24, and 44 (controllable) components respectively. As discussed in Section 4.11.3, each switch and WADM can contribute a large number of cross-talk terms of various types: interchannel, co-channel heterodyne, and multipath. Each one is a potential interferer on the path of interest. Because of the large number of terms, as well as incomplete information concerning their relative delays, phases, and polarizations, some compromise must be made in simulating cross-talk.

The technique used in the wavelength-domain simulation is to store the most important information about the interferers during the simulation: numbers and powers of dominant terms, and numbers only for "small" terms (i.e., interferers with nonnegligible power but below a given threshold).

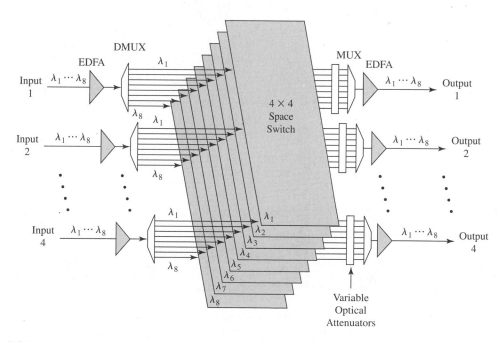

FIGURE 4.59 Wavelength-selective cross-connect.

Results of the simulation for the three different switch fabrics are considered now, focusing on cross-talk only.

4.12.3.1 Benes Switch

Histograms of the cross-talk terms affecting the selected path, as a function of their powers, are shown in Figures 4.60 and 4.61. In the first case, the elementary 2×2 switches in the WSXCs and the WADMs are of the high-cross-talk variety (e.g., LiNbO$_3$

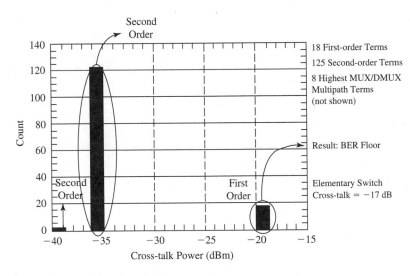

FIGURE 4.60 Benes switch cross-talk: I.

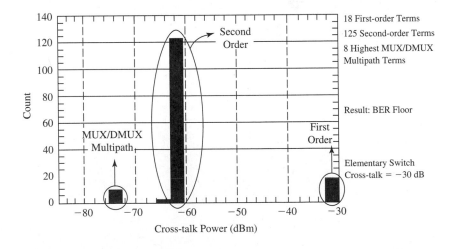

FIGURE 4.61 Benes switch cross-talk: II.

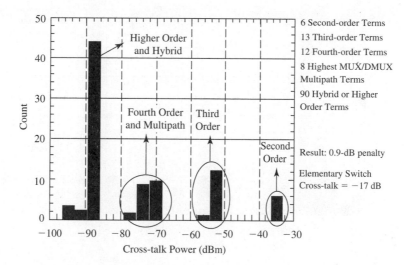

FIGURE 4.62   Router/selector switch cross-talk.

or polymer technology), with an assumed cross-talk of −17 dB, whereas in the second case they are low cross-talk (e.g., optomechanical), with a value of −30 dB. In each case the dominant terms are 18 first-order switch cross-talk terms and 125 second-order terms. The remaining nonnegligible interferers are eight multipath terms through the WMUX/WDMUX's. Note in comparing Figures 4.60 and 4.61 that the power levels of the various terms have been reduced considerably in the second case due to higher quality switches. Nevertheless, when all terms are taken into account, they represent an aggregrate interference that is enough to produce an unacceptable error floor, (above 10^{-9}), even in the case of the −30-dB switches.

4.12.3.2   Router/Selector Switch
The cross-talk terms in this case are shown in Figure 4.62.[32] (Only the case of −17-dB elementary switches is shown.) The switch fabric has now eliminated all first-order terms. As a result, satisfactory performance can be achieved on the selected path, but with a 0.9-dB power penalty. If −30-dB elementary switches had been used, the power penalty would have been unobservable.

4.12.3.3   Enhanced Performance Switch
The cross-talk terms when the enhanced performance WSXC is used (with −17-dB elementary switches) are shown in Figure 4.63. The extra stages have now eliminated all second-order terms. As a result, the highest power interferers are less than −50 dBm. This means that the WMUX/WDMUX multipath terms become relatively

---

[32] The hybrid terms in the figure are due to combinations of switch and WMUX/WDMUX cross-talk.

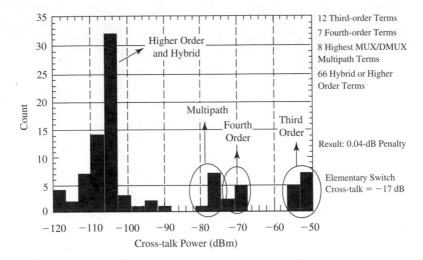

FIGURE 4.63 Enhanced performance switch histogram.

more significant. The power penalty has now been reduced to 0.04 dB, showing that cross-talk effects are now negligible. A price has been paid, however, in additional switch complexity. This result is comparable with the performance of the router/selector switch with −30-dB elementary switches. Which one is preferred depends on additional factors such as component cost, flexibility, reliability, maintainability, and so forth.

Examining these results, we find that the simulation has made it possible to compare the performance of various switch architectures and technologies in a network setting. In cases when acceptable and comparable performance results were obtained, the simulation results offer choices to the network designer, involving trade-offs between switch fabric complexity and component cost, as well as other important but less quantifiable criteria.

4.12.4 Study of Performance Degradations Due to Cross-talk

Both of the previous case studies involved wavelength-domain simulation only; that is, the first step of a two-step process. We now continue with the final, time-domain step, which makes use of the results of the wavelength-domain cross-talk study of Section 4.12.3 [Antoniades+98b].

Consider the selected path through the network that was studied for accumulated cross-talk and noise in the previous section. We now wish to determine how these effects influence the BER. The case considered is the router/selector switch with various cross-talk levels for the elementary switching elements.

The intended signal plus six dominant, second-order cross-talk terms are simulated as shown in the block diagram of Figure 4.64. Each is assigned a phase, an

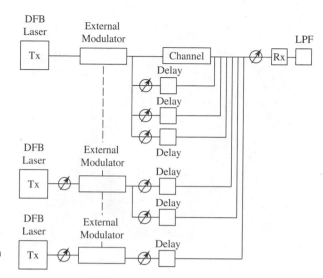

FIGURE 4.64 Time-domain simulation.

optical frequency, and a polarization, all distributed randomly with respect to the signal. A 10-Gbps pseudorandom data sequence intensity modulates each cross-talk term, with different sequence phases for each term, indicated by the external modulator blocks in the figure. Phase noise is included in the resultant signals, and the combined fields are incident on the photodetector. Although the noise due to the ED-FAs is also simulated, its effect is separated from the cross-talk effects, as explained later.

To reduce the computation time, a combined Monte Carlo method (for the cross-talk) and quasi analytical technique (for the noise) is used to determine eye diagrams and BERs. First, a set of noiseless time-domain simulations are run to determine the signal waveforms on the selected path, each run resulting in an eye diagram of the form of Figure 4.65. In each simulation run, the optical frequency, phase, and delay of the various cross-talk components in Figure 4.64 are chosen randomly, as signified by the circled arrows in the figure.

Based on wavelength-domain results for signal, cross-talk, and EDFA noise powers, the receiver noise power is calculated. It includes shot noise, thermal noise, ASE–ASE and signal–ASE beating terms, as well as smaller cross-talk terms not simulated in the time domain. The BER is calculated using a Gaussian assumption for the aggregate photocurrent statistics.

A factor, $Q = \Delta/2\sigma$, is calculated based on choosing the sampling time and the decision threshold optimally, as indicated in Figure 4.27(a). In the expression for Q, Δ is the eye opening $(y_1 - y_2)$, and σ^2 is the noise variance at the output of the low-pass filter, LPF in Figure 4.64. The actual BER calculations are based on Equation 4.41, where Q is replaced by a mean value $\bar{Q}$, averaged over all of the Monte Carlo runs.

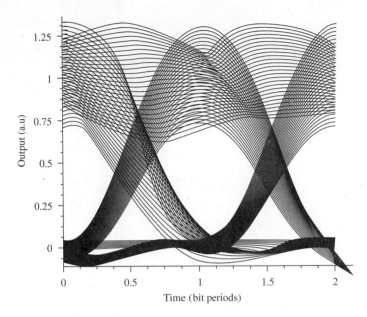

FIGURE 4.65 Eye diagram due to switch cross-talk.

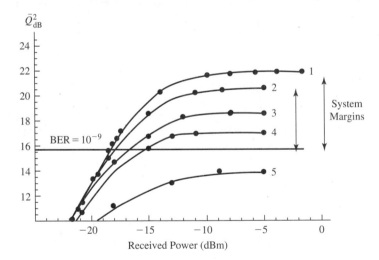

FIGURE 4.66 Calculated Q-factor versus received optical power.

Some typical results of this approach are shown in Figures 4.65 and 4.66 (see [Antoniades+98b]). The eye diagram (see Figure 4.65) corresponds to the case of −13-dBm cross-talk and −5.2-dBm received power. (The received signal power is varied in the simulation by placing an attenuator in front of the photodetector.) The maximum eye opening in the absence of cross-talk interferers is set equal to unity. Due to the effects of multipath cross-talk, the received waveform is distorted, causing the observed eye closure. The thickening of the eye is due to the long data sequence.

In Figure 4.66, $\bar{Q}^2_{dB}$ (rather than BER) is plotted as a function of received signal power for different elementary switch cross-talk levels ranging from -17 dB (curve 2) to -11 dB (curve 5). By examining the values of received power corresponding to BER $= 10^{-9}$ ($\bar{Q}^2_{dB} = 15.4$ dB), we find a power penalty of 2.8 dB for curve 3 (corresponding to -13-dB cross-talk switches). As received power is increased, the curves reach plateaus, which indicate *system margins* for the various cases. Thus, for example, curve 1 (corresponding to no cross-talk) shows a system margin of 5.5 dB. Curve 5, for the poorest elementary switch (cross-talk, -11 dB), falls below the value required for BER $= 10^{-9}$ by approximately 3 dB, and thus indicates an *error floor* above this BER for that case.

These examples, using both wavelength-domain and wavelength/time-domain methodologies, illustrate the role that simulation can play in estimating the performance of large systems subject to complex transmission and switching impairments. (The system in this case study involved 2,558 modules.) Because simulation is accomplished rapidly and efficiently, the results can be used to provide considerable insight to the network designer. To paraphrase Richard W. Hamming [Hamming62], the purpose of simulation is insight, not numbers.

4.13 Problems

1. What is the critical angle, the acceptance angle, and the numerical aperture of a step-index fiber with a core refractive index of 1.47 and a cladding refractive index of 1.44?

2. (Intermodal dispersion) Consider a multimode step-index fiber of length L and refractive indices of n_1 and n_2 for the core and the cladding respectively. The broadening of a pulse injected in such a fiber can be estimated by considering the time difference in the propagation of rays following the shortest and the longest paths to the receiver. If this time difference must be limited to a fraction of the bit period, find the maximum bit rate that can be transmitted through a fiber with the following parameters: $n_1 = 1.47, n_2 = 1.44$, and $L = 10$ km.

3. (Resolution of the Helmholtz equation) Consider a step-index fiber of radius a and refractive indices of n_1 and n_2 for the core and the cladding respectively; assume unbounded cladding. Using separation of variables to solve Equation 4.11, show that any field component can be written in the form

$$U(r, \phi, z, \omega) = \begin{cases} AJ_l(\kappa r)\exp(-jl\phi)\exp(-j\beta z) & r \le a \\ BK_l(\gamma r)\exp(-jl\phi)\exp(-j\beta z) & r > a \end{cases}$$

where A and B are arbitrary amplitude constants, β is the propagation constant, $\kappa^2 = (k^2 - \beta^2)$, $\gamma^2 = \left(\left(\frac{kn_2}{n_1}\right)^2 - \beta^2\right)$, and $J_l(.)$ and $K_l(.)$, respectively, are the Bessel function of the first kind and the modified Bessel function of the second kind of integer order l. (Note that U is a function of ω through the dependence of the solution parameters on the wave-number k.)

4. For a cascade of N independent sources of PMD, where the ith source contributes an average time differential of $\Delta \tau_{\text{PMD}i}$, the overall average time differential is

$$\Delta \tau_{\text{PMD}} = \sqrt{\sum_{i=1}^{N} \Delta \tau_{\text{PMD}i}^2}$$

Suppose an optical path passes through several WSXCs, each one containing a cascade of four lithium niobate switches ($\Delta \tau_{\text{PMD}} = 2$ ps each). What is the maximum number of WSXCs that can be traversed before the PMD becomes significant, if the signals are OC-48? OC-192?

5. A transmission link is composed of fiber with an attenuation of 0.3 dB/km, with EDFAs spaced every 60 km. All EDFAs are identical, with amplifier gain equal to fiber loss on the preceding fiber segment. The amplifier spontaneous emission factor is 1.5. Bandwidths of any optical filters in the link are large compared to the bandwidth (5 GHz) of the low-pass electrical filter preceding the electrical detector. Assume that thermal noise in the receiver is negligible, and that the signal-ASE beat noise is dominant.

   (a) What is the maximum distance a signal with transmitter power of -13 dBm and wave-length of 1,550 nm can propagate before the electrical SNR drops below 20 dB?

   (b) Repeat the calculation if the EDFAs are spaced every 30 km and their gain is adjusted to compensate for the new fiber loss. Assume the same spontaneous emission factor. Comment on the results.

6. (Upper bound on EDFA gain) An optical signal, with average power P_s^{in} and wavelength λ_s and an optical pump with average power P_p^{in} and wavelength λ_p, enter an Erbium-doped fiber. From energy conservation show that an upper bound on the EDF gain is

$$G \leq 1 + \frac{\lambda_p}{\lambda_s} \frac{P_p^{\text{in}}}{P_s^{\text{in}}}$$

7. (APD SNR) A receiver is composed of an avalanche photodiode and a high-impedance front-end. The APD is illuminated with constant optical power, P. The average photocurrent is enhanced by an average multiplication factor $\bar{M}$ compared to the PIN photodiode case.

   The shot noise generated in the photodetection process can be approximated as white Gaussian noise, with a power-spectral density of $q \bar{M}^{2+x} R P$, where q is the electron charge, R is the PIN photodiode responsivity given by Equation 4.35, and x is an excess-noise factor depending on the material (e.g., $x = 0.3$ to 0.5 for silicon APDs). Both the shot and thermal noise are filtered by the low-pass filter composed of the parasitic capacitance of the APD and the load resistance.

Derive the expression for the signal-to-noise ratio at the input of the electronic amplifier and show that there is an optimum value of the average multiplication factor $\bar{M}$ for which the SNR is maximized. Also show that at the shot-noise limit, the PIN photodiode provides better SNR performance than the APD.

8. Suppose that the n ports of the device shown in Figure 4.37 are grouped into n_1 input ports and n_2 output ports, where $n_1 + n_2 = n$. Assume that when optical signals are applied to the input ports only, there are no reflected waves at those ports.

   (a) Derive the relation between the $n_2 \times n_1$ power matrix, A (Equation 2.4), and the scattering matrix.

   (b) Now suppose that the input and output ports are interchanged, and that when optical signals are applied to only the (new) input ports, there are no reflected waves at those ports. Again, derive the relation between the new power transfer matrix, A', and the scattering matrix.

   (c) If the device is reciprocal, show that $A' = A^t$.

9. Consider a passive reciprocal element with $n + 1$ ports. Suppose that when the first port is used as an input and the others are used as outputs, it acts as a $1 : n$ power splitter. Show that, operated in the opposite direction, it is an $n : 1$ combiner with a combining loss of $1/n$.

10. Redo the previous problem in the case in which the element is a $1 : n$ demultiplexer. Show that it is a multiplexer when operated in the opposite direction.

11. (Filter cascading) In large networks, an end-to-end path often traverses many optical filters contained in WSXCs and other components along the path. In this problem, we study the bandwidth-narrowing effects of cascading for two types: FP and MI filters. The (low-pass equivalent) amplitude transfer function of an FP filter can be modeled using a first-order Butterworth function, while an MI filter can be modeled using a third-order Butterworth. The general nth order Butterworth function is defined as

$$|H(f)| = \frac{1}{\sqrt{1 + \left(\frac{f}{f_c}\right)^{2n}}}$$

where f_c is the (3 dB) cut-off frequency.

   (a) Assuming cascades of 10, 20, 30, and 50 filters, plot the overall power-transfer function of the cascades in dB for each filter type.

   (b) Compare the narrowing effects for the two filter types. Which seems more suitable for large-scale networks?

   (c) What is the cut-off frequency of a chain of MI filters with individual cut-off frequency of 100 GHz?

   (d) Comment on the effects of random filter center-frequency misalignments on the effective bandwidth of a cascade of filters. Which of the two types do you think would exhibit the best performance as a result of filter misalignments?

   (e) Comment on how bandwidth narrowing and filter misalignment affect tolerances to laser-tuning errors.

4.14 Bibliography

[Agrawal95] G. P. Agrawal. *Nonlinear Fiber-Optics Communication Systems, Second Edition*. New York: Academic Press, 1995.

[Agrawal97] G. P. Agrawal. *Fiber-Optic Communication Systems: Second Edition* (Wiley Series in Microwave and Optical Engineering). New York: John Wiley & Sons, 1997.

[Amann94] M. C. Amann. Wide tunable lasers for WDM applications. In *Fifth Optoelectronics Conf. Tech. Digest*, pp. 208–209, Makuhari Messe, Japan, July 1994.

[ANSI88] American National Standards Institute. Z136.2: Safe use of optical fiber communication systems utilizing laser diodes and LED sources. ANSI, 1988.

[Antoniades+97] N. Antoniades, I. Roudas, R. E. Wagner, and S. F. Habiby. Simulation of ASE noise accumulation in a wavelength add–drop multiplexer cascade. *IEEE Photonics Technology Letters*, 9(9):1274–1276, 1997.

[Antoniades+98a] N. Antoniades, I. Roudas, R. E. Wagner, J. Jackel, and T. E. Stern. Cross-talk performance of a wavelength selective cross-connect mesh topology. In *Proc. IEEE/OSA Optical Fiber Commun. Conf.*, pp. 61–62, San Jose, February 1998.

[Antoniades+98b] N. Antoniades, I. Roudas, R. E. Wagner, T. E. Stern, J. L. Jackel, and D. H. Richards. Use of wavelength- and time-domain simulation to study performance degradations due to linear optical crosstalk in WDM networks. *OSA Trends in Optics*, 20:288–293, 1998.

[Chraplyvy90] A. R. Chraplyvy. Limitations on lightwave communications imposed by optical fiber nonlinearities. *IEEE/OSA J. Lightwave Technology*, 8:1548–1557, 1990.

[Chraplyvy+95] A. R. Chraplyvy, et al. One-third terabit/s transmission through 150 km of dispersion-managed fiber. *IEEE Photonics Technology Letters*, 7(1):98–107, 1995.

[Clesca+94] B. Clesca, et al. Gain flatness comparison between erbium-doped flouride and silca fiber amplifiers with wavelength-multiplexed signals. *IEEE Photonics Technology Letters*, 6(4):509–512, 1994.

[Delorme+98] F. Delorme, G. Alibert, C. Ougier, S. Slempkes, and H. Nakajima. Sampled-grating DBR lasers with 101 wavelengths over 44 nm and optimized power variation for WDM applications. In *Proc. IEEE/OSA Optical Fiber Commun. Conf.*, pp. 379–381, San Jose, February 1998.

[Desurvire+87] E. Desurvire, J. R. Simpson, and P. C. Becker. High-gain erbium-doped traveling-wave fibre amplifier. *Optics Letters*, 12(11):888, 1987.

[Desurvire94] E. Desurvire. *Erbium-Doped Fiber Amplifiers: Principles and Applications*. New York: John Wiley & Sons, 1994.

[Dias+88] A. R. Dias, R. F. Kalman, J. W. Goodman, and A. A. Sawchuk. Fiber-optic crossbar switch with broadcast capability. *Opt. Eng.*, 27:955–960, 1988.

[Dragone+91] C. Dragone, C. A. Edwards, and R. C. Kestler. Integrated optics $n \times n$ multiplexer on silicon. *Photonics Technology Letters*, 3(10):896–899, 1991.

[Garrett+98] L. D. Garrett and A. H. Gnauck. 8 × 20 Gb/s–315 km, 8 × 10 Gb/s–480 km WDM transmission over conventional fiber using multiple broadband fiber gratings. In *Proc. IEEE/OSA Optical Fiber Commun. Conf.*, p. PD18, San Jose, February 1998.

[Gimlett+89] J. L. Gimlett and N. K. Cheung. Effects of phase-to-intensity noise conversion by multiple reflections on gigabit-per-second DFB laser transmission systems. *IEEE/OSA J. Lightwave Technology*, 7(6):888–895, 1989.

[Gnauk+97] A. H. Gnauk and R. M. Jopson. Dispersion compensation for optical fiber systems. In *Optical Fiber Telecommunications IIIA*. New York: Academic Press, 1997.

[Goldstein+94] E. L. Goldstein, L. Eskildsen, and A. F. Elrefaie. Performance implications of component cross-talk in transparent lightwave networks. *IEEE Photonics Technology Letters*, 6(5):657–670, 1994.

[Hamming62] R. W. Hamming. *Numerical Analysis for Scientists and Engineers*. New York: McGraw-Hill, 1962.

[Henry+88] P. S. Henry, R. A. Linke, and A. H. Gnauk. Introduction to lightwave systems. In *Optical Fiber Telecommunications II*. New York: Academic Press, 1988.

[Hinton93] H. S. Hinton. *An Introduction to Photonic Switching Fabrics*. New York: Plenum Press, 1993.

[Hjelme+98] D. R. Hjelme, H. Storey, and J. Skaar. Reconfigurable all-fiber all-optical cross-connect node using synthesized fiber Bragg gratings for both demultiplexing and switching. In *Proc. IEEE/OSA Optical Fiber Commun. Conf.*, pp. 65–66, San Jose, February 1998.

[Iannone+98] P. P. Iannone, K. C. Reichmann, and N. J. Frigo. Wavelength-dependent modulation effects of light-emitting diodes in multiple-subband passive optical network. In *Proc. IEEE/OSA Optical Fiber Commun. Conf.*, pp. 401–403, San Jose, February 1998.

[Inoue+93] K. Inoue, T. Hasegawa, K. Oda, and H. Toba. Multichannel frequency conversion experiment using fiber four-wave mixing. *Electron. Letters*, 29:1708, 1993.

[Jaggi+98] P. Jaggi and H. Onaka. Optical ADM and cross-connects: Recent technical advancements and future optimal architectures. In *NFOEC*, pp. 311–321, Orlando, September 1998.

[Jopson+91] R. M. Jopson and A.A.M. Saleh. Modeling of gain and noise in erbium-doped fiber amplifiers. *SPIE, 1581 Fiber Laser Sources and Amplifiers III*:114–118, 1991.

[Kaminow+97] I. P. Kaminow and T. L. Koch (editors). *Optical Fiber Communications IIIA and IIIB*. New York: Academic Press, 1997.

[Kato+98] M. Kato, K. Kurokawa, and Y. Miyajima. A new design for dispersion-shifted fiber with an effective core area larger than 100 mum^2 and good bending characteristics. In *Proc. IEEE/OSA Optical Fiber Commun. Conf.*, pp. 301–302, San Jose, February 1998.

[Kazovsky+96] L. Kazovsky, S. Benedetto, and A. Willner. *Optical Fiber Communication Systems*. Norwood, MA: Artech House, 1996.

[Korotky+88] S. K. Korotky and R. C. Alferness. Waveguide electrooptic devices for optical fiber communications. In *Optical Fiber Telecommunications II*. New York: Academic Press, 1988.

[Lee+94] E. A. Lee and D. G. Messerschmitt. *Digital Communication, Second Edition*. Norwell, MA: Kluwer Academic Publishers, 1994.

[Lin98] L. H. Lin. Micromachined free-space matrix switches with submillisecond switching time for large-scale optical cross-connect. In *OFC'98 Technical Digest*, pp. 147–148, San Jose, February 1998.

[Mears+87] R. J. Mears, L. Reekie, I. M. Jauncey, and D. N. Payne. Low-noise erbium-doped fibre amplifier operating at 1.54 μm. *Electron. Letters*, 23(19):1026, 1987.

[Meslener84] G. J. Meslener. Chromatic dispersion-induced distortion of modulated monochromatic light employing direct detection. *IEEE J. Quantum Electronics*, 20(10):1208–1216, 1984.

[Midwinter93a] J. E. Midwinter. *Photonics in Switching, Volume I: Background and Components*. New York: Academic Press, 1993.

[Midwinter93b] J. E. Midwinter. *Photonics in Switching, Volume II: Systems*. New York: Academic Press, 1993.

[Miller+88] S. E. Miller and I. P. Kaminow. *Optical Fiber Telecommunications II*. New York: Academic Press, 1988.

[Mollenauer+92] L. F. Mollenauer, E. Lichtman, G. T. Harvey, M. J. Neubelt, and B. M. Nyman. Demonstration of error-free soliton transmission over more than 15,000 km at 5 Gbit/s, single channel and over 11,000 km at 10 Gbit/s in a two-channel WDM. In *Proc. IEEE/OSA Optical Fiber Commun. Conf.*, Paper PD10, p. 351, Washington, DC, 1992.

[Murashige+98] K. Murashige, T. Miyakawa, H. Taga, et al. Sixty 5.3 Gbit/s 1650 km straight-line WDM transmission. In *Proc. IEEE/OSA Optical Fiber Commun. Conf.*, pp. 48–49, San Jose, February 1998.

[Murphy+97] E. J. Murphy, et al. Enhanced performance switch arrays for optical switching networks. In *Eighth European Conf. on Integrated Optics*, Paper EFD5, Stockholm, April 1997.

[Otani+97] T. Otani, T. Kawazawa, K. Goto, N. Takeda, and S. Akiba. 16 Channel 2.5 Gbit/s WDM transmission experiment over 9000 km by using gain equalised amplifier repeaters. *Electron. Letters*, 33(4):309–310, 1997.

[Patel+95] J. S. Patel and Y. Silberberg. Liquid crystal and grating-based multiple-wavelength cross-connect switch. *IEEE Photonics Technology Letters*, 7(5):514–516, 1995.

[Ramo+94] S. Ramo, J. R. Whinnery, and T. Van Duzer. *Fields and Waves in Communication Electronics, Third Edition*. New York: John Wiley & Sons, 1994.

[Rotolo+95] S. Rotolo, S. Brunazzi, R. Cadeddu, et al. Strategy for a computer-aided analysis of all-optical multiwavelength transparent networks. In *Proc. IEEE/OSA Optical Fiber Commun. Conf.*, pp. 205–206. City??, 1995.

[Roudas+97] I. Roudas, N. Antoniades, R. E. Wagner, and L. D. Garrett. Influence of realistic optical filter characteristics on the performance of multiwavelength optical networks. In *Proc. IEEE/LEOS Annual Mtg.*, pp. 542–543, San Francisco, November 1997.

[Saleh+90] A.A.M. Saleh, R. M. Jopson, J. D. Evankow, and J. Aspell. Modeling of gain in erbium-doped fiber amplifiers. *IEEE Photonics Technology Letters*, 2(10):714–717, 1990.

[Saleh+91] B.E.A. Saleh and M. C. Teich. *Fundamentals of Photonics*. New York: John Wiley & Sons, 1991.

[Scobey+96] M. A. Scobey and D. E. Spock. Passive DWDM components using microplasma optical interference filters. In *OFC '96 Technical Digest*, pp. 242–243, San Jose, February 1996.

[Sharony+92] J. Sharony, K. W. Cheung, and T. E. Stern. Wavelength dialated switches (WDS)— A new class of high-density, suppressed cross-talk, dynamic wavelength routing cross-connects. *IEEE Photonics Technology Letters*, 4(8):933–935, 1992.

[Smith+90] D. A. Smith, J. E. Baran, J. J. Johnson, and K. W. Cheung. Integrated-optic acoustically tunable filters for WDM networks. *IEEE J. Select. Areas Commun.*, 8:1151–1159, 1990.

[Soole+94] J. B. D. Soole and Chung-En Zah. Multiwavelength semiconductor lasers advance rapidly. *Laser Focus World*, June:S9, 1994.

[Spanke87] R. A. Spanke. Architectures for guided-wave optical space switching systems. *IEEE Communications Mag.*, 25(5):42–48, 1987.

[Srivastava+98] A. K. Srivastava, et al. 1 Tb/s transmission of 100 WDM 10 Gb/s channels over 400 km of TrueWave fiber. In *Proc. IEEE/OSA Optical Fiber Commun. Conf.*, Paper PD10, San Jose, February 1998.

[Stern60] T. E. Stern. Some quantum effects in information channels. *IRE Transactions on Information Theory*, IT-6:435–440, 1960.

[Stolen+73] R. H. Stolen and E. P. Ippen. Raman gain in glass optical waveguides. *Appl. Phys. Letters*, 22:276–278, 1973.

[Tsang87] W. T. Tsang. Quantum confinement heterostructure semiconductor lasers. In *Semiconductors and Semimetals*. New York: Academic Press, 1987.

[Vengsarkar+96] A. M. Vengsarkar, et al. Long-period gratings as band-rejection filters. *IEEE/OSA J. Lightwave Technology*, 14(1):58–64, 1996.

[Wagner+96] R. E. Wagner, R. C. Alferness, A.A.M. Saleh, and M. S. Goodman. MONET: Multiwavelength optical networking. *IEEE/OSA J. Lightwave Technology*, 14(6):1349–1355, 1996.

[Yoo+95] S.J.B. Yoo, C. Caneau, R. Bhat, and M. A. Koza. Wavelength conversion by quasi-phase-matched difference frequency generation in AlGaAs waveguides. In *Proc. IEEE/OSA Optical Fiber Commun. Conf.*, paper PD14-2, San Diego, February 1995.

[Yoo96] S.J.B. Yoo. Wavelength conversion technologies for WDM network applications. *IEEE/OSA J. Lightwave Technology*, 14(6):955–966, 1996.

[Yoo+96] S.J.B. Yoo, C. Caneau, R. Bhat, et al. Wavelength conversion by difference frequency generation in AlGaAs waveguides with periodic domain inversion achieved by wafer bonding. *Appl. Phys. Letters*, 68(19):2609–2611, 1996.

CHAPTER FIVE

Static Multipoint Networks

In static networks essentially all functionality resides in the network access stations (NASs). The performance of the network is therefore determined by how the NASs provide logical connectivity and throughput to satisfy the network's traffic requirements.

This chapter explores the performance issues in static networks, viewing them all as special cases of shared media, as described in Section 5.1. The multiplexing and multiple access techniques required to achieve multipoint logical connectivity in these networks are treated in Section 5.2. Sections 5.3 through 5.6 deal with capacity allocation and control to serve prescribed traffic requirements. We first point out some general flow conservation constraints that must be satisfied in any shared-channel system. Then the problems of traffic scheduling and control are discussed in settings with increasing degrees of complexity: dedicated connections (Section 5.4), demand-assigned connections (Section 5.5), and packet switching in the optical layer (Section 5.6). Section 5.7 is a brief description of some representative photonic packet switch proposals using the principles discussed in the chapter.

5.1 Shared Media: The Broadcast Star

The simplest form of a transparent optical network, the *static network*, was defined in Chapter 3 as a collection of fixed (passive) splitting/combining nodes without wavelength selectivity, interconnected by fibers that provide full or partial connectivity among a set of NASs. Of the static networks, the most elementary form is the broadcast star, in which all signals transmitted from the NASs are combined at a star coupler and broadcast to all receivers. We have seen, however, that many seemingly more complex topologies are functionally equivalent to the broadcast star, including folded buses, trees (see Figure 2.6), and embedded rooted trees (see Figure 3.27). Thus, we can consider the broadcast star a fairly general representation of a large family of static networks. Its essential feature is that it acts as a *shared broadcast medium*. This chapter explores in detail the properties of shared-medium networks operated in a broadcast-and-select mode, using the star as a prototypical example.

Before adopting abstract models for these networks, let us first examine a few ways in which a star network might be used in practice. Figure 5.1 shows examples of networks based on broadcast stars. Figure 5.1(a) shows the undirected and directed versions of the star, in which all NASs are connected directly to a star coupler through their access fibers. (These are identical to Figures 2.6(a) and 2.10, except that a general $M \times N$ star is shown in the directed case.) Each NAS may serve several co-located end systems.

When the stations are spread over a fairly wide area (say, 100 km), the most costly components of the network are its fiber links and its NASs. If there is a large number of stations, it may not be cost-effective to run a fiber link directly from the star coupler to each station. Instead, a more economical approach is to divide the overall network into a high-capacity backbone (the star coupler and its access links) and several lower capacity *local access networks*. This would be especially suitable for a network serving several separate but densely populated clusters of end users. Each access network connects a number of end systems through a tree to a point of access to the star backbone, as shown in Figures 5.1(b) and 5.1(c). At each node of the access network, traffic from two or more sources is multiplexed onto a link carrying it *upstream* to the star, so that all traffic generated in one access network is concentrated onto a single fiber accessing the star. Similarly, each outbound access fiber on the star carries traffic *downstream* to an access network, which in turn distributes it to the various destination points. The access network can be configured in several different ways.

An electronic approach is shown in Figure 5.1(b). The access network connects a set of end systems via electronic concentrating nodes to an NAS located at the access point to the star backbone. The traffic on the local access network might be in the form of continuous streams, ATM cells, or IP packets. In the undirected case, the network is bidirectional, and the concentrators perform an electronic multiplexing function upstream and a demultiplexing function downstream. Because demultiplexing is performed at the concentrators, each end system receives only the information destined for it. A directed star would be accessed by unidirectional concentrating networks serving the transmitting nodes, and distribution networks serving the receiving nodes.

An optical approach is shown in Figure 5.1(c). Comparing Figure 5.1(c) to Figure 5.1(b), we see that the electronic concentrators and the NAS accessing the backbone are replaced by optical network nodes, which (in the undirected case) are comprised of pairs of fixed (passive) optical splitters and combiners. The end systems are now interfaced to the local access network through NASs. Signals from the end systems are multiplexed and converted to optical form in the NASs, and the optical signals from the NASs are combined in the tree so that all transmitted traffic from an access network is concentrated on a single upstream fiber accessing the star coupler. Conversely,

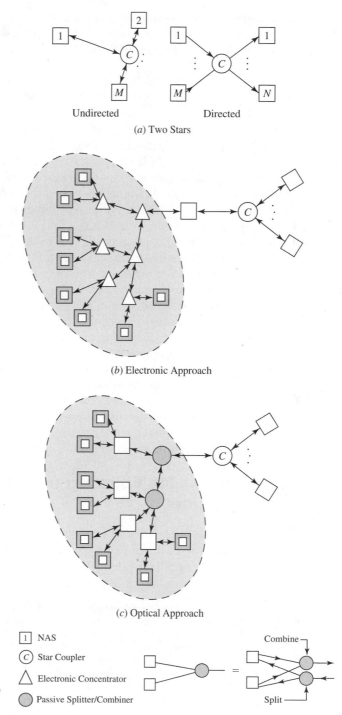

(a) Two Stars

(b) Electronic Approach

(c) Optical Approach

FIGURE 5.1 Local access to star networks.

optical signals carrying traffic on a downstream fiber from the star are distributed to all stations on the access network connected to that fiber, using fixed splitters at each node of the tree.[1] (A directed version of this network would use separate combining and splitting trees.)

Although we have assumed that the star coupler and its access nodes are fixed devices, the whole backbone network might be *embedded* on a larger optical infrastructure, as in Figure 3.27. In this case the star coupler and its access nodes would be linear divider combiners (LDCs) configured to create the equivalent of a broadcast star. Using waveband-selective LDCs, the embedded star could be arranged to operate on a prescribed portion of the available optical spectrum (one or more wavebands), with the spectrum allocation chosen to suit the traffic requirements.

It is important to observe the differences between the access configurations as far as network operation is concerned. In the case of either no local access network or an electronic access network—see Figures 5.1(a) and 5.1(b)—the backbone network sees essentially the same thing: a set of NASs connected directly to its star coupler, with the same number of NASs in each case. The required logical connectivity among the NASs may be either point to point or multipoint, with multipoint connections generally required in the case of Figure 5.1(b) because many individual end systems are connected to each NAS.

Things are very different when the local access network is purely optical. The backbone network sees all NASs in the access networks as if they were connected directly to the star coupler. The result is an equivalent broadcast star with a much larger number of NASs. The optical multiplexing and multiple access techniques used on the star in its original form must now be extended back to the stations on all the leaves of the access trees. This arrangement would normally be more costly than the electronic one, assuming that NASs are more expensive than electronic concentrators. However, this approach would have more capacity and flexibility because there are no electronic bottlenecks in the access networks.

5.2 Representative Multiplexing and Multiple Access Schemes

Multiplexing and multiple access play an essential role in a shared-medium network because this is the only way multiple logical connections (LCs) can be supported by the network. Therefore, as a prelude to a more general discussion of shared-medium

---

[1] One technical problem associated with the optical approach is the fact that the signal powers from each transmitting NAS may not be equal after they are combined on the upstream access fiber, due to the fact that they may experience different combining losses at the access network nodes and different attenuation along the access network fibers. In principle it is possible to adjust the combining ratios at each node and/or insert optical amplifiers to ensure power equality and maintain satisfactory power levels. However, it may be impractical to do so (see Section 6.5.7). This problem occurs in all passive tree networks.

networks, we first discuss some typical multiplexing and multiple access techniques in an optical broadcast-and-select environment.

Although multiplexing and multiple access have a long history, it is important to review their essential characteristics in the context of optical networks. Because the constraints of optical and electronic technologies are quite different, the advantages and disadvantages of various techniques in the optical domain are quite different than in the traditional electronic domain. Time– and wavelength–division multiplexing and multiple access were introduced in Section 3.2.1, where it was pointed out that wavelength–division techniques alone cannot provide the degree of logical connectivity that is required in a large network. Of the many possibilities for creating high logical connectivity, we consider four representative schemes here: TDM/TDMA, TDM/T-WDMA, subcarrier multiplexing and multiple access (SCM/SCMA), and code–division multiple access (CDMA).

The first two are treated together because TDM/TDMA is a special case of TDM/T-WDMA operating on one λ-channel. All of these except CDMA are orthogonal techniques, characterized by the fact that signals accessing a common medium are nonoverlapping in time and/or optical frequency. CDMA is a quasi orthogonal technique, requiring considerably more signal processing and transmission bandwidth than the other three techniques, but which is sometimes advantageous in situations involving large numbers of low-throughput users (typical of optical packet-switching applications).

Our discussion focuses on dedicated connections carrying stream-type traffic, with some digressions for packet-switched traffic when appropriate.

5.2.1 Time–Wavelength–Division Multiplexing/Multiple Access

In Section 3.2.1 we showed how several LCs can be maintained simultaneously on a 3×3 broadcast star by time sharing one or more λ-channels. To illustrate the fundamental features of TDM/T-WDMA, we expand on that example now.

Let us recall from Section 3.2.1 that the four ingredients necessary for realizing multipoint logical connectivity in a TDM/T-WDMA system operating on a shared broadcast medium are

- Transmission channel multiplexing in the transmitting stations using TDM
- Optical broadcast on the shared medium
- Optical multiple access using T-WDMA
- Transmission channel demultiplexing in the receiving stations

Suppose the shared medium is an $M \times N$ directed star, and we have C λ-channels available to carry the connections. For simplicity we focus on the case in which all optical transmitters (OTs) operate at a common bitrate R_t bits per second, and each

LC is point to point. This still allows for one-to-many and many-to-one logical connectivity, but rules out logical multicast connections. Each connection carries stream traffic at a prescribed bitrate, and we wish to provide dedicated connections by allocating fixed transmission capacities that match the flow requirements. In this case the traffic may be characterized by a set of MN prescribed flows, described in terms of an $M \times N$ *traffic matrix*: $\Gamma = [\gamma_{ij}]$. Each entry γ_{ij} represents the flow requirement on an LC between the source i and destination j in bits per second. (The matrix Γ alone is *not* sufficient to characterize logical *multicast* connections [see Section 5.4.1.4].) The total traffic represented by Γ is

$$\bar{\gamma} \equiv \sum_{ij} \gamma_{ij} \qquad (5.1)$$

The connections are carried on transmission channels multiplexed according to a fixed-frame schedule with L equal-size time slots. The channel–slot allocations can be expressed as a $C \times L$ *channel allocation schedule* (CAS). If c_{ij} is the number of channel–slots allocated to connection $[i, j]$, then this represents a capacity allocation of $R_t c_{ij}/L$ bits per second, which is the effective bitrate of that connection. Because c_{ij} is an integer, the basic quantum of capacity available in a fixed-frame system with frame length L is R_t/L bits per second.

To avoid information loss the CAS must be collisionless (no more than one transmitter may use the same channel in the same time slot) and conflict free. For stations equipped with single receivers, conflicts occur if more than one station transmits to the same receiver in the same time slot. (For a destination station with β receivers, as many as β transmissions are allowed to that station in the same time slot, but they must all be on distinct channels.)

The parameters R_t and C are limited by technological constraints. Thus, there is a limit on transmitter bitrate: $R_t \leq R_{max}$, set by the speed of the electronics, the modulation bandwidth of the laser transmitters, and the capacity of the λ-channels. Similarly, the number of channels, C, is limited by the available optical spectrum and the feasible channel-packing density. Finally, the functionality of the NASs (number of transmitters/receivers and their tunability) determines the scheduling options within a frame. The totality of these constraints determines whether it is possible to find a CAS that satisfies a given traffic requirement, Γ. To illustrate this point we return to the undirected 3×3 network of Figure 3.5, redrawn for convenience in Figure 5.2.

Let the traffic matrix be expressed as $\Gamma = R_0 T$, where Γ has been decomposed into a normalized (dimensionless and integer-valued) traffic matrix T multiplied by a scalar constant R_0 (bits per second), called the *basic bitrate*. We denote the total normalized traffic as

$$\bar{T} \equiv \sum_{ij} t_{ij} \qquad (5.2)$$

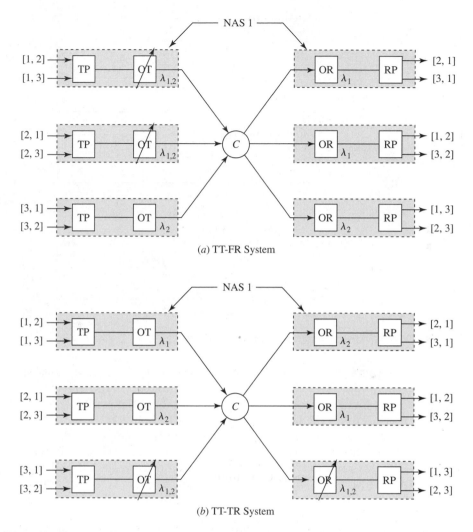

FIGURE 5.2   A 3 × 3 example.

Three cases of normalized traffic matrices and their corresponding CASs are provided in Figure 5.3. In each case, the number of channel–slots c_{ij} allocated to an LC is equal to the normalized traffic requirement t_{ij}. Now, equating the capacity allocation $R_t c_{ij}/L$ to the flow requirement $R_0 t_{ij}$, and using the fact that $c_{ij} = t_{ij}$, we find that to provide the required capacity, each transmitter must operate at a rate

$$R_t = R_0 L \tag{5.3}$$

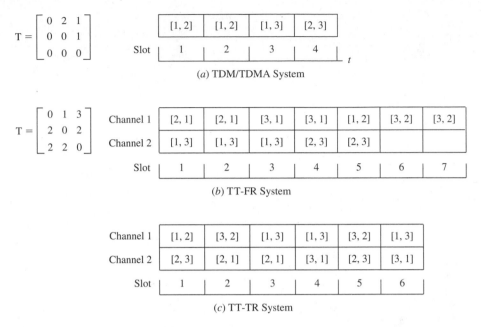

FIGURE 5.3 TDM/T-WDMA channel allocation schedules.

Equation 5.3 represents an acceleration of R_t relative to R_0. This results in a "speed-up" factor, R_t/R_0, which is equal to the frame length L for the channel–slot allocation; in other words, the longer the frame the higher the required transmitter speed. Let us see how this works out for the cases presented in Figure 5.3.

In Figure 5.3(a), the normalized traffic specified in the matrix T is to be carried using TDM/TDMA; that is, using a single λ-channel. A suitable CAS is shown in the figure. (Note that the traffic distribution and slot schedule corresponds to that shown in Figure 3.7.) Because this CAS requires a frame of length $L = 4$, each transmitter must operate at a bitrate of $R_t = 4R_0$. If this value exceeds R_{max}, the traffic cannot be supported by the network.

The remaining two cases in Figure 5.3 represent TDM/T-WDMA networks with different traffic requirements, and with two channels, operating on wavelengths λ_1 and λ_2. Stations are considered with varying degrees of tunability, and it is assumed in all cases that each station has a single transceiver.

A nonuniform normalized traffic matrix is shown in Figure 5.3(b). The objective now is to focus on the tunability options when $C = 2$ channels are available. The figure shows a possible CAS for a TT-FR system in which receivers 1 and 2 are both permanently tuned to channel 1, and receiver 3 is tuned to channel 2. Transmitting stations 1 and 2 tune over both channels, and transmitter 3 is fixed–tuned to channel 2. Figure 5.2(a) shows the system, indicating the tuning of the various OTs and ORs.

Note that the schedule has a length $L = 7$, and that two channel-slots are empty. Because they are both tuned to the same channel, the ORs in stations 1 and 2 capture all data on channel 1. Thus, the information destined for each station must be selected at the electronic level using synchronized gates in their reception processors (RPs). This schedule requires a transmitter bitrate of $R_t = 7R_0$. For example, if the basic bitrate is $R_0 = 500$ Mbps, then each transmitter must run at a rate $R_t = 3.5$ Gbps.

For this example, no TT-FR schedule can produce a frame length shorter than 7, and no FT-TR schedule can produce a frame length shorter than 8. Why? To obtain a more efficient schedule we must move to TT-TR. In this case, a possible 6-slot schedule for the normalized traffic of Figure 5.3(b) is shown in Figure 5.3(c). Only the transceiver in station 3 is required to be tunable; transmitters 1 and 2 are tuned permanently to channels 1 and 2 respectively. Similarly, receivers 1 and 2 are tuned permanently to channels 2 and 1 respectively (see Figure 5.2[b]). The required transmitter bitrate of $R_t = 6R_0$ is an improvement over the TT-FR case, allowing the prescribed traffic to be carried with slower transmitters. Alternatively, the throughput can be "scaled up" by maintaining the same transmitter speed and increasing R_0 by a factor of $7/6$.

Whenever tunability is required, wavelength-selectable arrays of transmitters or receivers can be used instead of tunable devices. (These are arrays with only one transmitter or receiver enabled at a time.) Thus, in the TT-TR case, the same CAS can be realized with arrays of two transmitters and two receivers in station 3, and single fixed transceivers in the other stations.

In the previous examples, C was taken to be fixed. However, it is often of interest to consider trade-offs between the number of channels used and the resultant traffic-handling capacity of the network. For illustration, consider an undirected $M \times M$ broadcast star network, where $M = 81$. We require full logical connectivity (without loopback connections) with uniform traffic; in other words, the traffic matrix is $\Gamma = R_0 T$, where $t_{ij} = 1$ for $i \neq j$ and is zero otherwise. Using an FT-TR system with $C = 81$, a CAS can be obtained that is a direct generalization of the 3×3 case of Figure 3.8(b)—see Figure 5.4(a). In this case the traffic can be scheduled in a frame of length $L = (M - 1) = 80$.

Now, suppose only three channels are available. Continuing in the FT-TR mode, let us partition the set of stations into three subsets containing 27 stations each, and assign one channel to all transmitting stations in the same subset. For example, assign channel k to station j, where $k = 1 + [(j - 1) \bmod 3]$. With these assignments, each transmitting station owns a channel, but there is an r-fold *reuse* of the channels, where $r = M/C$. It is still possible to schedule the traffic, provided that we observe the constraint that all stations transmitting in the same time slot must use distinct channels. A possible CAS for this case is shown in Figure 5.4(b), where $r = 27$ and a frame of length $L = r(M - 1) = 2{,}160$ is now required. Because each station is active for only $1/r$ of the time, the distinct channel constraint, which is required to avoid collisions, translates into an r-fold increase in frame length. This results in a reduction of aggregate throughput by a factor of r unless transmission speed R_t is increased by the same factor.

These examples were designed to show how traffic can be scheduled in a TDM/T-WDMA system while accounting for the various system constraints. A general treatment of scheduling in shared-channel systems is presented in Section 5.4.

Channel 1	[1, 2]	[1, 3]	$\cdots$		$\cdots$	
Channel 2	[2, 3]	[2, 4]	$\cdots$			
Channel 3	[3, 4]	[3, 5]	$\cdots$			
Channel 4	[4, 5]	[4, 6]	$\cdots$			
	$\vdots$	$\vdots$				
Slot	1	2	3		$\cdots$	

t

(a)

Channel 1	[1, 2]	[1, 3]	[1, 4]	$\cdots$	[4, 1]	[4, 2]	[4, 3]	$\cdots$	[7, 1]	$\cdots$
Channel 2	[2, 3]	[2, 4]	[2, 5]	$\cdots$	[5, 2]	[5, 3]	[5, 4]	$\cdots$	[8, 2]	$\cdots$
Channel 3	[3, 4]	[3, 5]	[3, 6]	$\cdots$	[6, 3]	[6, 4]	[6, 5]	$\cdots$	[9, 3]	$\cdots$
Slot	1	2	3	$\cdots$	81	82	83	$\cdots$	161	$\cdots$

(b)

FIGURE 5.4 Illustrating channel reuse in an FT-TR system.

5.2.1.1 Scheduling Efficiency

The previous section illustrates certain relations among traffic requirements, network resources (available channels), and station functionality (maximum bitrates and transceiver tunability) in shared-channel systems. There is an obvious trade-off between bitrates and the number of available channels. More channels means lower required bitrates, with the pure TDM/TDMA (single-channel) system requiring the highest bitrate. However, the required value of R_t also depends on how efficiently the traffic is scheduled. To quantify this idea, let us define *scheduling efficiency* η_s as the ratio of the total traffic requirement to the total capacity used to carry it:

$$\eta_s \equiv \bar{\gamma}/R_t C \tag{5.4}$$

Using Equations 5.3 and 5.2 we find that Equation 5.4 can also be expressed as

$$\eta_s = \bar{T}/LC \tag{5.5}$$

It can be seen from these expressions that $\eta_s = 1$ when the available channels are fully occupied; that is, when there are no idle slots in the frame. All schedules presented earlier had $\eta_s = 1$ except for the TT-FR network of Figure 5.3(b), which had $\eta_s = 6/7$. A well-balanced traffic matrix and/or a high degree of transceiver tunability permit CASs with high scheduling efficiency. Maximizing η_s minimizes the frame length L, and hence minimizes the transmitter bitrate required to support the given aggregate traffic. The interrelations among traffic requirements, system resources, and scheduling efficiency are discussed more generally in Section 5.4.1.

5.2.1.2 Transmission Constraints: Optical Spectral Efficiency

We have seen that the total capacity of a shared-channel system is given by $R_t C$ (in bits per second). Assuming that this capacity is realized within a limited optical bandwidth, a high capacity requires high-speed channels *and* a high channel-packing density. Both of these parameters are limited by many physical constraints. They include the following (see Chapter 4):

- *Laser characteristics:* modulation bandwidth, linewidth, chirp, and wavelength stability
- *Transmission impairments:* fiber dispersion, nonlinearities, and attenuation
- *Receiver characteristics:* optical filter imperfections, and receiver noise and detection method (direct or coherent)
- *Signal processing:* electronic speed limitations and modulation techniques used in the TPs/RPs

Even though these represent a complex set of interrelated constraints, their overall effect at the network level can be subsumed into a single parameter: the *optical spectral efficiency*, which we define as

$$\eta_{\text{op}} \equiv R_t C / B_{\text{op}} \quad \text{(bps/Hz)} \tag{5.6}$$

where B_{op} is the total optical bandwidth occupied by the shared-channel system. The parameter η_{op} represents the throughput of the shared-channel system *per unit of optical bandwidth*, assuming that all channels are utilized fully (i.e., $\eta_s = 1$). Combining scheduling efficiency and optical spectral efficiency we have a relation between total throughput and system bandwidth:

$$\bar{\gamma} = \eta_s \eta_{\text{op}} B_{\text{op}} \tag{5.7}$$

To understand the factors influencing optical spectral efficiency in the context of TDM/T-WDMA, we must examine the spectral characteristics of the signals at several points in the system. Suppose a set of access stations shares a set of C λ-channels running at optical frequencies $v_1, v_2, \ldots, v_C$. Figure 5.5(a) shows the structure of station j, where a number of LCs, $[j, 1], [j, 2], \ldots, [j, k], \ldots$ are time–division multiplexed onto a common transmission signal at point a in the figure. The multiplexed signal is used to modulate the laser transmitter OT. Any digital modulation format can be used as long as it is compatible with the characteristics of the laser modulator and the ORs. Consider a single LC $[j, k]$, and assume that it occupies one or more slots on a fixed λ-channel at optical frequency v_n. Also assume for simplicity that the data symbols are binary, so that each transmitted symbol carries 1 bit

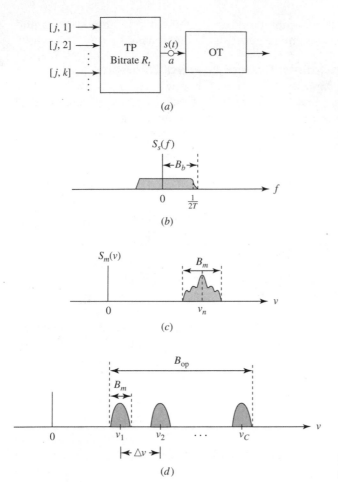

FIGURE 5.5 Illustrating optical spectral efficiency.

of information in a symbol interval of T seconds for a *symbol rate* of $1/T = R_t$. Then the baseband power spectral density (PSD) $S_s(f)$ of a signal $s(t)$ carrying one of the multiplexed connections appears as shown in Figure 5.5(b). Note that it occupies an electrical bandwidth $B_b > 1/2T$, where $1/2T$ is the Nyquist frequency, which determines the minimum possible spectral width for this signal. The PSD $S_m(v)$ of the modulated optical signal at the output of the laser transmitter is shown in Figure 5.5(c).

The shape of $S_m(v)$ and its bandwidth B_m varies considerably, depending on effects at the electrical (transmission channel) level and the optical level. At the electrical level, the bandwidth of the signal modulating the laser depends on the modulation format used for the original data. Some formats (e.g., OOK and phase-shift keying [PSK]) are bandwidth conserving; others (e.g., frequency-shift keying [FSK] and CDMA) are bandwidth expanding. Furthermore if this signal is used to intensity modulate the optical carrier, there will be a bandwidth expansion introduced by the nonlinearity of the modulation process (see Section 5.2.2.2). To this must be added additional bandwidth expansion factors introduced by two laser characteristics: (1) the linewidth of the unmodulated laser and (2) the chirp (optical frequency modulation) introduced when the laser is modulated directly (see Section 4.5.2.1).

Given R_t and B_m, the spectral efficiency of a digital modulation scheme is defined as

$$\eta_m = R_t/B_m \quad \text{(bps/Hz)} \tag{5.8}$$

In "ideal" cases, in which bandwidth-conserving modulation methods are used, laser linewidth is negligible, external modulation is employed, and reception is via coherent detection, it is possible to obtain values of η_m on the order of 1 bps/Hz. On the other hand, typical implementations using direct intensity modulation and direct detection $(\text{IM/DD})^2$ have efficiencies that are small fractions of the ideal.

When multiple stations are active using WDMA, the complete system PSD appears as in Figure 5.5(d). Note that C separate spectral components are shown centered at the available optical frequencies, which are spaced equally at intervals of $\Delta\nu$ Hertz. In the case of fixed–tuned transmitters with distinct frequencies assigned to each transmitter, these would correspond to the spectra of individual transmitters. In other cases (tunable transmitters and/or fixed–tuned transmitters time sharing the same channels), each separate component might represent a superposition of signals from more than one station. The value of $\Delta\nu$ is chosen to ensure that the individual spectral components do not overlap ($\Delta\nu > B_m$), and to allow for a guardband, which is essential for providing tolerance for laser frequency drift and imperfections in receiver tuning and filtering. (In practice, the guardband might be one or more orders of magnitude greater than the signal spectral width to allow for component manufacturing tolerances and parameter drift over time.)

In this system the total occupied optical bandwidth is $B_{\text{op}} = C\Delta\nu$, so that we have an optical spectral efficiency of

$$\eta_{\text{op}} = R_t/\Delta\nu < \eta_m \tag{5.9}$$

Clearly, highest performance is achieved when both optical spectral efficiency and scheduling efficiency are high. However, these come at a price. The former requires high-quality optical transceivers, and the latter requires rapid transceiver tunability or the use of laser and/or detector arrays, all of which are costly.

Although TDM/T-WDMA has been discussed as a specific multiplexing and multiple access technique using the λ-channel as the basic information-carrying medium, the basic concepts used in this section apply to any multichannel scheme. The subcarrier and CDMA techniques discussed next provide alternative ways of "carving" channels out of the optical spectrum.

---

[2] Direct detection precludes the use of optical phase information, which prevents the use of certain bandwidth-conserving modulation schemes such as PSK (see Section 2.4.2).

5.2.2 Subcarriers

Combined TDM and T-WDMA techniques are effective ways of achieving a high degree of multipoint logical connectivity while maintaining high aggregate throughput. However, their station complexity (and cost) tends to increase rapidly with the number of required connections. High connectivity requires many (and therefore densely packed) λ-channels, and rapidly tunable, highly stable transceivers (or large transceiver arrays) and/or very high-speed channels. Each of these requirements is costly. Therefore it is important to seek ways of supporting multipoint LCs without expensive or highly replicated optical or electro-optic components. An interesting approach is SCM and SCMA. In subcarrier systems, an additional level of modulation/demodulation is introduced electronically using microwave subcarriers. In this way, operations that are costly at the optical level (e.g., rapid tunability) can be replaced by electronic operations at the transmission channel level. Replacement of optics by electronics is the main advantage of the subcarrier approach, especially when cost is the primary issue. Subcarriers were used in some of the earliest fiber optic transmission systems: most notably in distribution of multiplexed cable television (CATV) signals.[3] They are currently being proposed for use on optical backbones for wireless personal communication systems.

Subcarrier techniques can be used by themselves or in combination with other multiplexing/multiple-access methods. In this section we discuss several configurations in which subcarriers are used as part of a shared-channel multiplexed/multiple-access system to support multipoint logical connectivity. Three possibilities are described: TDM/T-SCMA, SCM/SCMA, and SCM/WDMA/SCMA. We begin with a description and analysis of SCMA.

5.2.2.1 Principles of SCMA

Subcarrier multiple access provides the means for supporting many-to-one logical connectivity using only electronic signal processing in the NASs. For illustration, consider a directed 4×4 broadcast star SCMA network in which all stations are configured to support potential full bipartite logical connectivity. Figure 5.6 shows an example in which each transmitting station operates on an optical frequency ν_j and a *subcarrier frequency* f_j. (The required values of the ν_js are discussed in Section 5.2.2.2.) As in any broadcast network, one-to-many connectivity is achievable because of the signal splitting at the star coupler. For many-to-one connectivity, the ORs must be wideband so that all optical signals are picked up by the receivers, and thus *all* subcarrier frequencies are present in the photocurrent at the output of the OR. Any desired LC can be created at a receiving station by selecting the corresponding subcarriers, an operation that is executed in the station's RP.

Figure 5.7 shows the structure of the transmitting and receiving stations in more detail for a 4×4 network. Each transmitting station, see Figure 5.7(a), has a fixed–tuned

---

[3] One of the reasons for the appeal of subcarrier techniques is that the supporting microwave technology is mature and inexpensive due to the fact that it has been used widely in CATV systems for many years.

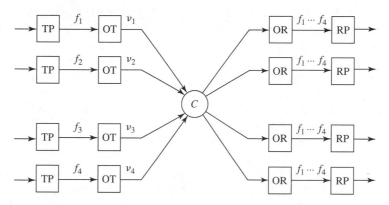

FIGURE 5.6 SCMA example.

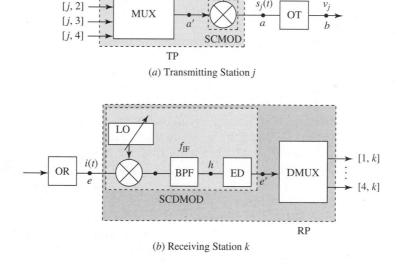

(a) Transmitting Station j

(b) Receiving Station k

FIGURE 5.7 Transmitting and receiving stations equipped for SCMA.

OT, with station j operating on a λ-channel at optical frequency ν_j. If transmitting station j is supporting full connectivity to all four receiving stations, then four LCs— $[j, 1]$, $[j, 2]$, $[j, 3]$, and $[j, 4]$—destined for the corresponding receiving stations are multiplexed onto a common data signal at point a' in Figure 5.7(a). (For the moment, the type of multiplexing used is irrelevant.)

The information carried may be digital, analog, or a combination of both in the case of multiple logical channels. Now, instead of using the data to modulate the laser directly, in SCMA it is first translated from baseband to a microwave subcarrier frequency by an electronic modulator (labeled SCMOD in the figure), which we consider to be part of the TP. The modulated subcarrier signal $s_j(t)$ appears at point a in Figure 5.7(a). A wide variety of modulation formats can be used in the modulator, employing standard electronic techniques. For analog signals, single sideband AM might be used to conserve microwave bandwidth, whereas FM would be used to reduce the effects of noise. For digital signals the options range from bandwidth-conserving techniques such as PSK to bandwidth-expanding methods including FSK and CDMA (see Section 5.2.3).

In typical SCMA systems, the signal $s_j(t)$ intensity modulates the laser, which is operating at a fixed optical frequency ν_j. (Direct modulation is currently most common because it is less costly, but external modulation is also used.) To fix ideas, suppose that digital data are impressed on the subcarrier using quadrature phase-shift keying (QPSK), so that the modulated subcarrier signal is of the form

$$s_j(t) = \sum_{l=-\infty}^{\infty} u(t - lT) \cos(2\pi f_j t + \phi_l) \tag{5.10}$$

where

$$u(t) = \begin{cases} 1, & -T/2 < t \le T/2 \\ 0, & \text{otherwise} \end{cases} \tag{5.11}$$

In Equation 5.10, T is the symbol interval, $u(t)$ is a rectangular pulse,[4] and the phase ϕ_l is drawn from the set $\{0, \pi/2, -\pi/2, \pi\}$ and carries 2 bits of data. The subcarrier frequency f_j (in Hertz) is assumed to be fixed at this point, so that the transmitted signal has a *pair* of carrier frequencies: f_j and ν_j. (Tunable subcarrier frequencies appear in some of the multiplexing and multiple-access methods described in Section 5.2.2.3.)

On the receiving side (illustrated by receiving station k in Figure 5.7[b]), an optical signal consisting of a superposition of all transmitted signals is received and converted to electrical form in a direct-detection OR using a wideband photodetector capable of detecting all transmitted λ-channels. (Because the photodetector is wideband, OR tunability is not an issue.) It is then the function of the subcarrier demodulator and demultiplexers in the RP to select the data signals destined for the receiver. The first stage of the selection process is subcarrier demodulation, translating the modulated subcarrier signal back to baseband at point e' in Figure 5.7(b). The photocurrent $i(t)$ is first downconverted by mixing with a signal generated by a tunable local oscillator so that the signal carried on a selected subcarrier frequency is translated to a fixed intermediate frequency f_{IF}. The desired signal is selected at point h using a bandpass filter centered at f_{IF}, and is then converted to baseband by an electronic detector. The combination of local oscillator, mixer, bandpass filter, and electronic detector constitute the tunable subcarrier demodulator. Depending on the details of the

---

[4] This is a slight simplification. In subcarrier systems it is important to conserve electrical bandwidth. But a rectangular pulse has infinite bandwidth, so that in real systems $u(t)$ would be "shaped" to produce a signal that is appropriately bandlimited.

multiplexing/multiple-access method being used, additional processing may occur in the demultiplexer shown in Figure 5.7(b). Note that this is the classical heterodyne configuration, similar to that used in both radio receivers and coherent optical receivers.

The modulated subcarrier signal $s_j(t)$ is a bandpass signal that occupies an *electrical* bandwidth B_j. Because the signals from all transmitting stations must be distinguishable in the photocurrent at the receiving station (point e in Figure 5.7[b]), some sort of orthogonality (or quasi orthogonality) must be maintained at the electrical level; i.e., the subcarrier level. (Orthogonality on the *electrical* level is required because the wideband photodetector cannot separate the superimposed signals at the optical level.) Typically, distinct subcarrier frequencies are used by all transmitting stations, with the frequencies spaced apart far enough so that the signal spectra from all transmitters are nonoverlapping in electrical frequency.[5]

Assuming that the electrical frequency bands do not overlap to ensure orthogonality, the aggregate bandwidth occupied by all active subcarrier signals combined is $B_T \geq \sum_j B_j$—see Figure 5.8(a) showing a case where $B_j = B$ for all j. The value of B_T cannot exceed the maximum modulation frequency of the laser (assuming direct modulation). The highest subcarrier frequency is also limited by fiber dispersion. Dispersion causes the relative phases of the sidebands in the optical signal to be modified as the signal propagates along the fiber. As a result, the subcarrier intensity modulation is attenuated and replaced by phase modulation (which cannot be observed in a direct-detection receiver [see Section 4.3.2.3]).

Each transmitting station can operate at a different bitrate and use a different subcarrier modulation format as long as the spectra of all modulated subcarriers fit into the total bandwidth B_T without overlapping. This is a fundamental limitation of SCMA, and it means that *the aggregate bandwidth of the signals from all transmitting stations is limited by the maximum allowable modulation frequency of the transmitter.* Thus, for subcarrier applications using direct modulation, lasers with especially large modulation bandwidths are required. (Typical values are 20 GHz, corresponding to aggregate network throughputs on the order of 20 Gbps.) This situation corresponds closely to TDMA, in which the aggregate throughput is limited by the maximum transmitter bitrate $R_{\max}$, which is in turn limited by the maximum allowable modulation frequency of the laser transmitter. But SCMA contrasts sharply with WDMA, in which the laser modulation bandwidth only limits the bandwidth of its own transmitted data signal, so that lasers with modulation bandwidths on the order of 1 GHz are sufficient.

5.2.2.2 Spectra

A quantitative performance analysis of subcarrier systems requires a closer look at their spectral characteristics. Let us continue with the 4×4 example, assuming that each modulated subcarrier $s_j(t)$ has bandwidth B. If all subcarrier frequencies are spaced equally, the spectral densities $S_s^{(j)}(f)$ of the modulated subcarriers appear as in Figure 5.8(a). Each signal $s_j(t)$ intensity modulates its laser to give the combined

---

[5] Orthogonality could be maintained in other ways. For example, the electrical spectrum could be shared among the different transmitting stations using TDMA, CDMA, or other techniques.

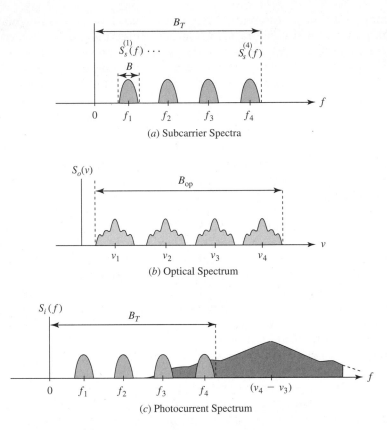

FIGURE 5.8 Subcarrier spectra.

optical PSD $S_o(\nu)$ shown in Figure 5.8(b). Although the optical carrier frequencies ν_j should be distinct, they play no role in the SCMA process, so their precise values are unimportant. This is a significant advantage of subcarrier techniques, because requirements for optical wavelength stability are not as stringent as in WDMA.

Although precise control of optical frequencies is unimportant, there *is* a requirement for wide spacing of optical carriers, because of *optical beat interference* (OBI) appearing at the output of the photodetector. Because the direct-detection receiver is a square-law device, and because a wideband receiver accepts signals from many different sources, pairs of optical signals from different lasers "beat" against each other in the detection process, producing "noiselike" OBI signals. The spectrum of each OBI signal is centered at an electrical frequency that is the difference between the optical frequencies of the pair of beating optical signals. If the transmitted signals are spaced too closely in optical frequency, some of the OBI power may fall in the microwave subcarrier band, possibly overwhelming the desired signals. As is shown later, this is the effect that usually determines minimum λ-channel spacing in an SCMA system.

To study the OBI effects in the general case, consider an $M \times M$ system with aggregate subcarrier bandwidth $B_T = MB$. On the optical level we assume that all λ-channels are separated by equal nominal spacings, $\Delta \nu$, fitting into a total optical spectrum of width $B_{op} = M\Delta\nu$—see Figures 5.8(a) and 5.8(b) for the 4×4 case. Of particular interest is the minimum value of spacing, and hence the minimum optical bandwidth required to achieve acceptable system performance. Let

$$\mathcal{E}(t) = \sum_k \mathcal{E}_k(t) \tag{5.12}$$

be the optical field present at the input of a receiver, where $\mathcal{E}_k$ is the contribution from the kth transmitter. Then, using complex envelope representation, $\mathcal{E}$ takes the form

$$\mathcal{E}(t) = \sum_k Re\left[E_k(t)e^{j2\pi\nu_0 t}\right] \tag{5.13}$$

where

$$\mathcal{E}_k = Re\left[E_k(t)e^{j2\pi\nu_0 t}\right] \tag{5.14}$$

In Equation 5.13, ν_0 is a nominal optical frequency for all transmissions. The kth complex envelope E_k is then defined as

$$E_k(t) = \sqrt{2I_k}(t)e^{j\Phi_k(t)} \tag{5.15}$$

with

$$I_k(t) = \frac{E_0^2}{2}[1 + m_k s_k(t)] \tag{5.16}$$

and

$$\Phi_k(t) = 2\pi(\nu_k - \nu_0)t + \phi_k(t) \tag{5.17}$$

Recall that *intensity* modulation (as opposed to *amplitude* modulation) is a nonlinear process due to the square root in Equation 5.15. This causes an irregular shape and spreading of the spectral components in Figure 5.8(b). This effect becomes more pronounced with increasing modulation index m_k.

In Equation 5.16, I_k is the intensity of the kth optical field, with a true optical frequency ν_k that appears in the phase function Φ_k of Equation 5.17. Now from Equations 2.17, 5.13, 5.15, and 5.17, the detected photocurrent is

$$i(t) = \frac{R}{2}\left|\sum E_k\right|^2 = R\sum_k I_k(t) + R\sum_{k \neq n} \sqrt{I_k I_n}e^{j2\pi(\nu_k - \nu_n)t + \phi_k - \phi_n} \tag{5.18}$$

where R is the responsivity of the photodetector.

The first summation in Equation 5.18 contains the desired detected intensities from the various transmitters, and the second summation contains OBI terms centered

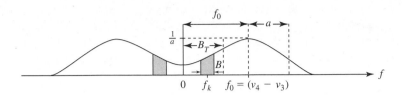

FIGURE 5.9 Effect of OBI.

around difference frequencies $(v_k - v_n)$.[6] Thus in a system with M transmitters there are $M(M-1)/2$ OBI terms.

Returning to our 4×4 example, the electrical spectrum $S_i(f)$ of the photocurrent at a receiver (see Figure 5.8[c]) contains the desired signal spectra $S_s^{(j)}(f)$ together with OBI. One OBI term from Equation 5.18 is shown, due to transmitters 3 and 4.

A more detailed picture of the two-sided electrical PSD at the input of the demodulator is shown in Figure 5.9. Again, only one OBI term is shown, centered at frequency $f_0 = (v_4 - v_3) = \Delta v$. Note that there is a "tail" of the OBI spectrum that extends into the subcarrier band B_T, overlapping the signal spectra. This overlapping OBI acts as noise, which degrades the signal at the input to the electrical detector (point h in Figure 5.7[b]). Normally, the intermediate frequency-filter has a bandwidth, B, equal to that of the modulated signal to eliminate as much noise and interference as possible. Thus, the interference affecting a particular received signal is the part of the total OBI spectrum falling within that signal's bandwidth (shown as the shaded area in Figure 5.9 for subcarrier f_k). In an $M \times M$ system with equally spaced optical carriers, the $M-1$ OBI terms due to beat notes between adjacent carriers, each centered at $f_0 = \Delta v = (v_{j+1} - v_j)$, produce the dominant noise in the subcarrier band. To maintain a satisfactory BER, this adjacent-channel beat noise must be kept small, which in turn implies making the λ-channel spacing Δv sufficiently large.

The minimum required optical spacing Δv_{min} for satisfactory performance depends on the spectral characteristics of the OBI terms and the vulnerability of the subcarrier-modulated signals to OBI noise. Each of these factors depends in a complex way on many physical parameters, including the channel bitrate, modulation format and bandwidth, the modulation index m, the acceptable BER, other sources of noise, the number of active OTs, the unmodulated laser line width, the type of laser modulation (direct or external), the subcarrier frequency, and so forth. These issues have been studied thoroughly in the literature (see, for example, [Darcie87], [Olshanksy+89], and [Saleh89]). In view of the complexity of the problem, we make a number of

---

[6] Note that when only two signals are present, this two-signal mixing process looks just like that in a heterodyne receiver. As in the heterodyne case, the intensities of the difference frequency terms depend on the relative polarizations of the contributing pairs of signals. In the heterodyne receiver, polarization alignment is necessary to produce the desired signal, whereas in the subcarrier case polarization alignment is detrimental, producing OBI. The OBI terms in Equation 5.18 represent the worst case, corresponding to perfectly aligned polarizations of the two beating signals.

simplifying approximations here to obtain a closed-form relation between $\Delta \nu_{\min}$ and the other system parameters. The development follows [Desem90]. The two basic assumptions are the following:

1. A suitable performance measure for OBI is the carrier-to-interference ratio (CIR) at the input to the electrical detector.

2. For CIR calculations, the spectrum of each of the OBI components can be approximated as Lorentzian.

By focusing on CIR, we avoid getting involved in the details of the modulation format and electrical detection process. A CIR of approximately 20 dB at the input of the detector is sufficient to produce a BER superior to 10^{-9} for binary digital modulation formats, while providing a reasonable margin for other sources of noise (see Section 4.6.3). For example, in the QPSK illustration of Equation 5.10, the signal is a sinusoid of unit amplitude and varying phase, so that the carrier power equals the signal power, and CIR is the same as SNR. Assuming that the OBI can be treated as independent Gaussian noise, the SNR sufficient to achieve a BER of 10^{-9} using QPSK is approximately 23 dB. (QPSK requires an increase of 3 dB in SNR over binary PSK for the same BER.)

Assuming $s_k(t)$ in Equation 5.16 is a sinusoid of unit amplitude, the carrier power for the kth signal present in $i(t)$ is $R^2 E_0^4 m_k^2 / 8$. The *total power* in the OBI due to the beating of signals k and n is $R^2 E_0^4 / 8$. To determine how much of this falls into a given signal band, we need an appropriate model for the PSD of the OBI. Given a signal $s(t)$ with modulation index m, the Lorentzian spectrum shown in Figure 5.9 (characteristic of a second-order resonant system) has been found empirically to model OBI well for small m (see [Antoniades+95]). For large m a more exact approach is required. The two-sided Lorentzian PSD of a signal centered at frequency f_0 and normalized to unity total power is given by

$$g(f) = \frac{a}{2\pi[a^2 + (f - f_0)^2]} + \frac{a}{2\pi[a^2 + (f + f_0)^2]} \qquad (5.19)$$

where a is one half the full width at half maximum (FWHM) of the OBI spectrum. Because each OBI term in the electrical spectrum is the result of convolving optical spectra from two signal sources, its width is the sum of the widths of the two convolved spectra. The width of each optical signal spectral component increases with laser linewidth and chirp (in the case of direct modulation of the laser). Furthermore, because of the nonlinearity of the modulation process, the spectral width is an increasing function of modulation index m and subcarrier frequency. However, the latter effects only become important for large modulation indices.

To compute an approximation for CIR, we assume a system of M transmitters with equal modulation indices m, equal signal bandwidths B, and with λ-channels at equal frequency spacings $\Delta \nu$. In computing the OBI power falling in the signal band, it is also assumed for simplicity that $\Delta \nu \gg B_T$, so that the integral of $g(f)$ over the signal band can be approximated as $2Bg(0)$. (The latter inequality is a fair assumption in systems in which some effort is made to maintain optical wavelength separation.)

Using Equations 5.16 and 5.18, the total OBI power for this system is

$$P_{\text{OBI}} = \sum_{k=1}^{M-1} \frac{(M-k)R^2 E_0^4 B a}{2\pi(a^2 + k^2 \Delta v^2)} \tag{5.20}$$

The summation in Equation 5.20 represents the effects of all superimposed OBI terms, with values of $k \geq 2$ corresponding to OBI from nonadjacent optical carriers. By retaining only the first (adjacent-channel) term in Equation 5.20, we obtain the following approximation for CIR[7]

$$CIR = \frac{m^2 \pi (\Delta v^2 + a^2)}{8(M-1)Ba} \tag{5.21}$$

It can be seen from Equation 5.21 that the CIR tends toward infinity for both large and small values of $a/\Delta v$. In the former case, the OBI spectrum is so spread out that little OBI power falls in the signal bandwidth, and the spacing Δv becomes unimportant. This suggests that when optical carrier spacing is very small, or when it cannot be controlled, the best line of defense against OBI is to increase a.[8] In the case of small a, the OBI spectrum is so concentrated that the tail that overlaps the signal bandwidth has negligible power. The worst case occurs for $a = \Delta v$, giving

$$CIR = \frac{m^2 \pi \Delta v}{4(M-1)B} \tag{5.22}$$

Equation 5.21 allows us to determine the minimum possible λ-channel spacing (that is, the maximum channel-packing density) for a given CIR. We have

$$\begin{aligned}
\Delta v_{\text{min}} &= \frac{2}{m} \sqrt{\frac{2(M-1)B\,a\,CIR}{\pi} - a^2} \\
&\approx \frac{2}{m} \sqrt{\frac{B_T\,a\,CIR}{\pi}}, \quad \text{for } M \gg 1, \quad a/\Delta v \ll 1
\end{aligned} \tag{5.23}$$

so that the total required optical bandwidth is

$$B_{\text{op}} \approx \frac{2M}{m} \sqrt{\frac{B_T\,a\,CIR}{\pi}} \tag{5.24}$$

---

[7] For small values of $a/\Delta v$, the error incurred by dropping OBI terms due to nonadjacent optical carriers increases with M, so that the OBI is underestimated by approximately 12.5%, 25%, and 56% for $M = 3$, 10, and 100 respectively.

[8] The fact that a large value of a reduces OBI has prompted a number of experiments in which the laser spectrum is widened intentionally to reduce OBI.

Equation 5.24 reveals an important relation between total optical bandwidth requirements in SCMA and two fundamental system parameters: B_T and M. The total subcarrier bandwidth B_T is a measure of aggregate system throughput, which is limited primarily by the laser modulation bandwidth and is independent of the number of stations. With B_T fixed, we see that for equally spaced optical carriers, B_{op} increases linearly with M. Thus in SCMA, as opposed to WDMA, increasing the number of stations increases the required optical spectrum *without* increasing the aggregate system throughput.

Using Equation 5.24 we can determine the optical spectral efficiency of SCMA. Assuming that all transmitting stations are modulated digitally at rate R_t bits per second with spectral efficiency η_m, we have

$$\eta_{op} = \frac{MR_t}{B_{op}} = \frac{B\eta_m}{\Delta\nu_{min}} \approx \frac{m\eta_m}{2}\sqrt{\frac{\pi B_T}{Ma \, CIR}} \tag{5.25}$$

The approximations in these OBI calculations conceal many interrelated physical phenomena. Although the minimum λ-channel spacing diminishes with increasing modulation depth, $\Delta\nu_{min}$ is *not* inversely proportional to m, as might be inferred from a cursory look at Equation 5.23. The previous development was based on the assumption of small m. As m increases it causes a to increase, and it changes the shape of the OBI spectrum. (As mentioned earlier, the Lorentzian approximation is no longer valid for large m.) This increase in a partially offsets the advantage of the increasing value of m.

The advantage of large m has been demonstrated empirically; experiments have been conducted with values of m up to 1.8 [Wood+93]. This corresponds to *overmodulation* of the laser, producing "clipping" of the subcarrier. This has little detrimental effect on signal quality provided that the subcarrier harmonics generated by clipping do not interfere with any useful signals.

Consider the following example, in which we study the performance of an $M \times M$ SCMA system, starting with empirical data for the case $M = 2$ and extrapolating to larger sizes.

In a system with $f_1 = 600$ MHz, $f_2 = 850$ MHz, and $m = 0.23$ for each transmitter, it is found empirically (see [Antoniades+95]) that the OBI spectrum is approximately Lorentzian, with $a = 100$ MHz. Assuming a modulation bandwidth $B = 100$ MHz, and an optical carrier spacing of $\Delta\nu = 7.6$ GHz, this gives a CIR of approximately 25 dB using Equation 5.21, compared with the measured value of approximately 21 dB in [Antoniades+95].

The laser can be modulated at frequencies as high as 1 GHz. This suggests that ten users can be fit into the modulation bandwidth, with subcarriers spaced 100 MHz apart, and each transmitting at $R_t = 100$ Mbps. (This implies a spectral efficiency at the subcarrier level of $\eta_m = 1$, which is accomplished easily using QPSK to modulate the subcarrier.) But for $M = 10$, we find from Equation 5.21 that the optical carrier spacing must be increased to $\Delta\nu = 22.8$ GHz to maintain the same CIR as in the case of two users. This gives a total throughput of 1 Gbps using an optical spectrum of approximately 228 GHz, resulting in optical spectral efficiency $\eta_{op} = 0.004$.

Now suppose the same throughput is divided among 20 users each occupying a bandwidth of $B = 50$ MHz while maintaining the same aggregate bitrate. In this case we find that $\Delta\nu$ and B_{op} must be increased to 33.1 GHz and 662 GHz respectively, reducing the spectral efficiency to $\eta_{op} = 0.0015$. The spectral efficiencies in these examples are relatively low because of the small value of m. Significantly better efficiencies are possible with larger m, but the analysis becomes more complex.

5.2.2.3 TDM/T-SCMA

In a TDM/T-SCMA system, the multiplexing function needed for one-to-many logical connectivity is realized using time–division methods, whereas the multiple access function (for many-to-one connectivity) uses a combination of time division and subcarrier multiple access. For illustration we return to the 4×4 system of Figure 5.6, shown in more detail in Figure 5.10. Transmitting station j transmits on a fixed and distinct optical frequency ν_j, with the optical frequency separation among the stations sufficient to make OBI negligible. (This condition is relaxed later.) To provide full logical connectivity, four logical channels are first time–division multiplexed to produce a single baseband data signal, which is then translated to a subcarrier frequency (in the boxes labeled MUX and SCMOD respectively in Figure 5.10[a]). In the multiplexed data signal, the LCs are assigned to designated channel–slots (assuming a fixed frame system), where *channel* now means *subcarrier channel*.

In an FT-TR subcarrier system, source station j is assigned a fixed subcarrier frequency f_j, and each destination station has a wideband OR together with a rapidly tunable subcarrier demodulator, as in Figure 5.10(a). The photocurrent at point e of each destination station contains all of the subcarriers, and hence all of the LCs are accessible at this point. Receiving station k selects information destined for it by tuning its demodulator to each transmitter's subcarrier frequency exactly at the times when that information is present. This is completely analogous to what takes place at the *optical* level in an FT-TR TDM/T-WDMA system. As in TDM/T-WDMA, the subcarrier system may also operate in a TT-FR or TT-TR mode. The demodulated information streams, at point e' in the kth receiving station in Figure 5.10(a), are processed by an array of synchronized gates in the DMUX box to extract the various LCs, $[*, k]$, and to route them to the proper output ports.

Like all shared-channel networks, subcarrier systems may operate using either fixed or dynamic capacity allocation. In the former case, channel–slots are allocated in a fixed periodic frame just as in TDM/T-WDMA, except that optical frequency tuning is replaced by subcarrier tuning. Similarly, in packet-switched systems, channel–slots are allocated dynamically, and contention for the shared channels must be resolved using an appropriate MAC protocol. All of the issues of synchronization, transmitter collisions, and receiver conflicts that are present in TDM/T-WDMA are also present here. Thus, for example, certain performance improvements and system simplifications can be achieved by replacing the tunable subcarrier demodulator by an array of demodulators, one tuned to each transmitted subcarrier frequency as shown in Figure 5.10(b). This allows a destination station to see all transmissions concurrently, eliminating receiver conflicts. Although this arrayed configuration is analogous to an

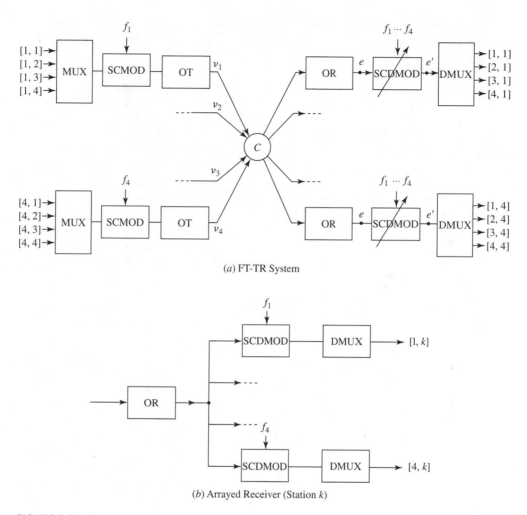

(a) FT-TR System

(b) Arrayed Receiver (Station k)

FIGURE 5.10   TDM/T-SCMA.

arrayed OR, there is an important practical difference: It is currently far less costly to replicate electronics than optics.

5.2.2.4   TDM/T-SCMA with Optical Spectrum Reuse

We have seen that the number of transmitting stations M in an SCMA network is limited by OBI and the related consideration: available optical spectrum. These limitations are predicated on the assumption that all M stations transmit simultaneously.

One way of circumventing the size limitation is by controlled optical spectrum reuse. Consider a system in which M is too large to be accommodated using distinct, dedicated optical frequencies for each transmitting station. Let $C = M/r$ equally spaced optical frequencies $\nu_1, \nu_2, \ldots, \nu_C$ be selected for allocation to the M stations, where r is the spectrum reuse factor. The number C is chosen to satisfy the constraints on OBI and spectrum availability. Now, following the TDM/T-WDMA illustration of Figure 5.4, the selected frequencies can be allocated among the M stations, with each frequency shared by r stations. As in TDM/T-WDMA, transmissions must be scheduled so that all stations with transmissions that overlap in time have distinct optical frequencies. In this way the OBI effects correspond to those for a system with C rather than with M transmitting stations.

The same scheduling method illustrated in Figure 5.4(b) for TDM/T-WDMA can be used here. As in that case, the distinct optical frequency constraint translates into a frame length that is longer by a factor of r than that required without optical frequency reuse. At first, one might think that the increase in frame length reduces the aggregate throughput of the subcarrier system by a factor of r, as is the case in TDM/T-WDMA. However, it turns out that *the achievable aggregate throughput of a TDM/T-SCMA system is independent of its degree of optical frequency reuse*. The difference in the WDMA and SCMA cases is due to the fact that it is the number of available λ-channels that limits aggregate throughput in WDMA, whereas it is the total subcarrier bandwidth B_T that limits aggregate throughput in SCMA.

Consider the following example. Suppose the 81×81 undirected star TDM/T-WDMA example of Figure 5.4 is to be implemented using FT-TR TDM/T-SCMA. We compare approaches without and with optical frequency reuse.

Without reuse, each transmitting station is assigned a subcarrier/optical frequency pair (f_j, ν_j), where all f_js are distinct and all ν_js are distinct. The traffic is scheduled in a frame with 80 slots, as was used for TDM/T-WDMA in Figure 5.4(a). Wideband ORs are used. Assuming that $B_T = 20$ GHz, each transmitting station is allocated a bandwidth of approximately 245 MHz, with the subcarriers spaced the same distance apart. At a spectral efficiency of 1 bps/Hz, the aggregate throughput for the system is 20 Gbps, or approximately 245 Mbps per transmitting station.

But is a system of this size feasible using subcarriers? Consider a typical set of system parameters: $m = 0.25$, $a = 100$ MHz, and minimum acceptable CIR $= 100$. We find from Equation 5.23 that $\Delta \nu_{\min} \approx 64$ GHz. In the 1,550-nm range this represents about 42 nm of optical bandwidth for 81 stations. Considering transmitter power limitations, losses in the star coupler and fibers, and receiver sensitivity, this system cannot be realized without optical amplification. However, the required bandwidth is beyond that of today's commercially available fiber amplifiers, so that it is questionable whether a system of this size can be realized with current off-the-shelf technology.

Now, consider spectrum reuse. Suppose an optical frequency reuse factor of $r = 27$ is applied, with subsets of 27 transmitters sharing the same optical frequency, so that only three transmitters are active at any one time. For simplicity, we use the same optical spacing as before. (To a first approximation, $\Delta \nu_{\min}$ is independent of the number of active transmitters.) Because only three distinct optical carriers are used, the spectrum required is approximately 200 GHz, or less than 2 nm.

To maintain maximum throughput in SCMA while reusing the optical spectrum, we reuse the *subcarrier* spectrum to the same degree as the optical spectrum. Because stations sharing the same optical frequency are not allowed to transmit at the same time, they can also share the same subcarrier frequency without any interference at the electrical level. Thus, each transmitting station can again be assigned one of three subcarrier/optical frequency pairs (f_j, v_j), where both the optical frequencies and the subcarrier frequencies are distinct. Subsets of 27 stations share the same pair. With this assignment the schedule of Figure 5.4(b) is valid for the TDM/T-SCMA case.

Without any other modifications of the system, there would be a factor of 27 loss in aggregate throughput because only three instead of 81 stations are active at any one time. This loss can be eliminated by a change in spacing at the subcarrier level. Because the aggregate bandwidth B_T available to all *active* stations has not changed, the subcarrier spacing and hence the microwave bandwidth allocated to each station can be increased by a factor of 27, giving a bandwidth of approximately 6.7 GHz for each station. As a result, the aggregate throughput for the system is exactly the same as it was without optical spectrum reuse.

Taking the idea of spectrum reuse to the limit, we may choose $r = 81$, in which case all transmitting stations share a common optical (and subcarrier) frequency. But this is nothing more than TDM/TDMA! In this case, two other difficulties arise. First, all transmitters must operate at $R_t = 20$ Gbps if the aggregate throughput is to be maintained at its original value, and this requires costly electronics. Second, the frame length for full connectivity is now $L = 6,480$, which may be too large in many applications.

In the case illustrated, a compromise was struck with a reuse factor of $r = 27$, wherein relatively high-speed electronics is required (for a transmitter bitrate of $R_t = B_T/3 = 6.7$ Gbps), but B_{op} has been reduced by a factor of more than 30. Clearly, optimum cost-effectiveness may be achieved for some other value of r depending on the relative costs of optical bandwidth and the station components.

5.2.2.5 Packet Switching Using SCMA

Subcarriers can also be used to implement packet switching in the optical layer. As mentioned in earlier chapters, packet-switched networks typically have large populations of bursty users with low average throughput per user. The fact that the population is large suggests that OBI may be a serious problem. However, the traffic characteristics of packet-switched networks suggest a different way of dealing with it: Just ignore it!

Consider an SCMA system operating in a packet-switched mode in which each station is active only when transmitting a packet. Now OBI only occurs when two or more transmitters operating on closely spaced optical frequencies are active simultaneously. But this event can be made reasonably rare by proper system design. This is the basis of the system proposed in [Shankaranarayanan+91]. The system uses a random access MAC protocol (see Section 5.6.1). M stations are assigned distinct subcarrier frequencies, but their optical frequencies are random and unknown. Stations are active only when they transmit a packet, and packet transmission times are random and uncoordinated. Thus, there is a non-zero probability that transmissions from two or more stations will overlap in time. Given a time overlap, there is also a non-zero probability of *outage* due to OBI. Outage occurs if the OBI power generated by the overlapping signals is large enough in the subcarrier band to mutilate the desired signals. Because the MAC protocol has a mechanism for retransmission of mutilated packets, this type of outage is not catastrophic provided that it occurs with sufficiently low probability.

The main advantage of this approach to SCMA is that it requires no special assignment or control of optical frequencies. However, the relatively high probability of outage for reasonable throughputs places a serious limit on the size and aggregate throughput of these systems.

5.2.2.6 SCM/SCMA

An alternative to TDM in providing one-to-many connectivity in subcarrier systems is SCM. Figure 5.11 shows a transmitting and receiving station supporting full logical connectivity in a directed 4×4 SCM/SCMA system. Transmitting station j, using an array of four subcarrier modulators, generates a microwave subchannel at carrier frequency f_{jk} for LC $[j, k]$ for $k = 1, 2, 3$, and 4. These are superimposed at point a in Figure 5.11(a) to modulate the OT. Thus, the signal at point a is of the form

$$s(t) = \sum_k m_k s_{jk}(t) \tag{5.26}$$

(If a single multicast LC—$[j, \{1, 2, 3, 4\}]$—is desired, only a single microwave modulator and single carrier frequency is needed.) Receiver k uses an array of four microwave demodulators, as shown in Figure 5.11(b), with demodulating frequencies f_{jk}, $j = 1, 2, 3$, and 4. Note that MN distinct subcarrier frequencies are needed in an

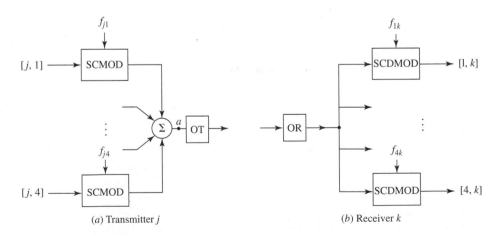

(a) Transmitter j (b) Receiver k

FIGURE 5.11 SCM/SCMA.

$M \times N$ system, but no time–division multiplexing/demultiplexing equipment is required. This represents a simple trade between time–division and frequency–division multiplexing techniques at the subcarrier level.

In some applications (e.g., multichannel analog video distribution in fiber backbone CATV systems), the frequency-domain approach is the natural one because the basic information must be delivered in analog form on sinusoidal carriers. Even when the information is digital, there may be a cost advantage for SCM/SCMA over TDM/ T-SCMA, in that relatively low-speed electronics can be used at the baseband level, and no rapid tuning or slot synchronization is required at any level.

There are important differences in using subcarriers for *multiplexing* as opposed to *multiple access*. In multiplexing, several subcarriers are superimposed on the *same* optical signal. Because there is only one optical signal, there is no OBI. However, impressing several microwave signals on one laser introduces intermodulation products caused by the inevitable nonlinearities in the modulation process.

Even if the relation between modulating signal and output intensity is linear, the overall modulation process is nonlinear due to clipping. Clipping occurs when the term in brackets in Equation 2.16 becomes negative. With a single signal modulating the laser, it is not difficult to avoid clipping by keeping the amplitude of $s(t)$ sufficiently small. However, when $s(t)$ consists of a sum of many independent signals, as in SCM, then clipping becomes unavoidable unless each individual modulating signal is kept at an unrealistically low level. If we admit the possibility of clipping, it is of interest to be able to predict the signal quality degradation due to this effect.

An analysis of carrier-to-noise ratio (CNR) appears in [Saleh89], who assumes that the modulating signal $s(t)$ consists of the sum of M sinusoidal carriers of unit amplitude. The CNR is the ratio of the signal power to the clipping noise power at the receiver. For the case of large M and random phases, $s(t)$ can be approximated as a Gaussian random process, in which case the resultant CNR is given by

$$CNR = \sqrt{\pi/2}\mu^{-3} \exp\left(1/2\mu^2\right) \tag{5.27}$$

where μ is a root mean square modulation index, defined as

$$\mu = m\sqrt{M/2} \tag{5.28}$$

For example, from Equation 5.27 we see that the maximum modulation index necessary to ensure a CNR of 25 dB is approximately $m = 0.6/\sqrt{M}$. (On the other hand, to avoid clipping altogether in the case of unit amplitude sinusoids, we need $m \leq 1/M$, a far more stringent condition for large M.) However, reducing the modulation index for large M to increase the CNR due to clipping reduces the CNR due to random noise. Thus, subcarrier-multiplexed system size is "boxed in" by these two effects.

Conversely, in SCMA, the transmitter clipping effects are absent because each laser is modulated by only one subcarrier. However, OBI occurs unless the λ-channel spacings are kept sufficiently large. The SCM/SCMA system just described is subject to both of these effects.

5.2.2.7 SCM/WDMA/SCMA

The constraint on throughput imposed by laser modulation bandwidth and the connectivity limit imposed by OBI in SCMA can be relaxed by using subcarriers in combination with optically tunable receivers to yield an SCM/WDMA/SCMA network. Basically, this is a generalization of SCM/SCMA, wherein optical tuning is used to enhance the spectral efficiency of the system at both the microwave and optical levels. The approach, first proposed by [Liew+89], is based on a two-level system implemented as shown in Figure 5.12. The underlying network is a directed broadcast star. The system is designed to operate in a circuit-switched mode, creating multiple LCs on demand. As in SCM/SCMA, no rapid tuning either at the subcarrier or the optical levels is required for one-to-many and many-to-one logical connectivity. (Tuning only changes during connection establishment so that millisecond or slower tunability is acceptable.)

As shown in Figure 5.12(a), each transmitting station is equipped with an array of tunable subcarrier modulators and a fixed–tuned OT, whereas each receiving station—

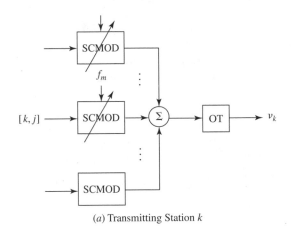

(*a*) Transmitting Station *k*

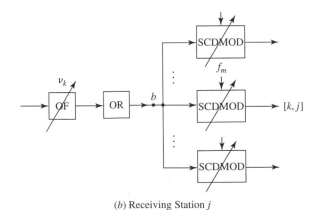

(*b*) Receiving Station *j*

FIGURE 5.12 SCM/WDMA/SCMA.

see Figure 5.12(b)—has a wideband OR preceded by a tunable optical filter, followed by an array of demodulators—point b in Figure 5.12(b). The filter is capable of independently selecting several (possibly nonadjacent) λ-channels, so it has the functionality of the multiwavelength switch described in Section 2.3.2.4.

Suppose that a distinct optical frequency ν_k is assigned permanently to transmitting station k. Then, whenever an LC of the form $[k, *]$ is needed, it is realized by assigning some subcarrier frequency f_m from a pool $\{f_1, f_2, \ldots, f_C\}$ to that connection. The number C of subcarrier channels available in the pool depends on the channel bandwidth B and the usable microwave spectrum bandwidth B_T. Any station can receive an LC from station k by tuning its optical filter to select the optical carrier frequency ν_k and tuning one of its subcarrier demodulators to receive the assigned subcarrier frequency f_m. If there are M transmitting stations, each with D modulators, the total number of possible simultaneous LCs is MD, a number that may be considerably greater than C. The interesting aspect of the two-level selectivity available in this system is that the active subcarrier frequencies do not have to be distinct, creating the possibility of reuse of the microwave spectrum. All that is required is that the set of subcarriers assigned to each transmitting station be distinct, and that the set demodulated by each receiving station be distinct.

Of course, adding tunable optical filters to a subcarrier system tends to nullify the cost advantages of the subcarrier approach. However, the fact that only slow tunability is required makes this a less costly approach than, say, TDM/T-WDMA.

To illustrate, suppose the connections $[1, 2]$, $[1, 3]$, $[2, 3]$, and $[2, 4]$ are to be set up in a 4×4 system. Let the subcarrier assignments be $[1, 2]_1$, $[1, 3]_2$, $[2, 3]_3$, and $[2, 4]_1$, where the subscript j on an LC indicates that subcarrier frequency f_j is assigned to that connection. Table 5.1 indicates the required receiver tuning. Note that the *accessible* LCs are those that appear (sometimes unintentionally) at the output of the ORs (point b in Figure 5.12[b]), whereas the *accepted* LCs are those selected after subcarrier demodulation. Figure 5.13 shows a system that is set up to carry the connections indicated in Table 5.1. The tuning of the optical filters is indicated by the notation ν_j associated with the optical filter, and the tuning of the demodulators is indicated by the notation f_j on the RPs. In this case f_1 is being reused and, in fact, appears twice (unintentionally) at receiver 3. However, this causes no interference because the only subcarriers being demodulated at that receiver are f_2 and f_3, carrying connections $[1, 3]$ and $[2, 3]$ respectively.

TABLE 5.1 SCM/WDMA/SCMA Example

Receiver Number	Optical Tuning	Accessible LCs	Subcarrier Tuning	Accepted LCs
2	ν_1	$[1, 2]_1, [1, 3]_2$	f_1	$[1, 2]$
3	ν_1, ν_2	$[1, 2]_1, [1, 3]_2, [2, 3]_3, [2, 4]_1$	f_2, f_3	$[1, 3], [2, 3]$
4	ν_2	$[2, 3]_3, [2, 4]_1$	f_1	$[2, 4]$

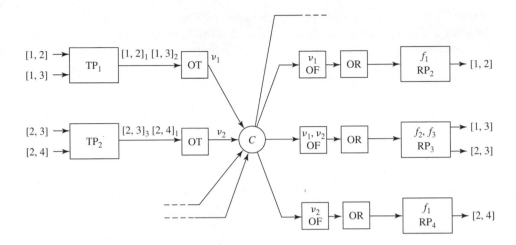

FIGURE 5.13 SCM/WDMA/SCMA example.

5.2.2.8 Summary

The following sums up the advantages and disadvantages of using subcarriers. The advantages include

- They make it possible to create multipoint logical connectivity using only fixed–tuned (or slowly tunable) optical transceivers, together with fairly inexpensive tunable microwave modulators and demodulators.
- More rapid and precise tuning is possible in the electronic domain than in the optical domain.
- The current subcarrier technology is more mature and less expensive than the corresponding WDM technology.

However, the disadvantages are

- Subcarriers make inefficient use of the optical spectrum because of the optical frequency spacing needed to avoid OBI.
- If direct modulation is used, lasers with wide modulation bandwidths are required to accommodate high subcarrier frequencies and to achieve a high aggregrate throughput for the system.
- Fiber dispersion severely limits the aggregate throughput of a subcarrier system.
- In the case of SCM, the modulation indices must be kept small to reduce intermodulation distortion, and this in turn reduces the resultant SNR at the receivers.

5.2.3 Code–Division Multiple Access

All multiple access techniques discussed thus far have used orthogonality to achieve channel distinguishability at the receivers. In contrast, CDMA is only quasi orthogonal, in the sense that (using linear processing) different channels are only "approximately" separable at the receivers, with the interference from unwanted channels appearing as background noise. CDMA is an example of a *spread-spectrum technique*, in which a modulation process is used that spreads the encoded signal spectrum over a much wider bandwidth than that of the original data signal. This spectral spread has many advantages in contexts other than optical networks: in particular, immunity to noise and interference. In shared-channel optical network applications, the most important advantage is that many simultaneous low-throughput logical channels can be accommodated on a shared medium with a minimum of coordination. (No time synchronization or precise optical tuning is required.) This makes it an attractive approach for packet switching, using either electronic or purely optical signal processing.

The basic idea of CDMA is to encode each bit in a data stream into a waveform that is unique for each LC. The unique code is analogous to a unique wavelength in a WDMA system, or a distinct time slot in TDMA. Thus, an LC is established between a source and a destination by "tuning" the transmitter and receiver to a common code. The transmitter generates bits with a unique waveform, and the receiver recognizes these bits only, filtering out all other waveforms. Quasi orthogonality means that the filtering is not perfect. As the number of superimposed CDMA channels is increased, the interference from the unwanted channels tends eventually to degrade the desired signal. However, the degradation in CDMA is "graceful," with the level of interference proportional to the number of superimposed channels.

In an FT-TR CDMA system using distinct assignments, each transmitter is assigned a distinct code, and receivers connect to a desired source by configuring themselves to capture only those bits with the assigned code. The usual problem of receiver conflicts arises when more than one source transmits to the same receiver. In a TT-FR system, the receivers are assigned distinct codes, and it is the source that must choose a code matched to the desired receiver. In this case, collisions and bit errors occur if more than one source transmits to the same receiver at the same time. Note that the CDMA codes act like source (destination) addresses in the case of FT-TR (TT-FR).

There are many possibilities for generating the CDMA waveforms. Two well-known methods use frequency hopping and pseudo random pulse sequences. In the former case the waveform is generated as a sinusoidal carrier with a frequency that is varied ("hopped") in a pseudo random manner over the bit duration. The wider the range of frequency variation, the more the spectrum is spread. In the latter case, the waveform consists of a pseudo random sequence of binary pulses, known as *chips*, with the chip duration $T_c = T/L$ much shorter than the bit duration T. The integer L is known as the *code length*. Because bits of duration T in the data signal are replaced by pulse trains with pulse widths T/L, this amounts to a bandwidth expansion of the data spectrum by a factor of L. As we shall see, other more elaborate codes are possible as well.

The signal processing creating the optical CDMA waveform may be performed either electronically or optically. For example, frequency hopping may be realized electronically using microwave subcarriers, or optically by varying the laser frequency. Similar alternatives are available for pseudo random pulses.

Let us examine optical CDMA in more detail. There are two basic approaches, using either intensity or phase variation, which are adapted to either direct-detection or coherent receivers respectively. In the case of intensity modulation, processing may be either electronic or optical.

5.2.3.1 Direct Detection Using Electronic Processing

In the direct-detection case using electronic processing, the CDMA signal intensity modulates the optical carrier, which is combined with others in a shared-channel system, and the combined signals are broadcast to all receivers. Each receiver's photodetector converts the combined signals to a photocurrent, which is processed by a CDMA decoder to extract the desired bitstream.

The block diagram of a typical FT-TR CDMA system based on pseudo random pulse sequences is shown in Figure 5.14. (Station j uses channel j.) The following notation will be used:

$x^{(j)}$ = Data signal at source station j

$h^{(j)}$ = Impulse response of the CDMA encoder for the jth channel

$s^{(j)}$ = CDMA encoded signal at source station j

$\mathcal{E}_j$ = Optical field at source station j

$\mathcal{E}$ = Optical field at a receiver

$g^{(k)}$ = Impulse response of the CDMA decoder for the kth channel

$y^{(k)}$ = Decoded signal at a receiver tuned to the kth channel

Note that the CDMA encoder is shown conceptually as a linear filter operating on the data signal. (This may not correspond to the actual implementation.)

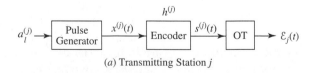

(a) Transmitting Station j

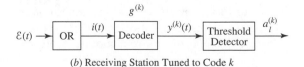

(b) Receiving Station Tuned to Code k

FIGURE 5.14 Block diagram of a direct-detection CDMA system.

Now suppose that the jth data signal is presented to the encoder in the form of rectangular pulses $u(t)$ of width T_c, spaced at the symbol interval T and carrying a binary data sequence $\{a_l^{(j)}\}$ (1s or 0s). Then we have

$$x^{(j)}(t) = \sum_l a_l^{(j)} u(t - lT) \tag{5.29}$$

and

$$s^{(j)}(t) = \sum_l a_l^{(j)} v^{(j)}(t - lT) \tag{5.30}$$

where

$$v^{(j)}(t) = \int u(\tau) h^{(j)}(t - \tau)\, d\tau \tag{5.31}$$

represents a single encoded pulse.

To generate the pseudo random chip sequence, we use an encoder with impulse response

$$h^{(j)}(t) = \sum_{n=0}^{L-1} c_n^{(j)} \delta(t - t_n) \tag{5.32}$$

where $t_n = nT_c$, and the c_n's are 0s or 1s chosen to make $h^{(j)}(t)$ look like a random sequence of impulses. Equation 5.31 then becomes

$$v^{(j)}(t) = \sum_{n=0}^{L-1} c_n^{(j)} u(t - t_n) \tag{5.33}$$

The effect of encoding on one data pulse is shown in Figure 5.15, in which the pulse $u(t)$ in Figure 5.15(a) is convolved with the CDMA impulse response $h^{(j)}(t)$ in Figure 5.15(b) to produce the encoded waveform $v^{(j)}(t)$ in Figure 5.15(c). The pulse positions in $v^{(j)}(t)$ are determined by the nonzero chip coefficients c_n. (CDMA codes with chip coefficients taking on only the values 1 and 0 are called *optical codes*.) The complete encoded signal $s^{(j)}(t)$ now has the appearance of a random sequence of narrow pulses.

The encoded signal can now be used to intensity modulate the laser using OOK, giving an optical field

$$\mathcal{E}_j(t) = Re\left[E_j(t) e^{j2\pi v_0^{(j)} t} \right] \tag{5.34}$$

where

$$E_j(t) = \sqrt{2I_j(t)} \tag{5.35}$$

and

$$I_j(t) = \frac{E_0^2}{2}[s^{(j)}(t)] \tag{5.36}$$

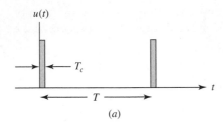

(a)

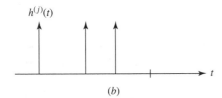

(b)

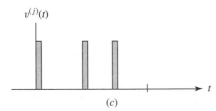

(c)

FIGURE 5.15 Waveforms for a direct-detection CDMA system.

The optical field at the input to the photodetector is

$$\mathcal{E}(t) = \sum_j \mathcal{E}_j(t) \tag{5.37}$$

so that the photocurrent $i(t)$ is proportional to $\sum_j s^{(j)}(t)$.[9] The receiver in Figure 5.14(b) is tuned to select the kth CDMA channel by making the impulse response of its decoder equal to that of the encoder for the kth channel, reversed in time (and delayed one symbol interval); that is,

$$g^{(k)}(t) = h^{(k)}(T - t) \tag{5.38}$$

This form of decoder is called a *matched filter*, and its effect is to correlate the incoming signal with a copy of the bit waveform for the kth channel. The signal at the

---

[9] This assumes that there is no OBI in the signal band.

output of the CDMA decoder is

$$y^{(k)}(t) = \sum_j \int s^{(j)}(\tau) g^{(k)}(t - \tau) \, d\tau = \sum_j y_j^{(k)}(t) \tag{5.39}$$

In Equation 5.39, $y_j^{(k)}(t)$ is the component of the output due to the signal from the jth transmitter and is given by

$$y_j^{(k)}(t) = \sum_l a_l^{(j)} w^{(k,j)}[t - (l+1)T] \tag{5.40}$$

where

$$w^{(k,j)}(t) = \sum_n w_n^{(k,j)} u(t - t_n) \tag{5.41}$$

and

$$w_n^{(k,j)} = \sum_m c_m^{(k)} c_{m+n}^{(j)} \tag{5.42}$$

The sequence $w_n^{(k,j)}$ in Equation 5.42 is the *correlation sequence* between the codes for channels k and j, which becomes an *autocorrelation sequence* when $k = j$. In an (unrealizable) ideal case, we would like to have

$$w_n^{(k,j)} = 0, \quad \text{for all } n \text{ when } k \neq j \tag{5.43}$$

$$w_n^{(k,k)} = 0, \quad \text{for } n \neq 0 \tag{5.44}$$

$$w_0^{(k,k)} = K \tag{5.45}$$

where K in Equation 5.45 is the number of nonzero chips in the code (called the *code weight*). In the ideal case all interfering terms ($w_n^{(k,j)}$ for $k \neq j$) in Equation 5.39 drop out, and the output of the CDMA receiver becomes

$$y^{(k)}(t) = K \sum_l a_l^{(k)} u[t - (l+1)T] \tag{5.46}$$

so that the desired data sequence is recovered perfectly (with a delay of one symbol interval).

In practice it is impossible to achieve the ideal conditions for perfect recovery. However, a class of codes, called *orthogonal optical codes* (OOCs), comes close. The OOCs obey the conditions

$$w_n^{(k,j)} \leq 1, \quad \text{for all } n \text{ when } k \neq j \tag{5.47}$$

$$w_n^{(k,k)} \leq 1, \quad \text{for } n \neq 0 \tag{5.48}$$

$$w_0^{(k,k)} = K \tag{5.49}$$

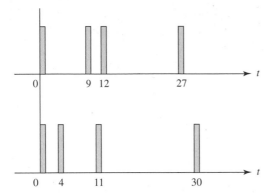

FIGURE 5.16 Orthogonal optical codes.

An example of a pair of OOCs with $L = 32$ and $K = 4$ is shown in Figure 5.16. These codes produce the lowest possible interference.

Equation 5.46 shows that by setting the threshold at the output of the decoder at a value slightly lower than K, it is possible to detect 1s while minimizing errors due to interference (0s are detected as the absence of 1s in a synchronous bitstream). In fact, using OOCs, a bit error can only occur (in the absence of random noise) if more than $K - 1$ stations interfere simultaneously with the desired station.

Unfortunately, only a relatively small number of OOCs exists for given values of L and K. It has been shown ([Salehi89]) that the maximum number of distinct OOCs of length L and weight K (and hence the maximum number of stations in an OOC-based system) is bounded by

$$M \leq \left\lceil \frac{L - 1}{K(K - 1)} \right\rceil \tag{5.50}$$

where $\lceil x \rceil$ is the smallest integer greater than or equal to x.

Thus, for example, the codes of Figure 5.16 are the only OOCs for $L = 32$ and $K = 4$. Equation 5.50 poses a dilemma: To accommodate a large number of stations, K should be made small. However, a small K makes the decoder vulnerable to noise and interference. A way out is to increase L, but then the point is soon reached when ultrashort pulses are required. This not only eats up optical bandwidth, but also makes the system highly vulnerable to fiber dispersion, limiting its application to LANs. Furthermore, implementation becomes difficult and expensive.

There are a few ways of improving the performance of the CDMA system just described. First, we note that interference is worst when all stations are active simultaneously. As in SCMA the interference problem is much less severe if the system is used for packet switching in the optical layer. In that case, the stations are active only when transmitting packets, so that interference can be kept under control by keeping the aggregate packet throughput sufficiently low.

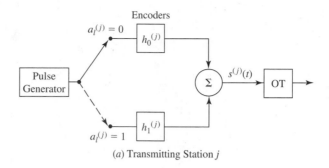

(a) Transmitting Station j

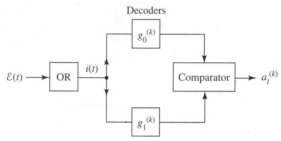

FIGURE 5.17 Parallel CDMA
transceiver structure.

(b) Receiving Station Tuned to Code k

Another way of reducing interference is by mutual synchronization of all stations to align their symbol intervals. In that case, the conditions for perfect detection reduce to

$$w_0^{(k,j)} = 0, \quad \text{when } k \neq j \tag{5.51}$$

$$w_0^{(k,k)} = K \tag{5.52}$$

Not only are these conditions realizable, but they can be achieved with a much larger number of codes (and thus with systems of larger size) than in the case of OOCs. Of course, synchronization presents its own difficulties, especially in cases of ultrashort pulses.

Finally, to improve discrimination between 1s and 0s, a *pair* of codes can be used for each CDMA channel. In this case, the transceiver structure takes the parallel form shown in Figure 5.17, in which the jth channel, 0s (1s) are encoded using the code $h_0^{(j)}$ ($h_1^{(j)}$). In the receiver, the photocurrent is decoded simultaneously using decoders $g_0^{(k)}$ and $g_1^{(k)}$, matched to the encoders for the kth channel, with a comparator detecting a 0 or a 1, depending on which decoder produces the largest output. This is a classic transceiver structure, and generalizes in an obvious way to q-ary data transmission: $q > 2$. The downside is that more codes are required, reducing the maximum number of stations that can be accommodated.

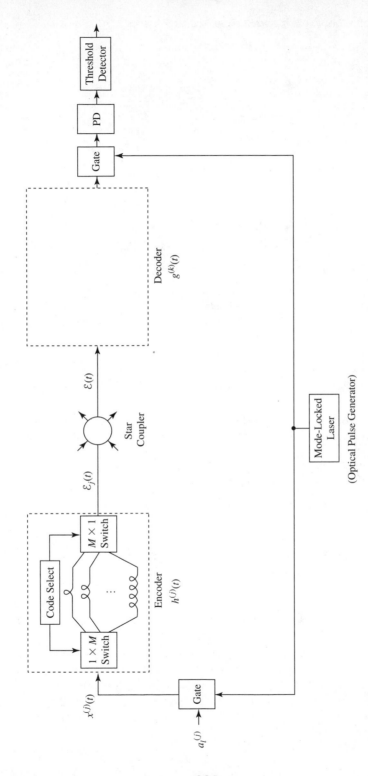

FIGURE 5.18 CDMA using optical processing.

5.2.3.2 Direct Detection Using Optical Processing

One of the earliest laboratory demonstrations of CDMA in an optical network used optical processing and direct detection, as shown in Figure 5.18 [Prucnal+86]. This is a synchronized system in which ultrashort optical pulses are generated by a mode-locked laser and are distributed to all transmitting and receiving stations. The pulses act as a system clock, and after gating by the data sequence, they provide the signals $x^{(j)}(t)$ in Equation 5.29. Because the signals are already in the optical domain, the encoding is performed optically through a parallel arrangement of fiber delay lines, each producing a delay of an integral number of chip times T_c to realize the impulse response $h^{(j)}(t)$. Different codes are programmed by selecting the appropriate combination of fiber delays. At the receiver, the matched decoder is realized in a similar fashion, with the output sampled at times synchronized with the symbol intervals. The samples are then converted to electrical form in a photodetector, with the photocurrent fed to a threshold detector.

The advantage of this system is that the high-speed signal processing is performed in the optical domain using simple components. However, because of problems of synchronization, dispersion, and signal attenuation, it is difficult to use this approach for large and geographically dispersed systems.

5.2.3.3 Coherent Detection

In systems using coherent detection, CDMA encoding can be accomplished at the level of the optical field [Salehi+90]. A conceptual block diagram is shown in Figure 5.19.

As shown in Figure 5.19(a), the signal $x^{(j)}(t)$ carrying the data at the jth transmitter is first converted to a series of short optical pulses, constituting the optical field $\mathcal{E}'_j(t)$. The field is then encoded optically to produce the transmitted field $\mathcal{E}_j(t)$, in which each narrow pulse is spread out in time to produce a noiselike waveform. The encoding is more easily understood in the frequency domain.

Let $\mathbf{E}'_j(v)$ and $\mathbf{E}_j(v)$ be the Fourier transforms of $\mathcal{E}'_j(t)$ and $\mathcal{E}_j(t)$ respectively, and let $\mathbf{H}^{(j)}(v)$ be the transfer function of the encoder for the jth channel (an optical filter operating on $\mathcal{E}'_j$). We then have $\mathbf{E}_j(v) = \mathbf{H}^{(j)}(v)\mathbf{E}'_j(v)$. At each receiving station, the combined field $\mathcal{E}$ is processed by a decoding filter $\mathbf{G}(v)$, where the frequency-domain condition for a filter matched to channel k is $\mathbf{G}^{(k)}(v) = \mathbf{H}^{*(k)}(v)$. The effect of the conjugate filter $\mathbf{H}^{*(k)}(v)$ is to "compress" the noiselike waveforms representing the

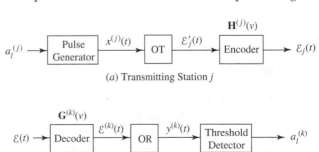

(a) Transmitting Station j

(b) Receiving Station Tuned to Code k

FIGURE 5.19 Block diagram for coherent CDMA.

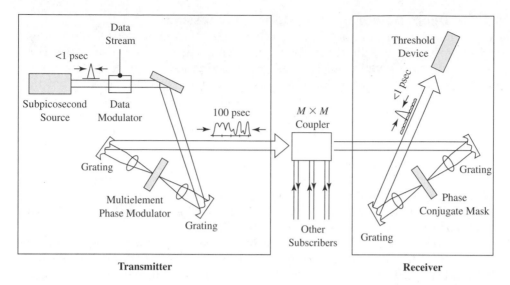

FIGURE 5.20 Realization of coherent optical CDMA. (From (Salehi+90, Figure 2). Copyright © 1990 IEEE. Used by permission of The Institute of Electrical and Electronics Engineers, Inc.)

selected bits back to narrow pulses, which are then converted to electronic form in the photodetector and are threshold detected.

A clever realization of coherent optical CDMA is shown in Figure 5.20. As in Figure 5.18 the data stream in the form of short optical pulses is first created by gating a periodic source of ultrashort (subpicosecond) pulses. The encoder is realized by first separating spatially the frequency components of the pulses using a grating, shifting the phases of the different frequencies pseudo randomly using a multielement phase modulator, or *phase mask*, and then recombining the components into a signal whose pulses are now spread out in time. As shown in Figure 5.20, the decoder has the same structure as the encoder, using a conjugate phase mask to compress the desired pulses, while the pulses from other channels pass through the decoder as low-level noise.

At this writing, coherent CDMA remains at the level of a laboratory demonstration. It has most of the problems of direct-detection CDMA together with an additional constraint: The source laser frequency must be tuned carefully so that the encoding and decoding filters are matched properly in the frequency domain.

5.3 Traffic Constraints in Shared-Channel Networks

Section 5.2 provided a detailed picture of a range of multiplexing and multiple access techniques suitable for shared-channel networks. We now step back from the details of data transmission to focus on the larger question of accommodating prescribed traffic requirements in general shared-channel networks. The objective is to derive some basic relations that determine whether a network with a limited pool of resources is capable of carrying a specified traffic load. Of particular interest is the issue of traffic imbalance and how it affects network performance.

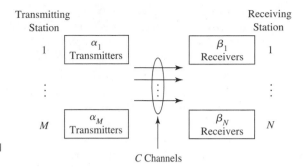

FIGURE 5.21 Shared-channel broadcast medium.

Figure 1.21 shows a model of a directed $M \times N$ shared medium. (If M is equal to N, and transmitting station i is co-located with receiving station i, then we have the undirected case.) As in Section 1.2.1, the network traffic is characterized by a set of MN prescribed flows, expressed as an $M \times N$ traffic matrix, $\Gamma = [\gamma_{ij}]$. Each entry γ_{ij} represents the flow on a point-to-point LC between the source i and destination j in bits per second (see Section 1.4.1.4 for the case of multicast connections).

The actual traffic can be modeled in various ways:

- Synchronous bitstreams requiring dedicated LCs
- Synchronous bitstreams requiring demand-assigned (circuit-switched) connections
- Asynchronous (packet) traffic

In the case of synchronous traffic on dedicated connections, a "fluid-flow" model is appropriate, in which the network capacity required to carry a specified traffic flow γ_{ij} corresponds exactly to the quantity of traffic being carried. In the other cases, the offered traffic is generally specified in terms of statistical averages. In these cases, a certain amount of "excess" capacity is required to accommodate random fluctuations exceeding the average. In this section we focus on the fluid-flow traffic model. The effects of random fluctuations in traffic flow are considered in Sections 1.5 and 1.6.

The network resources include the available channels and the station transmitters or receivers. Let

$C =$ the number of available channels

$\alpha_i =$ the number of transmitters in station i

$\beta_j =$ the number of receivers in station j

The ith transmitting station can transmit simultaneously on α_i distinct channels, and the jth receiving station can receive simultaneously on β_j distinct channels.

The channels are drawn from a pool containing a total of C channels. The precise meaning of *channel* may vary from one system to another. For example, in a WDMA system it would be a λ-channel, in an SCMA system it would be a microwave subcarrier, and in CDMA it would correspond to a distinct bit code assignment.

The transmitters and/or receivers may be rapidly tunable (on a submicrosecond time scale), slowly tunable (milliseconds), or not tunable at all. With rapid tuning, the pool of channels can be time shared to create multipoint LCs according to some fixed or dynamic time schedule, as in the examples of TDM/T-WDMA and TDM/ T-SCMA given in Sections 5.2.1 and 5.2.2.3. With slow tuning, LCs can be created on a demand-assigned (circuit-switched) basis, but each channel is dedicated to a single point-to-point LC for the duration of that connection.

The results of this section are derived from flow conservation conditions only, and are therefore independent of the multiplexing/multiple access methods used. However, to fix ideas, it is useful to think of the channels as λ-channels and to assume that the transceivers are rapidly tunable so that multipoint logical connectivity can be achieved using TDM/T-WDMA techniques.

Clearly, the larger C is, the larger the overall network throughput can be. Similarly, a large α_i (β_j) suggests that station i (j) is able to transmit (receive) a large aggregate data flow. But how are all of these quantities interrelated, and how do they limit the permissible traffic distributions in the network? This section addresses these questions in a general context, without requiring any detailed description of the channels, the transceivers, or the traffic. We assume only that the amount of network traffic is specified for all LCs linking the various source and destination stations.

As in Section 5.2.1, let us assume that all transmitters operate at a common, fixed bitrate, $R_t \leq R_{max}$.[10] Each channel can accommodate the flow from one transmitter, up to the maximum rate R_{max}. One question that is addressed is whether a given traffic matrix can be supported using a bitrate not exceeding R_{max}.

We begin with the following flow conservation inequalities:

$$
\begin{aligned}
\mathcal{T}_i &\leq R_t \alpha_i, \quad i = 1, 2, \ldots, M \\
\mathcal{R}_j &\leq R_t \beta_j, \quad j = 1, 2, \ldots, N \\
\bar{\gamma} &\leq R_t C
\end{aligned}
\tag{5.53}
$$

where

$$
\begin{aligned}
\mathcal{T}_i &= \sum_j \gamma_{ij} = \text{aggregate traffic from station } i \\
\mathcal{R}_j &= \sum_i \gamma_{ij} = \text{aggregate traffic to station } j \\
\bar{\gamma} &= \sum_{ij} \gamma_{ij} = \text{total traffic}
\end{aligned}
\tag{5.54}
$$

---

[10] Among the factors limiting the channel bitrate are the speed of the electronics in the TPs and RPs, the modulation bandwidth of the laser, the characteristics of the λ-channel and optical path it is using (bandwidth, dispersion, noise, interference, attenuation, nonlinearities), and the bandwidth and noise properties of the ORs. See Chapter 4.

The first inequality in Equation 5.53 expresses the limitation imposed by each station's transmitter capacity, and the second is the limit due to each station's receiving capacity. The third is the fundamental limitation imposed by the network capacity, relating the aggregate traffic to the aggregate transmission capacity available to carry it.

Combining the inequalities in Equation 5.53 we find a lower bound on the bitrate, R_t, needed to support a given traffic requirement:

$$R_{\min} = \max_{ij} \left[\frac{\mathcal{T}_i}{\alpha_i}, \frac{\mathcal{R}_j}{\beta_j}, \frac{\bar{\gamma}}{C} \right] \tag{5.55}$$

Equation 5.55 shows that a bitrate of at least $\bar{\gamma}/C$ is always necessary because of the aggregate traffic requirements, but this may not be sufficient. If one of the first two inequalities in Equation 5.53 is violated for some rate that satisfies the third, this signifies that there is a traffic imbalance with respect to the available station resources. This phenomenon can be expressed in terms of a *traffic balance factor*:

$$\eta = \frac{\bar{\gamma}/C}{\max_{ij} \left[\frac{\mathcal{T}_i}{\alpha_i}, \frac{\mathcal{R}_j}{\beta_j}, \frac{\bar{\gamma}}{C} \right]} \tag{5.56}$$

The parameter η attains a maximum value of unity when the traffic distribution is matched to the station resources, in the sense that the flow is limited only by the available capacity of the shared medium. The traffic is unbalanced ($\eta < 1$) when station transceiver limitations are the binding quantities. Another way of interpreting η is as the throughput of the network, $\bar{\gamma}$, normalized with respect to the total capacity $R_{\min}C$ needed to carry it. The two parameters $\bar{\gamma}$ and η subsume the key characteristics of the matrix Γ relative to the network resources. The lower bound on bitrate can be expressed in terms of these parameters as

$$R_{\min} = \bar{\gamma}/\eta C \tag{5.57}$$

The point to note in Equation 5.57 is that poorly balanced traffic necessitates an increased bitrate to support a given aggregate traffic requirement $\bar{\gamma}$. This in turn leads to inefficient use of the communication channels, as is shown in subsequent examples. It is not hard to conjure up extreme cases. For example, in a directed $M \times M$ shared-channel network with C equal to M channels, and with a single transmitter or receiver per station, the balance factor is $1/M$ if all traffic originates from one transmitting station or is destined to one receiving station. (This simply states the fact that $M - 1$ channels are superfluous in this case.)

A special case of Equation 5.56 arises when $C = 1$ and $\alpha_i = \beta_j = 1$ for all i, j, which corresponds to a TDM/TDMA network. In this case, $\eta = 1$ independent of the matrix Γ (because row and column sums of Γ are never greater than $\bar{\gamma}$).

To illustrate the significance of the traffic balance factor, we now examine η and $R_{\min}$ in a variety of situations. In each case the specified flows are expressed as

$$T = \begin{bmatrix} 1 & 1 & 1 & 1 \\ 1 & 1 & 1 & 1 \\ 1 & 1 & 1 & 1 \\ 1 & 1 & 1 & 1 \end{bmatrix} \qquad \begin{bmatrix} 0 & 2 & 2 & 0 \\ 0 & 0 & 1 & 3 \\ 2 & 0 & 1 & 1 \\ 2 & 2 & 0 & 0 \end{bmatrix}$$

$$(a) \qquad\qquad\qquad (b)$$

$$\begin{bmatrix} 0 & 2 & 1 & 0 \\ 0 & 0 & 2 & 3 \\ 2 & 0 & 1 & 1 \\ 2 & 2 & 0 & 0 \end{bmatrix} \qquad \begin{bmatrix} 0 & 2 & 2 & 0 \\ 0 & 0 & 3 & 1 \\ 2 & 0 & 1 & 1 \\ 2 & 2 & 0 & 0 \end{bmatrix}$$

$$(c) \qquad\qquad\qquad (d)$$

FIGURE 5.22 Normalized traffic matrices.

integer multiples of a basic bitrate R_0; that is, in the form $\Gamma = R_0 T$, where T is the normalized traffic matrix first introduced in Section 5.2.1. Figure 5.22 gives some examples of normalized traffic distributions in directed 4×4 systems. The total traffic in each case is $\bar{\gamma} = 16R_0$. We shall determine η and the value of $R_{\min}$ necessary to support these traffic distributions given several different sets of network resources.

5.3.1 Balanced Traffic

Figure 5.22(a) shows the case of uniform traffic. In this case, $\eta = 1$ for any $C \le 4$, so that $R_{\min} = \bar{\gamma}/C$. (This is true for any number of transmitters and receivers per station.) Thus, for a single-channel TDM/TDMA system, $R_{\min} = 16R_0$, and for a four-channel system, which can be operated in either an FT-TR or a TT-FR mode, $R_{\min} = 4R_0$.

The traffic matrix of Figure 5.22(b) represents nonuniform and incomplete multipoint connectivity. Nevertheless, $\eta = 1$ for all $C \le 4$ and any number of transmitters and receivers per station. Thus, once again, $R_{\min} = \bar{\gamma}/C$. The observation here is that traffic balance does not require uniformity of the traffic matrix.

5.3.2 Unbalanced Traffic

The next two examples, shown in Figures 5.22(c) and (d), illustrate traffic imbalances. In each case we start with the assumption that $C = 4$, with a single transmitter or receiver in each station. The normalized traffic of Figure 5.22(c) is a minor variation of the case of Figure 5.22(b), in which the entries t_{13} and t_{23} have been interchanged. As a result we now have $\mathcal{T}_2 = 5R_0$, which means that the balance factor is now $\eta = 4/5$. Because of the traffic imbalance, $R_{\min} = 5R_0$, an increase of 25% over the balanced case. However, if station 2 had two transmitters ($\alpha_2 = 2$), the balance factor would again be unity, returning $R_{\min}$ to $4R_0$.

Another unbalanced case is shown in Figure 5.22(d), which is obtained from Figure 5.22(b) by permuting entries t_{23} and t_{24}, with the result that $\mathcal{R}_3 = 6R_0$. Now when

$C = 4$, we have $\eta = 2/3$ and $R_{\min} = 6R_0$. Next, suppose that we reduce the number of channels to $C = 3$. Referring to Equation 5.57, we find that the balance factor increases to 8/9, but $R_{\min}$ remains at $6R_0$. If there are two receivers in station 3 ($\beta_3 = 2$) and $C = 3$, the balance factor returns to unity, reducing $R_{\min}$ to $16R_0/3$.

5.4 Capacity Allocation for Dedicated Connections

Each of the examples in the previous section determines a minimum value of the transmitter bitrate $R_{\min}$ that is *necessary* to support a specified traffic distribution. It has little practical meaning unless we can show that this minimum rate (or something close to it) is also *sufficient*. In this section we show that using fixed capacity allocations, a bitrate close to $R_{\min}$ can indeed support the specified traffic; that is, the lower bound on R_t is tight. A scheduling method is described for satisfying arbitrary traffic requirements in a variety of settings for both stream and packet traffic. The underlying optical infrastructure remains the $M \times N$ shared-channel broadcast medium of Figure 5.21.

5.4.1 Fixed-Frame Scheduling for Stream Traffic

The basic features of fixed-frame schedules for dedicated LCs in TDM/T-WDMA networks were presented in Section 5.2.1. A periodic time frame with L equal-size slots was used to multiplex the traffic onto C channels. The approach there was to present the ideas through some simple examples, limited to cases with a single transmitter or receiver per station. It remains to present a general method of determining fixed-frame schedules that are optimal for specified traffic flows and network resources, and to show that these schedules achieve a performance close to the best possible as indicated by the flow constraints of Section 5.3. As in the previous section, our results apply to shared-channel broadcast media based on a wide range of multiplexing/multiple-access techniques, of which TDM/T-WDMA is but one concrete example. We consider networks with multiple transmitters or receivers per station and with all transmitters running at a common bitrate R_t.

As in Section 5.3, the capacity of the broadcast medium is to be shared among a set of up to MN point-to-point LCs carrying stream traffic at bitrates specified by a traffic matrix Γ. The algorithm used for optimal scheduling is a generalization by [Gopal82] of a technique by [Inukai79]. For illustration, CASs are exhibited for the examples in Section 5.3.

In the scheduling problem, there are three interrelated parameters of particular interest:

1. $L_{\min}$ = the minimum number of slots required to schedule the traffic
2. $R'_{\min}$ = the minimum transmitter bitrate that accommodates the required traffic
3. η_s = the scheduling efficiency of the CAS (defined in Equation 5.5)

The frame time F and slot time F/L (in seconds) do not enter into the analysis. Once a frame schedule is determined, any value of F consistent with other system requirements can be used.

Clearly, a schedule with a minimum value of R_t is desirable to accommodate as much traffic as possible without exceeding R_{max}. The purpose of keeping L small is that there is a fixed overhead (the guard time) associated with each time slot. (In the case of multichannel systems involving rapid transceiver tuning, the guard time must include an allowance for transmitter and/or receiver tuning time.) Increasing the number of slots in a frame while keeping the frame time small (to limit latency) means that the slot size diminishes relative to the overhead, eventually producing a prohibitive reduction in transmission efficiency.

Following Section 5.2.1, to construct a traffic schedule we first decompose the traffic matrix into the product $\Gamma = R_0 T$, where the elements t_{ij} of the normalized traffic matrix T are relatively prime integers. A capacity of $c_{ij} = t_{ij}$ channel–slots is allocated to LC $[i, j]$ so that each channel–slot contains one unit of normalized traffic, which corresponds to $R_t F/L$ bits. (From now on we assume that the overhead due to guard times is negligible.)

Building on the terminology of Section 5.3, let us define the following quantities:

$$\mathcal{T}'_i = \sum_j t_{ij} = \mathcal{T}_i/R_0 = \text{aggregate normalized traffic from station } i$$

$$\mathcal{R}'_j = \sum_i t_{ij} = \mathcal{R}_j/R_0 = \text{aggregate normalized traffic to station } j \qquad (5.58)$$

$$\bar{T} = \sum_{ij} t_{ij} = \bar{\gamma}/R_0 = \text{total normalized traffic}$$

Using these definitions, it can be shown (see [Gopal82]) that the minimum number of time slots necessary to create a collisionless conflict-free schedule accommodating a normalized traffic matrix T, with one unit of normalized traffic per channel–slot, is

$$L_{min} = \max_{ij} \left(\left\lceil \frac{\bar{T}}{C} \right\rceil, \left\lceil \frac{\mathcal{T}'_i}{\alpha_i} \right\rceil, \left\lceil \frac{\mathcal{R}'_j}{\beta_j} \right\rceil \right) \qquad (5.59)$$

This number is also sufficient, as demonstrated in Appendix B, where an optimal scheduling algorithm is presented. The schedule is found by decomposing the normalized traffic matrix into L_{min} $M \times N$ matrices, $C^{(s)} = [c_{ij}^{(s)}], s = 1, 2, \ldots, L_{min}$, where $c_{ij}^{(s)}$ is a nonnegative integer representing the number of channels assigned to LC $[i, j]$ in time slot s, and $c_{ij} = \sum_s c_{ij}^{(s)}$.

To match the traffic requirements, the $C^{(s)}$'s must satisfy

$$\sum_{s=1}^{L_{min}} C^{(s)} = T \qquad (5.60)$$

Each $C^{(s)}$ must also satisfy the system constraints

$$\sum_j c_{ij}^{(s)} \le \alpha_i, \quad i = 1, 2, \ldots, M \tag{5.61}$$

$$\sum_i c_{ij}^{(s)} \le \beta_j, \quad j = 1, 2, \ldots, N \tag{5.62}$$

$$\sum_{ij} c_{ij}^{(s)} \le C \tag{5.63}$$

Note that the inequality in Equation 5.63 ensures that the allocation in each slot does not exceed the number of available channels, Equation 5.61 ensures that there are enough transmitters available for the allocation, and Equation 5.62 ensures that there are no receiver conflicts.

From flow conservation, we find that the traffic specified by a matrix Γ can be transmitted in a schedule with L_{min} slots using a value of transmitter bitrate:

$$R'_{min} = L_{min} R_0 \tag{5.64}$$

Equation 5.64 gives the minimum possible bitrate sufficient to carry the traffic Γ. The efficiency of the schedule with L_{min} slots can be expressed as

$$\eta_s = \frac{\bar{\gamma}}{R'_{min} C} = \frac{\bar{T}}{L_{min} C} \tag{5.65}$$

Because there are $L_{min} C$ channel–slots in the frame, the value of η_s is unity when all channel–slots are fully utilized. Otherwise, $\eta_s < 1$, indicating that there are some idle channel–slots.

These scheduling results parallel closely and complement the development of Section 5.3, which led to an expression for R_{min}—the minimum bitrate *necessary* to carry a specified traffic. In this case we have a method for scheduling a prescribed traffic matrix, together with a bitrate R'_{min} *sufficient* for transmitting that schedule. Using Equations 5.56, 5.58, and 5.65, we find that

$$\frac{R_{min}}{R'_{min}} = \frac{\eta_s}{\eta} = \frac{\max_{ij} \left[\frac{\bar{T}}{C}, \frac{\mathcal{T}'_i}{\alpha_i}, \frac{\mathcal{R}'_j}{\beta_j} \right]}{\max_{ij} \left(\lceil \frac{\bar{T}}{C} \rceil, \lceil \frac{\mathcal{T}'_i}{\alpha_i} \rceil, \lceil \frac{\mathcal{R}'_j}{\beta_j} \rceil \right)} \le 1 \tag{5.66}$$

with equality if and only if $\max_{ij} \left[\frac{\bar{T}}{C}, \frac{\mathcal{T}'_i}{\alpha_i}, \frac{\mathcal{R}'_j}{\beta_j} \right]$ is an integer. The schedule of length L_{min} requires a bitrate $R'_{min} \ge R_{min}$, with equality when $\eta_s = \eta$. Otherwise a higher bitrate is required to make up for the inefficiency caused by the fact that $\eta_s < \eta$.[11]

---

[11] In some cases the difference between η_s and η may be large. If this is bothersome, and if one is not concerned about keeping L small, then the matrix T can always be "scaled up" through multiplication by an integer (with a corresponding scaling down of R_0) until $\eta_s \approx \eta$, and a schedule can be found with $R'_{min} \approx R_{min}$. Thus, the scaling of T is a compromise between keeping L small (to reduce overhead and latency) and keeping scheduling efficiency high. (Another aspect of scaling appears in Section 5.4.1.3.)

Noting that $R'_{\min}$ cannot exceed the maximum permissible transmitter bitrate $R_{\max}$, we find that a sufficient condition for a network to be able to carry a prescribed traffic distribution is

$$R_{\max} \geq \frac{\bar{\gamma}}{\eta_s C} \tag{5.67}$$

5.4.1.1 Channel Assignments: Tunability

Although the matrices $C^{(s)}$ defined earlier give a feasible set of channel–slot allocations to match a given traffic matrix in a minimum-length schedule, only the *number* of channels assigned to each LC in each slot is prescribed. The issue of specific channel *assignment* (i.e., transceiver tuning) is not addressed. In general, once the $C^{(s)}$'s are determined, any arbitrary assignment of channels yields an acceptable CAS, provided that all assignments in a given slot are *distinct* (to avoid collisions). This freedom of choice in making channel assignments can be used to an advantage in satisfying other system limitations: in particular, constraints on transceiver tunability.

An arbitrary set of channel assignments generally produces a TT-TR CAS. Because tunability is costly, a natural question arises. Is it always possible to find an FT-TR or a TT-FR CAS with $L_{\min}$ slots for a prescribed traffic matrix? The answer is no, and this leads to a number of related questions that we address now.

In the case where $C \geq \sum_i \alpha_i$, enough channels are available to dedicate a distinct channel to each transmitter so that an FT-TR CAS is possible. (For the case where all source stations have a single transmitter, this corresponds to a system with $C \geq M$.) Similarly, if $C \geq \sum_j \beta_j$, enough channels are available to dedicate a distinct channel to each receiver so that a TT-FR CAS is possible. (For the case where all destination stations have a single receiver, this corresponds to a system with $C \geq N$.) We shall call these cases, systems with a "full complement" of channels. For smaller numbers of channels, as might be expected, a TT-TR system is usually required to produce a CAS with a minimum number of slots.

The next question is, what is the minimum frame length for an FT-TR or TT-FR system with a prescribed traffic matrix, and with less than a full complement of channels? We answer this now for a restricted class of systems: those with a single transmitter or receiver per station.

Consider an $M \times N$ shared-channel system with a single transmitter per station, and with $C = \hat{M} < M$. We seek a minimum-length FT-TR CAS for this system for a normalized traffic matrix T. Because there is less than a full complement of channels for an FT-TR system, a channel assignment must be chosen wherein some transmitters are necessarily tuned to the same channel. Let $\mathcal{P} = \{\mathcal{S}_1, \mathcal{S}_2, \ldots, \mathcal{S}_{\hat{M}}\}$ denote a partition of the set of source stations into $\hat{M}$ subsets, where each $\mathcal{S}_i$ is a set of source station numbers. In our FT-TR CAS, all stations in the same subset share a common dedicated channel. Let $\hat{T} = [\hat{t}_{ij}]$ be a normalized $\hat{M} \times N$ traffic matrix derived from T, where

$$\hat{t}_{ij} = \sum_{k \in \mathcal{S}_i} t_{kj} \tag{5.68}$$

The matrix $\hat{T}$ defines normalized traffic for a fictitious system with $\hat{M}$ source stations, where the ith fictitious source station has normalized traffic corresponding to the aggregate traffic from all (real) stations in the set S_i. Each source station in the fictitious system is assumed to have a single transmitter, and each destination station has the same number of receivers as it has in the original system. Under these assumptions we find that the minimum number of slots required to schedule this traffic in the fictitious system is

$$\hat{L}_{\min} = \max_{ij} \left(\left\lceil \frac{\bar{T}}{C} \right\rceil, \hat{\mathcal{T}}'_i, \left\lceil \frac{\mathcal{R}'_j}{\beta_j} \right\rceil \right) \tag{5.69}$$

where

$$\hat{\mathcal{T}}'_i = \sum_j \hat{t}_{ij} \tag{5.70}$$

By comparing Equation 5.69 with the value of $L_{\min}$ for the original system in Equation 5.59, we find that $\hat{L}_{\min} \geq L_{\min}$ with equality if and only if $\hat{\mathcal{T}}'_i \leq L_{\min}$ for $i = 1, 2, \ldots \hat{M}$.

Once a partition has been chosen, the scheduling algorithm of Appendix B can be used to find a channel–slot schedule for the fictitious system in the form of a set of $\hat{M} \times N$ matrices $\hat{C}^{(s)}, s = 1, 2, \ldots, \hat{L}_{\min}$. Because only one transmitter per station was assumed in this system, at the most one channel is allocated to fictitious source station i in each slot, with the total channel–slot allocation in the frame corresponding to the aggregate traffic for the source set S_i in the original system. Therefore, assigning a common channel to all stations in the set, the total channel–slot allocation is sufficient to schedule the aggregate traffic without collisions by distributing the channel–slot allocation among all stations in S_i. We have thus constructed an FT-TR CAS of length $\hat{L}_{\min}$ corresponding to the chosen partition of transmitting stations.

Clearly, $\hat{L}_{\min}$ depends on the choice of partition. By computing the minimum value of $\hat{L}_{\min}$ over all partitions, we find the shortest possible frame length for an FT-TR system with a given traffic matrix. In some cases (corresponding to traffic matrices with a high degree of imbalance) it is possible to find partitions (and hence channel assignments) with $\hat{L}_{\min} = L_{\min}$, so that no penalty is incurred in using FT-TR.

A completely parallel development is possible for systems operating in a TT-FR mode. In this case we assume that the destination stations have a single receiver per station and $C = \hat{N} < N$. Now the set of all destination stations is partitioned into subsets S_j, where all stations in a subset share a common dedicated channel. Letting $\hat{T} = [\hat{t}_{ij}]$ be a normalized $M \times \hat{N}$ traffic matrix, where

$$\hat{t}_{ij} = \sum_{k \in S_j} t_{ik} \tag{5.71}$$

it can be shown that a TT-FR CAS exists with minimum slot length

$$\hat{L}_{\min} = \max_{ij} \left(\left\lceil \frac{\bar{T}}{C} \right\rceil , \left\lceil \frac{\mathcal{T}_i'}{\alpha_i} \right\rceil , \hat{\mathcal{R}}_j' \right) \tag{5.72}$$

where

$$\hat{\mathcal{R}}_j' = \sum_i \hat{t}_{ij} \tag{5.73}$$

The details of the development leading up to this result are left as an exercise for the reader. The next section provides some examples that apply these scheduling principles.

5.4.1.2 Examples of Optimal Schedules

All the examples in this section except the last deal with 4×4 directed, shared-channel networks. In each case except Example 8 we use the normalized traffic matrices introduced earlier in Section 5.3, wherein the total traffic is $\bar{T} = 16$.

The first four examples illustrate optimal scheduling for systems with a single transmitter or receiver per station and a full complement of channels ($C = 4$). Although optimal schedules can be found using the algorithm of Appendix B, these examples are small enough to do the scheduling by inspection.

Example 1

Figure 5.23(a) shows a TT-FR CAS for the uniform traffic matrix of Figure 5.22(a), where receiver j uses channel j. It has a length $L = L_{\min} = 4$, so $R_t = R_{\min}' = 4R_0$. Reading down each column of the CAS we find the nonzero elements of the decomposition of T. Thus, for example, from column 2, $c_{21}^{(2)} = c_{32}^{(2)} = c_{43}^{(2)} = c_{14}^{(2)} = 1$.

Example 2

The traffic matrix of Figure 5.22(b) is nonuniform but balanced, and $\eta_s = \eta$. Thus a CAS can be found with $L = L_{\min} = 4$, as shown in Figure 5.23(b). The figure shows an FT-TR schedule where transmitter j uses channel j.

Example 3

Now consider the traffic of Figure 5.22(c), where $\eta_s = \eta = 4/5$, indicating a traffic imbalance. The minimum frame length is $L_{\min} = 5$, with $R_{\min}' = 5R_0 = R_{\min}$. An FT-TR CAS with minimum length is shown in Figure 5.23(c), in which the blanks in certain entries of the schedule indicate that channels and station equipment are idle in those channel–slots.

Channel 1	[1, 1]	[2, 1]	[3, 1]	[4, 1]
Channel 2	[2, 2]	[3, 2]	[4, 2]	[1, 2]
Channel 3	[3, 3]	[4, 3]	[1, 3]	[2, 3]
Channel 4	[4, 4]	[1, 4]	[2, 4]	[3, 4]
Slot	1	2	3	4

(*a*) TT-FR

Channel 1	[1, 2]	[1, 2]	[1, 3]	[1, 3]
Channel 2	[2, 3]	[2, 4]	[2, 4]	[2, 4]
Channel 3	[3, 4]	[3, 3]	[3, 1]	[3, 1]
Channel 4	[4, 1]	[4, 1]	[4, 2]	[4, 2]
Slot	1	2	3	4

(*b*) FT-TR

Channel 1	[1, 2]	[1, 2]	[1, 3]		
Channel 2	[2, 3]	[2, 3]	[2, 4]	[2, 4]	[2, 4]
Channel 3	[3, 1]	[3, 4]		[3, 1]	[3, 3]
Channel 4		[4, 1]	[4, 1]	[4, 2]	[4, 2]
Slot	1	2	3	4	5

(*c*) FT-TR

FIGURE 5.23 CASs for systems with a full complement of channels.

Example 4

Figure 5.22(d) gives another unbalanced normalized traffic matrix with $\eta = \eta_s = 2/3$, so that this traffic can be scheduled in $L_{min} = 6$ slots, as shown in Figure 5.24(a).

We continue with three more examples based on the normalized traffic matrix of Figure 5.22(d). The objective now is to illustrate how changing the system parameters affects the feasible CASs.

Example 5

Suppose only three channels are available to schedule the traffic of Figure 5.22(d), using a single transmitter or receiver per station. Despite this reduction of capacity, we find from Equation 5.59 that L_{min} remains at 6 slots. However, reducing C does pose a problem. Because we no longer have a full complement of channels, it is not clear whether a minimum-length FT-TR CAS can be found. To produce such a schedule

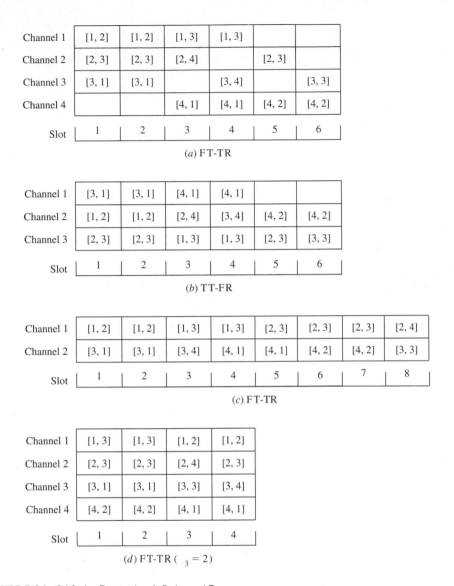

FIGURE 5.24 CASs for Examples 4, 5, 6, and 7.

we must assign the same channel to two transmitting stations with aggregate traffic that does not exceed $L_{min} = 6$. This is clearly impossible, and thus a minimum-length FT-TR schedule does not exist. On the other hand, we note that the aggregate traffic for *destination* stations 2 and 4 equals 6, so that a minimum-length TT-FR schedule is possible with those stations sharing a common channel. A feasible 6-slot CAS is shown in Figure 5.24(b) with receiver 1 operating on channel 1, receivers 2 and 4 on channel 2, and receiver 3 on channel 3.

Example 6

If an FT-TR CAS is required for the previous example, the frame length has to be increased. Because each source station has an aggregate traffic of 4, we have $\hat{L}_{min} = 8$, and η_s is reduced to 1/2. But by partitioning the source stations into two subsets, {1, 2} and {3, 4}, we find that the same frame length can be achieved with only two channels using FT-TR, with $\eta_s = \eta = 1$. A possible CAS is shown in Figure 5.24(c) with transmitters 1 and 2 sharing channel 1 and transmitters 3 and 4 sharing channel 2.

Example 7

This example shows the effect of increasing the station equipment in the case of the normalized traffic of Figure 5.22(d). Noting that it is receiving station 3 that carries the largest load, we shall add a second receiver to that station ($\beta_3 = 2$). Assuming that $C = 4$, this improves the balance factor to unity, and thus we now have $\eta = \eta_s = 1$, and $L_{min} = 4$. Figure 5.24(d) shows an FT-TR CAS with transmitter j using channel j, in which destination 3 is now allowed to appear as much as twice in each column of the schedule: $c_{13}^{(1)} = c_{23}^{(1)} = 1$ and $c_{13}^{(2)} = c_{23}^{(2)} = 1$.

Example 8

In this example, we use partitioning and FT-TR to accommodate a heterogeneous traffic mix on a small number of channels. Figure 5.25(a) shows a normalized traffic matrix for a 10×10 directed, shared-channel system in which source station 1 transmits 10 units of traffic while all others transmit 1 or 2 units. The total normalized traffic is $\bar{T} = 20$. We assume that all stations have a single transmitter or receiver and that $C = 2$, in which case the traffic is balanced: $\eta = \eta_s = 1$ and $L_{min} = 10$. Noting that the aggregate traffic from all the low-traffic stations is 10, a natural partition of the source stations to produce an FT-TR system is to assign channel 1 to source 1 and channel 2 to all others. A possible minimum-length CAS is shown in Figure 5.25(b).

This last example suggests that when there are many more users than available channels, an efficient way of assigning channels is to reserve one or more channels to be shared by the low-traffic population either on an FT-TR or a TT-FR basis, and to assign the remaining channels to the large users as needed.

5.4.1.3 Traffic Matrix Scaling

The first step in determining CASs for fixed frame systems involves the conversion of the traffic matrix Γ to a normalized traffic matrix T. In theory, if the elements of Γ are rational numbers, a unique decomposition of Γ in the form of a matrix T of relatively prime integers multiplied by a scalar R_0 is always possible.[12] In *practice* however, the decomposition involves approximations, and thus it is *not* unique. Furthermore, the way it is done can influence strongly the efficiency of the traffic schedule.

---

[12] Because any real number can be approximated arbitrarily closely by a rational, the decomposition is possible for all practical purposes for *any* Γ.

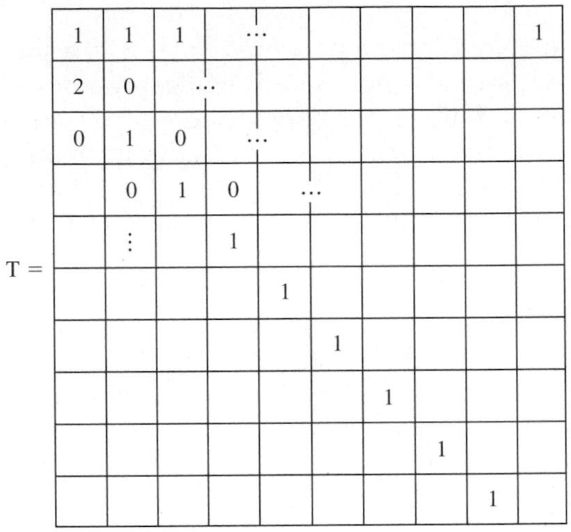

$$
T =
\begin{bmatrix}
1 & 1 & 1 & \cdots & & & & & & 1 \\
2 & 0 & \cdots & & & & & & & \\
0 & 1 & 0 & \cdots & & & & & & \\
 & 0 & 1 & 0 & \cdots & & & & & \\
 & \vdots & & 1 & & & & & & \\
 & & & & 1 & & & & & \\
 & & & & & 1 & & & & \\
 & & & & & & 1 & & & \\
 & & & & & & & 1 & & \\
 & & & & & & & & 1 & \\
\end{bmatrix}
$$

(a)

Channel 1	[1, 1]	[1, 2]	[1, 3]	⋯				[1, 8]	[1, 9]	[1, 10]
Channel 2	[3, 2]	[4, 3]	[5, 4]	⋯			⋯	[10, 9]	[2, 1]	[2, 1]
Slot	1	2	3	4	5	6	7	8	9	10

(b)

FIGURE 5.25 Heterogeneous traffic scheduling.

To illustrate the importance of a "good" approximation, consider the following 2×2 irrational traffic matrix:

$$
\Gamma =
\begin{bmatrix}
1 & \pi \\
1 & 1
\end{bmatrix}
\tag{5.74}
$$

Two possible approximations for γ_{12} are $10/3$ and $3.1416 = 3{,}927/1{,}250$. These are both rational numbers that overestimate π and thus represent the traffic conservatively. Using the first approximation, the decomposition is

$$
\Gamma = \frac{1}{3}
\begin{bmatrix}
3 & 10 \\
3 & 3
\end{bmatrix}
\tag{5.75}
$$

Using the second, it is

$$
\Gamma = \frac{1}{1{,}250}
\begin{bmatrix}
1{,}250 & 3{,}927 \\
1{,}250 & 1{,}250
\end{bmatrix}
\tag{5.76}
$$

Now suppose this traffic is to be scheduled in a single-channel system (e.g., TDM/TDMA). In this case each of these normalized matrices can be scheduled with $\eta_s = 1$, so that we have $L_{\min} = \bar{T}$. Thus, the first approximation gives a frame length of 19 whereas the second gives a length of 7,677! Clearly, the first approximation is much better in terms of frame length, even though approximately 7% of the capacity allocated to LC [1, 2] is wasted. What has happened here? In both cases we approximated Γ by "rounding up" γ_{12} to a rational number. But once the elements of Γ are approximated as rationals, the scalar constant R_0 in the decomposition becomes the reciprocal of the least common denominator of the γ_{ij}'s. A large denominator means a small R_0, which in turn implies a large $\bar{T}$, and hence a large $L_{\min}$. In the case at hand, the more accurate approximation of π produced a very long frame length. If we are willing to accept the poorer approximation, a much shorter frame can be used. Thus, two criteria must be considered in obtaining an "efficient" rational approximation of Γ: keeping the elements of T small while at the same time avoiding excessive rounding errors.

5.4.1.4   Multicast Logical Connections

If some of the LCs carried by a shared-channel broadcast medium are multicast instead of point to point, then the previous discussion of flow constraints and capacity allocation in the last two sections must be revised. In this section we present the necessary modifications.

The traffic requirements used for scheduling point-to-point LCs were defined in terms of a traffic matrix Γ. A property of any traffic matrix is the flow conservation condition:

$$\bar{\gamma} = \sum_i \mathcal{T}_i = \sum_j \mathcal{R}_j = \sum_{ij} \gamma_{ij} \tag{5.77}$$

which expresses the fact that the total traffic carried by the network equals the aggregate traffic transmitted, which equals the aggregate traffic received. But in a *multicast* LC the total traffic received *exceeds* the total traffic transmitted, because the traffic leaving the source arrives at more than one destination. Thus, a matrix description of multicast traffic is incomplete. Instead, the traffic parameters must be obtained directly from a prescribed set of LCs.

To formalize this, let $l_k = [\tau_k, \varrho_k]$ represent the kth LC in our shared-channel system, where τ_k is the transmitting station and ϱ_k is a set of receiving stations. As in the case of point-to-point connections, we assume that the traffic flows are normalized to integer values, so that if γ_k represents the flow requirement (in bits per second) on LC k, then

$$\gamma_k = R_0 t_k \tag{5.78}$$

$$\bar{\gamma} = \sum_k \gamma_k \tag{5.79}$$

$$\bar{T} = \sum_k t_k \tag{5.80}$$

where t_k is an integer, and $\bar{\gamma}$, $\bar{T}$, and R_0 represent the total *transmitted* traffic, the total normalized transmitted traffic, and the basic bitrate used for normalization respectively.

The aggregrate normalized traffic $\mathcal{T}'_i$, transmitted from station i, is found by summing the normalized traffic over all LCs emanating from i:

$$\mathcal{T}'_i = \sum_{\{k|\tau_k=i\}} t_k \qquad (5.81)$$

and the aggregate normalized traffic $\mathcal{R}'_j$, destined for station j, is found by summing the normalized traffic over all LCs with a receiving set that contains j:

$$\mathcal{R}'_j = \sum_{\{k|j\epsilon\varrho_k\}} t_k \qquad (5.82)$$

The relations among these quantities are

$$\sum_j \mathcal{R}'_j \geq \sum_i \mathcal{T}'_i = \bar{T} \qquad (5.83)$$

By substituting the values of $\bar{T}$, $\mathcal{T}'_i$, and $\mathcal{R}'_j$ given in Equations 5.80, 5.81, and 5.82 respectively into Equation 5.59, we find the minimum frame length for the multicast case. Note that it is the aggregate normalized *transmitted* traffic that determines the total traffic requirement $\bar{T}$ in Equation 5.59, and this quantity does not include the effect of multicast. However, the aggregate received traffic requirements $\mathcal{R}'_j$ needed for determining the minimum frame length are computed by taking into account the multicast connectivity.

To illustrate the changes in scheduling for multicast connections, let us revisit the schedule for the normalized (point-to-point) traffic matrix of Figure 5.22(c). Recall that for a four-channel network with one transmitter or receiver per station, this traffic was scheduled with $L = L_{min} = 5$ slots yielding $R_t = R_{min} = 5R_0$—see Figure 5.23(c) for an FT-TR CAS.

Now suppose some of the connections in that example are multicast, with the traffic flow prescribed in Table 5.2. Note that the connections [4, 1] and [4, 2], both carrying two units of traffic in the point-to-point system, have been replaced by the multicast connection [4, {1, 2}], and a similar replacement was made for two units of traffic originating at station 2. The eight LCs are visualized graphically in Figure 5.26(a) using a directed LCH, with connection l_k represented by hyperarc k in the LCH. (This tripartite representation of an LCH was first introduced in Figure 3.36.)

The multicast modifications result in revised values of the arguments of Equation 5.59, with $\bar{T}$ reduced from 16 to 12, and $\mathcal{T}'_2$ reduced from 5 to 3. The binding quantities in determining frame length are now $\mathcal{T}'_3 = \mathcal{R}'_1 = \mathcal{R}'_2 = \mathcal{R}'_3 = \mathcal{R}'_4 = 4$, so that the minimum number of slots is reduced from 5 in the point-to-point case to 4 in the multicast case. An FT-TR CAS with $L = 4$ slots is shown in Figure 5.26(b).

TABLE 5.2   Multicast Connections

Connection Number	τ_k	ϱ_k	t_k
1	1	2	2
2	1	3	1
3	2	4	1
4	2	{3, 4}	2
5	3	1	2
6	3	3	1
7	3	4	1
8	4	{1, 2}	2

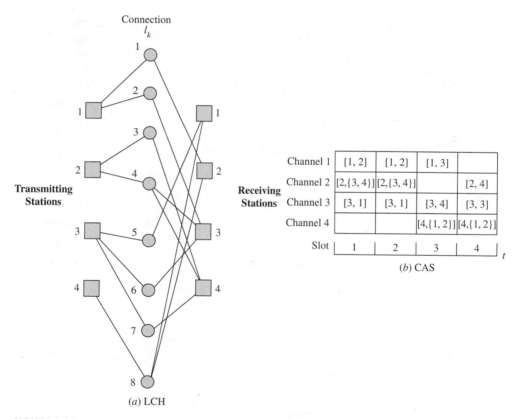

(a) LCH

(b) CAS

FIGURE 5.26   Logical multicast CAS.

Multicast receiving sets appear in certain entries of the CAS, indicating that all stations in the receiving set must tune simultaneously to the given channel. As before, for conflict-free operation each receiving station must appear no more than once in each column of the schedule. The reduction in frame length from the point-to-point to the multicast case reflects the fact that less information is being transmitted. Because of this reduction, the transmitter bitrates can be reduced by a factor of 4/5 to $R_t = 4R_0$.

It is interesting to compare three possible implementations of logical multicast in optical networks. In purely optical networks operating with only point-to-point optical connections (e.g., wavelength routed point-to-point networks) a k-fold multicast connection must be implemented on k individual LCs fanning out from the source to the receiving set, and all carrying the same information. This replication increases the traffic load on the network k-fold without carrying any additional information.

In logically routed networks (Section 3.5) an electronically switched logical topology is overlaid on the physical topology. In this case, the multicast connection can be realized at the logical level in the form of a multicast tree. Each logical switching node in the tree replicates the information for transmission on logical paths to the receiving nodes. This, however, requires conversion of information between the optical and electronic domain at each node of the tree. Furthermore, this still imposes an additional load on the physical layer, where the extent of the load augmentation depends on how the logical topology is embedded on the physical topology.

Finally, in networks in which the underlying optical connections can be broadcast or multicast (i.e., static broadcast networks or LLNs), a multicast LC can be implemented without any additional load on the network by exploiting the broadcast/multicast connectivity in the optical medium.[13]

5.4.2 Fixed-Frame Scheduling for Packet Traffic

In our discussion of fixed capacity allocation it was assumed that the traffic was in the form of synchronous bitstreams, so that the information flow on each LC was constant and known precisely in advance. In that case, all variables are deterministic, and fixed capacity allocations that are matched exactly to a prescribed traffic matrix produce maximum efficiency. With packet traffic we have the option of using either fixed or dynamic capacity allocations. In this section the fixed allocation approach is presented. Section 5.6, which is devoted to packet switching in the optical layer, explores the dynamic approach. (A brief review of the elements of random processes and queues that constitute the background for this and the next two sections is found in Appendix C.)

In scheduling packet traffic the slotted, fixed-frame structure used in the stream traffic case can still be employed. However, certain modifications are required to adapt

---

[13] To be fair in comparing efficiency of resource utilization, it must be recalled that a static broadcast or multicast medium always replicates each transmission optically on each link outbound from a broadcast/multicast optical node. Thus, in effect, it wastes capacity when used for point-to-point LCs and is most efficiently utilized for multicast LCs.

the capacity allocations to random traffic fluctuations. Returning to the example of Figure 3.5, let us assume that the traffic is now in packet form. Suppose that the LCs [1, 2] and [1, 3] constitute separate packet streams, transferred from external equipment to station 1 through two separate logical ports as shown in the figure. This implies that the packets destined for stations 2 and 3 have already been sorted and separated in a logical switch before being passed on to the NAS. In this case, the logical switch has already performed a packet-switching/routing function and sees the NAS as providing two separate point-to-point LCs—one to each destination. Referring back to the layered architecture of Figure 2.1, the packet-switching function is performed in the logical layer, which means that no additional packet encapsulation is required for addressing and control.

The traffic on an LC is now in the form of a sequence of packets possibly of random lengths, arriving at random points in time. Therefore, it must be characterized by statistical parameters, the most important of these being

Λ = the average packet arrival rate (in packets per second)

m = the average packet length (in bits)

This forces us to deal with traffic flow requirements stated as statistical averages (which are generally estimated imperfectly). In this case, how much capacity should be allocated to accommodate them? An exact match of capacity to estimated average traffic flows (which we considered to be ideal in the case of stream traffic) would be a disaster for random traffic. Any momentary increase of packet rate or packet size above the average value would cause an overload. The burstiness and unpredictability of packet arrivals in these systems is accommodated in two ways:

1. Buffering the packets awaiting transmission[14]
2. Allocating capacity in excess of that required to accommodate the average flow

To understand how these techniques can be implemented in a shared-channel system, let us focus on one LC. With static capacity allocation, the packet arrivals on the connection "see" the equivalent of a fixed-rate "pipe": the transmission channel carrying that connection. The capacity of the channel is determined by its channel–slot allocation, c_{ij}, giving an effective bitrate of $R_t c_{ij}/L$ bits per second.

We assume for simplicity that each channel–slot holds one data frame. This means that if the packets are of constant length (e.g., ATM cells), each channel–slot accommodates exactly one packet. If they have random lengths, the *maximum* packet length fits into one slot.[15] Because each packet now occupies one channel–slot regardless of its

---

[14] In the case at hand, the physical location of the packet buffers could be either in the external equipment or in the NASs.

[15] A more efficient arrangement is for long packets to be segmented and short packets to be concatenated to fit into the slots.

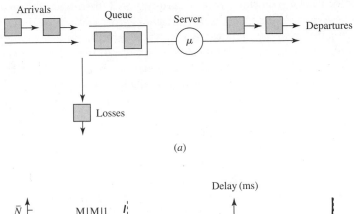

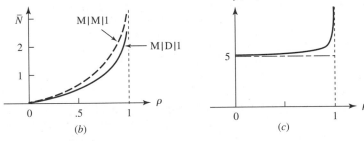

FIGURE 5.27 Single-server queue.

true length, the actual (possibly random) value of the packet length must be replaced by a fixed *effective* packet length m', where $m' \geq m$.

Using our slotted scheduling rule, the TP in each station places a packet belonging to a given LC in each channel–slot allocated to that connection. To allow for fluctuations in traffic flow, packets must be queued in buffers to wait their turn for transmission in allocated channel–slots. If no packets are awaiting transmission at the beginning of an assigned slot, the slot is left empty. This type of buffered transmission link can be modeled as a single-server queue as shown in Figure 1.27(a), in which the server is the slotted transmission channel. The behavior of the queue can be complex because of the random time each packet spends in the system and the possibility of buffer overflow. However, with a few reasonable assumptions, an adequate picture of its performance can be obtained.

A queue is characterized by its arrival process, service process, queue discipline, and buffer size. The buffer size is assumed to be *infinite* for the time being. We model the arrival process as a *Poisson process* with arrival rate Λ and assume a first-come-first-served (FCFS) queue discipline.[16] The service process is determined by the channel–slot assignments and frame time F. With c_{ij} channel–slots allocated to connection $[i, j]$

---

[16] Although the Poisson model is often a good one for packet traffic, it does not capture accurately the effect of packet segmentation. In that case each packet is converted into a "batch" of segments with random batch size. Our simplifying assumptions, which excluded segmentation, were designed to avoid the extra complications of batch arrivals.

in each frame, and with each channel–slot serving one packet, the *effective service time* for the queue is for all practical purposes *constant* at $\mu^{-1} = F/c_{ij}$, with a *service rate* of $\mu = c_{ij}/F = c_{ij}R_t/Lm'$ packets per second.[17]

The fundamental quantity determining the behavior of the queue is its *traffic intensity*, $\rho = \Lambda/\mu$, where $1 - \rho$ is the probability that the queue is empty. Assuming that the queue is operating in the statistical steady state, the main quantities of interest in describing its behavior are the average queue length $\bar{N}$ (which includes the packet in service as well as the buffered packets) and average delay $\bar{D}$ that a packet experiences in the system. These can be expressed as

$$\bar{N} = \rho\frac{1 - \rho/2}{1 - \rho} \tag{5.84}$$

$$\bar{D} = \left(\frac{\rho}{2\mu}\right)\left(\frac{1}{1 - \rho}\right) + \frac{1}{2\mu} + \frac{F}{L} \tag{5.85}$$

Equation 5.84 is the formula for the average queue length of an M|D|1 queue (see Appendix C for queueing terminology), which is a fairly good approximation of our slotted transmission channel.

The first term in Equation 5.85 represents the average waiting time in an M|D|1 queue with service time μ^{-1}. The second term is a correction on the M|D|1 formula to account for the average latency incurred while waiting for the arrival of the next assigned time slot. The third term is the effective packet transmission time (one slot time).

The expression for average queue length is plotted as a function of traffic intensity in Figure 5.27(b). The obvious observation is that queue length (and consequently queueing delay) both become infinite as $\rho \to 1$, at which point the queue becomes unstable and a statistical steady state no longer exists. (Note that the queue is stable *only* if $\rho < 1$, implying that it must be empty occasionally.) This behavior is characteristic of virtually all types of queues with infinite buffers. In practice, the capacity allocation (proportional to the transmission rate R_t) must be large enough so that the traffic intensity ρ is *significantly* less than unity to maintain stable operation of the queue. This is one source of inefficiency in systems operating with bursty traffic. Assigning capacity so that ρ is very close to unity (say, 0.95) is risky. A temporary deviation in average traffic of 5% from its prescribed value is enough to overload the system.

Also plotted in Figure 5.27(b) is the average queue length for a simpler Markovian model: the M|M|1 queue. In the M|M|1 model, the packet length is assumed to be random and distributed exponentially[18] with mean m', giving an average queue length of

$$\bar{N} = \frac{\rho}{1 - \rho} \tag{5.86}$$

---

[17] Strictly speaking, the service time is constant if the assigned time slots are spaced regularly in the frame, but irregular spacing normally makes little difference in system performance.

[18] The random packet length assumption is actually a good approximation of situations in which slots are small compared with actual packet lengths, and long packets are divided into batches of fixed-length slot-size segments for transmission over several slots.

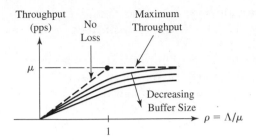

FIGURE 5.28 Throughput versus traffic intensity.

To make these ideas concrete, a numerical example is presented in Figure 5.27(c). The figure shows the average time delay from source to destination for a packet on LC $[i, j]$ arriving to the modified $M|D|1$ queue, which has an average length that is plotted in Figure 5.27(b). The total delay includes $\bar{D}$ plus propagation delay P at the speed of light in the fiber medium. Because all quantities in Equation 5.85 are inversely proportional to the transmission rate R_t, and because R_t is normally high in optical networks, the queueing delay is normally very small. (Consequently, the differences in computed delay resulting from using different queueing models are minor.)

The parameter values used in this illustration are $R_t = 10^9$ bps, $F = 125$ μs, $L = 100$ (so that $m' = 1{,}250$), $c_{ij} = 1$, and $P = 5$ ms, corresponding to transmission over a distance on the order of 1,000 km. This delay plot illustrates the relative *lack of importance* of queueing delay in *wide area* optical networks.[19] Propagation delays clearly dominate all others as long as the queue is stable. For example, if we maintain $\rho < 0.9$, then $\bar{D}$ remains less than 626 μs in this case.

In addition to queueing delays, a more important issue is buffer overflow. Because buffer capacity is always finite in any real system, there is always a nonzero probability that the buffer will be full when a packet arrives (even if ρ is small), in which case the packet is lost. Packet loss due to buffer overflow becomes larger as ρ increases and as the traffic becomes more bursty.

When there is loss one must distinguish between *offered traffic* Λ and *carried traffic* or *throughput*, which is the offered traffic reduced by the packet loss. The value of the throughput is thus $(1 - P_L)\Lambda$, where P_L is the probability of packet loss. For values of $\rho > 1$, flow conservation dictates that packet loss must always be large enough so that the throughput is less than the service rate μ. For realistic buffer sizes, the probability of packet loss generally becomes unacceptably high when ρ is close to unity. Thus whether buffers are finite or not, performance deteriorates unacceptably as $\rho \to 1$. A typical family of curves of throughput versus traffic intensity is shown in Figure 5.28. Note how throughput is reduced as buffer size is decreased.

To keep packet loss under control when buffer capacity is limited, enough capacity must be allocated to reduce ρ to an acceptable value. How much of a margin of

---

[19] Queueing delays may still be important on lower speed access links funneling traffic into a wide area optical backbone network.

security is needed in allocating capacity depends not just on packet arrival rate but on the detailed statistical behavior of the source, especially the "burstiness" and statistical dependencies of the arrival process. Burstiness is often expressed as the ratio of peak-to-average arrival rate. In very bursty systems the statistical fluctuations of packet arrivals may cause extreme excursions of queue length and very high packet loss rates. In some cases these may cause system deadlocks and failures.

Statistical dependencies can cause similar effects. For example, a packet source that generates packets in a statistically dependent manner is frequently modeled as a *Markov-modulated process*. The source may alternate randomly between two states—active and idle—where the underlying two-state modulating process is a Markov chain (see Appendix C). In the active state it generates packets at some specified rate, and in the idle state it generates no packets. The queue holding the packets is stable as long as the *average* arrival rate is less than the service rate.[20] However, even if the queue is stable, extreme queue excursions may occur if the average duration of an active state is very long. This leads to high packet loss rates and the other consequences mentioned earlier. In these cases traffic intensities much less than unity may be required to avoid these problems.

Having explored the performance of a single LC, let us now adapt the fixed-frame scheduling results for an $M \times N$ shared-channel network to the case of buffered packet traffic. An $M \times N$ framed system acts like a set of MN independent queues, each associated with one LC. To maintain a fixed capacity allocation for each connection, we follow the methodology of Section 5.4.1. Point-to-point LCs are to be scheduled with traffic requirements that are defined by an $M \times N$ traffic matrix $\Lambda = [\Lambda_{ij}]$ (in packets per second), with effective packet length m'. We consider the general case of a system with C channels and multiple, fully tunable transmitters or receivers per station.

Following Equation 5.56, the traffic balance factor is now defined as

$$\eta = \frac{\bar{\Lambda}/C}{\max_{ij} \left[\frac{\mathcal{T}_i}{\alpha_i}, \frac{\mathcal{R}_j}{\beta_j}, \frac{\bar{\Lambda}}{C} \right]} \tag{5.87}$$

where

$$\mathcal{T}_i = \sum_j \Lambda_{ij} = \text{aggregate traffic from station } i$$

$$\mathcal{R}_j = \sum_i \Lambda_{ij} = \text{aggregate traffic to station } j \tag{5.88}$$

$$\bar{\Lambda} = \sum_{ij} \Lambda_{ij} = \text{total traffic}$$

---

[20] In this case, the average arrival rate is equal to the fraction of time the source is active multiplied by the arrival rate in the active state.

The traffic matrix can be expressed in the form $\Lambda = \Lambda_0 T$, where a basic packet rate Λ_0 (in packets per second) is chosen so that the elements of the normalized traffic matrix T are relatively prime integers, representing the number of packets to be scheduled in one frame. Then a suitable frame schedule over $L_{\min}$ slots can be found, with $L_{\min}$ defined as in Equation 5.59, and with $c_{ij} = t_{ij}$.

Because the traffic intensity for each LC must be strictly less than unity, it is clear that *excess* capacity must be allocated to each connection. This can be done by scaling the underlying bitrate R_t to allow for some desired value $\rho < 1$. (The development that follows could easily be carried out using different values of traffic intensity ρ_{ij} for each LC. However, for simplicity, ρ is assumed to be identical for all connections.)

If each point-to-point connection is to operate with traffic intensity ρ, then the following constraints must be respected:

$$\Lambda_{ij} m' = \frac{t_{ij} \rho R_t}{L_{\min}}, \quad i = 1, 2, \ldots, M, \quad j = 1, 2, \ldots, N \tag{5.89}$$

Summing Equation 5.89 over i and j and solving for R_t, we find a minimum bitrate requirement of

$$R'_{\min} = \frac{\Lambda_0 L_{\min} m'}{\rho} \tag{5.90}$$

which gives a scheduling efficiency of

$$\eta_s = \frac{\bar{\Lambda} m'}{R'_{\min} C} = \frac{\bar{T} \rho}{L_{\min} C} \leq \rho \tag{5.91}$$

As in the case of stream traffic, the scheduling efficiency in the packet case can never exceed the traffic balance factor. In defining η_s, it is always assumed that for the given bitrate the *carried* traffic equals the *offered* traffic, defined by the matrix Λ; in other words, there is no traffic *loss*, even though there may be delays. If $\eta_s < \rho$, this means that there are some *unscheduled* channel–slots due to a balance factor $\eta < 1$. In this case the empty slots can be allocated as desired to reduce traffic intensities. A *scheduled* channel–slot is unused whenever the corresponding LC queue is empty, and this happens with probability $1 - \rho$. Because a common traffic intensity has been chosen for each LC, the average queue length is the same for all connections. However, the delay for the higher traffic connections is *less* than that for the lower traffic ones, due to the fact that the former are allocated more capacity than the latter (see Equation 5.85).

The point to keep in mind in this discussion is that when traffic is bursty, a fixed capacity allocation for each LC is satisfactory as long as ρ is kept sufficiently small. However, a conservative capacity allocation producing a small value of ρ reduces scheduling efficiency. If high efficiency is important, traffic arrival rates and perhaps other characteristics of the traffic must be controlled carefully for each logical channel to maintain satisfactory performance. Traffic control has two aspects:

1. Limitation of average offered traffic on each LC through admission control
2. "Shaping" of packet flow fluctuations using access and flow control

Implementation of these functions resides in the higher layers of the network architecture and is beyond the scope of this text.[21]

When dealing with a large number of low-throughput bursty users, the most effective way of dealing with packet traffic is through aggregation of traffic streams together with dynamic capacity allocation. These functions require moving the packet-switching function down into the optical layer. This is discussed in Section 5.6.

5.5   Demand-Assigned Connections

In Section 5.4 capacity allocation was treated as a deterministic problem, wherein a prescribed set of dedicated LCs was scheduled into channel–slots within a periodic frame. Fixed capacity "pipes" were assigned to connections, with the capacity allocation proportional to the number of assigned channel–slots. The fixed-pipe approach was used regardless of whether the actual traffic was subject to random fluctuations. Thus, we used the same basic procedure for asynchronous (packet) traffic in Section 5.4.2 as we did for stream traffic, and the random fluctuations in the packet case were accommodated by buffering and by assigning excess capacity.

In this section we treat the case of capacity allocation for *demand-assigned* (circuit-switched) LCs. In a circuit-switched environment we deal typically with a large number of stations, each of which is connected (active) only a portion of the time. Because these connections are established and released in response to a random sequence of connection establishment and termination requests, it is the statistical nature of the connection process that is of prime concern here. Again, what happens "inside" the connections is ignored, so that regardless of whether a connection carries stream or packet traffic it is treated as a fixed-bitrate pipe, which requires a corresponding fixed-capacity allocation. Depending on the state of the network (i.e., the number and type of active connections and their channel assignments), a connection request may be accepted or blocked. (Unless otherwise mentioned, it is assumed throughout this section that a connection request is blocked only if it is impossible to establish the desired connection.) The key performance parameter in this type of system is *blocking probability*—a quantity that depends on the offered traffic, the network resources, and the connection control algorithms.

---

[21] The interested reader should see, for example, [Schwartz96].

5.5.1 Blocking Calculations in WDMA Networks

We now study the blocking performance of the shared-channel network of Figure 1.21 under demand-assigned traffic. Because analysis of random traffic is a far more complex problem than the deterministic case, we shall only do a complete analysis of some special cases. The main objective is to present, through a series of illustrations, a methodology that can be extrapolated to more general situations.

Assume that each of the M source stations has a single transmitter and makes connection requests at random. If a request is accepted, the connection is held for a random length of time and is then released. To fix ideas, let us assume that each connection occupies one full λ-channel for the duration of a call, in which case we are discussing a WDMA network. (The results are equally applicable to any other type of channel, such as subcarrier or CDMA.) On the destination side, we consider two possibilities: nonblocking stations and stations equipped with a single receiver. In the former case, each destination station has C ORs, one tuned to each channel. This allows for many-to-one logical connectivity and eliminates connection blocking due to a busy receiving station. Although this may be unrealistic, we shall see that it is a good approximation to many real situations, and it allows us to separate blocking effects due to *busy channels* from those due to *busy destinations*. In the case of single-receiver stations, blocking may occur either because the requested destination station is busy or because of limitations in tunability. Varying degrees of tunability are considered for the single-receiver case: TT-TR, TT-FR, and FT-TR.

5.5.1.1 Nonblocking Destination Stations

We shall use Markovian traffic models for performance analysis. They are simple, mathematically tractable, and more often than not provide good approximations to real-world traffic statistics. Each source station is modeled as a two-state, continuous-time Markov chain, as shown in Figure 1.29(a). When the station is in the idle state, it generates connection (call) requests at a rate of λ requests per second, and if a request is accepted, it moves to the active state. If a request is blocked, it "forgets" that

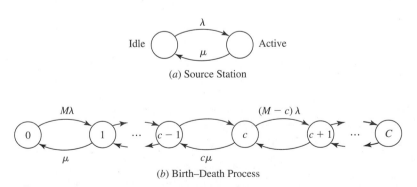

(a) Source Station

(b) Birth–Death Process

FIGURE 5.29 Markov chain model for demand-assigned traffic.

request and remains in the idle state, continuing to generate requests at the rate λ. This corresponds to a *lost calls cleared* (LCC) traffic model. (In the case of nonblocking receivers, a call request is accepted whenever there is at least one idle channel.) An active station releases calls at a rate μ releases per second, which implies that the call holding time is distributed exponentially with a mean value μ^{-1}.

In circuit-switched systems it is convenient to express traffic flow in terms of a dimensionless unit, the *Erlang*, which is the product of call arrival rate and average call holding time. In the absence of blocking, our two-state model generates $\rho/(1+\rho)$ Erlangs of traffic, where $\rho = \lambda/\mu$. Thus, the *offered traffic* in the network is $G = M\rho/(1+\rho)$ Erlangs, which represents the average number of sources that would be active at any one time in the absence of blocking. The *carried traffic* is $S = (1 - P_L)G$, where P_L is the probability of call loss.

Assuming that $M > C$ (otherwise there is no blocking), the complete Markov chain model for this system is the birth–death process shown in Figure 5.29(b), in which the state c represents the number of calls in progress (i.e., the number of occupied channels). The birthrate (call arrival rate) from state c for this case is

$$\lambda_c = (M - c)\lambda, \quad c = 0, 1, \ldots, C - 1 \tag{5.92}$$

and the death rate (call departure rate) from state c is

$$\mu_c = c\mu, \quad c = 1, 2, \ldots, C \tag{5.93}$$

The equilibrium probability distribution for the number of calls in progress in this system (see Appendix C) is

$$\pi_c = \binom{M}{c} \rho^c \left[\sum_{j=0}^{C} \binom{M}{j} \rho^j \right]^{-1} \tag{5.94}$$

Equation 5.94 is known as the *Engset* distribution.

The throughput, measured in terms of active calls, is equal to the average number of occupied channels $\bar{C}$, and the probability P_B that an arriving call request is *blocked* is just the equilibrium probability π_C that the chain is in state C when the request arrives:

$$P_B \equiv ENG(M, \rho, C) = \binom{M}{C} \rho^C \left[\sum_{j=0}^{C} \binom{M}{j} \rho^j \right]^{-1} \tag{5.95}$$

The probability P_L that a call is *lost*[22] is given by

$$P_L = ENG(M - 1, \rho, C) \tag{5.96}$$

The nonblocking receiver model simplifies further if we assume that $M \gg C$. This might correspond to the situation of Figure 5.1(c), in which a large number of NASs

---

[22] It turns out that in systems such as this one, with state-dependent call arrival rates, the probability that an arriving request is blocked, P_B, is not generally equal to the fraction of calls lost, P_L (see [Schwartz87, p. 520]).

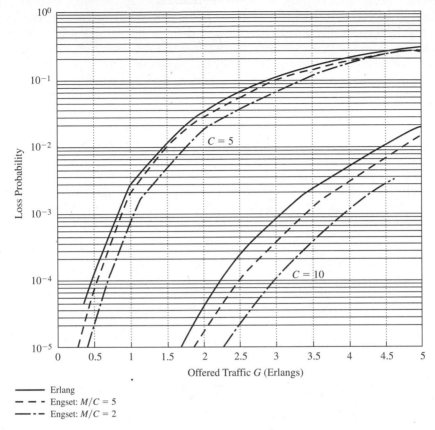

FIGURE 5.30 Comparison of Engset and Erlang models.

are interfaced to a broadcast star through optical local access networks. In this case, if the network is to operate with a reasonably low blocking probability, the rate λ at which any one station issues connection requests must be small enough so that the aggregate offered traffic G is equal to or less than the network capacity C. Under these circumstances we can approximate the *finite population* (Engset) model of Figure 5.29(b) by an *infinite population* (Erlang) model, by letting $M \to \infty$ and $\lambda \to 0$, with $M\lambda \equiv \Lambda$ held constant. The result is a simpler birth–death Markovian model in which there is no longer any state dependence on the call arrival rate. Without state dependence, $P_B = P_L$. The aggregate call arrival process is now a *Poisson process* with rate Λ. Departures occur at a rate μc when the chain is in state c, and the offered traffic is $G = \Lambda/\mu$. The Erlang distribution for the number of calls in progress in this model is

$$\pi_c = \frac{G^c}{c!} \left[\sum_{j=0}^{c} G^j/j! \right]^{-1} \tag{5.97}$$

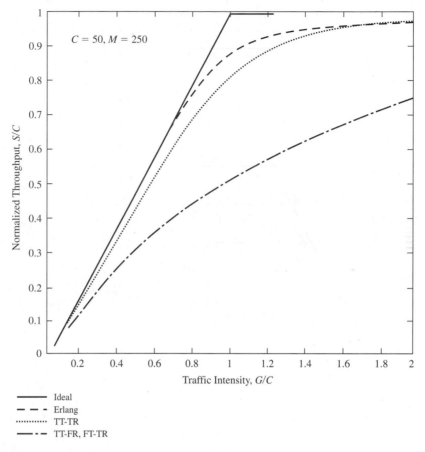

FIGURE 5.31 Normalized throughput versus traffic intensity.

This model leads to the well-known *Erlang-B* formula for blocking probability[23]:

$$P_B = P_L = \pi_C \equiv B(G, C) = \frac{G^C}{C!} \left[\sum_{j=0}^{C} G^j/j! \right]^{-1} \tag{5.98}$$

Figure 5.30 compares P_L computed with the Engset and Erlang models as a function of offered traffic G. The upper (lower) set of curves shows the convergence of the Engset loss model to the Erlang model with increasing M/C for the case $C = 5$ ($C = 10$). Note that, for the case $M/C = 5$, the Erlang-B formula is a fairly good approximation of the finite-population case.

Instead of using blocking probability, the performance of a circuit-switched system can also be displayed as a curve of normalized throughput, S/C, versus normalized offered traffic G/C, or *traffic intensity*. The dashed curves in Figures 5.31 and 5.32

---

[23] For curves of the Erlang-B formula see, for example, [Briley83].

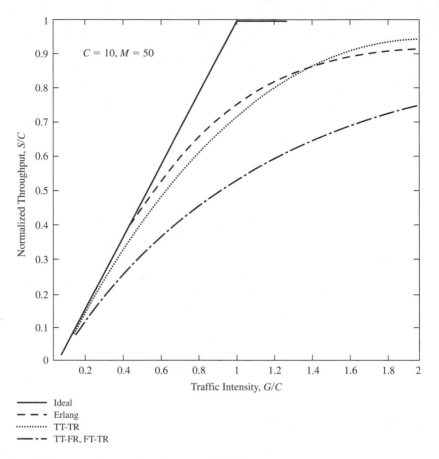

FIGURE 5.32 Normalized throughput versus traffic intensity.

respectively show the probabilistic effects of call blocking (using the Erlang-B model) for the cases $M = 250, C = 50$ and $M = 50, C = 10$. Thus in Figures 5.31 and 5.32 we compare large and small systems with the same ratio M/C. In each case $M \gg C$, so the Erlang-B approximation is a reasonable one. Loss probability can be deduced as the difference between traffic intensity and normalized throughput.

Ideal performance, represented by the solid line in both figures, is the throughput that would be obtained if the connection process was deterministic, with connection requests arriving at regular intervals of exactly Λ^{-1} seconds and connections held for exactly μ^{-1} seconds each. The deviation of actual performance from the ideal is due to the random fluctuations of the connection process; as in the case of packet traffic, randomness reduces traffic carrying capacity. Note that the large system achieves performance that is closer to the ideal than the small one, a consequence of the effect of the law of large numbers in "smoothing out" the fluctuations in the connection process.

This is a well-known effect in all circuit-switched systems: Scaling up a system while maintaining the same traffic intensity reduces the blocking probability significantly.

5.5.1.2 The Single-Receiver-per-Station Case

The previous results were based on the assumption of transmitter tunability and non-blocking destination stations, which simplifies the analysis but may not always be feasible. In [Ramaswami+90], the authors examine the influence of tunability on performance. In their analysis, an $M \times M$ system is assumed, with one transmitter in each source station and one receiver in each destination station, and with $C < M$ channels shared among the M stations. Each idle station is assumed to generate call requests at a rate λ, with uniformly distributed destinations. Three cases are considered: TT-TR, TT-FR, and FT-TR. A modified Engset model is appropriate in this case, in which the call arrival rates must include blocking effects dependent on the tuning rules. In the TT-TR case the call arrival rate in state c is given by

$$\lambda_c = \lambda(M - c)\left(1 - \frac{c}{M}\right) \tag{5.99}$$

The last factor, which is missing in the nonblocking receiver model of Equation 5.92, reflects the fact that a call is blocked if its destination is busy, and this happens with probability c/M. The call departure rates are the same as those for the nonblocking receiver model $\mu_c = c\mu$. Given the birthrates and death rates for this chain, it is straightforward to find the equilibrium probability distribution, which we denote by $\pi_c^{(TT-TR)}, c = 0, 1, \ldots, C$. The throughput is then given by

$$\bar{C} = \sum_{c=1}^{C} c\pi_c^{(TT-TR)} \tag{5.100}$$

and the loss probability is

$$P_L^{(TT-TR)} = 1 - \bar{C}/G = 1 - \frac{\sum_{c=1}^{C} c\pi_c^{(TT-TR)}}{G} \tag{5.101}$$

The dotted curves in Figures 5.31 and 5.32 show normalized throughput $\bar{C}/C$ versus normalized offered traffic $G/C = M\rho/(1 + \rho)C$ for $C = 50$ and $C = 10$ respectively, and $M/C = 5$ in both cases. Note that they are very close to the Erlang-B curves. This is to be expected, because when $M \gg C$, the birthrates for this model are close to those for the Engset (and Erlang) model. Thus, receiver blocking is a negligible factor and our simplified nonblocking receiver model is a good one.

In the TT-FR case, each channel is assumed to be assigned permanently to a set of M/C destination stations. Therefore, a connection request is blocked if it is directed to a receiving station tuned to an occupied channel. This leads to a modification of the call arrival rate for the chain of Figure 5.29(b) to

$$\lambda_c = \lambda(M - c)\left(1 - \frac{c}{C}\right) \tag{5.102}$$

The extra factor of $1 - c/C$ is due to the fact that when the chain is in the state c, call blocking at a receiver occurs with probability c/C.

In the FT-TR case each transmitter is assigned a fixed channel using the same rule as in the TT-FR case. To avoid collisions on occupied channels, a connection request generated at a transmitter tuned to an occupied channel is blocked. Now, when the chain is in state c, source stations generate requests on *idle* channels at a rate $\lambda M(1 - c/C)$, where the factor $1 - c/C$ represents the fraction of source stations tuned to idle channels. These requests are blocked if they are directed to a busy receiver, which happens with probability c/M. As a result, the state-dependent call arrival rate for this case is identical to that for the TT-FR case, yielding the same state probabilities and same throughput for both cases.

Normalized throughput curves for the TT-FR and FT-TR cases are shown as dotted–dashed lines in Figures 5.31 and 5.32. Note that normalized throughput is now significantly less than that for the TT-TR case.

5.5.2 Blocking in Combined Time–Wavelength–Division Networks

By abandoning the channel–slot frame structure in Section 5.5.1, the additional channelization possibilities afforded by combined time–wavelength–division techniques were sacrificed. We now examine the circuit-switched shared-channel network in the framed context. As before, the channels can be taken as λ-channels, which would make this a TDM/T-WDMA network.

Consider an $M \times N$ system with C channels, one tunable transmitter in each source station, and one tunable receiver in each destination station. Each source station generates connection requests at random, distributed uniformly to all destinations, and all transceivers run at a fixed bitrate R_t bits per second, where each active LC is assigned one channel–slot in a frame of length L. As a result, each connection is allocated the same bandwidth, running at an effective bitrate $R_0 = R_t/L$ bits per second. In this case, one-to-many (many-to-one) logical connectivity is possible by assigning more than one slot in a frame to a given source (destination) station, and multicast LCs can be created if more than one receiver tunes to the same channel in the same time slot. Furthermore, with the random connection request model, there are cases where more than one slot is assigned to the same source–destination pair. This can be interpreted as assigning additional bandwidth on demand to a given LC.

The framed TDM/T-WDMA system uses the time dimension to reduce the "granularity" of the shared-channel system. Thus, if L is large, a system is created in which the effective bitrate R_0 assigned to each LC is much less than the transmitter bitrate R_t. This is often desirable because circuit-switched connections frequently require lower bitrates than dedicated connections. The former would typically be used for individual user applications running at relatively low speeds, whereas the latter would most

	1	2	3	4	5	6
Channel 1		[1, 4]				
Channel 2		[2, 3]		[2, 1]	[2, 2]	
Channel 3					[3, 4]	[3, 4]
Channel 4	⋮					
Slot	1	2	3	4	5	6

FIGURE 5.33 Matching time slots.

likely be used in a semipermanent optical infrastructure for provisioning large, high-throughput logical networks. At the same time, by dividing each λ-channel into many small channel–slots, the "size" of the system in terms of the number of elementary information-bearing entities is made much larger.

In the model used here, call requests are generated as a Poisson process with the same rate λ for each source, and a common call holding time μ^{-1}.[24] To allow us to remain in the continuous-time framework of the Erlang model, it is assumed that the frame time F is much less than the call holding time (a realistic assumption). Also, to avoid unnecessary complications, we shall rule out multicast connections.

Suppose $M \leq N$. Then with $C = M$, the system can be run in an FT-TR mode using distinct channel assignments for each source station.[25] In this case, a call request generated at source station i for an LC $[i, j]$ is accepted if there is at least one slot in the frame which *neither* station i nor j is using. Otherwise it is blocked. This slot-matching condition is illustrated in Figure 5.33, in which a connection between source station 2 and destination 4 is requested in a frame of length $L = 6$. Figure 5.33 shows calls in progress from source 2 to destinations 3, 1, and 2, and calls in progress from sources 1 and 3 to destination 4, where the connection [3, 4] uses two units of bandwidth. Slots 1 and 3 are available for the new connection.

Assuming that slots are assigned independently and at random, it can be shown that the probability that a connection $[i, j]$ will be blocked for lack of an available slot in a frame of length L, given that sources i and j have m and n active connections respectively, is

$$p_b(m, n) = \begin{cases} \frac{m!n!}{L!(m+n-L)!}, & m + n \geq L \\ 0, & \text{otherwise} \end{cases} \tag{5.103}$$

Note that a call is blocked with certainty if either the source or the destination has an active connection in every slot. Also, a call is *never* blocked if $m + n < L$.

Our objective is to explore how the various system parameters influence the blocking probability for this system. Because of the Poisson assumption, call arrival rates

---

[24] The analytic approach used here is adapted from and extends what appears in [Humblet+93].

[25] The development applies equally well to the case of systems with $M \geq N$ and $C = N$ (using the TT-FR mode).

are state independent, which means that the loss probability for a connection request between stations i and j is given by

$$P_L = P_B = \sum_{m=0}^{L} \sum_{n=0}^{L} p_b(m, n)\pi(m, n) \tag{5.104}$$

where $\pi(m, n)$ is the steady-state joint probability that source station i and destination station j have m and n calls in progress respectively.

The difficulty with Equation 5.104 is that in systems of this kind, everything is dependent on everything else. For example, the slot allocations are *not* independent (as was assumed), so the state of an *exact* system model must include details of the slot assignments for all source and destination stations. Even for relatively small systems this poses a "state explosion" problem, making the model intractable. Thus, an exact calculation of P_L is out of the question for systems of any realistic size. Nevertheless, a few additional assumptions lead to an approximate model that is manageable and quite accurate for large-size systems.

Assume that the number of calls in progress at each source station and each destination station can be described approximately by an independent Erlang model. With a call arrival rate λ at each source station, and uniform traffic, each source has a traffic intensity $\rho_s = \lambda/\mu$, and each destination has a traffic intensity $\rho_d = M\lambda/N\mu$.

This simplified model implies that the effects of blocking on the state probabilities are ignored, and the state probabilities for all sources and destinations are mutually independent. Because ignoring blocking produces an overestimate of the probabilities of the higher slot occupancies, this approximation tends to overestimate P_L.

Under these assumptions we have $\pi(m, n) = \pi(m)\pi(n)$, where the individual state probabilities $\pi(c)$ are given by Equation 5.97 with $C = L$, $G = \rho_s$ for the sources, and $G = \rho_d$ for the destinations. As a result, Equation 5.104 reduces to

$$P_L = \left[\sum_{j=0}^{L} \rho_s^j/j!\right]^{-1} \left[\sum_{j=0}^{L} \rho_d^j/j!\right]^{-1} \sum_{m=L-n}^{L} \sum_{n=0}^{L} \frac{\rho_s^m \rho_d^n}{L!(m+n-L)!} \tag{5.105}$$

If $M = N$, then $\rho_s = \rho_d = \rho$, and Equation 5.105 simplifies further to

$$P_L = \left[\sum_{j=0}^{L} \rho^j/j!\right]^{-2} \sum_{u=L}^{2L} \frac{(2L-u+1)\rho^u}{(u-L)!L!} \tag{5.106}$$

If blocking due to slot mismatches is ignored, Equation 5.105 becomes

$$P_L = B(\rho_s, L) + B(\rho_d, L) - B(\rho_s, L)B(\rho_d, L) \tag{5.107}$$

Figure 5.34 shows curves of blocking probability as a function of normalized offered traffic ρ/L for $M \times M$ systems with several values of frame size L. The normalization

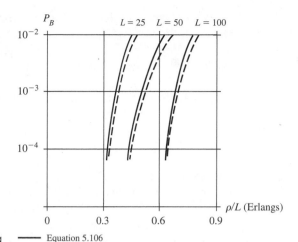

FIGURE 5.34 Framed system blocking probabilities.

——— Equation 5.106
— — · Equation 5.107

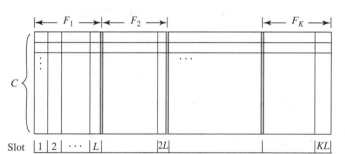

FIGURE 5.35 Superframe for $M = KL$.

is obtained by dividing the total offered traffic $G = M\rho$ by the total channel–slots available to carry it, ML, so that the system size M is eliminated. Two sets of curves are presented:

1. P_L using Equation 1.106
2. P_L ignoring slot mismatches (Equation 1.107)

Note that slot mismatch has a fairly minor effect on blocking, reducing the allowable offered traffic for a given loss probability by approximately 10%.

As mentioned earlier, the framed system is "fine grained," which means that the laws of large numbers work in our favor. This effect is clearly observable in Figure 1.34, in which the blocking probability is seen to decrease sharply with increasing L.

A generalization to systems with less than a full complement of channels is straightforward. Suppose, for example, that $M = KC$, where K is an integer. In this case, the frame of length L can be replaced by a "superframe" of length KL, containing frames $F_1, F_2, \ldots, F_K$, each of length L, as shown in Figure 1.35.

Then if an FT-TR system is desired, the stations can be partitioned into subsets with $M' = M/K$ stations each, for which distinct channels can be assigned to one subset in frame F_1 and reused for the other subsets in the remaining frames. Each frame now operates as an $M' \times N$ system that can be analyzed using the previous development.

In the system defined so far, the *positions* of active slots in a frame as well as their number can produce call blocking. There are a number of ways of eliminating slot mismatch altogether by changing the connection control procedures. We present two next.

5.5.2.1 Limited-Connection Systems

Equation 5.103 suggests a way of eliminating mismatches by constraining the permissible number of connections in a frame. Continuing with our $M \times N$ FT-TR system, suppose an admission control rule is applied in which each source station is limited to N simultaneous connections and each destination station is limited to M connections. (Repetitions are allowed, but are counted as distinct connections.) We shall refer to this as the *limited-connection case*. Furthermore, set

$$L = M + N - 1 \tag{5.108}$$

For this frame length, blocking of a connection request occurs only if either the source or the destination is already at its connection limit.[26] Constraining the number of connections in this way limits the maximum carried traffic to approximately 50% of the system capacity.

Using the Erlang model for source and destination slot occupancies, the loss probability in the limited connection case becomes

$$P_L = B(\rho_s, N) + B(\rho_d, M) - B(\rho_s, N)B(\rho_d, M) \tag{5.109}$$

Unfortunately, because M or N is approximately half as large as L in the limited-connection case, the blocking due to connection limits is higher than that in the original system. Nevertheless, the limited-connection system might be of interest for other reasons, such as fairness: Limiting connections to and from each station tends to prevent stations from "hogging" the shared-channel system.

5.5.2.2 Rearrangeability Revisited

Another way of eliminating mismatches is by channel–slot rearrangement. To illustrate, consider a 4×4 directed star network with $C = 4$, operating in an FT-TR mode.

Suppose the following sequence of connection requests is to be scheduled: [1, 2], [3, 1], [2, 2], [1, 3], [4, 4], [2, 4], [4, 3]. All LCs require one channel–slot except [3, 1],

---

[26] The condition in Equation 5.108 is identical to a well-known nonblocking result for traditional time-multiplexed electronic switches [Schwartz87].

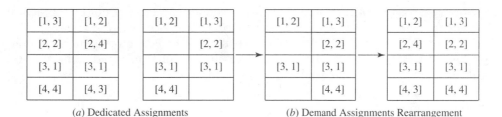

[1, 3]	[1, 2]
[2, 2]	[2, 4]
[3, 1]	[3, 1]
[4, 4]	[4, 3]

(*a*) Dedicated Assignments

[1, 2]	[1, 3]
	[2, 2]
[3, 1]	[3, 1]
[4, 4]	

[1, 2]	[1, 3]
	[2, 2]
[3, 1]	[3, 1]
	[4, 4]

[1, 2]	[1, 3]
[2, 4]	[2, 2]
[3, 1]	[3, 1]
[4, 3]	[4, 4]

(*b*) Demand Assignments Rearrangement

FIGURE 5.36 Illustrating rearrangeability.

which requires two; that is, we are allowing multiple effective bitrates. If this is considered as a dedicated connection assignment problem, it can be stated in terms of a normalized traffic matrix:

$$T = \begin{bmatrix} 0 & 1 & 1 & 0 \\ 0 & 1 & 0 & 1 \\ 2 & 0 & 0 & 0 \\ 0 & 0 & 1 & 1 \end{bmatrix} \tag{5.110}$$

This is clearly a balanced traffic matrix, and since $\bar{T} = 8$, it can be scheduled in a frame of length $L = 2$, as shown in Figure 5.36(a). On the other hand, if demand-assigned scheduling is used, the first CAS in Figure 5.36(b) shows the schedule as it would look after the first five connections are scheduled. The scheduling rule used to produce this result is the following: Place a connection in the first time slot if possible; if not, use the second slot. A slot mismatch problem now arises when the last two connection requests arrive. Neither can be scheduled without a conflict at the receivers, so they must be blocked. There is no way to avoid this situation without knowing the sequence of requests in advance. Thus, just as the statistical fluctuations of the call request arrival process reduce the traffic carrying capacity of a shared-channel network, the random *order* of these requests also reduces the carried traffic. However, if *rearrangement* is permitted, this problem can be circumvented.

In this example, the conflict is eliminated by moving connection [4, 4] to the second time slot, as shown in the second CAS in Figure 5.36(b). Thus, the issue of rearrangeability, which appeared in permutation switches in Section 2.3.2.1 and in WRNs in Section 3.3.1.1, reappears once more in time-multiplexed shared-channel systems. In general, scheduling with slot rearrangeability is equivalent to dedicated connection scheduling, so that blocking of a new connection request only occurs if it is impossible to accommodate the complete list of active connections plus the new request using the existing frame length. In this case, as long as the minimum frame length for the active connections plus the new request (computed using Equation 5.59) does not exceed $L = 2$, all connections can be accommodated with rearrangement. As in the previous discussions of rearrangeability, this option may or may not be a practical alternative.[27]

The framed TDM/T-WDMA system can be operated in more general circuit-switched contexts as long as the usual constraints required to avoid collisions and conflicts are observed. Some generalizations include

- Multicast connections
- Multiple transmitters/receivers per station
- Effective bitrate selected on demand
- More elaborate admission control rules

Although tractable mathematical models are hard to come by in these cases, the lack of analytical models should not be a deterrent from using TDM/T-WDMA systems under these more complex operating conditions. On the contrary, the flexibility offered by TDM/T-WDMA makes it an excellent choice when operations become more complex.

5.6 Packet Switching in the Optical Layer

So far we have considered the capacity allocation problem for shared-channel systems using either dedicated or demand-assigned connections. Thus the focus has been on connection-oriented transmission, and the capacity allocation has always been fixed for the duration of a connection. This type of service is appropriate for applications requiring a guaranteed bandwidth, which includes all synchronous traffic applications and some (typically real-time) asynchronous (packet) traffic applications. It is less appropriate in an environment consisting of a large population of low-throughput bursty users who require a high degree of logical connectivity. In this case, packet switching is the natural way of carrying the traffic. The most efficient way of implementing the packet-switching function in a purely optical network is to extend it downward to span the logical and optical layers. The properties of the shared-channel broadcast medium make it a particularly effective support for packet switching in the optical layer.

The general features of this approach were presented in Section 3.2.2. Recall that in packet switching, as opposed to dedicated or demand-assigned (circuit-switched) capacity allocation, addressing, scheduling, and capacity allocation are implemented on a packet-by-packet basis. This entails extensive communication, control, and processing functions, which are absent in the dedicated or circuit-switched case. Nevertheless, a number of benefits accrue from the additional communication and processing load,

---

[27] Rearrangement of time slots in a shared broadcast medium is normally possible with less disruption than, say, reassigning wavelengths and optical paths in wavelength routed networks because it is possible to "swap" time slots with little or no information loss.

the two most significant being:

1. High connectivity realized using packet header information for routing
2. High throughput and low delay realized through dynamic capacity allocation

Dynamic capacity allocation is an implicit by-product of the MAC protocols designed for packet switching on shared-channel media. The protocols that are discussed here are, in most cases, direct generalizations of those used in traditional LANs and MANs, and must address the same problems: contention resolution, packet loss, and retransmission if required.

A large number of MAC protocols have been devised for optical broadcast-and-select networks, representing various trade-offs among performance, overhead, hardware cost, and processing complexity [Mukherjee92, Ramaswami93]. Practical M station systems generally require anywhere from one to M separate control channels for dynamically scheduling packets. This represents significant out-of-band communication overhead and transceiver hardware. Furthermore, packet scheduling requires a considerable amount of real-time processing. As the size of the system grows, both in number of stations and geographical spread, channel collisions, receiver conflicts, signaling overhead, and propagation delays, as well as protocol processing overhead can reduce the efficiency of these systems substantially, increasing packet loss and/or delay and reducing throughput. Thus, our objective here is to study a number of representative protocols, focusing on how cost–performance trade-offs change with the structure of the system.

A good MAC protocol achieves the two objectives of high logical connectivity and high performance, and it does so by aggregating traffic and allocating capacity dynamically. Recall from Section 5.4.2 that when fixed allocations were used for packet traffic, estimates of average traffic requirements on each LC were needed at connection establishment time to produce a fixed-frame schedule with the required capacity allocation. The performance of a fixed-capacity system is vulnerable to unpredictable traffic fluctuations as well as errors in the estimated requirements. In the dynamic case we hope to achieve better performance and efficiency by using knowledge of the *actual* (rather than the estimated) traffic during the information transfer phase. Ideally, this knowledge can be used to allocate channel–slots "instantaneously," while at the same time coordinating transmissions among all stations to resolve contention for resources.

Thus, the fundamental difference between capacity allocation in the fixed and dynamic cases is that scheduling is done once and for all at connection setup time in the former case, and during information transfer in the latter case. Clearly, the more knowledge each station has of the instantaneous "global" state of the traffic in all other stations, the more efficiently the traffic can be scheduled. But this information is distributed geographically throughout the network, so to establish a dynamic schedule, a certain amount of control information concerning packets awaiting transmission must be communicated among the stations, and this information must be processed to produce scheduling decisions. Various degrees of control are exercised in typical packet-switched shared-channel protocols. We categorize these as[28]

- Uncontrolled scheduling (random access)
- Scheduling with loss
- Lossless scheduling (reservations)
- Perfect scheduling

In the descriptions that follow, the optical infrastructure is taken as an $M \times M$ undirected broadcast star with each station having a single transceiver for data.[29] (There may be additional transceivers for control.) Let us assume that all stations are equidistant from the star coupler, so that the propagation time from source to destination (the time required for a signal to propagate to the star coupler and back) is the same for all stations. The systems all operate in a slotted mode, with transmitters picking up slot synchronization as well as other control information by seeing all transmissions (including their own).

The transmitted data are assumed to be in the form of fixed-length packets, with the packet length equal to the slot size. The traffic is assumed to be distributed uniformly, and connection oriented, with all connections point to point. However, connectionless transmission as well as multicast connections are handled easily in the systems treated here.

As indicated in Section 3.2.2, most protocols for packet switching in the optical layer involve some probability of lost packets. Thus we must keep track of two types of traffic: original and retransmitted. Let

$S =$ the normalized throughput (average packets per channel–slot)

$G =$ the total normalized traffic offered to the network (average packets per channel–slot)

$E =$ the average number of retransmissions of a packet until success

$p_s =$ the probability that a transmission is successful

The total traffic G contains both originally generated packets (the normalized throughput S) and retransmitted packets. We are particularly interested in $S_{\max}$— the maximum normalized throughput the system can support. No matter what the protocol, the loss mechanism (e.g., collisions or conflicts), or the retransmission rule,

---

[28] In reality, an enormous number of protocols have been proposed that do not always fit neatly into these categories (see, for example, [Mukherjee92]). It is beyond the scope of this text to cover all of them.

[29] The undirected case is most appropriate for optical layer packet switching because of the ease of distributing control information.

the quantities defined here are related by[30]

$$G = S(1 + E) \tag{5.111}$$

$$S = p_s G \tag{5.112}$$

$$E = (1 - p_s)/p_s \tag{5.113}$$

5.6.1 Uncontrolled Scheduling: Random Access

The simplest possible MAC protocol is random access, with the earliest implementation being the ALOHA system [Abramson73]. In the slotted version, based on a slot-synchronized, single-channel shared broadcast medium, any station having a packet to transmit sends it in the next available slot. A copy of the transmitted packet is held in the transmitting station in case a retransmission is needed. The RP in each station reads all packet headers, performing a packet-filtering operation to select those destined for it. (Multicast destination addresses can be used in the case of multicast LCs.) Channel collisions occur when more than one packet is transmitted in the same time slot, in which case all collided packets are lost. The collisions are detected by the RPs in the stations that transmitted the collided packets, and this information is used to reschedule those packets at a later time.[31]

Although ALOHA is probably the oldest MAC protocol, and not a very efficient one at that, it serves as a useful point of comparison for more sophisticated techniques. Two performance parameters are of interest: the maximum normalized throughput, $S_{\max}$, and the average delay until successful receipt of a packet, $\bar{D}$. The key parameter in computing these quantities is the probability of successful transmission p_s. In general, an exact value of p_s is difficult to obtain because of statistical dependencies among original and retransmitted packets. However, with a few simplifying assumptions, a fairly simple, accurate, and tractable mathematical model can be obtained (see [Lam74]).

In the model, we assume that each station transmits into each slot with probability p, so that $G = Mp$, and the transmission is successful with probability p_s, where p and p_s for each slot and each station are independent of activity in previous slots. (One implication of this model is that there is no packet queueing in the transmitting stations, and hence no queueing delay.) This state of affairs approximates quite well a system with a large number of stations, in which collided packets are retransmitted after random delays, averaging about three or more slots. In this case, we have

$$p_s = (1 - p)^{M-1} \approx e^{-G}, \quad \text{for } M \gg 1 \tag{5.114}$$

---

[30] These relations apply only to systems in which lost packets are retransmitted. In some applications lost packets are simply dropped without attempts at retransmission (see Section 5.6.2).

[31] In contrast to wired LANs, collisions are normally detected in optical networks long after the packet transmission has been completed, so that protocols using carrier sense (e.g., CSMA/CD) are unusable (see Section 3.2.2).

Then from Equations 5.112 and 5.114 we have

$$S = Ge^{-G} \tag{5.115}$$

which is maximized for $G = 1$, giving $S_{max} = e^{-1} = 0.37$ and $E = 1.7$. For all values of throughput less than S_{max} there are two possible values of G. However, the larger value ($G > 1$) corresponds to a larger value of E, and to unstable operation of the network. This illustrates the well-known difficulty with all systems involving packet loss: The retransmitted traffic puts an extra load on the network, which may reduce significantly the maximum throughput. To avoid congestion and instabilities, offered traffic must be kept well below the value that maximizes throughput, and special retransmission control algorithms must be used to maintain stability. (Similar problems arise in CSMA/CD.)

The average delay until successful reception of a packet is expressed in units of time slots as

$$\bar{D} = 1 + P + E(P + \bar{K}) \tag{5.116}$$

where P is the source-to-destination propagation time (in slots) and $\bar{K}$ is the average time before retransmission of a collided packet (in slots). In a typical optical network, P is the dominant quantity in Equation 5.116, so that

$$\bar{D} \approx (1 + E)P \tag{5.117}$$

Because E is 1.7 at maximum throughput in slotted ALOHA, the average packet delay is approximately two to three propagation delays, corresponding to one to two retransmissions. Throughput and delay curves for slotted ALOHA as a function of total traffic G are shown in Figure 5.37. (The unstable region corresponding to $G \geq 1$ is omitted.) The delay is plotted in Figure 5.37(b) in units of propagation delay P. Note that the delay is less than $3P$ throughout the stable region.

In generalizing random access to a multichannel system, a number of channel assignment options are available. For example, a system with a full complement of channels can be operated in TT-FR mode, with each receiver assigned a distinct

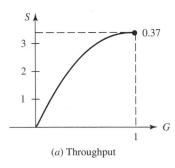

(*a*) Throughput

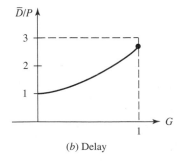

(*b*) Delay

FIGURE 5.37 Slotted ALOHA.

channel. There are no receiver conflicts, and packet filtering is not necessary because only those packets destined for a given station are captured by its optical receiver.

In a TT-FR system, collisions occur when more than one station transmits to the same receiver in the same time slot. Because each station only sees the packets destined for it, and therefore cannot monitor its own transmissions, collision detection requires additional control information. The *automatic repeat request* (ARQ) scheme, used in common DLC protocols, can be used here. Each destination station sends a positive acknowledgement back to the source on successful receipt of a packet (either on a separate control channel or by piggybacking the information on data packets). The source retransmits any packet for which it has not received an acknowledgment. This, however, requires a "timeout" of at least $2P$ before a packet loss is detected by the source station. The effect of the timeout is to replace P in Equation 5.116 by $2P$.

Many other variants are possible, involving sharing channels among multiple stations grouped on each channel, combined fixed schedules and random access, and so forth (see [Mukherjee92]). Typically, the maximum throughput of a C-channel system can be made C times that of a single-channel system. For example, a C-channel WDMA slotted ALOHA system can be operated with each source station selecting one of the C channels at random each time it transmits. Assuming that each destination can listen to all channels (with a tuned receiver array), the maximum throughput of the system is increased C-fold over a single-channel system.

In summary, random access has the virtue of simplicity, but suffers from low throughput and relatively high delays. To improve throughput and delay, additional protocol complexity must be introduced.

5.6.2 Scheduling with Loss: Tell-and-Go

In this section the performance improvement produced by the availability of certain limited global state information is investigated. Consider an $M \times M$ system with $C = M$ channels and a single transceiver per station, operating in FT-TR mode with a distinct channel assigned to each source station. New packets awaiting transmission are queued in each source station together with copies of packets that were transmitted previously but not received.

Now suppose that each station with a packet to transmit first communicates to all receivers the destination of the packet, and then sends the packet in the next time slot.[32] This is known as a *tell-and-go protocol*. Because capacity is allocated dynamically, this is also called *dynamic* T-WDMA (DT-WDMA). Because it takes one source-to-destination propagation time P for the information about transmissions to reach the receivers, and the data packet is transmitted before that time elapses, the transmitting stations have no way of knowing whether others are also transmitting when they send their packets. Furthermore, they have no confirmation that the intended destination

---

[32] Of course, the mechanism by which this control information is communicated is an essential feature of the protocol, but at this point it suffices to assume that the information is conveyed correctly "somehow" before the arrival of the packet.

station will be ready to receive the packet when it arrives. (Waiting for a confirmation would delay the transmission an additional propagation time.) This "haste" is the advantage (and disadvantage) of tell-and-go. It keeps delay to a minimum, which is especially important in networks with large propagation times; however, it also leads to conflicts, which arise when more than one station transmits a packet destined for the same receiver. In that case, the receiver must tune to one of the active transmitters, causing losses of the other packets.

In tell-and-go, these packet losses are inevitable.[33] But assuming that all stations know the rules by which the receiving stations choose among conflicting packets, the source stations all know which packets were received correctly and which were dropped. In this manner, each station knows after an interval P whether it must retransmit a packet. Although there are conflicts with this system, the use of FT-TR with a full complement of channels avoids collisions, and thus it is an improvement over TT-FR multichannel random access.

As an illustration, consider the 4×4 example in Figure 5.38(a). Each station maintains a single queue. The figure shows a "snapshot" of the state of the queues in the four transmitting stations at one instant in time. Each queue contains four packets awaiting transmission, labeled in the figure with their source/destination addresses and LC sequence numbers (subscripts). The distribution of destination addresses has been chosen to match the normalized traffic matrix in Figure 5.22(b). Recall that the fixed frame FT-TR CAS of Figure 5.23(b) accommodates these packets in four time slots. The stations normally schedule their transmissions FCFS, with each packet at the head of its queue transmitted in the next available channel–slot. This is shown in the schedule of Figure 5.38(b), in which slots are now allocated dynamically rather than in a fixed frame. In the case of conflicts, the best the designated receiver can do is to tune to one of the contending packets, losing the others. Figure 5.38(b) shows a case in which each receiver tunes to the lowest numbered transmitter having information for it, resulting in the loss of the five crossed-out packets.

The schedule is implemented in four time slots, which is sufficient for conflict-free packet delivery in a fixed frame system. However, the loss due to conflicts occurs because of the order in which the packets happened to be queued (and served). Comparing fixed scheduling to tell-and-go, we note that in both cases packets within each LC are *transmitted* in the correct order. However, because of the pipelining that occurs in tell-and-go, the loss of a packet is not likely to be detected until several packets behind it have been transmitted. Thus, the MAC protocol does not guarantee reliable and ordered packet delivery to the higher layers of the network. If loss-free, ordered delivery is required in an application, it must be realized through appropriate retransmission protocols (which include keeping track of sequence numbers) in the higher layers of the network architecture: the logical link layer and higher.

---

[33] Conflicts can be avoided if each station has an array of M fixed receivers, and conflicts can be reduced if each station has an array of a few tunable receivers. Another proposal for avoiding conflicts is to use optical delay lines to buffer conflicting packets at the destinations, and then direct the buffered packets to the tunable receiver when it is idle (see [Chlamtac+91]).

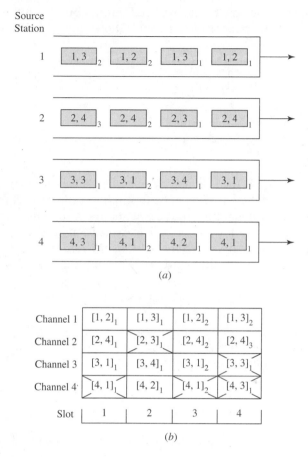

FIGURE 5.38 Tell-and-go.

For the random access system of Section 5.6.1, it was seen that collisions produce nonmonotonic relations between throughput and total traffic, together with tendencies toward instability. How do the performance relations work out in tell-and-go?

Consider a simplified model for our undirected $M \times M$ slotted system in which each source station transmits into a slot with probability p, with packets destined equiprobably to the $M - 1$ other stations. The total normalized traffic is $G = p$ (packets per channel–slot), and we wish to determine the relation $S(G)$ together with the average delay $\bar{D}$. (Note that in this model, as opposed to that used for random access, the maximum value of G is 1.) Following the methodology for the case of random access, the transmission probabilities and destinations are assumed to be independent from slot to slot. Because the total transmitted traffic includes retransmissions as well as the effects of queueing, these assumptions are only approximations.

Now we can calculate the normalized throughput S as follows. Let p_n be the probability that no one transmits to a given station j in a given time slot. We have

$$p_n = \left[(1-p) + p\frac{(M-2)}{(M-1)}\right]^{M-1} = \left(1 - \frac{p}{(M-1)}\right)^{M-1} \tag{5.118}$$

and

$$\lim_{M \to \infty} p_n = e^{-p} \tag{5.119}$$

In Equation 5.118, the brackets contain the probability that a specific station is not transmitting to station j, where the first term in the brackets is the probability that the station is not transmitting in the slot and the second term is the probability that it is transmitting, but not to station j. The expression in brackets is raised to the power $M-1$ to give the probability that no stations are transmitting to j. From Equation 5.119 we find that for large M, the normalized throughput is given approximately by

$$S = 1 - p_n = 1 - e^{-p} = 1 - e^{-G} \tag{5.120}$$

so that S increases monotonically to $S_{max} = 1 - e^{-1} = 0.63$ as $G \to 1$. (Monotonicity ensures that the relation $G(S)$ is single valued, so no instabilities occur.)

Now from Equation 5.111 we have

$$E = \frac{G}{S} - 1 = \frac{G - 1 + e^{-G}}{1 - e^{-G}} \tag{5.121}$$

so that in cases where propagation delay dominates all other delays we have

$$\bar{D} \approx \frac{PG}{1 - e^{-G}} \tag{5.122}$$

The normalized throughput and delay for tell-and-go are plotted in Figure 5.39 for large M. Note that at maximum throughput, $\bar{D}/P = 1/(1 - e^{-1}) = 1.58$.

Although the analysis has assumed that all lost packets are retransmitted, not all applications require this. For example, in real-time applications such as packet (variable bitrate) video, the retransmission delay for lost packets would normally be unacceptable, but a small probability of dropped packets may be permissible. By running the network at sufficiently low throughput, acceptable loss probability for real-time applications can be achieved.

5.6.3 A Dynamic T-WDMA Protocol

Tell-and-go protocols can be implemented in a wide variety of forms, depending on the tuning properties of the transceivers and the way control information is exchanged. As

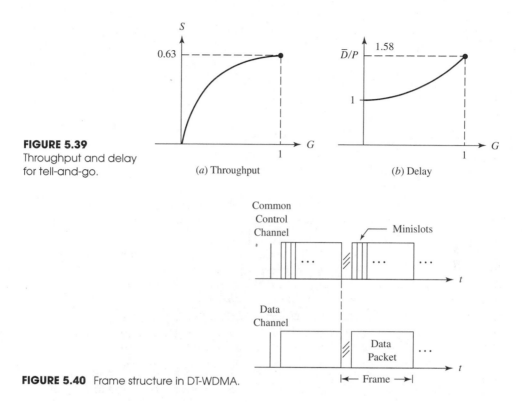

FIGURE 5.39
Throughput and delay
for tell-and-go.

(a) Throughput   (b) Delay

FIGURE 5.40 Frame structure in DT-WDMA.

an illustration we describe a protocol dubbed DT-WDMA. The development follows [Chen+90].

The system uses two transceivers in each station, one for data and one for control. The data transceivers operate in FT-TR mode using a distinct channel (wavelength) for each data transmitter. The tuning of the control transceivers is fixed to a common control channel so that $M + 1$ channels are required for an $M \times M$ network. The system operates using fixed time frames in both the control and data channels. As shown in Figure 5.40, the control channel frame is divided into M equal-size "minislots" followed by an idle period to allow time for receiver tuning in the data channel. Each minislot is "owned" by a given source station and is used to announce the destination of the packet it is to transmit in the next data slot, as well as priority information. The priority information is used in conflict resolution. For example, the priorities might be based on the "age" of a packet since its arrival at the source station. Each receiver faced with a conflict tunes to the highest priority packet and loses the others. As in all tell-and-go schemes, all stations see (and process) the control information from all others, so that they know whether their packets have been lost in a conflict and can take appropriate action.

The data frames consist of a single time slot for data, preceded by an idle period for receiver tuning. Synchronization is required between control and data channels to

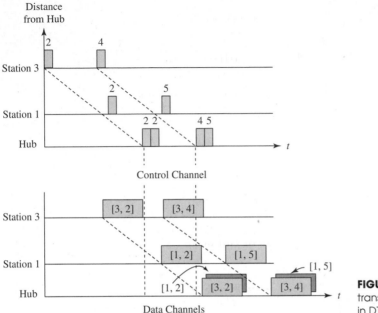

FIGURE 5.41 Data transmission scenario in DT-WDMA.

ensure that announcements of packets about to be transmitted arrive sufficiently in advance of the actual transmission so that the data receivers can tune to the desired channels.

A typical scenario for data transmission is shown in Figure 5.41, where stations 1 and 3 are shown at different distances from the hub of the network (a star coupler), as indicated by the vertical axis. They synchronize themselves to place control information into their assigned minislots, with both stations 1 and 3 announcing that they will transmit to station 2. Their data transmissions are timed to arrive in the next data slot (but on distinct data channels), causing a conflict, which must be resolved by the receiver. In the next pair of control and data frames, a similar sequence of events takes place, but this time the packet destinations are distinct and thus no conflict occurs.

The performance of this system is governed by the throughput and delay relations derived in Section 5.6.2. Assuming that receiver tuning time is short compared with packet transmission time (not always the case), DT-WDMA is efficient in its use of bandwidth. On the other hand, there are four negative features that limit its scalability:

1. The number of required minislots equals the number of stations.

2. Each station must process all control information.

3. The required optical bandwidth is proportional to the number of stations.

4. Two transceivers are required per station.

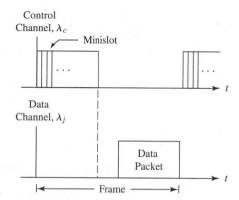

FIGURE 5.42 Single-transceiver DT-WDMA.

Some of the disadvantages of DT-WDMA can be circumvented by varying the protocol. For example, station equipment can be reduced by operating the system with a single tunable transmitter and receiver to be time shared between control and data functions. Suppose the control channel operates on wavelength λ_c and the jth data channel operates on wavelength $\lambda_j, j = 1, 2, \ldots, M$. As shown in Figure 1.42, the control minislots and one data slot now appear sequentially in each frame, and each station's transceiver tunes to λ_c during the first part of the frame. (Because the time scales in Figure 5.42 refer to the hub, the *actual* times when each station's transmitter and receiver retune are generally staggered with respect to each other.)

In the second part of the frame, each station's transmitter tunes to its own data channel, and its receiver tunes to a data channel selected on the basis of the previously received control information. Because the single transceiver is switching between control and data channels, the control information and the data must appear sequentially without time overlap at the hub. This reduces the bandwidth efficiency and throughput of the system. Thus, station complexity reduction is achieved at the cost of reduction in throughput.

Because optical spectrum limitations eventually constrain the size of the DT-WDMA system, it is of interest to find ways of using less than a full complement of channels and thereby breaking out of the spectrum limitation. One way of doing so is by following the approach of Figure 1.35. If only $C = M/K$ data channels are available, the DT-WDMA frame can be replaced by a superframe containing K smaller frames, F_k. The stations are partitioned into K equal-size subsets, and in each frame a subset of M/K stations is allowed to transmit using the protocol just described, with each data transmitter assigned a distinct channel. (All stations may receive during each frame.) The channels are reused in each frame for a new subset of stations so that all stations are allocated an equal part of the superframe.

In this case dynamic data slot assignments are made using tell-and-go among the stations within each individual subset, so there are no collisions among stations using the same data channel, but there are still conflicts within a slot, as before.[34] Of course, cutting down the number of channels reduces the effective capacity allocated to each transmitting station by a factor of K.[35] Also, confining subsets of sources to limited segments of the superframe amounts to a fixed partition of the transmission capacity, which tends to reduce the advantages of dynamic capacity allocation.

Further variants are possible by combining optical bandwidth reduction with station equipment reduction (i.e., using a single transceiver per station and less than a full complement of channels).

5.6.4 Lossless Scheduling: Reservations

The conflicts incurred using dynamic capacity allocation and tell-and-go can be avoided while maintaining an FCFS queue discipline, but this requires extending the schedule over more than the minimum number of slots. To construct a lossless schedule, global information concerning the packets at the head of each station's queue is required. This entails the distribution of additional control information among all transmitting and receiving stations, involving more communication overhead, more processing, and longer packet delays than tell-and-go. (A minimum of one propagation time P is required to communicate the global state to all stations before transmission begins.)

In a conceptually simple arrangement, each transmitting station broadcasts in each time slot (on a separate control channel) the destination address of the packet at the head of its queue. All stations receive this information and execute a distributed algorithm that determines which stations are allowed to transmit in the next available slot. (The next available slot in this case is delayed somewhat more than P from the time the address information is broadcast to leave sufficient time for the control information to be received and processed.) In an FT-TR system with distinct channel assignments, a packet selection rule must be followed to eliminate conflicts. It might be as simple as selecting the conflicting packet with the lowest numbered source address, but a better arrangement would be to select the packet at random or based on some other fairness criteria. In systems with less than a full complement of channels, the protocol must determine which stations should transmit and what channel they should use to avoid both conflicts and collisions.

Choosing a limited number of packets for transmission in the next slot amounts to *reserving* channels on a slot-by-slot basis—an example of dynamic scheduling using reservations.[36] In a slot-by-slot reservation system, packet loss is replaced by delay.

---

[34] The probability of packet loss due to conflicts is reduced in this case because transmissions from M/K sources are spread among M destinations.

[35] For a system accommodating a large number of low-throughput stations, this should not be a problem.

[36] More elaborate schemes have been proposed that involve reserving several channel–slots in advance, piggybacking control information on data packets, combining static and dynamic slot assignments, and so forth (see [Mukherjee92]).

	Slot 1	Slot 2	Slot 3	Slot 4	Slot 5	Slot 6
Channel 1	$[1, 2]_1$	$[1, 3]_1$	$[1, 2]_2$	$[1, 3]_2$		
Channel 2	$[2, 4]_1$		$[2, 3]_1$	$[2, 4]_2$	$[2, 4]_3$	
Channel 3	$[3, 1]_1$	$[3, 4]_1$	$[3, 1]_2$		$[3, 3]_1$	
Channel 4		$[4, 1]_1$		$[4, 2]_1$	$[4, 1]_2$	$[4, 3]_1$

FIGURE 5.43 Lossless scheduling.

An extra delay of at least P is incurred by each packet. This is a penalty incurred for ensuring lossless and ordered delivery.

Figure 5.43 shows how a lossless schedule for the packets queued in Figure 5.38(a) can be achieved in 6 slots. Note the relation between tell-and-go and reservations. In the tell-and-go case, whenever the packets at the head of the queues created conflicts, they were transmitted and all but one were lost. In the reservation system, potential conflicts were resolved by holding back transmissions, creating idle channel–slots. These idle slots are caused by a phenomenon known as head-of-the-line (HOL) blocking, which reduces throughput.[37] In fact, it can be shown [Hui90], using arguments similar to those we used for tell-and-go, that HOL blocking limits the maximum normalized throughput in these lossless systems to 0.63, the same value for tell-and-go! Thus, the use of extra control information has not improved the throughput of the system, but it has solved the problem of ensuring ordered delivery.[38]

5.6.5 Perfect Scheduling

In both tell-and-go and lossless scheduling, performance is less than optimal from the point of view of loss and/or delay because of a lack of complete information concerning the state of the source queues. Now suppose that complete information was available to all source and destination stations. How should capacity be allocated, and how well could the system perform?

In principle, if global queue information is available to all stations, *and* if packets are permitted to be scheduled in other than FCFS order, then a "perfect" schedule can be computed in which there is no packet loss, packets are delivered in correct order, and the channels are used with maximum efficiency; that is, a minimum number of

---

[37] This type of blocking can be avoided by taking packets out of order. For example, the packet at the head of the queue in station 4 could not be scheduled simultaneously with the others in the first time slot without a conflict. However, referring to Figure 5.43, the packet from the same station with destination 3 could have been transmitted without a conflict if it had been taken out of order. (Delivery within each logical channel would still occur in correct order.) The other three packets ahead of it in the queue blocked this possibility because of the FCFS queue discipline.

[38] The phenomenon of HOL blocking has been observed and analyzed in the context of electronic packet and cell switch fabrics, including crossbars and multistage switches.

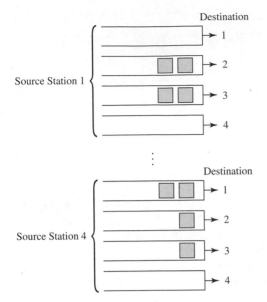

FIGURE 5.44 Queues for perfect scheduling.

channel slots are idle. The operation of such a system is illustrated conceptually in Figure 5.44. We continue with a 4×4 FT-TR system with distinct channels assigned to the source stations. The figure shows a modification of Figure 5.38(a), in which the system is in the same state as in Figure 5.38(a), but its waiting packets are now stored in four separate queues per station.

Assuming that this global-state information is available to all stations, an algorithm can be executed in each station that determines a conflict-free schedule for the waiting packets in a minimum number of time slots. (The channel–slot allocation algorithm of Appendix B can be used in which each waiting packet represents one unit of traffic in a normalized traffic matrix T.) Assuming that the global queue information is updated and distributed on a slot-by-slot basis, the schedule can be extended continuously in time and modified if necessary as new packets arrive. The longer the queues, the longer the schedule can be extended forward in time, and the more efficient it will be.

Of course, an extra delay P is incurred to distribute global information, as in the case of reservations. More importantly, the processing time in the perfect scheduling case can be considerable for large systems.

Depending on the queue states, it may not always be possible to fill all channel–slots. For example, occasionally some or all queues in a station are empty. (This is inevitable in a stable queueing system.) That station's channel may then be idle in the next slot. However, in the heavy-traffic case, when a queue is rarely empty, the channel–slot occupancy approaches the scheduling efficiency η_s dictated by the average traffic distibution. For balanced traffic $\eta_s \to 1$ as $\rho \to 1$.

Is perfect scheduling a practical objective in real networks? Clearly, it produces less average packet delay and higher throughput than the lossless case of Section 5.6.4, because it avoids HOL blocking. Furthermore, it ensures reliable and ordered delivery (assuming no channel errors) because packets in the *same* LC are transmitted in order even though packets in *different* LCs may be served out of order. However, the extra communication overhead, more complex data structure (for multiple queues), and additional processing must be weighed against potential performance improvement.

Several protocols have been proposed in which some attempt is made to approach perfect scheduling (see [Chen+91, Chipalkatti+92]). They all involve keeping track of the states of all queues and computing either optimal or suboptimal transmission schedules. For large M these techniques pose significant problems in terms of the volume of control information, the required databases, and the processing required in each station.

5.6.6 Dynamic versus Fixed Capacity Allocation

All of the procedures discussed previously for dynamic scheduling tend to adjust capacity allocations to the instantaneous traffic demand. Ignoring the issue of communication and processing overhead, the procedure with the highest performance is perfect scheduling. How does this compare with fixed-capacity allocation? Because of the complex interactions among all of the source queues, an exact analysis of performance of perfect scheduling is very difficult. However, certain general statements can be made.

Looking at the system from the point of view of flow conservation, it should be clear that the conditions relating traffic requirements and network resources for an $M \times N$ system using fixed capacity assignment apply to the dynamic case as well. Flow conservation requires that certain aggregate average flow conditions are satisfied. Let us assume a slotted system with fixed packet lengths of m' bits fitting into one slot and all transmitters operating at R_t bits per second. Furthermore, let the *aggregate* traffic intensity at each source station be limited to $\rho < 1$. Then, using the definitions in Equation 5.88, the traffic is constrained by

$$\mathcal{T}_i m' \leq \rho R_t \quad i = 1, 2, \ldots, M \tag{5.123}$$

$$\mathcal{R}_j m' \leq \rho R_t \quad j = 1, 2, \ldots, N \tag{5.124}$$

$$\bar{\Lambda} m' \leq \rho R_t C \tag{5.125}$$

Comparing Equations 5.123 and 5.124 to the constraints in Equation 5.89, we see that dynamic scheduling of packets imposes only $M + N$ constraints on source and destination flows rather than MN constraints in the case of fixed-frame scheduling. Furthermore, the constrained flows in the former case are *aggregate* traffic, all of which leads to a more flexible system with better performance in the face of unpredictable variations in flow.

5.7 Some Photonic Packet Switch Examples

Because static multipoint networks were the first practical optical network realizations, there have been a wide variety of proposals for LANs, MANs, and photonic switches based on this structure; many were implemented in the laboratory and a few were deployed as operational networks.[39] Most of them fit into the basic framework discussed in this chapter, executing packet switching in the optical layer. But each has its special characteristics and innovations. We provide a few representative examples to indicate some special features not discussed earlier.

Some optical LANs based on unidirectional buses operate using *sense taps*, which enable them to use protocols similar to CSMA/CD (called *attempt-and-defer*). A station taps a small amount of power from the bus, and if it senses activity on the fiber, it delays transmitting until the fiber is idle (see [Banerjee+93, Chalmtac+88]). A protection-against-collision (PAC) network (see [Karol+91]) bases its operation on collision avoidance. Using a broadcast star, stations that wish to transmit packets first send preambles to "probe" the network. An electrical signal is generated in response to the preambles, which controls a PAC switch, preventing transmissions that would lead to collisions.

Static multipoint networks are effectively distributed photonic switches. The NASs are the input/output ports and the fiber network is the switch fabric. When spread over an area of more than a few kilometers, propagation delays limit the performance of typical MAC protocols. However, there have been many photonic switch proposals based on star couplers as switch fabrics. Because the physical dimensions of a switch (as opposed to a LAN or MAN) are small, control is much easier. Some examples are Star-Track [Lee+90], FOX [Arthurs+88a], and HYPASS [Arthurs+88b]. These typically use separate networks (e.g., a token ring or an auxiliary star) to distribute control information.

More recently, photonic packet/cell switches have been proposed, which include optical buffering for the purpose of contention resolution.[40] An example is a broadcast-and-select switch that consists of a first stage of wavelength converters, a second stage of optical buffering using fiber delay lines, and a third stage of switching, implemented via WSSs [Renaud+97].

Optical buffering clears the way to purely optical packet-switched networks. At this writing, there is increased interest in these networks, in which packet/cell headers are read either electronically or optically, and packets are buffered optically in a network node and then forwarded on outbound links determined by a routing table. Although these networks are highly speculative at this time, the rapid progress of optical technology suggests that it is unwise to predict which way optical networks will evolve in the future.

---

[39] Unfortunately, most of the work on these networks has been on MAC protocols and performance analysis—the easy part. Implementation and deployment has fallen far behind analytical work.

[40] Optical buffering can also be used to deal with synchronization problems in a purely optical packet-switched network.

5.8 Summary

This chapter provided an overall picture of how static multipoint networks are structured, what their constraints are, and when they are useful and when they are not. The prototypical physical example used throughout was the broadcast star, operated as a shared communication medium.

The basic constraints that must be considered when designing a network are the station functionality (at both the optical and electronic levels) and the available optical spectrum. Within those constraints we demonstrated how one can design and optimize a network to satisfy given traffic requirements, taking into account various alternatives for trading off cost versus performance. The main objective was to obtain maximum connectivity and throughput at minimum cost and complexity.

It was seen that the highest efficiency is achieved when the design problem is deterministic; that is, when dedicated connections are implemented for synchronous traffic. Randomness generally reduces performance and increases cost: More sophisticated control is required and more resources (bandwidth in the fibers and processing power in the stations) are needed to provide a given quality of service. One way of mitigating effects of random fluctuations is by increasing system size and by aggregating traffic whenever possible. This effect appeared several times in this chapter. In packet-switched systems, packet loss is reduced by increasing buffer size, and vulnerability to traffic fluctuations is reduced by dynamic capacity allocation. In systems with demand-assigned connections, blocking probability at a given traffic intensity is reduced by scaling up the system.

Randomness is always present in the real world because of imprecision in predicting demand, statistical fluctuations of demand-assigned connection requests, or burstiness of packet traffic. Thus, the mathematical models introduced here to deal with random traffic are particularly important in a wide range of network applications.

As mentioned in Chapter 3, larger networks can be constructed using embedded broadcast stars as subnets. For this reason, the development of this chapter provides a foundation for the more complex WANs discussed in the remainder of the book.

5.9 Problems

1. A three-node directed star is configured with *optical* local access subnets. One node consists of a concentration subnet for "servers" (e.g., video juke boxes), and the other two are distribution subnets for end systems.

    (a) Show the fiber arrangements for these subnets.

    (b) Because the transmission through the subnets is unidirectional from servers to end systems, there will be a problem in network control (i.e., in implementing and controlling requests from the end systems for server-to-end system connections). Suggest a reasonable network control and management arrangement, including provisions for signaling.

2. It is indicated in Section 3.2.1 that TDM/TDMA or TDM/T-WDMA requires guard times between successive bursts from different transmitters.

   (a) Explain the operations the receivers must perform during guard times and during the initial portions of each transmitted burst.

   (b) How is receiver synchronization affected when different transmitters use different bitrates?

   (c) How is NAS operation simplified when it has an array of ORs?

3. In the case of the normalized traffic matrix of Figure 5.3(b), why is it that no TT-FR schedule can produce a frame length shorter than seven, and no FT-TR schedule can produce a frame length shorter than eight?

4. Revise the TDM/T-WDMA development of Section 5.2.1 for the case in which different transmitters use different bitrates R_{t_i}. Apply this to the case of the 3×3 system of Figure 5.3(b), using TT-TR with two channels available. Assume that the bitrate R_{t_1} for transmitter 1 is twice as fast as for the other two transmitters. Find the required bitrates for the system as well as a feasible CAS.

5. Compare the SCMA receiver of Figure 5.7(b) with the coherent optical receiver of Figure 2.34. Point out the similarities, differences, and technological problems of each. Comment on relative costs.

6. For the case $M = 50$, determine the error incurred in neglecting the nonadjacent channel OBI terms to give the approximation of CIR in Equation 5.21.

7. Derive Equation 5.22.

8. Redo the example at the end of Section 5.2.2.2 for $M = 10$ and 20 using a modulation index of $m = 1$ and assuming that the Lorentzian shape of the OBI spectrum is maintained with a width broadened to $a = 200$ MHz.

9. Give an example of how a packet-switched CDMA system could be implemented at the subcarrier level, along the lines of Section 5.2.2.5. Compare this to an IM/DD CDMA system without subcarriers. How does the subcarrier packet-switched approach change the type of codes that are applicable, the effect of OBI, and the resultant overall system performance? For example, how might the correlation properties of the codes differ in the two cases? (Hint: In a subcarrier CDMA system based on pseudo random pulse sequences, the coefficients in a chip sequence can have negative as well as positive signs, or can even be complex.)

10. Redo the numbers in the example at the end of Section 5.2.2.4 using $C = 9$ optical channels.

11. For the SCM/WDMA/SCMA system of Section 5.2.2.7, devise an algorithm for "static" subcarrier frequency assignment. Assume a general $M \times M$ system with C available subcarrier channels with fixed and distinct optical frequency assignments at the transmitters. Based on a list of required LCs, the algorithm should determine whether a feasible subcarrier frequency assignment can be found, and should give a possible assignment.

12. For the traffic matrix γ shown here, plot the balance factor, η, as a function of X, assuming that $C = 3$ and each station has a single transceiver.

$$\gamma = \begin{bmatrix} 0 & 1 & 1 & 0 \\ 0 & 1 & 1 & 0 \\ 3 & 0 & 0 & 0 \\ 0 & 0 & 0 & X \end{bmatrix}$$

13. Consider the following normalized traffic matrix:

$$T = \begin{bmatrix} 1 & 0 & 2 & 0 \\ 0 & 4 & 0 & 3 \\ 2 & 0 & 1 & 0 \\ 0 & 1 & 0 & 1 \end{bmatrix}$$

   (a) For an FT-TR system with a full complement of channels and a single transmitter or receiver per station, find L_{min} and an optimal CAS.

   (b) Repeat the previous part when $\alpha_2 = 2$.

   (c) Repeat the first part for the case $C = 2$, finding an optimal schedule for an FT-TR, TT-FR, and TT-TR system.

   (d) Assume that the traffic from station 2 consists of a point-to-point connection, [2, 2], carrying one unit of traffic, and a multicast connection, [2, {2, 4}], carrying three units. Redo the first part for this case.

14. Program the scheduling algorithm of Appendix B. Try out your program on some test cases.

15. In the example of Section 5.4.1.3, approximate π by $22/7$ and determine the minimum frame length L_{min}. How much capacity is wasted in this case?

16. In the queueing delay example of Figure 5.27, let all parameters be the same as before except the propagation delay. Take the speed of light in the fiber to be 2×10^8 m/sec. Determine the fiber distance at which the propagation delay in the fiber equals the average system delay $\bar{D}$ when $\rho = 0.5$. ($\bar{D}$ includes all delays except propagation delay.)

17. In the tell-and-go example of Figure 5.38, assume that all packets in transmitting station 4 are destined for receiving station 3.

   (a) Show how Figure 5.38(b) would look in this case, indicating conflicts and lost packets.

   (b) Show how the lossless schedule of Figure 5.43 would look in this case.

   (c) Show a perfect schedule for this case.

18. Consider the throughput performance of the system described in Section 5.5.1.2 and plotted in Figures 5.31 and 5.32. Compute a set of curves similar to those in the figures, with the parameters changed to $C = 5$ and $M = 25$. Plot the curves and compare them with the aforementioned figures.

5.10 Bibliography

[Abramson73] N. Abramson. The ALOHA system. In *Computer Networks*. Englewood Cliffs, NJ: Prentice-Hall, 1973.

[Antoniades+95] N. Antoniades, W. Xin, B. Pathak, E. Yang, and T. E. Stern. Use of subcarrier multiplexing/multiple access for multipoint connections in all-optical networks. In *SPIE Conf. on All-Optical Communications Systems: Architectures*, Philadelphia, October 1995.

[Arthurs+88a] E. Arthurs, J. M. Cooper, M. S. Goodman, et al. Multiwavelength optical cross-connect for parallel-processing computers. *Electron. Letters*, 24:119–120, 1988.

[Arthurs+88b] E. Arthurs, M. S. Goodman, H. Kobrinski, and M. P. Vecchi. HYPASS: An opto-electronic packet switching system. *IEEE J. Select. Areas Commun.*, 6:1500–1510, 1988.

[Banerjee+93] S. Banerjee and B. Mukherjee. Fairnet: A WDM-based multiple channel lightwave network with adaptive and fair scheduling policy. *IEEE J. Select. Areas Commun.*, 11:1104–1112, 1993.

[Briley83] B. E. Briley. *Introduction to Telephone Switching*. Reading, MA: Addison-Wesley, 1983.

[Chen+90] M. S. Chen, N. R. Dono, and R. Ramaswami. A media-access protocol for packet-switched wavelength-division metropolitan area networks. *IEEE J. Select. Areas Commun.*, 8(6):1048–1057, 1990.

[Chen+91] M. Chen and T-S. Yum. A conflict-free protocol for optical WDMA networks. In *Proc. IEEE Globecom.*, pp. 1276–1281, Phoenix, December 1991.

[Chipalkatti+92] R. Chipalkatti, Z. Zhang, and A. S. Acampora. High-speed communication protocols for optical star networks using WDM. In *Proc. IEEE Infocom.*, City??, 1992.

[Chlamtac+88] I. Chlamtac and A. Ganz. A multibus train communication architecture for high-speed fiber optic networks. *IEEE J. Select. Areas Commun.*, SAC-6:903–912, 1988.

[Chlamtac+91] I. Chlamtac and A. Fumagalli. Quadro-stars: High performance optical WDM star networks. In *Proc. IEEE Globecom.*, pp. 1224–1229, Phoenix, December 1991.

[Darcie87] T. E. Darcie. Subcarrier multiplexing for multiple-access lightwave networks. *IEEE/OSA J. Lightwave Technology*, LT-5:1103–1110, 1987.

[Desem90] C. Desem. Optical interference in subcarrier multiplexed systems with multiple optical carriers. *IEEE J. Select. Areas Commun.*, 8(7):1290–1295, 1990.

[Gopal82] I. S. Gopal. *Scheduling Algorithms for Multibeam Communications Satellites*. PhD thesis. New York: Columbia University, 1982.

[Hui90] J. Y. Hui. *Switching and Traffic Theory for Integrated Broadband Networks*. Norwell, MA: Kluwer Academic Publishers, 1990.

[Humblet+93] P. Humblet, R. Ramaswami, and K. N. Sivarajan. An efficient communication protocol for high-speed packet-switched multichannel networks. *IEEE J. Select. Areas Commun.* 11:568–578, 1993.

[Inukai79] T. Inukai. An efficient SS/TDMA time slot assignment algorithm. *IEEE Trans. Commun.*, 27(10):1449–1455, 1979.

[Karol+91] M. J. Karol and B. Glance. Performance of the PAC optical packet network. In *Proc. IEEE Globecom.*, pp. 1258–1263, Phoenix, December 1991.

[Lam74] S. S. Lam. *Packet Switching in a Multi-access Broadcast Channel*. PhD thesis. Los Angeles: Department of Computer Science, UCLA, 1974.

[Lee+90] T. T. Lee, M. S. Goodman, and E. Arthurs. A broadband optical multicast switch. In *IEEE Conf. Record ISS '90*, Stockholm, 1990.

[Liew+89] S. C. Liew and K-W. Cheung. A broadband optical network based on hierarchical multiplexing of wavelengths and RF subcarriers. *IEEE/OSA J. Lightwave Technology*, 7(11): 1825–1838, 1989.

[Mukherjee92] B. Mukherjee. WDM-based local lightwave netwroks—Part I: Singlehop systems. *IEEE Network Mag.,* 6(3):12–27, 1992.

[Olshanksy+89] R. Olshanksy, V. A. Lanzisera, and P. M. Hill. Subcarrier multiplexed lightwave systems for broadband distribution. *IEEE/OSA J. Lightwave Technology,* 7(9):1329–1342, 1989.

[Prucnal+86] P. Prucnal, M. A. Santoro, and T. R. Fan. Spread spectrum fiberoptic local area network using optical processing. *IEEE J. Lightwave Technology,* 4:547–554, 1986.

[Ramaswami93] R. Ramaswami. Multi-wavelength lightwave networks for computer communication. *IEEE Communications Mag.,* 31(2):78–88, 1993.

[Ramaswami+90] R. Ramaswami and R. Pankaj. *Tunability Needed in Multi-channel Networks: Transmitters, Receivers or Both?* IBM Technical Report No. RC-16237, 1990.

[Renaud+97] M. Renaud, F. Masetti, C. Guillemot, and B. Bostica. Network and system concepts for optical packet switching. *IEEE Communications Mag.,* 35(4):96–102, 1997.

[Saleh89] A.A.M. Saleh. Fundamental limit on number of channels in subcarrier-multiplexed lightwave CATV system. *Electron. Letters,* 25(12):776–777, 1989.

[Salehi89] J. A. Salehi. Code division multiple-access techniques in optical fiber network—Part I: Fundamental principles. *IEEE Trans. Commun.,* 37(8):824–833, 1989.

[Salehi+90] J. A. Salehi, A. M. Weiner, and J. P. Heritage. Coherent ultrashort light pulse code-division multiple access communication systems. *IEEE/OSA J. Lightwave Technology,* 8(3):478–491, 1990.

[Schwartz87] M. Schwartz. *Telecommunication Networks: Protocols, Modeling and Analysis.* Reading, MA: Addison-Wesley, 1987.

[Schwartz96] M. Schwartz. *Broadband Integrated Networks.* Englewood Cliffs, NJ: Prentice-Hall, 1996.

[Shankaranarayanan+91] N. K. Shankaranarayanan, S. D. Elby, and K-Y. Lau. WDMA/subcarrier-FDMA lightwave networks: Limitations due to optical beat interference. *IEEE/OSA J. Lightwave Technology,* 9(7):931–943, 1991.

[Wood+93] T. H. Wood and N. K. Shankaranarayanan. Operation of a passive optical network with subcarrier multiplexing in the persence of optical beat interference. *IEEE/OSA J. Lightwave Technology,* 11(10):1632–1640, 1993.

Wavelength/Waveband Routed Networks

In Chapter 5 we discussed shared-channel networks, and the emphasis was on satisfying traffic requirements on a static, multipoint physical topology (a broadcast star or its equivalent). The traffic requirements were expressed in terms of flows on *logical connections* (LCs), and satisfaction of these requirements involved multiplexing and multiple access to share the available channels efficiently. When combined time– and wavelength–division techniques were employed, the *optical connections* supporting the LCs were set up and time shared by rapidly tuning the transceivers over a given set of wavelengths. Because all optical connections shared a common broadcast medium in a static configuration, all optical paths supporting these connections were permanently in place. We now move on to optical connection routing and wavelength/waveband assignment—issues that were absent in the static case.

6.1 Introduction

In this chapter we focus on the optical layer of the architecture shown in Figure 2.1(a); that is, we treat purely optical networks with *reconfigurable* optical paths, in which reconfiguration is achieved by space switching together with wavelength and/or waveband routing. The earliest proposals for wavelength routed networks (WRNs) appeared in [Brain+88] and [Hill88].

In much of the subsequent work on these networks, a recurring issue has been to determine the number of wavelengths required to achieve a desired degree of connectivity as a function of network size and functionality of network nodes (e.g., static wavelength routers, static wavelength interchangers, or WSXCs). This is a critical issue because the available bandwidth of a fiber is not infinite, and the imperfections of the supporting optical technology place a lower limit on the feasible wavelength spacings.

In some cases some very general results on wavelength requirements have been obtained. For example, it has been shown (see [Barry93a, 93b; Barry+93]) that in a static N-node network (basically a network with nodes that are limited to static routers) with tunable transmitters and receivers, at least $\sqrt{N}/e$ wavelengths are required to support all permutations of connections from inputs to outputs (i.e., full permutation connectivity). Wavelength and switch requirements in switched WRNs were presented in [Barry+94].

As indicated in Section 3.5, when the connectivity limits of purely optical networks are reached, it is necessary to turn to logically routed networks (LRNs). In this case, the purely optical network is responsible for the transport of bulk flows (e.g., gigabits per second per λ-channel), whereas the logical switching node (LSN) does fine-grained (e.g., ATM cell or IP packet) switching. This is the essence of the multihop concept, in which data packets reenter the optical layer several times and are switched multiple times in the LSNs before reaching their final destination [Acampora94]. Chapter 7 focuses on the logical layer properties of LRNs. But what is the wavelength requirement in the optical layer supporting an LRN? Using a model similar to that used by [Barry93b], it has been shown that for a cell/packet-switched LRN [Bala+96a], a fixed number of wavelengths is sufficient to build a scalable network that supports full permutation connectivity on a packet basis. This demonstrates the power of combining electronics with optics for achieving both high connectivity and high throughput.

Bounds on wavelengths required for achieving full permutation connectivity in linear lightwave networks (LLNs) were obtained by [Pankaj92] and [Pankaj+95]. In one result, lower bounds on the number of wavelengths required for full permutation connectivity, given a constraint on nodal degree, were found. Because they are based on "counting" the network resources used in the connections, they are similar to the aggregate network capacity bound of Section 6.3.1.1. In additional results, special network topologies were sought that achieve full permutation connectivity with a minimum number of wavelengths. The chosen topologies are similar in structure to the multistage switch fabrics (e.g., Benes) discussed in Chapter 2 and the multihop networks (e.g., ShuffleNet) discussed in Chapter 7.

Although the general approaches to bounding wavelengths are important for indicating basic relations between network structure and performance limits, they are often asymptotic in nature and/or tied to unrealistic topologies. Thus, they are not very helpful in guiding the network designer, who deals with control and performance optimization in networks with realistic sizes and topologies.

This chapter focuses on these more realistic issues. We begin with a review of some general properties of physical topologies, stressing their relation to network performance. Then the problem of achieving a prescribed logical connectivity and throughput is studied in both WRNs and LLNs. Various network configurations and various methods of control are considered. If the traffic patterns are reasonably well-known in advance, the most effective technique for assigning optical resources (paths, wavelengths/wavebands, and channels) to LCs is by using static routing and channel assignment (RCA) rules. For example, static routing is appropriate for provisioning a list of specified, dedicated LCs; that is, for "semipermanently" embedding a specified logical topology onto a given physical topology. (As we shall see, static routing rules may also be useful for demand-assigned connections.) For more flexibility and efficiency in the face of random traffic, dynamic assignments are preferable. In Section 6.3

we explore static RCA in wavelength routed networks. The dynamic case is treated in Section 6.4. Sections 6.5 and 6.6 treat routing, waveband, and channel assignment for LLNs in the static and dynamic cases respectively. (In WRNs a *channel* is always a λ-channel, whereas in LLNs channels may take many different forms.) The chapter concludes with some case studies of economic trade-offs in multiwavelength networks.

6.2 Physical Topologies

The topological features of the fiber interconnections play a fundamental role in determining the key performance indices of a network. They influence optical signal quality, optical spectral efficiency, potential connectivity, maximum throughput, and survivability. Thus we begin with a brief description of common network topologies and their distinctive features.

Let $G(V, E)$ be a graph representing the topology of a network (excluding its access stations) with a set of vertices V representing the network nodes and a set of edges E representing the network links. The degree Δ of a vertex (or node) is the number of internodal links connected to the corresponding network node. Because the cost of a node (e.g., a static router or optical cross-connect) grows rapidly with the number of ports, it is desirable to keep Δ small.

The graph diameter D gives the longest distance between pairs of network nodes (in optical hops). Because long optical paths lead to poor signal quality, network congestion, and vulnerability to network faults, it is important to use topologies that have small diameters. Thus, good topologies are as "dense" as possible, in the sense that they have a high order (number of nodes) for a small diameter. To be cost-effective, this high order should be achieved with reasonably small node degrees. The well-known Moore bound gives the maximum order $N_{\text{Moore}}(\Delta, D)$ of a graph of maximum degree Δ and diameter D:

$$
\begin{aligned}
N_{\text{Moore}}(\Delta, D) &= 1 + \Delta \sum_{i=0}^{D-1} (\Delta - 1)^i \\
&= \frac{\Delta(\Delta - 1)^D - 2}{\Delta - 2}, \quad \Delta > 2
\end{aligned}
\tag{6.1}
$$

Graphs that achieve this bound are known as *Moore graphs*. There are an infinite number of Moore graphs of diameter 1 (the fully connected graphs of any degree). Also, Moore graphs of degree 2 and any diameter exist (all rings with an odd number of vertices). However, Moore graphs of small diameter grow scarce as Δ increases. For $D = 2$ there is only one Moore graph of degree 3 (the Petersen graph, with $N = 10$, Figure 6.38), and only one of degree 7 [Hoffman+60]. Moore graphs of diameter 2 and 3 do not exist for any other degrees except possibly $\Delta = 57$, for which the jury is still out.

Of course, graphs that come close to the Moore bound are also good candidates as physical topologies of optical networks. Figure 6.1 gives the number of vertices in

Δ \ D	2	3	4	5	6	7	8
3	10	20	38	70	128	180	280
4	15	40	95	364	731	(1081)	(2943)
5	24	60	174	532	2734	2988	7600
6	32	105	317	820	7817	10920	16385
7	50	122	420	1550	8998	31248	54168
8	57	200	807	2550	39223	40593	154800

FIGURE 6.1 Number of vertices in known maximal graphs.

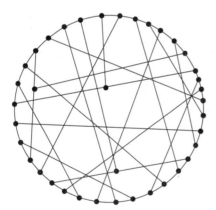

FIGURE 6.2 Thirty-eight-vertex graph.   (From (Ghafoor85, Figure 2.5). Copyright © 1985, A. Ghafoor, Reprinted by permission.)

known graphs of maximal order for degrees and diameters up to 8.[1] Some of these are "almost" Moore graphs. For example, the maximal graph with 38 vertices shown in Figure 6.2 has $\Delta = 3$ and $D = 4$, so its order is within 8 of the Moore bound of 46.

---

[1] With the exception of the numbers in parentheses in Figure 6.1, these are the graphs that were known as of 1982 [Bermond+82]. The numbers in parentheses correspond to Cayley graphs, discussed by [Chudnovsky+88] and [Arden+91].

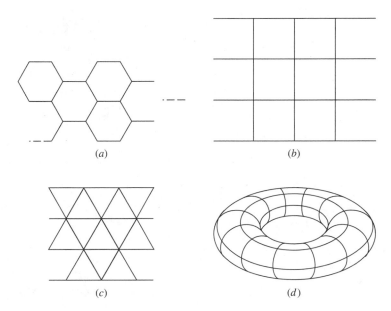

FIGURE 6.3 Tesselations of the plane.

For purposes of physical topology design and performance evaluation, it is generally easier to work with topologies that have a high degree of symmetry. For example, Figures 6.3(a), (b), and (c) show the three regular tesselations of the plane: the hexagonal, square, and triangular grids, of degree 3, 4, and 6 respectively. Each of these is made into a finite regular graph by closing it back on itself on two pairs of opposite sides, producing a torus as in Figure 6.3(d) for the square grid. It is then completely symmetric (i.e., it looks the same when viewed from any vertex).

The more common regular networks typically fall far short of the Moore bound. Thus, the n-cube has degree $\Delta = D = n$ and order $N_{n\text{-cube}} = 2^D$, whereas the square grid (as a torus) has $\Delta = 4$ and $N_{\text{torus}} = n^2$ for $D = n - 1$, where n is odd.

Two families of networks that are considerably more dense than the grids and the hypercubes are the *deBruijn* and *Kautz networks*.[2] Their directed versions (in the form of regular digraphs) are useful candidates for topologies of LRNs, where the values of Δ and D can be specified arbitrarily.[3] The undirected versions (which are not regular) provide a wide range of possibilities for physical topologies of purely optical networks. Figure 6.4 shows the undirected deBruijn and Kautz graphs with maximum degree $\Delta = 4$ and diameter $D = 3$.

---

[2] An extensive discussion of these networks and their properties appears in [Bermond+89].

[3] Construction procedures for deBruijn and Kautz graphs and their generalizations are presented in Section 7.1.2.

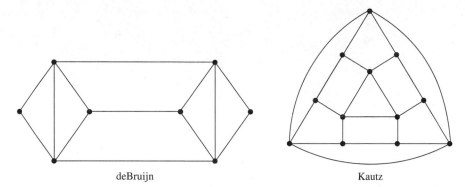

deBruijn   Kautz

FIGURE 6.4 Undirected deBruijn and Kautz graphs.

TABLE 6.1 Orders of Some Graphs

$D = \Delta$	*n*-cube	deBruijn	Kautz	Maximal	Moore
4	16	16	24	95	161
6	64	729	972	7,817	23,437
8	128	65,536	81,920	154,800	7,686,401

The orders of undirected deBruijn and Kautz graphs of diameter D and maximum degree Δ are given respectively by

$$N_{\text{deBruijn}}(\Delta, D) = \left(\frac{\Delta}{2}\right)^{D} \tag{6.2}$$

$$N_{\text{Kautz}}(\Delta, D) = \left(\frac{\Delta}{2}\right)^{D} + \left(\frac{\Delta}{2}\right)^{D-1} \tag{6.3}$$

A comparison of the orders of the *n*-cube, and deBruijn and Kautz physical topologies, is presented in Table 6.1. The known maximal graphs are also shown in the table together with the Moore bound.[4] Note that the deBruijn and Kautz graphs are far more dense than the *n*-cube, and they come within an order of magnitude of the sizes of the known maximal graphs.

---

[4] Only cases with $D = \Delta$ are listed so that comparisons can be made with the *n*-cube.

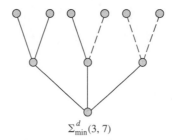

$\Sigma^d_{\min}(3, 7)$

FIGURE 6.5 Construction for $\Sigma^d_{\min}$.

The diameter of a network only gives the "worst case" internodal distance. It is more important, from the point of view of network performance, to have some measure of the *average* internodal distance $\bar{d}$. For a regular N-node network of degree Δ, it can be shown (see [Cerf+74]) that a lower bound on $\bar{d}$ is

$$\bar{d}_{\min}(\Delta, N) = \frac{1}{(N-1)} \Sigma^d_{\min}(\Delta, N) \tag{6.4}$$

where

$$\Sigma^d_{\min}(\Delta, N) = \Delta \sum_{j=1}^{D} j(\Delta - 1)^{j-1} - D \left[1 + \Delta \sum_{j=1}^{D} (\Delta - 1)^{j-1} - N \right] \tag{6.5}$$

In Equation 6.5, $\Sigma^d_{\min}$ is a lower bound on the sum of the distances (shortest paths) from any vertex of a regular graph of degree Δ to its $N - 1$ closest vertices. (D is the smallest integer for which $N_{\text{Moore}}[\Delta, D] \geq N$.) An example of the construction for $\Sigma^d_{\min}(3, 7)$ is shown in Figure 6.5. It is based on the assumption of a Moore graph topology. The figure shows a tree of depth $D = 2$, where $\Sigma^d_{\min} = 9$. Note that the same tree, completed with the dashed lines, can be used to find $\Sigma^d_{\min}(3, 10) = 15$. The Petersen graph shown in Figure 6.38 later in this chapter satisfies this bound exactly because it is a Moore graph. Although the bound in Equation 6.4 is not always very tight, it is a useful starting point for determining other important network properties. (See the aggregate network capacity wavelength bound in Section 6.3.1.1.) Figure 6.6 is a plot of $\Sigma^d_{\min}$ as a function of N, with Δ as a parameter.

Because physical topologies for real WANs usually have irregular and somewhat random structures, it is of interest to seek estimates of internodal distances for random graphs. The distance properties of "connected, semirandom" directed networks have been studied by [Rose92]. These are networks of N nodes and L directed links, in which every node is reachable from every other on a directed path, each node has p links emanating from it (i.e., its out-degree is p, its average in-degree

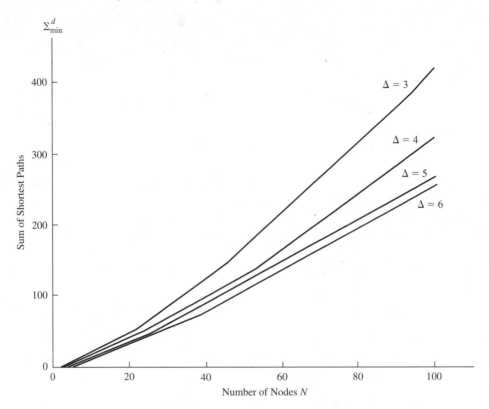

FIGURE 6.6 Plot of Σ_{min}^{d} as a function of N.

is p, and $L = Np$), and the topology is completely random otherwise. Figure 6.7 shows plots of the number of nodes reached from a single node in k hops for a random ensemble of 100 such networks, with $N = 4{,}608$ and $p = 2$.[5] This curve can be viewed as a probability distribution for internodal distances, in which distance is now measured in optical hops on *directed paths*. Note the striking resemblance to a Gaussian distribution. The mean of this distribution corresponds to $\bar{d}$ for the ensemble. In this case the curves show a mean of $\bar{d} \approx 11$ and standard deviation of $\sigma_d \approx 2$. (The standard deviation decreases with increasing p, remaining relatively independent of the order of the network.) The narrow Gaussian shape in Figure 6.7 suggests that individual node–pair distances in large random networks

---

[5] To ensure connectedness, these networks are constructed as random chordal rings (i.e., each network is a directed ring containing all nodes, with chordal links added at random).

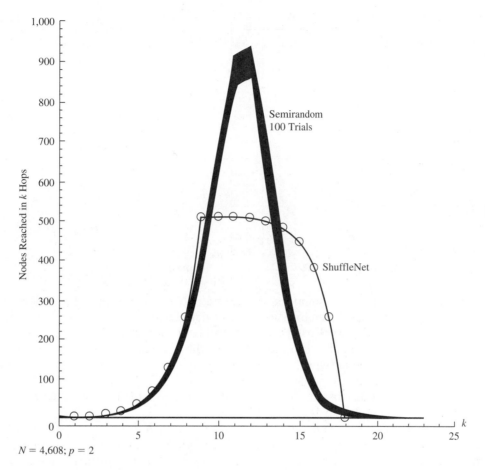

FIGURE 6.7 Internodal distances in random networks.   (From (Rose92, Figure 11a). Copyright © 1992 IEEE. Used by permission of The Institute of Electrical and Electronics Engineers, Inc.)

deviate very little from $\bar{d}$ (i.e., most node pairs are about the same distance apart!).

For comparison, the distribution of internodal distances for a $k = 9$ stage ShuffleNet (with the same values of N and p) is also shown in Figure 6.7. The figure illustrates the surprising fact that the regular and highly symmetric structure of the ShuffleNet actually produces a wider distribution of internodal distances with a slightly larger mean ($\bar{d} \approx 12$).

Applying these results to undirected networks, we note that if link directions are ignored, a random directed network with L links and with nodes of average out-degree

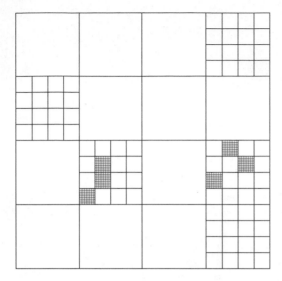

FIGURE 6.8 Recursive grid.

and in-degree p becomes a random undirected network with L links and average degree $\Delta = 2p$. It should therefore be expected that the internodal distances for random directed networks can be used as a guide to those in random undirected networks. Because there are no constraints on directions in the latter case, the hop distances for the derived undirected networks are bounded above by those for the corresponding directed networks. For example, the curves of Figure 6.7 represent "conservative" estimates of internodal distance distributions in an undirected network with 4,608 nodes and an average node degree $\Delta = 4$.[6]

Another useful approach to developing a good physical topology is recursive design. Often it is desirable, when planning a network, to start with a basic topology and then "grow" it to larger sizes matched to the evolution of traffic demand. Two approaches to recursive design are shown in Figures 6.8 and 6.54. The first begins with a square grid, which is refined recursively in neighborhoods in which demand has increased [Brown94]. The second is a hierarchical design based on growing new Petersen networks recursively out of the nodes of an existing network. The first has good survivability (many alternative paths), but rather poor distance properties. The second has good distance properties, but poor survivability. (Variations on these themes can ameliorate their shortcomings (see Problems 1 and 2 at the end of this chapter).

As we illustrate how to utilize network resources efficiently in this chapter and the next, the examples used are based frequently on dense topologies of the type presented here.

---

[6] An indication of differences between the directed and undirected case can be obtained by studying families of regular graphs. For example, for ShuffleNets ranging from $N = 8$ to 81, the undirected version has a $\bar{d}$ approximately 18% less than the directed version, on the average.

6.3 Wavelength Routed Networks: Static Routing and Channel Assignment

In this section, we consider static RCA in wavelength routed networks. Unless stated otherwise, the networks under discussion are assumed to operate *without* wavelength interchange. (Thus the constraint of wavelength continuity must be observed.) Because a WRN has a single λ-channel (wavelength) in each waveband, we shall use the term *wavelength* to denote both wavelength and waveband. (In Section 6.5, which treats wave*band* routed networks, these two terms have a different significance.)

In static routing, the traffic requirements are given as a prescribed set of point-to-point LCs between pairs of access stations. The set of connections defines a logical topology; that is, a directed logical connection graph (LCG). These connections are assumed to remain in place for relatively long periods of time, so it is worthwhile to attempt to optimize the way in which they are embedded onto the physical topology, even if optimization requires considerable computation.

The physical topology of the WRN may either be given or left free for the network designer. In the former case it most likely corresponds to the deployment of cables in some existing fiber infrastructure. In the latter case, the physical topology may be custom tailored to a prescribed logical topology (see Section 6.3.6).

In exploring RCA we begin with some general bounds on the number of wavelengths required to satisfy prescribed traffic requirements, followed by a general formulation of RCA as a graph coloring problem. We then treat some special physical topologies: rings and combinations of rings in Sections 6.3.4 and 6.3.5, and multistars in Section 6.3.6. In Section 6.3.7 general mesh topologies are considered, using optimization techniques. It turns out that the complexity of the optimization approach limits its applicability to fairly small networks. For larger problems, computational efficiency is the most important issue, suggesting the use of heuristic solution techniques for RCA. Two particularly effective heuristics are presented in Section 6.3.8. They are quite simple computationally and often achieve surprisingly good (and frequently optimal) results. The heuristic algorithms used for the static case are actually closely related to the dynamic rules discussed in Section 6.4.

The specification of the RCA problem begins with the traffic requirements, given as a set of M point-to-point LCs $\{l_1, l_2, \ldots, l_M\}$, where $l_i = [s_i, d_i]$, and s_i and d_i are the network nodes accessed by the source and destination stations respectively.[7] Unless stated otherwise, we assume that each LC requires the full capacity of one λ-channel. Therefore, each LC l_i is supported by a dedicated point-to-point optical connection

---

[7] There is no restriction on the LCs, so more than one can exist between the same source and destination nodes. This could happen either because several stations are accessing the same source–destination node pair or because several optical transceivers are being used in one source–destination station pair. When more than one NAS is attached to a node, the source s_i and destination d_i must refer to a station rather than a node. However, in most cases we assume that a single station is associated with each node, so that node designations are sufficient.

$c_i = (s_i, d_i)_k$, which is in turn supported by a dedicated point-to-point optical path $p_i = \langle s_i, d_i \rangle_k$. The subscript k indicates that c_i and p_i operate on wavelength k. For purposes of RCA, logical and optical connections are equivalent, so we shall frequently drop the adjectives, referring to both of them simply as connections.

Setting up an optical connection in a WRN requires two operations:

1. Creation of a source–destination optical path on a chosen wavelength (by setting the optical cross-connects along its route)
2. Creation of an optical connection by tuning the source transmitter and destination receiver to the chosen wavelength

An optical path p consists of a *fiber path* π; that is, a sequence of fibers directed from source to destination, and a wavelength assignment on that fiber path. Thus, several optical paths may share the same fiber paths as long as they use different wavelengths (to avoid violating the DCA condition).

In a WRN with a given physical topology, solving the RCA problem consists of finding an appropriate optical path for each connection. This means finding a fiber path (routing) together with a wavelength (channel or wavelength assignment). Static RCA is equivalent to finding an embedding of a prescribed logical topology onto a given physical topology while observing the constraints of the network.

In some cases the network resources may not be specified completely, so RCA may include specification of certain design parameters. For example, the number of wavelengths may be left free, in which case a "spectrally efficient" solution might be sought using a minimum number of wavelengths. In other cases we may be free to adjust the number of fiber pairs on each link to match the expected traffic, and hence reduce the number of required wavelengths. In this case the problem consists of combined RCA and link capacity (fiber) assignment. In still other cases, additional constraints might be imposed, such as a limit on the optical path lengths. Also, an incomplete solution might be acceptable, in which only most of the prescribed connections are established. All of these represent variants of the basic problem that appear in subsequent sections.

The RCA problem often can be solved in an efficient manner by taking advantage of special features of the network's topology, such as symmetry. This is the case for rings and other symmetric networks that are used here as illustrative examples. For more general topologies, RCA can be cast as a general optimization problem and solved using various combinatorial optimization techniques. However, due to the complexity of the problem, optimal solutions can be found only for relatively small networks, and suboptimal heuristics must be used in the larger cases.

Because of its complexity, it is usually necessary to separate the joint RCA problem into its two components. Solving the routing problem separately from the channel assignment problem frequently gives suboptimal results, but is much easier to accomplish and is generally satisfactory for engineering purposes.

Before going into the details of the RCA problem, it is helpful to obtain an overall picture of the relations between logical layer requirements and physical layer resources. From these relations we derive certain important connections between network "flows" and optical spectrum (wavelength) requirements.

6.3.1   Flow Bounds: Matching the Physical and Logical Topologies

Suppose a wavelength routed network has a given physical topology with N nodes and L links, and each link has the same number of fiber pairs F. If the network operates with an available spectrum of W wavelengths, the product WF represents the one-way capacity of a link, expressed in units of λ-channels. By varying either F or W, we vary the link capacity.[8] The ability of the network to support a prescribed set of LCs depends principally on the

- Form of the logical topology
- Form of the physical topology
- Link capacities WF

Assuming that all other network parameters are fixed, it is important to be able to determine the number of wavelengths required to support a prescribed logical topology. As we shall see, making an exact determination of this number by obtaining an optimal solution to the RCA problem is generally extremely difficult. When suboptimal heuristics are used, it is desirable to have some idea of how close the solution is to optimal. For this reason, bounds on W can be very useful. We now present two simple lower bounds based on network flows.

6.3.1.1   Aggregate Network Capacity Bound

Consider a prescribed set of M logical/optical connections $\{c_i\}$. Now if $d(s_i, d_i)$ is the distance between the source and the destination nodes for connection c_i (in optical hops), we call $\Sigma^d = \sum_{i=1}^{M} d(s_i, d_i)$ the *total internodal distance* for the connection set. The network capacity used in carrying this traffic must be at least Σ^d "link–channels," but the aggregate capacity of L links in the network is $2LFW$ link–channels. Comparing the two, we find that the number of wavelengths necessary to support all connections is bounded below by

$$W \geq \frac{\Sigma^d}{2LF} \tag{6.6}$$

Equation 6.6 is satisfied with equality when all connections are routed on shortest paths and all fibers are saturated; that is, when W wavelengths are used on every fiber. If connection c_i is routed on an optical path having H_i hops, we define the

---

[8] However, as pointed out in Section 3.3.1, F and W are not interchangeable quantities. Because of the wavelength continuity constraint, capacity in the form of fibers is more valuable than capacity in the form of wavelengths.

total hop count for the connection set as $\Sigma^H = \sum_{i=1}^{M} H_i$, and the average hop count as $\bar{H} = \Sigma^H / M$. Also we denote the average node degree by $\bar{\Delta} = 2L/N$. Then a lower bound on W to support all connections becomes[9]

$$W_{\text{Netcap}} = \frac{\Sigma^H}{2LF} = \frac{M\bar{H}}{\bar{\Delta}NF} \geq \frac{\Sigma^d}{\bar{\Delta}NF} \tag{6.7}$$

Suppose we apply the wavelength bound to a case in which the logical topology is fully connected, with one connection per node pair; in other words, $M = N(N-1)$. If the physical topology is regular of degree Δ, Equation 6.7 gives

$$WF \geq \frac{(N-1)\bar{H}}{\Delta} \geq \frac{\Sigma^d_{\min}(\Delta, N)}{\Delta} = \frac{(N-1)\bar{d}_{\min}(\Delta, N)}{\Delta} \tag{6.8}$$

where $\bar{d}_{\min}$ and $\Sigma^d_{\min}$ are defined in Equations 6.4 and 6.5 respectively.

Equation 6.8 was written with WF on the left side to express the bound in terms of required link capacity in units of λ-channels. Because the bound was obtained using flow conservation only, the wavelength continuity condition was not used. The bound therefore makes no distinction between capacity in the form of fibers and capacity in the form of wavelengths. In reality, as has been stated previously, a network in which each link has a total capacity of k λ-channels generally performs better if that capacity is provided by $F = k$ fiber pairs per link and $W = 1$ wavelength, than if the capacity is provided by $F = 1$ fiber pair per link and $W = k$ wavelengths.

These bounds clearly indicate the importance of packing the network nodes into a dense (small-diameter) topology to reduce the required number of wavelengths. For example, increasing Δ decreases the bound directly (in the denominator of Equation 6.8) as well as indirectly by reducing $\bar{d}_{\min}$. How closely the bounds can be approached depends on (1) the effectiveness of the RCA algorithm and (2) the uniformity of the link loading.

Uniformly distributed link loads can occur only if the prescribed traffic distribution is "matched" correctly to the physical topology. To obtain a bound that reflects this matching condition we need to look more closely at the network flows.

6.3.1.2 Limiting Cut Bound

The limiting cut bound is based on the Max Flow–Min Cut Theorem, which is well-known in operations research (see Appendix A).

Consider a connected N node network supporting a prescribed set of LCs. Suppose the nodes are partitioned into two subsets containing K_i and $N - K_i$ nodes. Let $\mathcal{C}_i$ be the *cut* separating the network into the two disconnected subnets induced by this node partition. Let F_i be the total number of fiber pairs in the links comprising the

---

[9] Equation 6.7 can be modified easily to apply to networks with different numbers of fiber pairs in different links.

cut and let M_i be the number of LCs from the first to the second subnet. Then a lower bound on the number of wavelengths W required to support these connections is

$$W \geq \frac{M_i}{F_i} \qquad (6.9)$$

It follows that a lower bound on W to support all connections is

$$W_{\text{Limcut}} = \left\lceil \max_i \frac{M_i}{F_i} \right\rceil \qquad (6.10)$$

where the maximum is taken over all cuts in the network. A cut that maximizes the right side is called a *limiting cut*. A necessary condition for this bound to be achieved is that traffic be distributed evenly among all fibers in each limiting cut.

In the case of a fully connected logical topology, Equation 6.10 becomes

$$W_{\text{Limcut}} = \left\lceil \max_i \frac{K_i(N - K_i)}{F_i} \right\rceil \qquad (6.11)$$

Let us apply this bound to the N node ring network of Figure 6.14. Taking the case N odd, we cut the ring almost in half, so that K_i and $N - K_i$ in Equation 6.9 are, respectively, $(N - 1)/2$ and $(N + 1)/2$. With $F_i = 2$ (a single-fiber-pair bidirectional ring), the bound becomes $W \geq \frac{N^2 - 1}{8}$, verifying that the wavelength assignments described in Section 6.3.4.2 are optimal. For the case N even, we have $W \geq \frac{N^2}{8}$, which is tight if and only if N is divisible by four (see Equation 6.12).

The limiting cut bound is very useful in detecting poor matches between logical and physical topologies. In [Baroni+97] the authors use network cuts effectively for this purpose. Figure 6.9 shows limiting cuts (indicated by dashed lines) in four real or hypothetical WANs: ARPANet, UKNet, the European Optical Network (EON), and NSFNet. For each of these networks, W_{Limcut} and the ratio $W_{\text{Limcut}}/W_{\text{Netcap}}$ are given, together with various other network parameters. For example, for the ARPANet, the limiting cut has three links, and for full connectivity a total of $11 \times 9 = 99$ connections pass across this cut. Hence, assuming $F = 1$, the minimum number of wavelengths required is 33 and is achieved when the routing algorithm divides the connections equally among the three links. A routing algorithm that fails to distribute the connections evenly requires more than the minimum number of wavelengths. Thus, the right choice of routes determines the efficiency of the wavelength assignment process. Furthermore, when routing is done independently of channel assignment (as is done when RCA is separated into two subproblems), inefficiencies and increased wavelength requirements may result.

The ratio of W_{Limcut} to W_{Netcap} indicates the degree of match between logical and physical topologies. A high ratio, as in the ARPANet, indicates a relatively poor match, suggesting a bottleneck at the limiting cut. (The fact that all ratios in these examples are less than two indicates that the networks are fairly well designed.)

Network	N	L	α	$\overline{H}$	D	$(\delta_{min}, \delta_{max})$	W_{Limcut}	N_λ	W_{Limcut}/W_{Netcap}
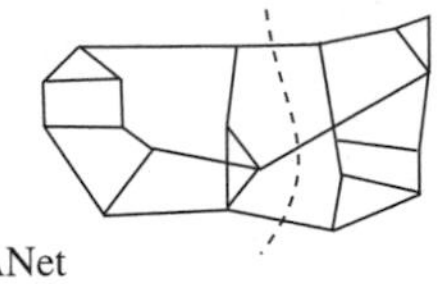 ARPANet	20	31	0.16	2.81	6	(2, 4)	33	33	1.92
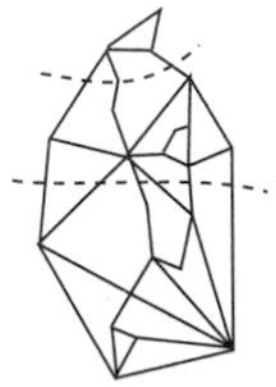 UKNet	21	39	0.19	2.51	5	(2, 7)	19	22	1.41
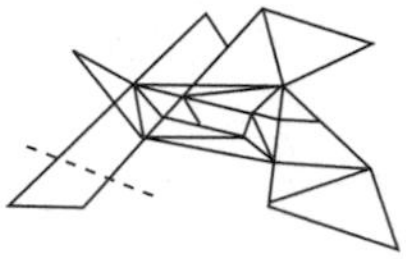 EON	20	39	0.2	2.36	5	(2, 7)	18	18	1.57
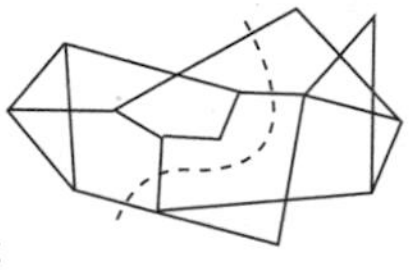 NFSNet	14	21	0.23	2.14	3	(2, 4)	13	13	1.40

FIGURE 6.9 Limiting cuts for four networks.   (From (Baroni+97, Table 1). Copyright © 1997 IEEE. Used by permission of The Institute of Electrical and Electronics Engineers, Inc.)

The limiting cut bound on wavelengths suggests a simple and cost-effective method of link capacity assignment in wide area WRNs, to match a given logical topology. Starting with a given fiber topology, and assuming a single fiber pair per link, the limiting cut bound can be calculated based on the prescribed LCs. If the resultant W_{Limcut} is too large, a reduction can be achieved by augmenting the number of fiber pairs on the links in the limiting cut(s). Because fiber cables normally contain many fiber pairs, this is a fairly efficient way of conserving the optical spectrum. As the number of fiber pairs in a limiting cut is increased, a point is reached when some other cut becomes limiting. This procedure can then be continued on the new limiting cut until it is no longer possible (or cost-effective) to improve the bound by increasing the fibers in the links.[10] Essentially, this amounts to a heuristic for assigning link capacities to match a prescribed

---

[10] The room for improvement of W_{Limcut} can be ascertained by comparing new values of W_{Limcut} and W_{Netcap} at each stage of the fiber augmentation process.

traffic distribution. Of course there is no guarantee that the actual wavelength assignments in the network can achieve the bound. The actual number of wavelengths used depends on the routing and channel assignments. Once RCA is complete, another iteration of fiber assignment can be executed to reduce the number N_λ of wavelengths actually used. This combination of RCA and fiber assignment on the "bottleneck" links comprises a combined RCA and capacity assignment problem. Although an optimal solution cannot be expected, empirical results (see [Baroni+97]) indicate that simple RCA heuristics together with some judicious increase in link fibers at strategic locations produce excellent results in minimizing N_λ. More details are provided in Section 6.3.8.

We have seen that the limiting cut bound can be an extremely useful tool for network design, provisioning, and other related problems. However, the expression for W_{Limcut} in Equation 6.10 is deceptively simple. The computation of M_i/F_i for each cut is trivial. However, the enumeration of all cuts in a large network is out of the question, because the total number of cuts to be examined in an N-node network is $2^N - 2$; in other words, it grows exponentially with the number of network nodes. Thus it is important to be able to find a good lower bound on W_{Limcut} for large networks using a minimum of computation. A computationally efficient heuristic that produces a tight lower bound, $\underline{W}_{\text{Limcut}}$, on W_{Limcut} is provided in Appendix D.[11]

6.3.2 Nonblocking Stations

As mentioned in Section 3.3.2, constraints on wavelength assignments are dependent on the way an NAS is connected to its network node. Thus, to separate station and access link constraints from network constraints, we reintroduce the concept of a nonblocking access station, first proposed in Section 3.3.2. (It is assumed here that each access station is attached to only one network node.)

We call an NAS with a single-fiber-pair access link, as shown in Figure 2.29, an *elementary station*. A station is called *nonblocking* if it can terminate all optical connections arriving at or departing from its network node. Thus, in a network with single-fiber-pair internodal links, a nonblocking NAS takes the form shown in Figure 3.16. It has as many access fiber pairs as the degree Δ of its node, and thus it is equivalent to Δ elementary stations in the same box.[12] Each access fiber pair is attached to its own input/output port on the network node so that it can be switched independently by the node. This implies that nonblocking stations require Δ access ports on their attached network node, compared with a single port for elementary stations. (In the case of networks with F fiber pairs on each link, a nonblocking access station requires ΔF access fiber pairs and access ports.) Assuming that the network operates on W

---

[11] A tighter fluid flow bound on W using linear programming is formulated in Section 6.3.7.4. However, the linear programming approach requires considerably more computation.

[12] Recall that the degree of a node is defined here as the number of *internodal* links incident on the node. The access links are not counted.

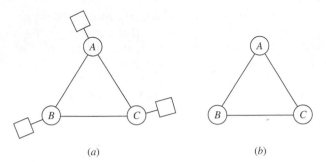

FIGURE 6.10 Three-node network.

(a) (b)

wavelengths, the nonblocking station must contain an array of W transceivers connected to each access fiber pair, with one transceiver in each array operating on each wavelength.

To remove the constraints of the access stations from the RCA discussion, we shall frequently assume that one nonblocking station accesses each network node, in which case the network can be represented by a model containing only the network nodes and the internodal fiber links, suppressing the NASs.[13] The difference between elementary and nonblocking stations is illustrated in Figure 6.10(a). If the NAS at node A is an elementary station, only one optical connection on each wavelength can originate at that station. However, if it is nonblocking, two connections per wavelength can originate at the station because node A has degree 2. With the assumption of nonblocking stations, the network can be represented by a graph containing only the vertices A, B, and C as in Figure 6.10(b). When the characteristics of the stations and access links are pertinent to the RCA problem (as in the case of elementary stations), we include them as additional vertices and edges in the network graph.

6.3.3 RCA as a Graph Coloring Problem

In this section we cast the RCA problem in terms of a *path interference graph, G_{PI},* incorporating all of the admissible RCA choices and the network constraints.[14] Determination of routing and channel assignments then reduces to the coloring of selected vertices of G_{PI}, subject to certain *interference* constraints. Section 6.3.7 provides alternatives such as mixed integer programming (MIP) or integer linear program (ILP) formulations. All of these formulations are equivalent, but depending on the particular problem, one formulation may be more convenient than another.

As before, we assume that each required logical/optical connection is supported by an optical path. Let $\pi_k = a, b, \ldots, z$ denote a *fiber* path using a sequence of fibers

---

[13] The nonblocking NAS is used here as a mathematical convenience. In practice, it would probably not be cost-effective to equip each station with $W\Delta F$ transceivers.

[14] Interference graphs have been used by [Gopal82] for channel assignment in satellite systems, and by [Chlamtac+89] and [Bala+91b] for proving NP-completeness of the channel assignment problem in WRNs and LLNs respectively.

$ab \ldots z$, and let $p = \langle A, B \rangle_{j, \pi_k}$ denote an optical path between source–destination pair (A, B) using a wavelength j on fiber path π_k.[15] Then, a *feasible* solution of the RCA problem consists of a choice of an optical path (OP) (i.e., a fiber path and wavelength) for each prescribed connection so that all network constraints are satisfied. An optimal solution of the RCA problem consists of a feasible solution that minimizes some cost function; for example, the number of wavelengths used.

Because we assume no wavelength interchange at this point, the channel assignments are constrained by wavelength continuity (as well as by the DCA condition). Two optical paths in a WRN violate DCA, and thus interfere if they share a common fiber and are assigned the same wavelength. In formulating the RCA problem, it is essential to identify interfering optical paths. This is done by means of G_{PI}, which exhibits potentially interfering OPs. Wavelength continuity is included in the network model by assigning the same wavelength to all fibers on a given OP.

For a given physical topology and prescribed connection set $\{c_i\}$, a path interference graph, G_{PI}, is constructed by identifying each vertex of G_{PI} with an *admissible* fiber path. Assuming that there is at most one connection required for each source–destination pair, and that there are K_i admissible paths for connection c_i, there will be $\sum_i K_i$ vertices in G_{PI}. Admissibility of paths is arbitrary; for example, the admissible paths for a given source–destination pair might be all minimum-hop paths, all paths less than a given physical length, or all possible paths. Two vertices of G_{PI} are joined by an edge (i.e., are adjacent) if their paths share a common fiber in the network. (Adjacent vertices represent potentially interfering OPs.)

Having constructed G_{PI}, solving the RCA problem consists of selecting one vertex of the graph (a fiber path) for each prescribed connection and choosing a color for each selected vertex (corresponding to a wavelength for the connection) so that adjacent vertices are assigned different colors. If the assignments are made with a minimum number of wavelengths, this is known as *minimal vertex coloring* of the subgraph induced by the selected vertices. It is a classic (and difficult) problem in graph theory (see Appendix A). In cases in which several connections are required between the same source–destination pair, they may be routed on different fiber paths and/or on the same fiber path provided that connections on the same fiber path are assigned different wavelengths. The latter case corresponds to a vertex coloring of G_{PI} using multiple colors per vertex.

For illustration, consider the network of Figure 6.11(a). We wish to determine a routing and channel assignment for the connection set $\{(A, C), (A, F), (A, E), (C, E)\}$. To simplify matters we assume that a single nonblocking station is attached to each node so that multiple optical connections using the same wavelength can begin and end on any node without risk of interference on the access fibers. We also assume that only minimum-hop paths are admissible, to reduce the number of possible routing

---

[15] When the network links carry more than one fiber pair, the specification of the path must distinguish a particular fiber on each link.

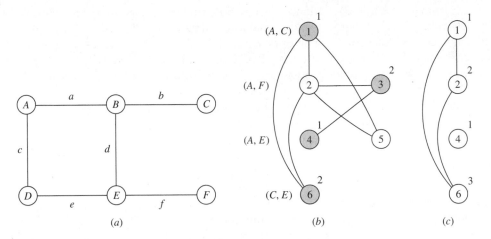

FIGURE 6.11   Illustrating RCA in a wavelength routed network.

alternatives. All admissible fiber paths that support the required connections are as follows:

$$\pi_1 = ab$$
$$\pi_2 = adf$$
$$\pi_3 = cef$$
$$\pi_4 = ce$$
$$\pi_5 = ad$$
$$\pi_6 = bd$$

Connection (A, C) is supported by π_1, connection (A, F) is supported by π_2 or π_3, connection (A, E) is supported by π_4 or π_5, and connection (C, E) is supported by π_6.

These produce the path interference graph shown in Figure 6.11(b). The vertices of the graph are arranged in the figure so that all fiber paths for a given connection appear in the same row. To satisfy the connection requirements, one vertex must be chosen from each row. Now suppose our objective is to minimize the number of wavelengths used to carry all connections. In that case the vertices must be chosen so that a minimum number of colors are used. The figure indicates a choice of paths π_1, π_3, π_4, and π_6 (shaded), which are assigned colors (wavelengths) 1, 2, 1, 2, respectively, so that a total of $W = 2$ wavelengths are needed. Using the limiting cut bound of Section 6.3.1.2, it is easy to show that this is the minimum possible number of wavelengths.

In this case, the joint routing and wavelength minimization problem was solved easily by inspection. However, even in networks with small numbers of nodes, RCA is an extraordinarily complex combinatorial problem. To obtain some idea of its complexity, consider the following "brute force" approach.

1. Make an arbitrary choice of vertices of G_{PI} (a routing assignment) to satisfy the connection requirements. Form the subgraph of G_{PI} induced by these vertices.

2. Determine the chromatic number of this subgraph.[16]

3. Repeat this process for all choices of vertices of G_{PI}, and select a routing assignment that produces a subgraph with a minimum chromatic number.

4. Do a minimal vertex coloring (wavelength assignment) of the selected subgraph.

The complexity of this approach is mind-boggling. For a set of M connections, the number of subgraphs that must be examined is $S = \prod_{i=1}^{M} K_i$, and each subgraph has M vertices. For full connectivity, $M = N(N-1)$. Determining the chromatic number of each subgraph is itself an NP-complete problem (see [Garey+79]), and this must be done S times. Finally, once a routing assignment is selected, a minimal vertex coloring must be found—again, an NP-complete problem.

A particularly disagreeable feature of the joint RCA problem is that the number of possible paths (and hence S) grows exponentially with the number of nodes and fibers in the network. One way of keeping the paths under control is to place bounds on the admissible path lengths, as was done in the previous example. This is important from performance considerations as well, as pointed out in Section 6.2. Long paths not only lead to poor signal quality because of accumulated noise, distortion, and cross-talk, they also cause congestion in the network. Thus a path that requires two optical hops consumes twice as much network capacity as one that requires only one hop.

In addition to reducing the size of the admissible path set, the RCA problem on G_{PI} can be simplified further by decoupling routing and channel assignment as follows:

1. Choose paths for the required connections according to some desired routing criterion, and form the subgraph of G_{PI} induced by this choice.

2. Do a minimal vertex coloring of the chosen subgraph (a minimal wavelength assignment).

This decomposition does not lead necessarily to a minimum-wavelength solution of the RCA problem. For example, in the network of Figure 6.11 the routing criterion might be to choose the lowest numbered path when more than one minimum-hop path exists. This produces the subgraph shown in Figure 6.11(c). The chromatic number

---

[16] The chromatic number of a graph is the number of colors required for a minimal vertex coloring of the graph. It is equal to or greater than the size of the maximum clique of the graph (see Appendix A).

of this subgraph is three, with a possible minimal coloring shown in the figure. In separating the routing and wavelength assignment problem in this case, optimality was sacrificed.

Fortunately, some good heuristics have been developed for solving the decoupled RCA problem, so that brute force techniques are not generally required. Many of these are very simple, and computational experience has shown that they yield optimal or close to optimal results in wide ranges of cases.[17] Heuristic approaches are examined in Section 6.3.8. The concept of the interference graph appears in a somewhat different setting when we consider channel assignment for LLNs in Section 6.5.6.

6.3.4 Rings

As mentioned earlier, networks with some degree of symmetry make the RCA problem simpler. Rings are an especially good choice for physical topologies because they are symmetric and they are Moore graphs. Fiber networks in the form of SONET rings have been deployed widely in the telecommunications industry for the past decade due to their advanced protection and network management capabilities. As a consequence, wavelength–division multiplexed (WDM) rings are expected to be the next step in the evolution of WDM from its current use in point-to-point transmission facilities to deployment in wavelength routed networks.

We therefore analyze static RCA in rings in this section before moving on to more general topologies. The development is prefaced by a brief explanation of automatic protection in rings. This digression is inserted because fault protection is such an important issue in optical networks and because the method of protection influences the way wavelength assignment must be performed in a WDM ring. The section ends with some ideas on extrapolating the RCA methods for rings to more general mesh topologies, using ring decomposition techniques.

6.3.4.1 Shared-Protection Rings

Shared-protection rings (SPRINGs) have been used for many years in traditional networks to provide for rapid fault recovery using automatic protection switching (APS). At this point we briefly describe a few basic features of a WDM SPRING as a prelude to discussing the RCA problem. (Chapter 8 treats the issue of fault recovery in rings in more depth.)

Figure 6.12 shows an example of a four-fiber WDM SPRING. It has a bidirectional fiber pair in each link, used as working fibers, paralleled with another pair used for protection. Stations access the ring through WADMs at each node. Section 8.3.2.2 describes the protection properties of this ring. Under normal operation, using shortest path routing, traffic from node 1 to node 2, for example, is carried in the outer (clockwise) working fiber, and traffic from node 2 to node 1 is carried in the inner (counterclockwise) working fiber.

---

[17] A good heuristic for minimal vertex coloring is provided in Appendix A.

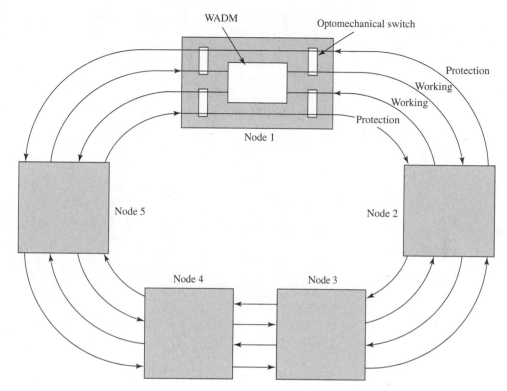

FIGURE 6.12 A four-fiber SPRING.

To recover from link or node failures the optomechanical switches close, sealing off the failed element, and reroute the affected connections the "long way" around the ring using the protection fibers.[18] Figure 6.13 shows a two-fiber WDM SPRING. Because there are two working fibers and no protection fibers, each working fiber reserves half of its capacity for failure restoration. This is done by using no more than half the number of available wavelengths on each fiber. The unused wavelengths serve as protection when traffic is looped back under fault conditions. To ensure that no distinct channel assignment (DCA) violation occurs in case of failure, the working wavelengths in each direction must be distinct.

In this section we focus on four-fiber SPRINGs, so that the wavelength assignments on the two counterrotating working fiber rings can be made independently, reusing the optical spectrum on each ring. It is easy to show that a two-fiber SPRING requires exactly twice the number of wavelengths as a four-fiber SPRING to support the same logical connectivity.

---

[18] Another protection technique, called *path protection,* maintains an additional connection on a different path for each active connection (see Section 8.2.2.1).

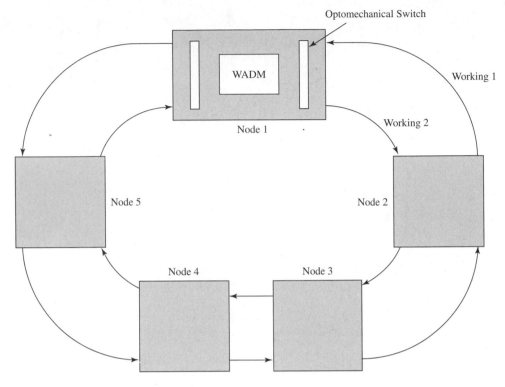

FIGURE 6.13   A two-fiber SPRING.

6.3.4.2   RCA in WDM Shared-Protection Rings

We examine the RCA problem in an N-node, four-fiber shared-protection ring; that is, a network with working fibers that form a bidirectional ring, as shown in Figure 6.14. The objective here is to determine routing and wavelength assignments over the ring to provide prescribed logical connectivity among the N nodes using a minimum number of wavelengths. A related objective is to do the assignments so that the ring can be scaled up without disturbing existing assignments. As usual in WRNs, each LC is carried by a dedicated optical connection, so it is not necessary to distinguish between logical and optical connections.

In most of this section it is assumed that each node is associated with a nonblocking NAS; that is, the station accesses its node through a two-fiber-pair access link.[19] The bidirectional ring was first encountered in Section 3.3.2. A typical node–station configuration is shown in Figure 3.18, in which each access fiber pair connects to a 2×2 multiwavelength switch acting as a WADM. (There is no λ-interchange in the nodes.)

---

[19] We shall, however, introduce a single-fiber-pair access link at one point in the development to illustrate the effect of elementary NASs.

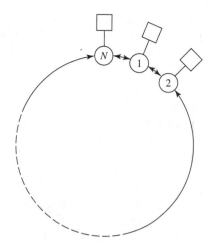

FIGURE 6.14 Bidirectional ring.

In effect, the bidirectional ring in Figure 3.18 is equivalent to two unidirectional rings, each containing N WADMs accessed by elementary stations.

We present a routing and wavelength assignment algorithm that achieves full bidirectional connectivity among all stations using a minimum number of wavelengths. The algorithm is scalable in the sense that the size of the ring scales gracefully without disturbing the existing wavelength assignments [Ellinas+98b]. The routing is always the shortest path.

Number of Wavelengths Required for Full Connectivity   In determining the minimum number of wavelengths required for full connectivity, we distinguish three cases: N odd, $N/2$ odd, and $N/2$ even. It can be shown [Ellinas+98a] that the number of wavelengths *necessary and sufficient* for full connectivity is

$$W = \begin{cases} \dfrac{N^2 - 1}{8}, & N \text{ odd} \\[2mm] \dfrac{N^2 + 4}{8}, & N/2 \text{ odd} \\[2mm] \dfrac{N^2}{8}, & N/2 \text{ even} \end{cases} \tag{6.12}$$

For example, the number of wavelengths required for the $N(N-1)$ connections on rings of size $N = 7, 8, 9$, and 10 are, respectively, $W = 6, 8, 10$, and 13.

Recall that lower bounds on W for the cases N odd and even were derived in Section 6.3.1 using the limiting cut bound. Equation 6.12 indicates that those bounds are tight for all cases except $N/2$ odd. If we replace the assumed nonblocking access stations with elementary stations (with single-fiber-pair access links), and apply the limiting cut bound to the access links, we find that at least $W = N - 1$ wavelengths are required for full connectivity on any N node network. This implies that for $N \leq 5$

a single-fiber-pair access link causes a bottleneck, necessitating a larger number of wavelengths on the ring than required with nonblocking stations. The difference between the two cases was illustrated in Figures 3.17 and 3.18, in which RCA tables were given for a fully connected five-node ring with single- and double-fiber-pair access links respectively. These assignments are optimal, requiring four and three wavelengths respectively.

Scalable Wavelength Assignment: *N* odd   Because the network is symmetric and shortest path routing is used, it is sufficient to focus on connections using one direction of the ring. Half of the shortest paths between node pairs use each direction. For N odd, shortest paths are unique, eliminating any routing decisions. (The case of N even has a minor complication due to the fact that there are two routing alternatives for the longest connections.) To avoid unnecessary complications, we limit the development here to the case N odd. A matrix approach to RCA, valid for all three cases and having desirable scalability properties, can be found in [Ellinas+98b].

The wavelength assignment methodology proposed here is recursive: A wavelength assignment for a ring with $K + 2$ nodes (K odd) is constructed by adding two nodes and their connections to a K-node ring with a known wavelength assignment using $(K^2 - 1)/8$ wavelengths. The old connections are not disturbed and the new connections require $(K + 1)/2$ new wavelengths. With the addition of the two nodes and their connections, a $(K + 2)$-node ring is created using a total of $\left((K + 2)^2 - 1\right)/8$ wavelengths. This constitutes an inductive proof of the fact that $(N^2 - 1)/8$ wavelengths is sufficient for an N-node ring.

The steps are as follows (all steps refer to the clockwise ring):

1. Start with $K = 3$ nodes and assign a common wavelength to the three shortest path (one-hop) connections.

2. To find clockwise connections for $K + 2$ nodes, assume that connections for K nodes are in place and thus require $(K^2 - 1)/8$ distinct wavelengths.

   (a) Insert two new nodes into the ring, one preceding node 1 and the other following node $(K + 1)/2$. Label them $K + 1$ and $K + 2$ respectively. This divides the original K nodes into two regions: region 1, containing nodes $1, 2, \ldots, (K + 1)/2$, and region 2, containing nodes $(K + 3)/2, \ldots, K$ (Figure 6.15). The new nodes are assumed not to disturb the connections among the original nodes. In other words, the original connections are assumed to "pass through" the new nodes without any add–drop operations.

   (b) Make all clockwise connections for the two new nodes using a total of $(K + 1)/2$ new wavelengths as follows (Assume the new wavelengths are labeled $\lambda_1, \lambda_2, \ldots, \lambda_{(K+1)/2}$.):

      1) *Region 1:* Assign λ_1 from node $K + 1$ to node 1, λ_2 from node $K + 1$ to node 2, ..., and $\lambda_{(K+1)/2}$ from node $K + 1$ to node $\frac{K+1}{2}$. Similarly, assign λ_1 from node 1 to node $K + 2$, λ_2 from node 2 to node $K + 2$, ..., and $\lambda_{(K+1)/2}$ from node $\frac{K+1}{2}$ to node $K + 2$.

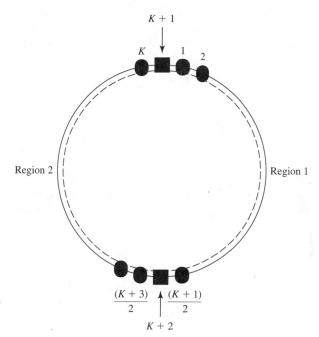

FIGURE 6.15 Recursive construction for RCA on the ring.

2) *Region 2:* Assign λ_1 from node $(K+3)/2$ to node $K+1$, λ_2 from node $(K+5)/2$ to node $K+1, \ldots$, and $\lambda_{(K-1)/2}$ from node K to node $K+1$. Similarly, assign λ_1 from node $K+2$ to node $\frac{K+3}{2}$, λ_2 from node $K+2$ to node $\frac{K+5}{2}, \ldots$, and $\lambda_{(K-1)/2}$ from node $K+2$ to node K. Note that the same wavelengths are reused for the second case because the connections are in different regions and do not overlap. Also, observe that wavelength $\lambda_{(K+1)/2}$ is left unused within region 2.

3) To complete the new connections, assign $\lambda_{(K+1)/2}$ from node $K+2$ to node $K+1$.

The identical procedure is followed on the counterclockwise ring (in the reverse direction), reusing the same wavelengths. Figures 6.16 and 6.17 show how this procedure is used to scale the ring up from $N=3$ to $N=5$ to $N=7$. (Only the clockwise direction is shown.) Note that the nodes have been renumbered in going from Figure 6.16 to 6.17.

The previous procedure produces optimal wavelength assignments (for N odd) for rings with *nonblocking* two-fiber-pair access stations. It is easy to verify that the resultant assignments do *not* work for elementary single-fiber-pair access stations. Yet, the limiting cut bound suggests that it might be possible to find feasible wavelength assignments for the elementary access station case using no more wavelengths than in the nonblocking case, provided that $N \geq 6$. We leave it as a (highly nontrivial)

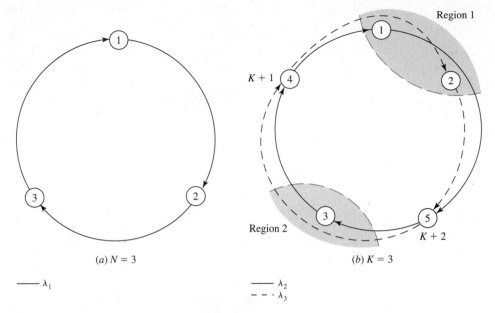

(a) N = 3

(b) K = 3

——— λ_1

——— λ_2
– – – λ_3

FIGURE 6.16 Scaling the ring from $N = 3$ to $N = 5$.

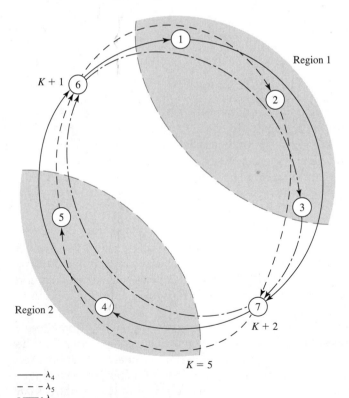

——— λ_4
– – – λ_5
–·–· λ_6

FIGURE 6.17 Scaling the ring
from $N = 5$ to $N = 7$.

396

exercise for the reader to find a general solution to the RCA problem with a minimum number of wavelengths for $N > 5$, using single-fiber-pair access links.[20]

Arbitrary Connectivity on the Ring: One Wavelength Interchanger   The previous development assumed full logical connectivity on the ring, with a single bidirectional connection between each node pair. Now suppose that an arbitrary LC pattern is desired instead. Of course, if the desired connections are a subset of the full connection pattern, the wavelength assignment rule presented for full connectivity can be applied to the subset. But can we make do with fewer wavelengths in this case? It turns out that this is often possible, *provided that one wavelength-interchanging node is included in the ring.*

In general it can be shown that with one wavelength interchanging cross-connect (WIXC) in the ring, any set of connections can be set up using a number of wavelengths determined only by the link capacity bounds (i.e., the DCA constraint). This constraint requires only that enough wavelengths must be available to accommodate the maximum number of connections carried on any fiber. Because this does not take into account wavelength continuity, the implication is that a single wavelength interchanger in a ring provides the same performance benefits achievable by putting WIXCs everywhere!

The reason why this is so is that a WIXC "breaks" the ring into an open linear chain as far as the wavelength continuity condition is concerned. But for a prescribed set of connections on an open-chain network there always exists a wavelength assignment that satisfies the DCA and wavelength continuity conditions, such that the required number of wavelengths is equal to the number of connections on the maximally loaded link [Bala+96a]. We do not provide a proof here; we leave that as an exercise for the reader.

To illustrate, consider the five-node WDM ring shown in Figure 6.18(a). Five connections are shown with a maximum link loading of two. Because of the wavelength continuity constraint, the number of wavelengths required is three. Now if a WIXC is present at node 1, as shown in Figure 6.18(b), the same five connections require only two wavelengths.

The economic implications of this result are substantial, suggesting that the benefits of wavelength interchange technology can be obtained for a modest increase in overall cost, by installing this technology at only a few nodes (e.g., less than 10%) in a large network. If the wavelength interchange results applied only to rings, they would be of limited value. However, in the next section we show that results for rings can sometimes be generalized to much wider classes of networks.

---

[20] A general algorithm has been found for determining wavelength assignments in rings with $N > 6$ stations and single-fiber-pair access links [Liu98]. It requires the same number of wavelengths as given in Equation 6.12 for the double-fiber-pair access case.

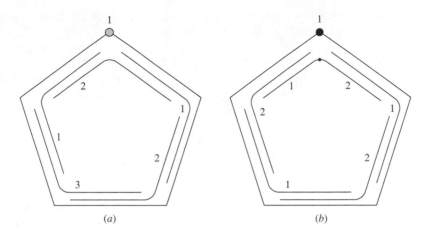

(a)   (b)

FIGURE 6.18 Five-node WDM ring.

6.3.5 Ring Decomposition of General Mesh Networks

As already mentioned, rings have a number of desirable properties that make them attractive in numerous applications. An application already mentioned is the use of a ring as a basic topological structure for public carrier networks, as in the case of SONET rings. Another is as a high-speed local or metropolitan area data network. Examples of the latter are the early token rings and their later higher speed counterparts: the Fiber Distributed Data Interface (FDDI) [Ross89] and the Distributed Queue Dual Bus (DQDB) [IEEE91].[21]

Although the topology of a general mesh network is richer than a ring, there are some advantages in decomposing a general network topology into a set of rings that "cover" the network. Two examples are shown in Figure 6.19. Figure 6.19(a) shows a network with $N = 9$ nodes and diameter $D = 4$. A bidirectional ring decomposition of the network is shown as dashed lines in the figure. Figure 6.19(b) shows a unidirectional ring decomposition of a hexagonal grid. The grid contains $N = 24$ nodes and has a diameter of $D = 7$. Note that "bridge" nodes (indicated as shaded circles in each network) are placed at strategic points in the network, linking two or more rings. The placement of the bridge nodes is chosen so that a path can be found through each network between any node pair, which consists of a concatenation of segments confined to rings (intraring segments). An end-to-end path between nodes on different rings hops from ring to ring at the bridge nodes. As indicated later, the network's performance can often be improved by equipping bridge nodes with special functionality.

Ring decompositions of networks can be derived from the following general properties of graphs.

---

[21] DQDB is actually an open-bus network that can be configured physically as a ring to aid in fault recovery.

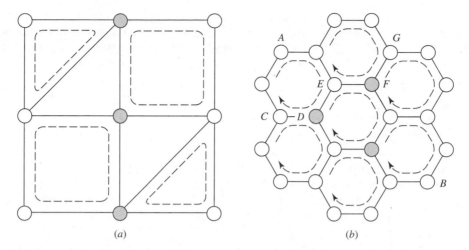

FIGURE 6.19 Ring decomposition.

Eulerian Networks   A large class of networks, the *Eulerian networks,* are amenable to decomposition into bidirectional rings. This is done by finding a closed *Eulerian trail* through the network.[22] (Algorithms for finding Eulerian trails can be found in [Fleischner90].) Because an Eulerian trail usually passes through some nodes more than once, it can generally be broken into sets of smaller cycles. By using both directions on each cycle (that is, "double tracing" it), an Eulerian network with a single fiber pair in each link can be decomposed into a set of bidirectional rings, intersecting at some of the network nodes—see Figure 6.19(a) for an example.

General Networks: Cycle Double Covers   The unidirectional ring decomposition of Figure 6.19(b) is derived from the concept of an *orientable cycle double cover*. A well-known conjecture in graph theory is that every bridgeless graph possesses an orientable cycle double cover: a set of cycles that "covers" all edges, traversing each exactly once in each direction. (A more precise definition is given in Appendix A.) The double-traced cycles in an Eulerian graph are a special case of an orientable cycle double cover. The unidirectional rings in Figure 6.19(b) are a subset of a cycle double cover of that graph. (Note that the graph in Figure 6.19(b) is not Eulerian, so it cannot be covered using an Eulerian trail.)

In wavelength routed networks, all nodes are WSXCs so that end-to-end connections can, in principle, be made directly through the network without any additional equipment. These wavelength routed connections can often be made on paths shorter

---

[22] An Eulerian network is a connected network, all nodes of which are of even degree. An Eulerian trail is a trail that traverses every node in the network at least once and every link exactly once (see Appendix A for properties of Eulerian graphs). The existence (or nonexistence) of Eulerian trails is at the heart of the famous Konigsberg bridge problem, which marked the birth of graph theory [Harary72].

than those confined to concatenated rings. (For example, a path from node A to node B using the unidirectional ring decomposition in Figure 6.19(b) requires 11 hops, whereas the shortest path between the nodes is only of length seven.) Nevertheless, the ring decomposition of a general network is useful as a basic structure to support a number of performance enhancements.

Sparse Wavelength Interchange   A network with bridges that are wavelength interchangers implements sparse wavelength interchange throughout the network. If the bridges are located at well-chosen points, they have the ability to nullify the wavelength continuity constraint and thereby reduce the number of wavelengths required to support a given logical connectivity. Each bridge effectively breaks all rings to which it belongs into open linear chains, as was explained in Section 6.3.4.2. Under static routing rules it is only the maximal link load that determines the wavelength requirement on each "broken" ring. Wavelength interchange is also important in reducing connection blocking under dynamic (demand-assigned) traffic conditions (see Section 6.4). It has been verified by numerous simulation experiments that networks with large diameters can benefit most from wavelength interchange, because long paths tend to interfere with many other paths. In these cases it is reasonable to expect that wavelength-interchanging bridges may be useful in breaking up long paths into smaller segments to find wavelength assignments that satisfy DCA on each fiber.

To illustrate, suppose the bridges in Figure 6.19(b) are WIXCs. Any connection between nodes on different rings can be considered a concatenation of segments within rings, joined at the bridges along the path. Note that it is possible to move among all rings using the bridges. Because all rings are broken, wavelength continuity does not constrain the wavelength assignments under static routing conditions.

Now consider a case of dynamic traffic in which the following optical connections are in place using the wavelengths indicated by the subscripts: $(C, D)_1$, $(D, E)_2$, $(E, F)_3$, and $(F, G)_2$. Assume that wavelength rearrangement is not permitted, shortest path routing is required (i.e., we ignore the orientations of the ring decomposition), and there is a total of three wavelengths available. Then if a new connection (C, G) is requested, it would have to be blocked if there were no wavelength interchangers. However, on the network with wavelength-interchanging bridges, the new connection can use wavelength 2 on the first link, and wavelength 1 on the remaining links.

Bridges as Overlay Processors   Another possible use for ring decomposition is in providing convenient regeneration points for long paths. For example, in the network of Figure 6.19(b), it may be that some of the paths in the network are too long for acceptable signal quality. In that case, placement of regenerative repeaters at the bridge nodes may solve the problem (see Section 2.5). Using the indicated unidirectional ring decomposition, the longest path between bridges is five hops, as opposed to seven hops for end-to-end connectivity on the complete grid. Assuming that a five-hop purely optical path is acceptable but seven hops is not, the longer paths can be realized as concatenations of segments on the rings, with regeneration at the bridges ensuring end-to-end signal quality. (Shorter end-to-end paths can bypass the repeaters using purely optical switching.) For example, a connection (A, B) requires seven hops without repeaters and 11 hops on four segments in the ring decomposition, but no segment has more than four optical hops.

Bridges as Logical Switches   As noted, rings are a preferred topology in traditional voice and data networks. Thus, to provide some "backward compatibility" in evolving wavelength routed networks, it may be worthwhile to set aside a portion of the optical spectrum to configure a ring decomposition of a network as a logically switched overlay (see Section 2.6). This can be particularly useful for exploiting the management capabilities that have been highly refined for ring structures. In this case, the bridges are in the form of LSNs, in which traffic hopping from one ring to another is processed electronically before being passed to the next ring.

As an example, in the case of bidirectional rings, one wavelength, λ_d, in each direction might be set aside to configure the overlay as a data network (e.g., an FDDI network). In that case each FDDI station would access an ONN using λ_d in both directions on its ring, forming the usual bidirectional FDDI configuration. For traffic moving from one ring to another, the bridges would access each ring to which they are connected, performing a routing function as is done in typical LAN and MAN bridges or routers (see, for example, [Halsall96]).

As shown in the example of Figure 6.20, traffic from ring 1 in the form of data frames flows through the bridge, which "filters" the frames, reading destination addresses and detecting those addressed to stations on ring 2. It copies those frames and transmits them onto ring 2. The reverse process from ring 2 to ring 1 is also executed. Note that only the clockwise direction has been shown on each ring, but both directions are present using the same wavelength, so that shortest path routing can be used. Each

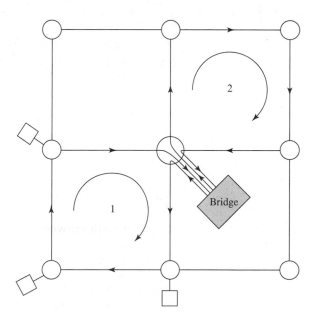

FIGURE 6.20   Bridged ring overlay.

node performs an add–drop operation on wavelength λ_d, so all optical connections are only one hop: from each station to its neighbor on each side. (In general, a bridge can access more than two rings, and the filtering and routing functions are basically the same.)

Although FDDI was used as an example, any logically switched overlay could be configured in the same fashion. One possible application of the data ring overlay on a general optical network might be as a means of distributing information for network control and management.

In a ring decomposition of a network, the optimal size of the rings is an open question. If a network is decomposed into many small rings, there are many routing alternatives, so that routes limited to concatenated ring segments might approach shortest path routing. However, a large number of rings means many intersections, which in turn requires many bridges. Conversely, a few large rings imply long paths, high link loading, and a larger number of required wavelengths. But fewer bridges are needed.

6.3.6 Multistar Wavelength Routed Networks

The multistar topology illustrated in Figure 6.21 is a direct generalization of the star configuration, discussed extensively as a shared broadcast medium in Chapter 5. As shown in the figure, each station transmits to several stars through separate outbound access fibers and receives signals from several stars through a separate inbound access fiber for each star. In the case shown, each subnet is a 3×3 star, and there are four stars connecting six stations. Each station has two transceivers. The convention used throughout this section is that like-numbered transmitters and receivers belong to the same access station.

In a general (static) multistar WRN we assume that the central nodes of the stars are wavelength routers providing full bipartite connectivity between their transmitting

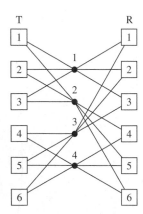

FIGURE 6.21 A multistar network.

and receiving sets.[23] That is, an optical connection is created from any transmitter on a star to any receiver on the same star by tuning to a unique wavelength associated with that connection. This is known as *permutation routing.* If the stars provide full fiber connectivity between all transmitting and receiving stations, then any station can connect to any other station by finding a star to which they are both attached and tuning to the wavelength supporting a connection between that source–destination pair.

We first encountered permutation routers in Section 2.3.1.2, where an $n \times n$ router was exhibited (Figure 2.9) with the following routing rule. A signal on input port j, carried on wavelength λ_k, is routed to output port i, where $k = (i - j) \mod n$. In the permutation router, full connectivity among all input and output ports is achieved using n wavelengths.

Now consider a general, regular multistar network containing M stars based on $r \times r$ permutation routers operating on $W = r$ wavelengths, where we call r the *size* of the star. The network has N stations, each transmitting to and receiving from Δ stars, where $M = N\Delta/r$. It turns out that a multistar configuration of this type, with full fiber connectivity among N stations, using M stars of size r exists, provided that certain relations hold among the parameters M, Δ, r, and N. Systematic design procedures for these networks are given in Sections 6.5.9 and 7.4.2.2.

Assuming that a full *fiber* connectivity pattern exists among the stations in a multistar wavelength router-based WRN, full *optical* connectivity is established by equipping each station with Δ arrays of r fixed–tuned transceivers. Each transmitter array is connected to one outbound access fiber, and each receiver array is connected to one inbound access fiber (not necessarily on the same star). In this way each station acts as the source and destination of Δr optical connections, so that full connectivity (including loopback connections) is achieved.

To illustrate, the network of Figure 6.21 has $N = 6$, $M = 4$, $\Delta = 2$, and $r = 3$. With $W = 3$ wavelengths, each star provides nine connections between its transmitting and receiving sets, which are enough to provide full bipartite connectivity between the sets. All nine connections are necessary on stars 2 and 3 because the subnets are *directed* stars with disjoint transmitting and receiving sets. However, the transmitting and receiving sets for stars 1 and 4 are identical, and thus three of the connections are loopback connections. Excluding these, the total number of useful connections is 30, which is just enough for full connectivity.

Multistar networks are very efficient in utilizing the optical spectrum (they provide M-fold spectrum reuse) because their fiber topology is tailored to the desired connectivity pattern. Furthermore, they offer high throughput, but at the (inevitable) expense of using large numbers of optical transceivers. A negative feature of the multistar structure is that it requires very long fibers, and the fibers are not arranged in

---

[23] In a simpler configuration, each central node in Figure 6.21 is a star coupler, so that each transmitting station multicasts to three receiving stations and shares each star with two other transmitting stations, creating a hypernet logical topology embedded on an LLN. Multistar LLNs based on optical multicast are discussed in Sections 6.5.9 and 7.4.2.2.

a fashion that enhances survivability. (There are no alternate paths between pairs of stations.) For example, suppose we wish to connect N stations with geographic locations that are on a circle of diameter D. Comparing the total fiber length for a large multistar, a single star, and a ring, we find the approximate values, $N\Delta D$, ND, and $2\pi D$ respectively.[24] Clearly, the multistar is the worst from the point of view of fiber length, but it has the best optical efficiency. This suggests that multistars are best for use as LANs interconnecting high throughput end systems over short distances; for example, as interconnection networks for high-speed processors (see, for example, [Birk91]).

6.3.7 RCA as an Optimization Problem

In this section we consider the static RCA problem in its most general form. Any network topology is allowed, and networks with and without wavelength interchange are considered. Routing and channel assignment are considered together as an optimization problem using MIP formulations. These turn out to have extremely large numbers of variables, and are intractable for large networks. For tractability the variables must typically be "pruned" by limiting the admissible solutions. This can be done, for example, by allowing only shortest path routing.

Joint routing and channel assignment can be cast as an optimization problem in a number of different ways using various cost functions. Some possibilities are the following:

- Establish all connections using a minimum number of wavelengths.
- Establish all connections using minimum path lengths.
- Maximize the number of connections established, subject to a constraint on the number of wavelengths and/or the path lengths.

The following is an MIP formulation for solving the RCA problem. The network's physical topology is modeled as a set of nodes, $\mathcal{N} = \{1, 2, \ldots, N\}$ and a set of links $\mathcal{L} = \{l_{xy}\}$, where l_{xy} denotes a unidirectional link from node x to node y. The elements of $\mathcal{N}$ may be either the ONNs alone or the ONNs and the access stations. In these two cases, the elements of $\mathcal{L}$ are, respectively, the internodal links alone or both the internodal and access links. The available spectrum consists of a set of wavelengths $\Lambda = \{1, 2, \ldots, W\}$, where $W = |\Lambda|$. Two versions of the problem are presented: for networks without and with wavelength interchange. We refer to these as RCA-I and RCA-II respectively.

---

[24] This assumes that the stations on each star are positioned randomly around the circle, so that the best placement of the central node is at the center.

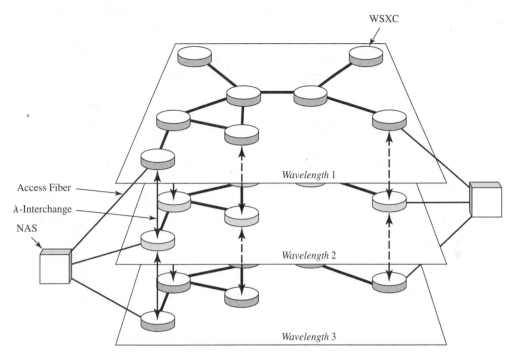

FIGURE 6.22   Layered view of RCA.

6.3.7.1 No Wavelength Interchange: RCA-I

The prescribed traffic on the network is given in the form of a logical topology to be realized by a set of optical connections $\mathcal{C} = \{c_k\}$, where $c_k = (s_k, d_k)$ is a connection with a fiber path and wavelength that are to be determined.[25] In the case considered here, the objective is to find an embedding of the prescribed connections, which minimizes a linear combination of total wavelengths and total path lengths. Each ONN consists of a WSXC, and there are no wavelength interchangers in the network. (In the case when the model includes access stations, the stations are assumed to be equipped with arrays of optical transceivers that cover the full set of available wavelengths.)

The wavelength continuity constraint is represented by replicating the network topology into as many layers (copies of the network) as the number of available wavelengths. To use wavelength w for a connection, the source and destination stations access the wth copy of the network, as visualized in Figure 6.22. Note that in this representation of the topology the number W of available wavelengths must be known in advance, so the number of variables and equations in this formulation increases in proportion to W. There is, therefore, a trade-off involved in the choice

---

[25] Note that more than one c_k may have the same source–destination pair, indicating that several parallel connections are required for that pair.

of W: Too large means too many variables, but too small means that a solution may not exist.

In designating parameters and variables, subscripts are used to indicate physical layer entities (e.g., nodes, links, and wavelengths), and superscripts are used to indicate connections. The network parameters used in this formulation are

- f_{xy}: The number of fibers on link l_{xy}
- d_{xy}: A weight assigned to link l_{xy}; a positive constant "length" chosen for design purposes
- D^k: The maximum permissible path length for connection c_k (a positive constant)

The variables used are

- Ω_w^k: A binary variable equal to one if connection c_k is carried on wavelength w, and zero otherwise
- $a_{w,xy}^k$: A flow variable equal to one if connection c_k is carried on wavelength w on link l_{xy}, and zero otherwise
- e_w: A binary variable equal to one if wavelength w is used for at least one connection, and zero otherwise

Now RCA-I can be formulated as follows.

Minimize

$$m \sum_w e_w + \sum_k \sum_{w,xy} d_{xy} a_{w,xy}^k \tag{6.13}$$

With

$$\sum_{j \neq x} a_{w,xj}^k - \sum_{j \neq x} a_{w,jx}^k = \begin{cases} \Omega_w^k, & \text{if } x \text{ is the source of } c_k \\ -\Omega_w^k, & \text{if } x \text{ is the destination of } c_k \\ 0 & \text{otherwise} \\ \qquad \forall w \in \Lambda, \ c_k \in \mathcal{C}, \ x \in \mathcal{N} \end{cases} \tag{6.14}$$

$$\sum_{w,x,y} d_{xy} a_{w,xy}^k \leq D^k, \quad \forall c_k \in \mathcal{C} \tag{6.15}$$

$$e_w = \min\left(1, \sum_k \Omega_w^k\right), \quad \forall w \in \Lambda \tag{6.16}$$

$$\sum_k a_{w,xy}^k \leq f_{xy}, \quad \forall w \in \Lambda, \ x, y \in \mathcal{N} \tag{6.17}$$

$$\sum_w \Omega_w^k = 1, \quad \forall c_k \in \mathcal{C} \tag{6.18}$$

$$a_{w,xy}^k \in \{0, 1\}, \quad e_w \in \{0, 1\}, \quad \Omega_w^k \in \{0, 1\} \tag{6.19}$$

In Equation 6.13, a large value of m is chosen to emphasize wavelength minimization, and a small one is selected to emphasize total path length minimization.

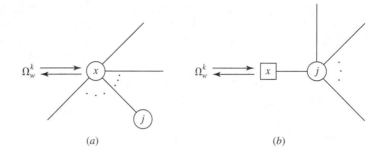

FIGURE 6.23 External traffic in flow conservation equations.

(a)　　　　　　　　　　　　(b)

Equation 6.14 is the flow conservation equation, which states that a connection c_k entering a node x on wavelength w must leave the node on the same wavelength, thus ensuring wavelength continuity. If x is a source (destination) node for c_k, the flow conservation relation is completed with the additional term Ω_w^k $(-\Omega_w^k)$ to account for flow entering (leaving) the network.

Figure 6.23 illustrates how external traffic is modeled in the cases when access stations are either excluded from or included in the model. In Figure 6.23(a), node x is an ONN, and Equation 6.14 describes flow conservation including external flow. In Figure 6.23(b), node x is an NAS accessing the network through node j. Now for node x, Equation 6.14 reduces to the form:

$$
a_{w,xj}^k = \begin{cases} \Omega_{w'}^k & \text{if } x \text{ is the source of } c_k \\ -\Omega_{w'}^k & \text{if } x \text{ is the destination of } c_k \\ 0 & \text{otherwise} \\ & \forall w \in \Lambda, \ c_k \in \mathcal{C} \end{cases} \tag{6.20}
$$

Inclusion of access stations in the model is useful for dealing with the constraints of elementary access stations, wherein the presence of an access link containing a single fiber pair limits the number of connections that can be supported. Also, extra constraints, such as limited tunability of transceivers, are accommodated easily when access stations are included in the model. For example, the variables Ω_w^k can be constrained to exclude forbidden wavelengths.

The inequality in Equation 6.15 specifies a limit on the length of any path. (It can be relaxed if there is no limit on the path length.) The limit can be used in a number of ways. For example, if all link weights are set to one, and $D^k = d(s_k, d_k)$—the optical hop distance between source and destination—then the inequality specifies that only minimum-hop paths can be used. In this case, the inclusion of the path length summation in Equation 6.13 is redundant. However if $D^k > d(s_k, d_k)$, some opportunity is left for choices of longer paths, and inclusion of path lengths in the objective function may be appropriate.

A very important role of these path length constraints is to reduce the complexity of the problem by reducing the number of possible choices of fiber paths. For example, if only shortest paths are allowed, a list of all shortest paths can be computed before proceeding with the rest of the optimization problem. If the shortest paths happen to be unique, the routing problem is solved, and what remains is channel assignment. Relating this to the two-step formulation of the RCA problem described in Section 6.3.3, the computation of the unique shortest paths completes the first step.

The second step is solved by coloring the resultant subgraph of G_{PI}. If the shortest paths are not unique, we still have a joint RCA optimization problem, but of considerably reduced dimensionality. In effect, the paths satisfying the inequality in Equation 6.15 define a reduced set of alternatives for the flow variables $a_{w,xy}^{k}$, forcing most of them to zero. In this case it is generally more efficient to reformulate the problem using a set of permissible paths rather than the flow variables.[26] Optimization then reduces to choosing a subset of the permissible paths and assigning wavelengths to them, as is done in the path interference graph approach. The details are left as an exercise for the reader (see Problem 11).

The significance of the remaining equations in the optimization formulation is as follows:

- Equation 6.16 indicates whether a wavelength w is used for the embedding.

- Equation 6.17 is a constraint that limits the number of connections on a link and a wavelength to the number of fibers on that link.

- Equation 6.18 requires that each connection be assigned to one and only one wavelength.

When used with care, this formulation can be a useful optimization tool. However, without any constraints to reduce its complexity, the number of variables and constraints can become enormous even for problems of relatively small size. Thus, for a network with L bidirectional links, N nodes, and M connections, there are $2LMW$ flow variables and NMW flow conservation equations. Another difficulty with this and most other MIP formulations of the RCA problem is that solutions are not unique. Given an optimal routing and channel assignment, another one can be found by relabeling the wavelengths. Thus, there are at least $W!$ optimal solutions. Nonuniqueness of solutions can sometimes wreak havoc on optimization algorithms.

To illustrate the importance of pruning the number of choices in an optimization calculation, consider the problem of embedding optimally a fully connected ten-node logical topology into a Petersen network (Figure 6.38). If elementary access stations are used, the limiting cut bound indicates that this requires at least $W = 9$ wavelengths. Modeling the physical topology to include the access stations, we have $L = 25$ and $M = 90$. Taking the minimum possible value for W yields 40,500 flow variables in this formulation! This problem was run on a SPARC 20 computer, which produced a feasible but not optimal solution after about two days. (RCA assignments using nine wavelengths were found, but the path lengths were not minimum.) In contrast, an optimal solution to the problem was found by hand in less than an hour using shortest

---

[26] A set of K shortest paths between all node pairs can be found in polynomial time.

paths and exploiting the symmetry of the network (see Table 6.6).[27] This experience was, to say the least, humbling for the computer but gratifying for the human!

6.3.7.2 Full λ-Interchange: RCA-II

Introduction of wavelength interchange at each node makes the WRN equivalent to a traditional electronically switched telecommunication network in which each λ-channel is equivalent to a "trunk." When full λ-interchange is allowed, the RCA problem can still be visualized in terms of the layered picture of Figure 6.22. However, in this case, optical paths are allowed to move between the layers. The vertical lines in the figure represent the links between different wavelength layers created by λ-interchangers.

Because wavelength continuity is absent in this case, the separation of the wavelength layers in the MIP formulation is no longer necessary. This means that the number of wavelengths W need not be fixed in advance, nor do we need separate flow variables for each wavelength. Therefore, the formulation of RCA-II simplifies to

Minimize

$$mW + \sum_k \sum_{l_{xy}} d_{xy} a^k_{xy} \tag{6.21}$$

With

$$\sum_{j \neq x} a^k_{xj} - \sum_{j \neq x} a^k_{jx} = \begin{cases} 1, & \text{if } x \text{ is the source of } c_k \\ -1, & \text{if } x \text{ is the destination of } c_k \\ 0 & \text{otherwise} \end{cases} \tag{6.22}$$

$$\forall c_k \in \mathcal{C}, \ x \in \mathcal{N}$$

$$\sum_{l_{xy}} d_{xy} a^k_{xy} \leq D_k, \quad \forall c_k \in \mathcal{C} \tag{6.23}$$

$$\sum_k a^k_{xy} \leq W f_{xy}, \quad \forall x, y \in \mathcal{N} \tag{6.24}$$

$$a^k_{xy} \in \{0, 1\}, \quad w \text{ integer} \tag{6.25}$$

Comparing RCA-I with RCA-II, we see that the subscript w is missing from all variables in RCA-II because there is no need to maintain counts of flows for each wavelength. Instead, Equation 6.24 places a global limit on the number of connections using each link. Another difference is that a feasible solution always exists for the problem with wavelength interchange, provided that the path length constraints are sufficiently loose. This is not the case in the formulation without wavelength interchange because the choice of W may be too small to admit a feasible solution.

---

[27] Because the Petersen network has unique shortest paths between all node pairs, the RCA problem reduces to channel assignment alone if a shortest path constraint is imposed.

6.3.7.3 Sparse λ-Interchange

Although networks with full wavelength interchange may have better performance than networks without wavelength interchange, the improvement may not be worth the price. (WIXCs are considerably more complex and hence currently more costly than WSXCs.) A middle ground is proposed by [Subramaniam+96b] and [Bala+97], who show that by placing WIXCs judiciously at a small number of sparsely dispersed locations in the network, the full performance benefits of this technology can be obtained. An example of this approach is the use of wavelength-interchanging bridges in the ring decompositions discussed in Section 6.3.5. This suggests that with a small increase in overall network cost, the performance benefits associated with wavelength interchange can be obtained. Another variant of this approach is to install "limited" wavelength interchange at all the nodes in the network [Gerstel+97, Yates+96]. In this case, the wavelength interchange function is limited to a small set of permutations (i.e., it is not nonblocking). Of course, the two concepts can be combined to provide sparse and limited wavelength interchange in the network.

The RCA-I formulation for optimal routing and wavelength assignment can be adapted to networks with sparse wavelength interchange. Referring back to Figure 6.22, the inclusion of a WIXC at a given network node corresponds to the inclusion of the vertical lines as sets of extra links, allowing paths to move from one layer to another. With appropriate modifications of the flow conservation Equation 6.14 to take into account the possibility of switching wavelengths at the WIXC nodes, the RCA-I formulation is still valid. An alternative approach in this case is to include wavelength interchangers everywhere, but assign weights to the wavelength-interchanging links to penalize the use of wavelength interchange. In this way, connection patterns are created that tend to avoid wavelength interchange if possible, thereby allowing the elimination of many of the original WIXCs.

The issue of wavelength interchange is revisited in the context of dynamic traffic in Section 6.4.

6.3.7.4 The Fluid Flow Bound

One additional simplification is possible to make the optimization problem of RCA-II much more tractable: removal of the integer constraint. So far, Equations 6.21 through 6.25 constitute an MIP. Relaxation of the integer constraint in Equation 6.25 and replacement by $a_{xy}^k \geq 0$ converts the MIP to an ordinary linear program, which is much easier to solve. In this case the connections are treated as fluid flows, and thus the optimal flow variables generally are not integers. Because each connection requires one unit of capacity (one λ-channel), a fractional value of a_{xy}^k indicates a bifurcated flow, which is not physically realizable in a WRN. The value of W found in solving the linear program represents the minimum capacity of each fiber (in units of λ-channels) required to accommodate the aggregate flow in the network with optimized (bifurcated) routing. This value generally is not an integer so it also is a nonphysical result.

The fluid flow formulation is an example of a "multicommodity" flow problem (see Appendix D). In this version we are attempting to optimize routing to minimize required capacity for prescribed flows, but various alternatives are possible. For example, we might wish to maximize carried traffic subject to a bound on capacity, or minimize the average path length (by setting $m = 0$ in Equation 6.21).

Although noninteger solutions of the fluid flow problem are nonphysical, they can be useful in placing a lower bound on the wavelength requirement. Thus, if we let $W_I^* = \sum_w e_w$ be the number of wavelengths found in solving RCA-I (no λ-interchange), W_{II}^* be the number of wavelengths found in solving RCA-II for the same problem (with λ-interchange), and W_{LP}^* be a solution of the fluid flow version of the same problem, we then have

$$W_I^* \geq W_{II}^* \geq \lceil W_{LP}^* \rceil \geq W_{\text{Limcut}} \geq \underline{W}_{\text{Limcut}} \tag{6.26}$$

These inequalities follow directly from the fact that in proceeding from left to right, each value is the solution of a problem that is a relaxed version of the previous one. In the case of W_{Limcut}, its value (and the value of its lower bound, $\underline{W}_{\text{Limcut}}$) is obtained by assuming that traffic (as a fluid flow) is distributed equally among the fibers in the limiting cut. But this distribution is a "best case," and may not be possible given the flow constraints within the partitioned network.

One way of interpreting the linear programming problem is as a limiting case of a network in which the number of connections and wavelengths increases without bound, while their granularity (required bitrate) becomes infinitely small. Thus, imagine that each connection, c_k in our original formulation, is replaced by n connections, with each new connection operating at $1/n$ times the bitrate of the original connection. In this way the total throughput remains constant in going from the original formulation to the new one. Then if W_{II}^* is a solution of RCA-II, a *feasible* solution $W^{(n)}$ of the new MIP (with an n-fold increase in required connections) exists with $W^{(n)} = nW_{II}^*$, because for each wavelength in the original problem there are now n wavelengths available to route the n replicated connections in the new problem. However, for an *optimal* solution $W^{(n)*}$ of the new problem we typically have $W^{(n)*} < nW_{II}^*$, because the n replicated connections can be spread over as many as n parallel optical paths, allowing for more routing options.

So far, all we have done is increase the wavelength requirement. To complete the fluid flow picture it is conceptually reasonable to imagine that the n-fold increase in connections and wavelengths is accompanied by an n-fold decrease in the optical spectrum occupied by each wavelength because each λ-channel now requires only $1/n$ times the capacity required in the original problem. This would be the case under ideal conditions (no guardbands between λ-channels). Now, as $n \to \infty$, the granularity of the connections becomes infinitely fine and the connections resemble a fluid. The solution W_{LP}^* of the linear programming problem now represents the total optical spectrum occupied by these infinitely fine channels.

Because of technological limitations (e.g., finite guardbands), this conceptual decrease in granularity cannot be pursued to any significant degree in WRNs. However, in Section 6.5 it is shown that in LLNs it is possible to refine the granularity of LCs to almost any degree through the use of multipoint optical connections. (Unfortunately, granularity refinement in LLNs does not necessarily improve routing alternatives.)

6.3.7.5 Maximizing Carried Traffic

Another formulation of the RCA problem distinguishes between offered and carried traffic, maximizing the carried traffic subject to network resource constraints [Ramaswami+95]. We shall henceforth refer to this as the *RS version* of the RCA optimization problem.

The network consists of L single-fiber-pair links and M source–destination $(s–d)$ pairs. It operates on W wavelengths. All prescribed connections are assumed to be full duplex, with both directions of a connection routed on the same path using the same wavelength. The topology of the network is described in terms of its $(s–d)$ pairs, the set of fiber paths between them, and the path–link incidence matrix B, which gives the links on each path. The paths can be precomputed before the rest of the optimization process is executed.

The parameters describing the network are

- P: The total number of available paths on which connections can be routed
- $A = [a_{ij}]$: The $P \times M$ path $(s–d)$ pair incidence matrix, where

$$a_{ij} = \begin{cases} 1, & \text{if path } i \text{ is between source–destination pair } j, \\ 0, & \text{otherwise} \end{cases} \qquad (6.27)$$

- $B = [b_{ij}]$: The $P \times L$ path–link incidence matrix, where

$$b_{ij} = \begin{cases} 1, & \text{if link } j \text{ is on path } i, \\ 0, & \text{otherwise} \end{cases} \qquad (6.28)$$

The traffic requirements are specified as a total offered load ρ, with $p_i\rho$ being the offered load between $(s–d)$ pair $i, i = 1, \ldots, M$. Thus the p_i's define the distribution of the offered traffic. In [Ramaswami+95], both deterministic and stochastic interpretations of the offered load are considered. We focus on the deterministic (static) traffic case here, and thus the offered load represents the number of connections available to be routed.

The objective of the RS formulation is to maximize the *carried* traffic for a given value of ρ, with a constraint W on the number of wavelengths. This is the dual of RCA-I, which (for large m) minimizes the number of wavelengths for a given carried traffic. The variables used in RS are

- m_i: The number of connections carried between $(s–d)$ pair $i, i = 1, \ldots, M$
- $C = [c_{ij}]$: A $P \times W$ path–wavelength assignment matrix containing the RCA variables, where

$$c_{ij} = \begin{cases} 1, & \text{if wavelength } j \text{ is assigned to path } i \\ 0, & \text{otherwise} \end{cases} \qquad (6.29)$$

The optimization problem is then stated as

Maximize

$$\sum_{i=1}^{M} m_i \tag{6.30}$$

With

$$\sum_{k=1}^{P} c_{ki} b_{kj} \le 1, \quad i = 1, \dots, W, \quad j = 1, 2, \dots, L \tag{6.31}$$

$$m_i \le \sum_{j=1}^{W} \sum_{k=1}^{P} c_{kj} a_{ki}, \quad i = 1, \dots, M \tag{6.32}$$

$$m_i \le p_i \rho, \quad i = 1, \dots, M$$

$$m_i \ge 0, \quad \text{integer}, \ i = 1, \dots, M \tag{6.33}$$

$$c_{ij} \ge 0, \quad \text{integer}, \ i = 1, \dots, P \ \ j = 1, \dots, W$$

Equation 6.31 expresses the fact that no wavelength can be used more than once on any link, Equation 6.32 is a bound on the amount of carried traffic for $(s$–$d)$ pair i, and Equation 6.33 expresses the relation between carried and offered traffic. The optimal values of the RCA variables c_{ij} can be interpreted as the result of executing an RCA algorithm that maximizes carried traffic.

Several other versions of the RS problem are given in [Ramaswami+95], including a formulation with λ-interchange as well as a linear programming fluid flow bound found by relaxing the integer constraints. They also present an alternative and equivalent MIP formulation based on the path interference graph G_{PI}, which we refer to as RS'.

The first step in the RS' formulation is to determine the set of all maximal independent sets of G_{PI} (see Appendix A). Wavelengths are then assigned to vertices in these sets, with each assignment representing an optical path for one connection. Each wavelength assigned to an independent set can be reused in that set to support as many connections as there are vertices in the set. This assignment problem is equivalent to vertex coloring a graph with multiple colors per vertex. In this case the objective is to maximize the carried load, which corresponds to assigning as many colors (wavelengths) as possible to the vertices subject to the constraints on offered traffic and available wavelengths. Because this formulation is based on graph coloring, it becomes quickly intractable as the number of vertices of G_{PI} (i.e., the number of admissible paths) becomes large. Thus, as in other formulations, either shortest path routing or similar path limitations must be imposed to make the problem tractable.

The various RCA formulations in [Ramaswami+95] are used to obtain bounds on carried traffic in a variety of scenarios, with and without wavelength interchange. The reader is referred to the cited reference for more information.

As in the case of problems RCA-I and RCA-II, the usefulness of the RS formulations depends on their dimensionality. Considering all possible source–destination paths is out of the question because there are PW RCA variables in RS, and the number of paths P can be exponential in the number of network nodes or links. The situation in RS' is still worse, because the number of maximal independent sets can be exponential in P. Because the path list is arbitrary, some subset of all paths can be used. This would correspond to a predetermined static routing rule. For example, if single shortest paths are selected, this is similar to our two-step separation of the RCA-I problem in Section 6.3.3. Of course, this approach gives a suboptimal solution of the complete RCA problem.

Although the RS formulation with a complete set of fiber paths generally has far more variables than the RCA-I formulation, the number of variables can be reduced drastically by using a reduced set of paths. Thus, the number of RCA variables is PW in RS, and the number of flow variables is $2LMW$ in RCA-I. Now suppose K shortest paths are used for each source–destination pair in the RS form. We then have KMW RCA variables in the RS version compared with $2LMW$ flow variables in the RCA-I form. In this case the RS form normally has fewer variables for reasonably small values of K. However, as mentioned earlier, path pruning can also be done in RCA-I, reducing the number of flow variables.

In making comparisons of RS and RCA-I, it must be understood that we are comparing apples and oranges. The former formulation maximizes carried traffic using a fixed number of wavelengths, whereas the latter minimizes the number of wavelengths used for fixed offered (and carried) traffic. For example, in the versions of each involving single shortest paths, both problems reduce to wavelength assignment only. In RS this is equivalent to coloring a maximum number of vertices in G_{PI} with a fixed number of colors, but in RCA-I it is equivalent to coloring *all* vertices of G_{PI} with a minimum number of colors. The former will generally use fewer wavelengths than the latter if the same number of connections are assigned in both cases. The difference is caused by the fact that in attempting to maximize carried traffic, as in RS, one is free to drop the "difficult" connections (i.e., those involving long paths) in favor of "easy" (short) ones. This makes the problem easier but tends to produce unfairness, with discrimination against the longer connections. In RCA-I, all traffic must be carried so that everyone is treated equally.

6.3.8 Heuristics for Static RCA

A large number of heuristic RCA algorithms have been proposed for WRNs. Some representative examples can be found in [Chlamtac+89, Bala+91a, Ramaswami+94, Nagatsu+95, Ayanoglu+96, Banerjee+96, Chen+96, Karasan+96, Mukherjee+96, Wauters+96, Baroni+97, Subramaniam+97, Mokhtar+98].

Most of these attack the RCA problem by separating it into the two subproblems of routing and channel assignment, resulting in an enormous simplification of the overall problem. Some, such as that by [Banerjee+96], do some loosely coupled iterations of both subproblems. In some cases (e.g., [Baroni+97]), the admissible paths are constrained, and in others (e.g., [Banerjee+96]), any paths are allowed. Although the latter unconstrained approach might appear to be better, empirical results over a wide range of examples show that this is not the case. Allowing paths of any length in heuristic algorithms tends to congest the network, leading to an increase in the required number of wavelengths. Thus, heuristics restricted to shortest paths or "almost-shortest paths" tend to give better results in terms of spectrum usage, as is illustrated next.

Two heuristics are described in this section. They have been chosen because they exhibit superior performance in a wide variety of test cases, and at the same time are computationally simple and efficient. The first is a minimum-hop algorithm presented in [Baroni+97], and the second is a Monte Carlo approach [Bouillet98].

6.3.8.1   A Minimum-Hop Heuristic

The algorithm in [Baroni+97] separates RCA into its two subproblems and confines all routes to shortest (minimum optical hop) paths. It has been shown to give optimal or close to optimal results (in terms of wavelength usage) in fairly extensive experiments with both actual and randomly generated network topologies.

Given a list of M prescribed LCs, the routing portion of the algorithm attempts to minimize fiber congestion (the number of paths using any one fiber), which tends to minimize the number of required wavelengths. It operates as follows:

1. List all connections in random order and compute all minimum-hop paths for each connection.

2. Assign any minimum-hop path to each connection.

3. For each connection on the list, substitute an alternative minimum-hop path for the one previously assigned if and only if the number of connections (congestion) on the most loaded link in the alternative path is lower than the congestion of the most loaded link in the previously assigned path.

4. Repeat the previous step until no further substitutions are possible.

Once the paths are assigned, a wavelength assignment algorithm is executed, making assignments to the longest paths first. The steps are as follows:

1. Group paths with same lengths into common sets and rank the sets in decreasing order of length. Assign a numerical order to the wavelengths.

2. Select a path randomly from the first set.

3. Assign to the selected path the lowest numbered wavelength previously unused on any link in the path.

4. Continue this wavelength assignment process for all paths in the first set. Then repeat for the next and subsequent sets until all assignments have been made.

It should be noted that the total number of wavelengths used in this process is unknown until the algorithm terminates. Thus, the RCA process may fail if it results in a wavelength requirement greater than the total number of available wavelengths.

These algorithms are noteworthy for their simplicity. Comparing them with the brute force techniques of Section 6.3.3, we see that the complexities of the routing and wavelength assignment algorithms are $O(M)$ rather than being exponential or worse in the number of connections when graph coloring is used.

In [Baroni+97], the RCA heuristic is applied to a large number of networks including the four shown in Figure 6.9. Recall that these networks were used in Section 6.3.1.2 to illustrate an application of the limiting cut bound. For the networks shown, the figure gives the number of wavelengths, N_λ, needed to support full connectivity using the heuristic RCA algorithms stated here. For comparison, W_{Limcut} and the ratio of the two lower bounds on wavelengths $W_{\text{Limcut}}/W_{\text{Netcap}}$ are also included. The topological parameters listed in the figure are

$$N = \text{number of nodes}$$
$$L = \text{number of links}$$
$$\alpha = \frac{2L}{N(N-1)} = \text{physical connectivity}$$
$$\bar{H} = \text{average path length}$$
$$D = \text{network diameter}$$
$$\delta_{\min} = \text{minimum node degree}$$
$$\delta_{\max} = \text{maximum node degree}$$

Note that the heuristics either achieved or came very close to $N_\lambda = W_{\text{Limcut}}$ in all cases. Besides the fact that the algorithms are very effective, there are at least two other explanations for this excellent performance. First, the networks are of fairly small diameters, with $\bar{H} < 3$ in all cases so that long paths, where considerable path interference might be expected, are rare. This means that sophisticated RCA algorithms and/or wavelength interchange are not necessary to conserve wavelengths. Second, $W_{\text{Limcut}}/W_{\text{Netcap}}$ ranged from approximately 1.4 to 1.9 in these networks. A large ratio suggests that the network contains bottlenecks, forcing an increase in N_λ to provide for the connections on the bottleneck (limiting cut) links. But this increase in turn produces idle channels on the nonbottleneck links: 40% to 90% idle λ-channels in this case. Thus, if it is possible to optimize RCA on the bottleneck links, the RCA problem for the remaining connections is simplified considerably. Hence, it should not be necessary to exceed the W_{Limcut} limit for these connections.

In Section 6.3.1.2 it was pointed out that one way to reduce the number of wavelengths required to support a given traffic is to add capacity in the form of extra fibers to the links in the limiting cut. This approach is used by [Baroni+97]. The results of selective increase in fiber capacity for the four networks of Figure 6.9 are shown in Figure 6.24. Because ARPANet has the highest $W_{\text{Limcut}}/W_{\text{Netcap}}$ ratio, it is the best candidate for capacity augmentation. For example, the number of wavelengths used is reduced from $N_\lambda = 33$ to $N'_\lambda = 22$ by adding one additional fiber pair to six of the

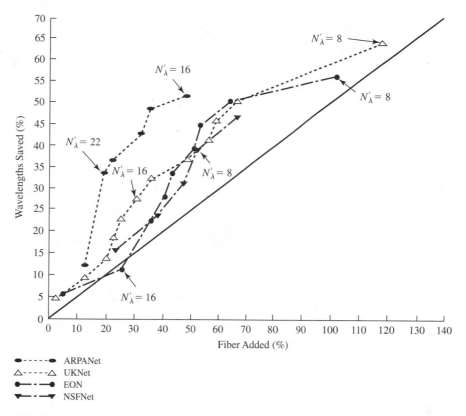

FIGURE 6.24 Wavelength savings by increasing fibers.   (From (Baroni+97, Figure 11).
Copyright © 1997 IEEE. Used by permission of The Institute of Electrical and Electronics
Engineers, Inc.)

network links, following the reasoning in Section 6.3.1.2. This results in a 33%
reduction in required wavelengths achieved by a 19% increase in fiber (and no change
in the physical topology).

In addition to studying real network topologies, [Baroni+97] gives empirical results
on N_λ for randomly connected networks (RCNs). Families of RCNs are generated by
picking values of N and the physical connectivity parameter α, and constructing
random (but connected) networks for these values.

The parameter α represents the ratio of L, the number of links in the network,
to $L_{FC} = N(N-1)/2$, the number of links in a fully connected network with the
same number of nodes. Noting that the average node degree is $\bar{\Delta} = 2L/N$, we have
$\bar{\Delta} = \alpha(N-1)$. An intriguing aspect of the empirical RCA results is that α seems to be
a key parameter for large classes of networks, predicting quite accurately the mean
number of wavelengths $\bar{N}_\lambda$ and minimum number of wavelengths $N_{\lambda_{min}}$ needed to

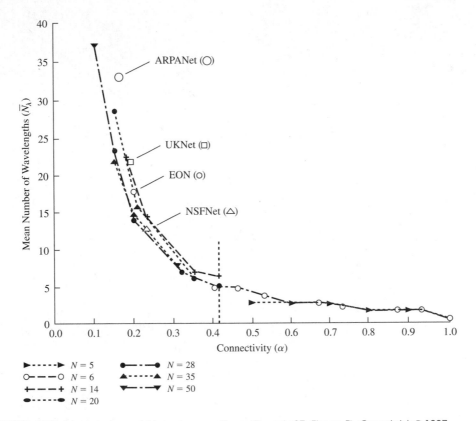

FIGURE 6.25 Mean values of N_λ versus α.   (From (Baroni+97, Figure 5). Copyright © 1997 IEEE. Used by permission of The Institute of Electrical and Electronics Engineers, Inc.)

support full connectivity over a wide range of network sizes.[28] Figures 6.25 and 6.26 show the mean and minimum values of wavelengths respectively for a large set of networks as a function of α. The networks in the figures include the four real networks of Figure 6.9 as well as RCNs for $N = 5$ through 50. Note that the curves for $N_{\lambda_{min}}$ are of the approximate form $N_{\lambda_{min}} \approx 2.4/\alpha$. Very similar results were obtained for N_λ in *regular* networks—undirected ShuffleNets and deBruijn networks over the range $N = 8$ to 125. This suggests that regularity and symmetry of the physical topology do not necessarily improve performance. In fact, they inhibit the network designer because they prevent modular network growth.

These empirical results can be related neatly to the wavelength bound W_{Netcap}. Substituting $\bar{\Delta} = \alpha(N - 1)$, $M = N(N - 1)$, and $F = 1$ into Equation 6.7, we have

$$W_{Netcap} = \bar{H}/\alpha \tag{6.34}$$

---

[28] $N_{\lambda_{min}}$ is the minimum value of N_λ over the ensemble of RCNs tested.

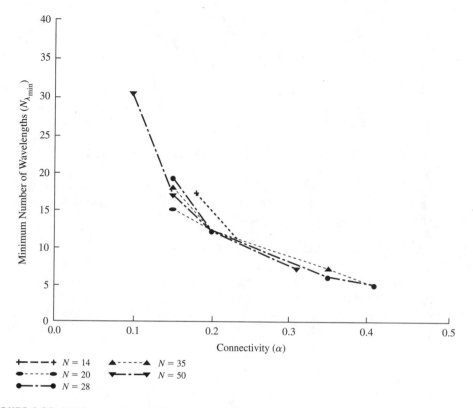

FIGURE 6.26 Minimum values of N_λ versus α. (From (Baroni+97, Figure 8). Copyright © 1997 IEEE. Used by permission of The Institute of Electrical and Electronics Engineers, Inc.)

This suggests that spectrum usage for the best cases of RCNs is close to the bound W_{Netcap}, and that over the range of sizes examined, the RCNs have $\bar{H} \approx 2.4$ independent of α and N. (The value of $\bar{H} = 2.4$ for the RCNs is consistent with the known value $\bar{H} = 2.33$ for the regular network examples.)

Without looking carefully at these results, one might conclude that using a fixed number of available wavelengths, WRNs can be "grown" to large sizes while maintaining full connectivity. There is only one problem with this: α must be held fixed as N increases, which implies that $\bar{\Delta}$ must grow linearly with N. That kind of growth cannot be sustained because the cost of each network node grows faster than $\bar{\Delta}$. In fact, it is unreasonable to expect to maintain full optical connectivity among all nodes in large networks because that means that $N - 1$ simultaneous optical connections must be supported by each station (assuming one station per node) no matter how large N is. This in turn means that the number of optical transceivers in each station, and hence its cost, increases linearly with the size of the network.

A more reasonable assumption is that each station supports some fixed number M_{STA} of optical connections independent of network size. In that case, we have from Equation 6.7

$$W_{\text{Netcap}} = \frac{M_{\text{STA}}\bar{H}}{\bar{\Delta}} \qquad\qquad (6.35)$$

so that with a fixed average node degree the lower bound on wavelengths does not grow with network size as long as the average internodal distance is kept under control.[29] But with fixed M_{STA}, how do we maintain full connectivity among the stations? The only way to do this is to provide a logically switched overlay on the wavelength routed network; that is, turn it into an LRN. This is a fundamental motivation for LRNs.

Our overall conclusion concerning RCA in wavelength routed networks is, therefore, *wavelength routed networks cannot by themselves achieve full connectivity among a large number of nodes in a cost-effective manner!*

6.3.8.2 A Monte Carlo Approach

The RCA algorithms and optimization procedures discussed earlier are all deterministic. A fixed set of rules is applied to determine routes and channel assignments for a set of prescribed connections, with the outcome determined uniquely by the procedures used. However, with optimization and design problems as complex as these, experience has shown that stochastic approaches using simulated annealing, genetic algorithms, or neural networks often give better results than deterministic ones, and require less computation [Aarts+97, Reeves93, Rayward-Smith+96].

We now present a stochastic approach to the static RCA problem. Its objective is to minimize the number of wavelengths required for a prescribed connection set while observing a given set of constraints on allowable fiber paths. (The constraints can be chosen to suit the needs of the designer.) In a large number of test problems, a small sample of which appear in Table 6.2 (see also page 424), the stochastic method outperforms the best deterministic heuristics that have appeared to date, and does so with considerably less computation. It is a Monte Carlo technique, wherein the static problem is converted to a dynamic one. The prescribed set of LCs is replaced by a stochastic offered load on the network, where a sequence of connection requests is drawn at random from the prescribed set.

An attempt is made to assign a fiber path and a λ-channel to each requested connection using a simple shortest path RCA rule. The characteristics of the algorithm are "adjustable" in the sense that path constraints and link weights (or "lengths") may be assigned dynamically depending on link utilization and possibly other factors. Thus, "shortest path routing" does not necessarily mean minimum hop. (General dynamic RCA rules are discussed in Section 6.4.) If no feasible path exists given the constraints of the algorithm, the request is blocked and tried again later. Requests that are accepted are held for a random time and then released. Statistics on connection

---

[29] Of course, $\bar{H}$ does grow, albeit slowly (logarithmically), with network size, so that something has to give (either M_{STA} or $\bar{\Delta}$) to keep the bound, and hence N_λ, from growing.

TABLE 6.2 Comparative Performance of Three RCA Heuristics.

Case	N	L	M	D	$\bar{d}$	$\bar{\Delta}$	σ_{Δ}^2	$\underline{W}_{\text{Limcut}}$	W_{mc}	W_{Bar}	W_{BC}
1	30	45	870	6	3.133	3	0	38	40	42	48
2	30	36	870	9	4.064	2.4	0.24	72	72	83	78
3	30	38	870	10	4.306	2.53	0.249	88	89	89	94
4	40	60	1560	6	3.546	3	0	57	63	70	74
5	40	61	1560	8	3.464	3.05	0.498	59	61	62	73
6	40	54	1560	9	4.038	2.7	0.46	91	93	143	111
7	51	62	2550	10	4.898	2.43	0.245	126	138	156	158
ARPANet	20	31	380	6	2.805	3.1	0.19	33	33	33	36
UKNet	21	39	420	5	2.505	3.71	1.823	19	19	22	25
EON	20	39	380	5	2.363	3.9	2.99	18	18	18	20
NSFNet	14	21	182	3	2.143	3	0.286	13	13	13	16
Atlantis	66	107	4290	14	5.135	3.24	1.94	173	175	212	250

blocking probability are kept, and link weights are fine-tuned to select paths and to assign wavelengths depending on blocking statistics. Lists of "good" paths for each connection are also accumulated as the process proceeds so that the algorithm "learns" about the network topology and the load distribution resulting from the prescribed connections. Connection holding times are adjusted dynamically, increasing the holding times of the connections having highest blocking probability. In this way the more "difficult" connections tend to become "sticky," remaining in place for longer periods of time than the "easy" connections.

The algorithm starts with a light Erlang load and a minimum number of available wavelengths W. As it proceeds, the load is increased and, if necessary to reduce blocking, W is increased. At convergence all connections are accommodated and the algorithm terminates. Because the performance of the algorithm depends on the specific RCA rule and constraints that are applied, this is not one algorithm but rather a class of algorithms.

The execution of the algorithm, in the form of an event-driven simulation, is described in more detail in the flow chart of Figure 6.27. The notation used in the figure is as follows:

l_i = an LC

P_i = a set of paths used previously for l_i

P_i^* = a subset of feasible fiber paths in P_i

W = the number of available wavelengths

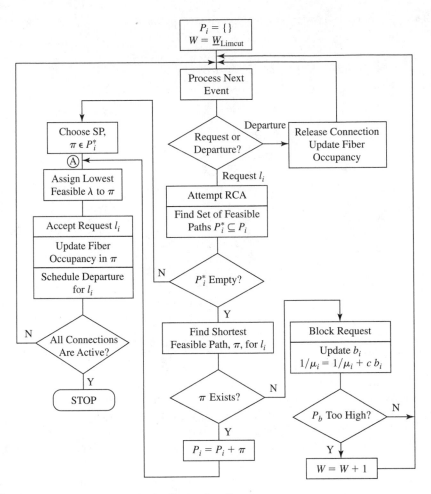

FIGURE 6.27   Flow chart of the Monte Carlo algorithm.

π = a feasible fiber path for l_i

μ_i = the departure rate for connection l_i

b_i = the current blocking probability for l_i

P_b = the current blocking probability for all connections

Referring to Figure 6.27, the simulation is initialized with all path sets, P_i, empty. The initial number of available wavelengths, W, is set equal to $\underline{W}_{\text{Limcut}}$, which can be calculated using an algorithm in Appendix D. Events (either connection requests or releases) are scheduled and processed according to the following rules:

1. Connection requests are generated for all *inactive* connections, with exponentially distributed interarrival times. The average interarrival times and holding times determine the Erlang load on the system. The simulation begins with a light load, which is increased as it proceeds. A connection, l_i, is released after an exponentially distributed holding time with mean μ_i^{-1}. The simulation keeps track of the fiber path π occupied by each active connection as well as the wavelength it uses.

2. If the next event is a departure, the fiber occupancy is updated by removing the wavelength used by the released connection from each fiber on its path, and the simulation processes the next event.

3. If the next event is a connection request, l_i, an attempt is made to assign an optical path to it. First, the set of feasible fiber paths, $P_i^* \subseteq P_i$, is examined. (A feasible path is a fiber path in P_i for which a λ-channel is available that satisfies wavelength continuity.[30]) If P_i^* is non-empty, a "shortest path" (SP) in P_i^* is chosen based on any appropriate link weight criterion. For example, link weights might be adjusted dynamically for congestion, current blocking probability, or some other phenomenon. Having chosen a fiber path, the algorithm proceeds to the channel assignment phase (point A in Figure 6.27).

4. If a feasible path is not found in P_i, a shortest feasible fiber path for l_i is sought outside of P_i, satisfying specified path constraints. The feasible paths might be limited to minimum-hop paths or they might be constrained in any other way. If an acceptable fiber path π is found, it is added to the path set P_i, and the algorithm again proceeds to the channel assignment phase.

5. If no feasible fiber path can be found that satisfies the path constraints, the request is blocked, its blocking probability b_i is updated, and its average holding time μ_i^{-1} is incremented by an amount proportional to b_i. The overall blocking probability P_b is also incremented, and if it is deemed to be too high, the number of available wavelengths is increased by one. The next event is then processed.

6. Once a fiber path, π, has been chosen, the lowest numbered feasible wavelength is assigned to the connection.[31] The request is accepted, the fiber occupancy on path π is updated, and the departure for that connection is scheduled. If all connections are active, the algorithm terminates. Otherwise, the next event is processed.

Figure 6.28 shows a typical time trace of a Monte Carlo experiment. The fraction of active connections is plotted as a function of the cumulative number of connection requests. With the initial value of W, the fraction of accepted requests quickly reaches approximately 0.94, after which a transient period ensues, with the value of W

---

[30] We assume that there is no wavelength interchange in the network. However, a simple modification of the algorithm at this point would allow for full or sparse wavelength interchange.

[31] A feasible wavelength is a free wavelength that satisfies wavelength continuity.

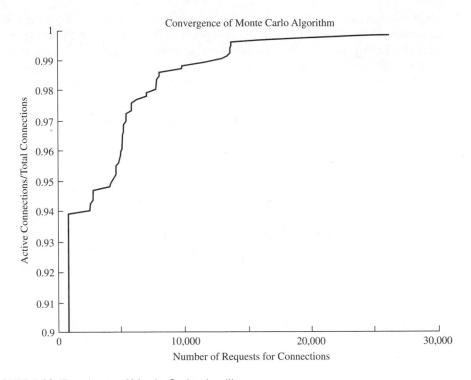

FIGURE 6.28 Time trace of Monte Carlo algorithm.

incremented several times until convergence occurs, with all requests satisfied. In this example, convergence required 25,000 connection requests.

Table 6.2 gives the results of 12 computational experiments with the Monte Carlo algorithm, with comparisons with two other heuristics. Seven random networks of orders ranging from $N = 30$ to $N = 51$ nodes are listed, together with the four networks of Figure 6.9, and a 66-node version of Atlantis—a more detailed version of the network in Figure 3.38(b). As indicated in Table 6.2, networks with various numbers of links L, diameters D, average node–pair distances $\bar{d}$, average degrees $\bar{\Delta}$, and degree variances σ_Δ^2 were studied. In each case a routing and channel assignment was determined for a set of $M = N(N-1)$ connections (full connectivity) using W_{mc} wavelengths. The objective of the experiments was to determine how close W_{mc} was to optimum, considering a range of network sizes and topologies. The optimality of W_{mc} was checked by comparing it with $\underline{W}_{Limcut}$.[32] Because $\underline{W}_{Limcut} \leq W_{Limcut}$, and the latter is a lower bound on the required number of wavelengths for the prescribed

---

[32] The value of W_{mc} could not be checked against the true optimum, or even against W_{Limcut}, because neither one of these quantities could be computed in a reasonable amount of time for problems of the size being tested.

connection set, a small difference between W_{mc} and $\underline{W}_{Limcut}$ indicates a good solution, and perhaps an optimal one.

To compare this stochastic approach with some good deterministic algorithms, the performance of the Monte Carlo algorithm was compared with the deterministic heuristic of [Baroni+97] and with the algorithm of [Banerjee+96] as shown in the columns labeled W_{Bar} and W_{BC} respectively. Note that in all cases W_{mc} is the lowest of the three, with $W_{Bar} = W_{mc}$ in only four of the cases, and W_{BC} always greater than W_{mc}. In five of the cases in Table 6.2, $W_{mc} = \underline{W}_{Limcut}$, which implies that the value of W_{mc} is optimal and that the limiting cut heuristic of Appendix D computed the true value of the limiting cut wavelength lower bound, $\underline{W}_{Limcut} = W_{Limcut}$.

Because full connectivity was required (and achieved) in all experiments, the solutions obtained for this *static* RCA problem can be applied directly to the *dynamic* case. All that is required is to keep a table of the route and wavelength obtained for each (*s–d*) pair, and to use table look-up to do routing and wavelength assignment on demand. However, for networks operating with less than full connectivity, this will generally produce a less efficient utilization of the optical spectrum than the dynamic algorithms described in the next section.

There is an important observation that comes as a byproduct of these experiments. Because all results on the required number of wavelengths W either meet or come close to $\underline{W}_{Limcut}$, and because $\underline{W}_{Limcut}$ is a lower bound on W obtained ignoring the constraint of wavelength continuity, the results demonstrate empirically that wavelength interchange is *unnecessary* in the networks studied in these experiments.

6.4 Wavelength Routed Networks: Dynamic Routing and Channel Assignment

Under dynamic traffic conditions, a sequence of LC requests arrives to a network controller in some random fashion, and these requests may or may not be accommodated, depending on the current state of activity in the network. The network state consists of all active connections together with their optical path (route and wavelength) assignments. The state evolves randomly in time as new connections are admitted and active connections are released. In performing routing and channel (wavelength) assignment under dynamic traffic conditions, an algorithm must be executed in real time to accommodate each request if this is feasible. If a request cannot be accepted (either because of physical constraints or admission control limitations), it is blocked. Because of the real-time nature of the problem, algorithms for RCA in a dynamic traffic environment must be very simple.

The performance of a dynamic RCA algorithm is generally measured in terms of blocking probability. However, we shall see that blocking probability as a single parameter may hide some other very important aspects of network behavior—in particular, *fairness*. Both blocking probability and fairness are influenced by the presence or absence of wavelength interchangers in the network. These effects are examined in the context of some specific examples.

Because connections among the various node pairs all share the same sets of links, there are statistical dependencies among all fiber and wavelength occupancies, and these influence blocking strongly. These dependencies make it impossible to perform an exact analysis of blocking probabilities and fairness in networks containing more than a few nodes. Instead, we present some case studies of special topologies (rings and interconnected rings) through simulation and through some approximate analytical models. For more general topologies, some simple but highly approximate expressions for blocking probabilities are presented.

6.4.1 Some Basic Routing and Channel Assignment Algorithms

Most RCA algorithms for wavelength routed networks have the following general form:

- Arrange all *admissible* fiber paths for a given source–destination pair in some prescribed order in a *path list*.

- Arrange all wavelengths in some prescribed order in a *wavelength list*.[33]

- Attempt to find a feasible route and wavelength for a requested connection starting with the path and wavelength at the top of the list.

The specific nature of an RCA algorithm is determined by the constraints used in defining admissible paths, the order in which paths and wavelengths are listed, and the order in which the path and wavelength lists are accessed.

6.4.1.1 Characterization of Routing

In a *static* routing algorithm the admissible paths are chosen and ordered independently of the network state, whereas in an *adaptive* algorithm admissibility and ordering may vary according to the current network state. A *fixed* routing algorithm is a static algorithm in which every source–destination pair is assigned a unique path (i.e., the path list for each node pair contains only one admissible path). In a fixed routing algorithm, a connection is blocked if there is no wavelength available on the designated path, even if a different route for the connection exists with a free wavelength at the time of the connection request.[34] In *alternate* routing each connection is assigned a set of admissible paths for which the ordering of the path list, and hence the choice of paths, typically depends on the state of the network: the adaptive routing case.[35]

In most practical cases, path admissibility and ordering is based on *path length*. The paths typically are listed in increasing order of path lengths, and path length is

---

[33] This assumes no wavelength interchange.

[34] A slight variant of fixed routing is a procedure in which only one shortest path is considered, but a random choice is used when more than one shortest path exists [Chlamtac+89].

[35] Alternate routing schemes can also be state independent (i.e., static). For example, if a path is selected from the list by random choice, the alternate routing rule is state independent and therefore static (but probabilistic).

normally defined as the sum of link weights along the path. The link weights are typically chosen using some desirable routing criterion, and because they can be assigned arbitrarily, they offer a wide range of possibilities for selecting path priorities. Link weights may reflect the load or "interference" on a link (i.e., the number of active connections sharing the link [Bala92, Ayanoglu+96]), or they may reflect the interference lengths of the paths sharing the link (i.e., the number of hops shared by pairs of interfering paths).[36] Many other weighting functions are possible. By assigning small weights to least loaded links, for example, we place the paths with the maximum number of free channels on their links at the head of the path list, producing a least loaded routing algorithm. Paths that are congested become longer and are moved farther down on the list. This tends to avoid heavily loaded bottleneck links.

For example, in a static routing algorithm, the path list might consist of all minimum-hop paths, listed in order of increasing geographic length. In an adaptive routing scheme, the path with the least interference might be placed at the head of the path list. Note that with static algorithms, the path lists can be computed and ordered off-line. On the other hand, in the adaptive case, real-time shortest path computation is required for each connection request, because link weights change with the network state.

Most routing algorithms are *constrained* in the sense that the admissible paths are selected as a predetermined subset of all possible paths. For example, the set of admissible paths for a given connection might be limited to those having no more than $d + 1$ hops, where d is the source–destination distance (in optical hops).

Among unconstrained algorithms, the simplest is shortest path routing. An example of an unconstrained shortest path algorithm is one that chooses a minimum-hop path from among all those that have at least one free channel available (see Section 6.4.1.4). More general shortest path algorithms comprise two parts: (1) the assignment of appropriate link weights ("lengths") and (2) the computation of a shortest path based on link weights.

Although shortest path routing would appear to be a very simple procedure, complications may arise because

1. The link weights may be state dependent

2. The path lengths may be influenced by the presence or absence of wavelength interchangers

3. The length of a path may not be equal to the sum of the link weights

The first item means that the routing algorithm is adaptive, which in turn implies that global state information must be stored at the site (or sites) executing the routing algorithm. If the algorithm is executed in a distributed fashion, this information must be exchanged among the various network nodes performing the computation,

---

[36] The term *interference* is used here in the sense of *potential interference*. That is, the connections sharing a link would interfere with each other, garbling their information *if* they were assigned the same wavelength.

creating significant control overhead. The significance of the last two items is explained in the least loaded routing algorithm, described in Section 6.4.1.5.

6.4.1.2 Characterization of Channel Assignment

The definition of a *free channel* depends on whether the network contains wavelength interchangers. If there is no λ-interchange, a free channel (wavelength) exists on a path only if at least one wavelength is unused on *every* fiber on the path (i.e., wavelength continuity and DCA must be observed throughout the path). If there is sparse λ-interchange, the wavelength continuity condition is relaxed at each node containing a wavelength interchanger so that different wavelengths may be assigned on different segments of a path. With full wavelength interchange, a free channel exists as long as there is at least one unused wavelength on each fiber on the path, but the wavelengths need not be the same (i.e., only the DCA constraint must be observed). A path is called *feasible* if a free channel exists on that path. (In the discussion that follows, wavelength interchange is excluded unless indicated otherwise.)

The wavelength list is typically ordered either by wavelength number (the static case) or by usage (the adaptive case). The usage of wavelength λ_i is defined here as the number of active connections using λ_i. In the adaptive case, wavelengths might be listed in either decreasing or increasing order of usage. We refer to the former case as the *maximum reuse method* (Max Reuse) and the latter as the *minimum reuse method* (Min Reuse). In the wavelength assignment phase of an RCA algorithm, an attempt is made to assign a wavelength to a chosen path, typically starting from the top of the wavelength list and working down.[37] Thus, in the Max Reuse case, the most used wavelengths are tried first, the rationale being to reuse active wavelengths as much as possible before trying others. This in turn makes it more likely that a channel that satisfies wavelength continuity is available on a long path. In the Min Reuse case, the idea is to spread the load as equally as possible over all available wavelengths. Experience with simulations has shown that the Max Reuse method usually works best in WRNs (see, for example, [Ramaswami+95] and [Bala+91a]).

There is no "universal" algorithm that performs best in all circumstances and under all performance criteria. Thus we shall present a few alternative approaches in this section, pointing out some of their pitfalls and advantages.

6.4.1.3 k Shortest Path

In the k shortest path (k-SP) algorithm [Bala+91a], the first k shortest paths for a connection are considered admissible and placed on the path list in increasing order of length. (For $k = 1$, this reduces to shortest path routing.) Assuming that path lengths are state independent, k-SP is a static routing algorithm. Each path is checked in order, and the first that is feasible is assigned the first free wavelength on the wavelength list.[38] If none of the k paths are feasible, the connection is blocked.

---

[37] Another technique is to pick wavelengths from the list at random [Ramaswami+95].

[38] A modified version of k-SP adapted to LLNs is discussed in Section 6.6.1.2. It uses a minimum interference criterion to choose a path from the admissible list.

Note that if k-SP is used, there is no limit on the length of the admissible paths. If k is large and if the network is congested, the first feasible path might exceed a reasonable length limit. Furthermore, if k is small, there is a significant possibility that the path list does not contain *any* feasible paths, resulting in a high blocking probability. For example, in the case $k = 1$, a connection is blocked if the unique path on the list does not have a free wavelength.

6.4.1.4 Shortest Path with Deletions

To reduce the risk of blocking using the k-SP algorithm, an adaptive version can be used: shortest path with *deletions* (SPD). In SPD, shortest paths are computed taking feasibility into account. A copy of the network topology is examined for each wavelength, following the layered model of Figure 2.5(b). (The order in which the wavelengths are selected is arbitrary.) All fibers carrying active connections on a particular wavelength are *deleted* from the corresponding copy of the network, and a shortest path is computed on the resultant "deleted topology." (This is equivalent to finding a shortest path on a given wavelength when the occupied fibers are assigned infinite weights.) At least one path exists for a given connection request on a given wavelength unless the source and destination nodes fall into two disconnected subgraphs for that wavelength. After scanning all wavelengths, the lengths of all resultant paths are compared, and the shortest among them is selected using the corresponding wavelength. If a feasible path exists for the given source–destination pair, at least one path and wavelength are found. Otherwise the connection is blocked.

An example of the operation of SPD is shown in Figure 6.29. The network has five nodes, operates on two λ-channels, and all link weights are assumed to be one. A sequence of states (deleted topologies) of the network is shown in Figure 6.29, with the complete topology (the network with all fibers idle) shown as the initial state on both wavelength copies. A request for connection (A, E) arrives. It can be satisfied by two-hop paths on both copies. To break the tie, the lower numbered wavelength, λ_1, is used, producing the second state in the sequence. A request for connection (A, C) arrives next and is placed on the shortest path, A–C, using λ_2. Finally, a request for connection (A, D) arrives and is placed on the only feasible path, A–B–C–E–D, on λ_2. If shortest path routing had been used *without* deletions, the path A–C–E–D would have been chosen for the connection (A, D), but the connection would have been blocked because the link A–C is saturated, making the chosen path infeasible.

The SPD algorithm always finds the shortest *feasible* path for a connection, *given the current state of the network*. It therefore results in a blocking probability that is as good or better than k-SP for any given connection request. However, its *overall* performance may be worse in some cases because it tends to produce longer average path lengths than k-SP, thereby creating more network congestion.

6.4.1.5 Least Loaded Routing

A constrained least loaded routing algorithm has been proposed by [Ayanoglu+96]. A set of admissible paths is precomputed for each source–destination pair, and the

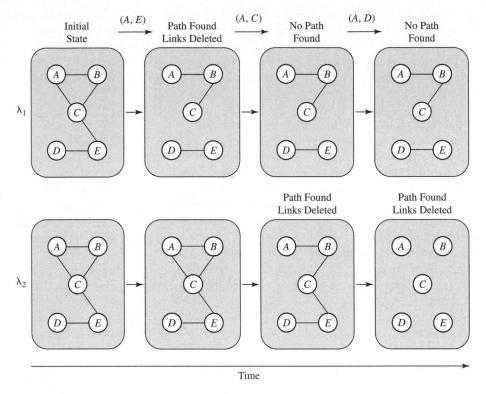

FIGURE 6.29 An example of SPD routing.

admissible path with the maximum free capacity (MFC) is chosen for a connection. The admissible paths might be a set of k minimum-hop paths for the source–destination pair, which can be computed off-line. Thus, this is a static constraint. Complications arise in this algorithm due to the definition of free capacity. For a given connection, let

$\Pi =$ the set of admissible paths

$\pi =$ a path in Π

$M_l =$ the number of fibers on link l

$A_{lj} =$ the number of fibers on link l for which wavelength j is active

$U_l = \sum_j A_{lj} =$ total number of channels active on link l (the link utilization)

$\Lambda = \{\lambda_1, \lambda_2, \ldots, \lambda_W\}$, the set of wavelengths available in the network, where $W = |\Lambda|$

The least loaded path is chosen as follows:

1. Without wavelength interchange, let

$$MFC = \max_{\pi \in \Pi} \max_{\lambda_j \in \Lambda} \left[\min_{l \in \pi} (M_l - A_{lj}) \right] \tag{6.36}$$

The path and wavelength assigned are those that achieve the indicated maximizations.

2. With full wavelength interchange,

$$MFC = \max_{\pi \in \Pi} \left[\min_{l \in \pi} (WM_l - U_l) \right] \tag{6.37}$$

The path assigned is one that achieves the indicated maximization.

In both cases the quantity in brackets is the free capacity on a path π. The link l, which has the minimum free capacity over all the links on the given path π, is the "bottleneck" link. The inverse of the free capacity of a path can be thought of as the *effective path length*. In the case without wavelength interchange, the algorithm finds the path (and wavelength) on which this free capacity is greatest (i.e., the path/wavelength with the shortest effective length). In the wavelength interchange case the wavelength is not involved. In either case, a connection is blocked if MFC is zero. (This corresponds to all admissible paths having infinite effective length.)

The fact that a small, precomputed set of admissible paths, Π, is used in the computation means that the maximization can be performed easily. In an unconstrained case, the admissible set includes all possible paths, meaning that the maximization process is considerably more complex. A simple shortest path algorithm such as Dijkstra's (see [Tarjan83]) does not suffice here because the effective path lengths are not sums of link weights.

6.4.1.6 Fairness

In general, any network has the property that longer paths are likely to encounter more blocking than shorter ones. Depending on the network topology and the routing rules, this can result in unfair treatment of the connections between more distant node pairs. Blocking of the longer connections leaves more network resources free for shorter paths, so that the paths allocated in the network tend to be short ones. Unfortunately, these shorter paths "fragment" the wavelength mapping, making it less likely that the same wavelength is available throughout the network for longer paths. It is useful to quantify these fairness relations so that the influence of effects such as path constraints and wavelength interchange on fairness can be measured. To this end we define the *unfairness factor*, U_f, as the ratio of the blocking probability on the longest path to that on the shortest path under a given RCA rule.

The problem of unfairness is more pronounced in networks without wavelength interchange because finding long paths that satisfy the wavelength continuity constraint is more difficult than without the constraint. To quantify the effect of wavelength

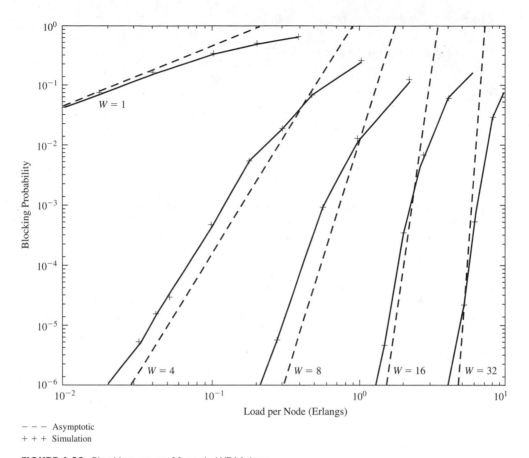

− − − Asymptotic
+ + + Simulation

FIGURE 6.30 Blocking on an 11-node WDM ring.

interchange on unfairness we define the *fairness ratio* as

$$F_r = \frac{U_f(\text{without } \lambda\text{-interchange})}{U_f(\text{with } \lambda\text{-interchange})} \tag{6.38}$$

A related quantity, the *average gain in blocking probability*, G_p, is defined in [Ayanoglu+96] as the ratio of overall blocking probability without λ-interchange to that with λ-interchange. In defining both F_r and G_p, the Max Reuse wavelength assignment rule is assumed here for the case without wavelength interchange.

The influence of various network parameters on fairness is examined through simulation and asymptotic analysis in some case studies that follow. One important observation is that networks with wavelength interchange sometimes exhibit *orders of magnitude* improvement in fairness compared with networks without the wavelength

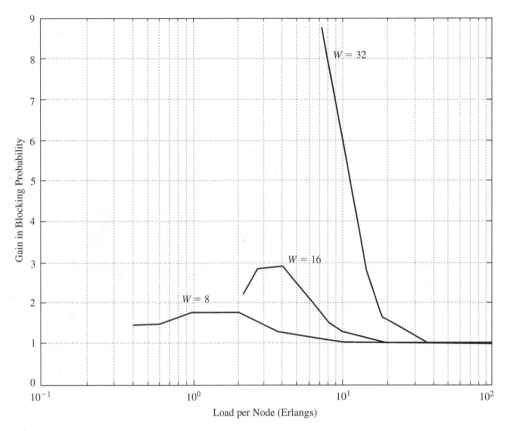

FIGURE 6.31 Gain in blocking; 11-node WDM ring, simulation.

interchange capability. The improvement in overall blocking probability due to wavelength interchange is much less pronounced.

6.4.2 Case Study: Bidirectional Rings

Figures 6.30 through 6.33 show the results of a case study of a bidirectional ring under dynamic channel assignment rules. Shortest path routing is used, and channels are allocated using the Max Reuse rule.

Each node on the ring generates connection requests in a Poisson fashion, with an average arrival rate α, and connections have exponentially distributed holding times with mean $1/\mu$. Under *uniform traffic*, each request is directed equiprobably to all other nodes. Under a *worst case* traffic distribution, each source node generates connection requests equiprobably to the two most distant destination nodes—$(N-1)/2$ hops away for N odd. Blocking and fairness are studied as a function of offered load per node ($\rho = \alpha/\mu$), available wavelengths (W), and wavelength interchange capability.

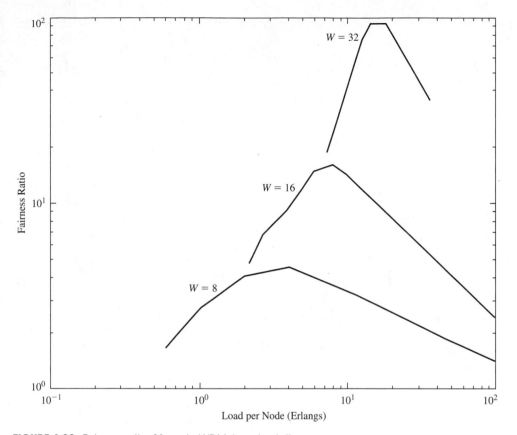

FIGURE 6.32   Fairness ratio; 11-node WDM ring, simulation.

In the case $W = 1$, it can be shown (see Problem 18 at the end of the chapter) that for rings of size N (odd), where $N \geq 5$, the blocking probability under a worst case traffic scenario is given by

$$P_b = \frac{\beta(N-2) + N\beta^2}{1 + N\beta + N\beta^2} \tag{6.39}$$

where $\beta = \rho/2$. Blocking calculations under uniform traffic are far more difficult. Thus, although the worst case is somewhat artificial, it leads to some simplifications.

For larger values of W, the following asymptotic formula provides a simple and fairly good "back-of-the-envelope" estimate of blocking probability on the ring in this worst case scenario:

$$P_b \approx \left(\frac{\alpha d}{\mu W}\right)^W, \quad \text{for} \quad \frac{\alpha d}{\mu W} < 1 \tag{6.40}$$

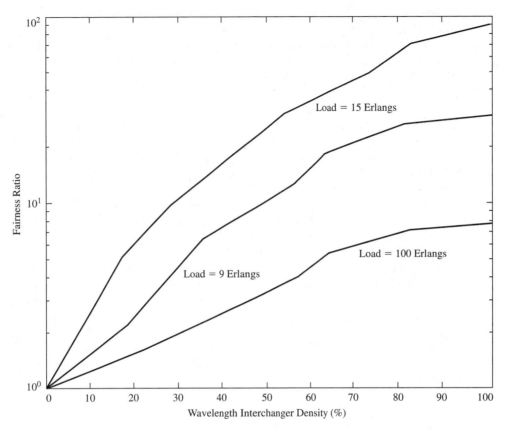

FIGURE 6.33 Fairness ratio improvement versus interchanger density; 11-node WDM ring with 32 wavelengths.

where $d = (N-1)/2$ is the ring diameter. This approximation can be derived directly from the Erlang-B formula, which gives low blocking for cases when total load offered to a set of channels (in this case $\alpha d/\mu$) is less than the number of channels in the set (in this case W).

Simulation results, together with the asymptotic approximation, are shown in Figure 6.30 for the case $N = 11$, using a worst case traffic distribution. Considering the simplicity of the asymptotic model, it works reasonably well, providing a simple way to estimate the blocking probability for general WDM rings.

6.4.2.1 Rings with Full Wavelength Interchange

The effect of full wavelength interchange capability in an 11-node WDM ring is presented in Figures 6.31 and 6.32. These and subsequent results dealing with fairness and wavelength interchange were obtained by simulation using uniform traffic distributions.

Figure 6.31 shows the average gain in blocking probability, G_p, due to wavelength interchange for the ring with 8, 16, and 32 wavelengths. It is clear that for 8 and 16 wavelengths there is limited improvement in blocking. However, with 32 wavelengths the improvement reaches a peak of an order of magnitude at a fairly high load and then drops.[39]

The case study of Section 6.4.4 shows that for ring interconnection with a large number of wavelengths, the value of G_p is even larger. In general for WDM rings (or ring interconnections), G_p increases with the number of wavelengths and the lengths of the paths (i.e., the ring sizes).

The fairness ratio, F_r, obtained by simulation for the 11-node WDM ring is shown in Figure 6.32. Observe that for 32 wavelengths, F_r reaches a peak of approximately 100. As in the case of G_p, the peak is attained at fairly high loads, after which F_r drops.

The significance of this fairness improvement becomes clearer when we examine some of the numbers more closely. Consider the case with 32 wavelengths at a load of 12 Erlangs, giving an F_r of 80.

In this case, without wavelength interchange the simulation yields blocking on the longest paths of 4.5×10^{-2}, whereas it is 1.4×10^{-4} on the shortest paths. (The average blocking is 2×10^{-2}.) Thus, the unfairness factor, U_f, is 320 at this load. On the other hand, with wavelength interchange the blocking on the longest paths is 8×10^{-3} and the blocking on the shortest paths is 2×10^{-3}, with an average blocking of 5×10^{-3}, giving a U_f of 4. Clearly, wavelength interchange results in a very large improvement in the blocking of long paths in this case.

6.4.2.2   Rings with Sparse λ-Interchange

Given the current cost of wavelength interchangers, it is important to determine whether it is possible to achieve the benefits of wavelength interchange by introducing it sparsely, at a few strategic places in the network [Subramaniam+96a, Bala+97].

In the case of a ring carrying uniform traffic, best results are obtained when the interchangers are placed uniformly around the ring. Figure 6.33 shows the results of simulations of the fairness ratio for approximate uniform placement on an 11-node ring, with Erlang load per node as a parameter. The improvement is a roughly linear function of the λ-interchange density (on the semilog scale). Improvement peaks at a fairly high load. (Note that the 15-Erlang curve shows the highest fairness ratio.)

---

[39] Intuition suggests that the improvement in blocking is small with very light and very heavy loads. In the former case, wavelength interchange is not needed for good performance, and in the latter case links tend to saturate, and thus wavelength interchange does not help.

6.4.3 Performance of Dynamic Routing Rules on Meshes

Even in the case of simple topologies such as rings, using fixed routing rules, the calculation of blocking probabilities in multiwavelength networks is extremely difficult. In networks with arbitrary mesh topologies, and using alternate routing, the problem is much more complex. The network typically has many alternate paths between a source–destination pair, so that a connection that is blocked on one path can be carried on another. Once paths have been chosen however (e.g., using a fixed routing rule), the blocking problem is similar in structure to that in rings, although the dependencies among interfering connections are generally more complicated.

In view of the complexity of the problem of predicting blocking in general mesh networks, it is doubtful that mathematical models can be found that are accurate, general, and tractable. Nevertheless, some progress has been made in recent work. In [Subramaniam+96a], a Markovian model is used to capture the effect of link dependency on connection blocking. In [Birman95], a more accurate method for calculating the blocked traffic in a mesh topology is proposed. However, this method is limited to fixed routing schemes with routes of three hops or less.

Probably the simplest and most intuitive approach is due to [Barry+95]. The model they use is similar to that used for finding approximate blocking probabilities in traditional telephone networks and circuit switches. As in telephone network models, the key assumption is that the channel (wavelength) occupancies on each link are *mutually independent* random variables.

Consider a network with W available wavelengths, with a single fiber pair on each link, and without wavelength interchangers. Suppose the probability ρ that a wavelength is used on a link is known and equal for all links. Then, subject to the aforementioned independence assumption, the probability that a connection is blocked on a specific H hop path is

$$P_b = [1 - (1 - \rho)^H]^W \tag{6.41}$$

The result is derived easily. The term $1 - \rho$ in Equation 6.41 is the probability that any given wavelength is free on any given link. Raised to the power H, it represents the probability that the wavelength is free on every link of the given path. Thus, $1 - (1 - \rho)^H$ is the probability that the wavelength is occupied on at least one link on the path, and therefore is unusable on the given path. Equation 6.41 therefore gives the probability that all W wavelengths are unusable, so that the connection is blocked on the given path.

The independence assumption, on which the previous argument is based, is approximately valid in cases when there is a high degree of "mixing" at each node (i.e., the nodes are of high degree and/or W is large), so that many connections enter and leave a node in many different directions and on many different channels (wavelengths). This is often the case in telephone applications. Unfortunately,

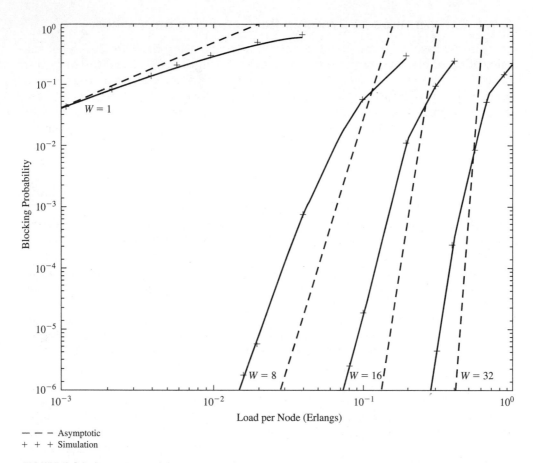

— — — Asymptotic
+ + + Simulation

FIGURE 6.34 Simulation and asymptotic analysis; 195-node interconnected WDM rings.

the independence assumption is less valid in networks with small nodal degree and few wavelengths (less mixing), which is more typical of current optical networks. A ring is an extreme case, in which the nodal degree is only two. (To check validity in the case of a ring, the reader should try to match some of the simulation points in Figure 6.30 with Equation 6.41. See Problem 19 at the end of the chapter.)

How does Equation 6.41 change in the presence of wavelength interchangers? With full wavelength interchange, a mesh optical network behaves like a traditional network, without any wavelength continuity constraint. In this case, a connection request is blocked on a given H hop path only if all wavelengths are used on one of the links. Under the same assumptions as stated earlier, an expression for blocking

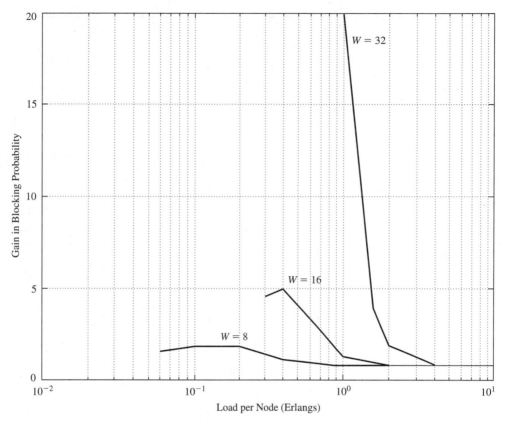

FIGURE 6.35 Blocking improvement with wavelength interchange; 195-node interconnected WDM rings.

probability in this case is [Barry+95]:

$$P_b = 1 - (1 - \rho^W)^H \qquad (6.42)$$

6.4.4 Case Study: An Interconnected Ring

In the case of rings, various reasonable approximations of blocking probabilities are possible. In the case of meshes, the simple formulas of Equations 6.41 and 6.42 are useful in gaining some insight into how connection blocking is related to the various network parameters. However, they are not very useful in obtaining quantitative results. To obtain more accurate results in realistic networks, simulation is currently the only viable approach.

Interconnected rings are examples of practical topologies going beyond rings, which are frequently used by telecommunications carriers. Figures 6.34 through 6.36

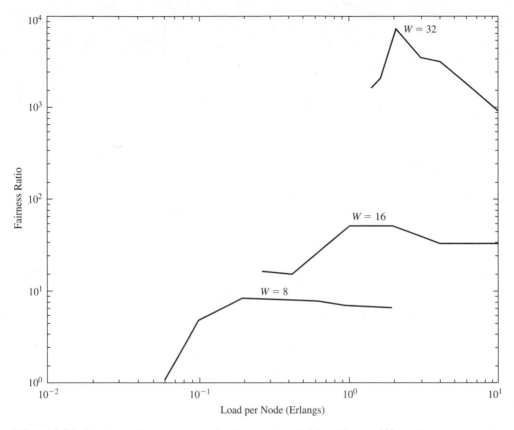

FIGURE 6.36 Fairness ratio improvement with wavelength interchange; 195-node interconnected WDM rings.

show simulation results for blocking and fairness ratios in an interconnected ring network with 195 nodes. The results are qualitatively similar to those for the 11-node ring, with more significant improvements in fairness.

In this example, the rings are interconnected pairwise, using WSXCs, some of which are replaced by WIXCs when wavelength interchanging is introduced. The overall network resembles a "necklace" with 15 "beads" (the rings). Each ring has 13 nodes. The traffic distribution is uniform, and shortest path routing is used.

A good placement for sparse wavelength interchange in the network under study is at the ring interconnection nodes, where the path interferences are the highest under uniform traffic. As the density of wavelength interchangers increases, the interchangers are placed approximately uniformly throughout the network. As shown in Figure 6.37, most of the benefits from the use of wavelength interchange are achievable by installing this capability at 10% to 20% of the nodes in the network.

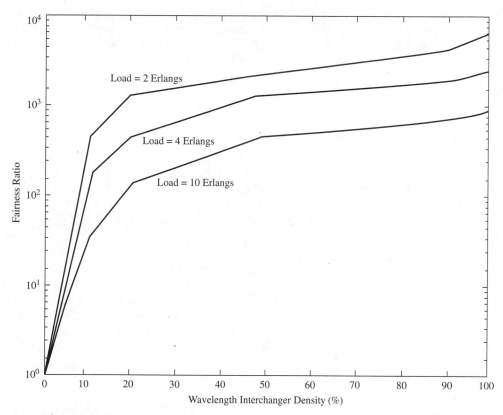

FIGURE 6.37 Fairness ratio improvement versus interchanger density; 195-node interconnected WDM ring, 32 wavelengths.

6.5 Linear Lightwave Networks: Static Routing Rules

The basic structure of the LLN was described in Section 3.4. Recall that the difference between a wavelength routed network and an LLN lies in the functionality of the network nodes. In the former, the node is a wavelength-selective *permutation* switch (optical cross-connect) whereas in the latter, it is a wave*band*-selective linear divider combiner (LDC) (i.e., a *generalized* switch).[40] As illustrated in Section 3.4, the extra functionality of the LDC offers both opportunities and challenges in allocating resources to optical connections.

---

[40] The LLN is assumed to have no wavelength interchange.

In an LLN, an optical *path* consists of a fiber path carried on a designated *waveband*. An optical *connection* is created on a designated optical path by allocating a λ-channel within the path's waveband to that connection. Thus, connection establishment in an LLN is a resource allocation problem at three levels.

1. Waveband selection

2. Fiber path allocation (routing)

3. Channel assignment (including λ-channels and transmission channels)

As we shall see, this three-level separation is needed because of the extra complications at the optical path level caused by multicast paths and the inseparability constraint.

This section treats LLNs operating under a static routing regime (see Section 6.6 for the dynamic routing case). Under static routing rules, optical paths, acting as fixed "pipes" on designated wavebands, are established on selected routes. Once the optical paths are in place, optical connections can be directed through the pipes by assigning them to λ-channels on the corresponding wavebands. This amounts to *waveband routing* of the connections. This approach applies equally well to dedicated and demand-assigned optical connections. In other words, we can have static routing rules in the optical path layer, supporting either dedicated (static) or on-demand (dynamic) optical connection assignments. Furthermore, several LCs can be multiplexed on a given optical connection by assigning them to distinct *transmission channels*.

Resource allocation in LLNs is viewed best from the bottom up, starting in the optical path layer. As shown in Figure 2.5(c), the LLN can be visualized as several independently controlled copies of a network with the same physical topology, one copy for each waveband. The optical spectrum is divided into W wavebands with C λ-channels per waveband. Establishing an optical path between NASs consists of choosing a route from source to destination stations on a selected waveband and setting the LDCs in the network nodes to direct signals in that waveband along the chosen route. Thus, creation of an OP is a routing and waveband assignment (RWA) problem. For point-to-point OPs this is similar to the RCA problem in wavelength routed networks, except that we are now routing a "bundle" of λ-channels instead of one. But in LLNs, as opposed to WRNs, optical paths, optical connections, and logical connections may be multicast as well as point to point. This means that the LLN has considerably more connectivity options. In particular, a large number of LCs (both point to point and multicast) can be carried on each OP. (The other side of the coin is that the routing, waveband, and channel assignment problems become considerably more complex.)

Examples of static routing in LLNs were presented in Section 3.4.2 in the form of multipoint subnets (MPSs). The optical paths for the MPSs were embedded on the physical topology in the form of directed trees. These trees were capable of supporting multipoint logical connectivity using wavelength–division techniques (at the optical connection level) and/or time–division techniques (at the transmission channel level).[41]

Once an OP is established on a given waveband, one or more optical *connections* can be activated on the path by assigning λ-channels to them within the waveband and tuning the optical transceivers in the source and destination stations to the selected wavelengths. Finally, each LC is established by assigning a transmission channel to it on the supporting optical connection and configuring the TPs/RPs in the source station and destination stations to operate on that channel.[42]

Because of its complexity, it is helpful to partition the three-part resource allocation problem into two subproblems: RWA and channel assignment. In this section RWA is considered a static problem, and channel assignment is treated both statically and dynamically. (Section 6.6 considers the case of dynamic routing.)

Let us use the network of Figure 6.38 as a point of departure to illustrate various facets of the resource allocation problem. The physical topology for this network (excluding the attached stations) is known as a *Petersen graph*, and it has a number of properties that are useful in the discussion that follows. It is a regular graph with $N = 10$ vertices (network nodes) and $L = 15$ edges (network links). Each vertex has degree $\Delta = 3$. It has diameter $D = 2$, and it is completely symmetric (i.e., its topology looks the same as seen from each node). Also, it is a Moore graph. The symmetry of the network enables us to deduce the important performance parameters without extensive computation, and provides some insight into the effects that limit performance.

6.5.1 Routing of Optical Paths

In selecting routes for OPs, we must observe the four routing constraints in LLNs. As first presented in Sections 3.3 and 3.4, these are

1. Wavelength continuity
2. Inseparability
3. Distinct channel assignment
4. Distinct source combining (DSC)

Once the LDCs in a network are set to establish an OP, the laws of physics (embodied in the first two constraints) determine how signals propagate over it. When several

---

[41] It should be observed here that even in the case of spectrum partitions with $C = 1$ (i.e., single-wavelength-per-waveband LLNs), bundling of LCs can take place at the transmission channel level. Thus, using TDM/TDMA on a multipoint OP, several sources can share a single λ-channel to produce multipoint logical connectivity.

[42] In WRNs the distinction between an optical connection (carried on a λ-channel) and an LC (carried on a transmission channel) is unimportant, because there is no opportunity for sharing λ-channels.

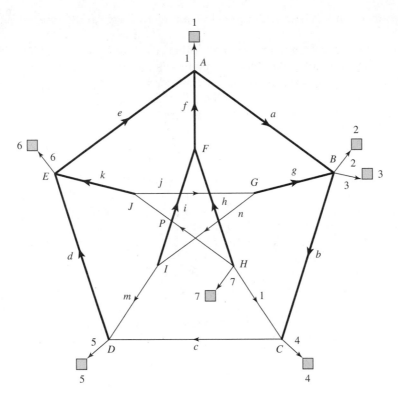

FIGURE 6.38 Petersen network.

OPs are established on the same waveband, signals may propagate in unintended ways, as we first encountered in Section 3.4. The last two constraints are imposed to ensure that when several signals are present on one or more OPs, they do not interfere, and thus destroy useful information.

In LLNs, as in WRNs, it is important to separate station/access constraints from network constraints. To this end we once again distinguish between nonblocking and elementary NASs. Figure 6.39 illustrates a possible structure for a nonblocking NAS in an LLN. The station is attached to a network node of degree 3 through an access link containing three fiber pairs: c_1, c_2, and c_3—see Figure 6.39(a). It is equipped to operate on two wavebands, w_1 and w_2, with four λ-channels in each waveband. The station can be "resolved" into three elementary stations—C_1, C_2, and C_3—one for each access fiber pair, as shown in Figure 6.39(b). Within an elementary station C_i, there are two arrays of four OTs, one operating on waveband w_1 and the other operating on w_2—Figure 6.39(c). Each transmitter is fixed–tuned to a λ-channel in its waveband. Signals from all transmitters in an array for one waveband are first multiplexed onto

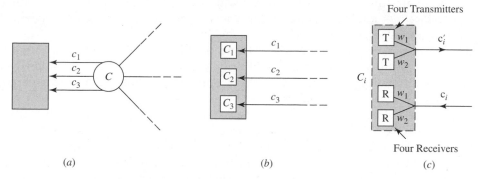

FIGURE 6.39 Structure of a nonblocking access station for an LLN.

a fiber, and then the combined signals for the two wavebands are multiplexed onto the access fiber c_i', serving elementary station C_i.[43]

Similarly, on the receiving side of elementary station C_i, optical power from fiber c_i is waveband demultiplexed, with signals on each waveband sent to a different array of ORs. Note that the elementary components of a larger station behave, from an optical point of view, exactly as if they were independent NASs. Therefore, no distinction is made between an elementary (single-access fiber pair) station and an elementary component of a larger station. Following this pattern, a nonblocking station in an LLN with F fiber pairs on its internodal links contains $F\Delta$ elementary stations, each on its own access fiber pair, where Δ is the degree of the node being accessed. Each elementary station contains an array of W transceiver sets, one set operating on each waveband, and each set contains an array of C fixed–tuned transceivers, one for each channel in its waveband. In this way, the station is capable of terminating all optical connections arriving at or departing from its ONN.

We define the source (destination) of an optical path operating on a waveband w to be the set of *all* transmitters (receivers) operating on waveband w in an *elementary* NAS. Thus, for example, the nonblocking NAS in Figure 6.39 can act as the source of up to six different OPs, one for each waveband and each outbound access fiber.

In contrast to sources of OPs, the source of an optical *connection* is one OT generating a signal on that connection. The destinations of the connection are all of the ORs reached by the source signal.

The differences in definitions of optical paths and optical connections are due to the fact that an optical *path* routes the aggregate power on one waveband on a fiber, which

---

[43] Following the terminology first introduced in Section 3.4.1.2, we use unprimed link labels to designate fibers carrying signals in the direction of the link reference arrow, and primed link labels for fibers carrying signals in the opposite direction.

could originate from several transmitters within the waveband, whereas an optical *connection* defines a relation between one transmitter and one or more receivers, all operating on the same wav*elength*.

Using these definitions, each station may contain several entities that serve as sources and destinations of optical paths and connections. Nevertheless, to avoid cumbersome notation, a source or destination is identified using the label of its station whenever there is no risk of ambiguity.

Having defined our terms, we now present an example that illustrates the difference between feasible and infeasible routes for OPs, using the Petersen network of Figure 6.38. In our first look at this network we assume that it has seven attached *elementary* stations, with single fiber pairs on all internodal links. It is also assumed initially that the network operates on a single waveband, so that the RWA problem reduces to OP routing only.

The notation $p_i = \langle s_i, D_i \rangle$ is used to denote an OP from a source s_i to a destination set D_i. The *fiber* path for an OP takes the form of a directed tree composed of all fibers carrying signals from s_i to the set D_i.

Suppose the following optical paths are to be routed on the network:

$$p_1 = \langle 1, \{5, 7\} \rangle$$
$$p_2 = \langle 2, 6 \rangle$$
$$p_3 = \langle 4, 1 \rangle \qquad\qquad (6.43)$$
$$p_4 = \langle 4, 5 \rangle$$

Assuming that shortest path routing is used, Figure 6.40 shows the evolution of the fiber paths and LDC settings as each OP is established. The role played by the LDCs in linking the fibers is indicated by intranodal connection matrices for the network nodes in Figure 6.40.[44] Figure 6.40(a) shows that the multicast OP p_1 is produced by setting node A to split the signal arriving on fiber $1'$ to fibers f' and e'. Figure 6.40(b) shows the state of the network after addition of p_2. Now, p_2 shares fiber e' with p_1, and thus the two OPs coalesce into a directed tree that contains all sources and destinations of the constituent OPs. As a result of inseparability, fortuitous destinations are added to both OPs, as explained in Section 3.4.1.1.

When OP p_3 is added, the coalesced optical paths are extended as shown in Figure 6.40(c). At this point the three OPs become

$$p_1 = \langle 1, \{5, 7, \underline{6}\} \rangle$$
$$p_2 = \langle 2, \{6, \underline{1}, \underline{5}\} \rangle \qquad\qquad (6.44)$$
$$p_3 = \langle 4, \{1, \underline{5}, \underline{6}\} \rangle$$

---

[44] Each entry in an intranodal connection matrix corresponds to a path within the LDC from an input fiber to an output fiber, where the rows and columns correspond to inputs and outputs respectively.

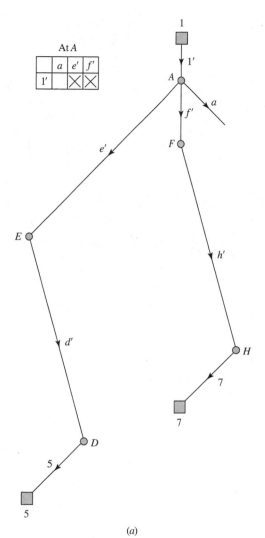

FIGURE 6.40 Optical paths.   (a)

The notation used in Equation 6.44 represents *expanded* OPs, of the form $p_i = \langle s_i, \mathcal{D}_i \rangle$, where $\mathcal{D}_i$ is the destination set of the original OP, expanded to include its fortuitous destinations (underlined). The coalesced OPs are still in the form of a directed tree. However, without looking "inside" the LDCs, it is impossible to determine the way the signals are routed. In particular, the setting of node A indicates that the OPs from sources 2 and 4 continue on to fibers 1 and e' without splitting to fiber f', whereas the OP from source 1 is split between e' and f'. Thus, to specify each optical path uniquely, the internodal *and* intranodal connections are required.

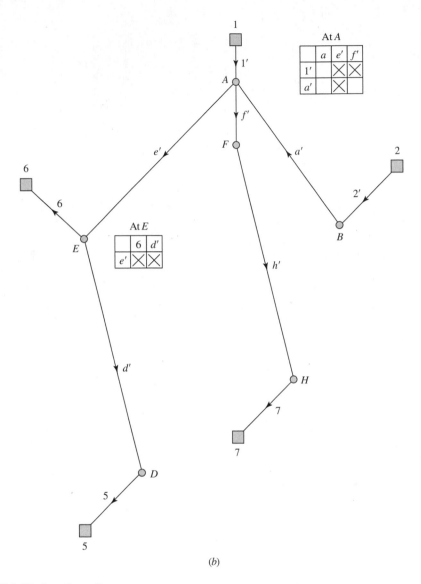

At A

	a	e'	f'
1'		✕	✕
a'		✕	

At E

	6	d'
e'	✕	✕

(b)

FIGURE 6.40 (*continued*)

Now when we attempt to add OP p_4, originating at station 4 and routed on fiber c (the shortest path), two things happen. First, because station 4 is an elementary station operating on a single waveband, it can be the source of only one path, and thus paths p_3 and p_4 must coalesce to a single path originating at station 4. Second, examining the settings of nodes C and D, as shown in Figure 6.40(d), we find that

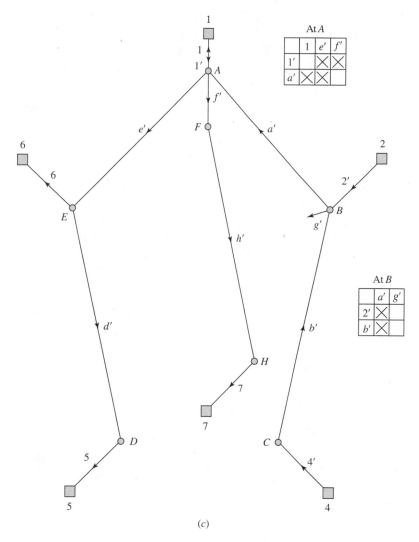

At A

	1	e'	f'
1'		✕	✕
a'	✕	✕	

At B

	a'	g'
2'	✕	
b'	✕	

(c)

FIGURE 6.40   (*continued*)

the complete set of coalesced OPs no longer forms a tree: There are two parallel paths from source 4 to destination 5, violating the DSC condition.[45] Therefore, the new OP cannot be routed on fiber c. The reason for the DSC violation is that the *intended* destination for the new OP has already been included in p_3 as a *fortuitous* destination. As a result, there is no need to add another OP to create a path from station 4 to

---

[45] This type of difficulty was first brought out in the example of Figure 3.22.

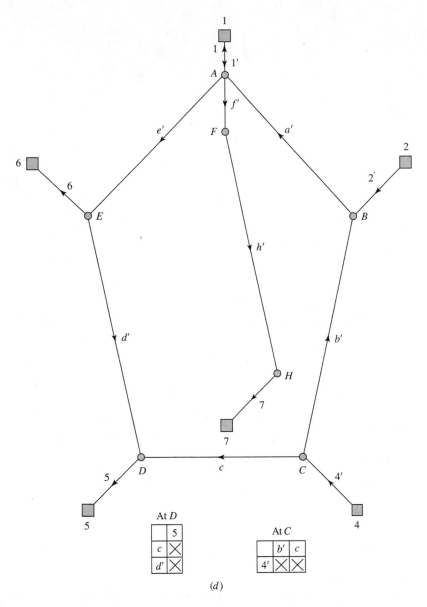

FIGURE 6.40 *(continued)*

station 5. Because the labeling of a destination as intended or fortuitous is arbitrary, we simply redesignate destination 5 as *intended*, so that p_3 in Equation 6.44 becomes an intentionally multicast OP: $p_{34} = \langle 4, \{1, 5, \underline{6}\} \rangle$—which replaces the two point-to-point OPs $p_3 = \langle 4, 1 \rangle$ and $p_4 = \langle 4, 5 \rangle$.

In general, to ensure that all optical paths on the same waveband satisfy the DSC conditions, *the graph of all coalesced optical paths within one waveband (including intranodal paths) must form a set of directed trees.* (The trees need not be disjoint.) That is, there can be no directed cycles or parallel paths. The graph of the coalesced OPs defines a transformation from the set of original OPs $\langle s_i, D_i \rangle$ to their expanded counterparts $\langle s_i, \mathcal{D}_i \rangle$, where $D_i \subseteq \mathcal{D}_i$. In $\langle s_i, \mathcal{D}_i \rangle$, the destination set $\mathcal{D}_i$ consists of all destinations "downstream" from s_i in its optical path tree. Note that there are generally fewer OPs in the coalesced set than in the original set because all OPs originating from the same source coalesce to a single OP rooted at that source. For example, in this case the two OPs from source 4 coalesced into one.[46]

Because all routing discussions up to this point concerned a single waveband, the waveband assignment problem was absent. Extending these ideas to a network with several wavebands, the RWA problem consists of choosing a route and a waveband for each required optical path so that the coalesced OPs assigned to each waveband consist of collections (forests) of directed trees. In making routing and waveband assignments, it is generally desirable to keep the number of fortuitous destinations to a minimum. As we shall see, this tends to minimize the number of distinct wavelengths required in allocating λ-channels to the optical connections supported by the OPs. Static routing rules should be designed to achieve this and other performance objectives independent of the type of optical and logical connectivity that is embedded onto the optical paths.

6.5.2 Optical Connections: λ-Channel Assignment

Having established optical paths, the next issue is channel assignment. This problem is examined in detail for both optical and logical connections in Section 6.5.6. To lay the groundwork for the channel assignment problem, this section focuses on certain basic relations between optical path selection and channel (wavelength) assignments for optical connections. Because the DSC condition must be observed at the optical path level, the only remaining constraint that needs attention now is distinct channel assignment. We examine this issue now, limiting attention once again to connections within a single waveband. (In the multiwaveband case, the channel assignment procedures are executed independently for each waveband.)

Following the notation for optical paths, we specify optical connections (OCs) in the form $c_i = (s_i, D_i)$, where D_i is the intended destination set. The OC has the expanded form $c_i = (s_i, \mathcal{D}_i)$, where $\mathcal{D}_i$ is the expanded destination set of its supporting OP. Thus, all destinations of the OP that are not intended destinations of the carried OC become the optical connection's fortuitous destinations.

---

[46] When two OPs coalesce into a single, expanded OP, the naming of intended and fortuitous destinations becomes ambiguous. We shall adopt the convention that when two OPs p_i and p_j, with intended destination sets D_i and D_j respectively, coalesce into a single OP p_k, the set of intended destinations for p_k is $D_k = D_i \cup D_j$.

Suppose the following optical connections are to be established in one waveband on the Petersen network:

$$c_1 = (1, \{5, 7\})$$
$$c_2 = (2, 6)$$
$$c_3 = (4, 1)$$
$$c_4 = (4, 5)$$
$$c_5 = (6, 3)$$
$$c_6 = (7, 1)$$

(6.45)

Except for the last two, these can all be carried on the OPs of Equation 6.44. By adding two more paths—$p_5 = \langle 6, 3 \rangle$ and $p_6 = \langle 7, 1 \rangle$—all connections can be accommodated.

A list of the routes used for these OCs appears in Table 6.3. Each OC uses one of the five OPs defined earlier, and each table entry indicates the sequence of fibers carrying a signal from a source to one of its destinations (including the access fibers). Correspondence between OCs and OPs is determined by their sources. Thus, both c_3 and c_4 are carried on p_{34}. There is one entry in each row for each intended destination and one entry (underlined) for each fortuitous destination. The fortuitous destinations are "inherited" from the destination set of the OP carrying the OC. (The signal power on each OC fans out to all the destinations of its supporting OP, and the destinations it reaches unintentionally become its fortuitous destinations.)

With the inclusion of the fortuitous destinations, the OCs of Equation 6.45 expand to

$$c_1 = (1, \{5, 7, \underline{6}\})_1$$
$$c_2 = (2, \{6, \underline{1}, \underline{5}\})_2$$
$$c_3 = (4, \{1, \underline{5}, \underline{6}\})_3$$
$$c_4 = (4, \{5, \underline{1}, \underline{6}\})_4$$
$$c_5 = (6, 3)_2$$
$$c_6 = (7, 1)_1$$

(6.46)

TABLE 6.3   Routing Table

Connection	Source	Destination						
		1	2	3	4	5	6	7
c_1	1	—	—	—	—	$1'e'd'5$	$\underline{1'e'6}$	$1'f'h'7$
c_2	2	$\underline{2'a'1}$	—	—	—	$\underline{2'a'e'd'5}$	$2'a'e'6$	—
c_3	4	$4'b'a'1$	—	—	—	$\underline{4'b'a'e'd'5}$	$\underline{4'b'a'e'6}$	—
c_4	4	$\underline{4'b'a'1}$	—	—	—	$4'b'a'e'd'5$	$\underline{4'b'a'e'6}$	—
c_5	6	—	—	$6'ea3$	—	—	—	—
c_6	7	$7'hf1$	—	—	—	—	—	—

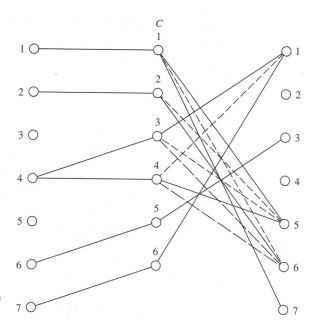

FIGURE 6.41 Optical connection
hypergraph.

A useful way of visualizing these connections is as a directed optical connection hypergraph (OCH), whose tripartite representation is shown in Figure 6.41. In the OCH, each hyperedge represents an optical connection, and the fortuitous destinations are indicated by dashed lines. (Sources are listed on the left, destinations on the right, and connection labels are in the middle.) Because our sources and destinations are assumed to be contained in elementary stations in this example, all OCs terminating at the same destination station (fortuitous or not) are carried on the same access fiber and may therefore interfere with each other. (A station may contain several optical receivers, and thus it may terminate more than one OC.) Because more destinations tend to produce more potential interference, it is important to keep the number of fortuitous destinations small. To do so requires intelligent routing decisions at the optical path level.

Note that the list of optical connections (or, equivalently, the OCH) defines completely the optical connectivity of the network *within a given waveband* while suppressing the details of the the network's physical topology and the specific routes taken by the connections. Thus, in moving up from the optical path layer to the optical connection layer, the details of the former are left behind.

Once the expanded destination sets for all prescribed OCs are determined, these contain the information necessary to determine λ-channel assignments that satisfy the DCA condition. A systematic procedure for making these assignments is given in Section 6.5.6.1. As we shall see, the connections in the example of Equation 6.46 can be realized using four distinct wavelengths, with a possible λ-channel assignment indicated by the subscripts on the connections.

6.5.3 Significance of Nonblocking Access Stations in LLNs

We have seen that the feasible optical paths in an LLN, and the feasible optical connections and channel assignments, are constrained by the access links as well as the internodal network topology, just as they were in WRNs. This introduces an added and sometimes unnecessary level of complexity into the network model. For example, OP coalescing, fortuitous destinations, and potential interference of OCs all depend on how the stations access the nodes. It was for this reason that a distinction had to be made between general and elementary NASs.

To understand the significance of a nonblocking station, let us return to the question of OP routing on the Petersen network operating on a single waveband. Recall that we had attempted to use shortest path routing for all OPs in the list of Equation 6.43, but were unable to route p_4 via the shortest path without violating the DSC constraint. Now, suppose we replace elementary station 4 by a nonblocking station resolved into the three elementary stations C_1, C_2, and C_3, as shown in Figure 6.39. This allows us to split the single source at station 4 into two separate sources, say C_1 and C_2. Using these for the two paths originating at station 4, we now obtain the following OPs:

$$
\begin{aligned}
p_1 &= \langle 1, \{5, 7, \underline{6}\}\rangle \\
p_2 &= \langle 2, \{6, \underline{1}, \underline{5}\}\rangle \\
p_3 &= \langle C_1, \{1, \underline{5}, \underline{6}\}\rangle \\
p_4 &= \langle C_2, 5\rangle
\end{aligned}
\tag{6.47}
$$

where p_4 is now shortest path routed on fiber c. The change in routing is possible because the two OPs that originated at source 4 are no longer superimposed on the same access fiber, so they do not coalesce at the source.[47] This is a simple illustration of the fact that nonblocking stations increase routing options by eliminating the inseparability constraint on the access fibers.

When analyzing a large network, it is often convenient to assume that all traffic sources and destinations are contained in nonblocking access stations, with one station at each node. (This is true for WRNs as well as LLNs.) In this way, a "stripped down" network model can be used that consists only of the ONNs and internodal links. Because there is a one-to-one correspondence in this case between nodes and stations, all optical paths and optical connections can be identified in terms of source and destination nodes rather than stations. In making this identification, the assumption is that in extending each internodal path backward to a source and forward to a destination, paths on the same waveband are always routed on different access fibers. Consequently, using one nonblocking station per network node,

- Optical paths on the same waveband coalesce *only* if they share a common internodal fiber

---

[47] They still coalesce at destination station 5 if it is an elementary station. However, this does not violate the DSC constraint. Why?

- Optical connections are potentially interfering only if they share a common internodal fiber

As we shall see in subsequent examples, the use of nonblocking stations can often lead to significant improvement in network performance.

6.5.4 Local Access to LLNs

As in traditional networks, good designs for optical networks are often based on hierarchical principles. We suggested this first in Section 5.1, in which a star network was used as a backbone for a larger network, and clusters of end systems accessed the backbone nodes via concentrating networks, which will henceforth be called local access subnets (LASs). The same hierarchical principle applies to any wide area LLN. The backbone might consist of a network with general mesh topology, and the LASs would be in the form of trees, as in Figure 5.1.

An example of three LASs concentrating traffic onto nodes A and C in the Petersen network is shown in Figure 6.42. Each LAS is assumed to connect to a "gateway" network node via a single-fiber-pair access link. Of particular interest here is the purely optical version of the LAS—see Figure 5.1(c), in which the access subnet consists of two parallel directed trees. Traffic from the stations is routed upstream to the gateway on one tree, and traffic from the gateway is routed downstream to the stations on the other tree.

In an LLN, the nodes within the LAS might be either fixed optical splitters and combiners or controllable LDCs. The net effect of the LAS is to concentrate the traffic from all attached stations onto the link accessing the gateway. We denote each LAS using a subscripted node label: A_1 for the LAS attached to node A, and C_1 and C_2 for those accessing node C in Figure 6.42. Superscripts are used to identify stations within an LAS. Thus, LAS C_1 contains stations $C_1^{(1)}$, $C_1^{(2)}$, and $C_1^{(3)}$.

Because signals from all stations within the LAS are multiplexed onto a common fiber accessing its gateway node, some sort of control must be exercised to coordinate transmissions within the LAS. For example, the gateway node might be equipped with an optical network manager (ONM) as shown at node C in Figure 6.42, which processes requests for demand-assigned logical connections from stations within the LASs accessing its node. This might include managing admission control, assigning transmission channels, providing synchronization, and executing various other functions required for efficient utilization of the optical bandwidth.

To illustrate the operation of the ONM, suppose an optical path $\langle C_1, A_1 \rangle$ is set up to carry LCs from stations in LAS C_1 to those in LAS A_1. (Because all stations in the LAS are attached to the same access fiber, the complete set of stations constitutes the source of the optical path.) If the waveband supporting the path contains several λ-channels, fixed frame TDM/T-WDMA might be used for multiplexing the LCs onto the optical path, where each station is assigned the number of channel–slots needed for its traffic. Node C then acts like a directed star coupler, broadcasting all traffic

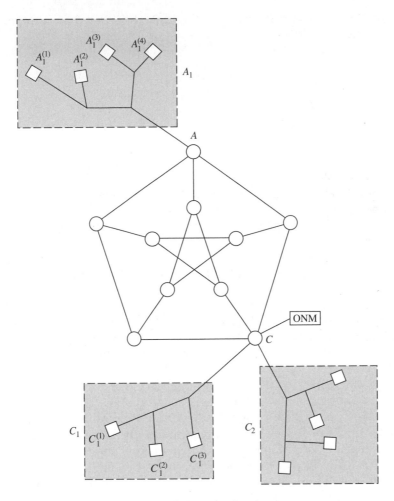

FIGURE 6.42 Local access subnets on the Petersen network.

from C_1 to all stations in A_1.[48] Because stations do not see their own transmissions, a separate bidirectional channel might be set aside for signaling and synchronization purposes. In this case the ONM would receive connection requests from the stations on the upstream signaling channel and would monitor the transmissions from all stations to verify synchronization. It would broadcast commands to all stations on the downstream channel, which would include channel–slot assignments as well as

---

[48] If the LDC at the gateway node is set to combine all signals from C_1 and C_2, then the transmitting set for the directed star includes both LASs, and all stations in both subnets constitute the source of the optical path.

synchronization signals. Other optical paths on other wavebands would allow C_1 to communicate with other gateway nodes.

Provided that the necessary coordination is exercised by the ONM, all LASs accessing a gateway are seen by the network as one elementary access station. As we shall see in Section 6.5.8, the equivalence between an LAS and an elementary NAS is especially useful in designing and controlling more complex hierarchical networks.

6.5.5   Routing and Waveband Assignment on the Petersen Network

In this section we evaluate and compare several static RWA rules in some more elaborate contexts, continuing with the Petersen network as an illustrative example.

6.5.5.1   Single Waveband

Suppose a static routing rule is to be defined on the Petersen network when the available spectrum contains a single waveband. We continue with the assumption that all internodal links are comprised of single fiber pairs, and the stations are elementary NASs. A simple rule accommodating full connectivity among stations attached to all nodes is the following: Route all optical connections on any spanning tree—say, $T = \{a, e, f, d, k, b, g, i, h\}$—shown in heavy lines in Figure 6.38. Although the tree has been specified, the routing paths have not. Two possible approaches for routing the optical connections are

1. Rooted routing using an embedded broadcast star [Kovacevic+92]

2. Shortest-path-on-tree routing

Rooted Routing   In the rooted routing approach, the optical paths on the tree are configured as an embedded broadcast star network with a root at node A in Figure 6.38. The LDC at node A is set to emulate a star coupler joining the links a, e, f, and 1. The other LDCs are set to route signals from all attached stations to node A and back. In this way a broadcast optical path of the form $\langle s_i, D \rangle$ exists from any source station s_i to the destination set D, containing all stations including s_i. We shall refer to this setting of the LDC at node A as a *reflecting star*. (A *nonreflecting star* is described in Section 6.5.5.2.)

Once the routes for the OPs are established by the LDCs, their internodal link settings remain fixed, with optical and logical connections set up through the actions of the stations only (transceiver tuning and multiplexing/multiple access).[49] The stations then see the network as a static broadcast star with an available optical spectrum equal to the width of the waveband carrying the paths. Because a waveband can be channelized in various ways, all of the techniques discussed in Chapter 5 for shared-channel operation in a broadcast network apply to this case. Either dedicated

---

[49] Changes in LDC settings for the access links may be required to disconnect stations or add new ones.

or demand-assigned LCs can be used, and capacity can be allocated according to the requirements of each connection, using either fixed multiplexing/multiple-access schemes or dynamic methods (i.e., packet switching in the optical layer).

To illustrate, suppose that the following LCs are to be established in the Petersen network: [1, {5, 7}], [2, 6], [4, 1], [4, 5], [6, 3], and [7, 1]. Assuming that WDM/WDMA is used to carry these connections, with a full λ-channel used to carry each LC, the list of optical connections in Equation 6.45 supports the required LCs. For example, LC [1, {5, 7}] is carried by OC (1, {5, 7, 1, 2, 3, 4, 6}), which is in turn supported by the OP, $\langle 1, \{5, 7, \underline{1, 2, 3, 4, 6}\} \rangle$. Because all λ-channels must be distinct in the case of the embedded star, this would require six wavelengths, with each signal fanning out to all attached stations.[50]

This approach has the virtue of simplicity, but is inefficient in its usage of the fibers and the optical spectrum: All optical connections must be routed to node A (the root node) and back, some fibers are not used at all, and there is no reuse of the optical spectrum.

Shortest-Path-on-Tree Routing In the second approach, routing is still confined to T, but now each connection is routed on the shortest path on the tree, so that the LDC settings depend on the active optical connections. (This stretches our definition of static routing a bit because optical paths are established based on the desired optical connections.)

The development of Section 6.5.2 showed how the six optical connections of Equation 6.45 could be carried on five optical paths while satisfying the DSC condition. The paths used are

$$p_1 = \langle 1, \{5, 7, \underline{6}\} \rangle$$
$$p_2 = \langle 2, \{6, \underline{1}, \underline{5}\} \rangle$$
$$p_{34} = \langle 4, \{1, 5, \underline{6}\} \rangle \qquad (6.48)$$
$$p_5 = \langle 6, 3 \rangle$$
$$p_6 = \langle 7, 1 \rangle$$

where p_{34} is the coalesced combination of $\langle 4, 1 \rangle$ and $\langle 4, 5 \rangle$. All these OPs are routed on the shortest path on T so that they conform to the shortest-path-on-tree routing rules. In fact, all except p_{34} are shortest path in the *network* (not just on the tree). (As explained in Section 6.5.1, the path $\langle 4, 5 \rangle$ cannot be routed shortest path if elementary stations are used.)

A λ-channel assignment for the OCs using (and reusing) four wavelengths was given in Equation 6.46. This gives a spectrum reuse factor of 1.5, compared with no reuse using rooted routing.

Unfortunately, any routing scheme based on an embedded spanning tree runs out of wavelengths rapidly as the number of connections increases. (Full connectivity among all ten nodes in the Petersen network using rooted routing requires 90 wavelengths if

---

[50] This requires arrayed OTs and ORs because some stations are the source or destination of more than one optical connection. Using TDM/TDMA, only one optical transceiver would be required in each station, and a single λ-channel would be shared by all users.

one λ-channel is used for each connection.) Thus, to accommodate larger numbers of connections within a limited optical spectrum, more efficient use must be made of the fibers and the spectrum. We propose several different approaches now, illustrating and comparing them using the Petersen network. Of course, this network is a special case because of its density and regularity. However, many of the conclusions we draw from this simple example can be extrapolated, at least qualitatively, to larger networks.

6.5.5.2 Multiple Wavebands and Fiber Pairs

The problem we pose now is to determine static routing and waveband assignments in the Petersen network to support full connectivity in cases in which several wavebands are available or in which each internodal link contains more than one fiber pair. In each case all routing is shortest path. According to these routing rules, the internodal LDC settings remain fixed. However, usage of the optical paths may vary dynamically depending on station activity.

We make the following four assumptions:

1. Each LC is point to point and uses the full capacity of a λ-channel.

2. A single access station is attached to each network node.

3. The network operates on W wavebands, with C λ-channels per waveband.

4. Each internodal link contains F fiber pairs.

The second assumption allows some simplification of notation; we use the same label for a station and the node it accesses.

Networks using different values of W and F are compared. The routing rules to be explored are all based on trees, so they are generalizations of the spanning tree treated earlier. In this case we use multiple nonspanning trees to exploit network resources more efficiently. Each tree, T_i, is a star centered at node i and consisting of three links as follows (refer to Figure 6.38):

$$
\begin{aligned}
T_A &= \{a, f, e\} \\
T_B &= \{b, g, a\} \\
T_C &= \{c, l, b\} \\
T_D &= \{d, m, c\} \\
T_E &= \{e, d, k\} \\
T_F &= \{f, h, i\} \\
T_G &= \{g, n, j\} \\
T_H &= \{h, l, p\} \\
T_I &= \{i, n, m\} \\
T_J &= \{j, p, k\}
\end{aligned}
\tag{6.49}
$$

Although these are not spanning trees, their union "covers" the network in the sense that each node can reach every other node using paths confined to one of the trees to which it belongs. Furthermore, routing on these trees is necessarily shortest path.

Four cases are considered:

1. $W = 3$, $F = 1$: Multicast optical paths
2. $W = 5$, $F = 1$: Point-to-point optical paths
3. $W = 9$, $F = 1$: A Latin router
4. $W = 1$, $F = 2$: Multicast optical paths

Case 1: $W = 3$, $F = 1$; Multicast Optical Paths   In this case each internodal link consists of a single bidirectional fiber pair, and we assume that all stations are non-blocking. Because the trees are not fiber disjoint, we cannot route connections independently on each tree. However, if each tree is assigned its own waveband, the trees can be made "waveband disjoint" (i.e., if two trees share a fiber, they are assigned different wavebands so that they lie on different "copies" of the network). It turns out that the minimum number of wavebands needed to accomplish this "tree coloring" is $W = 3$. A possible assignment is T_A, T_G, and T_H on waveband 1; T_B, T_D, T_F, and T_J on 2; and T_C, T_E, and T_I on waveband 3.

We now configure the *exterior* nodes of each tree as an MPS, as described in Section 3.4.2. As shown in Figure 6.43(a) for T_A, a broadcast star joining nodes B, E,

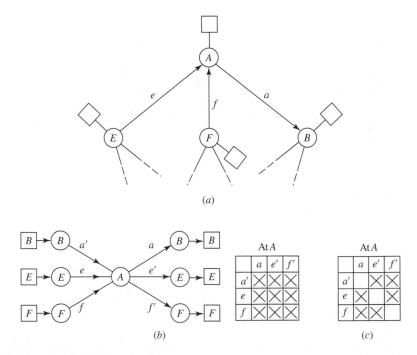

FIGURE 6.43 Embedded star on tree T_A.

and F is embedded on the tree by setting the LDC at the central node to emulate a star coupler. The emulation can be in the form of either a reflecting or a nonreflecting star. In the former case, illustrated in the intranodal connection matrix in Figure 6.43(b), the LDC is set to combine all signals arriving at node A on fibers a', f, and e, and then "reflect" them back along all outbound fibers. In the nonreflecting star, illustrated in the intranodal connection matrix in Figure 6.43(c), the set of signals on an outbound fiber includes all signals *except* the signal on the corresponding input fiber; that is, there are no loopback connections. As we shall see, network performance changes significantly depending on which option is used.

Note that all OPs in Figure 6.43(b) are two-hop paths (excluding the access links), and the LDC settings apply to waveband 1 only. For reasons to be explained later, station A attached to the central node has been excluded from the broadcast star. The resultant OPs on T_A are then

$$p_1 = \langle B, \{E, F, \underline{B}\}\rangle$$
$$p_2 = \langle E, \{B, F, \underline{E}\}\rangle \qquad (6.50)$$
$$p_3 = \langle F, \{B, E, \underline{F}\}\rangle$$

for the reflecting star, and

$$p_1 = \langle B, \{E, F\}\rangle$$
$$p_2 = \langle E, \{B, F\}\rangle \qquad (6.51)$$
$$p_3 = \langle F, \{B, E\}\rangle$$

for the nonreflecting star.

A number of options are possible for channel assignment, depending on station equipment and LDC settings. These are explored in detail in Section 6.5.6. For now, let us assume that each node is configured as a nonreflecting star. Under our assumptions, a full point-to-point OC must be dedicated to each LC. Then, to provide full logical connectivity among the exterior nodes, the following optical connections are established on tree T_A:

$$c_1 = (B, \{E, \underline{F}\})_1$$
$$c_2 = (E, \{B, \underline{F}\})_1$$
$$c_3 = (B, \{F, \underline{E}\})_2$$
$$c_4 = (F, \{B, \underline{E}\})_2 \qquad (6.52)$$
$$c_5 = (E, \{F, \underline{B}\})_3$$
$$c_6 = (F, \{E, \underline{B}\})_3$$

Because these are all to be used as point-to-point connections even though they each have two destinations, only one destination is shown as *intended*. (Only the three connections—c_1, c_2, and c_4—would have been required if each optical connection was shared between two LCs.) The subscripts on the connections indicate λ-channel (wavelength) assignments obeying DCA, found using the procedures of Section 6.5.6.1. This requires $C = 3$ λ-channels to support the six connections. Thus, there is a twofold spectrum reuse within the tree.

In contrast to the two-hop exterior node paths, the paths from the central node, A, to the other nodes on the tree are all one-hop paths. Although they could have been included in the embedded star, it is more efficient to route them outside the tree. This can be done without using any additional spectrum. Note that the waveband assignments used for all trees only allocate two wavebands to each fiber, leaving the third free. We use this for the single-hop connections. For example, referring to Figure 6.38 and Equation 6.49, fibers a and f both have waveband 3 free because T_A operates on waveband 1, and T_B and T_F operate on waveband 2. Similarly, fiber e has waveband 2 free. The unassigned wavebands can be used to route the one-hop connections on these fibers.

Using the RWA rules just described, a possible waveband assignment for this case is constructed as shown in Table 6.4. (Note that the routing assignments are symmetric.) Using Table 6.4 and the list of trees in Equation 6.49, we can deduce how optical connections are distributed on each path and waveband. For example, focusing on node A and continuing with the assumption of a nonreflecting star at each node, we find from row A in Table 6.4 that the OPs originating at station A are

$$
\begin{aligned}
p_{CG} &= \langle A, \{C, G\}\rangle_2 \\
p_{HI} &= \langle A, \{H, I\}\rangle_2 \\
p_{E} &= \langle A, E\rangle_2 \\
p_{DJ} &= \langle A, \{D, J\}\rangle_3 \\
p_{B} &= \langle A, B\rangle_3 \\
p_{F} &= \langle A, F\rangle_3
\end{aligned}
\tag{6.53}
$$

TABLE 6.4 Waveband Routing in Petersen Graph: $W = 3$, $F = 1$

Source	Destination									
	A	**B**	**C**	**D**	**E**	**F**	**G**	**H**	**I**	**J**
A	—	3	2	3	2	3	2	2	2	3
B	3	—	1	3	1	1	3	3	1	1
C	2	1	—	1	2	1	2	2	2	1
D	3	3	1	—	1	3	1	1	1	3
E	2	1	2	1	—	1	2	2	2	1
F	3	1	1	3	1	—	3	3	1	1
G	2	3	2	1	2	3	—	2	2	3
H	2	3	2	1	2	3	2	—	2	3
I	2	1	2	1	2	1	2	2	—	1
J	3	1	1	3	1	1	3	3	1	—

where a subscript $\langle * \rangle_j$ indicates that the OP is carried on waveband j. Although all of these paths originate from the same NAS, the paths on the same waveband do not coalesce because they use disjoint internodal fiber paths, and the source station is non-blocking. For similar reasons, paths assigned to the same waveband and converging on the same destination do not coalesce.

There are nine point-to-point optical connections originating at station A:

$$
\begin{aligned}
c_C &= (A, \{C, \underline{G}\}) \\
c_G &= (A, \{G, \underline{C}\}) \\
c_H &= (A, \{H, \underline{I}\}) \\
c_I &= (A, \{I, \underline{H}\}) \\
c_E &= (A, E) \\
c_D &= (A, \{D, \underline{J}\}) \\
c_J &= (A, \{J, \underline{D}\}) \\
c_B &= (A, B) \\
c_F &= (A, F)
\end{aligned}
\tag{6.54}
$$

The OP carrying each connection is determined by matching the path subscript in Equation 6.53 and the connection subscript in Equation 6.54. Thus, for example, c_C and c_G are both carried by p_{CG}. Note that the two-hop connections are on multicast OPs, whereas the one-hop connections are on point-to-point OPs.

All nine OCs originating from A are supported by six OPs, divided equally between two wavebands. We shall see in Section 6.5.6.1 that all 90 connections in the network can be supported using three λ-channels per waveband. (For example, all two-hop connections on T_A can be supported on three channels on waveband 1, as indicated in Equation 6.52.) Each single-hop OP has the capacity of a complete waveband available to it (three λ-channels), but only supports one connection. Thus, the capacity of the one-hop LCs can be tripled by assigning all available channels to them without requiring any increase in the optical spectrum.

Case 2: $W = 5$, $F = 1$; Point-to-Point Optical Paths   In the previous example, the use of both multicast and point-to-point optical paths resulted in a nonuniform capacity available for LCs. We change that situation now by making all OPs point to point, thus eliminating all fortuitous destinations. Each internodal link again contains a single fiber pair, and we initially use nonblocking access stations.

It turns out that it is possible to create point-to-point optical paths if three wavebands are allocated to the six two-hop paths on each tree, with a total waveband complement of $W = 5$ sufficient for the network. (The tree no longer exists as an entity carried on a single waveband, having been replaced by point-to-point paths.) An example of a suitable RWA for two overlapping trees, T_A and T_B, is shown in Figure 6.44.

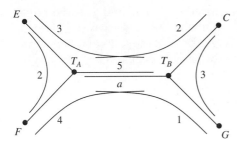

FIGURE 6.44 Waveband assignments: $W = 5$.

TABLE 6.5 Waveband Routing in Petersen Graph: $W = 5$, $F = 1$

					Destination					
Source	A	B	C	D	E	F	G	H	I	J
A	—	5	2	1	5	5	1	3	1	4
B	5	—	1	5	3	4	4	4	5	2
C	2	1	—	2	3	4	3	3	4	5
D	1	5	2	—	4	3	1	1	5	5
E	5	3	3	4	—	2	4	5	2	3
F	5	4	4	3	2	—	2	5	5	1
G	1	4	3	1	4	2	—	3	3	5
H	3	4	3	1	5	5	3	—	4	4
I	1	5	4	5	2	5	3	4	—	4
J	4	2	5	5	3	1	5	4	4	—

The wavebands are assigned symmetrically. For example, optical connections (E, B) and (B, E) use the same waveband, and all waveband assignments on each fiber are distinct. For example, on fiber a, wavebands 3 and 4 support two-hop connections on T_A; wavebands 1 and 2 support two-hop connections on T_B; and waveband 5 supports the single-hop connections (A, B) and (B, A). A similar pattern is followed throughout the network, with the complete waveband assignment shown in Table 6.5.

It is easily verified from Table 6.5 and Figure 6.38 that each fiber carries five distinct wavebands. Using nonblocking stations (each containing three elementary stations), nine separate OPs can be set up from each source station to all others, with the destination station associated uniquely with an elementary source station–waveband combination. For example, station A contains elementary stations A_1, A_2, and A_3, which can be used for paths to B, E, and F respectively, all using waveband 5. Thus, to reach station E, for example, an optical connection is made from A_2 using a λ-channel on waveband 5. Because its optical path is point to point, the optical connection has no fortuitous destinations. Similar arrangements must be made at destination stations. Thus, for example, station B is the destination for paths on waveband 4 from stations

F, G, and H. To avoid violations of the DCA constraint, these paths should be routed to different elementary stations: say, B_1, B_2, and B_3 respectively. In this way, station B can select a signal from any other station using a unique elementary station–waveband combination. Because all optical connections are either fiber or waveband disjoint, one λ-channel per waveband is sufficient to support all connections without violating the DCA condition.

With a single λ-channel per waveband, the LLN is equivalent to a WRN because all connections are point to point (there is no signal dividing or combining), and a waveband is equivalent to a wavelength. All connections are on shortest paths, and the average optical path length is $\bar{H} = 5/3$. Using this value in the bound, W_{Netcap}, of Equation 6.7 we find that $W = 5$ is the minimum possible number of wavelengths for full connectivity in this network. The fact that this assignment achieves the bound indicates that all links are fully loaded.

The situation becomes more interesting if the nonblocking stations are replaced by elementary stations. Now all OPs originating at a common station on a common waveband coalesce to a single OP. For example, the 24 point-to-point paths on waveband 5 coalesce to ten (mostly) multicast paths:

$$
\begin{aligned}
p_A &= \langle A, \{B, E, F\}\rangle \\
p_B &= \langle B, \{A, D, I\}\rangle \\
p_C &= \langle C, J\rangle \\
p_D &= \langle D, \{B, I, J\}\rangle \\
p_E &= \langle E, \{A, H\}\rangle \\
p_F &= \langle F, \{A, H, I\}\rangle \\
p_G &= \langle G, J\rangle \\
p_H &= \langle H, \{E, F\}\rangle \\
p_I &= \langle I, \{B, D, F\}\rangle \\
p_J &= \langle J, \{C, D, G\}\rangle
\end{aligned}
\tag{6.55}
$$

The optical connections on each multicast OP now inherit fortuitous destinations from the OP. For example, p_E supports optical connections $(E, \{A, \underline{H}\})$ and $(E, \{H, \underline{A}\})$. The fortuitous destinations produce limitations on the feasible λ-channel assignments, with the result that three wavelengths instead of one are now required to satisfy the DCA constraints (see Section 6.5.6.1).

Case 3: $W = 9$, $F = 1$; A Latin Router In the last example, nonblocking access stations were needed to operate the network with only five wavebands and one λ-channel per waveband because each station reused at least some wavebands to support all LCs to the other stations. This reuse required extra access fiber pairs to satisfy the DCA condition. However, by using more wavebands it is possible to achieve full connectivity using only *elementary* access stations while maintaining point-to-point OPs. The minimum number of wavebands required for creating full connectivity using point-to-point OPs is nine, because each station needs a connection to each other station on a distinct waveband. A feasible routing table using nine wavebands is shown in

TABLE 6.6 Waveband Routing in Petersen Graph: $W = 9$, $F = 1$

Source	Destination									
	A	**B**	**C**	**D**	**E**	**F**	**G**	**H**	**I**	**J**
A	—	8	4	2	5	9	7	6	1	3
B	8	—	7	6	1	5	4	9	3	2
C	4	7	—	9	3	8	1	5	2	6
D	2	6	9	—	7	3	8	1	5	4
E	5	1	3	7	—	4	6	2	8	9
F	9	5	8	3	4	—	2	7	6	1
G	7	4	1	8	6	2	—	3	9	5
H	6	9	5	1	2	7	3	—	4	8
I	1	3	2	5	8	6	9	4	—	7
J	3	2	6	4	9	1	5	8	7	—

Table 6.6.[51] The table entries are in the form of a Latin square, so the resultant connections constitute a Latin router (see Section 2.3.1.2).

Again, this example is equivalent to a WRN. Applying the network capacity bound of Equation 6.7 to this case, we obtain the tightest version by including the access links and stations, because these are the bottlenecks. We then have $L = 25$ and $\sum^H = 330$, giving $W_{\text{Netcap}} = 6.6$. The difference between W_{Netcap} and the actual number of wavelengths used reflects the fact that the internodal links are not saturated.

By applying the bound of Equation 6.10 to a cut consisting of any access link, we verify the obvious requirement of nine wavelengths for full connectivity.

Table 6.6 is symmetric with each row or column containing a permutation of the nine wavebands. Because there is no repetition, routing can be accomplished by waveband-selective LDCs, with all optical signals to and from each station superimposed on a single access fiber pair. Because each signal on a fiber uses a different waveband, one λ-channel per waveband is sufficient to support all connections.

By checking the fibers used by each path (under shortest path routing) we see that all OPs carried on a given fiber use distinct wavebands, thus ensuring that each path is point to point and can be routed independently through the nodes as required.

Case 4: $W = 1$, $F = 2$; Multicast Paths   The use of routing trees can be extended to the case in which all channels are grouped onto a single waveband, provided that we double the number of internodal fibers in the network by running two fibers in each

---

[51] This assignment was found by first assigning wavebands to the one-hop connections using an edge coloring of the graph, and then filling in the two-hop connections to observe the DCA condition (see Appendix A).

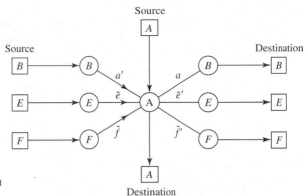

FIGURE 6.45 Realization of a routing tree.

direction in every link. This is not a serious drawback because optical cables typically carry many fibers. Essentially we are trading the waveband routing techniques in the previous cases for space–division routing. Each link label, x, in Figure 6.38 now represents four fibers, denoted x, x', $\tilde{x}$, and $\tilde{x}'$.[52] The network now has 30 fiber pairs, which will be grouped into ten trees containing three links each, as follows:

$$T_A = \{a, \tilde{f}, \tilde{e}\}$$
$$T_B = \{b, \tilde{g}, \tilde{a}\}$$
$$T_C = \{c, l, \tilde{b}\}$$
$$T_D = \{d, m, \tilde{c}\}$$
$$T_E = \{e, \tilde{d}, k\}$$
$$T_F = \{f, \tilde{h}, \tilde{i}\}$$
$$T_G = \{g, n, \tilde{j}\}$$
$$T_H = \{h, \tilde{l}, p\}$$
$$T_I = \{i, \tilde{n}, \tilde{m}\}$$
$$T_J = \{j, \tilde{p}, \tilde{k}\}$$

(6.56)

Note that these are essentially the same trees as in Equation 6.49, except that they are now fiber disjoint. This means that they can each be operated as independent MPSs using an embedded broadcast star to define each MPS. It is interesting to note that doubling the number of fibers is sufficient to create *fiber*-disjoint trees, whereas the realization of waveband-disjoint trees required *tripling* the number of wavebands. This is a reflection of the fact, first noted in Section 3.3.1.2, that a network with multiple fiber pairs per link offers more routing flexibility than one with multiple wavelengths.

Routing on the fiber-disjoint trees is illustrated on the tree T_A in Figure 6.45. An embedded star is located at node A. (This time the central node is included in the star

---

[52] Because each bidirectional link is now replaced by two parallel bidirectional links, the graph of the network becomes a multigraph, with two parallel edges representing each link. The degree of each node is therefore $\Delta = 6$, which means that each LDC must have six internodal input/output ports (but it need not be waveband selective), and a nonblocking access station must have six access fiber pairs.

because there is no advantage in routing the one-hop paths elsewhere.) If a nonreflecting star is used with nonblocking access stations and with one λ-channel dedicated to each LC, six distinct wavelengths are required on each star. These wavelengths can be reused on each tree, for a tenfold reuse of the spectrum.

Of the LCs sharing each star, the six two-hop connections have only one routing choice. However, the six one-hop connections each belong to two stars, and thus there are some choices. Each one-hop connection might be routed on the tree based at its source node. Another possibility is to route on the tree based at the destination node, and a third possibility would be to route on parallel optical connections using both trees.

Each tree in this configuration of the Petersen network acts as a shared medium, in which capacity can be shared fully among all stations on the tree. This corresponds to a hypernet, with ten hyperedges corresponding to the ten trees (see Sections 3.4.3 and 7.3. An LCH representing the Petersen hypernet appears in Figure 6.46. Note that this is an *undirected* hypergraph, because the transmitting (source) and receiving (destination) sets of each hyperedge are identical. Its diameter is 1 because each station can reach all others via a single logical hop, using one of the hyperedges to which it belongs.

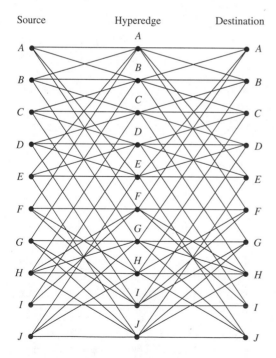

FIGURE 6.46 Logical connection hypergraph for Petersen hypernet.

6.5.6 Channel Assignment

In an LLN, channels must be assigned at two levels:

1. Each optical connection must be assigned a λ-channel.
2. Each LC must be assigned a transmission channel.[53]

The objective of a good channel assignment procedure is to satisfy traffic requirements while making efficient use of the available optical bandwidth. We now give
a systematic approach to channel assignment that achieves that objective in the case
when optical paths are in place based on *static* RWA rules. It is important to recognize at the outset that channel assignments in an LLN are made *independently* for
each waveband. The discussion that follows applies to channel assignments *within
one waveband*.

6.5.6.1 λ-Channel Assignment

We begin at the λ-channel level, focusing on wavelength assignments for optical connections that are assigned without any channelization at the transmission channel
level (i.e., without dividing a λ-channel into subchannels). This implies that there is
no rapid tuning of transceivers while a connection is active, so that the system is
purely WDM/WDMA.

   To determine the feasible wavelength assignments, we must revisit the DCA condition, which was first discussed in the context of WRNs in Section 3.3.1.2. To this end, a
definition is needed to clarify the notion of interference between optical connections:

> Two optical connections are *potentially interfering* if they are on the same waveband and the
> intersection of their destination sets contains an element that is an intended destination for
> at least one of the connections.[54]

The DCA condition can now be restated as follows:

> All potentially interfering optical connections must be assigned λ-channels on distinct
> wavelengths.

   A few explanations are in order.

---

[53] Depending on how the wavebands and optical connections are channelized, assignment alternatives
may or may not exist at each level. For example, if each waveband contains only one λ-channel, as in a
WRN, there are no λ-channel alternatives. Similarly, if each LC uses the full capacity of a λ-channel, there
is no channelization of optical connections and therefore no transmission channel alternatives.

[54] Note that two connections that are on the same waveband and share a fiber *necessarily* have identical
destination sets and therefore are potentially interfering according to this definition.

1. Two connections do *not* interfere when their only common destinations are fortuitous. (In this case no problems are caused by assigning them the same λ-channel.)

2. Two optical connections destined for the same nonblocking NAS on the same waveband do not interfere if they do not share any internodal links. (The extra access fibers on nonblocking stations eliminate interference.)

3. Two optical connections originating from the same *elementary* station on the same waveband are always potentially interfering. Because they share a common access fiber, they are necessarily supported by the same optical path, which makes their destination sets identical except for the labeling of the intended destinations.

We now present a procedure for assigning λ-channels to a prescribed set of optical connections within a common waveband to minimize the number of required channels while satisfying the DCA constraints. (In a multiwaveband network, the procedure is applied independently on each waveband.) It is based on the construction and vertex coloring of a *connection interference graph* G_{CI}, similar to G_{PI} defined in Section 6.3.3.

Each optical connection on a given waveband is represented by a vertex of G_{CI}, and a pair of vertices is joined by an edge if their connections are potentially interfering. Then, a feasible λ-channel assignment is equivalent to a vertex coloring of G_{CI}.

To illustrate the procedure, we apply it to the optical connections of Equation 6.46, shown graphically in the OCH of Figure 6.41. These represent six connections on a spanning tree in the Petersen network. The graph G_{CI} for these connections is shown in Figure 6.47. Because we have assumed that the access stations are elementary, the existence of an edge between two vertices i and j of G_{CI} is determined by checking whether the connections c_i and c_j have a common destination. If so, and if the destination is not fortuitous for both of them, an edge is placed in G_{CI}. For example, there is an edge joining vertices 1 and 2 in G_{CI} because c_1 and c_2 both have the destination 6, and it is an intended destination for c_2.

This graph is colored easily by inspection using four colors, indicated by the numbers next to the vertices. (This is the channel assignment that appears in Equation 6.46.) Furthermore, it is a minimum coloring because the largest clique in G_{CI} is of size four (see Appendix A).

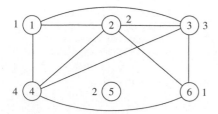

FIGURE 6.47 Connection interference graph.

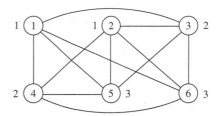

FIGURE 6.48 Connection interference graph for Equation 6.52.

The connection interference graph is a useful tool in comparing different scenarios for operating an LLN because it reveals how different routing configurations (e.g., reflecting versus nonreflecting stars), different station structures (e.g., nonblocking versus elementary), and different optical connection alternatives (point to point versus multicast) affect channel assignments. We now illustrate its application using several of the RWA examples treated in the previous section.

Petersen Network: $W = 3$ In the Petersen network for the case $W = 3$, six two-hop point-to-point optical connections are routed on each tree using a nonreflecting star. Equation 6.52 lists the connections routed on tree T_A using waveband 1. They produce the interference graph of Figure 6.48. Note that G_{CI} can be colored using three colors, leading to the λ-channel assignments indicated as subscripts in Equation 6.52. Because nonblocking stations are used in this example, each tree can be treated in isolation. The same analysis on each tree indicates that $C = 3$ λ-channels per waveband is sufficient for all connections in the network. It is left as an exercise for the reader to show that with *reflecting stars*, six wavelengths are required.

It is interesting to reexamine the channel assignments in the case in which multicast optical connections are used for each pair of destinations on the tree. In this case Equation 6.52 is replaced by

$$c_{13} = (B, \{E, F\})$$
$$c_{25} = (E, \{B, F\}) \tag{6.57}$$
$$c_{46} = (F, \{B, E\})$$

where each optical connection carries two LCs, which now must share one λ-channel. For example, c_{13} carries LCs $[B, E]$ and $[B, F]$, which could share a common λ-channel using TDM. This connection set clearly requires three different wavelengths. Although the same number of wavelengths are used in both the point-to-point and multicast case, the latter makes less efficient use of the optical spectrum because there is no channel reuse. As a result, each LC receives only half as much capacity as in the point-to-point case. On the other hand, an advantage of optical multicast is that only half as many OTs are required for these connections.

Petersen Network: $W = 5$ All optical paths are point to point in this case, provided that the stations are nonblocking. Thus there are no potentially interfering optical connections, and channel assignment is trivial: one λ-channel per waveband is sufficient.

As explained in Section 6.5.5.2, elementary stations can also be used here, but they produce multicast OPs. The required number of λ-channels per waveband then increases, because there are less opportunities for spectrum reuse. In the case of multicast OPs, there are a number of channel assignment options depending on the performance criteria that are most important. We consider two possibilities:

1. Multicast optical connections (most economical)
2. Point-to-point optical connections (highest throughput)

Considering the first option, and focusing on waveband 5, we note that there are 24 optical paths, which coalesce to a set of ten, listed in Equation 6.55. We identify each coalesced OP with one optical connection, where the optical connection is multicast whenever its supporting OP is multicast. For example,

$$c_F = (F, \{A, H, I\}) \tag{6.58}$$

is supported by p_F in Equation 6.55. It is left as an exercise for the reader to show that in this case three wavelengths are sufficient to support all ten optical connections (see Problem 22).

Because we are interested in setting up full point-to-point logical connectivity, each multicast optical connection is required to carry several point-to-point LCs. For example, c_F carries $[F, A]$, $[F, H]$, and $[F, I]$. Because multiplexing of LCs onto an optical connection is a transmission channel issue, it can be separated from the issue of optical connection assignments (see Section 6.5.6.2).

This approach does not offer the full capacity of a λ-channel to each logical channel. If that is required, we must use the option of point-to-point optical connections. For example, p_F now must carry $(F, \{A, \underline{H}, I\})$, $(F, \{H, \underline{A}, I\})$, and $(F, \{I, \underline{A}, I\})$—each assigned a distinct wavelength and each originating at a separate OT. To determine the minimum number of wavelengths required in each waveband in this case, a minimal coloring of G_{CI} for the resultant connections on that waveband must be determined. (One more exercise for the reader!) The complexity of the channel assignment (graph coloring) problem will become apparent to the courageous reader because there are now 24 connections on waveband 5.

Although an optimal λ-channel assignment is more difficult when each multicast optical connection is replaced by a set of point-to-point connections, it is easy to find an upper bound on the required number of wavelengths in this case, together with a suboptimal channel assignment meeting the bound. We note that each threefold multicast connection that previously required one λ-channel now needs three λ-channels on distinct wavelengths, because it is broken down into three point-to-point optical connections sharing the same OP. Because threefold multicast is the worst case in this example, an upper bound on the number of λ-channels on waveband 5 for point-to-point optical connections is $C = 9$ (three times the number of channels used in the multicast OC case). This reasoning can be applied generally whenever comparing multicast optical connections and their point-to-point counterparts.[55]

Summarizing these examples, we see that more throughput is obtained with point-to-point optical connections because λ-channels do not have to be shared. However, multicast connections require fewer OTs and usually use less optical bandwidth.

6.5.6.2 Shared Channels: Transmission Channel Assignment

There are many opportunities in LLNs for sharing λ-channels among several LCs using multiplexing/multiple-access techniques at the transmission channel level. These possibilities exist because of the multipoint nature of the optical paths. (The broadcast star, which was explored thoroughly in Chapter 5, is the simplest and the most effective example of the power of multipoint optical connectivity.)

Channel sharing provides a number of advantages:

- More flexibility in allocating capacity to LCs
- Finer granularity of LCs (see Section 6.5.6.4)
- More efficient use of the optical spectrum
- Transfer of the burden of equipment replication from the optical level to the electronic level

In most cases the discussion of multiplexing/multiple access in Chapter 5 applies directly to channel sharing in LLNs. However, extra complications arise in certain special situations, so it is helpful to treat the following three cases separately:

1. Multicast optical connections
2. Many-to-one optical connections
3. Many-to-many optical connections

Multicast Optical Connections An N-fold multicast OC creates an embedded $1 \times N$ shared-channel broadcast medium, which can be used to support several LCs (either point to point or multicast). The LCs can be multiplexed onto a common λ-channel at the source station using a wide variety of techniques. One possibility is TDM, in which each LC is assigned a transmission channel consisting of one or more time slots in a fixed-frame schedule. (Other methods discussed in Chapter 5 can also be used.) Because multiplexing occurs at the electronic level in the case

---

[55] The worst case can be overly pessimistic. For example, we found that the point-to-point connections of Equation 6.52 required no more wavelengths than the twofold multicast connections of Equation 6.57, both of which were derived from the OPs of Equation 6.50.

of multicast optical connections, there is an N-fold savings of OTs and the optical spectrum. Furthermore, the multiplexed connections can share the capacity of the λ-channel in a way that matches their traffic requirements. There is no free lunch, however! Whenever there is a saving in transmitters and spectrum there is generally an equivalent reduction in aggregate throughput. In this case, the total throughput of all LCs supported by one optical connection cannot exceed the capacity of one λ-channel.

On the receiving side, each receiver demultiplexes and selects the information destined for it. Thus, the optical equipment in the receivers remains the same as for point-to-point optical connections, but it is not fully utilized.

Applying these ideas to the case of the Petersen network with $W = 5$, using elementary stations we note from Equation 6.55 that there are ten optical paths on waveband 5, eight of which are multicast due to the coalescing of paths from common sources. Each of these can support a multicast optical connection, which in turn must carry several LCs. For example, station F is the source of the threefold multicast connection c_F in Equation 6.58, which must carry three point-to-point LCs. On the receiving side, each station must use one receiver for each optical connection destined to it, and extract the desired LCs using TDM in its reception processor. Thus on waveband 5, station A requires three receivers tuned to λ-channels 2, 1, and 3 to receive LCs $[B, A]$, $[E, A]$, and $[F, A]$ respectively (see Problem 22). Following this reasoning for the remainder of the connections, we find that by using optical multicasting, only 48 OTs are required for the whole network, but 90 ORs are needed (as in the point-to-point case).

Many-to-One Optical Connections   The reasoning for many-to-one connections is similar to that for multicast or one-to-many connections. Recall that in discussing λ-channel assignment in Section 6.5.6.1, whenever several optical connections had the same intended destination they had to be assigned distinct λ-channels. This was a consequence of the assumption that each LC required the full capacity of a λ-channel. We now relax that assumption, admitting the possibility of using multiple access (i.e., channel sharing) when several optical connections are destined for the same receiving station. An objective is to save on ORs and optical spectrum.

Continuing with the example of the Petersen network with $W = 5$, let us return to the case of nonblocking stations using point-to-point optical connections. Originally, this required placing nine ORs in each station, one for each LC from another station. Now, let us use a multiple-access method to reduce the number of receivers. Suppose each station is equipped with only one receiver on each waveband it uses. In cases when several optical connections reach a station on the same waveband, any multiple-access method (say, TDMA) can be used to distinguish the connections.[56] For example, Table 6.5 shows that station A receives signals from stations B, E, and F on waveband 5. Using a fixed-frame TDMA system, the LCs $[B, A]$, $[E, A]$, and $[F, A]$ can be assigned time slots according to their traffic requirements, so that a single receiver at A, equipped with demultiplexing electronics, can separate them. The transmitting

---

[56] TDMA requires synchronization of the different transmissions, which may be accomplished by feeding back control signals from each destination station to the sources it sees.

stations must use one OT for each LC, as in the point-to-point case. As a result, a total of 90 OTs and 48 ORs are required in the network when multiple access is used. (Not all wavebands are used at each station.)

Many-to-Many Optical Connections   In the many-to-many case, we must combine multiplexing with multiple access. One approach that comes to mind is TDM/T-WDMA. But will this work? Let us try it on the Petersen network with $W = 5$. To reduce optical equipment we employ optical multicast, allowing the use of elementary stations. We assume an FT-TR system using a single transceiver per station on each waveband. Figure 6.49 shows a portion of the OCH on waveband 5 for this case. Only transmitting nodes E and F and receiving nodes A and H are shown. Note that each transmitting station multicasts to both receiving stations, and that additional connections exist (shown as dashed lines in the figure). The transmissions associated with the additional connections are ignored. The optical connections $c_E = (E, \{A, H\})$ and $c_F = (F, \{A, H, I\})$ use λ-channels 1 and 3 respectively, corresponding to the assignments in Problem 22. Referring to Figure 6.38, it can be seen that the four physical paths involved are all different, and hence have different propagation delays.

Figure 6.50 illustrates how the time frames might appear in a fixed-frame schedule with $L = 3$ slots, where LCs $[E, H]$ and $[F, A]$ are assigned two units of capacity.

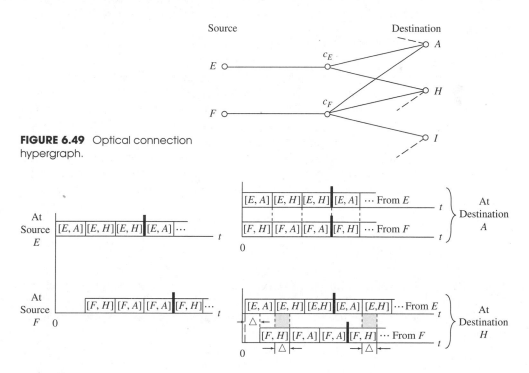

FIGURE 6.49 Optical connection hypergraph.

FIGURE 6.50 Fixed-frame scheduling for four LCs.

The frames are shown at the sources and destinations, and the relative timing has been adjusted so that the frames on the two channels are aligned properly at receiver A. Note that all information can be extracted without conflicts at A. On the other hand, the transmissions arriving at H are misaligned by an amount Δ because the propagation delays are different. As a result, there are intervals (shown as shaded areas in the figure) during which conflicts occur. There is, in fact, no way to schedule these transmissions without conflicts using the given frame time and three slots.[57]

This is an example of what happens when many-to-many connections take multiple physical paths. Rooted routing is designed to avoid this problem by forcing all paths to pass through a common root, at which they can all be synchronized. However, in so doing, the optical path emulates a broadcast star, and hence sacrifices possibilities for spectrum reuse.

We now consider another multiplexing/multiple-access approach for many-to-many connectivity, continuing with the Petersen network example with $W = 5$ and elementary stations. Section 5.2.2 showed how TDM/T-SCMA can be used to move multiple access from the λ-channel level to the transmission channel level. This can be applied directly to the problem at hand. We again use one optical transceiver per station per waveband. Each OR captures all λ-channels within its waveband. The station structure is as shown in Figure 5.7. As before, each OT has a λ-channel assignment that satisfies the DCA conditions, and most optical connections are multicast, following the optical paths of Equation 6.55. (All λ-channel assignments in this illustration follow Problem 22.)

Now on the transmission channel level, let each station be assigned a fixed subcarrier frequency using the same pattern of frequency assignment as on the optical level. All outbound LCs are then multiplexed on the subcarrier. For example, station A is assigned the optical/subcarrier frequency pair (ν_2, f_2) on waveband 5, with LCs $[A, B]$, $[A, E]$, and $[A, F]$ multiplexed on the subcarrier using TDM. Because three distinct wavelengths were required for optical channel assignment on waveband 5, a total of three optical frequencies (corresponding to the wavelength assignments) and three subcarrier frequencies are required. (The distinct optical wavelengths are only needed to avoid OBI in this case, so there are no stringent tolerances on their exact values.)

On the receiving side, we assume that each station contains an array of three subcarrier demodulators following each OR (for a total of nine demodulators on all wavebands) to detect each LC. For example, station A receives signals on waveband 5 from three different sources: B, E, and F. These are carried on subcarriers 2, 1, and 3 respectively. By following the same pattern with subcarriers as with optical frequencies, the DCA condition is satisfied at both the optical and transmission channel levels. It is important to note that a reuse of the *subcarrier* spectrum is achieved here as well as reuse of the optical spectrum. This leads to a TDM/T-SCMA system with a higher throughput than would have been possible using a broadcast star.

---

[57] Some ways out of this dilemma are suggested in Problem 25 at the end of this chapter.

When demultiplexing the TDM signals emanating from each source, the receiving station experiences the same propagation delay problems as occurred in the TDM/T-WDMA case. It is generally impossible to synchronize all sources and destinations simultaneously. That is why a subcarrier receiver *array* is proposed here. In this way, sources can transmit without mutual synchronization. Each receiver processes the demodulated subcarriers from all sources it sees, separately and in parallel, so that no conflicts arise. Couldn't we have done the same thing using TDM/T-WDMA? Yes, but this would have required replication of tuned ORs—a much more expensive proposition.

Still more savings of ORs are possible if a single wideband receiver covering all wavebands is placed at each station. In this case, however, nine distinct subcarrier frequencies are required to satisfy DCA at the subcarrier level, eliminating the possibility of subcarrier frequency reuse. The same total number of subcarrier demodulators (nine) is required at each station.

Although rooted routing cannot be used to an advantage in the Petersen network examples for $W = 5$ and $W = 9$, it has a natural role in the case $W = 1, F = 2$. Figure 6.45 shows the routing for a typical tree, T_A, in this case. The optical paths are in the form of an embedded star, rooted at the central node of the tree, and serve four stations. All 12 LCs on the star can share fully the capacity of its waveband using multiplexing/multiple access at the transmission channel level. For example, a TDM/T-WDMA system can be used without any synchronization problems in this case because all signals pass through the central node of the tree. Furthermore, if the star is reflecting, mutual synchronization is achieved easily because each station sees all signals, including its own.

Multiplexing and Multiple Access in Hierarchical Structures   Another opportunity to use transmission channel multiplexing and multiple access occurs when a network has a hierarchical structure consisting of a backbone together with local access subnets. In this case it is often possible to use multiplexing/multiple access within the LASs to concentrate traffic efficiently for routing through the backbone. We illustrate with the network of Figure 6.42, in which the Petersen backbone is assumed to be configured as a Latin router using nine wavebands. Recall that in this case one λ-channel per waveband was sufficient to set up a single LC between each pair of nodes. However, there are now several stations accessing each backbone node through an LAS, so that many LCs may be active between each node pair. We may therefore wish to use several channels so that multiplexing can be used at both the λ-channel and the transmission channel levels.

Consider the traffic flowing between LAS A_1 and LASs C_1 and C_2 in Figure 6.42. Because all of this traffic passes through node A using waveband 4 (see Table 6.6), the LDC at that node can be set to act as a star coupler on that waveband, creating an embedded broadcast star for all traffic accessing that node on waveband 4. If the LDC is configured as an undirected star, it can support intra-LAS traffic as well as inter-LAS traffic. Another option is to configure node A (or nodes A and C) as two directed stars, one carrying traffic from LAS A_1 to LASs C_1 and C_2, and the other carrying traffic in the opposite direction. In this case only inter-LAS traffic can be supported, but the channels on the optical path can be reused in each direction.

With more than one λ-channel, TDM/T-WDMA can be used to share the capacity of the channels among all active LCs on the waveband. Furthermore, if the LCs are assigned on demand, the star node might also serve as a local network manager to coordinate transmissions as described in Section 6.5.4.

These multiplexing/multiple-access arrangements can be implemented on the appropriate waveband for each of the optical connections listed in Table 6.6, so that a combined fixed and demand-assigned connectivity is established. Waveband routed optical paths are fixed in place between all node pairs on the backbone, whereas demand-assigned LCs between stations within LASs are set up by multiplexing each connection onto the waveband corresponding to its gateway node pair. Using this approach, LCs can share the capacity of the backbone using the demand assignment procedures described in Section 5.5.

6.5.6.3 Performance Comparisons

The Petersen network served as a basic structure to illustrate RWA and channel assignment in LLNs. Because many different configurations were presented, we pull them together in this section to indicate how different scenarios affect performance. The following notation is used:

W = number of wavebands

R_t = transmitter bitrate (in bps) = capacity of one λ-channel

C = λ-channels per waveband

C_f = capacity of one fiber (in bps) = $WC\,R_t$

S = total network throughput normalized to the capacity of one λ-channel

ϱ = S/WC = spectrum reuse factor

B_λ = bandwidth occupied by one λ-channel, including interchannel guard band (in GHz)

B_g = guard band between wavebands (in GHz)

α = B_g/B_λ = guard band width normalized to λ-channel bandwidth

B_{op} = total optical bandwidth occupied on a fiber (in GHz)

β = $B_{\mathrm{op}}/B_\lambda$ = total optical bandwidth normalized to λ-channel bandwidth

η_f = C_f/B_{op} = fiber spectral efficiency (in bps/Hz)

η_N = SR_t/B_{op} = network spectral efficiency (in bps/Hz)

Using this terminology we have[58]

$$C_f = WC R_t = WC \eta_m B_\lambda \tag{6.59}$$

where $\eta_m = R_t/B_\lambda$ is the spectral efficiency of the λ-channel modulation scheme, taking into account the interchannel guard band, and

$$B_{\text{op}} = WC B_\lambda + (W - 1) B_g \tag{6.60}$$

The fiber and network spectral efficiencies can now be expressed as

$$\eta_f = \frac{\eta_m}{1 + \frac{W-1}{WC}\alpha} \tag{6.61}$$

$$\eta_N = SR_t/B_{\text{op}} = \varrho \eta_f = \frac{\varrho \eta_m}{1 + \frac{W-1}{WC}\alpha} \tag{6.62}$$

With all channels within a single waveband ($W = 1$), Equation 6.61 reduces to $\eta_f = \eta_m$, the best possible fiber efficiency. With several channels in each waveband and $W \gg 1$, efficiency drops to $\eta_f \approx \eta_m/(1 + \alpha/C)$. Because α may attain values of ten or more, it is desirable to group many λ-channels on each waveband to limit the wasted spectrum in the guardbands. However, we shall see that grouping channels to increase η_f tends to reduce the routing flexibility, which in turn reduces the reuse factor ϱ and therefore the network spectral efficiency η_N. Proper design of an LLN requires balancing these two factors.

The performance parameters of particular interest in an LLN are S, ϱ, η_f, and η_N; the latter three determine how efficiently the resources are being utilized. We now derive these parameters for the various cases considered in Section 6.5.5. Instead of assuming that each LC requires the full capacity of one λ-channel, as was done in most of the previous examples, we leave C arbitrary, on the assumption that the LCs might require varying capacities. Thus, more than one λ-channel might be used for an especially high-capacity LC, or several low-traffic LCs between the same source and destination nodes might share the capacity of one channel.

Case 1: $W = 3$, $F = 1$ We focus on the scenario using nonblocking stations, point-to-point optical connections, and nonreflecting stars. In this case, the six LCs routed on two-hop optical paths on each tree share the C λ-channels on its waveband with a twofold reuse of the λ-channels. Because there are ten trees with twofold reuse of a capacity R_tC on each tree, the 60 two-hop connections in the network are allocated an aggregate capacity of $20R_tC$. However, each of the 30 LCs routed on a one-hop path has the full capacity of a waveband available to it. Therefore, these LCs are allocated

---

[58] It is assumed that the waveband/channel grouping is the same on each fiber.

an aggregate capacity of $30R_tC$. (We assume that all allocated capacity is used, which in this case leads to an unbalanced traffic distribution.) This results in the following performance:

$$S = 50C$$

$$\varrho = 16.7$$

$$\eta_f = \frac{\eta_m}{1 + 0.67\alpha/C}$$

$$\eta_N = \frac{16.7\eta_m}{(1 + 0.67\alpha/C)}$$

Case 2: $W = 5$, $F = 1$ Again, assuming nonblocking stations, there are no multicast optical connections in this case, so we have

$$S = 90C$$

$$\varrho = 18$$

$$\eta_f = \frac{\eta_m}{1 + 0.8\alpha/C}$$

$$\eta_N = \frac{18\eta_m}{1 + 0.8\alpha/C}$$

Case 3: $W = 9$, $F = 1$ Comparing this case with the previous one, the number of wavebands has been increased and the NASs are now elementary stations. The net result is to simplify the access stations at the expense of reducing the reuse factor and spectral efficiency. The performance parameters are

$$S = 90C$$

$$\varrho = 10$$

$$\eta_f = \frac{\eta_m}{1 + 0.9\alpha/C}$$

$$\eta_N = \frac{10\eta_m}{1 + 0.9\alpha/C}$$

Case 4: $W = 1$, $F = 2$ In this case, an embedded nonreflecting star is assumed on each tree, which enables 12 LCs to be realized with 6 λ-channels, for a reuse factor on the tree of two. In addition, the complete capacity of the unique waveband is reused ten times on the ten trees. It can be allocated in any way among the LCs sharing a tree without affecting the total throughput. The performance parameters are, therefore,

$$S = 20C$$

$$\varrho = 20$$

$$\eta_f = \eta_m$$
$$\eta_N = 20\eta_m$$

Although the expressions for performance derived here provide useful qualitative information, the results cannot be compared without assuming some specific values for the system parameters. Let

$$B_\lambda = 20\,\text{GHz}$$
$$B_g = 100\,\text{GHz}\ (\alpha = 5)$$
$$B_{\text{op}} = 1{,}000\,\text{GHz}\ (\beta = 50)$$
$$\eta_m = 0.1$$

With these values of bandwidths, the values of C in the various cases are no longer arbitrary. From Equation 6.60, we have

$$C = \left\lfloor \frac{\beta - (W-1)\alpha}{W} \right\rfloor \tag{6.63}$$

Table 6.7 compares the performance of the representative cases discussed here. Recall that each case corresponds to full logical connectivity on the Petersen network. Also included in the table is the case ST, in which full connectivity is achieved using the spanning tree of Figure 6.38 on a single waveband. An asterisk in the comment column indicates that there are more channels available than the number of LCs sharing them. For example, in Case 1, 13 channels are available on each waveband. But only three stations access each tree, sharing the capacity of a full waveband. Thus to make full use of the capacity of the 13 channels, there must be at least 13 transceivers distributed among the three stations, with a suitable multiplexing/multiple-access method used for sharing capacity.

Table 6.7 illustrates that total throughput S and network spectral efficiency η_N are maximized by increasing reuse factor ϱ *and* by concentrating the channels into a

TABLE 6.7   Comparison of Performance of Various Configurations of the Petersen Network

Case	C	S	ϱ	η_f	η_N	Comments
$W = 3, F = 1$	13	650	16.7	0.08	1.33	*
$W = 5, F = 1$	6	540	18	0.06	1.08	*
$W = 9, F = 1$	1	90	10	0.07	0.7	—
$W = 1, F = 2$	50	1,000	20	0.1	2	*
ST	50	50	1	0.1	0.1	*

limited number of wavebands. Thus, observe that case 4 gives the largest throughput and spectral efficiency—a consequence of the fact that it has the highest reuse factor and uses only one waveband.

Although all cases considered in these comparisons used the Petersen topology, it is interesting to examine what happens when a less dense topology is used. For example, if we had tried to achieve full logical connectivity on a ten-station ring using point-to-point optical paths (i.e., operating it as a WRN), it would require $W = 13$ wavebands (see Equation 6.12). But with the values of bandwidths given earlier and $W = 13$, we find that Equation 6.63 gives $C = 0$. Thus, the available spectrum cannot support full connectivity on a ring operated as a WRN.

6.5.6.4 Demand-Assigned Logical Connections

In discussing multiplexing and multiple access in hierarchical structures we showed how demand-assigned LCs can be superimposed on an optical layer in which the optical paths provide a static connectivity pattern. In this way, connection management and control is concentrated in the logical layer, while ignoring the details of the underlying optical paths. Furthermore, demand assignments at the optical and transmission channel levels allow for LCs with arbitrarily fine granularity as well as varying capacities. In this section we investigate how the random nature of demand-assigned traffic, together with its granularity, affects system performance.

To model random activity in the network we assume that many elementary stations, each with a single tunable transceiver, access each node. (The stations might access the nodes directly or through LASs.) The station population is assumed to be sufficiently large so that the connection request arrivals can be approximated as a Poisson process. Assuming an LCC model, the blocking probabilities can then be deduced using the Erlang-B formula of Equation 5.98. As we shall see, the blocking performance depends on the way channels are shared in the LLN.

Let us assume that the collection of stations accessing each node generates an offered traffic G (Erlangs per node), where the destinations of the connection requests are distributed uniformly to N other nodes. (Any blocking because of busy destination stations is neglected.) Suppose that one point-to-point optical connection is in place for each of the N outbound paths to the other nodes; that is, one λ-channel is available for each destination. In this case, each path is offered G/N Erlangs, so that the Erlang formula reduces to $P_B = G/(N + G)$, which means that the offered traffic must be kept extremely low for acceptable blocking probability.

As an example, consider the Petersen network with $W = 9$ and $C = 1$, in which many elementary access stations are attached to each node possibly through LASs, as shown in Figure 6.42. Each node generates G Erlangs, distributed uniformly to nine other nodes, with one λ-channel available to each destination. Then we find that $G \approx 0.38$ for $P_B = 0.04$. This corresponds to a total normalized *carried* load (throughput) for the network of $S = 3.6$, compared with a maximum throughput of $S = 90$ in the deterministic case. The poor throughput for demand-assigned traffic is due to the fact that the number of channels is too small (the granularity is too large).

A "brute force" way of improving P_B is to assign many λ-channels (i.e., many parallel optical connections) to each path. For example, taking $C = 30$ in the previous example, we find that $G \approx 216$ for $P_B = 0.04$. This gives a carried load of $S = 2{,}074$, compared with $S = 2{,}700$ in the deterministic case. Although this is much better, the random nature of the connection activity still degrades throughput by more than 20% with a nonnegligible blocking probability.

Unfortunately, in multiwavelength networks, large numbers of λ-channels are not usually available. However, blocking probability can still be reduced using a limited number of λ-channels by refining the granularity of the LCs. Suppose that instead of occupying a full λ-channel, each LC requires a lower effective bitrate: R_t/K, where $K \gg 1$. In this case up to K LCs can be multiplexed on each λ-channel with each LC allocated one subchannel of a λ-channel. For example, if TDM/TDMA is used, a subchannel would correspond to a time slot. With several λ-channels allocated to each path, TDM/T-WDMA can be used so that the basic subchannel corresponds to one channel–slot.

This procedure is valid for refining the granularity of any LLN. We shall apply it to the cases of the Petersen network compared in Table 6.7. We determine the traffic-handling capacity of the "fine-grained" network, assuming that each LC requires one channel–slot. Let $f_E(C, P_B)$ be the solution of Equation 5.98 for G; that is, f_E gives the maximum offered traffic to C channels for a blocking probability not exceeding P_B. Then for the cases being considered, the offered traffic per node sustainable by the Petersen network with blocking probability not exceeding P_B, using K subchannels per λ-channel and C λ-channels per waveband, is

$$
\begin{aligned}
G &= 9f_E(KC/3, P_B), & \text{for } (W = 3, F = 1) \\
G &= 9f_E(KC, P_B), & \text{for } (W = 5, F = 1) \\
G &= 9f_E(KC, P_B), & \text{for } (W = 9, F = 1) \\
G &= f_E(KC, P_B), & \text{for } (W = 1, F = 2)
\end{aligned}
\tag{6.64}
$$

The constants multiplying f_E in each equation reflect the traffic splitting factor at each node. (In the last equation the assumption is that one-hop traffic is split equally on the two possible paths it can use.) The first argument of f_E indicates the number of subchannels available on each path. (In the first equation, the argument $KC/3$ reflects the fact that the C λ-channels in each waveband must be divided among three sets of connections to satisfy the DCA condition. Otherwise, we assume full sharing.)

Using the values of G from Equation 6.64, the maximum *carried* traffic sustainable by the Petersen network at a blocking probability P_B is

$$
S(K, C, P_B) = 10(1 - P_B)G/K
\tag{6.65}
$$

where division by K is necessary to normalize the traffic to the capacity of one λ-channel.

6.5.7 Power Distribution in LLNs

The settings of the signal power dividing and combining ratios in an LDC provide an additional degree of freedom in an LLN. Many different power distribution rules can be chosen. Which is best depends on many issues, including the architecture of the LDCs, the presence or absence of amplification, the complexity of the power distribution algorithm, and deleterious effects associated with unequal signal levels. We present two possible approaches in this section:

1. Equal power levels

2. Uniform power splitting

6.5.7.1 Equal Power Levels

In the first approach, which requires amplification, equal aggregate power levels are maintained on a fiber for each waveband. This is generally the best arrangement for simplifying network management, for optimizing signal quality at the receivers, and for adapting the signal power levels to the gain and noise characteristics of the amplifiers (see Section 4.4). For illustration, Figure 6.51 shows an $r \times n$ network node, assumed to be a waveband-selective LDC in the three-stage form of Figure 2.22, equipped with amplifiers on each outbound fiber. (Other arrangements might have amplifiers within the LDC fabric and/or on the input fibers.) To fix ideas, suppose that the middle-stage elements are crossbar space switches of the form of Figure 2.19, with continuously variable transmission constants. In this case, the power levels are given by

$$P_i'(w_k) = \sum_j a_{ij}(w_k) P_j(w_k) G(w_k) \tag{6.66}$$

where $P_j(w_k)$ and $P_i'(w_k)$ are, respectively, the power on input port j and output port i, both on waveband w_k, and $G(w_k)$ is the amplifier gain on waveband w_k. By choosing a desired power level, P_0, and setting

$$a_{ij}(w_k) = \frac{P_0}{P_j(w_k)G(w_k)} \tag{6.67}$$

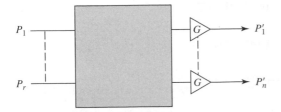

FIGURE 6.51 Power distribution with constant power levels.

all output powers at each node are maintained at a nominal level, P_0, irrespective of the transmitter power levels and any other effects upstream from the node, including signal splitting and combining, attenuation on the fibers, and losses in the LDCs. As a by-product, this rule automatically equalizes the wavelength-dependent gain characteristics of the fiber amplifiers. By monitoring power levels at critical points within the node and feeding back information to the LDC controller, the coefficients a_{ij} can be adjusted dynamically to correct for changes in input power levels and transmission characteristics.

6.5.7.2 Uniform Power Splitting

The objective of the second approach is to attempt to distribute signal power as uniformly as possible, subject to the limitations of passive components. It is most appropriate for systems that can be approximated as "ideal," in the sense that attenuation in the fibers and excess losses in the LDC components are negligible (or are compensated by amplification). We derive the uniform power-splitting rule for the case of LLNs using δ–σ LDCs. The discussion pertains to power control within a single waveband. However, the results are also applicable to multiwaveband networks containing waveband-selective LDCs. In the multiwaveband case, the dividing and combining ratios on each waveband are set according to the rules developed next.

We examine an appropriate power distribution rule for a single node first, and then show how this extrapolates to a general LLN. Consider a network that consists of a single, ideal δ–σ LDC to which are connected M transmitters and N receivers, as shown in Figure 6.52. (If $M = N$, and like-numbered transceiver pairs are located in the same station, this represents a network with N elementary stations accessing a common node.) Let P_j be the power generated by source j, and P_i' be the power delivered to destination i. Suppose source j maintains a multicast optical connection to N_j destinations, and destination i receives power from M_i sources. Then a natural way of distributing power is to set

$$\delta_{ij} = 1/N_j$$
$$\sigma_{ij} = 1/M_i \tag{6.68}$$

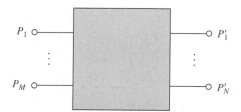

FIGURE 6.52 Single-node LLN.

With this rule, the power transfer relations become

$$P'_i = \frac{1}{M_i} \sum \frac{P_j}{N_j} \qquad (6.69)$$

where the sum is taken over all sources delivering power to i. For example, when all inputs are broadcast to all outputs, the power splits equally to each destination, with an attenuation factor of MN reflecting the combining losses $(1/M)$ and splitting losses $(1/N)$.

Generalizing this to an arbitrary network, consider the power transfer ratio between an input port j and an output port i on an LDC at any node in the network. Let

S_j = number of source signals superimposed at input port j

S'_i = number of source signals superimposed at output port i

D_j = number of destinations reached by the signals at input port j

D'_i = number of destinations reached by the signals at output port i

All of these coefficients pertain to a single waveband, and the signal destination sets include fortuitous destinations. Now, uniform power splitting throughout the network is obtained by setting $a_{ij} = \delta_{ij}\sigma_{ij}$, with

$$\delta_{ij} = \frac{D'_i}{D_j}$$
$$\sigma_{ij} = \frac{S_j}{S'_i} \qquad (6.70)$$

for all pairs ij for which an intranodal path exists. When no routing path exists, a_{ij} is set to zero.

It can be shown that the settings in Equation 6.70 can always be realized in an ideal δ–σ LDC. It can also be shown that in a network with ideal δ–σ LDCs and lossless links, the settings of Equation 6.70 yield the power-splitting rules of Equation 6.69 on a networkwide basis. That is, Equation 6.69 now represents the power delivered to destination station i, where the coefficient M_i in Equation 6.69 now refers to the number of source signals reaching destination i from anywhere in the network, and N_j refers to the number of destinations reached by the signal from source j. Thus, with this power distribution rule, the LLN is seen by the stations as one large LDC with power transfer matrix $A = [a_{ij}]$, where

$$a_{ij} = \begin{cases} 1/M_i N_j, & \text{when an optical path exists from } j \text{ to } i \\ 0, & \text{otherwise} \end{cases} \qquad (6.71)$$

The interesting feature of this rule is that the resultant end-to-end power transfer coefficients are independent of the routing paths through the network, the number of nodes they traverse, and the order in which signals are combined and split. They

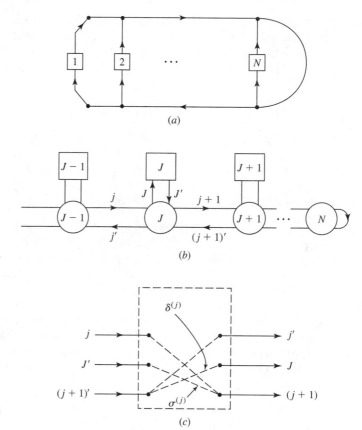

FIGURE 6.53 Folded bus power relations.

depend only on the number of destinations for each source and the number of sources reaching each destination.

The uniform splitting rule was used in an earlier example in Section 3.4.1.2. It is left as an exercise for the reader to complete the application of this rule to the network of Figure 3.25, verifying that the power relations of Equation 6.69 are satisfied.

The power distribution rules have useful applications in static as well as controllable networks. To illustrate, we apply them to the folded bus of Figure 6.53(a). The figure shows N stations accessing the folded bus through static signal combiners and dividers (taps). (All combiners and dividers are assumed to be ideal, and all fibers are lossless.) In Figure 6.53(b) the bus is redrawn to place each divider–combiner pair within a common node, and in Figure 6.53(c) the details of the connections within the jth node are shown, illustrating the labeling conventions. By abuse of notation we assign the label J to the jth node, the jth access fiber, and the jth station. (The lowercase label j is reserved for the jth internodal link.)

Assuming that each transmitter has the same output power P_0, we wish to determine the combining and dividing ratios for each station so that the signals delivered to the receivers all have the same levels. Denoting the combining coefficient for adding the signal from station J to the inbound bus as $\sigma^{(j)}$, and the dividing coefficient for tapping the signal from the outbound bus to station J as $\delta^{(j)}$, the power distribution rules of Equation 6.70 give

$$\delta^{(j)} = \sigma^{(j)} = \frac{1}{j} \quad j = 1, 2, \ldots, N \tag{6.72}$$

With these values, the power from each transmitter reaches each receiver attenuated by a factor of N^2, which is the best one can do if signals enter and leave the network through individual combining and splitting nodes.

6.5.8 A Hierarchical Optical Internet

Because the population served by a large network changes (and typically grows) with time, it is important to allow for growth in the fiber topology of the network to follow the projected growth in the user population. Many types of networks can be designed to grow in this fashion. One approach is illustrated in Figure 6.8 in which the basic topology, consisting of a square grid, is "refined" recursively in areas of population growth. In this section we illustrate a hierarchical approach. Although it is based on the Petersen graph, any other basic topological structure can be used.

Figure 6.54 shows a hierarchical optical internet, grown from repetitions of the Petersen graph of Figure 6.38. We begin with the original ten-node network of Figure 6.38, containing the set of nodes

$$\mathcal{N} = \{A, B, \ldots, J\} \tag{6.73}$$

(Because all subnets in the hierarchy have the same topology, it suffices to define the network by its nodes alone.) The original network forms level 0 in the hierarchy. At each of its nodes a subnet of the same form can be grown, as exemplified by the subnets $\mathcal{N}_C$, $\mathcal{N}_D$, and $\mathcal{N}_G$, which represent level 1. With these first-level subnets, the expanded network has the set of nodes

$$\mathcal{N} = \{A, B, \mathcal{N}_C, \mathcal{N}_D, E, F, \mathcal{N}_G, H, I, J\} \tag{6.74}$$

where

$$\begin{aligned}
\mathcal{N}_C &= \{CA, CB, \ldots, CJ\} \\
\mathcal{N}_D &= \{DA, \mathcal{N}_{DB}, DC, DD, \mathcal{N}_{DE}, DF, DG, DH, DI, DJ\} \\
\mathcal{N}_G &= \{GA, GB, \ldots, GJ\}
\end{aligned} \tag{6.75}$$

Note from Figure 6.54 that the level 1 subnet $\mathcal{N}_D$ in turn includes level 2 subnets:

$$\begin{aligned}
\mathcal{N}_{DB} &= \{DBA, DBB, \ldots, DBJ\} \\
\mathcal{N}_{DE} &= \{DEA, DEB, \ldots, DEJ\}
\end{aligned} \tag{6.76}$$

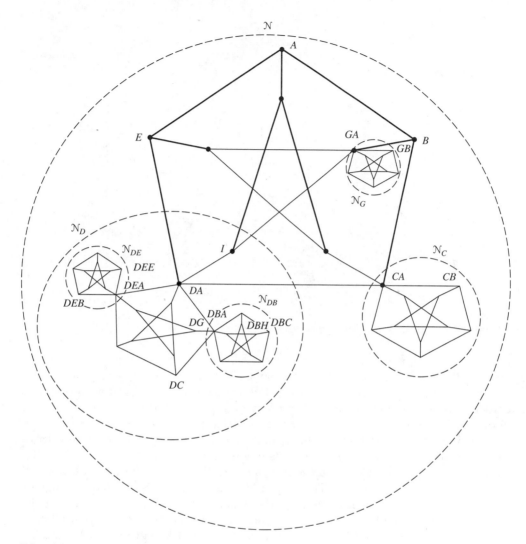

FIGURE 6.54 Hierarchical optical internet.

A node from which a higher level subnet is grown is called a *gateway node*. The nongateway nodes are called *end nodes*. To simplify the network structure, NASs are only connected to end nodes, and at most one higher level subnet is grown from each gateway. (This limits the degree of each gateway to six.) The relations in the hierarchy are shown more clearly in the tree representation of Figure 6.55.

The terminal vertices of the tree represent network nodes, and the nonterminal vertices represent subnets. Underlined terminal vertices correspond to gateway nodes. The vertices at level k of the tree represent level k subnets and level k nodes. All network

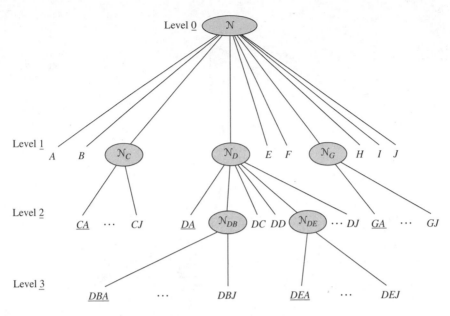

FIGURE 6.55 Tree representation of the hierarchy.

nodes that are shown as descendants of a given subnet vertex are contained in that subnet. (Level k nodes are contained in subnets of level $k-1$ and lower.)

The labeling convention is as follows. Subnets are identified by subscript strings corresponding to the identifier (ID) of the node from which they were grown. That node then becomes a gateway node, with a new ID formed from the old one by adding the suffix A. (By definition, the gateway node now belongs to the new subnet grown from it as well as the lower level subnets to which it previously belonged.) The IDs of all level k nodes are formed by adding suffixes $B, C, \ldots, J$ to the ID of the level $k-1$ subnet containing them. The length of a subnet or node ID string equals its level. Given any two node IDs, the longest matching left substring gives the ID of the smallest (highest level) subnet containing both of them. For example, $\mathcal{N}_D$ is a level 1 subnet. The ID of the level 2 gateway node from which it was grown is DA, and the remaining level 2 nodes in $\mathcal{N}_D$ are $DC, DD, DF, \ldots, DJ$. The suffix A on the nodes DBA and DEA indicates that they are level 3 gateways belonging to subnets $\mathcal{N}_{DB}$ and $\mathcal{N}_{DE}$ respectively. The smallest subnet containing both DDA and DEB is $\mathcal{N}_D$, but the smallest subnet containing both DBA and DBB is $\mathcal{N}_{DB}$.

A key feature of this hierarchy is that all subnets at the same level in the hierarchy (e.g., $\mathcal{N}_G$, $\mathcal{N}_C$, and $\mathcal{N}_D$, or $\mathcal{N}_{DE}$ and $\mathcal{N}_{DB}$) are mutually disjoint, which means that they can reuse the same wavebands.

Paths between two nodes belonging to different subnets must pass through all gateways leading to their highest level common subnet. This corresponds to the first common ancestor encountered in the tree of Figure 6.55. For example, nodes DBJ and DJ must communicate with each other via gateways DBA and DA, in $\mathcal{N}_D$.

Figure 6.54 is an example of an *incomplete* hierarchy of level 3. It can be completed by growing all possible level 2 subnets, which is achieved by converting all end nodes at level 2 or less to gateway nodes. The total number of level K end nodes in a complete hierarchy of level K is

$$N = 10\left(9^{(K-1)}\right) \tag{6.77}$$

The diameter of a hierarchy of level K (in optical hops) is

$$D = 4K - 2 \tag{6.78}$$

Clearly, for fairly small values of K, the network contains large numbers of end nodes while remaining quite dense, because the number of nodes grows exponentially with the diameter. For example, a four-level hierarchy contains 7,290 end nodes, each of which can serve many stations. It has a diameter of 14 and an average node degree of approximately 3.2.[59] In a complete hierarchy, all links except those in the highest level subnets serve to interconnect gateway nodes, so they can be considered the backbone network. The links within each highest level subnet represent the local distribution networks.

6.5.8.1 Waveband Routing

The hierarchical structure of this network suggests a natural method of using waveband routing to achieve a high degree of spectrum reuse. To illustrate, we focus on a three-level network exemplified by Figure 6.54. We use a strategy in which each waveband carries traffic at a given level of the hierarchy, numbering the wavebands 1, 2, and 3 to correspond to the levels. Thus, waveband 3 is used to carry intrasubnet traffic among the level 3 end nodes within a common level 2 subnet (e.g., among end nodes within subnet $\mathcal{N}_{DB}$). Similarly, all "middle-level" traffic between end nodes in a common level 1 subnet, but not within the same level 2 subnet, uses waveband 2. For example, traffic between DC and a node in $\mathcal{N}_{DE}$, such as DEB, would use waveband 2. Finally, all traffic between end nodes that are not within the same level 1 subnets uses waveband 1. An example would be traffic between node B and a node in $\mathcal{N}_G$ such as GB. We refer to the middle-level traffic as *long distance*, and the level 1 traffic as *very long distance*.

Another way of expressing these waveband assignments is in terms of the end node IDs. Thus, suppose the longest matching left substrings in the source and destination IDs are of length n. Then the connection uses waveband $n + 1$. This example generalizes in a natural way to a hierarchy of level K. Traffic between end nodes in a common level $k - 1$ subnet, but not within the same level k subnets, is carried by waveband $k, k = 1, 2, \ldots, K$. Following this technique, a hierarchy of level K requires

---

[59] For comparison, a square grid closed on itself as a torus and containing 85^2 or 7,225 nodes has a diameter of 84 for a node degree of 4.

K wavebands. This means that the total number of wavebands required for a full hierarchy containing N nodes is $W \approx \log_9 N$, and wavelength k is reused $10(9^{k-2})$ times in a full, level K hierarchy.

Let us examine how the waveband routing function would be carried out using static routing rules. Continuing with the example of Figure 6.54, waveband 3 is used for intrasubnet traffic within $\mathcal{N}_{DB}$ and $\mathcal{N}_{DE}$. Waveband 2 is used for intersubnet traffic between $\mathcal{N}_{DB}$ and $\mathcal{N}_{DE}$, and for intrasubnet traffic within $\mathcal{N}_C$, $\mathcal{N}_D$, and $\mathcal{N}_G$, excluding the traffic assigned to waveband 3. Finally, waveband 1 is used for all other traffic.

Given these waveband assignments, the routing paths remain to be determined. We consider a rooted routing approach next. Following that, a shortest path routing method is described, which uses additional wavebands.

6.5.8.2 Rooted Routing

In rooted routing, a level k embedded tree is established within each level k subnet, using waveband $k + 1$, and rooted at any convenient node in the subnet. The tree interconnects all end nodes within its subnet. All traffic between end nodes on the tree that are not in the same level $k+1$ subnet use that tree to communicate with each other. Using waveband $k + 1$, all traffic from the end nodes is routed to the root, and then broadcast back to the end nodes. Thus each embedded tree acts as a shared broadcast medium, and can be operated using any appropriate multiplexing/multiple-access scheme. For example, if C λ-channels are available in each waveband, each tree can be operated as a TDM/T-WDMA system.

In this way, each level k end node has access to routing trees at level $0, 1, \ldots, k-1$, each on a distinct waveband. Any end node can reach any other by selecting the proper waveband.[60] One disadvantage of rooted routing is that each tree concentrates all traffic from its attached end nodes onto a single equivalent broadcast star, so all of this traffic must share the capacity of a single waveband. (A remedy for this problem is presented in Section 6.5.8.5.)

To illustrate, we return to the example under discussion. To fix ideas, let us assume that each tree is rooted at a node with an ID with the last letter A. The links shown with bold lines in Figure 6.54 represent the level 0 routing tree operating on waveband 1. All end nodes in the network are included in this tree, and they are joined to the root by a minimum-hop path. Note that the routing tree is formed recursively. A shortest path tree is constructed from root node A to all nodes in the original Petersen network. It is joined to shortest path trees leading from the gateway nodes CA, DA, and GA to the nodes contained in their subnets. This process is repeated at gateway nodes DEA and DBA. Although the optical path configurations are static, individual demand-assigned LCs of varying capacity can be set up on each tree by assigning the desired number of channel–slots to each requested connection.

---

[60] Multicast is possible from any end node to any destination set by selecting the tree (waveband) corresponding to the highest level subnet containing all communicating end nodes.

The path for each higher level tree corresponds to the portion of the level 0 tree that is contained in a higher level subnet. Thus, the tree links within subnets $\mathcal{N}_C$, $\mathcal{N}_D$, and $\mathcal{N}_G$ represent level 1 trees rooted at gateway nodes CA, DA, and GA respectively. Although its fiber path coincides partially with that for the level 0 tree, each level 1 tree operates on waveband 2. Similarly, level 2 trees are included in subnets $\mathcal{N}_{DB}$ and $\mathcal{N}_{DE}$, operating on waveband 3.

Even though each tree is the shortest path to its root node, it does not provide shortest paths between end nodes. For example, traffic between $\mathcal{N}_C$ and $\mathcal{N}_D$ traverses six hops to and from root node A instead of a single hop on the shortest path between the subnets. The extra five hops are due to rooted routing. Furthermore, the concentration of all traffic on each routing tree at the root node creates bottlenecks, unnecessarily limiting the throughput. We now show how shortest path routing can be substituted for rooted routing at the cost of increasing the number of wavebands.

6.5.8.3 Shortest Path Routing

In the rooted routing plan discussed previously, all paths between communicating nodes are minimum hop until they reach the lowest level subnet they traverse. Thus, shortest path routing would be possible, provided that the paths are modified within that subnet.

To see how this might be done, consider first the level 0 tree in a full hierarchy. It concentrates traffic generated by end nodes in level 1 subnets and terminating in different level 1 subnets, routing that traffic to node A and back to the end nodes. The ten level 1 subnets generating this intersubnet traffic can be considered local access subnets offering a stream of concentrated traffic to their gateway nodes (see Section 6.5.4). It would be preferable if that traffic took the shortest path between the level 1 gateways. This requires setting up full point-to-point connectivity among all gateway nodes using shortest paths, and routing each connection from a given source gateway to the proper destination gateway. Now, in Case 3 of Section 6.5.5.2, this problem was solved for the case when all traffic was generated by elementary stations. It required nine wavebands (the minimum possible number).

Assuming that nine wavebands are available, each connection can be routed selectively on the shortest path to its destination gateway by assigning it to the unique waveband reaching that gateway. A possible waveband routing rule is presented in Table 6.6. (A similar routing rule can be followed at each higher level, assuming that nine wavebands are available for each level.) This shortest path routing rule replaces the single rooted routing tree by 90 directed trees joining all pairs of source and destination subnets. These trees require a total of only nine wavebands, indicating a tenfold spectrum reuse. Because all traffic is routed on shortest paths, the number of optical hops for each point-to-point connection equals the source–destination internodal distance.

Nine wavebands are required for intersubnet traffic using the level 0 tree because several connections destined for different subnets may enter a gateway from the same fiber. The only way to route the connections selectively in this case is to have one waveband available for each of the nine destination gateways. However, under the (reasonable) assumption that the stations accessing the end nodes in the network are nonblocking, some savings in wavebands can be achieved for intrasubnet traffic in the highest level subnets. In a full hierarchy, all end nodes are in these subnets. With nonblocking stations, only five wavebands are required to support full intra-subnet connectivity in the highest level subnets (see Case 2 of Section 6.5.5.2, and Table 6.5).[61]

This reasoning shows that full shortest path connectivity can be achieved in a full three-level hierarchy with nonblocking stations using a total of 23 wavebands. In re-turn for the increased number of wavebands, the network throughput is considerably improved, as we shall see.

6.5.8.4 Performance Comparisons

Performance is evaluated for the full three-level hierarchy using the parameters S (throughput), ϱ (spectrum reuse factor), and η_N (network efficiency), as defined in Section 6.5.6.3. It is assumed that C λ-channels are available on each waveband, and the total capacity may be distributed among all connections on demand. We compare the cases $W = 3$ and $W = 23$, assuming that all network capacity is used and that both cases use the same amount of total optical spectrum, with a finer waveband division in the latter case.

In the rooted routing scenario ($W = 3$), all local traffic (intrasubnet traffic on level 3) shares C λ-channels and there are 90 subnets, for a total local throughput of $90C$. Similarly, we find total long-distance and very long-distance throughputs of $10C$ and C respectively. Thus, the performance parameters in this case are

$$S = 101C$$
$$\varrho = 33.7$$
$$\eta_N = \frac{33.7\eta_m}{(1 + 0.67\alpha/C)}$$

For the shortest path case ($W = 23$) there are nine end nodes in each level 3 sub-net, so that 72 point-to-point optical paths are available with C' λ-channels on each. (Because this case corresponds to a finer waveband subdivision of the available spec-trum than the case $W = 3$, we have $C' < C$.) The local throughput in each level 3 subnet is therefore $72C'$, giving a total local throughput of $6,480C'$. Similarly, the total long-distance and very long-distance throughputs are $720C'$ and $90C'$ respectively.

---

[61] The table gives waveband assignments for all ten nodes of the Petersen network. However, we have assumed that access stations are only attached to nongateway nodes, so connectivity is only required among nine of the ten nodes.

This gives

$$S = 7,290C'$$

$$\varrho = 325$$

$$\eta_N = \frac{317\eta_m}{(1 + 0.96\alpha/C')}$$

A quantitative comparison of throughput in these two cases can be made if we choose some specific values of system parameters. Suppose

$$B_\lambda = 20 \text{ GHz}$$

$$B_g = 100 \text{ GHz } (\alpha = 5)$$

$$B_{\text{op}} = 5,000 \text{ GHz } (\beta = 250)$$

Then from Equation 6.63 we have $C = 80$ and $C' = 6$. This results in a throughput $S = 8,080$ and $43,740$ for the cases $W = 3$ and $W = 23$ respectively, which is a more than fivefold improvement for shortest path over rooted routing.

6.5.8.5 Traffic Patterns in Hierarchical Networks

A hierarchical topology such as that in Figure 6.54 has two related defects:

1. High degrees of traffic concentration at the lower levels of the hierarchy
2. Poor survivability, because failure of a gateway node cuts the network in two

Traffic concentration is caused by the fact that the total number of potential intersubnet connections at level k in a full K-level hierarchy grows exponentially with $K - k$. Thus, the traffic concentration at the lower levels would be overwhelming if the traffic distribution was uniform. However, hierarchical structures are usually based on traffic patterns that are also hierarchical.

To work well, the hierarchy should be organized into "communities of interest" so that demand for connections tends to diminish with optical hop distance between source and destination stations. If the decrease in demand is exponential with distance, this tends to compensate for the exponential traffic concentration. If the demand pattern does not solve the concentration problem, other measures can be taken to match the physical topology to the demand pattern. These include assigning extra wavebands and/or channels to the lower levels, as well as increasing the number of fibers in the backbone links.

The survivability problem requires additional measures. For example, the problem of node failure in the topology of Figure 6.54 can be alleviated by adding extra links joining some of the higher level nodes. These can also serve to offload some of the traffic that would otherwise concentrate at the lower levels (see Problem 2 at the end of this chapter).

6.5.9 Multistar Linear Lightwave Networks

Until now, all routing and waveband assignment problems in LLNs were treated on networks in which the physical topology was given. We now consider the case when a physical topology is designed for a network in the form of multiple broadcast stars. The multistar physical topology was discussed in the context of a WRN in Section 6.3.6, in which each star was based on a wavelength router, supporting point-to-point connections only.[62] In this section we take a broader view of the multistar network, as a physical support for a *hypernet*. Now each star acts as an MPS joining a cluster of network stations. The MPS is a generalization of a point-to-point network link, allowing all stations in the cluster to communicate with each other through multicast optical paths. Each MPS operates as a shared medium. Some of the early work on multistar-type networks appears in [Ganz+92] and [Birk91].

Our first illustration of this approach appeared in Section 3.4.3.4. There, a seven-node hypernet of diameter 1 is described, based on seven MPSs (see Figure 3.30). The LCs in the network are represented in Figure 3.30(a) as a logical connection hypergraph, in which each hyperedge represents an MPS containing three stations. Figure 3.30(b) gives an alternative tripartite representation of the LCH, in which each hyperedge appears in the form of a star. This representation can be viewed as a picture of a fiber topology designed specifically to support the given LCs. By identifying each hyperedge in the LCH with a multicast star in the network realization, we obtain a general methodology for realizing any logical hypernet on a multistar physical topology.

Our interest here centers on hypernets of diameter 1, which correspond to purely optical networks. (Recall that in a hypernet of diameter 1, every node can be reached from every other through one MPS [i.e., on one logical hop]). Larger diameter hypernets must be realized as hybrid LRNs, and these are treated in Chapter 7.

Consider a set of N stations that we wish to connect via an LLN. Suppose we are free to choose both the logical topology and the physical topology, subject to the resource constraints and performance objectives. The approach we take is to begin at the logical layer, and choose a hypernet logical topology that consists of sets of stations clustered into MPSs. The natural representation of the hypernet is an LCH $H(v, \varepsilon)$, in which the vertices v represent the stations, and the hyperedges ε represent the MPSs (see Appendix A). If each station is required to have a direct LC to any other, the LCH must have a diameter of 1. After a suitable LCH is chosen, we construct a multistar network patterned after the LCH, in which each star supports an MPS corresponding to a hyperedge in the LCH. Although the topological parameters of the multistar (star sizes and station degree) are taken from the LCH, the details of implementation and operation of each star (i.e., the multiplexing/multiple-access methods used) are a sep-

---

[62] Topologies that are generalizations of multistars, called *static light trees*, are studied in [Barry93b].

arate issue, independent of the logical layer design. Thus we have two subproblems that can be treated (almost) independently: logical layer design and physical layer design.

The hypernet (or, equivalently, its LCH) can be directed or undirected. In an undirected hypergraph the hyperedges are subsets of vertices. If the hypergraph is of diameter 1, each pair of vertices must belong to at least one hyperedge. In the undirected case, the MPSs can be realized as undirected stars, with the tripartite representation of the LCH defining the multistar network. All stations in an MPS communicate with each other, fully sharing the capacity of the star using any of the channel-sharing techniques described in Chapter 5. For example, the LCH of Figure 3.30 is an undirected hypergraph with vertex set $\nu = \{1, 2, \ldots, 7\}$ and hyperedges $\varepsilon = \{E_1, E_2, \ldots, E_7\}$, where

$$E_1 = \{2, 5, 7\}$$
$$E_2 = \{1, 2, 6\}$$
$$E_3 = \{2, 3, 4\}$$
$$E_4 = \{1, 4, 5\} \tag{6.79}$$
$$E_5 = \{1, 3, 7\}$$
$$E_6 = \{4, 6, 7\}$$
$$E_7 = \{3, 5, 6\}$$

In Equation 6.79 each hyperedge defines a 3×3 star.

In the directed case, each hyperedge (now called a *hyperarc*) is of the form $E = (E^-, E^+)$, where E^- and E^+ are, respectively, the in-set and out-set of E. These correspond respectively to the transmitting and receiving stations of an MPS. In realizing a directed hypernet, an MPS corresponding to a hyperarc E is implemented as a directed $s^- \times s^+$ star, where $s^- = |E^-|$ and $s^+ = |E^+|$ are the sizes of the in-set and the out-set of E respectively. This allows all stations in E^- to multicast to all stations in E^+, fully sharing the capacity of the star. Note that E^- and E^+ need not be disjoint, nor do they have to be the same size.

Figure 6.56 shows a multistar realization of an eight-station directed hypernet of diameter 1, with transmitters and receivers on the left and right respectively. Four 4×4 directed stars provide full connectivity among the stations, and each station has two transmitters and two receivers. In the language of hypergraphs, the LCH has the vertex (station) set $\nu = \{0, 1, 2, \ldots, 7\}$. These vertices are clustered into four hyperarcs (MPSs), each with in-size and out-size 4, and each vertex has in-degree and out-degree 2. The in-degree and out-degree of a vertex correspond to the number of receivers and transmitters respectively in the station it represents. The hyperarcs are

$$E_0 = (\{0, 2, 4, 6\}, \{4, 5, 6, 7\})$$
$$E_1 = (\{0, 2, 4, 6\}, \{0, 1, 2, 3\})$$
$$E_2 = (\{1, 3, 5, 7\}, \{4, 5, 6, 7\}) \tag{6.80}$$
$$E_3 = (\{1, 3, 5, 7\}, \{0, 1, 2, 3\})$$

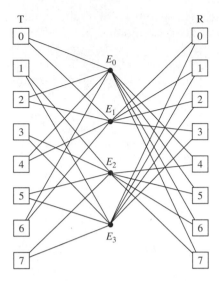

FIGURE 6.56 Directed hypernet *GKH* (2, 8, 4, 4).

Once the multistar realization has been determined, the flows on the stars can be adapted to a prescribed traffic pattern using suitable multiplexing/multiple-access methods. For example, if the available spectrum consists of $C = 4$ λ-channels, each star might be operated using TDM/T-WDMA in an FT-TR mode, in which the capacity of the four channels is shared among 16 point-to-point LCs according to traffic demand. Any value of $C < 4$ can also be used with a concomitant reduction in the total capacity of the MPS. In general, each hyperarc in the LCH can be viewed as a fully shared, directed medium with a capacity of C λ-channels. If the network consists of m stars, it achieves an m-fold reuse of the spectrum.

It should be noted that any hypernet configuration based on multicast stars, as described here, can be converted to a multistar WRN simply by replacing the star couplers with wavelength routers. Thus, the example of Figure 6.56 becomes a fully connected WRN if the central nodes of the stars are 4×4 permutation routers.

It is of interest to find multistar designs that make efficient use of network resources, accommodating a maximum number of stations with a minimum use of optical spectrum and transceivers. To this end, we make use of Moore bounds for hypergraphs.

For the undirected case, let $N_u(\Delta, D, r)$ be the number of vertices in a hypergraph of maximal degree Δ, diameter D, and maximal hyperedge size r. Then the Moore bound for undirected hypergraphs, given in Appendix A, reduces in the case $D = 1$ to

$$N_u(\Delta, 1, r) \leq 1 + \Delta(r - 1) \tag{6.81}$$

It turns out that this bound can only be attained for certain pairs (Δ, r). The existence of large hypergraphs of diameter 1 was studied thoroughly by [Bermond+84]. A few of their results are presented here.

For the case $\Delta = r$, undirected hypergraphs achieving the Moore bound exist when $q = r - 1$ is a power of a prime. (The seven-vertex hypergraph in Figure 3.30 is an example.) The bound is not attainable for certain other cases; for example, $r = 7$ and $r = 15$.

It is also shown in [Bermond+84] that undirected hypergraphs exist with

$$N_u(2, 1, r) = 2r - \lceil r/2 \rceil$$
$$N_u(3, 1, r) = 3r - \lceil r/3 \rceil \qquad (6.82)$$
$$N_u(4, 1, r) = 4r - \lceil r/4 \rceil$$

In the directed case, let $N_d(d, D, s)$ be the number of vertices in a directed hypergraph with maximal out-degree d, diameter D, and maximal out-size s. Then, in the case $D = 1$, the Moore bound for directed hypergraphs given in Appendix A reduces to

$$N_d(d, 1, s) \leq 1 + ds \qquad (6.83)$$

Systematic design procedures for directed hypergraphs exist for wide ranges of parameters. Because the construction methods yield classes of regular hypergraphs of arbitrary diameters, we discuss them more extensively in Chapter 7. In this section we illustrate the design methodology using one class, called *generalized Kautz hypergraphs*, considering only the case $D = 1$ [Bermond+97, Imase+83].

Let $GKH(d, n, s, m)$ denote a generalized Kautz hypergraph containing n vertices and m hyperarcs, where s is the out-size of each hyperarc and d is the out-degree of each vertex. A hypergraph in this class exists whenever the parameters obey the relations

$$dn \equiv 0 \pmod{m}$$
$$sm \equiv 0 \pmod{n} \qquad (6.84)$$

With the vertices labeled as integers modulo n and hyperarcs labeled as integers modulo m, the incidence rules are the following:

Vertex v is in the in-set of hyperarcs

$$e \equiv dv + \alpha \pmod{m}, \quad 0 \leq \alpha < d \qquad (6.85)$$

and the out-set of hyperarc e consists of vertices

$$u \equiv -se - \beta \pmod{n}, \quad 1 \leq \beta \leq s \qquad (6.86)$$

The diameter of the resultant hypergraph is bounded by

$$D \leq \lceil \log_{ds} n \rceil \qquad (6.87)$$

Equation 6.87 shows that if we take $ds = n$, these hypergraphs approach the Moore bound for $D = 1$ when n is large.

The in- and out-size of each hyperarc has the same value s, and the in- and out-degree of each vertex has the same value d if and only if $dn = sm$. The hypernet $GKH(2, 8, 4, 4)$ of Figure 6.56 is an example of this case. Another example is the wavelength routed multistar network of Figure 6.21, which was derived from the hypernet $GKH(2, 6, 3, 4)$ by replacing the directed MPSs based on star couplers by point-to-point connections based on wavelength routers.

Finally, it should be observed that the two-layered approach to network design taken here applies to realizations other than multistars. Thus, once the LCH is defined in terms of a hypergraph, the hyperedges/hyperarcs (MPSs) can be realized on *any* given physical topology by embedding each MPS into the given network topology. An example of this was shown in Table 3.1, in which a seven-node hypernet was embedded in a mesh topology. More general examples of embedding appear in Chapter 7.

6.6 Linear Lightwave Networks: Dynamic Routing Rules

In Section 6.5 we treated the case of static routing rules, in which a predetermined set of optical paths (fiber paths on designated wavebands) are put in place, acting as fixed pipes capable of supporting one or more LCs. The LCs are realized by allocating channels to them either on a fixed or demand-assigned basis. The static routing approach is suitable for cases in which a fixed arrangement of optical paths is sufficient for provisioning capacity for a known, quasi static traffic pattern. However, in cases when there is a high degree of uncertainty in the traffic demand, dynamic routing rules are required, and the OPs as well as the channels are assigned on demand. We consider the dynamic case in this section, dealing with point-to-point LCs in Section 6.6.1 and multipoint LCs in Section 6.6.2.[63] More complete presentations of the material contained in this section can be found in [Bala92, Bala+95a, Bala+91a].

6.6.1 Point-to-Point Connections

As in the static case, we break down the problem of establishing connections dynamically in an LLN into two subproblems:

1. Routing and waveband assignment
2. Channel assignment

Connection requests in a dynamically routed LLN are assumed to arrive sequentially at an ONM, which attempts to accommodate the requests as they arrive, given the

---

[63] To avoid unnecessary complications, it is assumed throughout that each LC uses a full λ-channel, so that LC $[s, d]$ is equivalent to OC (s, d).

current state of activity in the network. Active connections are held for random periods of time and then released. Requests that cannot be accommodated are blocked.

The principal performance measure for the RWA and channel assignment algorithms discussed later is blocking probability. Throughout the discussion of dynamic routing rules, it is assumed that rearrangement of currently active connections is not allowed. That is, neither the path, the waveband, nor the channel allocated to a connection in progress can be changed to accommodate a new connection.

In keeping with our picture of the LLN as multiple independent copies of the same network, one for each waveband, as shown in Figure 2.5(c), the RWA problem consists of first choosing a waveband (i.e., a copy of the network) to support a given connection request, and then attempting to find an optical path for the connection on that waveband. Once a path is found, a free channel on that path is assigned. Commands are then issued by the ONM to the various nodes along the path, which must set their LDCs to configure the path, and commands are issued to the terminating NASs to tune to the assigned channel, thereby completing the optical connection. The most difficult part of connection management in the LLN is the routing problem; that is, the selection of a feasible optical path within a chosen waveband, subject to the special LLN constraints: inseparability and DSC (see Section 3.4.1.1). In the approach presented here, routing is separated from waveband and channel selection to simplify the issue of path selection as much as possible.

6.6.1.1 Selection of a Waveband

Consider an LLN with K wavebands, $w_1, w_2, \ldots, w_K$. A simple, yet quite general, way of selecting a waveband for a given connection request is to maintain a sorted list of the K wavebands, and attempt to assign connections to wavebands in the order in which they appear on the list. They can be sorted using various criteria. Two rules that have been explored are *Maxband*, in which the list is sorted in decreasing order of usage, and *Minband*, in which it is sorted in increasing order of usage. Two wavebands with the same usage are sorted in ascending numerical order. The rationale behind Maxband is to attempt to reuse a waveband as much as is feasible before trying another one. Each waveband is loaded as heavily as possible and the "overflow" is offered to the next on the list. In contrast to Maxband, Minband attempts to load all wavebands equally by starting with the most lightly loaded waveband and working up.

Using the "list" approach, the steps in a connection allocation algorithm are as follows:

1. Select the waveband at the top of the list.
2. Try to allocate the connection on the chosen waveband using one of the routing and channel assignment algorithms presented later. (If allocation is successful, the connection is activated.)
3. If the connection cannot be allocated on the current waveband, then select the next waveband on the list and go to Step 2. (If the connection cannot be allocated on all wavebands in the list, it is blocked and the algorithm terminates.)

4. Update the order of the wavebands in the list whenever a connection is activated or released.

Simulations of the Maxband and Minband approaches to waveband selection have shown that the former outperforms the latter by a significant margin (approximately 20%) in typical cases. Thus, in the discussion that follows, the waveband selection algorithm used is always Maxband.

6.6.1.2 Routing within a Given Waveband

Having chosen a waveband, w, for a requested connection from source station s to destination station d, we seek an optical path $p = \langle s, d \rangle$ on w such that both the DSC constraint and the DCA constraints are satisfied *throughout the waveband* when the new connection is activated.[64]

Finding paths in an LLN that satisfy all constraints is complicated by the effects of inseparability. When the new connection is added, inseparability between the intended connection and those already active on waveband w may cause a coalescing of the intended path with other active paths. This in turn converts the intended point-to-point path p to an expanded point-to-multipoint path $p' = \langle s, \mathcal{D} \rangle$, where the expanded destination set $\mathcal{D}$ includes unintended (fortuitous) destinations as well as the intended destination d. The structures and destination sets of all other active paths that coalesce with p are expanded as well (see Section 6.5.1). We recall from Section 3.4.1.1 that this type of coalescing may cause violations of the DSC and DCA constraints in unexpected ways, affecting the original path and its expansion.

One phenomenon that can cause connection blocking frequently in an LLN is a "color clash": an inadvertent violation of the DCA constraint caused by the coalescing of a new path with preexisting paths on the same waveband. An example of a color clash produced by three interfering connections on a common waveband was presented in Figure 3.24, repeated here as Figure 6.57. In Figure 6.57(a), the optical connections $(1, 1^*)$ and $(2, 2^*)$ are both active using the same channel, λ_1, when the path for a new connection $(3, 3^*)$ is established by resetting the LDCs at nodes D, E, F, and G. As shown in Figure 6.57(b), the changes in the settings of those switches cause the signals S_1 and S_2 from the previously active connections to combine on fiber f, violating the DCA condition. Note that this violation of DCA occurs even before a channel is assigned to the new connection.

An optical path p for a requested connection is called *feasible* if the DSC and DCA constraints are satisfied on its waveband when it is configured, *and* if a free channel

---

[64] In this section all discussion pertains to activity within the same waveband unless stated otherwise.

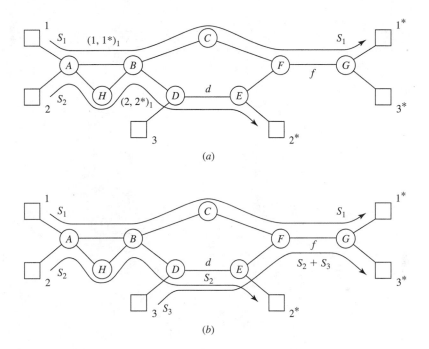

FIGURE 6.57 Color clash.

exists on p that can be assigned to the requested connection.[65] (For an intended path p to be feasible, the DSC and DCA conditions must satisfied on the expanded path p' as well as on p.)

Unfortunately, determining whether a feasible path exists for a given LC on a chosen waveband with a known pattern of existing connections is an NP-complete problem. It is much simpler to find a path for a connection while ignoring the DSC and DCA constraints, and check for feasibility later. To determine feasibility of a selected path, it is necessary to generate its expanded version and check whether it violates the constraints. A recursive algorithm for performing this task can be found in [Bala92].

Considering the complexity of the various possible approaches, our strategy is to select a path for a given connection on a chosen waveband that has some desirable properties, and then check to see whether that path is feasible. Because dynamic routing requires real-time computation, the algorithms for path selection must be simple and efficient.

---

[65] In the current context, a "channel" is a full λ-channel. In more general situations, a channel might be realized in some other way. For example, a low-rate LC might use one time slot in a λ-channel with a capacity that is subdivided into multiple time slots using T-WDMA.

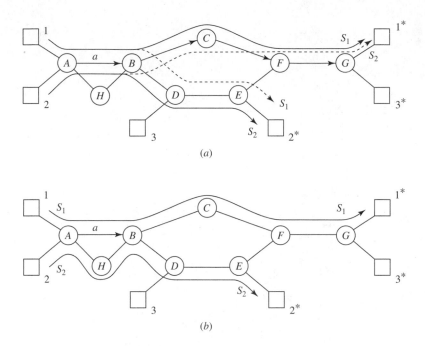

FIGURE 6.58 Illustrating inseparability.

We present two routing algorithms, called *k*-SP and Min-Int. Both of them attempt to find shortest paths on a chosen waveband (based on arbitrary link weights) while taking into account potential interference due to path coalescing. To define interference as it is used here, we return to the example of inseparability previously presented in Figure 3.20(a) and repeated for convenience as Figure 6.58. In Figure 6.58(a), suppose the connection $(1, 1^*)$ is active (denoted by signal S_1), and a new connection $(2, 2^*)$ is added on the intended path $p = \langle 2, 2^* \rangle = 2-A-B-D-E-2^*$ (denoted by signal S_2). Due to inseparability, a portion of S_2 appears at destination station 1^*, resulting in the expanded path $p' = \langle 2, \{2^*, \underline{1^*}\} \rangle$. The presence of the fortuitous destination 1^* means that the two active connections must use distinct channels to avoid interference at the receivers. We define the *interference* experienced by connection $(2, 2^*)$ on its intended optical path p as the number of additional independent signals it encounters on that path. In this example, the interference has a level of 1.

The two algorithms considered find paths that are short and that tend to reduce interference. Interference reduction in turn reduces the required number of channels for the connections, because a path with an interference of I requires $I + 1$ distinct channels for the connections sharing fibers on the path.

k-SP   The path allocation algorithm *k*-SP chooses a minimum-interference path from among a set of k shortest paths from source s to destination d. The steps are as follows:

1. Find k shortest paths from s to d.

2. Check each of the k paths for feasibility. If none of them are feasible, the connection request is blocked *on the chosen waveband*.[66]

3. From the subset of paths that are feasible, choose the one with the least interference for the connection.[67]

An efficient way to find k shortest paths is through a generalization of Dijkstra's label setting algorithm for finding shortest paths [Tarjan83]. Any meaningful link weight assignment can be used. For example, if power and noise limitations are an important consideration, the link weight might be chosen proportional to the attenuation on the link. (If the link weights are all equal, the shortest paths are minimum-hop paths.) If $k = 1$, then the selected path is always the shortest path. It is important to note that the k shortest paths are enumerated *before* feasibility is determined. Thus, all k paths might be infeasible either because there is no free channel on any of them or because they violate constraints.[68]

To illustrate the operation of k-SP, we return to the example of Figure 6.58(a), considering the problem of selecting a path for the connection $(2, 2^*)$, assuming that connection $(1, 1^*)$ is currently active on the indicated path. If minimum-hop routing is used with $k = 1$, signals S_1 and S_2 share fiber a, and inseparability causes them both to reach fortuitous destinations, as indicated by the dotted paths in the figure. Hence, the two connections must use two distinct channels to avoid DCA violations.

On the other hand, if 3-SP is used (assuming equal weight links), the following three paths for $(2, 2^*)$ would be found: $p_1 = 2–A–B–D–E–2^*$, $p_2 = 2–A–B–C–F–E–2^*$, and $p_3 = 2–A–H–B–D–E–2^*$. The first two have an interference level of 1, whereas p_3 has an interference level of 0 and would therefore be the selected path, as shown in Figure 6.58(b). In this case, $(2, 2^*)$ can reuse the same channel used by $(1, 1^*)$. Note that the selected path is not the shortest in this case.

Min-Int   Although the k-SP algorithm tends to find a path of reduced interference, it is not designed to find a path of minimum interference. Furthermore, it is constrained to examining only k paths. In contrast to the k-SP approach, the Min-Int algorithm finds a path for a new connection request that always has minimum

---

[66] If the connection request is blocked on the chosen waveband, other wavebands are tried according to the waveband selection algorithm being used.

[67] Evaluating the level of interference for a given connection is a simple operation.

[68] The performance of the k-SP algorithm can sometimes be improved by removing "saturated" fibers from consideration *before* executing the algorithm. Each saturated fiber (one that has all channels currently active on the chosen waveband) is eliminated from the graph of the network before finding shortest paths. In this way, paths chosen in Step 1 of the algorithm are never rejected because of link saturation (see Section 6.4.1.4).

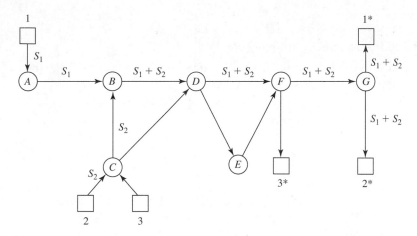

FIGURE 6.59 Illustrating Min-Int.

interference given the current activity in the network. The algorithm is not constrained to searching a limited number of paths, nor does it check for feasibility at the path selection phase. Once a minimum-interference path is selected, its expanded path is checked for feasibility. The connection is blocked on the chosen waveband if the path is not feasible. Because only one path is selected, it is especially important for it to have a good chance of satisfying the DSC and DCA constraints. Choosing a path of minimum interference tends to improve the likelihood that it satisfies these constraints.

An example of how the algorithm works is shown in Figure 6.59. Suppose connections $(1, 1^*)$ and $(2, 2^*)$ are active (using distinct channels) on the chosen waveband, and a connection $(3, 3^*)$ is requested. Assuming that the links are unidirectional in the orientation indicated by the arrows, there are four possible paths for the new connection: $p_1 = 3–C–D–F–3^*$, $p_2 = 3–C–B–D–F–3^*$, $p_3 = 3–C–D–E–F–3^*$, and $p_4 = 3–C–B–D–E–F–3^*$ in order of increasing length (assuming equal link weights). The respective levels of interference for the paths are $I_1 = 2$, $I_2 = 2$, $I_3 = 0$, and $I_4 = 2$, and therefore the Min-Int algorithm would choose p_3, which uses three internodal hops, compared with two hops for the shortest path.[69] The total number of channels required for the three connections in this case is only two, because connection $(3, 3^*)$ can reuse one of the channels used for the other active connections. (The selected path is clearly feasible in this case.)

---

[69] In this example the minimum-interference path is found easily by inspection. A Min-Int algorithm applicable to the general case is presented in Appendix E.

Comparing this to k-SP and assuming that there are at least three channels available on the chosen waveband, we find that the 2-SP algorithm would choose p_1, a shorter path with more interference. All three channels are required in the 2-SP case because the interference on the expanded path p_1' has a level of 2. (If only two channels are available, the connection would be blocked on the chosen waveband using 2-SP, whereas it would be accepted using Min-Int.) For $k \geq 3$, both Min-Int and k-SP give the same result.

Provided that the path $p = \langle s, d \rangle$ found by Min-Int satisfies the DSC constraint, it can be shown ([Bala92]) that it minimizes the additional interference on the entire waveband caused by the activation of the new connection (see Appendix E).

6.6.1.3   Channel Allocation

Having selected a feasible path for a connection, it remains to allocate a channel to that connection on the chosen waveband. (Feasibility implies that given the current state of activity in the network, at least one free channel exists on the selected path.)

A free channel is one that does not violate the DCA constraint on all fibers of the selected path. It is assumed that a list of all free channels for the selected connection is available. It would be produced typically as a by-product of a check for DCA constraint violations. Two simple allocation strategies are of interest: Max Reuse or Min Reuse channel allocation. In the former, the free channel that is most used on the chosen waveband is assigned to the connection. In the latter, the least used channel is assigned. The rationale here is similar to that behind the Maxband and Minband approach to waveband allocation. In the Max Reuse case, the objective is to reuse a channel as much as possible before trying another one. In the Min Reuse case, the objective is to distribute the load on all channels evenly. Although the two allocation problems would appear to be similar, it turns out that the best strategy for waveband allocation (Maxband) is not generally the best one for channel allocation. The Min Reuse channel allocation approach typically outperforms the Max Reuse approach because it creates fewer opportunities for color clashes.

6.6.1.4   Performance of Dynamic Algorithms:
Point-to-Point Connections

As indicated in Section 6.4, the performance of a dynamic routing algorithm is very difficult to evaluate analytically, even in the simpler case of wavelength routed networks. We therefore explore the performance of dynamic routing rules for LLNs in this section via simulation. (More details concerning performance of dynamic algorithms can be found in [Bala+91a, 91b] and [Bala92].

The network of Figure 6.60 is used in all simulations presented here. It has 20 nodes of average degree 2.7, and was generated randomly using the procedure presented in [Hagouel83]. Each link contains a single fiber pair unless indicated otherwise. Each node is assumed to serve one or more source stations as well as a nonblocking destination station. The activity of each source station is modeled as a two-state (idle

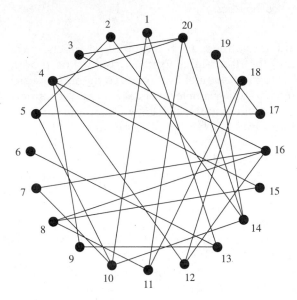

FIGURE 6.60 Random network.

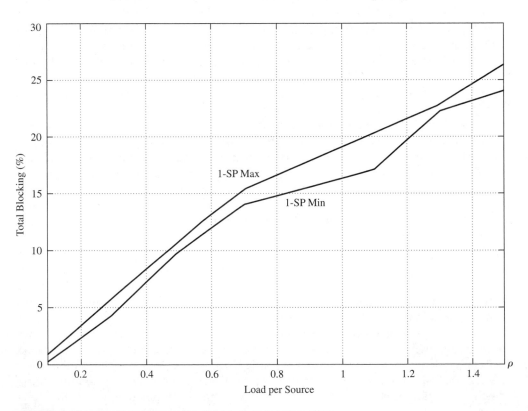

FIGURE 6.61 Max Reuse versus Min Reuse channel allocation.

and active) Markov chain, which generates connection requests at a rate λ when idle, with a connection holding time of μ^{-1} (see Figure C.1). The destinations of the connection requests are chosen at random and equiprobably. The activity of each source is then determined by the source load parameter $\rho = \lambda/\mu$, and the total load offered to the network (in Erlangs) is given by $S\lambda/(\lambda + \mu)$, where S is the total number of sources in the network.

The study focuses first on activity within a single waveband. Routing and channel allocation algorithms are compared based on their blocking performance. Networks with single-fiber-pair links as well as multifiber-pair links are studied. In all routing algorithms, equal link weights are used.

In the single waveband examples, blocking is high (typically as high as 20% for high offered loads) because of the restriction of all connections to one waveband. It must be recalled, however, that in a multiwaveband network, blocking of a connection on one waveband does not mean that the connection request is blocked. It merely means that additional wavebands must be tried for that connection. In the final example, the complete blocking performance of a multiwaveband network is examined.

Case 1: Single Waveband; Max Reuse versus Min Reuse Channel Allocation

Figure 6.61 shows the blocking performance of the two channel allocation algorithms discussed in Section 6.6.1.3 when there are three channels available. Blocking is plotted as a function of the source load parameter ρ, with a single source per node and a single fiber pair per link. Because $S = 20$, the maximum offered load to the network is 12 Erlangs in this example (when $\rho = 1.5$). The 1-SP routing rule is used with equal link weights, corresponding to minimum-hop routing.

As can be seen from Figure 6.61, the Min Reuse rule performs better than the Max Reuse rule for all values of load, with the blocking reaching approximately 25% for the highest offered load. It is also of interest to know which effects are dominant in producing blocking. It turns out that approximately half of the blocking is due to color clashes and the rest is due to the unavailability of a free channel. Blocking due to DSC violations is negligible in this example. The blocking due to color clashes is substantially diminished, especially at lighter loads, by using the Min Reuse rule. This is because the lower degree of channel reuse resulting from the Min Reuse rule decreases the chance that a color clash occurs. Blocking due to channel unavailability is slightly increased by using the Min Reuse rule, but not enough to offset the reduction of color clashes.

Case 2: Single Waveband; k-SP Routing   Figure 6.62 compares the performance of the k-SP algorithm for the cases $k = 1$ and $k = 2$ using the Min Reuse channel allocation rule. Again, there are three channels in the waveband. As is to be expected, the blocking performance for $k = 2$ is considerably better than for $k = 1$, with both color clashes and channel unavailability reduced as k is increased.

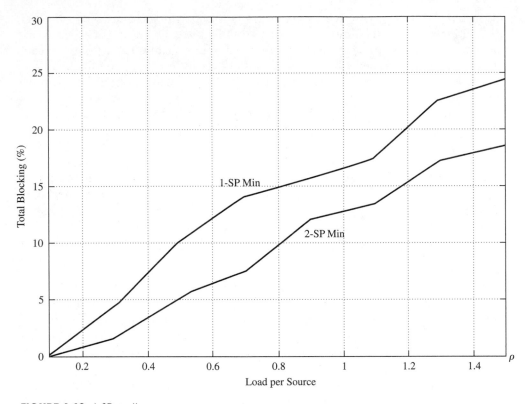

FIGURE 6.62 *k*-SP routing.

Case 3: Single Waveband; 2-SP versus Min-Int Routing

Figure 6.63 compares the performance of the 2-SP and Min-Int algorithms. Again the Min Reuse channel allocation rule is used with three channels. For this case, the range of the load parameter ρ is increased to 3.1 to observe differences in relative performance at high loads. As can be seen, Min-Int outperforms 2-SP at the lower loads, but the reverse is true at the higher loads. This effect can be explained by the fact that the number of hops on the selected paths is more tightly constrained in the 2-SP algorithm than in the Min-Int algorithm. As a result, the latter algorithm sometimes selects unusually long paths to avoid interference. This in turn tends to increase congestion in the network at high loads, increasing blocking probability.[70] In this example, the average path length using the Min-Int algorithm was approximately 3.6 hops, compared with 2.9 hops for 2-SP, indicating a moderate increase in congestion.

---

[70] A similar effect has been observed in dynamic routing algorithms in both wavelength routed optical networks and traditional communication networks. At the higher loads, routing rules that tend to produce longer paths typically lead to higher congestion and higher blocking probabilities, and can eventually cause instabilities in network operation (see, for example, [Schwartz87, page 630 f]).

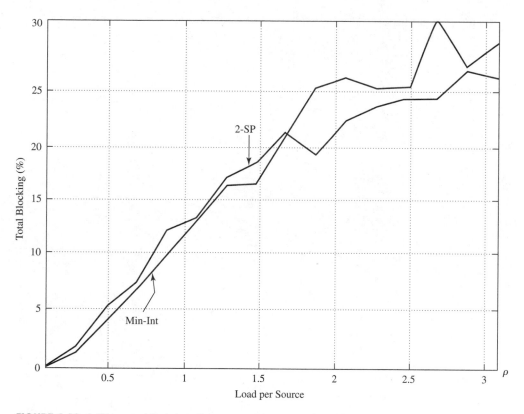

FIGURE 6.63 *k*-SP versus Min-Int routing.

Case 4: Single Waveband; Multifiber Links

The purpose of this example is to compare the performance of the routing algorithms when more than one fiber pair is available on a link. Each link in the network of Figure 6.60 now has five fiber pairs. To keep the load on the network roughly commensurate with the total fiber capacity, the number of sources per node is increased to four. The total number of available channels is still three. Figure 6.64 compares the blocking performance for three algorithms: 2-SP, 10-SP, and Min-Int, with the source load parameter ρ varied from 0 to 1.6, corresponding to a maximum offered load of approximately 50 Erlangs. Min Reuse channel allocation is used. The 2-SP algorithm performs very poorly; in fact, it performs significantly worse than in the case of Figure 6.62 with a comparable load. By increasing k to 10, performance improves to the range of blocking exhibited earlier for the single-fiber-pair cases. By contrast, the blocking for the Min-Int algorithm is far superior (less than 2%) throughout.

The comparison in this example reveals a significant difference in performance between algorithms that consider only a limited number of paths between source and destination (e.g., k-SP) and those that have no limitation (e.g., Min-Int). In the case at hand, the number of possible fiber paths between a given source–destination pair is increased enormously by increasing the number of fiber pairs per link. For

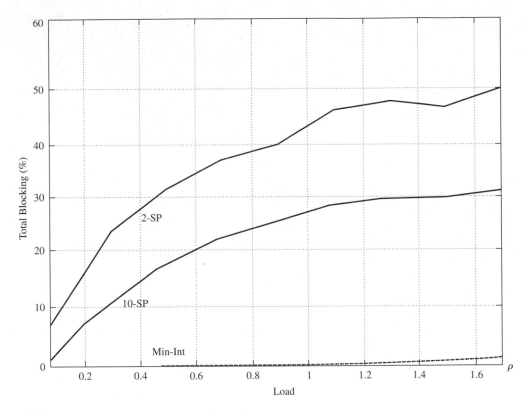

FIGURE 6.64 Blocking in networks with multifiber links.

example, one given three-hop path is replaced by 125 three-hop alternative paths on the same links when there is a choice of five fibers on each link. The 2-SP and 10-SP algorithms examine only a small fraction of these, whereas the Min-Int algorithm finds a minimum-interference path, taking all fibers into consideration. In general, for the multifiber case, Min-Int delivers better performance with less computational complexity than *k*-SP.

Another way of viewing this comparison is that the first step of the *k*-SP algorithm is *static*, in that it selects paths independent of the state of the network. The Min-Int algorithm is *adaptive*, in that the path is selected based on transnodal weights that are a function of network activity (see Appendix E).

Case 5: Single Waveband; Rooted Routing
In view of the complexity of the dynamic routing algorithms as well as the problems of satisfying the DSC constraint and avoiding color clashes, it is worthwhile to investigate whether there is much to be gained by dynamic routing rules in LLNs. In this example we compare the dynamic routing case using the Min-Int algorithm and Min Reuse channel allocation with a

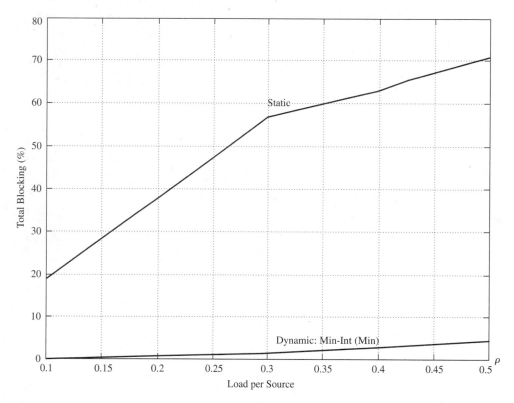

FIGURE 6.65 Static versus dynamic routing.

static approach using rooted routing (see Sections 6.5.5.1 and 6.6.2.3). The same 20-node test network is used, with a single fiber pair per link and three channels available on a single waveband.

The simplest way to avoid complications when routing connections on a common waveband is to choose a spanning tree of the network and to pick an appropriate node on the tree as its "root", setting that node to operate as a star coupler and setting the other nodes to confine all paths to the chosen tree. This is the rooted routing approach based on an embedded star. Because all connections are routed on a tree, there are no routing decisions. However, about one third of the links are unused when rooted routing is used in this example. Channel assignment is easy: Any available channel is assigned to each new requested connection. Because all connections are broadcast from the root, there is no channel reuse. Thus, the question at hand is to determine which is worse: lack of channel reuse (the static tree-based case) or LLN constraint violations (the dynamic case). The comparison is shown in Figure 6.65. The static curve for blocking probability is obtained using the Engset formula $P_B = ENG(20, \rho, 3)$, because this is equivalent to a 20-user shared-channel system with three channels (see Equation 5.95). The dynamic curve is repeated from Figure 6.63. Clearly, from the

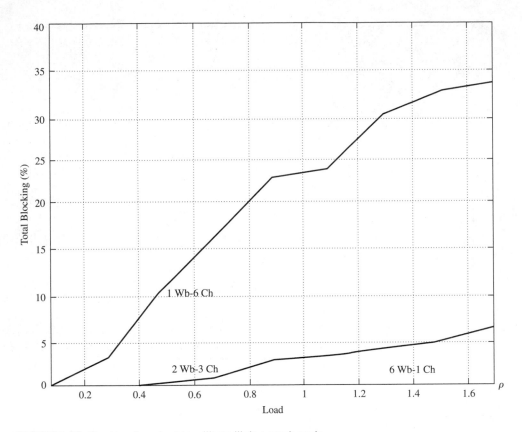

FIGURE 6.66 Blocking in networks with multiple wavebands.

point of view of blocking, the dynamic case is far superior. Even at very light loads ($\rho = 0.1$) the static approach is unacceptable.

Case 6: Multiple Wavebands   The available optical spectrum can be partitioned in various ways into wavebands and λ-channels. In this example we compare three different partitions, each containing the same total number of λ-channels. (The different partitions lead to different spectral efficiencies because of the guardbands between wavebands. This effect is examined at the end of the example.)

Figure 6.66 compares blocking probabilities in the case of a six-channel network in which the following spectrum partitioning is used:

- One waveband, six channels per waveband
- Two wavebands, three channels per waveband
- Six wavebands, one channel per waveband

The latter case corresponds to a wavelength routed network.

The Maxband rule is used for waveband selection, Min-Int for path selection, and Min Reuse for channel allocation. Two sources are used at each node to double the load on the network, consistent with the doubling of the total number of channels from three to six.

Note that blocking improves dramatically as the number of wavebands is increased. There is a factor of six improvement at high loads and still more at low loads, when two wavebands are used instead of one. There is negligible blocking for the case of a single channel per waveband. This illustrates the penalty incurred through LLN constraint violations when several channels are grouped into wavebands rather than operating the network as a WRN, with a single channel per waveband.

Other conclusions can be drawn from comparisons of Figure 6.66 with the Min-Int curve in Figure 6.63. We note that the latter shows a blocking of approximately 16% with $\rho = 1.5$ (for an offered load to the network of 12 Erlangs) when three channels are used on one waveband. Compare this with the curves of Figure 6.66 at the point $\rho = 1.5$ (giving 24 Erlangs offered load). In the case in which all six channels are confined to a single waveband, the blocking increases to approximately 32%. This case corresponds to "scaling up" both the offered load and the network capacity by a factor of two. Ordinarily, this upward scaling would *reduce* blocking because the laws of large numbers work in our favor in the larger network. However, the simulation shows that the upward scaling effect is more than overcome by additional blocking due to LLN constraint violations when all traffic is confined to one waveband.

Next consider the two-waveband case with three channels per waveband. Figure 6.66 shows approximately 5% blocking, which is a factor of three reduction in blocking compared with the system of Figure 6.63. In the two cases, the offered load to the network *per channel* is the same, but blocking is reduced in the two-waveband system by sending the overflow from the first waveband to the second one. Again, the advantage of partitioning into more wavebands is evident. The six-waveband case takes this approach to its ultimate limit.

It it clear from the last example that the more the spectrum is partitioned into wavebands, the better the blocking performance. However, spectrum partitioning results in an increase in optical spectrum usage (as well as requiring a more complex network node). Recall that to be able to discriminate between wavebands at the network nodes (LDCs), a guardband of width B_g is needed between wavebands, and B_g normally must be considerably greater than the λ-channel bandwidth B_λ (see Section 6.5.6.3). To quantify this effect, let $B_{op}(W, C)$ be the spectrum required to support W wavebands containing C channels each, so that $B_{op}(1, WC)$ is the spectrum required if all WC channels are grouped into a single waveband. Let $r(W, C)$ be the ratio of spectrum usage in the first case to that in the second case. Then, using Equation 6.60, we have

$$r(W, C) = \frac{B_{op}(W, C)}{B_{op}(1, WC)} = 1 + \frac{W - 1}{WC}\alpha \qquad (6.88)$$

where $\alpha = B_g / B_\lambda$.

Using Equation 6.88 and assuming $\alpha = 5$, we find that the two-waveband case requires a factor of $r = 1.83$ increase in bandwidth over the single-waveband case, whereas the six-waveband (WRN) case requires a factor of 5.16 increase in bandwidth. Thus, in partitioning the spectrum into an increasing number of wavebands, we incur a gain in performance in terms of blocking but a loss in terms of spectrum efficiency.

6.6.1.5 Summary of Point-to-Point Dynamic Routing in LLNs

The static and dynamic formulations of the connection allocation problem in LLNs differ in their design and performance objectives. In the static case, one is generally interested in allocating resources to a set of known connections to minimize the use of the optical spectrum; that is, the number of wavebands and channels required to support a given set of connections. In the dynamic case, because the connection set is not known a priori, one generally works under the assumption of a fixed available spectrum (wavebands and channels) and attempts to do the resource allocation in a way that maximizes performance, typically by minimizing blocking probability for a given offered load. The unpredictability of the connection request sequence makes it important for the dynamic algorithms to adapt to random fluctuations in demand.

Among the three parts of the connection allocation problem under dynamic routing rules (waveband selection, path allocation, and channel assignment), it is only the routing problem that is difficult, primarily because of the potential interference among optical paths sharing the same waveband. Simulation results suggest that routing algorithms (e.g., the Min-Int algorithm presented here) that tend to minimize interference (the number of fortuitous destinations) on each new connection perform best under most conditions. The simulations also show that it is best from the point of view of blocking to attempt to reuse each waveband as much as possible (the Maxband waveband selection rule) and to attempt to reuse each channel on a given waveband as little as possible (the Min Reuse channel selection rule).

The performance of LLNs under dynamic routing rules improves markedly as the spectrum is partitioned into an increased number of wavebands, and as the number of fiber pairs per link is increased. This is due to the fact that the special constraints of the LLN (inseparability and distinct source combining) are less troublesome in these cases.

6.6.2 Routing Multicast Connections

In the multicast case, under dynamic routing rules, each LC is in the form $[s, D]$, where the destination set $D = \{d_1, d_2, \ldots\}$ may contain any number of stations, up to the full broadcast case. An example of a multicast connection from source 1 to destination set $\{2^*, 3^*\}$ is shown in Figure 6.67. The links on the path $p = \langle 1, \{2^*, 3^*\} \rangle$ are shown as bold lines. The LDC in node A is set to split the optical signal generated at 1^*, directing portions of it (possibly amplified) to nodes B and C.

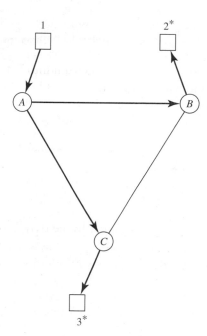

FIGURE 6.67 Example of a multicast
connection.

Generalizing the point-to-point case, a multicast connection allocation algorithm can be broken down into the following steps:

1. Choose a waveband for the connection according to some given selection rule.
2. Attempt to find a path for the connection on the selected waveband. If one is found that satisfies the LLN constraints, assign a channel to the connection. (If allocation is successful at this point, the algorithm terminates.)
3. If the connection cannot be allocated on the current waveband, go to Step 1. (If all wavebands have been tried at this point, the connection is blocked.)

For simplicity in this section we focus on the single-waveband case; that is, the emphasis is on Step 2, which is primarily a routing problem. The waveband selection rule, embodied in Steps 1 and 3, is arbitrary and independent of the routing rule. The Maxband approach, which was found to be best in the point-to-point case, is likely to perform best under multicast conditions as well.

6.6.2.1 Routing within a Given Waveband: Multicast Trees

Having chosen a waveband w for a requested connection from source station s to destination set D, we seek an optical path $p = \langle s, D \rangle$ on w such that both the DSC and DCA constraints are satisfied throughout the waveband when the new connection is activated. At the stage of path selection, satisfaction of the DCA condition implies that no color clashes occur and that a free channel exists on p that can be used for the requested connection. A path that satisfies all of these conditions is called a *feasible multicast path*.

In the multicast case, inseparability often causes path coalescing, which expands the path p to a path $p' = \langle s, \mathcal{D} \rangle$. The expanded destination set $\mathcal{D}$ includes fortuitous destinations in addition to the intended set D. The structures and destination sets of all other active paths that coalesce with p are also expanded. For the intended path p to be feasible, the DSC and DCA conditions must be satisfied on the expanded path p' as well as on p. The potential violations of the DSC and DCA constraints caused by path coalescing are more complex in the multicast case than in the point-to-point case, making routing more difficult.

The set of fibers forming a path p from source s to the intended destination set D must contain a directed path from s to each station in D. Furthermore, p and its expanded form p' must both satisfy the DSC condition, meaning they cannot contain any directed cycles or any directed parallel paths. We call a path that satisfies these conditions a *multicast tree*. A multicast tree that satisfies the DCA condition constitutes a feasible multicast path. Thus a routing algorithm for multicast connections in LLNs must (1) find multicast trees and (2) ensure that they satisfy the DCA constraint. Because the first step alone is already an NP-complete problem for the special case of a point-to-point connection, this is clearly a very difficult task.

Because of the extra complexity of the multicast case, we add a preliminary step to the routing procedure that greatly simplifies the problem: The network is initially decomposed into a set of edge–disjoint trees, and each optical path is confined to one of these "preselected" trees.[71] The remainder of the connection allocation algorithm is performed dynamically in response to each connection request. Thus the overall algorithm is a hybrid static–dynamic procedure. Because the fibers carrying the connection are confined to a tree, the intended path p as well as its expanded version p' (if the connection coalesces with other active connections on the tree) satisfies the DSC constraint automatically.[72]

A typical LLN operates on multiple wavebands. In the multiwaveband case, a tree decomposition is performed independently on each waveband, and the decompositions may be the same or different on the different wavebands. After the trees are preselected, the dynamic part of the algorithm consists of choosing a waveband for the optical path carrying the requested connection and determining whether a tree T, which can support the connection, can be found on that waveband.[73] A multicast

---

[71] Because the trees are preselected, this part of the routing algorithm is "static," and it can be performed offline when the network is initialized. Therefore, the computational complexity of the tree decomposition step is not a paramount issue.

[72] The DSC condition can be violated on a tree only if a connection is routed so that it doubles back on a link, forming a loop that circulates endlessly through both oppositely directed fibers on the same link—an obviously pathological routing decision.

[73] It should be noted that this procedure can be applied to dynamic connection allocation in the point-to-point case as well as in the multicast case. However, the extra constraint imposed by tree preselection makes this static–dynamic approach less efficient than unconstrained purely dynamic algorithms in the point-to-point case (see case 5 in Section 6.6.1.4).

connection [*s, D*] can be supported on a tree *T* operating on a given waveband if

1. *T* contains *s* and *D*
2. The optical path *p* supporting the connection causes no color clashes on *T*
3. A free channel exists for the connection on path *p*

We consider each of these issues next.

6.6.2.2 Preselecting Edge-Disjoint Trees on a Waveband

The discussion in this section applies to each waveband separately. On a given waveband, the network can be described as a multigraph. Each node in the network is represented by a vertex of the multigraph, and each link in the network is represented by *F* parallel edges, where *F* is the number of fiber pairs on the link. We include only the network nodes and *internodal* links in the multigraph model, excluding the access stations and their access links. Each station is assumed to be able to access all trees containing the node to which it is attached, by an appropriate setting of the LDC at that node.

In general, any network can be decomposed into a set of edge–disjoint trees in many different ways. The procedure used here for tree decomposition is as follows. The multigraph is first decomposed into a (hopefully large) number of edge–disjoint spanning trees. (It is assumed that the graph of the network is connected, so that spanning trees exist; otherwise, not all multicast connections are possible.) Then the remaining edges are grouped into the smallest possible number of (nonspanning) edge–disjoint trees. (Each tree is necessarily an ordinary subgraph, containing no more than one edge between each pair of vertices.)

In a tree decomposition of the network graph (or multigraph), there are two conflicting objectives. First, it is important to find as many spanning trees as possible, because each spanning tree can potentially accommodate any multicast connection. Second, it is desirable to keep the trees "dense" (i.e., of small diameter) so that the multicast paths are short, promoting channel reuse and reducing chances of color clashes.

The problem of decomposing a graph into the maximum number of edge–disjoint spanning trees is solved in [Gusfield83] using the method of partitioning of matroids. Unfortunately, in decomposing a graph into a large number of spanning trees, each tree tends to be of a large diameter. This is because the degree of each vertex in a tree must be kept small to allow other trees to include that vertex, thereby maximizing the number of trees containing each vertex of the graph. In the worst case, each spanning tree becomes a long chain, with vertices of maximum degree 2.

Another approach to tree decomposition is to seek the densest spanning trees (those with the smallest diameter). This, however, tends to produce a smaller number of spanning trees for the reason stated in the previous paragraph. Thus, some compromise is required to produce a "good" tree decomposition: one containing many dense spanning trees. For this purpose, a useful heuristic algorithm has been developed based on a *modified breadth-first search with parameter d* (MBFS-*d*; see [Bala+93]). The algorithm starts with one node and adds nodes using a breadth-first search until a spanning tree is formed. The parameter *d* represents the maximum number of neighboring nodes

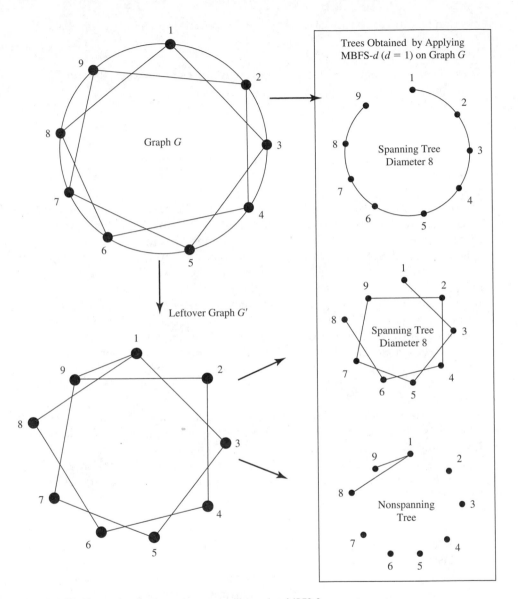

FIGURE 6.68 Example of a tree decomposition using MBFS-1.

that are considered for adding to the tree at each step. As *d* is increased, the algorithm tends to find trees of smaller diameter, but this usually produces fewer spanning trees.

Examples of the results of running the MBFS-*d* algorithm on an eight-node network with a single fiber pair per link are shown in Figures 6.68 and 6.69. In each case, the

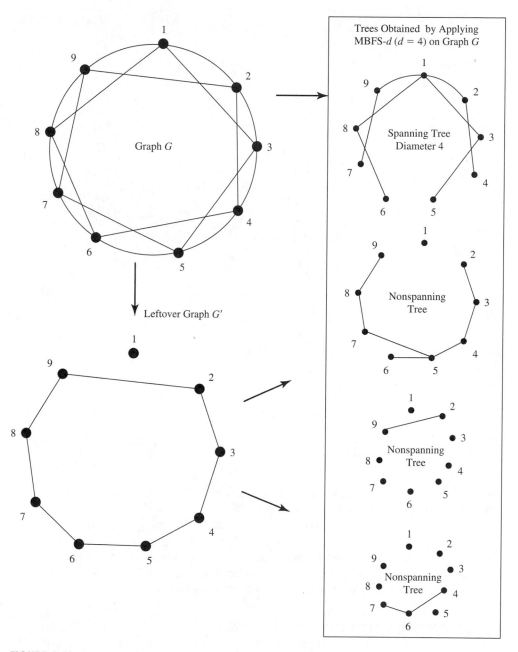

FIGURE 6.69 Example of a tree decomposition using MBFS-4.

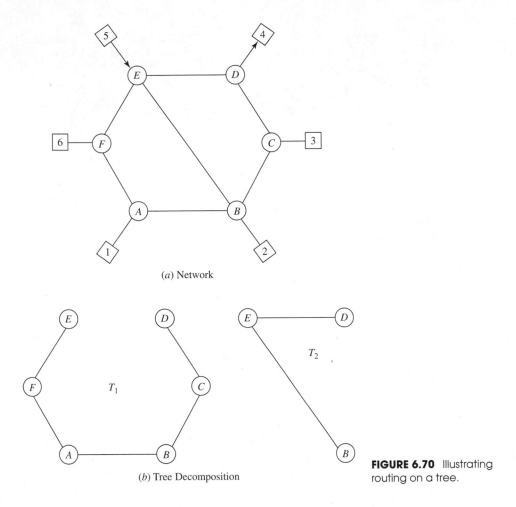

(a) Network

(b) Tree Decomposition

FIGURE 6.70 Illustrating routing on a tree.

first spanning tree is shown extracted from the original graph G, leaving a graph G', which is further decomposed into additional trees.

The examples illustrate the two extreme cases: $d = 1$ (finding a maximum number of spanning trees) and $d = 4$ (producing smaller diameter trees). In Figure 6.68, the MBFS-1 algorithm finds two spanning trees of diameter 8, and one nonspanning tree. The MBFS-4 case in Figure 6.69 yields only one spanning tree from a total of four in the decomposition, but the maximum diameter of the trees is 6.

6.6.2.3 Routing Connections on a Tree

Because each multicast connection is confined to a tree, its optical path is (almost) unique. We provide two alternative routing techniques in the following pages, each of which has some positive and negative features. Both techniques yield multicast trees as defined in Section 6.6.2.1.

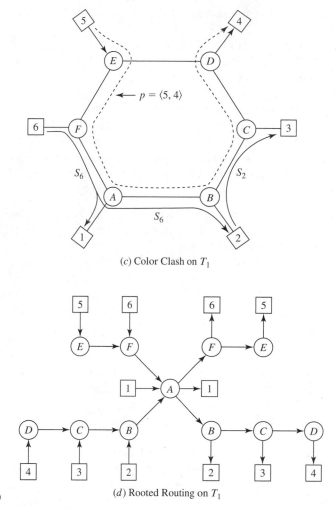

(c) Color Clash on T_1

FIGURE 6.70   *(continued)*   (d) Rooted Routing on T_1

Shortest Path Routing   If connections are not allowed to double back on links, then the path for any multicast connection on a given tree is unique and satisfies the DSC constraint automatically. (It is also the shortest possible path on the tree.) However, shortest path routing can lead to a problem we have observed earlier in LLNs: color clashes. To illustrate, consider the six-node, single-waveband, single-fiber-per-link network of Figure 6.70(a), which is decomposed into two trees, T_1 and T_2, in Figure 6.70(b). Suppose two connections, [6, {1, 2}] and [2, 3], are active on T_1 as shown by signals S_6 and S_2 in Figure 6.70(c) and are both assigned the same wavelength, λ_1. Now a new request arrives for connection [5, 4], which must also be placed on T_1. By inseparability, the intended path $p = \langle 5, 4 \rangle$ is expanded to $p' = \langle 5, \{4, \underline{1, 2, 3}\} \rangle$, carrying a portion of signals S_6 and S_2 with it to stations 3 and 4. Because these are both on the same channel, this results in a color clash on the last portion of the path.

The situation leading to the color clash in this example is an inevitable result of using the Max Reuse rule for channel allocation on the tree.[74] As indicated earlier, channel reuse in an LLN is a two-edged sword: It can economize on spectrum use, but it can also introduce unnecessary blocking (assuming that connection rearrangement is not allowed). In this example, even if there is a free wavelength available, there is no way to route the new connection on the tree, and it must be blocked.

One way of avoiding color clashes is to require all connections using a given tree to use distinct channels. Unfortunately, this eliminates any possibility of reusing channels on the tree. An approach that requires distinct channel allocation, but carries with it some offsetting advantages, is rooted routing, which is considered next.

Rooted Routing on a Tree   Rooted routing, as described in Sections 6.5.5.1 and 6.6.1.4, can be used for either point-to-point or multicast LCs. But it is especially effective in the multicast case.

Using rooted routing in our example, the tree T_1 is configured as an embedded star rooted at node A in Figure 6.70(d). Note that the LDCs at all nodes except the root node are configured to concentrate all transmitted signals at the root, and then broadcast the combined signals back to the receiving side of all stations—an arrangement used earlier in several other examples. It is important to note that the internodal link settings of the LDCs can be *fixed* once the tree decomposition is known, because all stations on each tree must have access to the root node.[75] The only LDC settings that must be changed when a connection enters or leaves the network are those connecting the affected access stations to a chosen tree. This is in contrast to shortest path routing, in which all LDC settings depend on the current state of the network and thus must be changed each time a new connection becomes active.

Another advantage of the rooted routing approach is that the total capacity of the waveband can be shared fully among all connections on the tree using any desired multiplexing/multiple-access technique, as described in Chapter 5. (Recall from Section 5.4.1.4 that shared-channel systems are readily adaptable to multicast LCs.) This means that the capacity allocated to each multicast connection need not be quantized to units of full λ-channels. However, the downside of rooted routing is that the capacity of the waveband supporting the tree cannot be reused.

Routing Rules and LDC Complexity   Under the routing rules defined here, the tree decomposition of a network is precomputed when the network is initialized, and it remains fixed thereafter (barring a failure or network reconfiguration). This means that on a given waveband, interconnections exist only among the internodal

---

[74] However, even if some other channel allocation rule is used, it is possible for the network state to evolve to that shown in Figure 6.70(c). Can you construct an example?

[75] Depending on the power distribution rule, some adjustments in dividing and combining ratios might be required as connections enter or leave the network (see Section 6.5.7).

links belonging to a common tree. If this arrangement remains static, the structure of the LDCs can be simplified to realize only the required internodal tree connections, implying that fewer LDC ports and switching elements are needed. A further simplification may be possible in the case of rooted routing, as mentioned earlier. Provided that means are included in the nodes for maintaining proper power levels, all internodal LDC settings can be held fixed, so that the only controllable elements in the LDCs are those required for connecting the access stations to the trees.

6.6.2.4 Completing Multicast Connection Allocation

After setting up preselected trees and choosing a waveband for a requested connection, it remains to choose a tree on the selected waveband and a channel on the selected tree for the connection.

Choosing a Tree for a Connection   Suppose a waveband is chosen on which to route a new connection. Intuitively, there are many criteria that might be used for selecting a tree for the connection on that waveband. Three reasonable possibilities are

1. Choose the smallest tree that can accommodate the connection.
2. Choose the most used tree (one with the most active connections).
3. Choose the minimum-interference tree.

Results of simulations using shortest path routing on trees show that the minimum-interference rule is superior to the other two from the point of view of blocking. However, the margin of superiority decreases with increasing degree of multicasting [Bala92, Bala+93].

In implementing the minimum-interference rule under shortest path routing, all preselected trees are checked to determine which ones contain a feasible multicast tree for the connection. Among the feasible trees, the one with the least amount of interference is chosen for the connection. Testing for feasibility requires checking for color clashes as well as checking for the existence of a free channel. (If rooted routing is used on each tree, a color clash check is unnecessary.)

Channel Allocation on a Tree   Recall that regardless of the degree of multicast, a single channel suffices for a multicast optical connection. Under shortest path routing, it is simplest to assume that each channel is a λ-channel. The rule used for allocating that channel can be important.[76] Recall that in the case of point-to-point connections allocated under dynamic routing rules, attempting to reuse λ-channels as much as possible on a given waveband may be a poor tactic because it leads to color clashes. The same holds true in the multicast case. Therefore, we shall assume henceforth that

---

[76] It is irrelevant under rooted routing.

the Min Reuse rule is used for channel allocation. In the context of tree routing, Min Reuse implies allocating the channel that is used least on the selected tree.

6.6.2.5 Results of Simulations

Given the number of factors interacting in dynamic allocation of multicast connections, simulation is the only reasonable approach to performance evaluation. This section examines blocking in a simulated multicast scenario, focusing on a single waveband. As in the point-to-point case, a multicast connection is blocked in a multiwaveband network only if it is blocked on each waveband.

In the simulation results presented in this section, the network has a randomly generated topology with 20 nodes, an average degree of 6, and two fiber pairs per link. The waveband contains three λ-channels. One source is attached to each node, with connection request generation governed by a two-state Markov chain with variable load parameter ρ (see Section 6.6.1.4). Each requested connection selects three receivers randomly. Shortest path routing is used with minimum-interference tree selection. All receivers are assumed to be nonblocking.

The MBFS-d algorithm is used for tree decomposition, with the results shown for various values of d in Table 6.8. The table lists the sizes of the trees found using the algorithm for each value of d ranging from 2 to the maximum nodal degree, 8. Among all values of d producing the maximum number of spanning trees ($d = 2, 3, 5, 6$), the decomposition for $d = 6$ gives the minimum average path length (in optical hops) when used as a basis for connection allocation in the simulation. Figure 6.71 shows that this value of d also produces the lowest blocking probability over almost the complete range of the load parameter ρ. (Values of d less than 6 are not shown. They produce higher blocking probabilities for all values of ρ.) While the blocking probabilities in this single waveband example are substantial, blocking using multiple wavebands would be much less, following the same pattern as in the point-to-point case (see Figure 6.66).

TABLE 6.8   Sizes of Trees Generated with the MBFS-d Algorithm

d	Sizes of Trees
2	20, 20, 20, 20, 18, 12
3	20, 20, 20, 20, 16, 5, 4, 2, 2, 2, 2, 2, 2
4	20, 20, 20, 18, 18, 7, 4, 2, 2, 2, 2
5	20, 20, 20, 20, 16, 6, 5, 2, 2, 2, 2
6	20, 20, 20, 20, 18, 6, 5, 2, 2
7	20, 20, 20, 19, 11, 7, 6, 6, 2, 2, 2
8	20, 20, 19, 19, 9, 9, 7, 7

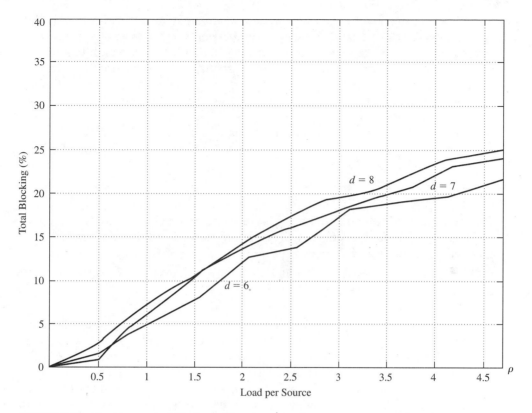

FIGURE 6.71 Blocking probability for multicast connections.

6.7 Economic Trade-offs in Multiwavelength Optical Networking

Several studies in recent years have addressed the economics of multiwavelength optical networking [Bala+96b]. On the transmission level there is a clear advantage with WDM. By replacing a single optical carrier on a fiber with 16 or more signals on distinct λ-channels, the inherent bandwidth of the fiber is utilized much more efficiently, and additional advantages are obtained through the use of optical rather than electronic amplification on long transmission links (see Section 4.4). However, WDM networking[77] also requires routing (switching). Some have suggested that WDM switching should be opaque [Bala+95b], and others have recommended that WDM routing should be performed using transparent optical approaches [Coathup+95].

---

[77] To conform to current usage in this section, we shall use the term "WDM network" for our generic WRN.

In addition to the obvious capacity expansion advantages of WDM transmission, the advantages of all-optical approaches going beyond transmission include transparency to signal formats, upgradability, and the ability to provide high-bandwidth "clear" channels directly to the users' end systems. As studied quantitatively in Section 4.12, a significant disadvantage of transparency is the accumulation of transmission and switching impairments, such as noise, dispersion, nonlinear distortion, and switch cross-talk.

Among WDM equipment that is commercially available at this time, there are varying degrees of transparency. Some examples, in decreasing order of transparency are:

- Purely optical cross-connects
- Optical transmission line-terminating equipment performing WDM multiplexing/demultiplexing functions as well as partial to full (electronic) regeneration (see Section 2.5)
- Fully regenerative terminal and switching equipment, with regeneration and switching performed electronically

In this section, we study some economic trade-offs for a range of applications and architectures—from point-to-point connections to rings to cross-connected mesh networks. The discussion is based on the availability and cost of commercial products as this is being written. The reader should be aware that these products are evolving very rapidly. Given the characteristics of current equipment, the primary advantage of multiwavelength *networking* (as opposed to transmission only) is the ability to route and switch signals at the line rate; for example, STS-48 (2.5 Gbps) or higher. Demultiplexing down to lower rates (as is usually done in electronic switches) is costly and often unnecessary.

WDM is currently being widely deployed by telecommunications network operators across the United States. The deployment has been led by long-distance or interexchange network operators. However, the local exchange is expected to follow soon. At present, the major deployments are in the form of point-to-point WDM transmission systems. These deployments are driven by a substantial increase in network traffic due to growth in internet and data communications, resulting in an increasing demand for capacity from the network operators.

Currently, the long-haul networks and some of the local exchange networks are running at near capacity exhaust. The terms capacity exhaust, fiber exhaust, conduit exhaust, and cable exhaust are used interchangeably in this book. In general practice, each term has its own significance with regard to the utilization of the fiber resources within a *conduit*—the physical structure in the ground carrying fiber cables. There might be several cables (e.g., four) in a single conduit. Each cable typically contains several fibers (e.g., 96). The term *fiber exhaust* implies that a single cable has run out of fiber. However, there might be room in the conduit for more cables to be installed. The term *conduit exhaust* implies that there is no room in the physical structure to carry more cables. This case has the greatest economic impact. It is both costly and time-consuming to dig up the ground to build new conduit facilities.

In such a scenario there are two ways to add capacity to the network:

1. Dig up the ground, install new fiber conduits, and continue to deploy traditional TDM systems: the "backhoe solution."
2. Upgrade the remaining fibers to higher capacity systems: TDM or WDM.

Let us consider the economic trade-offs associated with these options. The first case examined involves upgrading via point-to-point WDM transmission. Next, a ring architecture upgraded via both TDM and WDM switching is treated, and the final case studies the use of WDM cross-connects in an arbitrary mesh configuration.

The terminology and symbols used in these examples are chosen to reflect current usage in the telecommunication network community. It is worthwhile at this point to point out the correspondence between current usage and the generic terms used throughout this book. Central offices are typically large facilities that contain a variety of switching, multiplexing, transmission, and end system equipment. The switching and multiplexing equipment is largely electronic at present, including SONET DCSs, ADMs, and TDM multiplexers. These systems fit into our generic category of logical switching nodes, with associated optical transceivers (see Section 2.6). The WDM equipment currently being deployed includes WDM terminals, also called wavelength terminal multiplexers (WTMs) or WDM transport systems, WADMs, and optical cross-connects. The WDM terminals correspond to our generic network access stations, whereas the WADM and optical cross-connect (OXC), exemplify generic optical network nodes (see Sections 2.3 and 2.4). If they are limited to wavelength-selective permutation switching they fit under our category of WSXCs, the basic switching nodes in wavelength routed networks. If they have multipoint switching capability and/or switch on a wave*band* basis, they are examples of generic LDCs, which are the switches in LLNs.

6.7.1 WDM Point-to-Point Systems

Figure 6.72 shows a network with six central offices. Two of the offices are major hub switching offices. The figure shows a scenario in which the link between the hubs is running at capacity exhaust, and the remaining links have spare capacity.

Figure 6.73 shows a WDM point-to-point transmission system deployed between the hubs to alleviate the capacity exhaust between these nodes. The economic trade-off between the backhoe and WDM solution is as follows:

1. Laying new fiber in the ground currently costs about $60,000 per mile. For a distance of 100 miles between the central offices, the cost for installing new fiber is $6 million.

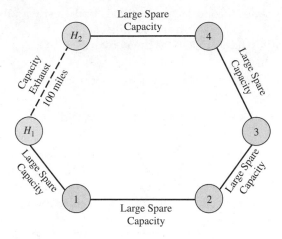

FIGURE 6.72 Six central offices, including two hubs, with capacity exhaust.

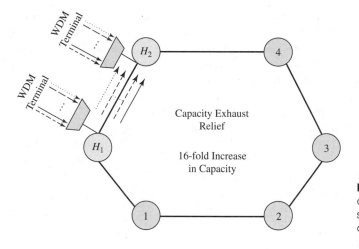

FIGURE 6.73 Application of WDM point-to-point systems to alleviate capacity exhaust.

2. Installing a WDM transmission system that increases the capacity of each fiber between the hubs by a factor of 16 or more is the other option in this case. The cost of a WDM terminal with 16 wavelengths can be less than $1 million. The total system cost (for two terminals in a point-to-point configuration) is less than $2 million.

In this type of capacity exhaust scenario, WDM increases the capacity of each fiber between the hubs by a factor of 16 or more, and is the clear winner among the two alternatives.

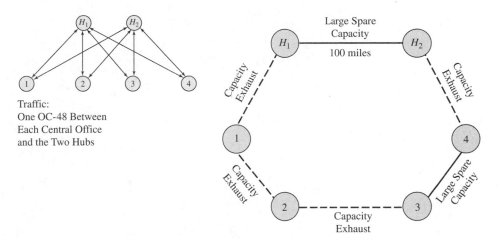

FIGURE 6.74 Six central offices, including two hubs, with capacity exhaust.

Even in cases in which there is no fiber exhaust, WDM can be a very attractive solution. This is especially true in the long-haul network scenario. A long-haul transmission link might be as long as 600 km, with several electronic regenerators en route (see Problem 38 at the end of this chapter). Electronic regenerators are required every 40 km, whereas optical amplifiers (e.g., EDFAs) currently can be spaced as far as 120 km. Furthermore, only one optical amplifier is required to amplify simultaneously all wavelengths multiplexed on a fiber, as opposed to one regenerator for each wavelength in the electronic case (together with wavelength multiplexing and demultiplexing equipment).

6.7.2 WDM Rings

Figure 6.74 shows a traffic scenario in which two hub nodes terminate an OC-48 (2.5-Gbps) signal from each central office, as shown on the left side of the figure. There are four links on the ring with capacity/cable exhaust, each with a length of 100 miles. Three options for network deployment are considered:

1. *Backhoe solution:* Dig up the fiber routes and install new fiber. This is a costly option. At $60,000 per mile for the four sections, this results in an overall cost of $24 million.

2. *Upgrade to OC-192 (10-Gbps) TDM:* In this case two OC-192 TDM rings are required, which results in a total of ten SONET ADMs. This results in a total cost of $3 million, assuming that each ADM costs $300,000.

3. *OC-48 2.5-Gbps WDM:* In this case six WADMs using a 16-wavelength system are required, for a total cost of $2.25 million (assuming that each WADM costs

1. Backhoe Solution:
   Very high cost—$24 Million

2. OC-192 TDM Solution:
   0% Spare Capacity
   in Network
   10 ADMs
   Cost = 10 × $300,000
        = $3 Million

3. OC-48 WDM
   16 λ Solution:
   50% Spare Capacity
   in Network
   6 WADMs
   Cost = 6 × $375,000
        = $2.25 Million

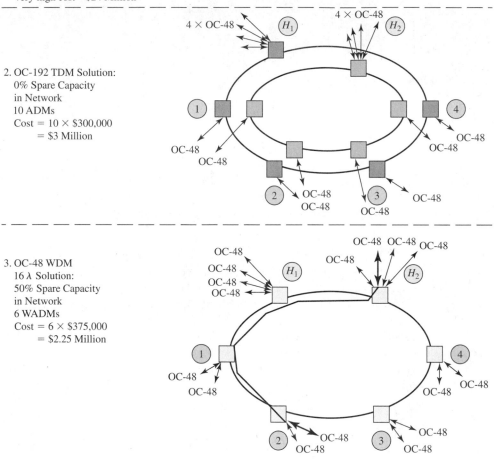

FIGURE 6.75 Economic case for WDM rings.

$375,000). In this case we assume that the WDM ring is path protected (see Chapter 8). The WDM ring has 50% spare capacity for future upgrades.

As shown in Figure 6.75, the WDM solution is clearly superior. It is less expensive on first-installed cost and has 50% spare capacity for upgrading network capacity.

6.7.3 WDM Cross-connect Networks

Figure 6.76 shows typical, traditional electronic switching and multiplexing equipment based on DCSs in a central office using WDM transmission. The central office

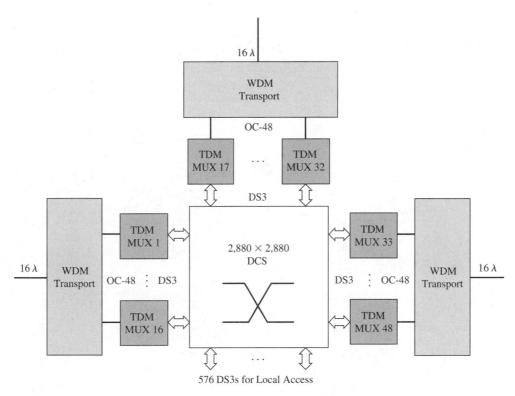

FIGURE 6.76 Node in central office: current mode of operation.

might represent a node in a mesh network architecture. In this case, WDM transport systems terminate the individual wavelengths at the central office. We compare an electronic switching scenario with an optical cross-connect approach in Figure 6.77.

In the example shown, each transport system carries 16 wavelengths, each of which terminates on a SONET TDM terminal (labeled TDM MUX in the figure). The wavelengths might be set at 100-GHz spacings in the 1.5-μm band (the grid recommended by the International Telecommunications Union). The interconnection between the TDM and WDM terminals is via a short reach 1.3 μm optical interface. Each TDM terminal demultiplexes the 2.5-Gbps (OC-48) signals into their constituent DS3 tributaries (48 DS3s in an OC-48). In the traditional mode of operation, the individual DS3s (running at 45 Mbps) are terminated onto a large digital cross-connect, which is responsible for grooming, provisioning, and protecting the individual DS3 channels (see Appendix F). This makes sense if there is a need to access these individual low-speed bitstreams; that is, if all of them terminate at the switching node at DS3 speeds, and none are terminated at higher speeds or passed through. However, in the emerging datacentric world, IP routers and ATM switches will be available with direct OC-48c (concatenated OC-48) or higher speed interfaces. It is therefore

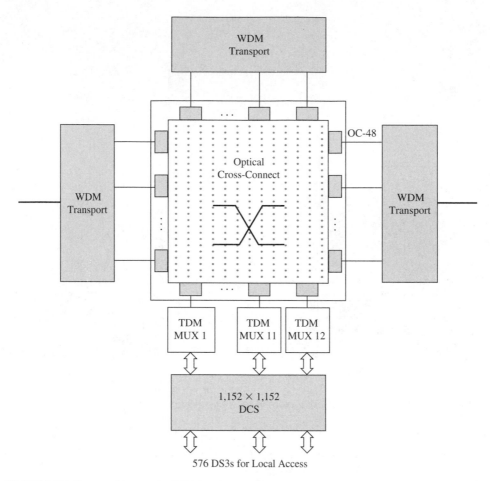

FIGURE 6.77 Economic case for WDM optical cross-connect.

unnecessary and costly to demultiplex these concatenated optical signals into their low-speed components.

To compare the optical and electronic switching approaches, let us assume that the network is dominated by data traffic that terminates on equipment (e.g., IP routers and/or ATM switches) with OC-48c interfaces, so that demultiplexing to DS3 speeds at the cross-connect is unnecessary. Let the cost of each DS3 termination on the digital cross-connect be $1,000, and let the cost of the SONET TDM terminal (unprotected; protection provided at the cross-connect) be $40,000.

In the electronic switching approach of Figure 6.76, a 2,880 × 2,880 DCS is required to switch signals at the DS3 level, assuming that most of the traffic is pass-through, with 576 DS3 local access ports.

Now compare this with the case in which an optical cross-connect is installed at the node to switch the high-speed optical signals without demultiplexing them to the DS3 level. The connections between the WDM terminals and the OXC are short lengths of fiber operating at 1.3 μm, as in the case of the electronic switching approach. As shown in Figure 6.77, the local traffic is now dropped at the node in the form of 12 OC-48s, which are then demultiplexed into 576 DS3s. Replacing the DCS by the optical cross-connect reduces the number of SONET TDM terminals from 48 to 12 and the size of the low-speed digital cross-connect from $2,880 \times 2,880$ to $1,152 \times 1,152$. (The smaller DCS is still needed for switching local traffic.) This can result in savings of more than \$3 million, depending on the cost of the cross-connect. Note that the combination of WDM transport systems and an optical cross-connect functions as a WIXC. The cross-connect alone is essentially a space switch without wavelength selectivity, because wavelength selectivity is handled in the WDM transport systems.

6.8 Problems

1. Suggest a way of adding links sparingly to the network of Figure 6.8 to reduce the average distance between nodes.

2. Suggest a way of adding links sparingly to the network of Figure 6.54 to improve its survivability.

3. Suppose that full logical connectivity is to be set up in the deBruijn network of Figure 6.4. Assuming a single fiber pair per link, find W_{Limcut}.

4. Solve the RCA problem of Figure 6.11 without the constraint of minimum-hop routing.

5. Write a computer program to implement the wavelength assignment algorithm for WDM rings (for N odd). Use it to determine an RCA for full connectivity on a seven-node ring.

6. Full logical connectivity is to be established in the six-node bidirectional WDM ring. According to Equation 6.12, this can be done with five wavelengths if the access stations are *nonblocking*.

   (a) Find an RCA for this case using five wavelengths.

   (b) Now suppose that elementary stations are used. Find an RCA for this case using as few wavelengths as you can. (It is still possible with five wavelengths!)

7. Find an RCA algorithm that produces full connectivity on a WDM ring with *elementary* access stations, and with $N > 6$. The algorithm must use the number of wavelengths specified in Equation 6.12. (This is not easy!)

8. Show that with one WIXC placed anywhere in a bidirectional ring wavelength routed network, any set of connections can be established using a number of wavelengths equal to the maximum number of connections traversing any fiber.

9. Devise a multistar network with eight stations, based on permutation routers and using four 4×4 stars. Compare your answer with Figure 6.56.

10. Program RCA-I and RCA-II.

    (a) Try out your programs on some small problems and compare results.

    (b) See if you can get as good or better results by inspection.

    (c) Compute W_{Limcut} in each case and compare it to the number of wavelengths used.

11. Reformulate RCA-I to include a prescribed set of permissible paths.

12. Consider a three-node unidirectional bus network with nodes $A, B,$ and C. Poisson-distributed connection requests arrive at node A at rate λ, with exponentially distributed holding times. There are two wavelengths available. Each connection is destined randomly for nodes B and C with equal probabilities. Calculate the blocking probability for each of the following cases.

    (a) Nodes $A, B,$ and C are WSXCs in a WRN.

    (b) Nodes $A, B,$ and C are WIXCs in a WRN.

    (c) Nodes $A, B,$ and C are LDC nodes using a single waveband containing both wavelengths.

    Are there any differences? Explain.

13. In Problem 12, Poisson-distributed connection requests arrive at node A at rate λ. Each connection is destined randomly for nodes B and C with equal probability. Also, Poisson-distributed connection requests arrive at node B, destined for C, at a rate of $\lambda/2$. Calculate the blocking probability for each of the following cases using approximations when necessary.

    (a) Nodes $A, B,$ and C are WSXCs in a WRN.

    (b) Nodes $A, B,$ and C are WIXCs in a WRN.

    (c) Nodes $A, B,$ and C are LDC nodes using a single waveband.

    Explain the results.

14. Give an exact Markov chain model for each case of Problem 13.

15. For each case of Problem 13, write a simulator that computes the blocking probability. Compare the simulations with the calculated results.

16. Derive Equation 6.40 from the Erlang-B formula.

17. Derive Equation 6.42.

18. Using a three-state Markov chain derive Equation 6.39.

19. Use Equation 6.41 to generate some points matching the simulation points in Figure 6.30. Assume $H = 5$ (the worst case traffic distribution), and compute ρ from the Erlang load per node. How good is the formula in this case?

20. Write a simulator to study dynamic RCA in wavelength routed networks. Use it to exercise the various algorithms discussed in this chapter and/or some of your own.

21. For the Petersen network example with $W = 3$, $F = 1$, consider the following variants:

    (a) Reflecting stars are used instead of nonreflecting stars.

    (b) Nonreflecting stars are used with elementary stations.

    (c) Reflecting stars are used with elementary stations.

    In each case, find the minimum number of required λ-channels per waveband, and give a feasible channel assignment for waveband 2. In the last case there is a violation of the DSC condition. Comment on its significance.

22. Consider the Petersen network example with $W = 5$, $F = 1$, using elementary stations.

    (a) In the case of multicast optical connections, let c_X denote the optical connection from station X. Show that a feasible channel assignment for the connections on waveband 5 is the following: c_E, c_D, c_H, and c_J use channel 1; c_A, c_B, and c_G use channel 2; and c_C, c_F, and c_I use channel 3.

    (b) If a point-to-point optical connection is used to carry each LC, find the minimum number of required λ-channels on waveband 5 and give a feasible channel assignment for waveband 5.

23. Find the minimum number of wavelengths required for the Petersen network example with $W = 1$, $F = 2$, assuming that nonblocking stations and reflecting stars are used. Consider three cases that correspond to different routing rules for the one-hop LCs between adjacent nodes:

    (a) Each connection is routed on the tree based at its source node.

    (b) Each connection is routed on the tree based at its destination node.

    (c) Each connection is routed on two parallel optical connections using both trees.

24. Repeat Problem 23 using elementary stations.

25. Show by an example that a possible (but not necessarily practical) solution of the propagation delay problem illustrated in Figure 6.50 is to choose the frame time to be a common divisor of the relative propagation delays to each receiver. Show by an example that another approach is to accept less than 100 scheduling efficiency.

26. Show that with nonblocking stations and nonreflecting stars, six wavelengths are sufficient to realize full point-to-point logical connectivity in the Petersen network with $W = 1$ and $F = 2$. Discuss the effects of using elementary stations.

27. Verify that the power relations of Equation 6.70 are satisfied at the node shown in Figure 3.25 for the network of Figure 3.23(b).

28. This problem concerns power distribution in the passive folded bus of Figure 6.53.

    (a) Verify that if the power distribution rules of Equation 6.72 are applied at each combining and dividing node, the power from each transmitter reaches each receiver attenuated by a factor of N^2.

    (b) If it is required that a common value of combining ratio α is used to combine power from each transmitter onto the bus, and the same value is used to split power to each receiver, find the value of α that maximizes the power from station 1 reaching the head end.

(c) With the value of α determined in (b), find the power transfer matrix for an N station bus. Compare this result to that obtained using the power distribution rules of Equation 6.72.

29. Consider a five-node four-fiber (two-working fiber) bidirectional ring network with the full mesh connectivity scenario described in Section 6.3.4. Suppose the ring is now operated as an LLN using a single waveband instead of as a WRN. The nodes are now LDCs instead of WADMs.

    (a) Is it possible to use shortest path routing for all connections in this case? Explain.

    (b) Find a routing and wavelength assignment using as few wavelengths as possible.

    (c) Compare with the WRN case.

30. Write a simulator to study dynamic routing and wavelength assignment in LLNs. Use it to exercise the various algorithms discussed in this chapter and/or some of your own.

31. Find the time complexity of the k-SP and Min-Int algorithms for allocating point-to-point connections in an LLN. Include the complexity of the waveband and the wavelength allocation algorithms.

32. In Figure E.1 add a new transmitter, 4, at node C and a new receiver, 4*, at node G. Now show the new image network. Assign the connection from 3 to 3* along the shortest path as determined by the Min-Int algorithm. Show the new weights on the intranodal links. Now, allocate a connection from transmitter 4 to receiver 4* using the shortest path as determined by the Min-Int algorithm. Show the upgraded values of the link weights.

33. Consider the results shown in Figure 6.66. Starting with the plot showing the blocking for one waveband containing six channels, estimate and plot the blocking probability for the same network under the assumption that two wavebands containing six channels each are now available. Assume the Maxband allocation policy and use reasonable approximations.

34. Find the complexity of the MBFS-d algorithm for tree decomposition.

35. Find the complexity of the overall multicasting algorithm. Include the waveband selection process, tree selection, the check for color clash, and channel allocation.

36. Consider the plot in Figure 6.71, which shows the blocking for dynamic multicast connections for $d = 6$ in an LLN operating on a single waveband with three λ-channels. Suppose that the same network operates under the same conditions, except that it now has two wavebands containing three channels each. Estimate the blocking probability as a function of load using simplifying assumptions when necessary.

37. Construct an example of a connection arrival and departure sequence in the network of Figure 6.70(a), which leads to the state of the network shown in Figure 6.70(c) when the Min Reuse channel allocation rule is used.

38. Consider a point-to-point bidirectional transmission link of length 600 km, with repeater huts every 40 km. Compare the costs of the following arrangements for implementing a 16×2.5-Gbps system.

(a) Sixteen OC-48 links with intermediate regenerators every 40 km

(b) A WDM system with 16 wavelengths and optical amplifiers. In this case the amplifiers must still be placed in repeater huts, but they may have longer spacings appropriate to the link characteristics and bitrates (see Chapter 4).

Assume the following costs:

(a) OC-48 SONET terminal = $100,000

(b) OC-48 regenerator = $60,000

(c) Optical amplifier = $200,000

(d) WDM terminal = $750,000

39. In the WDM cross-connect scenario described in Section 6.7.3, assume that the cost of the optical cross-connect is $500,000. Plot the savings using the optical cross-connect compared with the traditional low-speed digital cross-connect as a function of the pass-through traffic.

6.9 Bibliography

[Aarts+97] E. Aarts and J. K. Lenstra. *Local Search in Combinatorial Optimization*. New York: John Wiley & Sons, 1997.

[Acampora94] A. S. Acampora. Multi-wavelength transport networks. *IEEE Communications Mag.*, 32(12):36–43, 1994.

[Arden+91] B. W. Arden and K. W. Tang. Representations and routing for Cayley graphs. *IEEE Trans. Commun.*, 39(11):1533–1537, 1991.

[Ayanoglu+96] E. Ayanoglu and E. Karasan. Wavelength routing and selection algorithms for WDM optical networks. In *Proc. ICC '96: Workshop on WDM Network Management and Control*. Dallas, June 1996.

[Bala+91a] K. Bala, T. E. Stern, and K. Bala. Algorithms for routing in a linear lightwave network. In *Proc. IEEE Infocom '91*, Miami, April 1991.

[Bala+91b] K. Bala, T. E. Stern, and K. Bala. A minimum interference routing algorithm for a linear lightwave network. In *Proc. IEEE Globecom.*, Phoenix, December 1991.

[Bala92] K. Bala. *Routing in Linear Lightwave Networks*. PhD thesis. Columbia University, New York, 1992.

[Bala+93] K. Bala, K. Petropoulos, and T. E. Stern. Multicasting in linear lightwave networks. In *Proc. IEEE Infocom '93*, San Francisco, March 1993.

[Bala+95a] K. Bala and T. E. Stern. Routing in linear lightwave networks. *IEEE/ACM Trans. Networking*, 3(4):489–500, 1995.

[Bala+95b] K. Bala, R. R. Cordell, and E. L. Goldstein. The case for opaque multiwavelength optical networks. In *Proc. IEEE/LEOS Summer Topical Meeting on Optical Networks*, Keystone, CO, August 1995.

[Bala+96a] K. Bala, F.R.K. Chung, and C. A. Brackett. Optical wavelength routing, translation and packet/cell switched networks. *IEEE/OSA J. Lightwave Technology*, 14(3):336–343, 1996.

[Bala+96b] K. Bala, R. H. Cardwell, D. Feddor, et al. WDM network economics. In *Proc. National Fiber Optics Engineers Conference*, Denver, Sept. 1996.

[Bala+97] K. Bala, E. Bouillet, and G. Ellinas. The benefits of minimal wavelength interchange in WDM rings. In *Proc. IEEE/OSA '97 Optical Fiber Communication Conference*. Dallas, February 1997.

[Banerjee+96] S. Banerjee and C. Chen. Design of wavelength-routed optical networks for circuit switched traffic. In *Proc. IEEE Globecom.*, London, November 1996.

[Baroni+97] S. Baroni and P. Bayvel. Wavelength requirements in arbitrary connected wavelength-routed optical networks. *IEEE/OSA J. Lightwave Technology*, 15(2):242–252, 1997.

[Barry93a] R. A. Barry. An all-optical non-blocking $M \times M$ switchless connector with $O(\sqrt{M} \log M)$ wavelengths and without wavelength changers. *Electron. Letters*, 29(14):1252–1254, 1993.

[Barry93b] R. A. Barry. *Wavelength Routing for All-Optical Networks*. PhD thesis. Massachusetts Institute of Technology, Cambridge, 1993.

[Barry+93] R. A. Barry and P. A. Humblet. Latin routers: Design and implementation. *IEEE/OSA J. Lightwave Technology*, 11(5/6):891–899, 1993.

[Barry+94] R. A. Barry and P. A. Humblet. On the number of wavelengths and switches in all-optical networks. *IEEE Trans. Commun.*, 42(2/3/4):583–591, 1994.

[Barry+95] R. Barry and P. Humblet. Models of blocking probability in all-optical networks with and without wavelength changers. In *Proc. IEEE Infocom.*, Boston, April 1995.

[Bermond+82] J-C. Bermond, C. Delorme, and J. J. Quisquater. Tables of large graphs with given degree and diameter. *Information Processing Letters*, 15:10–13, 1982.

[Bermond+84] J-C. Bermond, J. Bond, and J. F. Sacle. *Graph Theory and Combinatorics* (chapter: Large Hypergraphs of Diameter 1), pp. 19–28. New York: Academic Press, 1984.

[Bermond+89] J-C. Bermond and C. Peyrat. deBruijn and Kautz networks: A competitor for the hypercube. In *Hypercube and Distributed Computers*, pp. 279–293. Amsterdam: Elsevier Science Publishers B.V., 1989.

[Bermond+97] J-C. Bermond, R. Dawes, and F. O. Ergincan. deBruijn and Kautz bus networks. *Networks*, 30:205–218, 1997.

[Birman95] A. Birman. Routing and wavelength assignment methods in single-hop all-optical networks with blocking. In *Proc. IEEE Infocom.*, Boston, April 1995.

[Birk91] Y. Birk. Fiber-optic bus-oriented single-hop interconnections among multi-transceiver stations. *IEEE/OSA J. Lightwave Technology*, 9(12):1657–1664, 1991.

[Bouillet98] E. Bouillet. Monte Carlo techniques for design of wavelength-routed all-optical networks. *Internal Report*. New York: Center for Telecommunications Research, Columbia University, 1998.

[Brain+88] M. C. Brain and P. Cochrane. Wavelength-routed optical networks using coherent transmission. In *Proc. IEEE Int'l Conf. Commun.*, Philadelphia, 1988.

[Brown94] G. Brown. *Internal Report*. New York: Center for Telecommunications Research, Columbia University, 1994.

[Cerf+74] V. G. Cerf, D. D. Cowan, R. C. Mullin, and R. G. Stanton. A lower bound on the average shortest path length in regular graphs. *Networks*, 4:335–342, 1974.

[Chen+96] C. Chen and S. Banerjee. A new model for optimal routing and wavelength assignment in wavelength division multiplexed optical networks. In *Proc. IEEE Infocom '96*, San Francisco, April 1996.

[Chlamtac+89] I. Chlamtac, A. Ganz, and G. Karmi. Purely optical networks for terabit communication. In *Proc. IEEE Infocom '89*, pp. 887–896, Ottawa, 1989.

[Chudnovsky+88] D. V. Chudnovsky, G. V. Chudnovsky, and M. M. Denneau. *Regular Graphs with Small Diameter as Models for Interconnection Networks.* IBM Technical Report RC-13484, 1988.

[Coathup+95] L. Coathup, C. Y. Lu, and P. Roorda. Economical applications of all-optical networks. In *Proc. IEEE/LEOS Summer Topical Meeting on Optical Networks,* Keystone, CO, August 1995.

[Ellinas+98a] G. Ellinas and K. Bala. Wavelength assignment algorithms for WDM shared protection rings. In *Proc. IEEE Int'l Conf. Commun.,* Atlanta, June 1998.

[Ellinas+98b] G. Ellinas, K. Bala, and G. K. Chang. Scalability of a novel wavelength assignment algorithm for WDM shared protection rings. In *Proc. IEEE/OSA '98 Optical Fiber Communication Conference,* San Jose, February 1998.

[Fleischner90] H. Fleischner. *Eulerian Graphs and Related Topics Part I: Vol. 1* (volume 45 of *Annals of Discrete Mathematics*). Amsterdam: Elsevier Science Publishers B.V., 1990.

[Ganz+92] A. Ganz and Y. Gao. Traffic scheduling in multiple WDM star systems. In *Proc. IEEE Int'l Conf. Commun.,* pp. 1468–1472. Chicago, June 1992.

[Garey+79] M. R. Garey and D. S. Johnson. *Computers and Intractability: A Guide to NP-Completeness.* New York: W. H. Freeman, 1979.

[Gerstel+97] O. Gerstel, R. Ramaswami, and G. H. Sasaki. Benefits of limited wavelength conversion in WDM ring networks. In *Proc. IEEE/OSA '97 Optical Fiber Communication Conference,* Dallas, February 1997.

[Ghafoor85] A. Ghafoor. *A New Database Allocation Scheme for a Class of Networks.* PhD thesis. Columbia University, New York, 1985.

[Gopal82] I. S. Gopal. *Scheduling Algorithms for Multibeam Communications Satellites.* PhD thesis. Columbia University, New York, 1982.

[Gusfield83] D. Gusfield. Connectivity and edge-disjoint spanning trees. *Information Processing Letters,* 16:87–89, 1983.

[Hagouel83] J. Hagouel. *Issues in Routing for Large and Dynamic Networks.* PhD thesis. Columbia University, New York, 1983.

[Halsall96] F. Halsall. *Data Communications, Computer Networks and Open Systems.* Reading, MA: Addison-Wesley, 1996.

[Harary92] F. Harary. *Graph Theory.* Reading, MA: Addison-Wesley, 1972.

[Hill88] G. R. Hill. A wavelength routing approach to optical communications networks. In *Proc. IEEE Infocom '88,* pp. 354–362, New Orleans, 1988.

[Hoffman+60] A. J. Hoffman and R. R. Singleton. On Moore graphs with diameter 2 and 3. *IBM J. Research and Development,* November:497–504, 1960.

[IEEE91] IEEE. *Standard 802.6, Distributed Queue Dual Bus (DQDB) Sub-network of a Metropolitan Area Network (MAN).* New York: IEEE, 1991.

[Imase+83] M. Imase and M. Itoh. A design for directed graphs with minimum diameter. *IEEE Trans. Comput.,* c-32(8):782–784, 1983.

[Karasan+96] E. Karasan and E. Ayanoglu. Effects of wavelength routing and selection algorithms on wavelength conversion gain in WDM optical networks. In *Proc. LEOS Summer Topical Meeting,* Keystone, CO, August 1996.

[Kovacevic+92] M. Kovacevic and M. Gerla. Rooted routing in linear lightwave networks. In *Proc. IEEE Infocom '92,* pp. 39–48, Florence, 1992.

[Liu98] G. Liu. Wavelength assignments in WDM rings. *Project Report for Course EE E6768.* New York: Department of Electrical Engineering, Columbia University, 1998.

[Mokhtar+98] A. Mokhtar and A. Azizoglu. Adaptive wavelength routing in all-optical networks. *IEEE/ACM Trans. Networking,* 6(2):197–206, 1998.

[Mukherjee+96] B. Mukherjee, S. Ramamurthy, D. Banerjee, and A. Mukherjee. Some principles for designing a wide-area optical network. *IEEE/ACM Trans. Networking*, 4(5):684–696, 1996.

[Nagatsu+95] N. Nagatsu, Y. Hamazumi, and K. Sato. Optical path accommodation designs applicable to large-scale networks. *IEICE Trans. Commun.*, E78-B(4):597–607, 1995.

[Pankaj92] R. K. Pankaj. *Architectures for Linear Lightwave Networks*. PhD thesis. Massachusetts Institute of Technology, Cambridge, 1992.

[Pankaj+95] R. K. Pankaj and R. G. Gallager. Wavelength requirements of all-optical networks. *IEEE/ACM Trans. Networking*, 3(3):269–280, 1995.

[Ramaswami+94] R. Ramaswami and K. N. Sivarajan. Routing and wavelength assignment in all-optical networks. In *Proc. IEEE Infocom '94*, pp. 970–979, Toronto, June 1994.

[Ramaswami+95] R. Ramaswami and K. N. Sivarajan. Routing and wavelength assignment in all-optical networks. *IEEE/ACM Trans. Networking*, 3:489–500, 1995.

[Rayward-Smith+96] V. J. Rayward-Smith, I. H. Osman, C. R. Reeves, and G. D. Smith. *Modern Heuristic Search Methods*. New York: John Wiley & Sons, 1996.

[Reeves93] C. R. Reeves. *Modern Heuristic Techniques for Combinatorial Problems*. New York: John Wiley & Sons, 1993.

[Rose92] C. Rose. Mean internodal distance in regular and random multihop networks. *IEEE Trans. Commun.*, 40(8):1310–1318, 1992.

[Ross89] F. E. Ross. An overview of FDDI: The Fiber Distributed Data Interface. *IEEE J. Select. Areas Commun.*, 7(7):1043–1051, 1989.

[Schwartz87] M. Schwartz. *Telecommunication Networks: Protocols, Modeling and Analysis*. Reading, MA: Addison-Wesley, 1987.

[Subramaniam+96a] S. Subramaniam, M. Azizoglu, and A. K. Somani. All-optical networks with sparse wavelength conversion. *IEEE/ACM Trans. Networking*, 4(4):544–557, 1996.

[Subramaniam+96b] S. Subramaniam, M. Azizoglu, and A. K. Somani. Connectivity and sparse wavelength conversion in wavelength-routing networks. In *Proc. IEEE Infocom '96*, San Francisco, 1996.

[Subramaniam+97] S. Subramaniam and R. Barry. Wavelength assignment in fixed routing WDM networks. In *Proc. IEEE Int'l Conf. Commun.*, Montreal, June 1997.

[Tarjan83] R. E. Tarjan. *Data structures and Network Algorithms*. Philadelphia: Society for Industrial and Applied Mathematics, 1983.

[Wauters+96] N. Wauters and P. Demeester. Design of the optical path layer in multiwavelength cross-connected networks. *IEEE J. Select. Areas Commun.*, 14(5):881–892, 1996.

[Yates+96] Y. Yates and S. Everitt. Limited range wavelength translation in all-optical networks. In *Proc. IEEE Infocom '96*, San Francisco, 1996.

CHAPTER SEVEN

Logically Routed Networks

In this chapter we explore the structure, design, and performance of purely optical networks with electronically switched overlays. These are the logically routed networks (LRNs) that were introduced in Section 3.5. Typical examples of LRNs are networks of SONET digital cross-connects (DCSs), networks of ATM switches or IP routers, and ATM networks carried on a SONET DCS layer. To provide maximum flexibility the LRN should be carried on top of a *reconfigurable* purely optical network.

The rationale for using logical switching on top of a purely optical infrastructure has been discussed at various points throughout the book. The number of stations in a purely optical network cannot be increased indefinitely without running into a connectivity bottleneck. The sources of the bottleneck are the resource limitations within the network (fibers and optical spectrum) and within the access stations (optical transceivers). Figure 7.1(a) illustrates the bottleneck in a purely optical network. Network access station (NAS) A has established logical connections (LCs) that fan out to stations $B, C,$ and D. If this is a wavelength routed network, each LC is carried on a separate point-to-point optical connection; that is, three optical transceivers and three distinct wavelengths are required (assuming that the stations have single-fiber-pair access links). If it is an LLN, fewer transceivers and wavelengths could be used for the same three connections. For example, using an optical multicast connection on an optical path in the form of a tree, a transmitter at A can reach stations $B,$ $C,$ and D using one wavelength, time shared via TDM to create the three LCs.

If we try to extend the purely optical approach to large networks, however, we soon run into problems. For example, if a wavelength routed network (WRN) is to support full logical connectivity among N stations, this would require a fan-out of $N - 1$ point-to-point optical connections from each station. Given the finite available optical spectrum, the number of fibers in the network would have to grow as N^2 to provide the necessary capacity, and each station would require $N - 1$ transceivers. For large N, this is an obvious impossibility.

Using the optical multicast and channel-sharing capabilities of an LLN helps. Full logical connectivity could be supported at an NAS using some mixture of fixed and rapidly tunable transmitters and receivers, combined with multicast optical connections. However, eventually the routing constraints of the LLN, the overhead associated with the multiplexing/multiple-access methods required for channel sharing, and

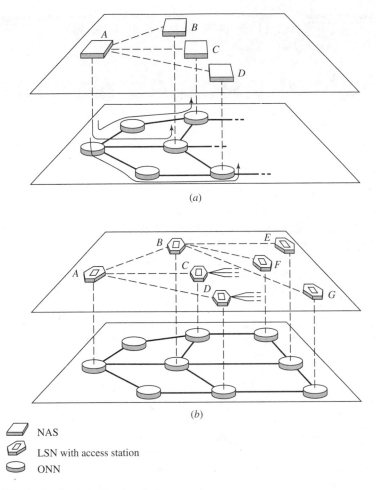

(a)

(b)

⬭ NAS

⬭ LSN with access station

⬭ ONN

FIGURE 7.1 Why logically routed networks?

the tuning requirements on the transceivers limit the number of stations that can be accommodated. Consequently, none of the purely optical approaches is practical for N on the order of 10^3 or more.

An additional limitation of both the WRN and the LLN approaches is the geographical "reach" limitation. A purely optical connection accumulates noise, distortion, and cross-talk over long distances, and eventually becomes unusable. Thus, electronic signal regeneration eventually becomes necessary.[1]

Although most applications do not require full logical connectivity among a large number of end systems, aggregation of traffic from many users at one access station

---

[1] Of course, all of the "nontransparent" operations we now relegate to electronics may eventually become cost-effective with purely optical processing. However, this does not appear likely in the near future.

tends to increase the connectivity requirements at that station. This is the case, for example, if a telephone central office aggregating traffic from many individual callers accesses an optical network through one NAS. Every destination must be potentially reachable from that central office. The high connectivity requirement carries with it a problem of low average usage of each LC. Many connections fanning out from one station necessarily generate a low average throughput per connection. This in turn leads to extreme inefficiency if the full capacity of one λ-channel is allocated to each connection, as is the case in WRNs, for example.

For a concrete illustration, let us revisit the "killer application" (LAN interconnection) of Section 1.5. A network that serves 10,000 LAN gateways was considered, so that the total number of connections for full connectivity is 99,990,000. Now if each LAN transfers an average aggregate traffic of 2 Gbps to all other LANs, then the total throughput is 20 Tbps, but the average flow on each connection is only 200 Kbps!

The most efficient way of meeting this combined requirement of high connectivity and low throughput per connection is through an LRN. If the LAN interconnection application is supported by an LRN, each connection between a pair of LANs is made at the *virtual connection level*. Recall from Section 3.5 that traffic from each virtual connection moves through an LRN on a *logical path* (LP), made up of a succession of LCs interconnected through electronic logical switching nodes (LSNs). The LSNs perform a routing function, ensuring that the traffic associated with a given source–destination virtual connection follows a prescribed LP through the LRN. Because each LC in general supports many multiplexed virtual connections, the load on a *logical connection* (and its supporting optical connection) is normally substantial even though each *virtual connection* might carry a mere trickle. At the same time, each LSN processes only the flow on LCs terminating on it. Thus, the electronic processing load on each LSN is, in general, much lower than the optical throughput at the ONN to which it is attached. In this way the LRN distributes the various processing and communications functions between the logical and physical layers in a manner that is matched to their capabilities.

The effect of this approach on virtual connectivity is illustrated in Figure 7.1(b). Now the LCs terminate on LSNs accessing the purely optical network through the NASs. Switching node A reaches nodes $B, C,$ and D through the same optical paths as before. But now, the virtual connections carried on those paths may extend still farther on the next set of LCs that fan out from $B, C,$ and D. In this way, an LP tree is built up, with the number of potential end-to-end *virtual* connections growing exponentially with the depth of the tree. The tree can be extended over any geographical distance without the accumulation of signal impairments, and the hardware and spectrum limitations of the purely optical network can be observed by choosing a logical topology that is consistent with the optical constraints.

Three important features of the LRN are the following:

1. The end systems communicate with each other using virtual connections, each of which typically carries relatively low traffic when compared to the capacity of a λ-channel.

2. Typical LRN topologies provide alternate LPs between all source–destination pairs for load distribution and survivability.

3. The logical topology can be designed almost independently of the supporting physical topology.

These characteristics suggest that sophisticated routing and protection strategies can be used in the logical layer, to adapt to changing load conditions and to address fault recovery in the logical layer.[2] Furthermore, there are several options for fault recovery in an LRN: at the virtual connection level by rerouting traffic around a failed LC or LSN, or at the logical level by rerouting LCs supported by a cut fiber or failed ONN onto different optical paths (optical layer protection).

In this chapter we study logically routed networks in detail, focusing first on point-to-point LRNs (multihop networks) and then on LRNs with multipoint logical connectivity (hypernets). As in Section 3.5, it is convenient to envision the traffic in these networks as asynchronous, in which case the LSNs would be packet or cell switches. All of the essential features of LRNs apply to stream (synchronous) traffic as well, except that addressing and routing are handled differently. In an asynchronous traffic LRN (e.g., an ATM network), routing is executed on a cell-by-cell basis (using VC/VP identifiers in cell headers), whereas in a synchronous traffic LRN (e.g., a network of SONET cross-connects), routing is performed on a synchronous transport signal (STS) basis (with addressing implicit in the position of slots in a SONET frame). Because packet-/cell-based networks offer more generality in traffic handling, we shall use this as our prototypical example.

The logical topology (LT) in an LRN can be viewed as an interface for matching a prescribed set of traffic requirements to a given physical infrastructure. Thus, based on some expected flow distribution among its nodes, an LRN must be constructed with a logical topology and LC capacities that are sufficient to support those requirements. But to complete the picture, the chosen LT and the logical connection capacities must be realizable using the resources of the given physical infrastructure: its physical topology (PT) and its fiber, node, and access station functionality.

Because of the complexity of the design problem, involving both logical and physical layer constraints, it is helpful to separate it into two subproblems:

1. Logical layer design (including routing and capacity assignment)
2. Physical layer design: embedding the LT on the PT

This chapter emphasizes performance and design issues. Thus, for a given logical topology we are interested in determining performance in terms of throughput and

---

[2] For example, bifurcated routing (i.e., assigning several parallel paths for traffic flow between a given source–destination node pair) makes it possible to distribute traffic loads evenly throughout a network. It also allows for "graceful" rather than catastrophic performance degradation in the event of a single failure on one of the paths, providing time for the affected traffic to be accommodated on alternate paths. Also, redundant LPs can be used for fault recovery (see Section 8.2).

connectivity, as well as other related features such as average LP length, adaptability to traffic imbalance, fault tolerance, and so forth. Concerning physical layer design, the basic problem is realizing a specified logical topology on a purely optical network infrastructure. As discussed in Chapter 1, the physical layer topology is typically fixed and may support several independent and disparate logical networks of which our LRN is but one. In this case physical layer design becomes a topological embedding problem, encountered previously in Section 3.5. In other cases, the physical topology might be chosen to match the logical topology of the LRN. A good choice in this case may be a multistar realization. Multistars were presented previously as physical supports for wavelength and waveband routed networks in Sections 6.3.6 and 6.5.9 respectively. Multihop LRNs and hypernets are treated separately in the sections that follow.

7.1 Point-to-Point Logical Topologies: Multihop Networks

In this section we examine the LRN concept in the context of point-to-point logical topologies. From a top-down point of view, the transport network is seen as a collection of LSNs (henceforth called nodes) joined by unidirectional internodal LCs. Thus, the logical connection graph (LCG) for the LRN is a digraph with vertices that represent the nodes and with arcs that represent the LCs. LCGs were used in earlier chapters to represent logical connectivity in both purely optical networks and LRNs. In the former case the vertices of the LCG represent the access stations, which serve as termination points for all LCs. In the case of the LRN, the vertices of the LCG represent LSNs, which serve as transit nodes for virtual connections.[3]

The virtual connections in an LRN are routed on generally multiple-hop LPs between end systems. A schematic view of a point-to-point LRN is shown in Figure 7.2. The virtual topology (VT) represents virtual connections in place among the end systems. These would typically be a mix of demand-assigned and dedicated connections, so the VT might change on a fairly short time scale (e.g., minutes). The logical topology is typically static (or quasi static), changing when changing traffic distributions or network faults necessitate reconfiguration. The physical topology is determined by the fiber cable layout, and remains fixed except when faults occur in the cables or the ONNs. Note that each of the topologies supports the one above it, but they all differ from each other.

Although the LRN must be realized on some physical (optical) infrastructure, the physical topology of the supporting network and its functionality (e.g., WRN or LLN) can be ignored in discussing logical layer performance characteristics. Of course when

---

[3] A logical layer node that serves as a terminal point only without any switching functions will be called a *logical terminal node* (LTN). Examples of LTNs appear in Figure 7.10.

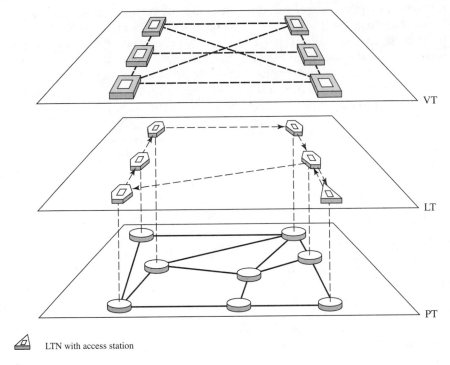

△ LTN with access station

FIGURE 7.2 A schematic of a point-to-point LRN.

it comes to network *design*, the structures of the logical and physical layers interact closely with each other.

The earliest proposal for an optically based LRN (using a perfect shuffle logical topology) appeared in [Acampora87], in which the term *multihop* was coined to denote a point-to-point LRN. Multihop networks based on a more general shuffle exchange logical topology (called *ShuffleNets*) are explored thoroughly in [Hluchyj+88, 91]. Extensions of these ideas to deBruijn graph LTs were presented in [Sivarajan+91]. Irregular topologies constructed to match traffic distributions were proposed in [Bannister90] and [Labourdette+91].

Although there is no necessity for LRNs to have regular topologies, almost all of the known results on these networks focus on the regular case, partly because it is difficult to draw any general conclusions concerning performance for irregular networks. Some of the advantages of regularity in both point-to-point and hypergraph LRNs are

- Simplified routing and congestion control mechanisms
- Potentially small network diameters and average internodal distances

- Highly symmetric topologies, simplifying load balancing and congestion reduction
- Identical structures for each network node, simplifying network implementation

Using arguments similar to those used for WRNs in Section 6.2, we can find certain important structural bounds on regular directed LCGs. Consider a regular digraph, $G(V, E)$, of maximum out-degree $\delta > 1$ and diameter D. Then its maximum order is

$$N_{\text{Moore}}^d(\delta, D) = 1 + \delta + \delta^2 + \cdots + \delta^D = \frac{\delta^{D+1} - 1}{\delta - 1} \tag{7.1}$$

Equation 7.1 is just the directed version of the Moore bound given in Equation 6.1.[4]

The average internodal distance in an LRN represented by a digraph $G(V, E)$ of order N is defined as

$$\bar{d} = \frac{1}{N(N-1)} \sum_{i \neq j} d(v_i, v_j) \tag{7.2}$$

where $d(v_i, v_j)$ is the length (in logical hops) of the shortest (directed) path from vertex v_i to v_j. For a regular directed network with in- and out-degree $\delta > 1$ and order N, $\bar{d}$ is bounded below by

$$\bar{d} \geq \frac{\delta - \delta^{D+1} + ND(\delta - 1)^2 + D(\delta - 1)}{(N-1)(\delta - 1)^2} \tag{7.3}$$

where D is the smallest integer such that

$$\frac{\delta^{D+1} - 1}{\delta - 1} \geq N \tag{7.4}$$

Now let us examine the relation between $\bar{d}$ and network throughput. Consider an LRN with N nodes and L unidirectional point-to-point LCs in which each logical connection has a capacity of one unit of flow. Its average nodal in-/out-degree is $\bar{\delta} = L/N$. Suppose ρ units of traffic are injected into each node for a total network throughput of ρN units, with uniform traffic distribution, and the average number of logical hops incurred by the traffic is $\bar{H} \geq \bar{d}$. To maximize the network throughput, the traffic should be routed over logical paths in a way that simultaneously minimizes $\bar{H}$ *and* loads all LCs equally. By flow conservation this would lead to a load on each LC of $\rho \bar{H} / \bar{\delta}$. This reasoning gives us the maximum throughput per node for the network:

$$\rho_{\max} = \bar{\delta} / \bar{d} \tag{7.5}$$

---

[4] In contrast to undirected graphs, there are no directed graphs that achieve the Moore bound.

which can be achieved only if all virtual connection routing is over the shortest LPs. Note that to realize the bound, the traffic distribution must be "matched" appropriately to the logical topology and routed optimally. Generally, the bound is not achievable.

This bound is useful in evaluating network performance in the sections that follow.

7.1.1 ShuffleNets

As mentioned earlier, the first regular topologies considered for LRNs were ShuffleNets. The LCG for a (δ, k)-ShuffleNet is a regular digraph of in- and out-degree δ, and of order $N = k\delta^k$. As illustrated in Figure 7.3 for the case $\delta = 3, k = 2, N = 18$, it is conveniently represented as an arrangement of k columns, each containing δ^k nodes. Each column connects to the next one on its right via δ^{k+1} arcs, in a generalization of a perfect shuffle pattern. As shown by the dashed line repetition of the first column in the figure, the LCG is closed back on itself in a cylindrical fashion to complete the regular structure. The complete network requires $k\delta^{k+1}$ point-to-point LCs. Although the regular structure of the ShuffleNet is useful in many ways, it carries with it a disadvantage: ShuffleNets do not exist for all values of N. Thus, a ShuffleNet

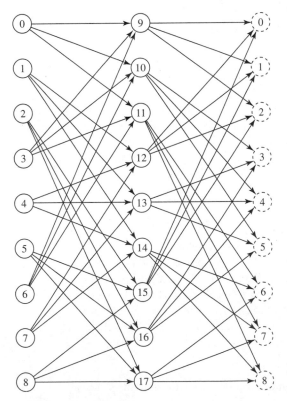

FIGURE 7.3 ShuffleNet: $\delta = 3, k = 2,$ $N = 18$.

(as well as all other network topologies possessing a high degree of symmetry) cannot be "grown" in a modular fashion, one node at a time.

End systems (not shown in Figure 7.3) accessing the switching nodes of the ShuffleNet communicate with each other by injecting sequences of cells into the nodes, which then sort and forward the cells over LPs to their destination nodes. For example, using shortest path routing, traffic from node 0 to node 7 would take the path 0–11–7, whereas traffic from 0 to 12 would use path 0–9–1–12, 0–10–4–12, or 0–11–7–12. (Shortest paths are not always unique.)

The diameter of a (δ, k)-ShuffleNet is $D = 2k - 1$, and thus the order of a ShuffleNet can be expressed as

$$N = \left(\frac{D+1}{2}\right)\delta^{\left(\frac{D+1}{2}\right)} \tag{7.6}$$

which shows that it is a moderately dense network, containing a large number of nodes for a given diameter and nodal degree.

The average internodal distance is given by

$$\bar{d} = \frac{k\delta^k(\delta - 1)(3k - 1) - 2k(\delta^k - 1)}{2(\delta - 1)(k\delta^k - 1)} \tag{7.7}$$

From Equation 7.7 it can be seen that for large ShuffleNets (large δ and/or k), we have $\bar{d} \approx 3D/4$. Substituting Equation 7.7 into Equation 7.5 leads to the following bound on throughput:

$$\rho_{max} = \frac{2\delta(\delta - 1)(k\delta^k - 1)}{k\delta^k(\delta - 1)(3k - 1) - 2k(\delta^k - 1)} \tag{7.8}$$

Figure 7.4 shows a plot of ρ_{max} as a function of N with δ as a parameter. Note that ρ_{max} decreases relatively slowly with increasing network size due to the roughly logarithmic dependence of $\bar{d}$ on N. Note also that ρ_{max} increases with δ due to the increased capacity available in the network. However, this increase in ρ_{max} is obtained at the cost of increased usage of physical layer resources—both transceivers and fiber capacity.

FIGURE 7.4 Maximum throughput per node for ShuffleNet. (From (Hluchyj+88, Figure 18). Copyright © 1988 IEEE. Used by permission of The Institute of Electrical and Electronics Engineers, Inc.)

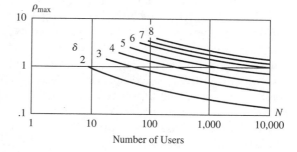

As we shall see (Section 7.3), by using shared rather than dedicated channels in the physical layer, it is possible to control network throughput and network connectivity (i.e., size) more or less independently, giving considerably more flexibility in network design.

7.1.2 Families of Dense Logical Topologies

In Section 6.2 we suggested a number of reasons for choosing dense physical topologies for purely optical networks. A similar case can be made for choosing dense logical topologies for LRNs. Dense logical topologies lead to fewer average logical hops and more alternate paths. These in turn produce a number of desirable results:

- The load on each LC is reduced.
- The processing load in each LSN is reduced.
- Opportunities for load balancing and congestion reduction are improved.
- Probability of information loss due to congestion and buffer overflow is reduced.
- Survivability is increased.

Logical topologies are typically specified as digraphs rather than undirected graphs. Two useful classes of regular digraphs, the deBruijn and Kautz digraphs, can be defined in terms of the state transition relations in finite state machines (shift registers).

A deBruijn digraph with in- and out-degree d and diameter D, denoted $B(d, D)$, has $N = d^D$ vertices. Its vertex labels can be defined as words of length D from an alphabet A containing d letters. If $(a_1, a_2, \ldots, a_D)$ is the label of vertex v, then there are arcs from v to all vertices with labels $(a_2, \ldots, a_D, \alpha), \alpha \in A$, representing a left shift of the vertex label. Note that a deBruijn digraph has self-loops for all vertices with labels that contain a D-fold repetition of a single letter. Omitting the self-loops results in an irregular LCG with the same order and diameter but with fewer arcs. Figure 7.5(a) shows $B(2, 3)$.

A Kautz digraph with in- and out-degree d and diameter D, denoted $K(d, D)$, has $N = d^D + d^{D-1}$ vertices. It is constructed in a manner similar to the deBruijn digraph. The vertices are labeled using all words of length D from an alphabet A containing $d + 1$ letters, such that no two consecutive letters are identical. (Thus it has no self-loops.) There is an arc from any vertex $(a_1, a_2, \ldots, a_D)$ to vertices $(a_2, \ldots, a_D, \alpha)$, where $\alpha \in A, \alpha \neq a_D$. Figure 7.5(b) shows $K(2, 3)$. Clearly both the deBruijn and Kautz digraphs are considerably denser than ShuffleNets. The density of the Kautz digraph comes very close to the Moore bound.

Families of digraphs that can be considered as generalizations of the deBruijn and Kautz digraphs were proposed by [Reddy+82] and [Imase+83]. The generalized versions have the useful property that they can be defined for any number of nodes. However, they are not necessarily regular.

The generalized Kautz digraph, denoted by $GK(d, n)$, has n vertices with integer labels modulo n where each vertex has out-degree d. There is an arc from vertex v to

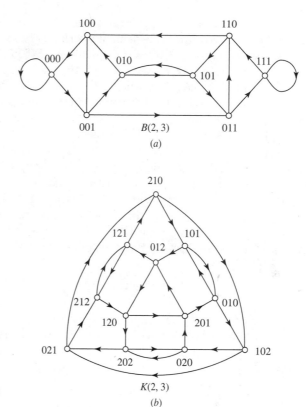

FIGURE 7.5 deBruijn and Kautz digraphs.

vertices $u \equiv -dv - \alpha \pmod{n}$ for $1 \leq \alpha \leq d$. The diameter of the resultant digraph is at most $\lceil \log_d n \rceil$. If $n = d^D + d^{D-k}$ for a positive integer k then the diameter is D, and if $k = 1$ then $GK(d, n)$ is isomorphic to $K(d, D)$.[5]

Not only are these digraphs useful as LCGs of point-to-point LRNs, but they can also be used to generate families of logical connection hypergraphs (LCHs) for hypernets (see Section 7.3).

The digraphs $B(2, 3)$ and $K(2, 3)$, of order 8 and 12 respectively, have the same diameter as a (2,2)-ShuffleNet, which has eight nodes. However, for larger networks the density of the ShuffleNet falls far short of the deBruijn and Kautz networks. Thus, for example, the ShuffleNet, deBruijn, and Kautz digraphs of in-/out-degree 6 and diameter 5 have orders of $N = 648$, $7{,}776$, and $9{,}072$ respectively, compared with the Moore bound of 9,331. The deBruijn and Kautz digraphs can be converted to undirected multigraphs by removing the arc orientations, and then to graphs by coalescing parallel edges and removing self-loops. For example, the undirected graph versions of the digraphs in Figure 7.5 are shown in Figure 6.4.

---

[5] Two graphs are isomorphic if one can be converted to the other by relabeling its vertices.

It turns out that for large deBruijn and Kautz digraphs, $\bar{d}$ is very close to D, indicating that all nodes are almost the same distance apart, as is the case for large random digraphs (see Section 6.2). For example, $B(4, 5)$, $B(5, 5)$, and $B(6, 5)$ have $\bar{d} = 4.56$, 4.70, and 4.77 respectively, compared with the (4,3)-, (5,3)-, and (6,3)-ShuffleNets (of diameter 5) with $\bar{d} = 3.69$, 3.76, and 3.81 respectively. This means that deBruijn and Kautz networks have slightly less maximum throughput than ShuffleNets with the same degree and diameter. Of course, the ShuffleNet being compared has far fewer nodes than the deBruijn and Kautz networks.

One of the useful features of logical topologies based on arithmetic operations is that routing rules can be defined conveniently in terms of node labels [Sivarajan+91, Jiang+95]. Thus, for example, in deBruijn and Kautz digraphs a simple shortest path "address shift" routing rule can be defined. Let $A = (a_1, a_2, \ldots, a_D)$ and $B = (b_1, b_2, \ldots, b_D)$ be, respectively, the source and destination addresses of a cell, and let $i > 0$ be the smallest integer for which $B = (b_1, b_2, \ldots, b_{D-i}) = (a_{i+1}, a_{i+2}, \ldots, a_D)$. Then we define the *shortest concatenation* of A and B as

$$(AB)^* = (a_1, a_2, \ldots, a_D, b_{D-i+1}, b_{D-i+2}, \ldots, b_D) \tag{7.9}$$

The value of i gives the length of the shortest path from A to B, and the $i + 1$ successive substrings of length D starting from the left in $(AB)^*$ give the sequence of nodes on that path. For example, in the Kautz digraph of Figure 7.5(b), the shortest path from node 210 to 021 is found by constructing the shortest concatenation, 21021, for $i = 2$, which gives the two-hop LP $210 \rightarrow 102 \rightarrow 021$.

7.2 Multihop Network Design

Ideally, design of an LRN should proceed simultaneously in both the logical and physical layers. However, as mentioned earlier, the complexity of the combined design problem makes this exceedingly difficult. Instead, we treat the logical layer design problem in the next section, followed by physical layer design in Section 7.2.2.

7.2.1 Logical Layer Design

The problem of logical layer design can be attacked by starting with a prescribed (typically highly symmetrical) LCG, say a ShuffleNet or deBruijn or Kautz digraph. A more general approach is also possible in which only certain basic constraints on the LCG are assumed, such as the in-/out-degree of the vertices (LSNs). In either case, the objective of logical layer design is to match the LCG to a given traffic distribution. The problem can then be treated as two subproblems:

1. *Configuring the logical topology:* In the case in which the LCG has been prescribed, completion of the LT configuration requires placement of stations (i.e., mapping of stations onto the vertices of the prescribed LCG). If the structure of the LCG is

left free, configuring the LT requires determining an LCG that is feasible in the sense that it can support the prescribed traffic, given the design constraints.

2. *Routing:* This entails finding a routing assignment for the prescribed traffic on the chosen LT that is "good" or best according to some performance criterion.

These subproblems are closely coupled. Determining whether an LCG will support a given traffic distribution subject to capacity constraints on the LCs generally requires solving the routing problem for the traffic flows; that is, solving a multicommodity flow problem. Furthermore, if an optimal solution is to be found, both the LT configuration problem and the routing problem must be solved simultaneously, resulting in a very complex combinatorial optimization problem.

Some solution techniques for the logical layer configuration and routing problems are presented in [Labourdette+91] and [Bienstock+93]. They assume that the optical infrastructure is a WRN, so that all logical and optical connections are point to point and there is no channel sharing. Given a set of LSNs, a prescribed traffic distribution among the nodes, and a fixed number δ of LCs to and from each node, a regular LCG of in-/out-degree δ is sought together with a routing assignment that minimizes the maximum flow on the LCs. The degree δ indicates the required number of optical transceivers at each node. Note that the structure of the nodes and their access stations remains fixed during the optimization, but the LCG is configured to match the offered traffic.

So far, link capacities have not been included in this formulation. Assuming all LCs have equal capacity, the flows corresponding to a solution of the minimax problem will accommodate a version of the prescribed traffic distribution, scaled up (or down) until the flow on the maximally loaded connection equals the link capacity. The smaller the maximum flow, the more aggregate throughput can be obtained by scaling upward.

The combined LCG design and routing problem can be cast as a mixed integer program (MIP) using the following variables [Labourdette+90, 91]:

- x_{ij}: A binary variable set to 1 if an LC is placed from node i to j, and set to 0 otherwise

- t_{sd}: The traffic injected into node s and destined for node d

- f_{ij}^{sd}: The traffic flow from source s to destination d, carried on connection $[i, j]$

- z: The maximum of the flows on all connections.

The MIP is given by the following equations:

Minimize z with

$$\sum_{j \neq i} x_{ij} = \delta, \quad \text{for all } i \tag{7.10}$$

$$\sum_{j \neq i} x_{ji} = \delta, \quad \text{for all } i \tag{7.11}$$

$$\sum_{s,d} f_{ij}^{sd} \le Mx_{ij}, \quad \text{for all } i \ne j \tag{7.12}$$

$$\sum_{j \ne i} f_{ij}^{sd} - \sum_{j \ne i} f_{ji}^{sd} = \begin{cases} t_{sd}, & \text{if } i = s \\ -t_{sd}, & \text{if } i = d \\ 0, & \text{otherwise} \end{cases} \tag{7.13}$$

$$\sum_{s,d} f_{ij}^{sd} \le z, \quad \text{for all } i \ne j$$

$$0 \le f_{ij}^{sd}, \quad \text{for all } s, d \text{ and all } i \ne j \tag{7.14}$$

Equations 7.10 and 7.11 incorporate the degree constraints. Making M in Equation 7.12 a sufficiently large quantity allows arbitrarily large flows, but only on connections that exist. Equation 7.13 provides the flow conservation relations, and Equation 7.14 sets z equal to the largest link load.

As might be expected from our earlier forays into the world of combinatorial optimization in Chapter 6, this MIP problem is extremely difficult computationally.[6] Recognizing this, [Labourdette+91] decomposes the problem into two subproblems: a preliminary heuristic for determining a good LCG, followed by solution of the (relatively easy) multicommodity flow problem (a linear programming problem). In the first subproblem the heuristic attempts to find an LCG which maximizes the single-hop traffic. The routing problem is then solved on this fixed LCG.

An example of a solution of an eight-node logical layer design problem is shown in Figure 7.6. Each node has $\delta = 2$.

A prescribed traffic matrix is shown in Figure 7.6(a). Note that the dominant terms, shown with bold lines, indicate that most of the traffic follows a unidirectional ring. The LCG optimized for the prescribed traffic matrix, together with traffic flows, found using the heuristics and routing of [Labourdette+91], are given in Figure 7.6(b). The LCG is in the form of a chordal ring, and the maximum flow values of 13.17 are underlined.

The LCG of Figure 7.6(b) can be viewed as an eight-node ShuffleNet (see Figure 3.33[a]) that has been "rearranged" by changing the source–destination interconnections of its stations to match a prescribed traffic distribution. This provides a useful comparison between a fixed and an optimized LCG. If the traffic matrix of Figure 7.6(a) had been routed on the ShuffleNet of Figure 3.33(a), the flow on the maximally loaded link would have increased to 22.1. Thus, the matched LCG with a maximum flow of 13.17 gives a 41% improvement in achievable throughput.

7.2.2 Physical Layer Design

In focusing on the logical layer design problem, the question of realization of the LT on an optical infrastructure was set aside temporarily. In the most general setting,

---

[6] The intractability of the problem is thoroughly documented in [Bienstock+93].

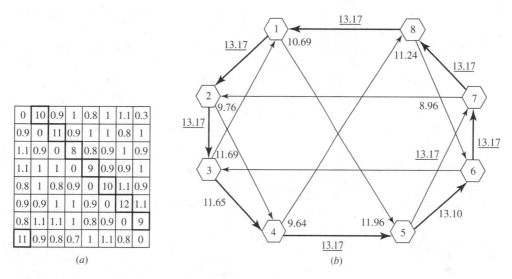

FIGURE 7.6 A traffic matrix and matched LCG. (From (Labourdette+91, Figure 5). Copyright © 1991 IEEE. Used by permission of The Institute of Electrical and Electronics Engineers, Inc.)

optical realization may include design of the physical (fiber) topology as well as embedding of the LT onto the physical topology. More commonly, the PT is given and it is embedding (i.e., optical path routing and wavelength/waveband assignment) that is of interest. Embedding of point-to-point LRNs has been considered by [Bannister90, Kovacevic93, Gerla+92]. We consider the problem of embedding on a given fiber topology next. Multistar realization is discussed in Section 7.4.2.2.

7.2.2.1 Embedding: Routing and Channel Assignment

Three possible classes of purely optical architectures have been examined in previous chapters: static, WRN, and LLNs. In a typical static network based on a tree fiber topology, as exemplified by Figures 2.6, 2.9, and 2.10, the embedding problem is straightforward. Assuming that each logical connection in the LT is supported by a dedicated λ-channel using a fixed–tuned transmitter and receiver, there is no routing problem (source–destination paths are unique). An embedding of the eight-node ShuffleNet of Figure 3.33(a) on a folded bus is shown in Figure 3.33(c). It requires 16 wavelengths, one for each of the LCs. If, instead, a star topology based on an 8 × 8 static router of the form of Figure 2.9 was used, with the wavelength routing rule given in Section 2.3.1.2, only five wavelengths would be required. (With a different static routing rule the number of wavelengths could be reduced to two.) Note that because there are no controllable ONNs in static networks, reconfiguration of the logical topology is simply a matter of retuning the optical transceivers in the access stations.

In a wavelength routed network with a given physical topology, embedding of the logical topology becomes an RCA problem, which was explored in some depth in Section 6.3. Optical paths and wavelengths are allocated to each LC using static RCA rules with some objective in mind, such as minimizing the number of wavelengths used or the optical path lengths.

In cases when LSNs connect to the network through elementary access stations, the DCA condition requires that all LCs originating on the same node be assigned distinct wavelengths, and the same holds true for connections terminating on a common node. In view of these DCA constraints, a lower bound on the number of wavelengths necessary to embed a given LCG on any physical topology is simply the largest vertex in- or out-degree of the LCG. This bound is not necessarily realizable because the structure of the physical topology may impose additional constraints.

As an example of WRN embedding, Figure 7.7 shows the eight-node ShuffleNet embedded on the Atlantis PT of Figure 3.38(b). Nodes 1 through 8 in the ShuffleNet LCG of Figure 3.33(a) are identified respectively with the NASs *A* through *H* in the optical network. Elementary access stations are assumed, which means that the minimum

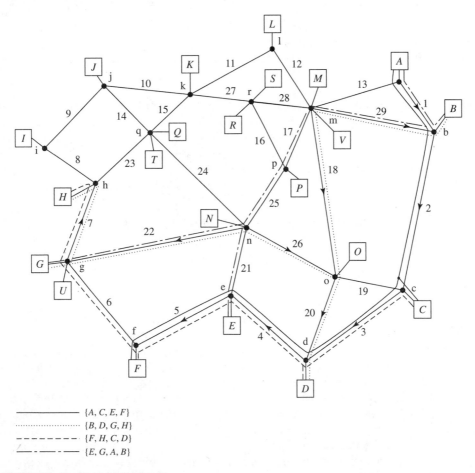

────────	$\{A, C, E, F\}$
··················	$\{B, D, G, H\}$
── ── ── ──	$\{F, H, C, D\}$
── · ── · ──	$\{E, G, A, B\}$

FIGURE 7.7 ShuffleNet on Atlantis.

TABLE 7.1 ShuffleNet Routing on Atlantis

Connection	Path	Wavelength
(A, E)	1, 2, 3, 4	1
(A, F)	1, 2, 3, 4, 5	2
(C, E)	3, 4	3
(C, F)	3, 4, 5	4
(B, G)	29', 18, 26', 22	1
(B, H)	29', 18, 26', 22, 7	2
(D, G)	20', 26', 22	3
(D, H)	20', 26', 22, 7	4

wavelength requirement is two (see Section 6.3.2). A feasible routing and wavelength assignment for the connections among the subsets $\{A, C, E, F\}$ and $\{B, D, G, H\}$ is indicated in Table 7.1. To simplify the routing, the four optical paths for the connections in each subset are confined to directed trees $\{1, 2, 3, 4, 5\}$ and $\{29', 18, 20', 26', 22, 7\}$ respectively, as shown in Figure 7.7.

The fiber orientations (primed or unprimed) on the paths in Table 7.1 are defined with respect to the link reference arrows in Figure 7.7. Four wavelengths are required to satisfy DCA for the four connections in subset $\{A, C, E, F\}$ because they all share fibers 3 and 4. The same wavelengths are reused in subset $\{B, D, G, H\}$ because the trees for the two subsets are fiber–disjoint. The optical paths among the remaining subsets $\{E, G, A, B\}$ and $\{F, H, C, D\}$ are also confined to fiber–disjoint trees, as indicated in Figure 7.7.[7] Thus, each subset of four connections can reuse the same four wavelengths.[8]

In this example the 16 connections on the eight-node ShuffleNet are realized in a WRN using two transceivers per station and four wavelengths, for a spectrum reuse factor of four. The maximum network throughput, normalized to the capacity of one λ-channel is $S = N\delta/\bar{H} = 8$, a value that is achieved if and only if shortest path routing is used and all LCs are loaded to saturation. (This corresponds to a maximum normalized throughput per node of $\rho_{max} = 1$.) Another possibility for embedding using shared channels is considered in Section 7.3.

The approach we have taken—separating the design problem into logical and physical layer design—may not always lead to a feasible physical layer embedding. If

---

[7] There are cases when two directed trees use the same link. However, they are fiber–disjoint because they use oppositely directed fibers on that link.

[8] Although a lower bound on the number of wavelengths necessary to realize this LCG on any physical topology is two, the additional wavelengths were required in this case because routing was confined to trees. It is left as an exercise for the reader to determine an embedding of the ShuffleNet on Atlantis with elementary access stations that requires fewer than four wavelengths.

it turns out that the designed LT cannot be embedded on a given physical topology without violating physical constraints, such as available wavelengths, available transceivers, and path length limitations, all is not lost! It may be possible to modify the logical layer design by taking the physical layer constraints that were violated into account. This amounts to a "loose coupling" of logical and physical layer design problems. Following this approach, several iterations of the two-step problem can be made with a goal of "fitting" the LT into the PT, if, indeed, such a fit is possible.

7.2.2.2 Hitless Reconfiguration

An essential feature of any large network is that it be reconfigurable in response to changing traffic conditions. As mentioned at the beginning of this chapter, LRNs are especially flexible in this respect because they can be reconfigured both at the virtual connection level and at the logical level. In this section we examine the problem of changing the LCG of an LRN, while it is in operation, to adapt to changing traffic *without disturbing the active connections*. This is known as *hitless reconfiguration*.

To fix ideas we consider an ATM network embedded on a WRN infrastructure. Each ATM switch accesses the WRN through an elementary access station. In a particular scenario, analyzed by [Bala+96], changes in traffic patterns are known in advance and are assumed to change in a cyclic order. The LCG that best matches each expected traffic pattern is determined off-line and is stored for use at the appropriate time.[9] A typical sequence of logical topologies in the form of LCGs T_i, is $T_0 \rightarrow T_1, T_1 \rightarrow T_2, \ldots T_i \rightarrow T_{i+1} \ldots T_{M-2} \rightarrow T_{M-1}$ and $T_{M-1} \rightarrow T_0$. Cyclic changes in logical topologies occur in a number of applications. For example, in a network that interconnects financial institutions, traffic patterns and intensities typically vary periodically on a daily basis. An LCG, T_0, might be used in the morning when the data traffic is relatively heavy, T_1 in the early afternoon when the traffic subsides, and T_2 at night when the institutions exchange data for the day's transactions and the data traffic is very heavy.

It is assumed here that

1. Each LCG remains in place for a long period of time (orders of magnitude longer than individual cell times)

2. The change $T_i \rightarrow T_{i+1}$ is completed before the next change begins

A hitless transition from T_i to T_{i+1} is achieved by first establishing all LCs in T_{i+1} without removing those from T_i. Thus, the links from both T_i and T_{i+1} are supported simultaneously. Then the links of T_i, which are not needed in T_{i+1}, are "emptied" (i.e., no new traffic is allocated to them and all active virtual connections are either allowed to terminate before the transition is completed or are transferred to the links of T_{i+1}). After all traffic has been transferred in this manner, the unwanted links of T_i are disconnected. The network has now completed its transition in a hitless fashion.

---

[9] The techniques of Section 7.2.1 might be used for this purpose.

Our objective is to determine requirements on LSN (ATM switch) ports and optical connections so that a known cyclic pattern of LCGs can be realized in this manner.

Sizing ATM Switches for Hitless Reconfiguration

An example of a four-node network that requires three different LCGs is shown in Figure 7.8. During the transition from the topology T_0 to T_1, the network's *transition* LCG is the union of the two *adjacent* LCGs, which we denote by $T_0^* = T_0 \cup T_1$. In general, for a cycle of LCGs of length M, $T_i^* = T_i \cup T_{[(i+1) \bmod M]}$. The four-node network with its transition LCGs is shown in Figure 7.9.

The switches must be sized to have sufficient ports to support all transition LCGs. If we denote the out-degree and in-degree of node u_j in T_i^* as $d^+\{(T_i^*(u_j)\}$ and $d^-\{(T_i^*(u_j)\}$ respectively, then the port requirements on the switches are

$$p^+(u_j) = \max_{i=1}^{M} d^+\{T_i^*(u_j)\}$$
$$p^-(u_j) = \max_{i=1}^{M} d^-\{T_i^*(u_j)\}$$

(7.15)

where $p^+(u_j)$ and $p^-(u_j)$ are the number of required output and input ports respectively. These correspond to the number of required optical transmitters and receivers in the supporting access stations. For example, in the system of Figure 7.9, the switches at nodes A, B, C, and D must be at least 4×3, 2×3, 2×2, and 3×2 respectively.

Optical Connections: Wavelength Requirements

Because each ATM switch accesses the WRN through a single elementary access station, during the ith transition the access station for the switch at node u_j must be capable of maintaining $d^+\{(T_i^*(u_j)\}$ outbound optical connections and $d^-\{(T_i^*(u_j)\}$ inbound optical connections. This

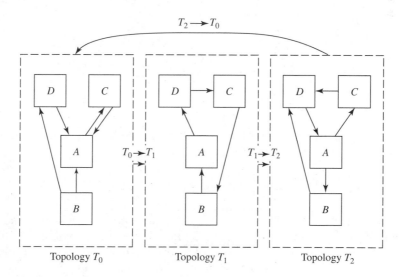

FIGURE 7.8 Reconfiguration of LCGs.

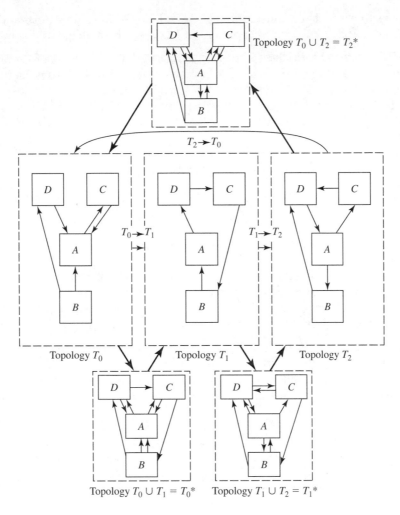

FIGURE 7.9 Union of adjacent LCGs.

gives the following lower bound on the number of wavelengths required to support hitless transmission over a complete cycle:

$$W_{min} = \max_{i=1}^{M} \left(\max_{j} \left[d^+\{T_i^*(u_j)\}, d^-\{T_i^*(u_j)\} \right] \right) \tag{7.16}$$

This bound applies independent of the physical topology on which the LRN is embedded. The constraints of the network may make it impossible to realize the bound. A determination of a feasible set of routing and wavelength assignments to support all LCGs in a cycle requires obtaining a "coupled" set of embeddings of each successive LCG on a given physical topology. *Hitlessness* means that rearrangeability of optical connections is not allowed from one LCG to the next; that is, in going from T_i to T_i^* new optical connections must be added without disturbing the old ones. This can be attacked as a static RCA problem, in which the complete cycle of routing and channel assignments is computed and stored, or as a dynamic problem, in which assignments are made sequentially, from one configuration to the next. The static case is more difficult because all assignments must be compatible over the closed cycle. Some simple heuristics for solving the embedding problem while attempting to minimize the number of wavelengths used can be found in [Bala+96].

7.3 Multipoint Logical Topologies: Hypernets

The hypernet paradigm was introduced through several examples in Sections 3.4.2 and 3.5.2—see Figures 3.26, 3.36, 3.38(a), and 3.39. A hypernet is a generalization of a multihop LRN, with point-to-point connections replaced by multipoint connections. The former can be represented by an LCG, and the latter by an LCH (see Appendix A for hypergraph definitions and terminology). The hypernet, together with its optical network infrastructure, is similar to the multihop network, as shown in the layered view of Figure 7.10. A virtual topology is supported by a logical topology, which is

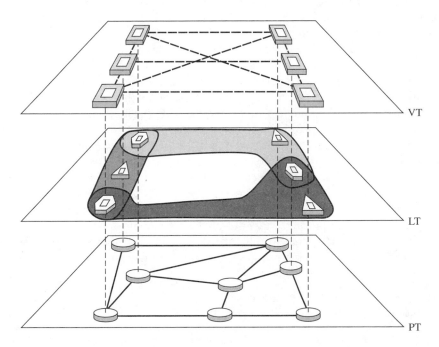

FIGURE 7.10 Layered view of a hypernet.

now in the form of a hypergraph, and the LT is in turn supported by the physical topology. The basic transport element in the hypernet is a multipoint LC, which may join together any number of network nodes. (Three multipoint LCs are shown in Figure 7.10.)

Multipoint networks and hypergraphs have been studied extensively as models for bus interconnection networks for parallel processors [Bermond+86, 83, 96; Birk86]. For applications to optical networks see [Birk91, Dowd92, Ofek87, Jiang+93, 95, Jiang95]. Hypergraphs have been applied in many other fields as well. (See, for example, [Shi92] for an application to integrated circuit layout.) In this section we study the basic structure and performance of networks with hypergraph logical topologies.

We define an *undirected (directed)* hypernet to be an LRN with connections that can be represented by an undirected (directed) LCH $H(\nu, \varepsilon)$. Figures 7.11(a), (b), and (c) show LCHs that represent undirected hypernets of orders 7, 12, and 24 respectively. The vertices of the LCH represent LSNs, and the hyperedges (hyperarcs in the directed case) represent the LCs, which are carried on multipoint subnets (MPSs).[10] The MPSs support multipoint logical connectivity and channel sharing through multipoint optical paths. This necessitates the generalized switching capabilities of a linear lightwave network (LLN). Thus it will be assumed henceforth that the underlying optical infrastructure for a hypernet is an LLN.

In the undirected case, a hyperedge $E = \{a, b, \ldots\}$ of size $r = |E|$ represents an undirected MPS containing r LSNs and providing full logical connectivity among all nodes in the subnet. Any node in the subnet is reachable from any other in one logical hop. A hyperedge of size $r = 2$ therefore represents an ordinary bidirectional point-to-point link, and a hyperedge of size r provides a logical connectivity equivalent to $r(r-1)$ point-to-point connections sharing the capacity of a common medium. A node of degree Δ transmits to and receives from Δ MPSs (hyperedges). In the hypernets of Figures 7.11(a) through (c), the hyperedges are of size 3, 4, and 4 respectively, and the nodes are of degree 3, 2, and 2 respectively.

In the directed case, a hyperarc $E = \{E^-, E^+\}$ represents a directed MPS, wherein the receiving set of the MPS, $\mathcal{R} = \{R_1, R_2, \ldots\}$, corresponds to E^+ (the out-set of E) and is reachable in a single logical hop from any node in the transmitting set, $\mathcal{T} = \{T_1, T_2, \ldots\}$ (the in-set, E^-, of E). The in-size, $s^- = |\mathcal{T}|$, of E indicates the number of nodes transmitting into E and the out-size, $s^+ = |\mathcal{R}|$, of E indicates the number of nodes receiving from E. A hyperarc of in-/out-size 1 represents a single (unidirectional) LC, and a general hyperarc is equivalent to $|\mathcal{T}||\mathcal{R}|$ point-to-point connections from the transmitting set to the receiving set, sharing the capacity of a common MPS.

---

[10] As indicated earlier, we classify the nodes of an LRN as either LTNs, which belong to a single MPS, or LSNs, which belong to at least two MPSs. Because LTNs are "dead ends" that do not participate in the routing functions of the network, we shall normally exclude them from the discussion that follows. (In the illustrations of Figure 7.11, all nodes are LSNs.)

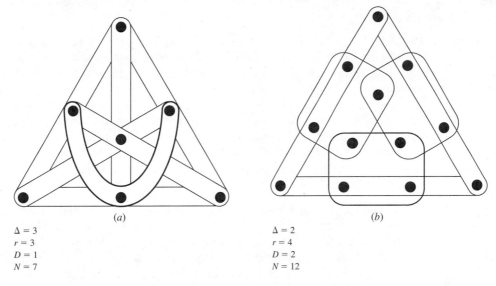

$\Delta = 3$
$r = 3$
$D = 1$
$N = 7$

$\Delta = 2$
$r = 4$
$D = 2$
$N = 12$

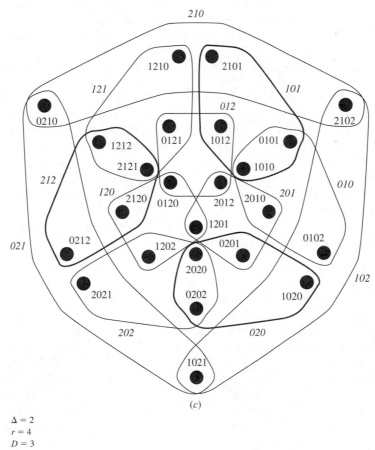

$\Delta = 2$
$r = 4$
$D = 3$
$N = 24$

FIGURE 7.11 Hypernets.

A directed MPS with $|\mathcal{T}| = M$ and $|\mathcal{R}| = N$ is called an $M \times N$ MPS. A node of out-degree d^+ transmits into d^+ MPSs (hyperarcs), and a node of in-degree d^- receives from d^- MPSs. (In the development that follows we shall often use the terms MPS and hyperedge/hyperarc interchangeably.)

To illustrate, consider the undirected hypernet of Figure 7.11(c) with nodes and hyperedges denoted by labels of length 4 and 3 respectively. It can be converted to a directed hypernet by assigning directions of transmission to each node (see arrows assigned in Figure 7.16). For example, MPS 101 has transmitting set $\mathcal{T} = \{2101, 0101\}$ and receiving set $\mathcal{R} = \{1012, 1010\}$. Each hyperarc is of in-/out-size 2 and each node of in-/out-degree 1.

The Underlying Graph of a Hypergraph   The connectivity in any hypergraph can also be achieved in an equivalent graph. Thus, an undirected hypergraph $H(\nu, \varepsilon)$ can be replaced by a graph $G(\nu, \varepsilon^*)$, in which each hyperedge $E \in \varepsilon$ of size r is replaced by $r(r-1)/2$ edges in ε^*, providing full connectivity among the vertices of E. The equivalent graph, $G(\nu, \varepsilon^*)$, is called the *underlying graph* of $H(\nu, \varepsilon)$. Similarly, a directed hypergraph can be replaced by an underlying digraph, in which each hyperarc of in-size s^- and out-size s^+ is replaced by $s^- \times s^+$ arcs in the digraph, providing full bipartite connectivity between the in-set and out-set of that hyperarc.

A multihop LRN with logical connection graph $G(\nu, \varepsilon^*)$ therefore has connectivity equivalent to a hypernet with LCH $H(\nu, \varepsilon)$ whenever $G(\nu, \varepsilon^*)$ is the underlying graph/digraph for the hypernet. The difference between the two is in the way capacity is allocated to the LCs. In the point-to-point case, each connection has a fixed capacity dedicated to it, determined by the bandwidth of its supporting optical channel and the constraints of the optical transceivers. In the hypernet, each MPS has a total capacity determined by the aggregate optical spectrum allocated to it, as well as the transceiver constraints. This capacity is shared among all LCs in the MPS. This difference between dedicated channels and shared channels is an important consideration in the development that follows.

7.3.1 Capacity of a Multipoint Subnet

To study throughput and routing issues in hypernets, it is important to have a measure of the *capacity* of an MPS. Because of the ability of an MPS to share its channels among several LCs, the definition of the capacity of an MPS is more complex than it is for point-to-point links, depending on the optical spectrum allocated to the MPS as well as the number of stations and transceivers accessing the MPS.

Each LSN in the hypernet accesses two or more MPSs through an access station, which may contain several optical transmitters/receivers. For simplicity, we assume here that each transmitter/receiver is capable of tuning over all optical channels available in its MPSs, and that all transceivers operate at a common bitrate R_t. Furthermore, we assume that the optical spectrum allocated to an MPS consists of one waveband. It may be a thin waveband consisting of a single λ-channel, or a thick waveband consisting of several λ-channels.

The physical mechanism of channel sharing is irrelevant at the logical level. However, the total available capacity in the MPS as well as any constraints on how it is shared do have an effect on the traffic-handling ability of the MPS. To define the key channel-sharing parameters for an MPS, we adopt the general model of a shared medium studied in Section 5.3. A directed $M \times N$ MPS is assumed to have the channel-sharing capabilities of a general shared medium with M transmitting stations and N receiving stations. In an undirected MPS, $M = N$ and a pair of like-numbered transmitting and receiving stations represent the transmitting and receiving sides of one node in the MPS.

We define the *capacity* of an MPS as the maximum possible value of the aggregate traffic that the MPS can carry. Recall from Section 5.3 (see Equation 5.57) that the maximum value of the aggregate traffic, $\bar{\gamma}$, is

$$\bar{\gamma}_{\max} = \eta R_t C \qquad (7.17)$$

where C is the number of λ-channels contained in the supporting waveband, and η, defined in Equation 5.56, is the *traffic balance factor* for the traffic distribution within the MPS. The parameter η reflects the "match" between the traffic distribution and the number of transmitters and receivers in the access stations. The traffic-bearing capability of an MPS therefore depends not just on the aggregate traffic, but also on its distribution. This dependence is to be expected because of the constraints imposed by the number and speed of the transceivers.

It was shown in Chapter 5 that, given a traffic distribution with aggregate traffic $\bar{\gamma}$ and balance factor η, a channel-sharing schedule can always be found, irrespective of the specific multiplexing/multiple-access techniques being used, that accommodates the given traffic distribution using a bitrate R_t arbitrarily close to $\bar{\gamma}/\eta C$ (see Equations 5.66 and 5.67). This suggests using $\eta R_t C$ as the capacity of the MPS. However, it is preferable to eliminate the balance factor from the definition of capacity. There are two additional observations that allow us to do so:

1. $\eta = 1$ when $C = 1$ independent of the traffic distribution.[11]

2. For any given traffic distribution and any value of C, η can be made equal to unity by providing a sufficient number of transmitters/receivers in each station.

Another way of stating these observations is that if an MPS is carried on a thin waveband, it is the channel that limits its capacity, whereas for a thick waveband the transceiver constraints limit the capacity. In light of this, it is clear that an MPS with a sufficient number of transmitters/receivers in its access stations can accommodate any traffic distribution provided that $\bar{\gamma} < R_t C$. Therefore, we shall henceforth assume,

---

[11] With $C = 1$, all stations accessing an MPS can share a single channel using TDM/TDMA. In that case, a single transceiver in each station is sufficient to share the channel fully, with $\eta = 1$ and $R_t C = \bar{\gamma}$ irrespective of the traffic distribution.

without any loss of generality, that $\eta = 1$ for each MPS in our LRNs. In this way each MPS can be considered to be a fully shared medium with capacity R_tC.[12]

If the MPSs supporting an LRN are *not* fully shared, then the network loses its hypernet characteristics. For example, suppose each MPS in a hypernet is operated on a thin waveband using TDM/TDMA on a single λ-channel. Suppose further that each LC between a pair of nodes in this MPS is allocated a fixed capacity by assigning it one slot in a fixed-frame system. In this case, when viewed at the logical level, the connectivity of the LRN is point to point rather than multipoint.

We find, therefore, that there are subtle differences in defining logical connectivity for LRNs supported by multipoint optical connections, depending on the way in which capacity is allocated. An LLN has the *capability* to create multipoint, shared-channel logical connectivity, in which case it provides support for a hypernet. However, if that capacity is channelized to create fixed-capacity point-to-point connections, the resultant logical topology is more properly described as a graph rather than a hypergraph. By channelizing in this way, a hypernet is reduced to a point-to-point network with a logical connectivity that is described by the underlying graph for the hypernet.

Another complicating issue is the matter of optical resource usage. Typically, a point-to-point LC in a multihop network would be supported by a dedicated λ-channel, requiring a dedicated optical transmitter/receiver pair. However, in a multihop network realized over an LLN, a single optical transmitter or receiver might support several multiplexed connections, each using only a portion of a full λ-channel. If the multiplexed connections are allocated fixed capacities, this configuration still behaves like a point-to-point LRN, but if dynamic capacity allocation is used (e.g., by packet switching in the optical layer), we have a shared-channel system that behaves more like a hypernet.[13] The conclusion is that in an LRN with an underlying optical connectivity that is multipoint, there are many options for assigning capacity to LCs. Thus, the distinctions between fixed-capacity and shared-capacity logical connectivity are blurred.

7.3.2 Families of Dense Hypernets

The performance benefits of dense point-to-point logical topologies that were listed in Section 7.1.2 are even more evident in hypernets, because hypergraphs can be made far more dense than graphs. Therefore, it is of interest to identify hypergraphs with large orders for given diameter D, maximum degree, and hyperedge size. For this purpose it is useful to have bounds on orders of hypergraphs similar to the Moore bounds for graphs.

We call an undirected hypergraph of diameter D, maximum vertex degree Δ, and maximum hyperedge size r a (Δ, D, r)-hypergraph, and denote its order by

---

[12] In cases in which the assumptions leading to this definition are violated, so that $\eta < 1$, the capacity must be reduced to an effective value of ηR_tC.

[13] In the literature these cases are often referred to as shared-channel multihop networks (see, for example, [Hluchyj+91, Kovacevic+95]).

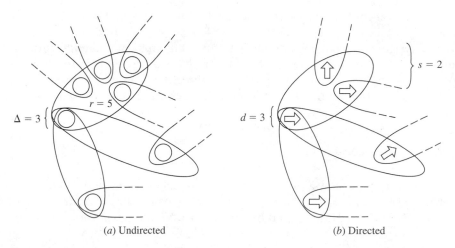

(a) Undirected   (b) Directed

FIGURE 7.12   Illustrating fan-out in hypergraphs.

$N(\Delta, D, r)$. A bound on the maximum number of vertices in a (Δ, D, r)-hypergraph is

$$N(\Delta, D, r) \leq 1 + \Delta(r - 1) \sum_{i=0}^{D-1} (\Delta - 1)^i (r - 1)^i \qquad (7.18)$$

Equation 7.18 is known as the *Moore bound for undirected hypergraphs*, and the hypergraphs that attain it are known as *Moore hypergraphs*.[14] Note that this reduces to the Moore bound for graphs (Equation A.2) when $r = 2$, and that the potential density of a hypergraph increases rapidly with hyperedge size r. Figure 7.12(a) illustrates the fan-out from a vertex in an undirected hypergraph, leading to the Moore bound.

A directed hypergraph of diameter D, maximum vertex out-degree d, and maximum out-size s is called a (d, D, s)-directed hypergraph, and its order is denoted by $n(d, D, s)$. A bound on the maximum number of vertices in a (d, D, s)-directed hypergraph is given by

$$n(d, D, s) \leq \sum_{i=0}^{D} (ds)^i \qquad (7.19)$$

Equation 7.19 is the Moore bound for directed hypergraphs, and the hypergraphs that attain it are known as *directed Moore hypergraphs*.[15] Note that Equation 7.19 reduces to the Moore bound for digraphs (Equation A.3) when $d = \delta$ and $s = 1$. Figure 7.12(b)

---

[14] It is known [Bermond+96] that for $D > 2$ (with the exception of rings of odd order [i.e., $r = 2$]), Moore hypergraphs cannot exist.

[15] It is known [Bermond+96] that directed Moore hypergraphs cannot exist for $ds > 1$ or $D > 1$.

illustrates the fan-out from a vertex in a directed hypergraph, leading to the Moore bound.

Dense hypergraphs have interested both the mathematical and engineering communities for some time. A survey of results up to 1983 can be found in [Bermond+83]. Hypergraphs can be constructed directly, or indirectly via a related graph. Two tools for construction of hypergraphs from graphs that are used here are

1. Edge grouping
2. Duality (see Section 7.3.3.1)

Edge grouping is a simple way of deriving a directed hypergraph from a digraph. The arc set of the digraph is grouped into *dicliques* (see Appendix A for a definition), and each diclique is replaced by a hyperarc in the derived hypergraph. For example, the shuffle hypernet with the LCH shown in Figure 3.36 was derived by grouping the 16 arcs of the ShuffleNet of Figure 3.33(a) into four dicliques. A larger example is shown in the LCH of Figure 7.13, in which the 18-node $(3, 2)$-ShuffleNet of Figure 7.3 is converted to a $(1, 3, 3)$-directed hypernet. In this transformation, the in-/out-degree of each node has been reduced from 3 in the ShuffleNet to 1 in the directed hypergraph, with a consequent 3:1 reduction in optical hardware requirements in the nodes.

7.3.3 Kautz Hypernets

In Section 7.1.2 we showed that Kautz and deBruijn graphs are examples of dense families of regular graphs. It is also possible to define families of Kautz and deBruijn hypergraphs and their generalizations, which have excellent topological properties, including very high density and good survivability. These hypergraphs also retain the simple addressing and self-routing properties of the corresponding graphs. We focus here on Kautz and generalized Kautz hypergraphs as the LCHs for Kautz hypernets. Although the emphasis is on basic performance indices such as throughput and processing load in the switches, it is important to note that hypernets with a high degree of symmetry, such as the Kautz families, also possess other useful properties such as even load distribution, ease of routing and multicasting, scalability, and fault tolerance (see [Jiang95]).

The families of graphs and hypergraphs that are of interest here are

- $K(d, D)$: The Kautz digraph, a regular digraph of in-/out-degree d and diameter D, defined for arbitrary positive integers d and D

- $GKH(d, n, s, m)$: The generalized Kautz hypergraph, a directed hypergraph of out-degree d, order n, out-size s, and number of hyperarcs m, where $d, n, s,$ and m are positive integers

- $DKH(d, D, s)$: The directed Kautz hypergraph, a regular directed hypergraph of in-/out-degree d, diameter D, and in-/out-size s, where $d, D,$ and s are arbitrary positive integers

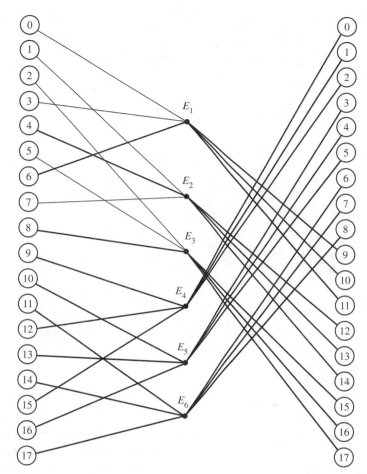

FIGURE 7.13 Shuffle hypernet.

- $KH(\Delta, D, r)$: The Kautz hypergraph, a regular hypergraph of degree Δ, diameter D, and hyperedge size r, where Δ and r are arbitrary *even* positive integers

Table 7.2 summarizes the key parameters for the corresponding Kautz hypernets. (In the case of directed hypernets, the node degree refers to the in-/out-degree.) As will be explained in Section 7.3.3.3, $KH(\Delta, D^*, r)$ is derived from $GKH(d, n, s, m)$ for special values of its arguments. The parameter D and the number of hyperedges in $KH(\Delta, D^*, r)$ are determined by the parameters of the corresponding generalized Kautz hypergraph. The table entry for $GKH(d, n, s, m)$ represents the special case of *symmetric GKHs* (see Section 7.3.3.3).

Note that these networks can be "grown" to large orders by increasing the size of the hyperedges (MPSs) while maintaining a small number of optical transceivers per node (the nodal degree) and a small logical diameter. An illustration of the effect of hyperedge size on order is shown in Figure 7.14, in which the order of $KH(2, D, r)$ is

TABLE 7.2   Kautz Hypergraphs

Network	Node degree	Nodes in MPS	Diameter D^*	Node label length	No. of nodes	No. of MPSs
$KH(2, D^*, r)$	2	r	$D^* \le D$	D	$(\frac{r}{2})^D + (\frac{r}{2})^{D-1}$	$(\frac{r}{2})^{D-1} + (\frac{r}{2})^{D-2}$
$DKH(1, D, s)$	1	$2s$	D	D	$s^D + s^{D-1}$	$s^{D-1} + s^{D-2}$
$KH(\Delta, D^*, r)$	Δ	r	$D^* \le D$	—	$(\frac{r\Delta}{4})^D + (\frac{r\Delta}{4})^{D-1}$	—
$GKH(d, n, s, m)$	d	$2s$	$D^* \le \lceil \log_{ds} n \rceil$	—	n	$m = dn/s$
$DKH(d, D, s)$	d	$2s$	D	—	$(ds)^D + (ds)^{D-1}$	—

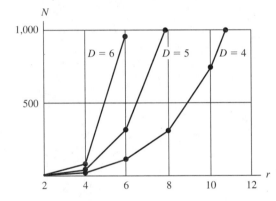

FIGURE 7.14   Orders of $KH(2, D, r)$.

plotted against r with D as a parameter. For comparison, the diameters $D = (2k - 1)$ of $(2, k)$-ShuffleNets must be much larger to produce networks of the same order as $KH(2, D, r)$. For example, the Kautz hypergraph $KH(2, 4, 8)$ has an order of 1,280 with a diameter of 4, whereas the $(2, 7)$-ShuffleNet has an order of 896 with a diameter of 13.

Each of the Kautz families can be defined in various ways. In particular, $DKH(1, D, s)$ and $KH(2, D, r)$ are derived conveniently from $K(d, D)$ by duality. The more general Kautz hypergraphs can be constructed from $GKH(d, n, s, m)$ by selecting special values of the parameters d, n, s, and m. These relations are studied in the following sections.

7.3.3.1 From Graphs to Hypergraphs: Duality

The dual of a hypergraph H is a hypergraph H^*, with vertices that correspond to the hyperedges of H and with hyperedges that correspond to the vertices of H. A vertex e_j^* of H^*, corresponding to a hyperedge E_j of H, is a member of a hyperedge V_j^* in H^* if and only if the vertex v_j in H, corresponding to V_j^*, is a member of E_j in H.

Bermond, Bond, and Peyrat [Bermond+86] observed the following relationship between a hypergraph and its dual:

> **Proposition** If H is a (Δ, D, r)-hypergraph, then its dual hypergraph H^* is an (r, D^*, Δ)-hypergraph where $D - 1 \leq D^* \leq D + 1$.

In particular, if G is a graph (or multigraph) of maximum degree r and diameter D, then its dual is a $(2, D^*, r)$-hypergraph.

$KH(2,D,r)$ by Duality   The duality relations between Kautz hypergraphs and Kautz digraphs work as follows. By removing arc orientations, the Kautz digraph $K(r/2, D - 1)$ becomes a multigraph of degree r with a dual that is $KH(2, D^*, r)$, with $D^* \leq D$. The hypergraph $KH(2, D^*, r)$ is of order $(r/2)^D + (r/2)^{D-1}$ with a degree of 2, whereas the digraph $K(r/2, D - 1)$ is of order $(r/2)^{D-1} + (r/2)^{D-2}$ with a vertex in-/out-degree of $r/2$. Thus we have gained a factor of $r/2$ in number of vertices while saving a factor of $r/4$ in degree. Although duality only produces hypernets of degree 2, this special case has considerable practical importance. It is economical in usage of optical transceivers (only two per LSN), and despite the limited number of transceivers these hypernets can still be grown to large sizes by increasing the size, r, of the MPSs.

Figure 7.15 illustrates the duality relation between the hypergraph $KH(2, 3, 4)$ and the digraph $K(2, 3)$. The latter is first converted to a regular multigraph with degree $\Delta = 4$ by ignoring the orientation of the arcs. The dual of the multigraph is $KH(2, 3, 4)$. Note the labeling convention in Figure 7.15. Each hyperedge in $KH(2, 3, 4)$ inherits its label, a word of length 3, from the dual vertex in $K(2, 3)$. Similarly, each vertex in $KH(2, 3, 4)$ derives its label, a word of length 4, from its dual arc in $K(2, 3)$, using the shortest concatenation of the labels of the vertices defining the head and tail ends of the arc. For example, vertex 1012 in $KH(2, 3, 4)$ obtained its label from the shortest concatenation of vertices 101 and 012.

The Kautz hypergraphs $KH(2, D^*, r)$ can also be defined directly using alphabets. The vertex labels are words of length D with no two identical consecutive letters, constructed on an alphabet $\mathcal{A}$ of $(r/2 + 1)$ letters. The hyperedge labels are the words of length $D - 1$ with no two identical consecutive letters. The vertex $(a_1, \ldots, a_D)$ belongs to two hyperedges: $(a_1, \ldots, a_{D-1})$ and $(a_2, \ldots, a_D)$. Each hyperedge $E = (b_1, \ldots, b_{D-1})$ contains r vertices of the form $(*, b_1, \ldots, b_{D-1})$ and $(b_1, \ldots, b_{D-1}, *)$.

$DKH(1,D,s)$ by Duality   The duality construction described earlier for undirected hypergraphs is extended easily to the directed case. Starting with a Kautz digraph $K(s, D - 1)$, we obtain a dual directed Kautz hypergraph $DKH(1, D, s)$ of order $s^D + s^{D-1}$, gaining a factor of s in number of nodes while saving a factor of s in nodal degree.

Figure 7.16 illustrates the construction based on $K(2, 3)$ and yielding $DKH(1, 4, 2)$. The labeling convention for the undirected case is followed here as well. The assignment of hypergraph vertices to hyperarc in- or out-sets is inherited from the orientations of their dual arcs in the digraph, and is indicated by arrows pointing in or out of each hyperarc. For example, the vertices 2101, 0101, 1012, and 1010 in the hyperedge E_{101} are duals of the four arcs incident on vertex 101 in the digraph. The first two are in E_{101}^- because their dual arcs are incident *to* vertex 101 in the digraph, and the last

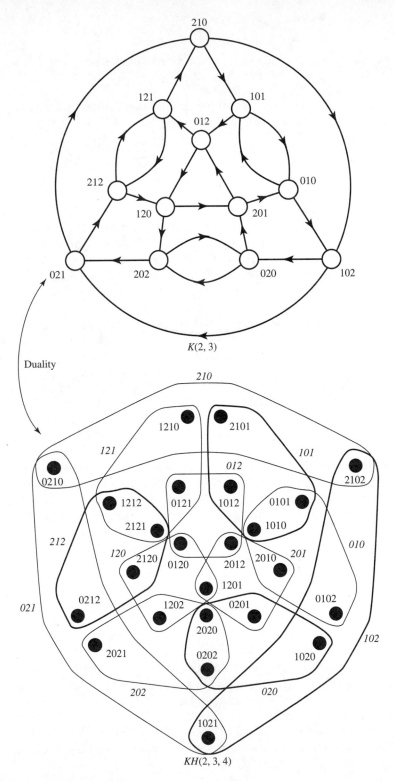

FIGURE 7.15 Duality construction.

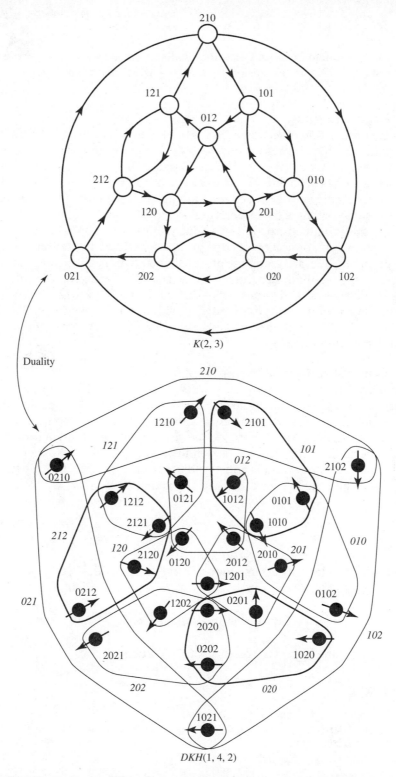

FIGURE 7.16 Directed hypergraph construction via duality.

two are in E_{101}^+ because their dual arcs are incident *from* vertex 101. This construction also suggests a multistar realization of $DKH(1, D, s)$ based on $K(s, D-1)$[16] (see Section 7.4.2.2).

7.3.3.2 Edge Grouping

The duality construction of Section 7.3.3.1 is limited to undirected hypergraphs of degree 2 and directed hypergraphs of out-degree 1. For more general cases we must turn to other techniques. One that is not limited in degree is *edge grouping*. This technique can be used to construct a directed Kautz hypergraph from an underlying Kautz or generalized Kautz digraph. Using edge grouping, the vertex set of the derived hypergraph is the same as that of the underlying digraph.

The edge grouping construction was illustrated for ShuffleNets in Section 7.3.2. Figure 7.17 shows an application of edge grouping to Kautz hypergraphs. The edges of the digraph $K(2, 3)$ are grouped into dicliques, with each diclique replaced by a hyperarc in the resultant hypergraph $DKH(1, 3, 2)$. For example, in the diclique with the shaded vertices, the four arcs—$201 \rightarrow 010, 201 \rightarrow 012, 101 \rightarrow 012$, and $101 \rightarrow 010$—correspond to the hyperarc E_{01}, with in-set $E_{01}^- = \{201, 101\}$ and out-set $E_{01}^+ = \{010, 012\}$. Although this example is of degree 1, edge grouping also yields hypergraphs of higher degrees.

7.3.3.3 Generalized Kautz Hypergraphs

The generalized Kautz hypergraphs $GKH(d, n, s, m)$ were defined in Section 6.5.9. The objective there was to find dense LCHs of diameter 1. These were implemented as purely optical multistar networks (LLNs) configured to provide connectivity among all pairs of nodes in one logical hop. We use the same family of hypergraphs here in the more general context of LRNs. The definition is repeated here for convenience.

Let n be the number of vertices and d be the vertex out-degree. Choose the number of hyperarcs m, and the hyperarc out-size s such that

$$dn \equiv 0 \pmod m$$
$$sm \equiv 0 \pmod n \tag{7.20}$$

The vertices are labeled as integers modulo n and the hyperarcs are labeled as integers modulo m. The incidence rules are as follows. Vertex v is incident to the hyperarcs

$$e \equiv dv + \alpha \pmod m, \quad 0 \le \alpha < d \tag{7.21}$$

and the out-set of the hyperarc e consists of the vertices

$$u \equiv -se - \beta \pmod n, \quad 1 \le \beta \le s \tag{7.22}$$

---

[16] The hypergraph $DKH(1, D, s)$ can also be defined directly, using alphabets, following the same general procedure as for $KH(2, D^*, r)$.

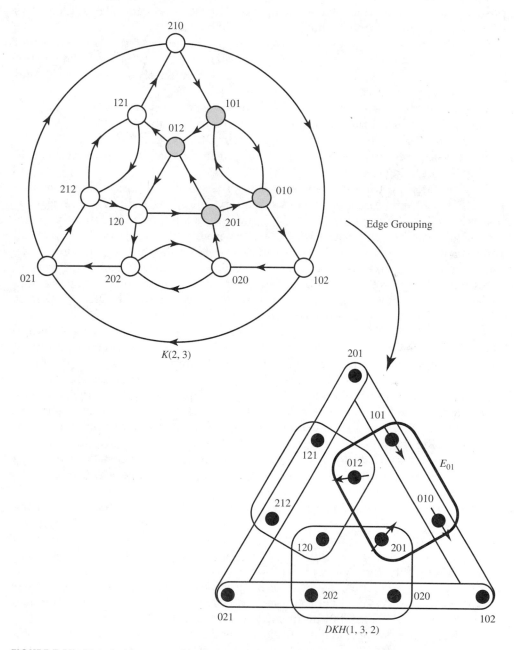

FIGURE 7.17 Directed hypergraph construction via edge grouping.

The diameter of $GKH(d, n, s, m)$ is at most $\lceil \log_{ds} n \rceil$. If $n = (ds)^D + (ds)^{D-k}$ for a positive odd integer k, then the diameter is D. Thus for $k = 1$ and $D = 2$, the orders of these hypergraphs come within 1 of the Moore bound.

In general the in- and out-size of a hyperarc of $GKH(d, n, s, m)$ will differ, as will the in- and out-degree of a vertex. However, there is a *symmetric* case, which is of particular interest here: The in- and out-size of all hyperarcs equals s, and the in- and out-degree of all vertices equals d if and only if $dn = sm$.

To simplify the discussion that follows, we focus on the symmetric case of GKH, assuming henceforth that $dn = sm$. Adding the condition that $n = (ds)^D + (ds)^{D-1}$, GKH reduces to the directed Kautz hypergraph $DKH(d, D, s)$, which has the maximum possible order for its diameter D. (Recall that $DKH[1, D, s]$ was derived in Section 7.3.3.1 using duality.)

To illustrate, the tripartite representation of $GKH(2, 42, 3, 28)$ is shown in Figure 7.18. Because it obeys the previous symmetry conditions and has $n = (ds)^2 + ds$, this is also $DKH(2, 2, 3)$. Its order is 42 and the Moore bound for these parameters is 43. Note how it forms a 28-fold multistar structure. Each star provides full connectivity between the three vertices in its in-set and the three vertices in its out-set, corresponding to nine LCs, or a 3×3 diclique in a digraph. This suggests an equivalence between the generalized Kautz hypergraph and an underlying digraph. In fact, the following relation exists: The underlying digraph of $DKH(d, D, s)$ is $K(ds, D)$.

Thus, each directed Kautz hypergraph is functionally equivalent to a Kautz digraph of the same order, with degree ds and the same diameter. This relation has important practical implications, showing more clearly how the hypernet approach economizes on optical hardware. The hypernet based on $DKH(d, D, s)$ can be realized using d transceivers in each LSN. Each transmitting node multicasts optically to s receiving nodes in the same MPS, and each receiving node is accessed by s transmitting nodes. Now suppose the same logical connectivity is realized as a point-to-point multihop network using the underlying digraph $K(ds, D)$ as its LCG. This would require ds transceivers in each node, for a factor of s increase in transceiver cost. (The increased number of transceivers in the point-to-point case carries with it the *potential* for higher throughput, provided that the necessary optical spectrum is available.)

By ignoring the orientation of the hyperarcs in $GKH(d, n, s, m)$ (i.e., by replacing each hyperarc E with a hyperedge with vertex set $E^- \cup E^+$), the directed hypergraph can be converted to an undirected hypergraph. In the important special case when $dn = sm$ and $n = (ds)^D + (ds)^{D-1}$, $GKH(d, n, s, m)$ is converted to an undirected Kautz hypergraph, $KH(\Delta, D^*, r)$, with degree $\Delta = 2d$ and edge size $r = 2s$. The diameter is $D^* \leq D$. Thus, the order of the undirected version can be expressed as $N = (r\Delta/4)^D + (r\Delta/4)^{D-1}$. For example, $GKH(2, 42, 3, 28)$ has the aforementioned properties, with $D = 2$, and its undirected version is $KH(4, 2, 6)$.

The Kautz hypergraph family provides a wide range of design alternatives for realizing large and dense hypernets with a variety of parameter values and hardware requirements. It is also worth mentioning in passing that these represent but one

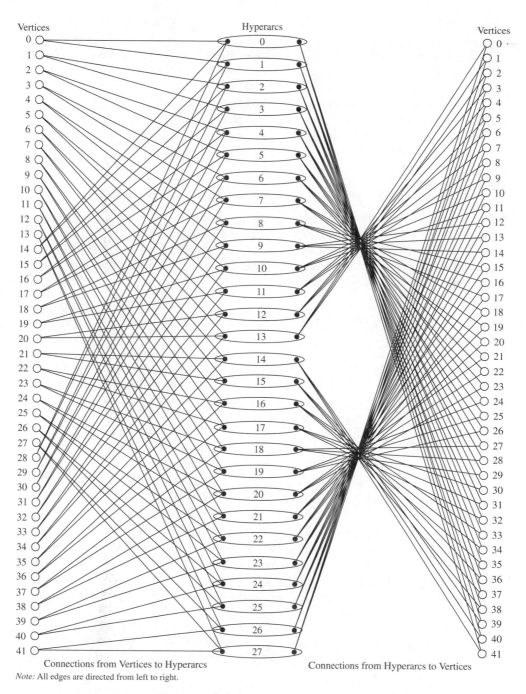

FIGURE 7.18 Tripartite representation of $GKH(2, 42, 3, 28)$. (From (Bermond+97, Figure 5). Copyright © 1991. Reprinted by permission of John Wiley & Sons, Inc.)

example of a dense family that can be grown to very large sizes with modest hardware requirements. Even in the special case of undirected hypergraphs of degree 2, there are many other possibilities. For example there exists a regular (2, 10, 16)-hypergraph of order 5, 368, 709, 120 [Bermond+86]. This compares with the corresponding Kautz hypergraph $KH(2, 10, 16)$ of order 1, 207, 959, 552.

In our discussion so far, high density has been the property of primary interest when considering hypergraphs as possible logical topologies for large networks. As is demonstrated next, hypernets—and especially families of regular hypernets—have other attractive features, including ease of routing and multicasting.

7.3.3.4 Routing

When node labels are defined in terms of alphabets, routing algorithms in Kautz hypernets can be defined and implemented conveniently using these labels. The algorithms to be described next are in that category. Thus, we now focus on the classes of Kautz hypernets that can be constructed using alphabets; that is, the undirected and directed Kautz hypernets of degree 2 and 1 respectively: $KH(2, D^*, r)$ and $DKH(1, D, s)$. The labeling is assumed to be defined either directly or through duality construction (see Section 7.3.3.1).

Address Shift Routing   Shortest path routing for directed Kautz hypergraphs can be implemented by address shifting in essentially the same way as for Kautz digraphs in Section 7.1.2. If $A = (a_1, \ldots, a_D)$ and $B = (b_1, \ldots, b_D)$ are, respectively, the source and destination node labels, then the shortest path from source to destination through the directed hypernet $DKH(1, D, s)$ is determined from the shortest concatenation $(AB)^* = (a_1, a_2, \ldots, a_D, b_{D-i+1}, b_{D-i+2}, \ldots, b_D)$, where $i > 0$ is the length of the shortest path from A to B in logical hops (see Equation 7.9). The sequence of nodes and hyperarcs along the path is given by

$$(a_1, a_2, \ldots, a_D) \xrightarrow{(a_2, \ldots, a_D)} (a_2, \ldots, a_D, b_{D-i+1}) \xrightarrow{(a_3, \ldots, a_D, b_{D-i+1})}$$
$$(a_3, \ldots, a_D, b_{D-i+1}, b_{D-i+2}), \ldots, \xrightarrow{(a_D, b_{D-i+1}, \ldots, b_{D-1})} (b_1, \ldots, b_D)$$

Note that the routing decision at any node along the shortest path is based only on a comparison of the destination address with the current node's address. This suggests implementing the algorithm in a distributed fashion with the aid of a routing record, as shown in Figure 7.19. We assume that the unit being routed is a cell, which contains a routing header, to provide self-routing information for transmission through the

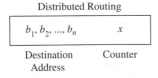

FIGURE 7.19 Routing header.

network. The routing header is generated at the source station and it consists of the destination address and a counter. The initial value of the counter, computed by the source node, is $x = i$. Each node $I = (i_1, i_2, \ldots, i_D)$ on the path, including the source node, performs the following operations:

1. If I is the same as the destination address, accept the cell.
2. If I is *not* the same as the destination address, check the value of the counter, route the message to node $(i_2, i_3, \ldots, i_D, b_{D-x+1})$, and decrement the counter by one.

To illustrate, consider $DKH(1, 4, 2)$ shown in Figure 7.16. Suppose a cell is to be routed from source $A = 1012$ to destination $B = 2010$. We have $(AB)^* = 1012010$ with path length $i = 3$ hops. The routing path then becomes

$$1012 \xrightarrow{012} 0120 \xrightarrow{120} 1201 \xrightarrow{201} 2010$$

Using self-routing, node 1012 places the destination address $(b_1, b_2, b_3, b_4) = 2010$ in the header in Figure 7.19, and the counter is initialized to $x = 3$. When the cell arrives at the next node on the path, $(i_1, i_2, i_3, i_4) = 0120$, the counter has been decremented to $x = 2$, so that the cell is forwarded to $(i_2, i_3, i_4, b_3) = 1201$.

This procedure can also be implemented without a counter by performing a shortest concatenation operation at each intermediate node. Thus, when a cell arrives at a node I, a shortest concatenation of the current node and destination addresses is formed, and the cell is forwarded to the next node on the path determined by the shortest concatenation. Continuing with the previous example, when a cell with destination $B = 2010$ arrives at node $I = 0120$, the expression $(IB)^* = 012010$ is computed, indicating that the next node on the address shift path is 1201.

Routing in the Undirected Case   In undirected hypernets $KH(2, D^*, r)$, both $(AB)^*$ and $(BA)^*$ can be evaluated, the former corresponding to left address shifts and the latter to right shifts. The source node then chooses the path defined by $(AB)^*$ if the length of $(AB)^*$ is less than or equal to that of $(BA)^*$, and chooses $(BA)^*$ otherwise. Although this may lead to shorter paths than in the directed case, it does not necessarily produce shortest path routing. We provide three examples to prove the point. In each case the network is $KH(2, 3, 4)$, derived from $DKH(1, 4, 2)$ by removing hyperarc orientation.

1. Routing from source $A = 1012$ to destination $B = 2010$ as in the previous directed case, we now have $(BA)^* = 201012$. Comparing $(AB)^*$ and $(BA)^*$, the latter is chosen as the shortest path, giving a path length $i = 2$. The routing path is

$$1012 \xrightarrow{101} 0101 \xrightarrow{010} 2010$$

2. Routing from source $A = 1012$ to destination $B = 2012$, we find that the shortest path via address shift routing is

$$1012 \xrightarrow{012} 0120 \xrightarrow{120} 1201 \xrightarrow{201} 2012$$

However, referring to the hypergraph in Figure 7.15, it can be seen that both source and destination nodes belong to the same hyperedge, so that the true shortest path is

$$1012 \xrightarrow{012} 2012$$

The problem here is that in $KH(2, D^*, r)$, vertices such as $(b_1, b_2, \ldots, b_{D-1}, x_1)$ and $(b_1, b_2, \ldots, b_{D-1}, x_2)$ where $x_1 \neq x_2$ belong to the same hyperedge—as do $(x_1, b_2, \ldots, b_D)$ and $(x_2, b_2, \ldots, b_D)$—so that the shortest path between them is one hop. However, the common hyperedge is not detected by the address shift algorithm.

3. Routing from source $A = 1012$ to destination $B = 0201$, we find that the shortest path via address shift routing is given by $(B A)^*$ and is three hops. However, the true shortest path is two hops:

$$1012 \xrightarrow{012} 2012 \xrightarrow{201} 0201$$

where the first hop is not an address shift hop.

These examples suggest that it is the hyperedge labels rather than the vertex labels that should be considered in the routing algorithm. In $KH(2, D^*, r)$ each vertex belongs to two hyperedges, so that four potentially shortest paths can be examined between any pair of source and destination vertices. This leads to a shortest path-on-edge algorithm (see [Jiang95]). Because $KH(2, D^*, r)$ is the dual of an undirected Kautz multigraph, the computation of a shortest path between a pair of hyperedges in the former is equivalent to shortest path vertex routing in the latter (see the shortest path algorithm for Kautz graphs given in [Bermond+89]).

7.3.3.5 An Implementation

At this point let us examine a concrete example of how a realization of a Kautz hypernet would look. Suppose $DKH(1, 4, 2)$ is to be implemented on some given physical topology operated as an LLN. Using the embedded tree approach of Section 3.4.2, the hypergraph logical topology is implemented as a set of directed MPSs, one for each hyperarc, and each MPS is realized as a directed tree embedded on the PT. An example of two intersecting MPSs, 120 and 201, is shown embedded in this fashion in Figure 7.20(a), in which the orientation of each MPS in the LT is shown by the arrows symbolizing the nodes. For example, node 1201 is in the receiving set of MPS 120 and

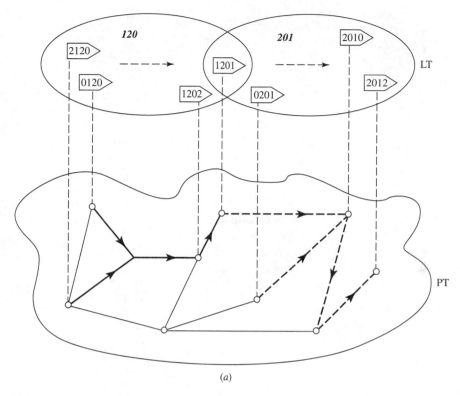

(a)

FIGURE 7.20 Implementation of *DK H*(2, 4, 4).

the transmitting set of 201. The tree supporting MPS 120 is shown in bold in the PT, and that supporting MPS 201 is shown dashed.

The details of a possible implementation of LSN 1201 and its access station are shown in Figure 7.20(b). The NAS contains a single optical transceiver, receiving transmissions from nodes 2120 and 0120. The configuration shown might represent a TDM/SCMA system, wherein each transmitting station, using a distinct subcarrier, injects a time–division multiplexed stream of cells into its MPS, and each receiving station picks up information from both transmitting stations using a single wideband optical receiver followed by an array of subcarrier demodulators (see Section 5.2.2.3). In this case we have two demodulators tuned to the subcarrier channels transmitted from nodes 2120 and 0120. The outputs of the demodulators consist of streams of cells that must be "filtered" by reading the addresses of the nodes to which they are destined in the MPS.

As in previous examples, we assume that the cells are encapsulated with an outer "local" address, which is the address of the node to which they are destined in the current MPS, and an "inner" address, which is their final destination address (see Section 3.5.2.1). Thus, each stream consists of cells addressed to nodes 1201 and 1202,

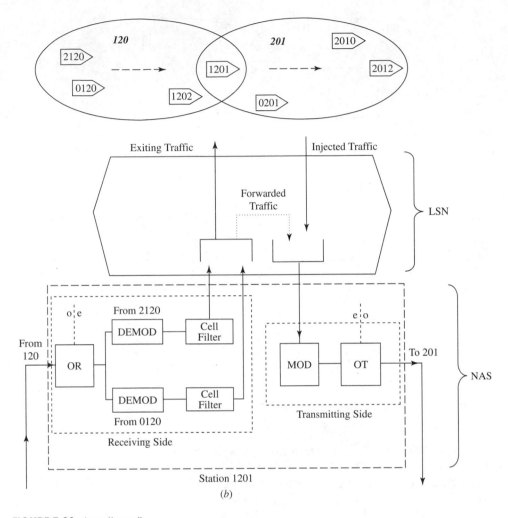

FIGURE 7.20 *(continued)*

and only cells with the local address 1201 are passed on to the LSN.[17] The outer encapsulation is then removed, and those with a final address of 1201 exit the network. The others are reencapsulated with the next node local address and forwarded to the transmitting side to be modulated onto its assigned subcarrier and injected into MPS 201 using the optical transmitter.

Two-level addressing is a convenient way of separating addressing functions associated with the logical and optical layers. In a different approach, the two-level

---

[17] Note that in a multicast LC, cells might be addressed to both 1201 and 1202, in which case both receiving stations send the cells to their LSNs.

scheme could be replaced by a single global address. However, this would require more processing in the cell filters.

7.3.3.6 Performance Comparisons

In this section we provide some comparisons of the principal performance indices for families of Kautz hypernets. The quantities that are compared include

- D: The network diameter
- $\bar{H}$: The average logical hop count
- γ_{avg}: The average hyperedge load
- μ_{avg}: The average load processed per node

The average logical hop count $\bar{H}$ for the traffic in an LRN is the key performance parameter. It determines three other performance indices:

1. *Throughput*: Because the communication link loading is proportional to the logical hop count, the maximum sustainable throughput is inversely proportional to the hop count.

2. *Time delay*: As explained in Section 5.4.2, the total delays in a wide area optical network operating in a packet-/cell-switched mode are dominated by propagation delays. (Queueing delays are minimal.) Thus, the average time delay through an LRN is essentially the sum of the propagation delays on each logical hop. Assuming that each hop has approximately the same propagation delay, the average time delay is proportional to the logical hop count.

3. *Processing load*: The hop count acts as a multiplier, determining how much processing (e.g., ATM cell routing) is required in the switches. Because switch processing power can be the limiting factor in an LRN, this also limits throughput.

The hyperedge load, γ, is the aggregate traffic injected into the hyperedge by all nodes transmitting into it. The load processed per node, μ, includes only that traffic forwarded by the node from an upstream node to a downstream node (i.e., it excludes traffic either entering or exiting the network at that node).

Performance of hypernets is examined under uniform carried traffic, with $1/(N-1)$ units of traffic flowing between each source-destination node pair in a network with N nodes. Thus, each source injects one unit of traffic into the network regardless of the network's size, and the total throughput is N. Under these conditions, flow conservation dictates the following relations among the performance indices:

$$\gamma_{\mathrm{avg}} = \frac{r\bar{H}}{\Delta} \tag{7.23}$$

for undirected hypernets $KH(\Delta, D^*, r)$,

$$\gamma_{\text{avg}} = \frac{s\bar{H}}{d} \tag{7.24}$$

for directed hypernets $DKH(d, D, s)$, and

$$\mu_{\text{avg}} = \bar{H} - 1 \tag{7.25}$$

for both the directed and undirected case.

Note that a uniform injected traffic distribution does not necessarily produce uniform hyperedge load. The exact hyperedge loading depends on the routing rule. In this case we use address shift routing, and resort to simulation to determine $\bar{H}$ and the maximum values of hyperedge load and processing load: γ_{max} and μ_{max} respectively. (The performance results are 10% to 15% better when shortest-path-on-edge routing is used. See [Jiang95].)

Table 7.3 gives the performance parameters for hypernets $KH(2, D^*, r)$ with orders ranging from 12 to 324. Their diameters D^* are either $D - 1$ or D, where D is the node label length.

It can be seen from Table 7.3 that $\bar{H}$ is approximately $0.75D^*$ in most of these cases, which is the same relation that holds for large ShuffleNets using shortest path routing (see Section 7.1.1). Both the hyperedge loads and the processing loads are essentially uniform in the smaller networks and are roughly uniform in the larger

TABLE 7.3   Performance of $KH(2, D^*, r)$

Node label length	r	N	Diameter D^*	$\bar{H}$	γ_{avg}	μ_{avg}
2	6	12	2	1.18	3.54	0.18
2	8	20	2	1.31	5.24	0.31
3	4	12	2	1.5	3	0.5
3	6	36	3	1.87	5.67	0.87
3	8	80	3	2.11	8.44	1.11
4	4	24	3	2.18	4.36	1.18
4	6	108	4	2.74	8.22	1.74
4	8	320	4	3.04	12.16	2.04
5	4	48	4	2.98	5.96	1.98
5	6	324	5	3.68	11.04	2.68
6	4	96	5	3.86	7.72	2.86

ones. (In $KH[2, 5, 4]$, the network exhibiting the least uniformity in loading, γ_{max} and μ_{max} were found to be 18% and 37% respectively above their average values.)

How do these numbers influence the optical resource requirements? Suppose that each hyperedge is realized as an MPS supported by a "thick" waveband containing $C = r$ λ-channels. In this case, the MPS might be operated as a multicast star, using TDM/T-WDMA in FT-TR mode, with one of the λ-channels dedicated to a transmitter in each node. Because the nodes are of degree 2 in all of these networks, each node must be equipped with two optical transceivers. Assuming that one unit of traffic corresponds to a bitstream running at some fixed basic bitrate R_0, and that the balance factor for the traffic in each MPS is $\eta = 1$, Equation 7.17 indicates that the N units of traffic can be carried by the network provided that its transceivers and λ-channels run at bitrates $R_t \geq R_0(\gamma_{max}/r)$. Note that γ_{max}/r represents the worst case load on an MPS normalized by the number of transmitters injecting traffic into it. We shall refer to γ_{max}/r as the *normalized maximum hyperedge load* or *speed-up factor* in a regular undirected hypernet.[18] It indicates how much the transmitter bitrate R_t must be increased over the basic rate R_0 to accommodate the hyperedge load, assuming that one λ-channel is available for each transmitter (i.e., $C = r$). (As indicated earlier, under uniform carried traffic the normalized maximum hyperedge load is typically close to the normalized *average* hyperedge load γ_{avg}/r.) If it is not possible to run the transceivers/channels at the required speed, there are two other possibilities: either scale down the traffic requirements proportionally to reduce the speed-up factor, or scale up the optical resources by providing extra transceivers and channels. These are general rules applicable to all LRNs—either point to point or multipoint.

7.3.4 Hypernet versus Multihop

Because hypernets require an LLN infrastructure but point-to-point (multihop) LRNs can operate over wavelength routed networks, it is worthwhile determining what (if anything) is to be gained by going with the hypernet/LLN approach rather than the simpler multihop/WRN approach. To this end, we make some performance comparisons between hypernets and multihop networks. First the undirected Kautz hypernet and the ShuffleNet are compared, then comparisons are made between some larger size multihop networks and directed hypernets.

Figure 7.21 shows a comparison between $KH(2, D, 6)$ and the $(2, k)$-ShuffleNets of the same order operating under uniform traffic with one unit of traffic injected into the network by each source. We assume the same general configurations as in the previous example. Each node is equipped with a number of transceivers equal to its degree, so that each of these networks requires two transceivers per node. Each transmitter in the ShuffleNet is allocated a full λ-channel, and the six transmitters operating in each MPS of the hypernet share the capacity of six λ-channels.

---

[18] The normalized maximum hyperarc load (and speed-up factor) for a regular *directed* hypernet is γ_{max}/s, where s is the hyperedge in-size.

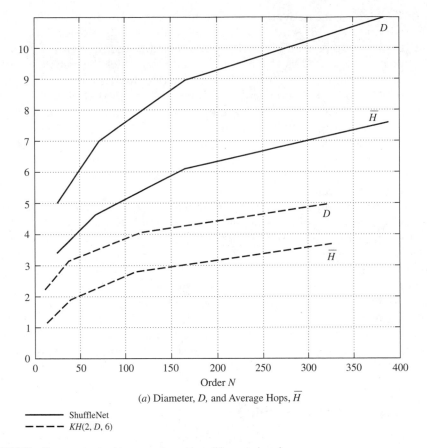

(*a*) Diameter, *D*, and Average Hops, $\overline{H}$

——— ShuffleNet
– – – *KH*(2, *D*, 6)

FIGURE 7.21 Comparison of hypernets and multihop networks.

In Figure 7.21(a), diameters *D* and average logical hops $\overline{H}$ are compared using shortest path routing. The hypernet is superior to the ShuffleNet by a factor of approximately 2. Figure 7.21(b) compares the normalized average hyperedge load, $\gamma_{avg}/6$, for the hypernet, with average link load in the ShuffleNet, again showing a factor of two reduction in load for the hypernet compared with the ShuffleNet. Figure 7.21(c) shows an improvement factor of more than two in processing load for the hypernet.

What about the relative costs of the two approaches in optical hardware and spectrum usage? Both systems use the same number of transceivers and the same total number of λ-channels: one for each transmitter. The actual spectrum usage depends on the degree of spectrum reuse, which in turn depends on the structure of the physical topology and the way in which the logical topologies are embedded in the physical layer. In the absence of any information on the physical layer, let us assume that there is no spectrum reuse. In that case, the number of *distinct* λ-channels is the same in both systems. However, the total *spectrum* occupied by those channels is less in

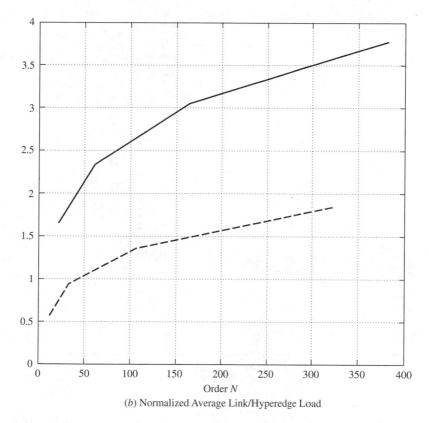

(b) Normalized Average Link/Hyperedge Load

FIGURE 7.21 (continued)

the hypernet because it bundles its channels into $N/3$ thick wavebands, whereas the ShuffleNet requires $2N$ thin wavebands. A more complete comparison of resource utilization in multihop networks and hypernets is undertaken in Section 7.4.2, in which embedding is examined in more detail.

As a final comparison, Table 7.4 illustrates the performance of larger size hypernets and multihop networks. Two multihop networks: a (2,11)-ShuffleNet (of diameter 21) and a Kautz digraph $K(2, 14)$ are compared with three directed Kautz hypernets $DKH(d, D, s)$. The orders of the networks range from 22,528 to 110,000. The average logical hops $\bar{H}$, normalized average hyperarc load γ_{avg}/s, and average node processing load μ_{avg} are listed for each case. Because simulation is out of the question for these sizes, we assume shortest path routing ($\bar{H} = \bar{d}$) to determine $\bar{H}$. The known formula (Equation 7.7) for average internodal distance $\bar{d}$ is used in the case of the ShuffleNet, and the approximation $\bar{H} = 0.75D$ is used for the other networks. The remaining quantities are derived using Equations 7.24 and 7.25.

In these large networks the advantage of the hypernet over the multihop approach is more pronounced. All of the networks require two transceivers per station except

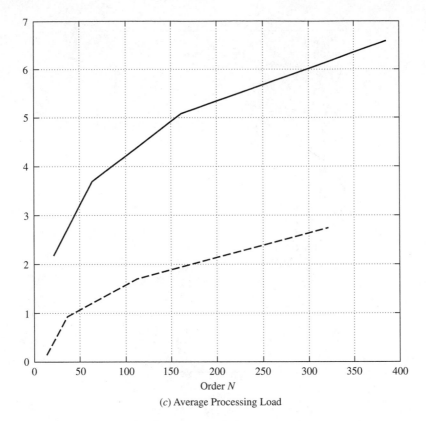

(*c*) Average Processing Load

FIGURE 7.21   (*continued*)

TABLE 7.4   Performance Comparison of *DK H*(*d*, *D*, *s*) to Multihop Networks

Case	*d*	*D*	*s*	*N*	$\bar{H}$	γ_{avg}/s	μ_{avg}
ShuffleNet	2	21	1	22,528	15	7.5	14
Kautz digraph	2	14	1	24,576	10.5	5.25	9.5
DKH	2	5	4	36,864	3.75	1.88	2.75
DKH	2	5	5	110,000	3.75	1.88	2.75
DKH	1	5	8	36,864	3.75	3.75	2.75

DK H(1, 5, 8), which requires only one. The hypernets serve a significantly larger number of nodes than the two multihop networks, with a factor of four improvement in logical hop count over the ShuffleNet, and an improvement of somewhat less than three over the Kautz digraph. The improvement in $\bar{H}$ carries with it corresponding reductions in normalized hyperarc load and processing load. As a consequence,

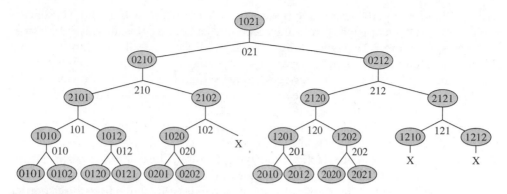

FIGURE 7.22 Multicast tree in $DKH(1, 4, 2)$.

the optical transceivers and LSNs can operate at significantly lower speeds in the hypernets.

7.3.5 Multicast Virtual Connections

Multicast connections are becoming increasingly important in large LRNs. For example, considerable effort has been invested in designing multicast protocols on the Internet and making them more efficient. In a multihop LRN, a multicast virtual connection is implemented by forming a multicast tree in the network, rooted at the multicasting node, and replicating the information transmitted from the root on each link in the tree. Because all links are point to point, the aggregate load generated in the network by the multicast connection equals the total number of links in the tree.

In a hypernet, all transmissions into an MPS are always multicast *optically* to all receiving stations in that MPS. This suggests that hypernets should be natural supports for multicast virtual connections.[19] Rather than doing a detailed analysis of multicasting in hypernets, we confine ourselves here to a simple example that illustrates the savings in usage of network capacity.

Suppose node 1021 in the directed hypernet $DKH(1, 4, 2)$ of Figure 7.16 wishes to broadcast to all other nodes in the network. A possible approach is shown in Figure 7.22. A multicast tree is formed with links that are hyperarcs (MPSs) rather than point-to-point connections. Each node in the tree (except the leaf nodes) logically multicasts to all nodes in the receiving set of the MPS to which it transmits. In an ATM network, for example, this can be implemented simply by using a multicast local address on each cell (see Section 7.3.3.5). Because $D = 4$ and $s = 2$ in this case, an incomplete tree of degree 2 and depth 4 is formed, containing the other 23 nodes. For example, node 1021 multicasts to the two nodes 0210 and 0212 in the receiving set of

---

[19] We have already seen an example of the economies attainable when multicast LCs are implemented on a broadcast star, which is just a hypernet composed of a single hyperedge (see Section 5.4.1.4).

MPS 021, and node 2102 unicasts to node 1020 in MPS 102. Note that in the latter case node 1021 has been "pruned" from the receiving set because it is already in the tree.

Although Figure 7.22 resembles an ordinary multicast tree, there is an important difference: Each connection from a transmitting node in the tree to all receiving nodes in the same MPS uses no more network capacity than if it had been unicasting to a single node. As a result, the total capacity usage in this example is roughly 50% of what it would have been in a multihop network.

A more complete discussion of multicasting in hypernets can be found in [Jiang95]. In general, a multicast connection in a directed hypernet can be compared with the same connection implemented in its underlying digraph. The two networks are equivalent to each other in terms of connectivity, but the underlying digraph represents a point-to-point LRN, and thus uses network resources less efficiently than the hypernet. The network capacity used for a multicast virtual connection in a directed hypernet is approximately a factor of s less than the usage in a digraph. Similar results hold for the undirected case. Thus, hypernets with large hyperedge sizes are especially efficient supports for multicast virtual connections.

7.4 Hypernet Design

As in the case of multihop LRNs, the hypernet design problem can be separated into a logical layer design subproblem followed by realization of the chosen logical topology on an optical infrastructure. The physical topology may be given or left free to the designer. In the case of hypernets, the division into subproblems is even more important than in the multihop case because hypernet design is more complex than point-to-point network design (which is already exceedingly complex).

7.4.1 Logical Layer Design

When viewed in its full generality, the logical layer design problem involves finding an LCH, together with a routing assignment on the LCH, which is capable of supporting a prescribed traffic distribution. This is a direct generalization of the multihop network design problem presented in Section 7.2. Following the approach in that section, the design problem can be cast as a combinatorial optimization problem in which the objective is to produce an LCH design and a routing assignment that minimizes some cost function. As in the multihop case, the objective here is to minimize the maximum flow on the LCs. We formulate this problem now as an MIP, for the case of regular undirected hypernets with node degree Δ and maximum hyperedge (MPS) size r. The variables used are

- x_{im}: A binary variable set to 1 if node i is placed in hyperedge E_m, and set to 0 otherwise

- y_{ijm}: A binary variable set to 1 if nodes i and j are in hyperedge E_m, and set to 0 otherwise

- t_{sd}: The traffic injected into node s and destined for node d
- f_{ijm}^{sd}: The traffic flow from source s to destination d, carried from node i to j on hyperedge E_m
- z: The maximum of the flows on all hyperedges

The MIP is given by the following equations:

Minimize z with

$$\sum_m x_{im} = \Delta, \quad \text{for all } i \tag{7.26}$$

$$\sum_i x_{im} \leq r, \quad \text{for all } m \tag{7.27}$$

$$y_{ijm} \leq \frac{1}{2}(x_{im} + x_{jm}), \quad \text{for all } i, j, m \tag{7.28}$$

$$\sum_{s,d} f_{ijm}^{sd} \leq M \, y_{ijm}, \quad \text{for all } m \tag{7.29}$$

$$\sum_m \sum_{j \neq i} f_{ijm}^{sd} - \sum_{j \neq i} f_{jim}^{sd} = \begin{cases} t_{sd}, & \text{if } i = s \\ -t_{sd}, & \text{if } i = d \\ 0, & \text{otherwise} \end{cases} \tag{7.30}$$

$$\sum_{s,d} \sum_{i,j \in E_m} f_{ijm}^{sd} \leq z, \quad \text{for all } m$$

$$0 \leq f_{ijm}^{sd}, \quad \text{for all } s, d, \text{ all } m \text{ and all } i \neq j \tag{7.31}$$

Equation 7.26 is the degree constraint. (It would be replaced by in- and out-degree constraints in directed hypernets.) Equation 7.27 is the hyperedge size constraint. Equations 7.28 and 7.29 permit flow only between stations belonging to the same hyperedge. (M is chosen as a large positive number in Equation 7.29.) The flow constraints appear in Equation 7.30, and Equation 7.31 sets z equal to the largest hyperedge load. Note that no assumptions have been made regarding MPS capacity or the numbers of optical transceivers in the stations supporting the network nodes. These quantities could be added as extra constraints.

In view of the difficulty of this problem, the MIP optimization approach will not be pursued further here. As in the multihop case, it is more prudent to retreat to a suboptimal approach, decomposing the logical design problem into the following three steps:

1. Choice of a logical topology
2. Node placement; matching the traffic matrix to the LT
3. Routing

In the first step a candidate logical topology is chosen from some family having desirable characteristics (e.g., regularity, symmetry, high density, etc). Following that, the network nodes are placed on the vertices of the chosen LT, attempting to reduce the aggregate network load by optimal placement of the nodes.[20] Thus, for example, sets of nodes having high traffic among each other are placed close together in the LT. At the same time the placements are chosen to spread traffic loads evenly over all hyperedges. After node placement, a routing algorithm is run with the objective of minimizing maximum hyperedge loading. These steps can then be iterated to improve the design by reducing the highest hyperedge loads.

7.4.2 Physical Layer Design

In this section we treat the last subproblem in hypernet design: realization of a given LCH on an optical infrastructure. The first version of the problem assumes that the physical topology (an LLN) is given, and we seek an embedding of the given hypergraph onto the prescribed PT. We then consider the (much easier) problem of realizing the hypernet on a multistar network designed to fit the LT.

7.4.2.1 Hypergraph Embedding: Routing and Waveband Assignment

In Section 3.5.2, we showed how a hypernet can be realized on an LLN with a given physical topology using collections of MPSs, in which each MPS is configured to support one of the hyperedges. A more general treatment of this approach is provided now.

To support full optical connectivity in a hyperedge, its supporting MPS must be realized as a connected subgraph of the PT, containing all nodes in the hyperedge. To fix ideas concerning MPS implementation, we continue with the earlier assumptions of Section 3.4.2 on the structure of the MPSs:

- Each MPS is realized on a tree.
- All transmissions within an MPS use λ-channels within a common waveband.
- The tree is configured as an embedded multicast star.

Although more general configurations of MPSs are possible, there is usually not much to be gained by violating these assumptions. By specifying the MPS as a multicast star embedded as a tree, considerable freedom is left in network design. The capacity of the MPS and the way in which it is shared can be adjusted by using either thin or thick wavebands, by using various numbers of optical transceivers in each node, and by using various capacity allocation techniques. Thus, for example, a waveband containing many λ-channels may be allocated to a given MPS to increase its capacity. Arrayed optical transceivers may be employed to ensure that the traffic balance factor remains high even though the traffic distribution seen by the MPS is

---

[20] More details on the node placement problem can be found in [Jiang+95].

nonuniform (see Equation 5.56). Packet switching in the optical layer may be used to provide for dynamic capacity allocation in each MPS, and so on.

The hypernet embedding problem is a static routing and waveband assignment problem in an LLN, wherein the optical paths being embedded are multipoint trees. Thus it is a direct generalization of the embedding problem for multihop networks, which is a static point-to-point RCA problem in a WRN. In an optimal solution to this problem one might wish to minimize the number of wavebands used (maximize waveband reuse), minimize the sum of the tree sizes, or minimize some combination of the two. In large networks, this problem is generally intractable, necessitating the use of suboptimal heuristics. A reasonable approach is to solve the tree-routing and waveband assignment problems separately. After trees are chosen for each MPS, wavebands are assigned in a fashion that minimizes the number of wavebands used.

Tree Routing   When selecting trees for a given set of hyperedges, it is desirable to choose fiber paths with at least two objectives in mind: making them short, and making them fiber–disjoint whenever possible. The first objective promotes economy in the use of network capacity, reduces congestion, enhances survivability, and improves signal quality. The second objective improves the waveband reuse factor. As in the case of point-to-point connections, the access links must be considered when determining whether fiber paths are fiber–disjoint.[21]

In an undirected hypernet, the tree-routing problem is closely related to the problem of routing of multicast optical connections on an LLN with a given physical topology. Any node in the tree can be considered as the source of a multicast optical connection to the other nodes. Thus, embedding a set of trees is equivalent to a static routing problem for a set of multicast optical connections. The heuristics of Section 6.6.2.1 can be used here with some modifications.

Selection of a shortest path (or more generally minimum cost) tree is known as the Steiner tree problem [Winter87]. Given a set $\mathcal{K}$ of vertices of a graph, with edges that have been assigned costs, a Steiner tree is a tree that spans $\mathcal{K}$ while minimizing the sum of its edge costs. It is well known that the Steiner tree problem is NP-complete. However, some efficient heuristics are available [Kompella+93, Waxman88]. The embedding of a hypergraph onto a graph can be thought of as constructing a "Steiner forest."

Embedding based on finding a Steiner forest does not take into account the question of waveband assignment and waveband reuse. However, it is possible to do combined routing and waveband assignment for a given LT by updating edge costs in the PT as the embedding process proceeds. The idea is to embed the hyperedges sequentially and update the costs of edges in the PT each time a new hyperedge is embedded using those edges. The cost of an edge is increased by one each time an embedded hyperedge

---

[21] The paths for two hyperedges embedded on an LLN *with elementary access stations* cannot be fiber–disjoint unless the hyperedges are disjoint. (If a node belongs to two hyperedges, its access fibers must be used in the MPSs supporting both hyperedges.) Similarly, the paths for two hyperarcs cannot be fiber–disjoint unless their in-sets are disjoint and their out-sets are disjoint.

uses that edge. In this way, successive trees tend to avoid previously used edges, thereby tending to increase the possibilities for waveband reuse. This is similar to static and dynamic routing techniques for WRNs that attempt to minimize congestion (see Sections 6.3.8 and 6.4.1).

The eight-node shuffle hypernet presented in Section 3.5.2 is a useful point of departure for exploring embedding. The discussion in Chapter 3 involved embedding on a ring. We extend that example here to a more general physical topology. (Because we are now dealing with network nodes at both the logical and optical levels, the LRN nodes will henceforth be referred to as LSNs, to distinguish them from the optical network nodes.) Figure 7.7 shows an embedding of the eight-node point-to-point ShuffleNet on Atlantis, and Table 7.1 indicates some of the wavelength assignments. Our objective here is to embed the corresponding eight-node shuffle hypernet on the same physical topology. (Note that the point-to-point ShuffleNet is the underlying digraph for the shuffle hypernet.) We shall assume that each LSN connects to an optical network node through an elementary access station, which means that distinct channel assignment must be observed on the access links as well as the internodal links.

The embedding of the point-to-point ShuffleNet (Figure 7.7) can be used as a basis for the hypernet embedding. Recall that the set of connections for each diclique in the ShuffleNet is confined to a tree, and each diclique of the ShuffleNet becomes a hyperarc in the shuffle hypernet. Thus, each tree supporting a set of four point-to-point connections in the ShuffleNet can be used to support the corresponding MPS in the embedded shuffle hypernet, using rooted routing. For example, the union of the fiber paths listed in Table 7.1 for the ShuffleNet connections (A, E), (A, F), (C, E), (C, F) forms the tree $\{1, 2, 3, 4, 5\}$. By setting the LDCs appropriately at the nodes, these fibers can be configured into a directed embedded tree rooted at a convenient node (say, C) that supports the hyperarc $(\{A, C\}, \{E, F\})$. (This embedding technique was described previously in the context of the ring PT in Table 3.4.) The trees for the embedding on Atlantis are Steiner trees, and it can be seen from Figure 7.7 that they are fiber–disjoint.[22]

In another example of tree routing, the embedding of the undirected 22-node hypernet of Figure 3.38(a) on Atlantis is given in Table 7.5. Each hyperedge E_i is listed with its tree t_i (excluding the access links). We again assume elementary access stations. The chosen trees are Steiner trees and they are edge-disjoint whenever their corresponding hyperedges are disjoint. (Because this is an undirected network, intersecting hyperedges use the same access fibers in this case, so their trees cannot be fiber-disjoint.)

Waveband Assignment   In making waveband assignments it is generally desirable to minimize the number of wavebands used. This must be done subject to observing the DCA condition, which requires that the same waveband can be assigned to two different trees if and only if they are fiber-disjoint. The waveband assignment problem

---

[22] When considering the access links, the trees are not *edge*–disjoint because each access link belongs to two different trees. However, they are *fiber*–disjoint because one tree is directed toward the access station and the other is directed away from the station.

TABLE 7.5 Hypernet Trees on Atlantis

Hyperedge number	Tree	Waveband
1	1, 2, 3	1
2	5, 21, 25	1
3	12, 13, 17, 18, 25	3
4	29, 28, 27, 15, 16	3
5	7, 8, 9	1
6	28	1
7	19, 26, 21, 22	2
8	4, 5, 6, 7, 23, 15, 27	2
9	18, 17, 25, 24, 14, 9	2
10	12, 11, 10	2

is equivalent to a graph/hypergraph coloring problem, and thus optimal assignment is very difficult for large networks. Still, simple heuristics of the type discussed in Appendix A produce fairly good results in moderate-size networks.

In the case of embeddings in networks *comprised of elementary access stations*, certain necessary conditions on waveband assignments can be deduced from the logical topology alone, even before the embedding is attempted. Following up on our observations concerning fiber–disjoint trees, we find that

1. For undirected hypernets, two hyperedges containing a common LSN must be assigned distinct wavebands

2. For directed hypernets, two hyperarcs containing a common LSN in their in-sets or in their out-sets must be assigned distinct wavebands

This constraint suggests that using elementary access stations, a *minimal edge coloring* of the LCH should be found as a preliminary to a final waveband assignment. An edge coloring of a hypergraph is an assignment of colors to its hyperedges such that two intersecting hyperedges are always colored differently. (If nonblocking access stations are used, the logical topology alone does not constrain waveband assignments, and thus this preliminary step serves no purpose.)

Applying these ideas to our examples, we find that in the case of the eight-node shuffle hypernet, all four trees are fiber–disjoint, and thus the same waveband can be reused on each. In the case of the 22-node hypernet, we note that the hyperedges E_1, E_2, E_5, and E_6 are mutually disjoint. Furthermore, their trees, as indicated in Table 7.5, are disjoint, so they can be assigned the same waveband. Similar observations hold for the sets E_7, E_8, E_9, E_{10} and E_3, E_4. As a result, a minimal waveband assignment can be made with three wavebands, as shown in Table 7.5.

The waveband assignment methodology just described can be formalized in terms of an auxiliary hypergraph as follows. Given an LT in the form of a hypergraph $H^l(v^l, \varepsilon^l)$, and a PT defined as a graph $G^p(V^p, E^p)$, let each hyperedge $E_i^l \in \varepsilon^l$ be embedded in the PT as a tree $t_i = \{e_{i_1}, e_{i_2}, \ldots\}$, where $e_{i_j} \in E^p$. Let $H^{em}(v^{em}, \varepsilon^{em})$ be a hypergraph with vertices that are the edges of the given PT and with hyperedges that are the trees; that is, $v^{em} = E^p$ and $\varepsilon^{em} = \{t_1, t_2, \ldots\}$. Then a minimal waveband assignment for H^l is equivalent to a minimal edge coloring of H^{em}. Note that even if $H^l(v^l, \varepsilon^l)$ is a graph, H^{em} is generally a hypergraph. Solving this waveband assignment problem by edge coloring the auxiliary hypergraph H^{em} is the counterpart of solving the λ-channel assignment problem in WRNs by vertex coloring the path interference graph G_{PI} (see Section 6.3.3).

A Cost–Performance Comparison We examined an embedding of a point-to-point ShuffleNet on a WRN in Section 7.2.2.1 and an embedding of the hypernet version on an LLN in this section. How do they compare in terms of network resource utilization versus performance? On the logical level they are identical except for the fact that the δ^2 LCs in each $\delta \times \delta$ diclique of a (δ, k)-ShuffleNet each operate on single dedicated channels, whereas in the hypernet, the capacity of the MPS carrying those connections is shared among all LCs. Because of this capacity sharing, MPS loading in the hypernet version is less sensitive to nonuniform traffic distributions than link loading in the point-to-point version. Otherwise, the performance in terms of average logical hop count and processing load is identical in the two cases.

On the other hand, the networks show significant differences in their use of network resources: optical transceivers and optical spectrum. To see this, we take a specific numerical example. Two cases are considered, the (2, 2)-ShuffleNet/hypernet (eight nodes), and the (3, 2)-ShuffleNet/hypernet (18 nodes). For simplicity, we assume that the traffic load is distributed ideally, in the sense that all links are loaded equally and the average logical hop count $\bar{H}$ equals $\bar{d}$, the average internodal distance.

On the optical level it is assumed that each LRN is embedded on the Atlantis PT, using a minimum number of wavebands; that is, $W = \delta^2$ in the point-to-point case and $W = 1$ in the hypernet case. (It is left as an exercise for the reader to verify that an embedding on Atlantis can be found with these values in the 18-node case.) The normalized guardband width is taken as $\alpha = 5$, and the spectral efficiency of the channel modulation scheme is taken as $\eta_m = 0.1$ (see Section 6.5.6.3). In the point-to-point case, the in-/out-degree of each node is δ, and each connection is carried on one λ-channel. In the hypernet, the in-/out-degree of each node is $d = 1$, the size of the transmitting/receiving set of each MPS is $s = \delta$, and C λ-channels are allocated to each MPS.

Using these assumptions and using the terminology defined in Section 6.5.6.3, we find that the total network throughput normalized to the capacity of one λ-channel is $S = N\delta/\bar{d}$ for the ShuffleNet and $S = NdC/\bar{d}s = NC/\bar{d}\delta$ for the shuffle hypernet. These expressions give a spectrum reuse factor of $\varrho = N\delta/W\bar{d}$ for the point-to-point case and $\varrho = N/W\bar{d}\delta$ for the hypernet case.

Note that in the hypernet there is an option of using different values of C (i.e., wavebands of varying thicknesses). We compare hypernets with three different values of C. The case $C = 1$ corresponds to a low-end system in which all stations in an

TABLE 7.6 Resource Utilization in 8-Node ShuffleNet Embeddings

Case	C	W	S	ϱ	η_f	η_N	OTs/ORs per node
ShuffleNet	1	4	8	2	0.021	0.042	2
Hypernet	1	1	1	2	0.1	0.2	1
Hypernet	2	1	4	2	0.1	0.2	1
Hypernet	4	1	8	2	0.1	0.2	2

TABLE 7.7 Resource Utilization in 18-Node ShuffleNet Embeddings

Case	C	W	S	ϱ	η_f	η_N	OTs/ORs per node
ShuffleNet	1	9	24.5	2.73	0.018	0.05	3
Hypernet	1	1	2.73	2.73	0.1	0.27	1
Hypernet	3	1	8.2	2.73	0.1	0.27	1
Hypernet	9	1	24.5	2.73	0.1	0.27	3

MPS share one channel using TDM/TDMA. In this case, the optical transceivers are underutilized, with each being idle most of the time. We also consider a second case, $C = \delta$ (with a traffic balance factor of $\eta = 1$), in which the transmissions can be scheduled so that both the channels and the transceivers are fully utilized. Both of these cases require only one optical transceiver per station as opposed to δ transceivers for the point-to-point case, but both cases have throughputs inferior to the point-to-point case. Finally, we set $C = \delta^2$ and use δ transceivers in each station. This makes both the throughput and the total complement of channels and transceivers in the hypernet equal to those in the point-to-point case. However, in the hypernet, the δ^2 channels are grouped into one waveband, whereas they are carried on δ^2 individual wavebands in the point-to-point case.

Tables 7.6 and 7.7 give the key performance and resource usage parameters for the eight and 18-node cases respectively. Note that when the transceivers are fully utilized,[23] the relative throughputs of the different cases depend only on the number of optical transceivers per node. Thus, the throughput is 4 units per transceiver in the 8-node case and 8.2 units per transceiver in the 18-node case. Because the traffic carried in an LRN is $\bar{H}$ times the injected traffic, the spectrum reuse factor in these examples is diminished by that factor. Thus in both the 8- and 18-node networks, ϱ remains relatively small. The main difference in resource utilization is in spectral efficiencies. Both the fiber spectral efficiency, η_f, and the network spectral efficiency, η_N, are approximately five times as large in the hypernets as they are in the point-to-point

---

[23] This excludes the hypernet case with $C = 1$.

implementations because of the grouping of λ-channels within a single waveband in the former case.

7.4.2.2 Multistar Realizations

In Section 6.5.9 it was shown that a multistar physical topology is a natural way to realize a hypernet of diameter 1. Hypernets of diameter 1 are purely optical networks (LLNs) configured to provide full logical connectivity between all pairs of nodes in one logical hop. In these multistar realizations, a set of undirected (directed) broadcast stars are arranged so that each star forms an undirected (directed) MPS, with each MPS supporting one hyperedge (hyperarc) in the network's LCH. The design of the multistar network is facilitated by the fact that its fiber connectivity is an exact replica of the tripartite representation of its LCH.

These ideas extend directly to LRNs defined by hypergraphs of a diameter greater than 1. The only difference is that the connectivity is incomplete on the optical level and must be completed on the logical level through an overlay of LSNs.

As an example, consider the directed hypergraph $GKH(2, 42, 3, 28)$ with a tripartite representation that is shown in Figure 7.18. Let each hyperarc be replaced by a corresponding 3×3 directed star joining the three LSNs in its transmitting set to three LSNs in its receiving set. For example, hyperarc 0 becomes a star multicasting from nodes {0, 14, 28} to {39, 40, 41}.[24] Because this network has an in-/out-degree of 2, each transmitter/receiver is connected to two stars. Like-numbered transmitting and receiving nodes are assumed to belong to the same LSN, and logical paths are set up by routing traffic through a series of LSNs from source to destination. In this case the LRN has a diameter of 2, so that in the worst case the traffic must transit one intermediate node on a source–destination path. For example, traffic from source 0 to destination 6 would take the two-hop path

$$0 \xrightarrow{0} 40 \xrightarrow{25} 6$$

In cases in which a hypergraph is constructed from a graph using duality, a multistar realization of the corresponding hypernet can be deduced directly from the dual graph. For example, Figure 7.15 shows the undirected Kautz hypergraph $KH(2, 3, 4)$ constructed from the Kautz digraph $K(2, 3)$. Each hyperedge (MPS) can be realized by a star connecting its vertices. The dual digraph gives the exact topology of the multistar network. Because each vertex of $KH(2, 3, 4)$ is the dual of an arc of $K(2, 3)$, an arc of $K(2, 3)$ corresponds to an LSN of the Kautz hypernet, and the terminal vertices of that arc represent star couplers to which the LSN is attached. (The LSN can be viewed as a box inserted in the middle of the arc.)

In the undirected case, each LSN transmits and receives from each star, so it must have two transceivers, and the links through which it accesses the stars are bidirectional fiber pairs. The construction can also be used for the directed case in which each

---

[24] The star connections can be determined from the definition of $GKH(d, n, s, m)$ in Section 7.3.3.3.

arc of the dual digraph represents an LSN with a single transceiver, with the transmitter and receiver oriented according to the direction of the arc. For example, node 1012 in the hypernet of Figure 7.15 is the dual of the arc $101 \rightarrow 012$ in the digraph. Thus, in the undirected case, LSN 1012 is connected to the two stars 101 and 012. Each of these is an undirected 4×4 star. In the directed case, LSN 1012 transmits into star 012 and receives from 101, where each is now a directed 2×2 star.

The prime advantage of the multistar physical topology is that it provides a very high degree of spectrum reuse. Each star makes the total usable optical spectrum available to the transceivers using it, and that spectrum is reused in every star. Thus, for example, in $GKH(2, 42, 3, 28)$, three transmitting nodes use each star so that the full spectrum is shared among them. Assuming that the transceivers in the nodes are connected directly to the stars, they access the network in a nonblocking fashion. That is, a node accessing several stars can reuse the same wavelengths on different stars.

The number of λ-channels allocated to a star is arbitrary, depending only on the required throughput. Because a broadcast star acts as a shared-channel medium, any number of channels can be shared among all nodes accessing the star using any of the multiplexing/multiple-access techniques described in Chapter 5. A reasonable allocation would be s λ-channels for a star with in-/out-size s, so that nodes equipped with one optical transceiver can exploit fully the channels and the transceivers.

In a high-throughput application, additional transceivers and channels might be appropriate. In our example, suppose the available spectrum consists of nine λ-channels per star. Then, to take advantage of the available channels, each node should be equipped with an array of six transceivers, three for each star it uses. Using these arrays in TDM/T-WDMA mode, it is possible to utilize the full capacity (nine units) of each star. The λ-channels in one star are reused in all stars, giving a reuse factor of 28 in this example.

Still more mileage can be obtained from the optical spectrum if the star couplers are replaced by permutation wavelength routers as in Section 6.3.6. In that case, using s λ-channels, each $s \times s$ star can support s^2 point-to-point LCs among its attached nodes, each running at the full capacity of one λ-channel. But this requires that each node be equipped with ds transceivers, where d is its in-/out-degree. The spectrum reuse factor of such a system is sm, where m is the number of hyperedges (wavelength routing stars). Using this approach for $GKH(2, 42, 3, 28)$, we obtain the same throughput using three λ-channels and permutation routers as we had using nine λ-channels and broadcast stars. The same number of transceivers are used in each case, and the reuse factor is increased to 84.

The major disadvantage of a multistar is that it uses a very large amount of fiber. (The number of stars is the same as the reuse factor.) This should come as no surprise because, as usual, there is no free lunch! Spectrum reuse comes at the inevitable expense of fiber replication. Another disadvantage of multistars that was cited in Section 6.3.6 is their poor survivability. In a multistar realization of a hypernet of diameter 1, when one star fails, communication is cut between the transmitting and receiving sets of that star. However, this disadvantage disappears in hypernets of larger diameter because there are alternate paths between LSNs in this case.

We have shown through examples that hypernets can accommodate easily on the order of 10^5 LSNs with relatively small node degrees, diameters, and hyperedge sizes. This means that multistar realizations can support hypernets of these sizes using only a moderate number of λ-channels and using limited optical hardware.

For example, the directed Kautz hypernet $DKH(2, 5, 5)$ has order 110,000. From Table 7.4 we find that for one unit of uniformly distributed traffic injected at each node, the average hyperarc load is 9.4 units. Thus, if this network is realized using 10 λ-channels per star, it can support a throughput of 110,000 (normalized to the capacity of a λ-channel).[25] This requires four optical transceivers per LSN and 11,000 stars.

7.5 Summary

Logically routed networks consisting of electronic LSNs superimposed on a purely optical network infrastructure comprise the widest and most versatile classes of multiwavelength optical networks. The model used to represent LRNs in this chapter is broad enough to include virtually any type of hybrid electronic/optical network, including networks of SONET cross-connects, networks of ATM switches or IP routers, ATM-over-SONET, and many more yet to be invented.

The LRNs examined here were divided into two classes: those with point-to-point logical topologies (multihop networks) and those with multipoint LTs (hypernets). The optical infrastructure for a multihop network can be either a WRN or an LLN. In the case of hypernets, the infrastructure must be a network capable of providing multipoint optical connectivity (i.e., an LLN). It was shown that these networks can be studied at two more or less independent levels: the logical layer, and the physical layer. Desirable properties of logical topologies were explored, and families of dense, regular LTs were studied in both the multihop and the hypernet cases.

The families of Kautz graphs and hypergraphs were chosen for special attention as logical topologies for LRNs. These have desirable properties in terms of density, load balancing, routing, and survivability. Cost–performance relations were compared within families of hypernets and for hypernets versus point-to-point LRNs. It was found that the most important performance parameter in LRNs is the average logical hop count $\bar{H}$ (related closely to the average internodal distance $\bar{d}$), and that this parameter can be kept under control cost-effectively by using dense hypernet logical topologies. A hypernet LT produces the smallest value of $\bar{d}$ for a given investment in optical resources: transceivers and optical spectrum.

The design of an LRN can be broken down into logical layer design and physical layer embedding. Although these two subproblems can, in principle, be solved simultaneously, this is possible in only very small networks. Logical layer design consists of finding a suitable logical topology and routing assignment to accommodate a given traffic distribution. The performance of a logical layer design when carrying a

---

[25] This allows a little slack for uneven traffic distribution.

prescribed traffic distribution may be evaluated by determining the communication link loads and switch processing loads. A well-matched LT will not have any "hot spots," so the loads will be distributed fairly evenly throughout the network. Some simulation results were exhibited to illustrate and compare typical communication and processing loads under uniform traffic conditions.

Physical layer embedding typically involves routing and wavelength assignment on a WRN in the multihop case, and routing and waveband assignment on an LLN in the hypernet case. In the case of uniformly distributed traffic, the maximum aggregate throughput of the embedded LRN is roughly proportional to the total number of optical transceivers used in the embedding, and is inversely proportional to $\bar{H}$.

The cost of the LRN in optical resource usage depends, to a large extent, on the optical spectrum reuse factor, which in turn depends on the richness of the physical topology. The reuse factor is largest when a multistar PT is used. However, multistars carry with them certain handicaps, the most significant of which is high fiber usage.

7.6 Problems

1. Show that five wavelengths are sufficient to realize the eight-node ShuffleNet using a star topology with a permutation router with routing rules defined in Section 2.3.1.2.

2. Show that two wavelengths are sufficient to realize the eight-node ShuffleNet using a star topology with a permutation router with routing rules different from those defined in Section 2.3.1.2.

3. Find an embedding of the eight-node ShuffleNet on Atlantis using elementary access stations and a minimum number of wavelengths.

4. For networks of the same diameter, compare the orders of $(2, k)$-ShuffleNets to the orders of the hypernets $KH(2, D, r)$ plotted in Figure 7.14.

5. This problem concerns the duality relations between graphs and hypergraphs.
   (a) Derive $KH(2, D^*, 6)$ from $K(3, 2)$ by duality and show its multistar realization.
   (b) Derive $DKH(1, 3, 3)$ from $K(3, 2)$ by duality and show its multistar realization.
   (c) Determine the diameter, D^*, of $KH(2, D^*, 6)$.

6. Prove that for $KH(2, D^*, 4)$ with node label length D, $D^* < D$.

7. Construct the tripartite representation of $GKH(2, 6, 2, 3)$. Is it symmetric? Find its diameter.

8. Find an embedding of the 18-node shuffle hypernet on Atlantis using Steiner trees and as few wavebands as possible. Assume elementary access stations, and map the LSNs onto the stations in Atlantis in numerical/alphabetical order.

9. Find an embedding of $DKH(1, 4, 2)$ on Atlantis using Steiner trees and as few wavebands as possible. Assume elementary access stations, and map the LSNs onto the stations in Atlantis in numerical/alphabetical order. (Add stations W and X to nodes i and j, respectively.)

10. Simulate one or more of the logical topologies used in Table 7.3 under nonuniform traffic conditions.

   (a) Compare your results on average hyperedge load and processing load per node with those in the table.

   (b) Determine the maximum values of these quantities and their percent deviation from the average.

7.7 Bibliography

[Acampora87] A. S. Acampora. A multichannel multihop local lightwave network. In *Proc. IEEE Globecom.*, pp. 1459–1467, Tokyo, November 1987.

[Bala+96] K. Bala, G. Ellinas, M. Post, et al. Towards hitless reconfiguration in WDM optical networks for ATM transport. In *Proc. IEEE Globecom.*, London, November 1996.

[Bannister90] J. A. Bannister. *The Wavelength-Division Optical Network: Architectures, Topologies and Protocols*. PhD thesis. University of California at Los Angeles, 1990.

[Bermond+83] J.-C. Bermond, J. Bond, M. Paoli, and C. Peyrat. Graphs and interconnection networks: Diameter and vulnerability. In *Surveys in Combinatorics*, pp. 1–30. Cambridge: Cambridge University Press, 1983.

[Bermond+86] J.-C. Bermond, J. Bond, and C. Peyrat. Interconnection networks with each node on two buses. In *Parallel Algorithms and Architectures*, pp. 155–167. Amsterdam: North-Holland, 1986.

[Bermond+89] J.-C. Bermond and C. Peyrat. de Bruijn and Kautz networks: A competitor for the hypercube? In *Hypercube and Distributed Computers*, pp. 279–293. Amsterdam: Elsevier Science Publishers, 1989.

[Bermond+96] J.-C. Bermond and F. O. Ergincan. Bus interconnection networks. *Discrete Applied Mathematics*, 68:1–15, 1996.

[Bermond+97] J.-C. Bermond, R. Dawes, and F. O. Ergincan. de Bruijn and Kautz bus networks. *Networks*, 30:205–218, 1997.

[Bienstock+93] D. Bienstock and O. Gunluk. Computational experience with a difficult mixed integer multicommodity flow problem. *Math. Programming*, 68:213–237, 1993.

[Birk86] Y. Birk. *Concurrent communication among multiple transceiver stations via shared media*. PhD thesis. Stanford University, Palo Alto, 1986.

[Birk91] Y. Birk. Fiber-optic bus-oriented single-hop interconnections among multi-transceiver stations. *IEEE/OSA J. Lightwave Technology*, 9(12):1657–1664, 1991.

[Dowd92] P. W. Dowd. Wavelength division multiple access channel hypercube processor interconnection. *IEEE Trans. Comput.*, 41(10):1233–1241, 1992.

[Gerla+92] M. Gerla, M. Kovacevic, and J. Bannister. Multilevel optical networks. In *Proc. IEEE Int'l Conf. Commun.*, pp. 1168–1172, Chicago, June 1992.

[Hluchyj+88] M. G. Hluchyj and M. J. Karol. ShuffleNet: An application of generalized perfect shuffles to multihop lightwave networks. In *Proc. IEEE Infocom.*, pp. 4B.4.1–12, New Orleans, 1988.

[Hluchyj+91] M. G. Hluchyj and M. J. Karol. ShuffleNet: An application of generalized perfect shuffles to multihop lightwave networks. *IEEE/OSA J. Lightwave Technology*, 9(10):1386–1397, 1991.

[Imase+83] M. Imase and M. Itoh. A design for directed graphs with minimum diameter. *IEEE Trans. Comput.*, c-32(8):782–784, 1983.

[Jiang95] S. Jiang. *Multicast Multihop Lightwave Networks: Design and Implementation.* PhD thesis. Department of Electrical Engineering, Columbia University, New York, 1995.

[Jiang+93] S. Jiang, T. E. Stern, and E. Bouillet. Design of multicast multilayered lightwave networks. In *Proc. IEEE Globecom.,* pp. 452–457, Houston, November 1993.

[Jiang+95] S. Jiang and T. E. Stern. Regular multicast multihop lightwave networks. In *Proc. IEEE Infocom.,* Boston, April 1995.

[Kompella+93] V. P. Kompella, J. C. Pasquale, and G. C. Polyzos. Multicast routing for multimedia communication. *IEEE/ACM Trans. Networking,* 1(3):286–292, 1993.

[Kovacevic93] M. Kovacevic. *HONET: An Integrated Services Wavelength Division Optical Network.* PhD thesis. University of California at Los Angeles, 1993.

[Kovacevic+95] M. Kovacevic, M. Gerla, and J. Bannister. Performance of shared-channel multihop lightwave networks. *Computer Communications,* 18(1):37–44, 1995.

[Labourdette+90] J.-F.P. Labourdette and A. S. Acampora. Wavelength agility in multihop lightwave networks. In *Proc. IEEE Infocom.,* pp. 1022–1029, San Francisco, June 1990.

[Labourdette+91] J.-F.P. Labourdette and A. S. Acampora. Logically rearrangeable multihop lightwave networks. *IEEE Trans. Commun.,* 39(8):1223–1230, 1991.

[Ofek87] Y. Ofek. *The Topology, Algorithms and Analysis of a Synchronous Optical Hypergraph Architecture.* PhD thesis. University of Illinois, 1987.

[Reddy+82] S. M. Reddy, J. G. Kuhl, S. H. Hosseini, and H. Lee. On digraphs with minimum diameter and maximum connectivity. In *Proc. 20th Allerton Conference,* pp. 1018–1026, Urbana, IL, 1982.

[Shi92] C-J. Shi. A signed hypergraph model of the constrained via minimization problem. *Microelectronics J.,* 23:533–544, 1992.

[Sivarajan+91] K. N. Sivarajan and R. Ramaswami. Multihop lightwave networks based on de Bruijn graphs. In *Proc. IEEE Infocom.,* pp. 1001–1011, Miami, April 1991.

[Waxman88] B. M. Waxman. Routing of multipoint connections. *IEEE J. Select. Areas Commun.,* 6:1617–1622, 1988.

[Winter87] P. Winter. The Steiner problem in networks: A survey. *Networks,* 17:129–167, 1987.

CHAPTER EIGHT

Survivability
Protection and Restoration

Survivability, together with fault protection and restoration, is a growing area of concern with increasing interconnection of high-bandwidth optical networks. More traffic is concentrated on fewer routes, increasing the number of customers that can be potentially affected by a failure. An analysis of failures in the Public Switched Telephone Network for the period April 1992 through March 1994 has shown that human error, acts of nature, and overloads are the major sources of failure [Kuhn97]. The impact of the failures was measured in terms of how many times a particular failure occurred, duration of the outage, and number of customers and number of customer minutes affected during that outage. During that period, the average number of customers affected due to cable cuts or cable component failures was 216,690, costing 2,643 million in customer minutes.[1] Similarly, the average number of customers affected by each equipment failure was 1,836,910, costing 3,544.3 million in customer minutes [Kuhn97]. Cable cuts and hardware/equipment failures account for approximately half of the failures encountered in the network during that period [Kuhn97].

Fiber cuts are considered one of the most common failures in fiber optic networks. Furthermore, the use of WDM over these fibers produces an extremely high volume of traffic on a cable. Commercially available fiber optic transmission systems can run at 10 Gbps per channel with eight or more channels (wavelengths) per fiber. This translates to more than 80 Gbps per fiber. If we take into account the fact that on the average each cable carries 100 fibers, there is a possibility that a cable cut will result in the loss of several terabits per second. The most prevalent form of communication failure is the accidental disruption of buried telecommunication cables. Aerial cables are also affected, but not as frequently as those in the ground. Fiber cuts may result from construction work ("backhoe fade"), lightning, rodent damage, fire, train derailments, vandalism, car crashes, human error, and so on [Grover89]. One of the main reasons why underground telecommunication cables are so susceptible to

---

[1] A *customer minute* is defined as the outage in minutes multiplied by the number of customers affected.

failure is the fact that they are buried in the same public right-of-ways as are other utility transport media (water pipes, gas pipes, television cables, etc.; [Wrobel90]).

Examples of fiber cuts that affected network operation severely can be found throughout the short history of fiber optic networks. During the 1980s in particular, when all the major telecommunications companies were laying their fiber in the ground, cable cuts were an almost everyday occurrence [Wrobel90]. One of the most devastating cable cuts happened in 1987 when a 12-fiber lightwave cable that was a major backbone carrier facility was severed. Because of that cut more than 125,000 trunks were put out of service and an estimated 100,000 connections were lost 2 seconds after the cut. It took more than 2 hours to restore manually some of the capacity on physically diverse routes, at a cost of millions of dollars [Grover89].

Equipment failures at network nodes, even though not as common, can have devastating consequences. In fact, in general, equipment failures affect many more people than cable cuts. If a switching node fails, for example, all the fibers and their connections through that node fail. Equipment failures can result from natural phenomena (earthquake, flood, fire), human error, and hardware degradation. Examples of well-known equipment failures that have had a devastating effect on the network include the 1988 fire that destroyed Illinois Bell's Hinsdale switching office, the 1987 fire that damaged New York Telephone's Brunswick switching office, and the 1987 AT&T switching computer failure in Dallas. The 1988 Illinois fire is rated as the worst telecommunications disaster in U.S. history because it happened on one of the busiest days of the year (Mother's day) and took more than a month to completely repair. All three failures cost the telephone companies millions of dollars in business, as well as revenue loss by their customers during the outage. Furthermore, they resulted in diminished customer confidence in the companies' services.

8.1 Objectives of Protection and Restoration

It is obvious from the enumeration of different failures and their impact on the networks described earlier that a fast and reliable carrier link and node protection and restoration method is required.[2] The objective of the restoration method should be to reroute the affected traffic accurately and rapidly using the redundancy provided in the network.

Even though failures cannot be avoided, quick detection, identification, and restoration make the network more robust and reliable, and ultimately increase the level of customer confidence. For this to be possible the network's topology must have inherent survivability properties, which determine its ability to survive single or multiple

---

[2] In the current literature, *protection* and *restoration* have different meanings. The former refers to a system involving 100% redundant capacity, using physical layer automatic protection switching (APS) to switch traffic from failed to protection facilities. The latter refers to a system based on reconfigurable cross-connects and spare capacity where a higher layer restoration scheme is used to reroute traffic around failures (typically in mesh networks). In this chapter, henceforth usually, we shall use the term *restoration* to encompass both of these.

link or equipment failures. For a network to be survivable, its topology must allow rerouting around a fault condition. This issue falls under the category of network design and planning. For example, for survivability in the face of single link failures, the network must at least be two-edge connected.

Even if a network has a survivable topology, and robust operating conditions have been established, redundancy is always necessary to ensure that a significant amount of information is not lost in the case of fiber or node failure. Together with redundancy, rapid failure detection, identification, and restoration features must be present. Service restoration time is important because faster restoration means that less data are lost during the outage. Speed is important not only because of the economic impact of the outage time but also because of the vital services that are currently supported in the network. Whereas previously an outage meant that a telephone caller had to hang up and try again later, an outage nowadays may affect banks, stock exchanges, airlines, or public safety.

Much of the research in fault restoration has been concentrated on point-to-point systems, self-healing rings (SHRs), and centralized/distributed restoration using digital cross-connect systems (DCSs). This chapter first reviews some of the important restoration techniques currently used for networks employing SONET and WDM technologies. It then presents some new methods for restoration in optical networks.

The chapter is organized as follows. Section 8.2 describes current fault restoration techniques used in networks based on SONET and DCS technologies. These are subdivided into point-to-point, ring (and ring interconnection), and mesh fault restoration techniques. Although the techniques presented in Section 8.2 focus on failure restoration using SONET equipment and DCSs, similar approaches have been studied for networks employing SDH, ATM, and a number of other technologies [Ayanoglu+96; Veitch+96; Nederlof+95; Kawamura+95, 94; May+95; Kajiyama+94, 92; Sato+90].

Section 8.3 concentrates on optical layer restoration techniques in networks employing WDM point-to-point and ring architectures. Shared optical layer protection in mesh topologies is covered in Section 8.4, and the chapter concludes with a brief discussion of a proposed technique for optical path protection in mesh topologies (Section 8.5).

8.2 Current Fault Restoration Techniques in the Logical Layer

Because of its well-developed protection mechanisms and widespread use, we use the SONET network architecture as an example of current practice. The SONET terminology is adopted throughout this section, and the key terms are defined and explained in Appendix F.

SONET standards specify an end-to-end two-way availability objective of 99.98% for interoffice applications (0.02% unavailability or 105 min/year maximum downtime) and 99.99% for loop transport between the central office and the customer's premises [Bell Communications Research91]. To conform to these standards, failure restoration times have to be short. For both point-to-point and SHR systems, automatic protection switching is used, enabling the network to perform failure restoration in tens of milliseconds (50 msec to detect the failure and to complete the switching process).

8.2.1 Point-to-Point Systems

APS is used to improve the reliability and availability performance of SONET transport systems by switching to standby equipment when failures occur. Systems for APS can be classified as *one-for-one* (1:1), *one-for-N* (1:N; more generally, M:N), or *one-plus-one* (1+1) [Hall+89]. Any single fiber cut can be restored using any of these techniques, as explained later. To protect against equipment failures (e.g., switches or terminals), spare equipment (*protection equipment*) is used. The protection equipment provided can be one-for-one (i.e., one protection system for one working system) or one-for-N (i.e., one protection system for N working systems). These are the same techniques as for link protection, with the difference that spare equipment is used instead of spare fibers. They can protect against any single node failure in the network.

SONET *linear* APS is the standard defined for $(1 + 1)$, (1:1), or (1:N) protection architectures in point-to-point systems.[3] An APS signaling channel is embedded in the SONET line overhead and carried on the protection facility using the K_1/K_2 bytes (see Appendix F).

Although redundancy is used to perform fault restoration, proper design of the fault monitoring and protection process ensures that the network is able to recognize and respond to fault conditions as soon as they occur. In SONET systems, BER thresholds are established that activate and deactivate the protection switches, time windows are specified for detecting a fault condition and activating the protection switch, and an APS protocol is specified to ensure smooth operation of the protection switching process [ANSI88; Bell94a, 91, 90].

8.2.1.1 (1 + 1) Facility Protection

In SONET terminology, in the context of point-to-point systems, a *facility* or *link* or *line* refers to a point-to-point transmission link with two terminals (i.e., without any intermediate terminals). The *route* or *physical path* taken by the facility is the physical structure on which the link is laid out. It may traverse several central offices, being "spliced" through these offices without terminating any data streams at those points. In contrast, a *path* in the SONET world is a tributary (e.g., STS-1, DS3 or VT1.5) within a SONET frame. Sometimes the word *channel* is used in place of *path*. A path may traverse many nodes in a large network.

Figure 8.1 illustrates the difference between SONET line and path restoration. To clarify the terminology we use the term *logical path* to refer to the sequence of nodes and links in the figure, and *SONET path* to refer to an end-to-end SONET tributary.

---

[3] SONET $(1 + 1)$ or (1:N) protection may be unidirectional or bidirectional.

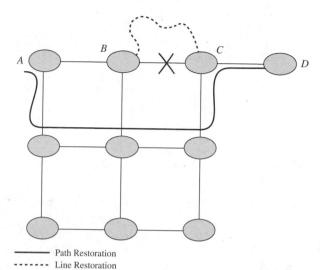

FIGURE 8.1 Path versus line
restoration.

—————— Path Restoration

-------- Line Restoration

Line restoration simply reroutes traffic normally carried between the line terminating equipment at each end of a failed link, to an alternate physical structure, detouring the traffic around the failed link. Path restoration (a higher level operation) allocates an alternate restoration SONET path between the terminal nodes (the path terminating equipment) of a failed path. (Path failure may be caused by the failure of one or more links or nodes.) Figure 8.1 shows both line and path restoration associated with a failed link, B–C. A SONET path is active on the logical path A–B–C–D between the path terminating equipment at nodes A and D. In line restoration, all traffic that normally would have traversed the failed link between nodes B and C is rerouted over the dashed protection facility, detouring the link failure. This includes the SONET path in question, as well as any other paths using that link. In path restoration, the SONET path between A and D detects the failure, and is rerouted on an alternate logical path, shown as the solid line. (Other paths using the failed link would detect the failure independently and be rerouted on their own restoration paths.) Note that path restoration requires many more operations than line restoration because many SONET paths generally share each link.

In a $(1+1)$ protection architecture, a protection facility is provided for every working facility, and the working and protection facilities are on two physically diverse routes between source and destination. Thus, if a fiber is cut, the signal uses the second facility to reach the destination. The traffic is bridged permanently at the electrical (i.e., logical) level to both the working and protection facilities at the transmit end (head end). At the receive end (tail end), the same data stream arrives from both facilities, and the received signals are continuously monitored identically and independently for failures [ANSI88; Bell94a, 93]. The receiving equipment then selects either the working or protection optical signal based on the switch initiation criteria. In the event of a link

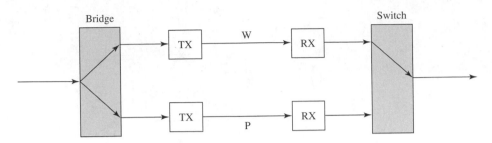

FIGURE 8.2 (1 + 1) SONET protection.

failure, an electrical switch at the receiver end immediately switches to the "other" facility, thus effectively restoring the service with minimum outage time. In this scheme, because the signal is bridged at the source, head end-to-tail end signaling is not required. The receiver simply selects the best of the two arriving signals. Figure 8.2 shows an example of a (1 + 1) electrical layer protection architecture. (In the figure, TX, RX, W, and P denote transmitter, receiver, working, and protection, respectively.)

The default mode of operation for a (1 + 1) system is the *nonrevertive mode*. This means that the receiver does not switch back to the working facility (the path along which it was receiving signals before the failure occurred) after the fault condition is cleared. Operation in the *revertive mode*, when the system reverts to its original configuration after the fault is cleared, is optional [Bell94a, 93].

For 100% survivability after a single link failure, each working fiber system needs a diverse route. Thus, as many diverse routes as working fiber systems are required. The physical path for the protection facility may be chosen to be the shortest path that is link– and node–disjoint from the working path.

8.2.1.2 (1:1) Facility Protection

A (1:1) APS system provides two diverse routes for the same connection so that if a fiber cut or a node failure occurs, the signal can reach the destination using an alternate physical path. The signal at the transmitter end is not bridged permanently but is switched onto a diversely routed facility depending on the state of the network. On detection of a failure, the receiver end signals the transmitter end, indicating that a failure has occurred, and requests the transmitter end to switch to the protection facility. The transmitter end complies with the request, switches the service to the protection facility, and sends a message to the receiver end that the service has been switched. The receiver end then switches to the protection facility and the service is restored. In the case of (1:1) APS systems, all switching is revertive (i.e., the head and tail ends switch back to the working channel after the failure condition is cleared [Bell94a, 93]).

In SONET linear APS, the APS signals are exchanged over the protection facilities between SONET line terminating elements (LTEs). The (1:1) architecture allows the

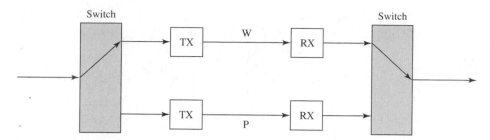

FIGURE 8.3 (1:1) SONET protection.

protection facility to carry low-priority traffic in the absence of a failure. This low-priority traffic is preempted in the event of a failure.

As in the (1 + 1) scheme, 100% survivability after a single link failure requires as many diverse routes as working fiber systems. The route for the protection facility can again be chosen to be the shortest path that is link–/node–disjoint from the working path. Figure 8.3 shows an example of a (1:1) SONET layer protection architecture. Note that the optical transceivers are included in the links being protected, so that a transmitter or receiver failure is detected as a link failure, and is restored.

8.2.1.3 (1:N) Protection

The (1:N) restoration method is the same as the (1:1) facility restoration method except that in this case one protection facility protects N working facilities; (N working channels can be switched to a single optical protection channel). Permissible values of N are from 1 to 14 [ANSI88]. Again, as in the case of (1:1) APS systems, all switching is revertive. In the case of two or more simultaneous failures, there is some contention for the use of the protection facility. This contention is resolved using priorities assigned to each working channel [Bell93, 90].

Figure 8.4 shows an example of a (1:N) electrical layer protection architecture. Again, as in the (1:1) case, the protection line can be used to carry low-priority traffic. This traffic is preempted when one of the working facilities initates a protection request [Bell90].

8.2.2 SONET Self-healing Rings

The techniques described in the previous section use dedicated, diversely routed physical paths to protect traffic against failures when only one of the paths is affected. Such techniques, however, impose limitations because of the extra capacity requirements.

Architectures composed of SONET ADMs interconnected in a ring provide an alternative method of APS that allows facilities to be shared while protecting traffic within an acceptable restoration time. Because these SONET rings protect automatically against failures, they are called *self-healing rings*. For SONET SHRs, the typical

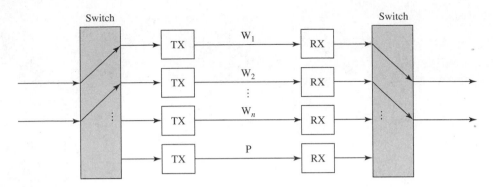

FIGURE 8.4 (1:N) SONET protection.

restoration process takes less than 50 ms. The importance of the SHR architectures stems from their ability to restore all traffic in the event of a cable cut, and part of the traffic in the event of a node failure.

Ring network architectures provide protection against service interruptions by having two diverse facility paths from each SONET ADM. If a cable is cut between any two ADMs, sufficient redundant capacity exists to reroute the affected circuits to their destinations. With APS, this rerouting can be done without any service interruption. Ring architectures can also reroute traffic around a failed node. However, traffic originating or terminating at a failed node cannot be restored unless there is appropriate node redundancy or diversity.

There are two types of SONET SHRs: the UPSR (unidirectional path-switched ring) and the BLSR (bidirectional line-switched ring). In a UPSR, the traffic is always routed in both directions around the ring (based on the [1 + 1] concept). In a BLSR, only the working traffic is assigned [Bell94a]. Comparison studies between the different architectures show that there are different areas of application in which each proves economical [Sosnosky+91]. Typically, unidirectional architectures are used in the collector portions of a network (where traffic is concentrated before it enters the core), and bidirectional architectures are used in the core part of a network.

8.2.2.1 Unidirectional Path-Switched Ring Architecture

The UPSR is a (1 + 1) single-ended, unidirectional, SONET path layer dedicated protection architecture. The nodes are connected in a ring configuration with one fiber pair connecting adjacent nodes. One fiber on a link is used as the working fiber and the other one is dedicated for protection. The working and protection fibers operate in opposite directions, so there is a working ring in one direction (e.g., clockwise) and a protection ring in the opposite direction (i.e., counter clockwise). For each SONET path, an STS or virtual tributary path signal is bridged permanently at the head end (i.e., the source or transmitter) to both outgoing fibers (working and protection), and is transmitted in both directions around the ring [Bell Communications Research 94a].

The tail end (i.e., destination or receiver) compares the incoming signals continuously at the SONET path layer and selects the better of the two based on signal quality. If a fiber is cut (or other transmission defects are detected), or equipment (a node) fails, the tail end just switches to the data stream coming from the operational direction and the failure is restored automatically. Because each end operates independently, and protection switching is solely the responsibility of the tail-end receiver, no notification or coordination with the head end is required. Thus, no APS signaling channel is required between the ring nodes, and thus the UPSR architecture is simple to operate and has a fast switching time. This architecture can work with either revertive or nonrevertive path switching. Nonrevertive switching minimizes the amount of information lost during the switching process because it switches only once due to a failure. On the other hand, revertive switching has the advantage that a default position always exists and is known. Clearly, nonrevertive switching is preferred when SONET systems with a large bandwidth are used, because even the smallest outage due to the switching time causes the loss of a large amount of information.

In the case of a bidirectional connection between two nodes on the ring, both directions of the working traffic travel in the same direction around the ring. The second (protection) ring carries duplicate copies of the path signals for both connections in the opposite direction. Thus, the full capacity of the protection ring protects the full capacity of the working ring. The total capacity available for carrying services around the ring is therefore limited to that of one fiber and is shared by all nodes on the ring [Shyur+94]. For example, in an OC-48 UPSR, the aggregate traffic injected into the ring by all nodes cannot exceed 48 DS3s. If a fiber cable is cut, only one direction of the two-way connection is affected and, for that direction, path switching is performed at the tail end. The other direction is unaffected by the failure, so no path switching is necessary.

The UPSR architecture can survive a single cable cut. If more than one cable is cut, the connectivity between the ring nodes is disrupted and some traffic is lost. The amount of traffic lost depends on the connectivity pattern at the time of the faults and the location of the multiple faults. Other fault restoration techniques at higher layers can then be used to provide alternate routes for the connections that could not be restored using path switching.

8.2.2.2 Bidirectional Line-Switched Ring Architecture

In a BLSR, a bidirectional connection between two nodes traverses the same intermediate nodes and links in opposite directions. A channel used in that portion of the ring can then be reused in another nonoverlapping part of the ring. Thus, the BLSR architectures have an advantage over the UPSR architectures in terms of the total traffic supported on the ring.

A BLSR is a bidirectional line-protected shared protection architecture. It is also referred to as a shared protection ring (SPRING). In contrast to the UPSR, in which the protection capacity is dedicated, the BLSR shares protection capacity among all the spans on the ring. Failure restoration is performed at the line layer (a lower layer than the path layer) and does not involve any path layer functions. Two types of BLSRs are defined in the SONET standard: two- and four-fiber BLSRs.

Two-Fiber Bidirectional Line-Switched Rings   In the two-fiber BLSR, adjacent nodes are connected using a single fiber pair. Each fiber is designated as a working fiber, but half the signal bandwidth on each fiber is dedicated for protection [Bell Communications Research95]. For example, a two-fiber OC-48 BLSR has 24 of the STS-1s assigned to working traffic and the other 24 (50% of the capacity) assigned to protection. If less than 50% of the capacity is reserved for protection, not all traffic can be restored in the event of a failure.

All protection switching is accomplished in the electronics of the SONET ADM via TSI. Each working slot on one fiber is preassigned to a protection time slot on the fiber going in the opposite direction. For example, for an OC-N ring, time slots 1 through $N/2$ can be used for working traffic on both fibers of an internodal link, with time slots $N/2 + 1$ through N used for protection traffic [Bell95]. In this case, time slot i of one fiber is protected with time slot $N/2 + i$ in the other. When a failure occurs, the working traffic from one fiber is looped back onto the opposite direction, carrying the working traffic in the opposite direction around the ring away from the failure [Harman+94, Bell95]. As in the case of (1:1) point-to-point APS, a signaling protocol using an APS channel carried in the SONET line overhead allows the ring nodes to effect a coordinated line switch when failure conditions occur.

The same procedure works in the case of a node (ADM) failure. In this case, only traffic that passes through the node can be restored. Traffic that is added or dropped at the failed node is lost. A node failure has the same effect as the failure of all the fibers connected to that node. The line switching is performed at both sides of the failed node to redirect traffic away from that node. Because the traffic that is added or dropped at a failed node cannot be restored, it may be misdirected to other erroneous destinations. To deal with this contingency, *squelching* has been proposed [Bell Communications Research95], wherein a path alarm indication signal (AIS) is inserted into these channels instead of the real traffic. This procedure can also be used when multiple links or nodes fail, and in general in all cases in which traffic cannot be restored but may be misdirected because of failure conditions in the network.

In BLSR architectures, switching is coordinated by the nodes on either side of a failure in the ring, so that a signaling protocol is required to perform a line switch and to restore the network. Thus, BLSR architectures are more difficult to operate than UPSRs (in which no signaling is required). The protection switching time with BLSRs depends on the time it takes for the signaling protocol to be completed.

Four-Fiber Bidirectional Line-Switched Rings   In a four-fiber BLSR (or SPRING), four fibers connect each adjacent pair of nodes, and the nodes are connected in a ring configuration. Two fibers are now used as working fibers (one in each direction) and two fibers are designated as protection fibers (one in each direction). In this case, the fibers are dedicated completely as either working or protection fibers. Thus, the ring capacity of a four-fiber BLSR is twice the capacity of a two-fiber BLSR. A bidirectional connection between two nodes travels on separate fibers (opposite directions) through the same intermediate nodes (typically on the shortest path around the ring).

As in the SONET linear APS architecture, the four-fiber BLSR APS channel is carried in the K_1 and K_2 bytes on the protection fibers. If both working and protection fibers are cut on the short path between two nodes, the service is restored using the long path. As in the two-fiber BLSR case, traffic that would normally be carried on a working fiber in the severed link is looped back on protection fibers to direct it away from the failure. The four-fiber BLSR can carry twice as much traffic as the two-fiber BLSR, but it requires twice as much fiber and electronics. An additional advantage of the four-fiber architecture is that it can support both *ring* and *span* switching. Ring switching was described earlier; it occurs when both the working and protection fibers are cut (cable cut). In this case, the protection switches on both sides of the cut engage, and the traffic is routed away from the cut with the help of an APS signaling channel. Span switching occurs when only the working fiber fails. In that case, the traffic is switched from the working to the protection fiber in the same direction as the working traffic [Bell95]. This architecture is preferred by long-haul carriers.

If a node fails, only the pass-through traffic can be restored. Squelching is used to account for the misdirected traffic in the case of node or multiple link failures.

8.2.3 SONET Self-healing Ring Interconnection Techniques

Figure 8.5 shows two possible interconnection configurations for SONET SHRs: single access and dual access. For the single-access configuration (Figure 8.5[a]), two rings are joined by a single access node, and for the dual-access ring configuration (Figure 8.5[b]), the ring interconnection point uses two common access nodes [Wu92]. Architectures consisting of many interconnected rings can be formed by employing several interconnection points on each ring. For the single-access ring interconnection configuration, a single node failure may disable the communication among the (possibly multiple) rings that are interconnected through this node.

The dual-access ring interconnection configuration avoids this problem by providing two points of contact between the rings, termed the *primary* and *secondary nodes*. In dual-access SONET SHR architectures, the traffic is dual fed to both rings using appropriate hardware and software techniques. Because dual access is currently the most popular method, the discussion that follows focuses on this technique.

One method for interconnecting SONET rings uses a *drop-and-continue function*, together with a *path selector* and/or a *service selector function*. The drop-and-continue function drops the traffic at a primary interconnecting node and continues a copy of that traffic to a secondary node where it is also dropped (i.e., the signal is bridged permanently and dual fed to the interconnecting nodes). The path selector function allows an interconnecting node to choose the best of two incoming signals independently to forward to the next ring. Drop-and-continue and path/service selector functions allow inter-ring traffic to survive coincident single fiber and node failures on both rings [Harman+94, Bell94b].

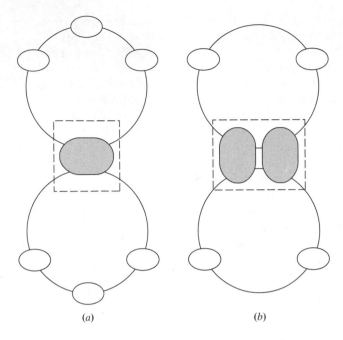

FIGURE 8.5 Single-
and dual-access ring
interconnection
configurations.

(*a*)   (*b*)

The following section illustrates the use of these interconnection techniques for SONET SHR architectures when either the same or different protection schemes (UPSR or BLSR) are used in each ring. The interconnections ensure that both the intra-ring traffic (traffic that stays within one ring) and the inter-ring traffic (traffic that crosses from one ring to the other) is protected in the event of a failure. For a more complete treatment of ring interconnection see [Harman+94, BeHannesey98, Siller+96, and Ester94].

8.2.3.1 Interconnected UPSR–UPSR Architectures

Interconnected UPSRs provide path protection as described in Section 8.2.2.1 for intra-ring traffic, and protect inter-ring paths using the drop-and-continue feature. The restoration mechanism is independent in each ring. Drop-and-continue together with path selection ensures that two copies of the signal are maintained between the rings [Bell94a]. In the event of a failure affecting one copy of the signal, traffic between the two rings is restored automatically using the other copy, as in the case of single UPSRs.

Figure 8.6 shows how a bidirectional SONET path between nodes in different UPSRs is protected. The traffic is duplicated at the transmitter as in a single UPSR, and the two copies are routed on different segments of the ring (in opposite directions). When it reaches the interconnection nodes, each copy is duplicated once more using the drop-and-continue function. The two signals reaching each path selector are those that were routed on different ring segments, so that a failure on one link in the ring causes only one of the two inputs to the path selector to drop out. The path

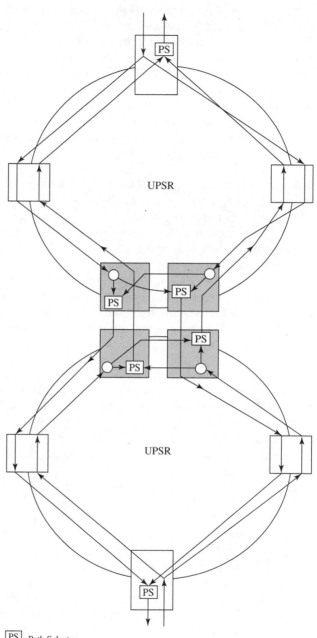

FIGURE 8.6 Two-fiber
UPSR-to-UPSR ring
interconnection.

selectors choose the best of their two input signals and inject them onto the second ring. Thus, two copies of the original signal enter the second ring on two different fibers traveling in different directions. This scheme provides protection from single failures on the interconnecting links and nodes. Recovery from a failure is therefore automatic, because the path selectors respond to a working signal degradation or failure and choose the signal coming from the protection path. The path protection technique just described is executed on a path-by-path basis for each SONET path traversing the two interconnected rings.

Note that the interconnection between the two rings is performed via SONET interfaces. This allows the alarms and maintainance signals to be preserved for connections crossing over from one ring to the other.

8.2.3.2 Interconnected BLSR–BLSR Architectures

As in the case of interconnected UPSRs, the restoration mechanisms in interconnected BLSRs are independent for each ring. A drop-and-continue function and a service selector (rather than a path selector) are now used to protect the rings.

Figure 8.7 illustrates the interconnection of two BLSRs. Again, the drop-and-continue function is used to duplicate the traffic at the interconnection points, and the two copies of the signal are injected into the second ring from two different points. A service selector at the destination node monitors the two duplicate signals. If it detects a failure, it switches immediately from the current channel to its duplicate. Link and node failures within each ring are protected by rerouting over protection fibers as described in Section 8.2.2.2.

8.2.3.3 Interconnected BLSR–UPSR Architectures

In this architecture, techniques used in both the UPSR and the BLSR are used to protect the traffic against failures. Drop-and-continue is used in both rings, and service and path selectors are used (in the BLSR and UPSR rings respectively) to restore the traffic if a failure occurs.

Figure 8.8 demonstrates the interconnection between a BLSR and a UPSR. For a connection from a BLSR to a UPSR, the drop-and-continue function at the interconnection points on the BLSR side creates two copies of the traffic that subsequently cross over to the second ring at the two different interconnection points. The interconnection nodes in the UPSR transmit the two copies of the traffic around the ring in opposite directions. A path selector at the destination node chooses one of the two signals. A slightly different technique is used when the signal travels from a UPSR to a BLSR. The signal is duplicated, using the drop-and-continue function at both interconnection points on the UPSR side. A path selector in each interconnection node compares two copies of the signal from the UPSR, choosing the best to pass on to the BLSR. A copy of the signal enters the BLSR from each interconnection node, and a service selector at one of the nodes selects one of the two signals to continue its path in the BLSR.

As explained earlier, in the case of interconnected SHRs, the self-healing mechanisms are independent for each of the interconnected rings. The interconnection

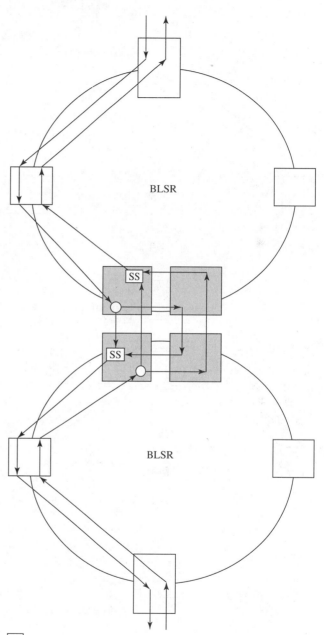

FIGURE 8.7 BLSR-to-BLSR ring interconnection.

SS Service Selector

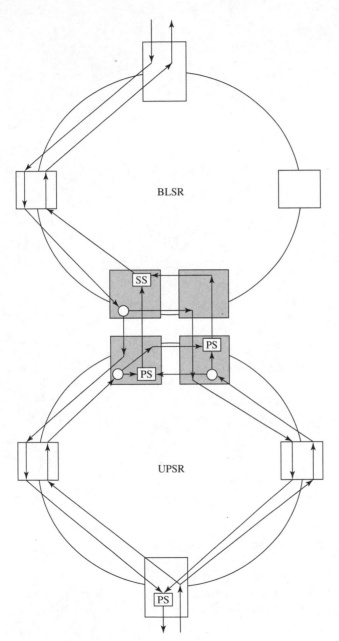

FIGURE 8.8 BLSR-to-UPSR ring interconnection.

is done in such a way that the rings can recover individually from a single failure in each ring. Multiple failures may result in the loss of the services that traverse several rings.

For interconnected SONET SHRs, the problem of the *ripple effect* has to be taken into account. This effect occurs due to the propagation of a path AIS from one ring to another if the self-healing mechanism in the ring in which the failure occurred does not engage quickly enough. The path AIS then causes the self-healing mechanism to engage in rings in which a failure hasn't occurred. This effect can occur in UPSR–UPSR and BLSR–UPSR interconnected rings. It is not a problem in BLSR–BLSR networks, in which path AIS is not detected. Because the ripple effect can increase the service restoration time as well as cause protection switching to engage in rings that do not have failures, it may compromise the "independence" of the various interconnected rings. This is especially troublesome when different rings belong to different service providers [Harman+94, Bell94b].

8.2.4 Architectures with Mesh Topologies

Various methods have been proposed to provide restoration and protection in networks that have mesh topologies. In this section we provide an overview of some of them. There are two basic approaches: (1) a generalization of ring protection techniques using ring covers, and (2) dynamic restoration based on reconfiguring DCSs at the network nodes to respond to failures. The latter approach may be implemented in either a centralized or a distributed fashion.

A *ring cover* is a set of closed paths that covers all links collectively in the network at least once. If these rings are composed of bidirectional fiber links, they can be made into self-healing structures that can protect the network against a cable cut or an equipment failure using the APS path or line techniques described in Sections 8.2.2.1 and 8.2.2.2. Restoration using the ring cover method can be achieved in a matter of milliseconds. A negative feature of ring covers is that they may require a significant amount of extra redundancy to ensure 100% protection against a link or an equipment failure (see Section 8.2.4.1).

When a failure occurs in the DCS restoration approach, connections are switched from the failed links and rerouted over others having spare capacity. Using centralized control, the reconfiguration necessary for restoration is computed by a single network manager, which issues commands to the various nodes involved in the restoration process. With distributed control, the restoration process is handled in an autonomous manner by the individual DCSs through the exchange of signaling messages. Distributed restoration requires complex protocols and high-speed signaling between the nodes as well as enhanced computational capabilities at each node.

The main disadvantage of DCS techniques is that the reconfiguration time may not be fast enough to meet user demands for service availability. An advantage is that they require much less spare capacity than ring-based schemes. Typically, the time required for a mesh architecture restoration using DCS equipment might be on the order of minutes if a centralized restoration algorithm is used, and on the order of seconds if a distributed restoration algorithm is used. Although centralized restoration is much slower than distributed approaches, it can restore the network more efficiently (in terms of overall network capacity requirements) because the network manager has a global view of the network. Thus, DCS restoration techniques have a place in networks in which the restoration speed is not as important as the redundant capacity required for protection.

8.2.4.1 Mesh Architectures Using a Ring Cover for Survivability

A simple choice of a ring cover for a network is a set of *fundamental cycles* (see Appendix A). The fundamental cycles "cover" the graph of the network in the sense that each edge is included in at least one cycle in the set. Each fundamental cycle can be treated as an independent SONET SHR. The mesh then "behaves" as a collection of SHRs, providing the advantages of simple control logic and speed in terms of failure restoration.

Any ring cover of the network requires at least 100% redundancy in terms of protection fibers.[4] But fundamental cycles, if they are not chosen carefully, may require much more than 100% redundancy, because a link included in multiple cycles must carry multiple protection fibers—one for each cycle traversing it.[5]

Because there are many different sets of fundamental cycles in a network, the design of "optimized" multiring networks is a complex problem. Studies have been performed in planning [May+91] and analyzing multiple SHR networks. Slevinsky et al. [Slevinsky+93] present an algorithmic approach that is near optimal in minimizing the required protection capacity. A related problem involves choosing a ring set so that most of the traffic has its source and destination in the same ring. The problem is addressed but not solved by [Slevinsky+93]. Gardner et al., in [Gardner+94], also address the ring cover problem and describe an algorithm that finds a minimum-cost ring cover for specific classes of networks, based on the Eulerian approach. The algorithm finds a ring cover that minimizes the equipment cost required to guarantee 100% restoration from a single link failure in arbitrary unidirectional rings. They also propose three heuristics that solve the same problem for bidirectional rings. A software tool called NetSolver, introduced by [Gardner+95], finds good ring covers and the routing paths for the point-to-point traffic in the network. It starts from an arbitrary ring cover and improves on it through a series of iterations. Other studies have also addressed the problem of analyzing ring cover designs. In [Wasem+92] and [Wasem91a,b], an algorithm for routing rings in a network is presented for the case when the topology of the network, the traffic matrix, and the nodes in each ring are known in advance. This algorithm can create cost-effective designs and increase network reliability at the planning stage.

---

[4] This assumes the four-fiber ring approach. With a two-fiber ring, the extra capacity would be in the form of spare channels.

[5] In the special case of Eulerian networks, an "ideal" ring cover can be found in the form of bidirectional ring decomposition of the network. In this case, each link is traversed by exactly one ring (see Section 6.3.5). A more general approach to "covering" a network uses *cycle decomposition*. This is applied to optical layer protection in Section 8.3.

8.2.4.2 DCS-Based Centralized Restoration Techniques

Various centralized restoration schemes have been proposed that use either predetermined restoration paths or on-line computation (assuming global knowledge of the network state) for failure restoration. These techniques assume a restoration time of a few minutes (compared with a few hours for manual restoration).

The FASTAR system used in AT&T's network operates at the DS3 transport network level, and combines centralized and distributed processes to provide failure restoration [Chao+91]. A central processor is used that receives and correlates alarm reports, and calculates, reroutes, and controls the restoration path implementation. The central processor maintains an extensive database including the network layout, cross-connect data, and the status of the network links. Local controllers are also used in each node for alarm gathering and reporting as well as various test functions. The controllers signal network conditions directly to the central processor.

For the FASTAR system, the restoration process is as follows. Alarm gathering is performed at various points in the network (line terminating equipment, DCS equipment), and these alarms are reported to the local controllers, which correlate them and pass the information to the central processor. The central processor waits until it receives all possible alarms, prioritizes the failed DS3s, and calculates the appropriate rerouting for each one. It then activates the restoration paths according to their priorities. Before transferring services to the restoration path, the central processor makes sure that the transfer does not disturb any current DS3s that are unaffected by the failure. After the service transfer, it also checks to verify that the transfer to the restoration path was successful.

Distributed intelligence is introduced into the network for fast alarm reporting. However, the central processor is essential for prioritizing the failed connections and rerouting them in an efficient manner. This approach is not as fast as the distributed schemes described next, but is satisfactory for users who do not require extremely fast restoration capabilities.

In the NETSPAR protocol [Tsai+90], the DCSs reroute the traffic (on the DS3 level) from failed physical facilities to surviving facilities with spare capacities. After a failure is detected, the surviving DCSs use a distributed protocol to determine which of the facilities are working. Based on these results, each DCS loads a new configuration table, rearranging the network to restore as much of the traffic as possible. These configuration tables can be calculated off-line (for example, for all single link faults) at a central node, saved at each individual DCS, and used when a failure occurs.

This is a combination of a centralized and a distributed approach. It uses a distributed topology update protocol to identify a fault and then downloads a precomputed rerouting table for that fault. Because it uses static, precomputed tables to achieve the reconfiguration of the network after a failure, the NETSPAR scheme is faster than the dynamic approaches presented in Section 8.2.4.3, generally achieving restoration in less than 100 ms. However, the technique becomes cumbersome when the networks considered have a large number of links and nodes [Coan+91]. Furthermore, the static nature of the rerouting tables presents problems when there are network topology changes, because all precomputed tables must be recalculated.

Centralized restoration requires a complete and accurate database of the state of the network at all times. Furthermore, even the most advanced centralized restoration techniques cannot restore a failure in less than a few minutes. This means that these techniques cannot be used by themselves to protect networks that carry applications with large bandwidth requirements. Furthermore, outage times of a few minutes are much longer than most timeouts in higher layer protocols. Consequently, higher layer connections are dropped when a failure occurs, and higher layer recovery procedures are invoked.

8.2.4.3 DCS-Based Distributed Restoration Techniques

Faster survivability schemes based on distributed restoration have been introduced to avoid the problems encountered by the centralized techniques.

A technique, called the *SelfHealing Network*, was introduced by [Grover87] for distributed, real-time restoration of high-capacity telecommunication transport networks. In this system, complex restoration plans are computed and are put into effect in real time in an entirely autonomous, distributed manner.

The SelfHealing process uses the DCS equipment in a SONET or DS3 transport network along with additional software features to achieve restoration of complete cable cuts in 1 to 2 seconds. These numbers correspond to the typical connection drop times. (If the traffic affected by a failure can be rerouted to the spare capacity in less than the connection drop times, the connections can be resumed.) This technique was the first attempt to use DCS equipment to support capacity-efficient restoration in real time and in a distributed manner without depending on large databases. It uses parallel, distributed interaction between the DCSs to achieve a very fast restoration mechanism.

The restoration process has two main components: (1) a network signature flooding wave and (2) a reverse signature linking sequence. After a failure occurs (e.g., a cable is cut), alarms are generated and are detected by the DCS equipment. The two nodes at the ends of the cable cut are aware of the failure and one becomes the *chooser* while the other one becomes the *sender* (predefined arbitrarily). The *sender* node then starts broadcasting appropriately indexed restoration signatures (signature flooding wave) out of its DCS. These signatures arrive at neighboring DCSs, which in turn reindex the restoration signatures and rebroadcast them to their neighboring nodes. Only spare DS3s are used for this process. Therefore, one or more signatures arrive at the *chooser* using the spare capacity in the network. The *chooser* then sends out a complementary signature on a link having a preferred arriving signature (reverse signature linking). This signature goes through a number of tandem nodes and finally arrives back at the *sender*. In this manner, a bidirectional connection between the *sender* and the *chooser* is established using spare capacity. This connection is used to restore the failure condition.

Multiple failures can also be restored using a slightly modified procedure. The basic SelfHealing protocol remains the same, but additional features are added to ensure that a node can now perform simultaneous SelfHealing tasks without experiencing any adverse interactions between concurrent tasks. Studies were performed to show that two SelfHealing tasks can be executed concurrently in a node to achieve restoration simultaneously.

The performance of the SelfHealing Network protocol was tested for various networks. It was shown that the scheme restored successfully any single failure in 2.5 seconds or less, and it found all the paths of an ideal k-shortest path restoration solution in one iteration [Grover+90].

The FITNESS (Failure Immunization Technology for Network Service Survivability) network protocol [Yang+88] uses DCSs in a SONET network to restore failures via distributed computation in less than 2 seconds. It uses the principle of the *sender* and *chooser* as the SelfHealing protocol and is based on the SelfHealing approach. The FITNESS protocol uses a selective flooding mechanism to limit the number of messages exchanged among the nodes. It attempts to find the restoration path with maximum available bandwidth. Several iterations are tried within a 2-second window, with the *chooser* responding only to the best route. In this protocol, the communication between nodes is done not through signatures but via the SONET embedded operations channel. As indicated, it requires multiple iterations to find all possible restoration routes. In contrast, the SelfHealing Network finds all required k shortest restoration paths in a single iteration (distributed process).

The RREACT distributed restoration protocol [Chow+92] again uses the *sender–chooser* method to perform the restoration function. It uses no prior network status or topology knowledge and supports multiple simultaneous link failure restorations. RREACT finds all the paths between the disrupted nodes by attaching path information in the broadcast request messages. This algorithm results in a significant increase in the number of message exchanges as the network grows. Contrary to the FITNESS protocol, it needs only one wave of request messages to perform a link restoration. The protocol also provides efficient utilization of network spare capacity resources. RREACT outperforms FITNESS in terms of both restoration time and spare capacity usage. Simulation results showed that it outperformed other similar restoration techniques, performing the restoration in less than 1 second.

Other similar restoration techniques have also been proposed. They are all based on a simple flooding algorithm to achieve the desired failure restoration. When a node detects a failure, it broadcasts a restoration message to adjacent nodes to find an alternate route. Every node except the *sender* and the *chooser* responds by rebroadcasting the message. When the restoration message reaches the *chooser*, the *chooser* responds by returning an acknowledgement to the *sender*. In this way, alternate restoration paths are found. By limiting the number of hops for the messages, the process can limit the distance these messages can travel in the network. [Bicknell+93] compared six algorithms in terms of time of restoration, level of restoration (number of lost working channels restored), utilization of spare channel resources, range of application (different kinds of failure cases to which the algorithm can respond), and message volume (number of restoration messages generated). FITNESS was the slowest of the algorithms because it uses a "multiwave" approach to find the restoration path. However, it has the lowest message volume because it chooses the restoration path with the largest bandwidth during each wave of messages. All algorithms restored most of the working traffic lost, and RREACT had the best capacity ultiliza-tion. As indicated later only the algorithm presented by [Chujo+90] can handle mul-tiple failures and node failures.

In [Chujo+90], a flooding algorithm is used that finds the shortest alternate route. As in the case of the FITNESS protocol, it requires multiple, succesive iterations to find all the possible alternate routes. Follow-up work in [Komine+90] uses multides-tination flooding (defining multiple *choosers*) and path route monitoring to address multiple link and node failures [Bicknell+93].

The NETRATS protocol (Network Restoration Algorithm for Telecommunication Systems) is described in [Sakauchi+90]. It provides both line and path restoration. During the line restoration process, a procedure similar to the SelfHealing Network and the FITNESS protocol is followed. In the path restoration process, a new proce-dure similar to that used for link failure is introduced. Because the path restoration approach releases each disrupted channel, and the source and destination ends of the channel reestablish their connections, path restoration requires more time than line restoration. It is also more complex to implement and requires more network in-formation and more switching. However, path restoration provides a better solution than line restoration in terms of the number of connections restored and the number of spare links used. Also, the path restoration procedure can handle both node and line failures.

Iraschko et al. [Iraschko+96] investigated the problem of capacity optimization for path restoration networks and attempted to quantify the benefits of path over line restoration in terms of capacity. Results showed that path restoration performed significantly better than line restoration for several case network studies (up to 19% less capacity required for protection).

The distributed mesh restoration techniques presented in this section are better than the APS point-to-point and SHR techniques presented earlier in terms of capacity requirements, but they are slower than APS. Clearly, there is a trade-off between restoration speed and spare capacity requirements. Rings require a 100% duplication of working capacity for full protection. Ring covers generally require quite a bit more. On the other hand, mesh techniques not based on SHRs can provide full survivability capabilities with redundancy that is typically proportional to the inverse of the average degree of the nodes in the network. For example, for networks with an average node degree between 3 and 4.5, 30% to 50% redundancy may be enough for full survivability capabilities. Case studies presented in [Grover92] demonstrate that a fully survivable mesh network requires approximately one third the total link redundancy of a ring cover design.

Various studies have been made to determine the minimum amount of spare ca-pacity needed for restoration in mesh-restorable networks. The applications are to networks in which cable cut restoration is possible via rerouting around the fault, us-ing either centralized or distributed restoration algorithms [Grover+91]. These stud-ies are useful in designing the network to ensure full survivability with minimum redundancy. When applied to various test networks, the studies showed that 100% survivable mesh networks are feasible with 50% to 70% redundancy.

8.3 Optical Layer Restoration and Protection: Point-to-Point and Ring Architectures

WDM transport systems are being deployed at an increasing rate in the backbone networks of several network operators. Eventually, optical layer protection and restoration will be introduced into these networks. In this section we present several techniques that are currently under consideration for point-to-point systems and rings. Sections 8.4 and 8.5, respectively, deal with shared optical layer protection and optical path protection in general mesh networks. Another possible approach to restoration in mesh networks uses reconfigurable optical cross-connects (OXCs). This is essentially the same as restoration using SONET DCSs, so it will not be discussed further here.

The point-to-point and SHR techniques reuse most of the concepts developed for SONET protection. Multiwavelength systems add extra complexity to the restoration problem and introduce several additional considerations (mainly at the physical layer). We shall assume the use of multiple wavelengths per fiber—the case in which optical restoration techniques are especially useful.

8.3.1 Point-to-Point Systems

With the growing use of WDM, protection switching for point-to-point systems at the optical level is a subject of great importance to the carriers.

8.3.1.1 (1 + 1) Optical Protection

With (1 + 1) optical facility protection, service is protected from link failures only, using an optical splitter to bridge the optical signal and dual feed it on diversely routed working and protection fibers. The protection switching is performed entirely in the optical domain. In the event of a single link failure, an optical switch at the receiving end switches to the protection fiber [Bonenfant+94, Wu92]. Because there are no duplicated electronics, a link failure can be restored but a transmitter or receiver failure leads to loss of service. Figure 8.9 shows an example of the (1 + 1) optical protection architecture for point-to-point systems. This arrangement is not the same as the (1 + 1) SONET protection architecture. In (1 + 1) SONET protection (Figure 8.2), both incoming signals are detected and can be compared continuously to select the better of the two. In the (1 + 1) optical protection architecture, with only one receiver at the tail end, a failure of the incoming signal is detected at the receiver. However, unlike (1 + 1) SONET protection, the receiver switches to the protection fiber without knowing anything about the state of the protection fiber. In the (1 + 1) SONET protection architecture, the duplicate electronics enables the receiving end to know the state of both signals.

Architectures are proposed in [Wu92] that can protect against both equipment and link failures. They use electrical layer protection to protect against equipment failures and optical layer protection to protect against link failures. The electrical protection

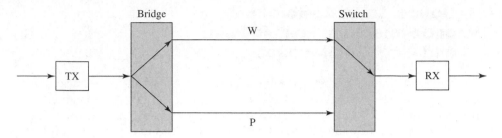

FIGURE 8.9 (1 + 1) Protection in the optical layer.

scheme can use a (1:N) technique in conjunction with (1 + 1) optical protection. (It is unlikely that more than one piece of equipment will fail at the same time.) Of course, the (1:N) protection procedure is considerably more cost effective than the (1:1) method.

8.3.1.2 (1:1) Optical Protection

The (1:1) optical protection scheme is similar to the (1 + 1) method in that diversely routed facilities protect against link failures. The service is not bridged permanently to both the working and protection fibers. Instead, a switch occurs once a failure has been detected [Bonenfant+94, Wu92]. Figure 8.10 shows an example of a (1:1) optical protection architecture.

An APS signaling channel (on the bidirectional path) is used to coordinate the protection switch in the event of a failure. In the (1:1) SONET protection architecture, there is an APS channel between the head and tail ends. This is implemented using the protection fiber and an APS signaling channel. In a (1:1) optical protection architecture, no communication path exists over the protection fiber because this architecture does not have duplicate electronics. A communication path is only established when the transmit and receive ends switch to the protection fiber. When a failure occurs, the receive end sends a message to the transmit end over the protection fiber without knowing whether the transmit end also switched to the protection fiber. Thus, initially it does not receive any reply. If the transmit end switches to the protection fiber, then

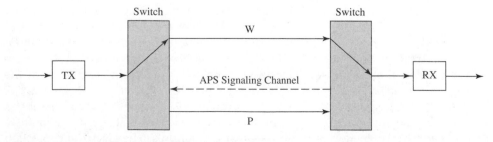

FIGURE 8.10 (1:1) Protection in the optical layer.

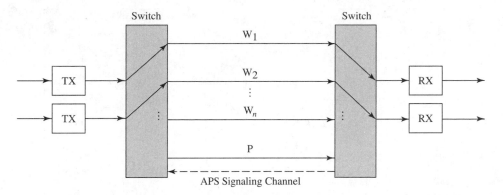

FIGURE 8.11 (1:N) Protection in the optical layer.

the service is restored. Otherwise, the traffic is lost. This difficulty can be avoided if a separate "out-of-band" optical service channel is provided to support signaling for protection switching.[6]

Note that although this is a (1:1) architecture, no spare traffic is supported, because the system lacks the duplicate transmitters and receivers necessary to support transmission and reception over the protection facility.

8.3.1.3 (1:N) Optical Protection

The (1:N) optical protection architecture is similar to the (1:1) technique. However, N working entities now share a single protection fiber. If several working fibers are cut, only the traffic that is carried on one of them can be restored. The failure with the highest priority is restored first. Figure 8.11 shows an example of a (1:N) optical protection architecture.

Figure 8.12 shows a combination of (1 + 1) optical and (1:N) equipment protection for a WDM system. It has significant economic benefits over (1:1) optical and equipment protection schemes. In this system, a spare wavelength λ_p, together with associated terminal equipment is set aside for equipment protection.

8.3.2 Self-healing Optical Rings

WDM ring networks are the subject of considerable interest because of their restoration capabilities. They provide 100% restoration capability for a single-fiber cable cut or equipment failure using a simple but fast protection-switching scheme [Wu+89].

The WDM SHR architectures proposed in the literature present various challenges that were not encountered in the SONET SHRs. For example, if the ring segments separating the WADMs are long, optical amplifiers are needed between the WADMs

---

[6] Currently, service channels are implemented on wavelengths outside the EDFA amplification band (e.g., at 1510 nm or 1300 nm).

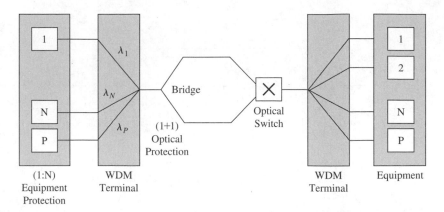

FIGURE 8.12 (1 + 1) Optical protection and (1:N) electronic protection for a WDM system.

on the working fibers. This means that optical amplifiers are required on the protection fibers as well. But when no faults are present, the protection fibers are configured in closed loops so that the amplified spontaneous emission noise from the fiber amplifiers recirculates in this closed protection path unless means are used to break these closed cycles. Several methods have been proposed to avoid this condition. They involve a topology based on properties of Eulerian graphs, as well as technological approaches [Bala+96, Iness+96].

As in the case of SONET SHRs, WDM SHRs can be either path switched or line switched. The path-switched rings are referred to as unidirectional path-protected ring (UPPR) architectures and the line-switched rings are referred to as SPRING architectures. Both of these types are discussed in the following sections. For both techniques, optical layer protection switches typically enable the restoration of failure conditions in a few tens of milliseconds—a time scale compatible with optomechanical switching technology. This time scale has been reduced by three orders of magnitude in recent testbed experiments, where lithium niobate protection switches have been used to achieve 10 μs restoration times in WDM SPRINGs [Xin+98].

8.3.2.1 Unidirectional WDM Path-Protected Ring Architecture

In a UPPR the nodes are connected in a ring using two fibers that propagate signals in opposite directions around the ring. One fiber is designated as a working fiber and the other is designed as a protection fiber. All the working traffic propagates around the ring in one direction while all the protection traffic propagates around the ring in the opposite direction. This architecture is very similar to the two-fiber SONET UPSR architecture. The self-healing capability is achieved by using 1 + 1 wavelength path selection. The signal is bridged on both fibers at the transmit end (using an optical splitter), resulting in two copies of the signal propagating in the ring in opposite directions. The receive end then switches to the protection fiber if a failure occurs. The counterpropagating signal thus provides network survivability when a link is cut [Elrefaie92, Wu+90]. All splitting and switching is done entirely in the optical domain. Because the receiving end does not need to notify the transmitting end that a failure has occurred, a signaling channel is not required. The decisions are all made at the receiver on a path-by-path basis.

Because there are no duplicate electronics in this architecture, a transmitter or receiver failure results in the loss of traffic. A node failure can be protected in the same way as in the SONET UPSR architecture (i.e., all pass-through traffic can be restored). Traffic that originates or terminates at the failed node cannot be restored. The UPPR architecture can restore a single cable cut or node failure.

8.3.2.2 Four-Fiber WDM Shared Protection Ring Architecture

A four-fiber SPRING is a bidirectional four-fiber ring: two fibers are designated as working fibers and the other two fibers are protection fibers (see Figure 8.13). In this case, the working traffic travels around the ring in both directions. For example, a bidirectional connection between two nodes is typically established on the short path connecting the nodes. The working fibers carry all the traffic under normal conditions and the protection fibers carry no traffic unless a failure occurs. For example, if we assume bidirectional connections, the traffic from node 1 to node 2 in Figure 8.13

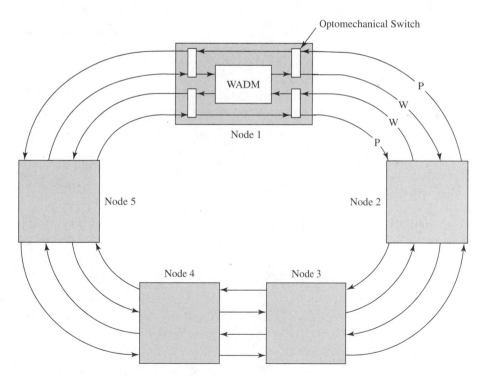

FIGURE 8.13 Four-fiber WDM SPRING architecture.

would be carried in the outer (clockwise) working fiber, and the traffic from node 2 to node 1 would be carried in the inner (counterclockwise) fiber.

To recover from failures the ring uses line protection switching (ring switching) to perform a loopback function [Elrefaie92, Wu+90], which requires an optical protection switch (typically optomechanical) at each node (the small white rectangles in Figure 8.13). This protection switching can be revertive or nonrevertive.

When a fiber segment of the ring is cut (a line that interconnects adjacent nodes), the two nodes at the ends of this segment close their protection switches and interconnect the working fibers to the protection fibers. The traffic is moved to the protection fibers, propagating away from the failure. The signals propagate around the ring on the protection fiber until they reach the other side of the failure, at which point they switch back to the original working fiber, thus restoring the traffic. For example, in Figure 8.14 the link between nodes 1 and 2 is cut so that the protection switches close, sealing off the failed link. Traffic that normally would have entered the link from the WADM in node 1 is switched to the counterclockwise protection fiber, and doubles back around the ring until it enters the closed protection switch in node 2, which directs it to the WADM in that node. The protection path taken by the traffic replaces the cut (clockwise) working fiber in the failed link. (A similar operation protects

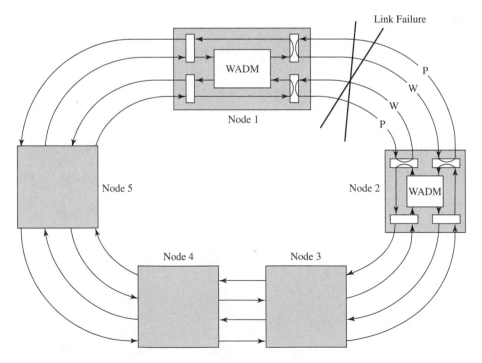

FIGURE 8.14 Four-fiber WDM SPRING surviving a link failure.

the counterclockwise working fiber.) An APS channel is required to coordinate the switching at both ends of the failure.

When a node fails, the protection switches in that node switch to interconnect the working and protection fibers on the incident links. The signal again propagates around the ring until it reaches the other side of the failed node, where it switches back to the working fiber, thus restoring the failure. Figure 8.15 illustrates how the ring survives a failure of node 1.

As in the SONET SHRs, only traffic that passes through a failed node can be restored. Traffic that originates or terminates at a failed node cannot be restored and is lost. Also, as in SONET some of the traffic may be misdirected and has to be squelched. (No specific methods have been developed at this time to deal with misdirected traffic in WDM SHR architectures.) Because no duplicate electronics are used, the SPRING architecture does not protect against a transmitter or receiver failure [Bonenfant+94, Manchester+96].

8.3.2.3 Two-Fiber WDM Shared Protection Ring Architecture

In the two-fiber WDM SPRING adjacent nodes are connected using two fibers. Each fiber is designated as working fiber but half the signal bandwidth on each fiber is

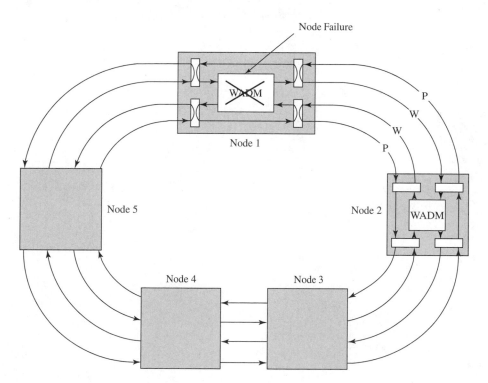

FIGURE 8.15 Four-fiber WDM SPRING surviving a node failure.

dedicated for protection [Wu92, Wu+90]. As for the four-fiber SPRING, a cable cut or a node failure causes the protection switches to interconnect the working and protection fibers to redirect the traffic away from the failure.

In the SONET two-fiber BLSR, 50% of the fiber capacity is reserved for protection, and TSI is used to switch the traffic from fiber 1 on a link to the oppositely directed fiber 2. Similarly, in the two-fiber WDM SPRING, only half of the wavelengths are used in each fiber. However, there is one important difference. In a SONET BLSR, a single bidirectional connection uses the same time slot in both directions. During protection switching, a TSI is performed at the protecting node, moving the working slots to the protection slots before transmission onto the fiber. In the two-fiber WDM SPRING, an analogous operation on the wavelengths would require the use of wavelength interchange, which is currently difficult to achieve while remaining in the optical domain. However, a simple wavelength assignment rule avoids this problem. It suffices to assign wavelengths from two disjoint sets to the two directions of a given bidirectional connection (Figure 8.16). For a network with N wavelengths, the working traffic in fiber 1 can use wavelengths 1 through N/2, and the remaining

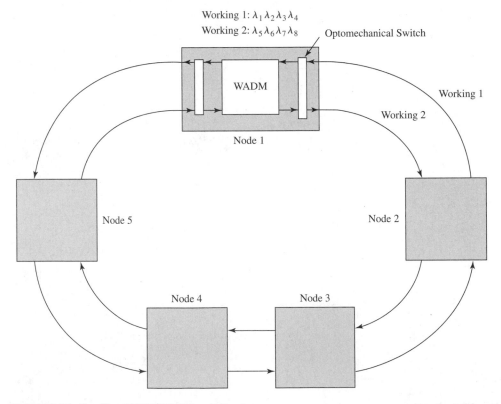

FIGURE 8.16 Two-fiber WDM SPRING architecture.

wavelengths can be reserved for protection traffic. In fiber 2, the assignments would be reversed. If a link failure occurs, the protection switch at the head end of fiber 1 on the concerned link closes, thereby looping working traffic onto fiber 2 of the preceding link. This traffic then moves in the opposite direction around the ring away from the failure [Bala96]. Because of the method of wavelength assignment, the rerouted traffic is on a vacant wavelength on fiber 2 in each link. Once again, node failures can be restored in a manner similar to SONET two-fiber BLSRs.

The SPRING architectures require coordination by the nodes on either side of the failure in the ring. A signaling protocol is required to perform a line switch and to restore the network. A detailed signaling protocol for the SPRING has not yet been provided but ITU studies are currently under way [Bonenfant+94]. SPRING architectures are much more difficult to operate than UPPR architectures, which require no signaling protocols for protection switching. However, they offer a substantial increase in the amount of carried traffic when compared with UPPRs.

WDM ring interconnection has not yet been addressed in any detail in the literature. This is an important topic that will receive more attention as the carriers start to deploy WDM optical rings.

8.4 Shared Optical Layer Protection: Mesh Topologies

In this section we present methodologies for APS in the optical layer of networks with arbitrary topologies. These are *shared optical protection* (line protection) techniques that can potentially restore failures within 50 ms by detouring traffic around a failed link or node. This speed is comparable with the specifications for restoration at the logical (path) level in SONET rings and similar networks. Although we present these protection techniques in the context of purely optical networks (WRNs using optical cross-connects as their switching nodes), they are also applicable to networks composed of point-to-point optical transmission links terminated by electronic switching equipment (e.g., digital cross-connects).[7]

8.4.1 Why Shared Optical Protection?

In traditional mesh networks, recovery from link or node failure is typically implemented in a centralized manner using path protection techniques. The protection is accomplished on a "fine-grained" basis; that is, the individual traffic units being restored are typically in the tens of megabits-per-second range (e.g., STS-1 or DS3). In $(1+1)$ mesh protection, for example, each signal is carried simultaneously on a working and a protection path, and a path selector at the receiver chooses one or the other based on the received signal quality. In a SONET network, there might be many individual connections using a failed link, each requiring its own protection path. This

---

[7] An approach to optical layer APS using path protection is discussed in Section 8.5.

leads to considerable wasted bandwidth in the network. In the (1:1) or (1:N) case, the required spare capacity is less. The protection paths are not active unless there is a fault, and they may be used for lower priority traffic, which is preempted when necessary. However, restoration in this case is a slower and more complex operation. Each of these techniques requires considerable coordination, processing, and delay, because many connections may be affected and have to be rerouted in the event of a single link or node failure.

In the currently evolving multiwavelength optical networks, the amount of traffic carried over each fiber is typically in the range of 10 Gbps to 100 Gbps. To be efficient, fault recovery techniques in these networks should deal with large units of capacity. Restoring connections on an STS-1 basis is wasteful in terms of bandwidth, time, complexity, and cost. To improve performance in the multiwavelength case, the path protection techniques described earlier can be implemented using a λ-channel as the basic unit to be rerouted. Nevertheless, the basic problems associated with coordination, centralized processing, complexity, and delay are still there, but on a somewhat reduced level.

The shared optical protection techniques discussed next are based on [Ellinas98]. They operate on a line- rather than path-protection basis, so that the fundamental unit being protected is a transmission link or switching node rather than an end-to-end connection. The protection methodology is, in a broad sense, a generalization of that used in SPRINGs. Each link carries a protection fiber for each working fiber, and thus the system requires 100% redundancy.[8] Fault recovery decisions are made locally, in a distributed fashion, and independent of the state of activity in the network. The implementation uses simple and reliable protection switches in each network node so that protection is accomplished without significant processing, transmission, or propagation delays.

Automatic protection switching for recovery from link failures in mesh networks is somewhat simpler than recovery from node failures. Thus, the two cases are treated separately, starting with link protection [Ellinas+96]. The discussion is also broken down according to network topologies—planar and nonplanar—because planar topologies are considerably simpler.[9]

8.4.2 Link Failure Restoration

Consider a wavelength routed optical network with a general mesh topology supporting a number of connections with optical paths that are determined by the settings of the optical cross-connects. Typically, each fiber in these networks carries several WDM connections. We assume that a network link consists of a pair of working fibers accompanied by a pair of protection fibers. This is similar to a link in the four-fiber WDM SPRING discussed earlier. Four 2 × 2 optical protection switches terminate the fibers

---

[8] In this section, all network links are assumed to be bidirectional four-fiber links.

[9] Various other special cases, such as Eulerian networks, offer additional possibilities for simplification. The reader is referred to [Ellinas98] for more details.

in each link as in a SPRING. Under fault-free operation, these switches connect the working fibers to the OXCs in the network nodes. If a link fails, the protection switches at the ends of the failed link move to their protection state. This automatically reroutes the affected traffic around the fault over a path consisting of protection fibers. These fibers are organized into *protection cycles*, with a configuration that depends only on the topology of the network and *not* on the current network state (i.e., its active connections). Thus, the protection cycle topology is computed off-line and set up when the network is originally activated.

Because protection switching is performed at individual switching nodes without instructions from a central network controller, the APS process is distributed and autonomous. However, a switching protocol implemented locally at each node is required to coordinate the protection switching process.

Figure 8.17 illustrates recovery from a link failure using protection cycles. A link terminated by four 2×2 protection switches is shown connecting optical switching nodes 1 and 2. The link consists of two working fibers W^+ and W^-, and two protection fibers P^+ and P^-. Before link failure, the switches are set in their normal position so that traffic between the OXCs traverses the link on the working fibers as shown in Figure 8.17(a). The protection fibers P^+ and P^- are interconnected with other protection fibers to form part of the protection cycles C_1 and C_2 respectively. (These cycles are completed on a sequence of other network links not shown in the figure.) When the link fails, the protection switches move to the protection position, shown in Figure 8.17(b). Now all traffic that normally would be routed from node 1 to 2 over the failed link is detoured around the link using protection cycle C_1, and similarly, traffic in the opposite direction is rerouted over C_2.

The key to the successful operation of this protection technique is the creation of a family of protection cycles that covers the network in a particular way. Using this approach, protection against all single link failures (and some sets of simultaneous failures) is possible in all networks with topologies (graphs) that are at least two-edge connected. A ring is a simple example of a two-edge connected graph (see Appendix A). Protection against all link failures is not possible in networks with graphs that are one-edge connected because they possess links called *bridges*. A fault in a bridge results in a disconnected graph, and any connections between the two components of the graph are lost. In [Ellinas+96], a systematic method is proposed for protecting any two-edge-connected network against link failures. The methods proposed also protect networks containing bridges against any link failure except the failure of a bridge. (In the following, whenever we refer to link failure recovery, it is to be understood that bridge failures are excluded.) The method is based on the following:

Proposition 1: Recovery from a single link failure in any optical network with arbitrary topology and bidirectional fiber links can be achieved using APS if a family of directed cycles using the protection fibers can be found so that

1. All protection fibers are used exactly once
2. In any directed cycle, both protection fibers in a pair are not used unless they are in a bridge

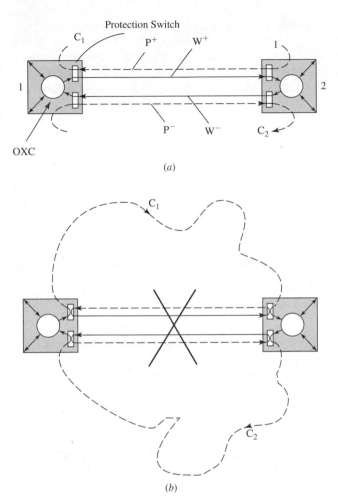

FIGURE 8.17 Rerouting around a failed link.

Figures 8.18 and 8.19 show examples of graphs with directed cycles covering each graph in the manner prescribed in Proposition 1. By interconnecting the protection switches appropriately in the corresponding network, these cycles can be implemented as protection cycles on the corresponding protection fibers. Methods are described next for finding an appropriate set of protection cycles in the planar and nonplanar cases. We then explain how these cycles can be used to protect against link failures using APS.

8.4.2.1 The Planar Case

Figure 8.18 shows a plane graph that is covered by five directed cycles. The figure suggests a systematic procedure for constructing the protection cycles in planar graphs to fulfill the requirements of Proposition 1. The graph is first embedded on the plane to

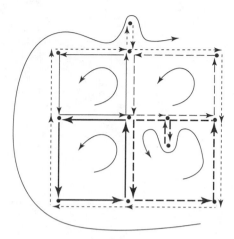

FIGURE 8.18 Directed cycles in a planar graph.

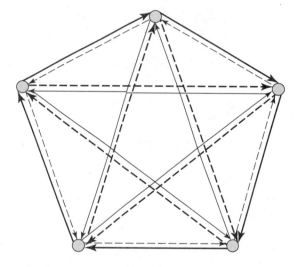

FIGURE 8.19 Directed cycles in a
nonplanar graph: K_5.

form a plane graph that contains $f-1$ inner faces and one outer face, where f is Euler's number (see Appendix A). The protection cycles are then the f face boundaries, with each oriented properly. This result is embodied in the following:

Proposition 2: Every planar graph can be decomposed into a family of directed cycles in which each edge is used exactly twice (once in each direction) and, in each directed cycle that does not include a bridge, an edge is used once at most. In each directed cycle including a bridge, the bridge is used twice (once in each direction) in the same directed cycle.

Algorithms are available [Gibbons85, Even79, Fisher65] that test a graph for planarity in linear time. A planarity testing, face traversal algorithm, which is a variation of

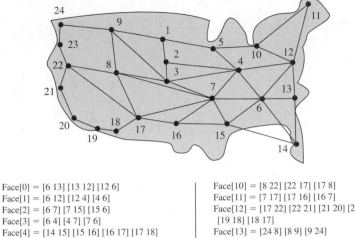

Face[0] = [6 13] [13 12] [12 6]
Face[1] = [6 12] [12 4] [4 6]
Face[2] = [6 7] [7 15] [15 6]
Face[3] = [6 4] [4 7] [7 6]
Face[4] = [14 15] [15 16] [16 17] [17 18]
 [18 19] [19 20] [20 21] [21 22] [22 23]
 [23 24] [24 9] [9 1] [1 5] [5 10] [10 11]
 [11 12] [12 13] [13 14]
Face[5] = [6 15] [15 14] [14 6]
Face[6] = [6 14] [14 13] [13 6]
Face[7] = [8 24] [24 23] [23 22] [22 8]
Face[8] = [15 7] [7 16] [16 15]
Face[9] = [7 8] [8 17] [17 7]

Face[10] = [8 22] [22 17] [17 8]
Face[11] = [7 17] [17 16] [16 7]
Face[12] = [17 22] [22 21] [21 20] [20 19]
 [19 18] [18 17]
Face[13] = [24 8] [8 9] [9 24]
Face[14] = [3 8] [8 7] [7 3]
Face[15] = [12 11] [11 10] [10 12]
Face[16] = [9 8] [8 3] [3 9]
Face[17] = [3 7] [7 4] [4 3]
Face[18] = [2 4] [4 5] [5 1] [1 2]
Face[19] = [5 4] [4 12] [12 10] [10 5]
Face[20] = [3 4] [4 2] [2 3]
Face[21] = [9 3] [3 2] [2 1] [1 9]

Number of faces = 22

FIGURE 8.20 Face traversal for a planar national network.

the path addition algorithm by [Gibbons85], is described in [Ellinas98]. This algorithm embeds the planar graph on the plane and traces the faces in the appropriate directions to create a family of cycles with the characteristics defined in Proposition 1. Figure 8.20 shows an embedding of a planar graph representing a "national network" for the contiguous United States, together with its protection cycles. All cycles except the outer one (face [4]) are traced counterclockwise, on the faces found using the algorithm.

Although the face boundaries of a planar network are a good choice for protection cycles, they are not the only possibility satisfying the conditions of Proposition 1. Other choices are generally possible, leading to families that contain smaller numbers of cycles with longer average lengths.[10] However, many short protection cycles are normally preferred over fewer longer cycles for reasons that become apparent as we proceed.

8.4.2.2 The Nonplanar Case

Extension of Proposition 2 to the nonplanar case requires certain results from graph theory dealing with *cycle double covers* (CDCs). A CDC of a graph *G* is a cycle decom-

---

[10] It can be shown that the face boundaries are the largest possible set of protection cycles.

position of G such that each edge appears in exactly two cycles (see Appendix A). There is a basic conjecture in graph theory on the existence of CDCs: *Every bridgeless graph has a CDC.*

The *CDC problem* has been studied thoroughly by graph theorists [Alspach+85]. However, the conjecture remains an open question, never having been proved or disproved. It is therefore extremely unlikely that a network will ever be discovered that does not possess a CDC!

A CDC is said to be *orientable* when it is possible to choose a circular orientation for each cycle of the CDC in such a way that each edge is taken in opposite directions in its two incident cycles [Alspach+85]. Figure 8.19 shows an orientable CDC consisting of four cycles, shown with solid, bold, dashed, and bold-dashed lines. An orientable CDC is exactly what we seek in constructing our protection cycles: a cycle decomposition such that each edge appears in exactly two protection cycles *and* each edge is used in opposite directions in the two cycles. A number of results in graph theory are strong evidence for the existence of orientable CDCs in any bridgeless graph. They obviously exist in all bridgeless planar networks because the face boundaries constitute an orientable CDC.

A heuristic presented in [Ellinas+97] is designed to find an orientable CDC of any given graph (planar or nonplanar). The heuristic includes modifications of the CDC to accommodate bridges, as indicated in Figure 8.18, and thus finds a family of protection cycles satisfying Proposition 1. It uses a backtrack (branch-and-bound) approach to find the family of protection cycles.

Figure 8.21 shows an orientable CDC for a nonplanar version of the ARPANet. It was found using the heuristic in [Ellinas+97]. When applied to planar graphs, this heuristic generally *does not* choose the face boundaries as protection cycles, and typically finds a covering with less than the maximum possible number of cycles (Euler's number). However, the number of cycles is usually close to the maximum, indicating that the cycles obtained are relatively short.

8.4.2.3 Implementation of APS for Link Failures Using Protection Cycles

Having shown how to determine a family of protection cycles with the characteristics defined in Proposition 1, we shall now explain how these cycles can be used to protect a network with an arbitrary topology against a single link failure.

As shown in Figure 8.22(a), the four fibers in each link are terminated by four 2×2 optical protection switches with switching speeds that are assumed to be on the order of tens of milliseconds, which is typical of optomechanical switches. In Figure 8.22(a) the switches are shown in their *normal* (or default) *position*, whereas in Figure 8.22(b) they are in their *protection position*, sealing off the failed link.

The designation of switch ports is indicated in Figure 8.22(c). Each switch has a working fiber input and output (ports p_w^i and p_w^o respectively), and a protection fiber input and output (ports p_p^i and p_p^o respectively). Within each node, the working ports are connected to the optical cross-connect as shown in the figure. The protection ports of the protection switches within each node are connected by intranodal fibers in

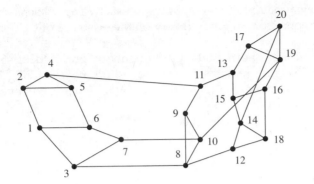

Cycle[0] = [5 6] [6 1] [1 2] [2 5]
Cycle[1] = [16 15] [15 14] [14 18] [18 16]
Cycle[2] = [9 10] [10 8] [8 12] [12 18] [18 14] [14 20]
[20 19] [19 10] [10 7] [7 6] [6 5] [5 4] [4 11] [11 9]
Cycle[3] = [5 2] [2 4] [4 5]
Cycle[4] = [8 9] [9 11] [11 13] [13 17] [17 20] [20 14]
[14 12] [12 8]

Cycle[5] = [13 15] [15 16] [16 19] [19 17] [17 13]
Cycle[6] = [3 1] [1 6] [6 7] [7 3]
Cycle[7] = [2 1] [1 3] [3 8] [8 10] [10 19] [19 16]
[16 18] [18 12] [12 14] [14 15] [15 13] [13 11]
[11 4] [4 2]
Cycle[8] = [17 19] [19 20] [20 17]
Cycle[9] = [7 10] [10 9] [9 8] [8 3] [3 7]

Number of cycles = 10

FIGURE 8.21   Orientable CDC of the ARPANet.

a way that creates the family of protection cycles described in Proposition 1. These intranodal connections are fixed when the network is set up, and remain unchanged thereafter, unless there is a permanent change in the network topology. Figure 8.23 illustrates the intranodal connections between protection switches in a seven-node planar network. Note that with the switches in their default positions, all protection fibers are interconnected into protection cycles (shown as dashed lines) coinciding with the face boundaries.

A protocol that can be used to control the settings of the protection switches uses the following commands to achieve signal restoration after a fiber link failure. These commands are similar to the APS commands used for unidirectional and bidirectional SONET rings [Bell91]:

- *Clear:* Clears all previous commands.
- *Lockout protection:* Prevents switching from working fiber to protection fiber.
- *Switch to protection:* Switches from normal to protection position.

In a link failure both the working and protection fibers normally fail in both directions. The objective of the APS process in this case is to restore the connections passing through the failed fiber link as rapidly as possible when a failure is detected.[11] This

---

[11] Various methods of detecting link failures are possible at both the optical and logical levels [Ellinas98].

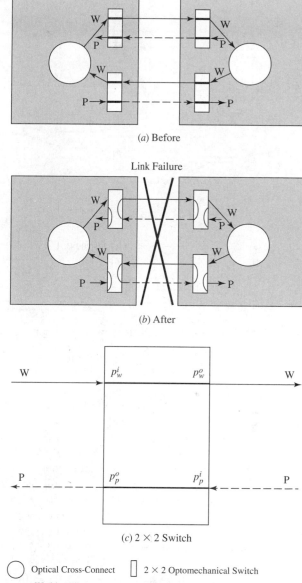

(a) Before

Link Failure

(b) After

(c) 2 × 2 Switch

FIGURE 8.22 Switching nodes before and after link failure.

○ Optical Cross-Connect   ▯ 2 × 2 Optomechanical Switch
— Working Fiber   − − − Protection Fiber

requires routing the signals from the node at one side of the failed link to the node at the other side using protection fibers on other healthy links. Note that the APS process restores all connections using the failed link in both directions.

As soon as the link fails, the failure is detected in the switching nodes on both sides of the failed link. The protection switches on this link then switch to their protection

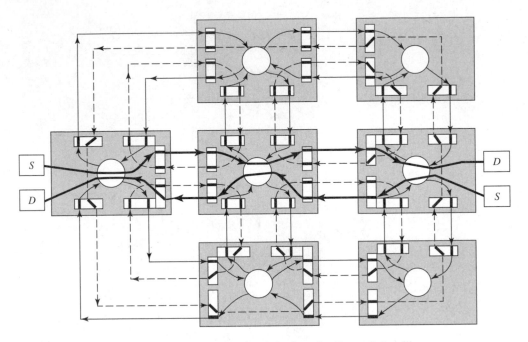

FIGURE 8.23 Seven-node planar network with default protection switch settings.

position. All other protection switches in the network remain in their default position and the optical cross-connects remain in their current states. After the failure is restored, a clear command is issued for the protection switches involved that restores them to their default state.

Figure 8.24 illustrates the protection scenario, showing the protection switch settings in the network of Figure 8.23 after a failure in the indicated link. A pair of bidirectional connections from S to D is depicted (with heavy solid lines) in Figure 8.23. After the failure, the path followed by the connections follows working fibers up to the protection switches, which have sealed off the failed link. The connections then switch to protection fibers, following the dashed, bold lines until they reach the other side of the failed link. There they switch back to the working fibers and continue on the same path that they used before the link failure. Note that the dashed segments of the routes (on the protection fibers) are carried on the two protection cycles that would normally traverse the failed link.

As illustrated in Figure 8.24, the path followed by each rerouted connection occupies the full length of a protection cycle less the one hop on the failed link. As a consequence, the overall physical path length for a signal using a protection cycle is increased by the length of the cycle less twice the length of the failed link. (This is generally a net length increase.) To maintain acceptable signal quality after a failure, this

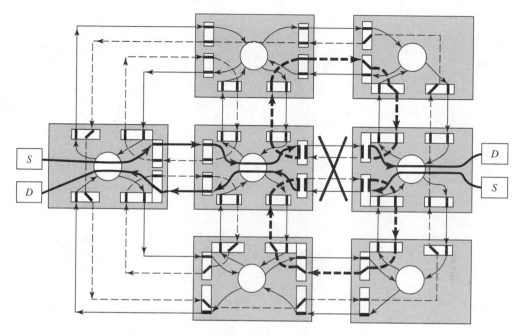

FIGURE 8.24   Seven-node planar network after a link failure.

path length increment should be kept small. Hence it is desirable to choose protection cycle families that consist of many short cycles rather than a few long ones.[12]

If multiple link failures occur with all failed links on distinct protection cycles, all failures can be restored. Figure 8.25 shows the recovery from two link failures for the seven-node network carrying unidirectional connections $S1$–$D1$ and $S2$–$D2$.[13]

8.4.2.4 Bounds on the Number of Restorable Link Failures

As mentioned earlier, the maximum number of protection cycles for a planar graph is the number of faces, f. When a link fails in a bridgeless network, its rerouted traffic uses two protection cycles. If another link in either of these protection cycles fails, recovery from both failures is not possible. Therefore, if all connections are bidirectional, the maximum possible number of simultaneous link failure recoveries

---

[12] For example, if the network happens to be Eulerian, a possible choice for protection cycles would be a double-traced Eulerian trail (see Section 6.3.5), but this consists of two very long cycles—a poor choice.

[13] APS covers the reverse connections as well, but they have been omitted so as not to clutter the figure.

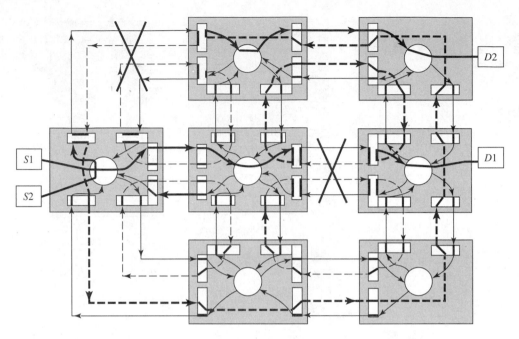

FIGURE 8.25 Seven-node network after two link failures.

in a bridgeless network is

$$R^b_{\max} = \left\lfloor \frac{f}{2} \right\rfloor \tag{8.1}$$

In the worst case (e.g., a bidirectional ring, which only has two cycles) only one fault can be restored. If every connection in the network is unidirectional, then the maximum possible number of link failure recoveries is

$$R^u_{\max} = f - 1 \tag{8.2}$$

Again, in the worst case ($f = 2$) only one fault can be restored.

For a graph (either planar or nonplanar) covered by a family of S protection cycles the same formulas apply, with the number S replacing Euler's number. In the case of planar networks, $S \leq f$, and thus there is no advantage from the point of view of link failure recovery in choosing protection cycles other than the face boundaries.

8.4.3 Node Failure Restoration

As we shall see, the basic concept of protection cycles can be extended to protect against switching node failure. However, it turns out that node failure restoration is a more complex issue than link failure restoration. In particular, the required protection switch hardware differs depending on the arrangement of the families of protection cycles, which in turn depends on the network topology. Planar topologies require 2×3 protection switches for link and node restoration rather than the 2×2 devices used for link restoration only. In nonplanar networks, 2×5 switches are required.

As in the previous section, it is assumed here that each link consists of a pair of working fibers and a pair of protection fibers, terminated by four protection switches that are interposed between the fiber link and the optical cross-connects. We also assume that the graph of the network is bridgeless and at least two-vertex connected. (If it is not two-vertex connected, failure of a single node may cut the network in half.) A node failure is interpreted here as failure of the OXC, leaving the protection switches and their interconnections intact.[14] (Because the OXC is a fairly complex subsystem, this is the most likely form of failure.)

Using the protection techniques described next, when an OXC fails, one of the active connections that use the failed OXC (called the *priority connection*) is restored immediately through the action of the protection switches and fibers. (Any connection traversing the switch can be designated as the priority connection.) For planar topologies this is the only connection that can be restored. The rest of the connections through that node must be restored using other, slower restoration techniques implemented in the logical (e.g., SONET) layer. For nonplanar topologies, restoration of more than one connection through the failed cross-connect node may be possible, but this requires more complex (2×5) protection switches. We focus here on the planar case, with a brief exposition of the nonplanar case at the end of the section. (See [Ellinas98] for a complete description of node failure restoration in nonplanar networks.)

8.4.3.1 Planar Networks

In a planar network, one active bidirectional connection passing through each node is designated as a priority connection, to be protected in case that node fails. Its two links are designated as priority links. Other connections (including those terminating on the failed node) are not restored. The protection methodology is based on a choice of protection cycles corresponding to the face boundaries of the network [Ellinas+99].

The arrangement of the protection switches in a typical node is shown in Figure 8.26. Note that each link is terminated by a 2×3 and a 3×2 protection switch, shown in their normal (default) positions in the figure. As shown in Figure 8.27(a), a 2×3 protection switch has working fiber input and output (ports p_w^i and p_w^o respectively), a protection fiber input (port p_p^i), and two protection fiber outputs (ports $p_{p_1}^o$ and $p_{p_2}^o$). A 3×2 protection switch has a working fiber input and output (ports p_w^i and p_w^o respectively), a protection fiber output (port p_p^o), and two protection fiber inputs (ports $p_{p_1}^i$ and $p_{p_2}^i$). Each switch has three states: default, priority link protection (P1), and node protection (P2).

---

[14] The protection procedures described here can, however, be extended to the case in which the node failure includes the failure of the protection switches as well [Ellinas98].

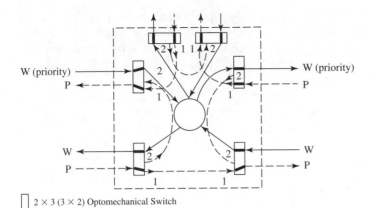

□ 2 × 3 (3 × 2) Optomechanical Switch

FIGURE 8.26 Switching node before an optical switch failure.

The default state appears in Figure 8.27(a), in which working port input p_w^i is connected to working port output p_w^o, and protection port p_p (input/output) is connected to port p_{p_1} (output/input). As shown in Figure 8.26, input/output port p_{p_1} of each protection switch is used for intranodal connection with a p_{p_1} port on another switch. With the switches in their default states, it is these connections that configure the protection fibers into a family of protection cycles in exactly the same way as explained previously for link protection.

The priority link protection state P1 is illustrated in Figure 8.27(b). In the event of a *node* failure, this state is used for the four protection switches associated with the two priority links (see links 1 and 2 in Figure 8.28). Note that in state P1, the protection switch seals off its link from the OXC. In the case of a node failure this causes the signal entering the node on a priority link (say link 1 in Figure 8.28) to double back on its outbound protection fiber. After detouring through a sequence of other protection fibers, that signal reappears on the inbound protection fiber of the other priority link (link 2 in this case), and this time it switches back to the working fiber of that link. This completes the detour around the failed node. A similar process takes place for the reverse priority connection. Switching the signal from the working to the protection fiber for the links that enter and leave the failed node ensures that the signals never enter the failed optical switch. The signals circumvent the failed node and, most importantly, they resume the same path as before on the working fiber leaving the failed node. Thus, none of the optical cross-connects have to be reset.

In the event of a *link* failure, state P1 is used for the switches at each end of the failed link. Now it is the healthy node that is sealed off from the failed link. All other protection switches at the nodes remain in their default positions. This configuration coincides with the link protection state described in Section 8.4.2, using 2 × 2 switches. In fact, if the protection ports p_{p_2} are left unused on the 2 × 3 and 3 × 2 switches, the system retains link protection functionality.

The node protection state P2 appears in Figure 8.27(c). In the event of a node failure, protection switches terminating all *nonpriority* links at that node are put in state P2.

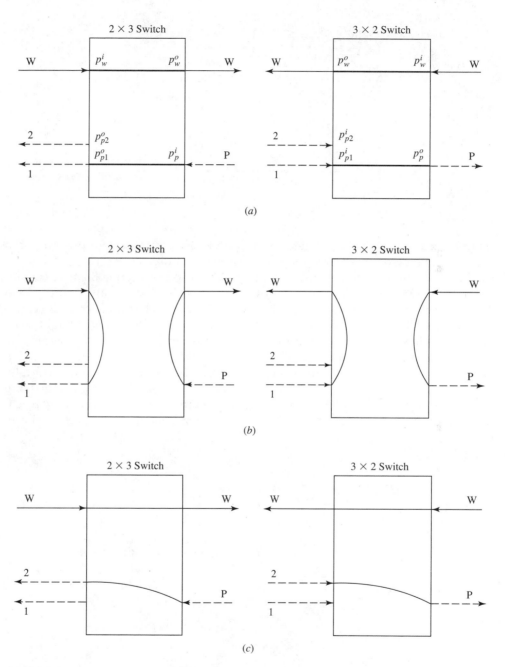

FIGURE 8.27 2×3 and 3×2 Protection switches.

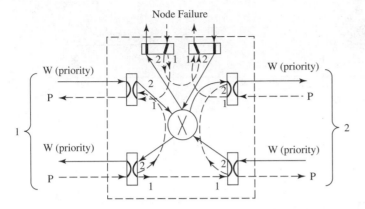

FIGURE 8.28 Switching node after an optical switch failure.

As indicated in Figure 8.28, in state P2 the intranodal connections for the protection ports p_{p_2} tie together the protection fiber pair on their link.

The combined function of the protection switches and protection fibers surrounding a failed OXC is illustrated in Figure 8.29. The priority links are 1 and m, and $C_1, C_2, \ldots, C_\Delta$ represent protection cycles (composed of protection fibers only) corresponding to all face boundaries including the failed node. (One of them might be an outer face boundary.) The interconnections among the fibers are shown in Figure 8.29 as they would be in the case of an optical switch failure. The effect of the protection switch connections is to break each protection cycle at the failed node and to concatenate the broken cycles into two paths joining pairs of working fibers. Signals arriving on inbound working fiber W_1^+ detour through one protection path, eventually reaching outbound working fiber W_m^-. A similar connection is made in the reverse priority direction.

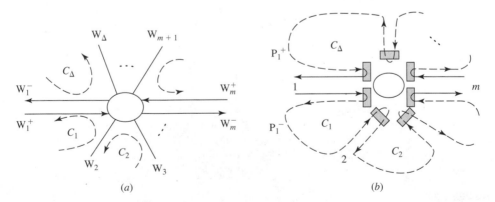

FIGURE 8.29 Node failure restoration in a network with a planar topology.

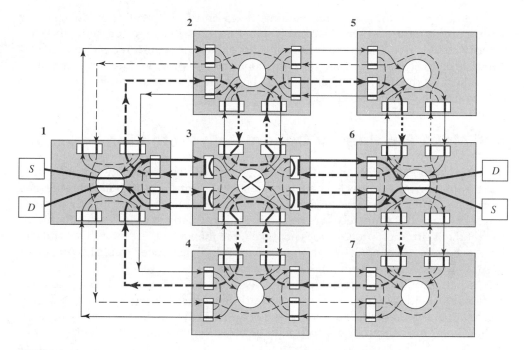

FIGURE 8.30 Seven-node network after a single switching node failure.

An example of rerouting a priority connection around a node failure is shown in Figure 8.30, in which the node labeled X has failed. The protection switches in the failed switching node, associated with the priority *S–D* connection, switch to state P1, and the others in the node switch to P2. The bold solid and dashed lines show the new path the signals follow from *S* to *D*. The protection cycle returns to and leaves the failed node on concatenated protection cycles without ever entering the optical cross-connect. Any other connections entering the failed node enter the failed OXC and are lost momentarily.[15] In this case, higher layer (e.g., SONET) fault recovery procedures would normally be invoked to restore them.

8.4.3.2 Nonplanar Networks

Because the node protection methodology for planar networks is based on using face boundaries as protection cycles, it fails in nonplanar networks or in planar networks in which a different set of protection cycles is chosen.

To deal with the nonplanar case, in which an arbitrary orientable CDC is used for the protection cycles, a more complex interconnection of protection cycles is required

---

[15] Trying to restore more than one bidirectional connection at the same time results in the loss of all connections.

in case of node failure, and this requires 2×5 and 5×2 protection switches. In return for this increased switch size, it is sometimes possible to restore more than one priority connection. The number of connections that can be restored simultaneously depends on the connections active on the node and any other restoration that may be in progress on the network when the node failure occurs. For a complete description of the nonplanar case, see [Ellinas98].

8.5 Mesh Topologies: Optical Path Protection

In optical path protection an end-to-end alternate path is set up between the source and destination of each affected path in the case of a failure. The original (working) and secondary (protection) paths must be edge– or node–disjoint to guarantee successful single link or node failure recovery respectively. These paths should be predetermined so that the restoration process does not take more than a few tens of milliseconds for low-speed (optomechanical) protection switches. If higher speed optical switches are used, even faster restoration times can be achieved.

The path protection approach presented earlier for $(1 + 1)$ and (1:1) point-to-point systems is extended in [Finn+97] and [Medard+99] to include networks with arbitrary mesh topologies. The assumption in this work is that when a link fails, both directions of that link fail. The proposed technique is based on creating redundant trees that provide two-edge or two-node connectivity to all other nodes. Assuming bidirectional connections, two directed spanning trees (a working and a protection tree) are found for every node, such that a failure does not affect the traffic upstream of that failure on the working tree, whereas the traffic downstream from that failure now uses the protection tree. Figure 8.31 shows an example of such a tree arrangement, protecting the leftmost node in the network.

Algorithms for both edge- and node-redundant cases have been developed [Medard+98]. It was shown that for any node- or edge-redundant graph, two directed trees can be found so that if any node or link fails, each node is connected by at least one of the trees.

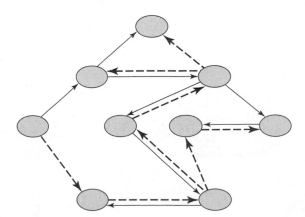

FIGURE 8.31 Spanning trees used in optical path protection.

8.6 Problems

1. A network is represented by a seven-vertex graph with the following edges: $(1,3)$, $(1,4)$, $(1,5)$, $(1,6)$, $(2,4)$, $(2,5)$, $(2,7)$, $(3,5)$, $(3,6)$, $(3,7)$, $(4,6)$, $(4,7)$, $(5,7)$, and $(6,7)$. Is it planar or nonplanar? If it is planar, embed it in the plane and obtain the protection cycles for the network as face boundaries. If it is nonplanar, find an orientable CDC.

2. A number of proposed failure protection schemes are based on the use of protection cycles using redundant protection fibers. What are some of the physical problems that can arise in these protection cycles if optical amplifiers are present in the protection fibers? Propose methods of eliminating these problems.

3. The fault protection/restoration schemes presented in this chapter require a system that detects the failures and responds appropriately.

   (a) Present a block diagram of a detection and control system that might be employed at the end of each fiber link in a purely optical network.

   (b) What are some of the detection problems that might be encountered in such a network and what are some possible solutions? (Consider the possibility of fiber amplifiers in the links.)

   (c) How can the system be configured so that both sides of a link react properly to a failure in case of a partial cable cut (e.g., only one working fiber, one protection fiber, or one working/protection fiber pair is cut).

4. The protection/restoration schemes presented in the latter part of this chapter are used for the survivability of the WDM transport layer. Assuming that the WDM layer lies below a SONET layer, which in turn lies below an ATM layer (i.e., this is an ATM/SONET/WDM architecture), and that all three technologies have their own protection/restoration schemes, certain interoperability problems may arise. Describe some of these problems and outline possible solutions.

5. A network is represented by a seven-vertex graph with edges $(1,2)$, $(1,3)$, $(1,4)$, $(1,5)$, $(1,6)$, $(2,3)$, $(3,4)$, $(4,5)$, $(5,6)$, $(6,7)$, and $(7,2)$. All links are bidirectional.

   (a) How many simultaneous link failures can be protected given the scheme of Section 8.4.2? (Consider the two cases of bidirectional and unidirectional connections.)

   (b) Give an example of multiple link failures in a case in which several unidirectional connections are active, and indicate the link failures and connections restored.

   (c) Repeat the previous part for bidirectional connections.

6. Consider a network represented by an eleven-vertex graph with edges $(1,2)$, $(1,3)$, $(1,5)$, $(1,7)$, $(2,3)$, $(2,4)$, $(2,8)$, $(3,4)$, $(3,5)$, $(3,6)$, $(4,7)$, $(4,8)$, $(4,11)$, $(5,6)$, $(5,7)$, $(6,8)$, $(6,9)$, $(7,9)$, $(7,10)$, $(8,9)$, $(8,11)$, $(9,10)$, $(9,11)$, and $(10,11)$. All links are bidirectional.

   (a) Assume that the ring cover method of Section 8.2.4.1 is used to obtain a family of protection cycles. Find a set of fundamental cycles and calculate the number of extra protection fibers required so the network can survive any single link failure.

   (b) Another method of finding a ring cover is by first obtaining a planar subgraph for the nonplanar graph. Describe this method and obtain the required ring cover as well as the number of extra protection fibers required for the network.

7. When an optical cross-connect fails in a multiwavelength network and shared protection is used to restore a priority connection using the methodology of Section 8.4.3, other connections passing through the failed node may be misdirected. Problems arise because the protection procedures do not distinguish between individual wavelengths on a fiber. There are two cases that arise—"unwanted" and "replacement" wavelengths—as illustrated in the following examples, based on Figure 8.30.

   (a) *Unwanted wavelength:* Suppose the following two unidirectional connections are active in the network: the priority connection (A, A') on path 1–3–6 using λ_1, and a nonpriority connection (B, B') on path 4–1–3–2 using λ_2. If node 3 fails, the priority connection is restored by rerouting over a protection cycle. During the process, the unwanted wavelength λ_2 supporting (B, B') is carried along with λ_1, appearing on link (3, 6) when it doesn't belong there.

   (b) *Replacement wavelength:* In the previous scenario, suppose a third connection, (C, C'), is added on path 4–3–6–7, reusing λ_2. Now when the failure of node 3 is restored, the signal from source C is blocked at node 3 and the signal from source B appears erroneously on link (3, 6), *replacing* the signal on the same wavelength from source C. It is routed through node 6 to destination C', creating the wrong connection, (B, C').

   Propose methods for solving these wavelength misdirection problems. (Note that one possibility is to make use of higher layers in the network architecture.)

8. A ten-node network is fully connected, with each of its links bidirectional. Find two spanning trees with the characteristics defined in Section 8.5 so that they can always protect node 1 of the network.

8.7 Bibliography

[Alspach+85] B. R. Alspach and C. D. Godsil. *Cycles in Graphs. Annals of Discrete Mathematics*, Vol. 115. Amsterdam: Elsevier Science Publishers B.V., 1985.

[ANSI88] American National Standards Institute. T1.105/1988. American Standard for Telecommunications—Digital Hierarchy—Optical Interface Rates and Formats Specification, 1988.

[Ayanoglu+96] E. Ayanoglu and R. D. Gitlin. Broadband network restoration. *IEEE Communications Mag.*, 34(7):110–119, 1996.

[Bala96] K. Bala. Multiwavelength optical network architecture. In *Proc. Seventh Workshop on Very High Speed Networks*, Baltimore, July 1996.

[Bala+96] K. Bala and C. A. Brackett. Cycles in wavelength routed optical networks. *IEEE/OSA J. Lightwave Technology*, 14(7):1585–1594, 1996.

[BeHannesey98] M. BeHannesey. Ring interworking and BLSR. In *Proc. National Fiber Optic Engineers Conf.*, Orlando, September 1998.

[Bell90] Bell Communications Research. *Automatic Protection Switching for SONET*. Technical Report No. SR-NWT-001756, October 1990.

[Bell91] Bell Communications Research. *Synchronous Optical Network (SONET) Transport Systems: Common Generic Criteria*. Technical Report No. TR-NWT-000253, December 1991.

[Bell93] Bell Communications Research. *Transport Systems: Generic Requirements*. Technical Report No. TR-NWT-000499, December 1993.

[Bell94a] Bell Communications Research. *SONET Dual-Fed Unidirectional Path-Switched Ring (UPSR) Equipment Generic Criteria.* Technical Report No. GR-1400-CORE, March 1994.

[Bell94b] Bell Communications Research. *SONET Ring Interworking Issues and Solutions.* Technical Report No. SR-3039, June 1994.

[Bell95] Bell Communications Research. *SONET Logical Ring Services—Network Element and Operations System Impacts.* Technical Report No. SR-3487, April 1995.

[Bicknell+93] J. Bicknell, C. E. Chow, and S. Syed. Performance analysis of fast distributed network restoration algorithms. In *Proc. IEEE Globecom.*, pp. 1596–1600, Houston, November 1993.

[Bonenfant+94] P. A. Bonenfant and C.M.C. Davenport. SONET optical layer protection switching. Bell Communications Research, Technical Report No. TM-24609, December 1994.

[Chao+91] C-W. Chao, P. M. Dollard, J. E. Weythman, et al. FASTAR—A robust system for fast DS3 restoration. In *Proc. IEEE Globecom.*, pp. 1396–1400, Phoenix, December 1991.

[Chow+92] C-H.E. Chow, S. McCaughey, and S. Syed. RREACT: A distributed protocol for rapid restoration of active communication trunks. UCCS, Technical Report No. EAS-CS-92-18, 1992.

[Chujo+90] T. Chujo, H. Komine, K. Miyazaki, et al. The design and simulation of an intelligent transport network with distributed control. In *Proc. Network Operations Management Symposium*, pp. 927–937. San Diego, February 1990.

[Coan+91] B. Coan, W. E. Leland, M. P. Vecchi, et al. Using distributed topology update and preplanned configurations to achieve trunk network survivability. *IEEE Trans. Reliability*, 40(4):404–416, 1991.

[Ellinas+96] G. Ellinas and T. E. Stern. Automatic protection switching for link failures in optical networks with bi-directional links. In *Proc. IEEE Globecom.*, London, November 1996.

[Ellinas+97] G. Ellinas, A. Hailemariam, and T. E. Stern. Creation of a family of cycles corresponding to the orientable cycle double cover. New York: Center for Telecommunications Research, Columbia University, Technical Report No. CU/CTR/TR 474-97-08, 1997.

[Ellinas98] G. Ellinas. *Fault Restoration in Optical Networks: General Methodology and Implementation.* PhD thesis. New York: Columbia University, 1998.

[Ellinas+99] G. Ellinas, A. Hailemariam, and T. E. Stern. Protection of a priority connection from an optical switch failure in mesh networks with planar topologies. In *Proc. IEEE/OSA Optical Fiber Commun. Conf.*, San Diego, February 1999.

[Elrefaie92] A. F. Elrefaie. Self-healing WDM ring networks with an all-optical protection path. In *Proc. IEEE/OSA Optical Fiber Commun. Conf.* (Paper ThL3), pp. 255–256, February 1992.

[Ester94] G. W. Ester. Can you talk to your SONET neighbor? *Telephony Mag.*, November, 1994.

[Even79] S. Even. *Graph Algorithms.* Rockville, MD: Computer Science Press, 1979.

[Finn+97] S. G. Finn, M. M. Medard, and R. A. Barry. A novel approach to automatic protection switching using trees. In *Proc. IEEE Int'l Conf. Commun.*, pp. 272–276, Montreal, June 1997.

[Fisher65] G. Fisher. *Computer Identification and Extraction of Planar Graphs.* PhD thesis. New York: Department of Electrical Engineering, Columbia University, 1965.

[Gardner+94] L. M. Gardner, M. Heydari, J. Shah, et al. Techniques for finding ring covers in survivable networks. In *Proc. IEEE Globecom.*, pp. 1862–1866, San Francisco, 1994.

[Gardner+95] L. M. Gardner, I. H. Sudborough, and I. G. Tollis. NetSolver: A software tool for the design of survivable networks. In *Proc. IEEE Globecom.*, pp. 926–930, Singapore, 1995.

[Gibbons85] A. Gibbons. *Algorithmic Graph Theory.* Cambridge: Cambridge University Press, 1985.

[Grover87] W. D. Grover. The SelfHealing network. In *Proc. IEEE Globecom.*, pp. 28.2.1–28.2.6, Tokyo, November 1987.

[Grover89] W. D. Grover. *SelfHealing Networks: A Distributed Algorithm for k-Shortest Link-Disjoint Paths in a Multi-Graph with Applications in Real-Time Network Restoration*. PhD thesis. Alberta: The University of Alberta, 1989.

[Grover+90] W. D. Grover, B. D. Venables, J. H. Sandham, and A. F. Milne. Performance studies of a SelfHealing network protocol in Telecom Canada long haul networks. In *Proc. IEEE Globecom.*, pp. 453–458, San Diego, December 1990.

[Grover+91] W. D. Grover, T. D. Bilodeau, and B. D. Venables. Near optimal spare capacity planning in a mesh restorable network. In *Proc. IEEE Globecom.*, pp. 2007–2012, Phoenix, December 1991.

[Grover92] W. D. Grover. Case studies of survivable ring, mesh and mesh-arc hybrid networks. In *Proc. IEEE Globecom.*, pp. 633–638, Orlando, December 1992.

[Hall+89] R. D. Hall and S. Whitt. Protection of SONET based networks. In *Proc. IEEE Globecom.*, pp. 821–825, November 1989.

[Harman+94] W. Harman, H. Kobrinski, and R. Kutz. *Interworking among Transport Network Architectures.* Bell Communications Research, Technical Report No. TM-24124, June 1994.

[Iness+96] J. Iness, B. Ramamurthy, B. Mukherjee, and K. Bala. Elimination of all-optical cycles in wavelength-routed optical networks. *IEEE/OSA J. Lightwave Technology*, 14(6):1207–1217, 1996.

[Iraschko+96] R. R. Iraschko, M. H. MacGregor, and W. D. Grover. Optimal capacity placement for path restoration in mesh survivable networks. In *Proc. IEEE Int'l Conf. Commun.*, pp. 1568–1574, Dallas, June 1996.

[Kajiyama+92] Y. Kajiyama, N. Tokura, and K. Kikuchi. ATM self-healing ring. In *Proc. IEEE Globecom.*, pp. 639–643, Orlando, December 1992.

[Kajiyama+94] Y. Kajiyama, N. Tokura, and K. Kikuchi. An ATM VP-based self-healing ring. *IEEE J. Select. Areas Commun.*, 12(1):171–178, 1994.

[Kawamura+94] R. Kawamura, K. Sato, and I. Tokizawa. Self-healing ATM networks based on virtual path concept. *IEEE J. Select. Areas Commun.*, 12(1):120–127, 1994.

[Kawamura+95] R. Kawamura and I. Tokizawa. Self-healing virtual path architecture in ATM networks. *IEEE Communications Mag.*, 33(9):72–79, 1995.

[Komine+90] H. Komine, T. Chujo, T. Ogura, et al. A distributed restoration algorithm for multiple-link and node failures of transport networks. In *Proc. IEEE Globecom.*, pp. 459–463, San Diego, December 1990.

[Kuhn97] D. R. Kuhn. Sources of failure in the public switched telephone network. *IEEE Computer Mag.*, April:31–36, 1997.

[Manchester+96] J. Manchester and P. Bonenfant. Fiber optic network survivability: SONET/ optical protection layer interworking. In *Proc. NFOEC*, Denver, September 1996.

[May+91] G. May and D. Jammu. A distributed architecture for survivable SONET transport networks. In *Proc. IEEE Globecom.*, pp. 2013–2017, Phoenix, December 1991.

[May+95] K. P. May, P. Semal, Y. Du, and C. Herrmann. A fast restoration system for ATM-ring-based LANs. *IEEE Communications Mag.*, 33(9):90–99, 1995.

[Medard+99] M. Medard, S. G. Finn, R. G. Gallager, and R. A. Barry. Redundant trees for automatic protection switching in arbitrary node-redundant or edge-redundant graphs. *IEEE/ACM Trans. Networking* (to appear), 1999.

[Nederlof+95] L. Nederlof, K. Struyve, C. O'Shea, et al. End-to-end survivable broadband networks. *IEEE Communications Mag.*, 33(9):63–71, 1995.

[Sakauchi+90] H. Sakauchi, Y. Nishimura, and S. Hasegawa. A self-healing network with an economical spare-channel assignment. In *Proc. IEEE Globecom.*, pp. 438–443, San Diego, December 1990.

[Sato+90] K. Sato, H. Hadama, and I. Tokizawa. Network reliability enhancement with virtual path strategy. In *Proc. IEEE Globecom.*, pp. 464–469, San Diego, December 1990.

[Shyur+94] C-C. Shyur, Y-M. Wu, and C-H. Chen. The capacity comparison and cost analyses for SONET self-healing ring networks. *IEICE Trans. Commun.*, E77-B(2):218–225, 1994.

[Siller+96] C. A. Siller Jr. and M. Shafi. *SONET and SDH—A Sourcebook of Synchronous Networking*. New York: IEEE Press, 1996.

[Slevinsky+93] J. B. Slevinsky, W. D. Grover, and M. H. MacGregor. An algorithm for survivable network design employing multiple self-healing rings. In *Proc. IEEE Globecom.*, pp. 1568–1573, November 1993.

[Sosnosky+91] J. Sosnosky, T-H. Wu, and D. L. Alt. A study of economics, operations and applications of SONET self-healing ring architectures. In *Proc. IEEE Globecom.*, pp. 2018–2024, Phoenix, December 1991.

[Tsai+90] E. I. Tsai, B. A. Coan, M. Kerner, and M. P. Vecchi. A comparison of strategies for survivable network design: Reconfigurable and conventional approaches. In *Proc. IEEE Globecom.*, pp. 49–55, San Diego, December 1990.

[Veitch+96] P. Veitch, I. Hawker, and G. Smith. Administration of restorable virtual path mesh networks. *IEEE Communications Mag.*, 34(12):96–101, 1996.

[Wasem91a] O. J. Wasem. An algorithm for designing rings for survivable fiber networks. *IEEE Trans. Reliability*, 40(4):428–432, 1991.

[Wasem91b] O. J. Wasem. Optimal topologies for survivable fiber optic networks using SONET self-healing rings. In *Proc. IEEE Globecom.*, pp. 2032–2038, Phoenix, December 1991.

[Wasem+92] O. Wasem, R. H. Cardwell, and T-H. Wu. Software for designing survivable SONET networks using self-healing rings. In *Proc. IEEE Int'l Conf. Commun.*, pp. 425–431, Chicago, June 1992.

[Wrobel90] L. A. Wrobel. *Disaster Recovery Planning for Telecommunications*. Norwood MA: Artech House, 1990.

[Wu+89] T-H. Wu, D. J. Kolar, and R. H. Cardwell. High-speed self-healing ring architectures for future interoffice networks. In *Proc. IEEE Globecom.*, pp. 801–807, November 1989.

[Wu+90] T-H. Wu and R. C. Lau. A class of self-healing ring architectures for SONET network applications. In *Proc. IEEE Globecom.*, pp. 444–451, San Diego, December 1990.

[Wu92] T-H. Wu. *Fiber Network Service Survivability*. Norwood, MA: Artech House, 1992.

[Xin+98] W. Xin, et al. Performance and operation of WDM layer automatic protection switching in a 1177 km reconfigurable multiwavelength ring network. In *Proc. IEEE/OSA Optical Fiber Commun. Conf.* (Paper PD25), San Jose, February 1998.

[Yang+88] C. H. Yang and S. Hasegawa. FITNESS: Failure immunization technology for network service survivability. In *Proc. IEEE Globecom.*, pp. 1549–1554, Hollywood, FL, November 1988.

Current Trends in Multiwavelength Optical Networking

Despite the fact that optical fiber communications has been an active area of research since the early 1970s, and optical transmission facilities have been widely deployed since the 1980s, serious activity in optical networking did not reach beyond the laboratory until the 1990s. It was in the early 1990s that a number of ambitious optical network testbed projects were initiated in the United States, Europe, and Japan. Although the testbeds were largely government-financed, they planted the seeds for subsequent commercial developments, many of which were spin-offs of the testbed activities. The commercial ventures benefitted from the knowledge accumulated from the testbeds as well as from the burgeoning demand worldwide for bandwidth. In this chapter we give an overview of developments in these two areas. The commercial activity is discussed first, after which we describe some of the major testbed projects in the United States and Europe.

9.1 Business Drivers for WDM Networks

Traffic growth in the Internet and other new data communications services and deregulation of the telecommunications industry have resulted in new business opportunities and challenges for telecommunications network operators. The number of Internet hosts grew 100-fold between 1990 and 1998 and the resulting demand is straining the capacity of the telecommunications network infrastructure. Traditionally, the markets of the inter-exchange carriers (IXCs) and the local exchange carriers (LECs) in the United States were separated by regulatory boundaries. The LECs (e.g., regional Bell operating companies [RBOCs] and GTE) were not allowed into the IXC (e.g., AT&T, MCI) market and the IXCs were not allowed to offer local services. Deregulation across the industry is currently resulting in the destruction of these boundaries, with each carrier trying to provide end-to-end network services under a single brand name. This implies that the IXCs and the LECs will build an infrastructure to compete effectively in each other's territories.

The increased demand and the competitive pressures of deregulation are driving the need for low-cost increased bandwidth. WDM is a proven method of increasing bandwidth by a factor of 30 at 50% of the cost of alternate methods. These cost advantages are particularly significant in cases in which new fiber builds are avoided by using WDM equipment. In particular, WDM optical networks allow for the following:

1. Duct, fiber, cable exhaust relief

2. Reduction in the number of regenerators

3. Equipment savings with advanced architectures

4. Reduced network deployment cost achieved by introducing flexibility and configurability into the optical layer of the network

Network operators have installed point-to-point WDM systems aggressively. Several long-haul carriers along with a few local exchange network operators have upgraded their fiber routes to WDM. The next step is the introduction of optical networking elements to create flexible networks that enable dynamic wavelength provisioning and protection. In the sections that follow, we examine the current evolutionary trends in optical networks from point-to-point installations to the next generation rings and meshes.

9.2　Point-to-Point WDM Systems

Point-to-point WDM systems have been deployed in large volumes by several carriers to increase the capacity of their existing fiber plant without costly installation of new fibers. The capacity of point-to-point WDM systems is increasing at a rapid pace. Whereas the first systems were deployed with eight wavelengths per fiber, the number of wavelengths carried by recently installed systems has increased to 40 wavelengths. Vendors have already announced the availability of as many as 128 wavelengths per fiber. The total span of these systems varies from tens of kilometers (local) to 1,000 km (long haul) with optical amplifiers at intermediate locations for boosting the signal level. Several network operators have already deployed these systems and are expecting to increase the number of wavelengths per fiber to even higher counts.

The ITU has specified a "grid" of wavelengths at 100-GHz frequency spacing in the 1,550 nm band. However, several equipment providers have announced products based on 50-GHz spacing and are considering 25-GHz spacings for adjacent channels. At the same time, the EDFA band has been flattened and increased by using dual-stage amplifiers with intermediate-stage filters. Recent advances in optical amplifiers [Rottwitt+98] and lasers suggest that there is still considerable room for growth in the number of wavelengths carried on a single fiber.

As shown in Table 9.1, the fiber exhaust problem is a serious one for network operators. As of 1995, several long-distance network carriers and LECs had less than 50%

TABLE 9.1 Fiber Utilization

Company	Total percentage
Percentage of lit fiber in 1995 for the RBOCs and GTE	
Ameritech	18.6
Bell Atlantic	40
BellSouth	22
NYNEX	38
Pacific Telesis	27
Southwestern Bell	19
US West	22
GTE	51
Average	30
Percentage of lit fiber in 1995 for AT&T, WorldCom, MCI, and Sprint	
AT&T	47
WorldCom	70
MCI	65 (approx.)
Sprint	77

spare fiber available in their cables. In addition, the long-haul carriers typically have a small number of fibers per cable. This exacerbates the fiber exhaust problem and has brought about a mass deployment of WDM into the network. For example, consider Sprint's fiber infrastructure. The average number of fibers per cable is approximately 20, and the portion of lit fiber is 77%. This leaves only 23% of the fibers for new network deployment. This situation is worsened by the fact that Sprint deploys mostly four-fiber ring architectures, which require two fibers out of four to be reserved solely for network protection.

As shown in Figure 9.1, these point-to-point systems are mostly deployed in "open" architectures using standard short-reach SONET interfaces operating at 1.3 μm. In the system shown in the figure, an optical cross-connect (OXC) is interfaced to three point-to-point links terminated by WDM transport systems (consisting of wavelength MUX/DMUXs and transponders converting optical signals between 1.3 μm and a wavelength in the ITU grid). The presence of the transponders makes this an "opaque" approach. The following are some advantages of this configuration:

- Multivendor interoperability using a standard 1.3 μm interface

- No cascading of physical impairments

- Wavelength conversion

On the other hand, as shown in Figure 9.2, some suppliers are supporting an "integrated" or closed system by providing "compliant" ITU grid wavelengths directly from their TDM (e.g., SONET terminal) equipment. There is a debate within the

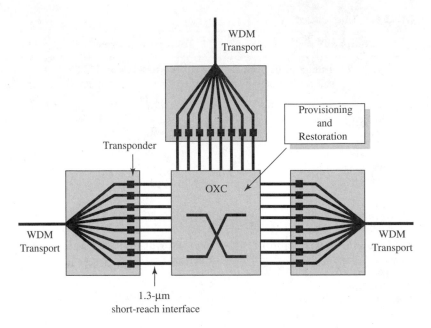

FIGURE 9.1 Open WDM network architecture: Opaque network.

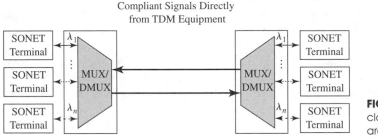

FIGURE 9.2 Integrated closed WDM network architecture.

industry on the "open" versus the "integrated/closed" WDM architecture. The open systems have the advantage that they enable competition among the suppliers on both TDM and WDM equipment. The open system allows network operators to obtain competitive pricing for their equipment. For example, in Figure 9.1 two suppliers compete to supply the TDM and the WDM equipment. The integrated approach generally results in a single-supplier solution. Although the number of components in the integrated system is lower (no transponders), the cost of this system can be higher due to the fact that the network operator is now locked into a single vendor environment. It is difficult to predict the direction that future network deployment will take. At the present time the trend is in favor of open systems.

9.3 WDM Optical Cross-connect Mesh Networks

The extensive deployment of point-to-point systems has resulted in large numbers of optical channels terminating at the central offices. This in turn has resulted in a pressing need to manage channels at the optical level without subrate demultiplexing of the individual connections. This proliferation of WDM transmission has made optical switching more attractive economically.[1] Several network operators have announced their intention to deploy optical cross-connects to interconnect these WDM transport systems, as shown in Figure 9.1. The idea here is to provision and to protect wavelengths directly at the optical layer. Network operators who have deployed open WDM transport systems with 1.3-μm short-reach SONET interfaces are considering the deployment of these cross-connects in an opaque architecture [Bala+95, Tkach+98, Young+98].

On the other hand, some network operators are planning to deploy the cross-connects in a transparent fashion [Davis+98]. The opaque architecture has the disadvantage that it has extra components (transponders) but has several advantages. The architecture clearly separates switching from transport and eliminates any cascaded impairments that accumulate during transmission, by providing signal regeneration. Furthermore, it enables wavelength interchange functionality between WDM transport systems by using the 1.3-μm interface as a common intermediate frequency between two WDM systems. In this fashion, it enables multi-vendor interoperability and allows different wavelength sets from different vendors to be interconnected by bringing them all to a common denominator (i.e., the 1.3-μm standard interface). In either case, the first applications of optical cross-connects are for wavelength interconnection, provisioning, and restoration.

It is possible that over time these separate WDM transport systems and optical cross-connects will be integrated to form wavelength selective (WSXCs) or wavelength interchange (WIXCs) cross-connects with both the transport and the switching subsystems integrated into one network element [Jackel+96, Jourdan+97]. This can potentially lower the cost of the cross-connect by eliminating duplicate components.

9.4 WDM Rings with Wavelength Add–Drop Multiplexers

The TDM rings described in Chapter 8 have been deployed by several network operators and the deployment of WDM rings is imminent. The LECs have installed both two-fiber unidirectional path-switched rings (UPSRs) and two-fiber bidirectional line-switched rings (BLSRs). Some long-haul carriers have installed four-fiber BLSRs in

---

[1] This is analogous to the situation that existed in the 1970s, when the widespread deployment of digital transmission systems in the telephone industry (e.g., the T1 carrier) led to the development of digital time-space-division switching equipment (e.g., AT&T's No. 4 ESS).

their networks for enhanced network survivability and increased bandwidth. Several carriers are planning to deploy WDM rings in architectural configurations similar to TDM SONET rings. Some equipment providers and network operators [Hatton+98, McCammon+98, Bala98] have proposed UPSR rings for the local exchange network using wavelength add–drop multiplexers (WADMs). Similar proposals have been made for the deployment of WDM BLSRs for the long-haul network. The Multiwavelength Optical Networking (MONET) consortium, which is partially funded by the Defense Advanced Research Projects Agency (DARPA) in the United States, is deploying two interconnected WDM optical rings in a testbed in the Washington, DC, area.

WDM rings offer enhanced survivability at the optical layer by reserving bandwidth (wavelengths and fiber) for protection purposes. WDM meshes can result in much higher network utilization than rings. However, as explained in Chapter 8, rings have simpler, well-developed protection switching protocols that allow them to protection switch in a short interval of time (e.g., 50 ms).

Algorithms for mesh restoration at the logical or SONET layer have received much attention in the literature over the past decade. Some of the carriers use mesh restoration techniques as a second line of defense against large failures. However, mesh restoration algorithms in the SONET layer can take several seconds to minutes to restore service mainly because the restoration is done at a subrate (e.g., DS1 or DS3) level. WDM meshes that are protected at the optical connection level have much fewer connections to reroute, resulting in an accelerated protection time, which can approach that in rings. (See Section 8.4.) Until the deployment of WDM mesh networks using optical level protection, it appears that network operators requiring millisecond protection time will continue to deploy ring architectures.

9.5 Multiwavelength Optical Network Testbeds

A picture of the current state of optical networking would be incomplete without a description of some recent wide area WDM network testbed efforts. Some of the recent projects are the Optical Networks Technology Consortium (ONTC) [Chang+96], Multiwavelength Transport Network (MWTN) [Hill+93, Joh96], RAINBOW [Hall+96], All Optical Network (AON) Consortium [Alexander+93, Kaminow+96], MONET [Wagner+96], National Transparent Optical Network Consortium (NTONC) [Wilt97], Optical Pan-European Network (OPEN) [Jourdan+97], and PROMETEO [Merli+97]. We give brief descriptions of a representative subset of these in the following sections.

9.5.1 Optical Networks Technology Consortium

The mission of the ONTC project was to investigate and to demonstrate WDM networking in a testbed environment. Formed in 1992 under partial sponsorship of DARPA in the United States, the consortium members included Bellcore, Columbia University, Hughes Research Laboratories, Lawrence Livermore National Labs, Nortel/BNR, Rockwell Science Center, Uniphase Telecommunications Products, Case Western Reserve University, and United Technologies Research Center. The work culminated in a successful demonstration of a four-wavelength WDM network at the Optical Fiber Communications Conference in 1995. The architectural approach was unique in that it used a combination of ATM and WDM networking to provide a data communications network for high-speed services. The fundamental architecture of the ONTC network was layered, separating the optical (WDM) layer from the logical switching (ATM) layer.

9.5.1.1 Demonstration Network

As shown in Figure 9.3, the demonstration system consisted of four network access nodes, distributed among two WDM optical fiber rings (totaling 150 km of single-mode fiber) joined by a 2×2 WDM cross-connect (marked 3 in Figure 9.3). Each ring had two WADMs (marked 1, 2, 4, and 5 in Figure 9.3), and each WADM had an access node attached to it. The WADM and the WDM cross-connects (labeled

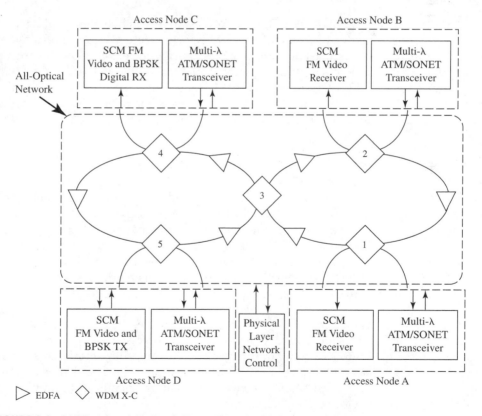

FIGURE 9.3 ONTC network testbed. (From (Chang+96, Figure 1). Copyright © 1996 IEEE. Used by permission of The Institute of Electrical and Electronics Engineers, Inc.)

"WDM X-C switch" in the figure) were implemented using a hybrid optomechanical switch approach and an acousto-optic tunable filter (AOTF) approach.

Both techniques were used to investigate different technologies for building the same network elements. Six EDFAs were used in the network to compensate for insertion loss of the optical switches and the fiber loss in the loops. Each access node had a multiwavelength laser array that accessed the network through a WADM. ATM switches attached to the access nodes provided cell-by-cell routing and sorting. This created a logically routed (multihop) overlay, which also offered an opportunity for wavelength interchange via optoelectronic conversion. Four optical channels at wavelengths of 1,546, 1,550, 1,554, and 1,558 nm were selected for the WDM layer. Three of the wavelength channels were modulated at SONET OC-3 rates, and the remaining one carried an SCM analog signal.

9.5.1.2 Key Network Components

There were five key network components, which are described in the following subsections.

Erbium-Doped Fiber Amplifiers   The EDFAs used in the testbed were evaluated in a series of experiments. Six EDFAs and six WDM switches were cascaded, and a signal was transmitted and examined at various stages. During the experiment the optical power was adjusted to be -20 dBm at every input stage of the EDFAs, and the observed gain was about 20 dB for every channel. After six amplifiers, the power penalty was less than 2 dB for a BER of 10^{-9}. However, it was concluded that without any signal level compensation or equalization, the scalability of the testbed was limited due to the fact that the EDFA gain is not flat (see Section 4.4.1).

Acousto-optic Tunable Filters   AOTFs were a key device technology for performing wavelength selection and routing (see Section 4.9.6). Although the AOTFs fabricated for the testbed had the advantage of allowing independent selection of channels from multiwavelength signals without demultiplexing, they had high co-channel cross-talk due to switch leakage. Experimental results showed that typical cross-talk was -15 dB with one radio frequency (RF) control channel turned on. However, this number worsened to -9 dB with all four RF channels turned on. These and other problems (oscillations in closed cycles—see Section 2.3.2) were eliminated by space-dilating the AOTF. The switching time for the device was in the microsecond range.

Hybrid WSXC Switches   To address the problems presented by the AOTF switch, a hybrid cross-connect was implemented. It was built in a three-stage architecture of the type illustrated in Figure 2.22, using multilayer dielectric thin-film interference filters for WMUX/WDMUXs and discrete 2×2 opto-mechanical switching elements in the middle stage. The hybrid WDM cross-connect had flat passbands and a low insertion loss. The typical width of the channel filter passband was 1 nm. The interchannel cross-talk was less than -30 dB, and the co-channel cross-talk was -60 dB. The switching time of the devices was on the order of 10 ms.

Multiwavelength Transmitter Module The WDM transmitters used integrated GaAs heterojunction bipolar transistor (HBT) laser drivers and multiwavelength DFB laser arrays. Functionally the module translated 1,310-nm signals to 1,550-nm band signals.

Multiwavelength Receiver Module A packaged four-channel InGaAsInP PIN-high electron mobility transistor OEIC receiver front end was fabricated at Bellcore. Also, an AlGaAs-GaAs HBT receiver integrated-circuit array, incorporating a four-channel integrated postamplifier, timing recovery, and decision circuits, was fabricated at Rockwell Sciences Center.

9.5.1.3 Network Signaling, Control, and Management

Signaling was implemented using in-band isochronous ATM data cells. The objective was to reconfigure the network with a minimal interruption of information flow and a maximal utilization of network bandwidth for data transport. Out-of-band optical layer signaling (at 1,310 nm) and electrical overlay signaling were also tested in the network.

A graphical user interface (GUI) network control program was installed on a workstation located at one of the access nodes. This served as the central controller for the testbed. The network controller was responsible for assigning communication routes between users. A software program monitored and controlled the switch configurations according to a routing table.

The network management system used commercial software (NetExpert), which was customized and implemented in the testbed to provide the required functions. The GUI was hierarchical and was set up to monitor the entire testbed. Various functions were implemented as a part of this network management system, including wavelength performance monitoring and per-channel power regulation.

The ONTC project was successful in designing, integrating, and demonstrating a reconfigurable optical network testbed using multiwavelength DFB laser arrays, multichannel integrated receivers, optical cross-connect switches, EDFAs, and ATM/SONET switches. The development of the ONTC testbed was extended into a second phase, during which the consortium developed advanced multiwavelength technology, including 20-wavelength DFB laser arrays and integrated laser driver arrays that were incorporated into an 8-wavelength transceiver module. This program also built larger scale AOTF-based switch structures and explored the network issues associated with switches of this type. The work of the consortium culminated in an 8-wavelength demonstration system that incorporated these elements.

9.5.2 All Optical Network Consortium

The AON Consortium was formed with DARPA funding in 1993 and included AT&T, Bell Laboratories, DEC, and MIT. Its objective was to develop architectures and technologies for high-speed WDM and TDM networks. A hierarchical three-level network architecture was proposed for the optical layer.

9.5.2.1 Network Demonstration

A testbed was set up in the Boston metropolitan area with a 20-channel WDM system running at a data rate per wavelength ranging from 10 Mbps to 10 Gbps. The network was all optical in that the transmitted data within the network did not undergo any opto-electronic and electro-optic conversions. The testbed used fast tunable laser transmitters and receivers. The levels of the network hierarchy are shown in Figure 9.4, with passive (static) broadcast LANs at level-0, static wavelength routed MANs at level-1, and a configurable wavelength routed WAN at level-2.

Ten wavelengths were allocated for use in the LANs, and the remaining ten were shared between the MANs and the WAN. Two all-optical services—type A, a dedicated channel circuit-switched service, and type B, a scheduled TDM service—shared the channels provided in the network. An additional service, type C, was used for network management, scheduling of wavelengths and time slots, and clock distribution. More details can be found in [Kaminow+96].

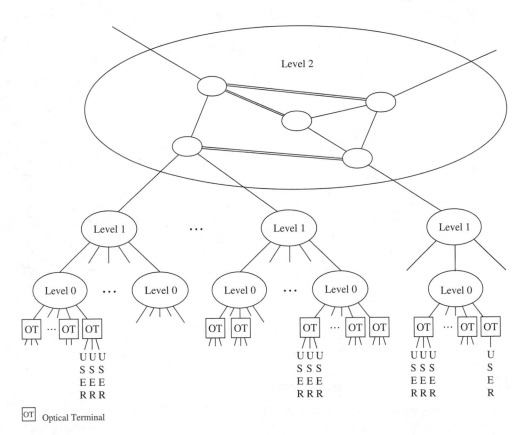

OT Optical Terminal

FIGURE 9.4 The AON hierarchical optical network. (From (Kaminow+96, Figure 1). Copyright © 1996 IEEE. Used by permission of The Institute of Electrical and Electronics Engineers, Inc.)

9.5.2.2 Technologies

Several technologies were demonstrated by the AON Consortium. Descriptions of four of them follow.

1. *Silica-on-Silicon Passive Devices* Silica waveguides can be formed in a planar geometry by several fabrication processes. The Lucent process, known as the *silicon optical bench*, uses a thick layer of SiO_2 glass on a silicon single-crystal substrate. A thin core layer of P-doped silica with an elevated refractive index is then deposited by metal–organic vapor phase technology. A waveguide pattern is formed by defining and etching the core layer photolithographically. Finally, a layer of silica is deposited over the waveguide cores. An efficient silica-on-silicon multiplexer based on an arrayed waveguide grating, a demultiplexer based on an optical phased array dispersive element, and a waveguide grating router were fabricated and demonstrated by the consortium.

2. *Tunable Lasers* Rapidly tunable distributed Bragg reflection (DBR) lasers were fabricated and tested by the consortium. These devices had a typical output of 10 dBm at a 30-mA drive current. The tuning speed was limited by the carrier lifetime to 10 ns. The lasers were tunable to 20 different frequencies at a 50-GHz spacing.

3. *Tunable Receivers* Tunable receivers were constructed based on a fiber Fabry–Perot filter made by AT&T. The filter was made with standard single-mode fiber, with multilayer dielectric mirrors coated on the fiber ends. Tuning was effected by varying the mirror spacing using a piezoelectric transducer. The tuning time was about 1 ms.

4. *Frequency Changers* Three options were pursued. The simplest one was a regenerator without retiming. The incoming data on a channel frequency f_i was detected and then remodulated on an output laser with channel frequency f_j. A second approach used the incoming signal to saturate an amplifier that served to impress the inverse data on a second laser at f_j. Another approach used FWM in a nonlinear medium.

9.5.2.3 Network Control, Management, and Scheduling

Control and management of the network and of individual devices in an optical terminal was available through a GUI and a command-level scripting interface, providing detailed telemetry and state information. Both the GUIs and the command–scripting interfaces communicated with the optical terminal, across the C-service control channel to the optical terminal processor, and (when necessary) across the backplane of the optical terminal to the individual daughter boards and devices. The optical terminal communicated with other (user) devices using standard commercial data communication interfaces.

GUI functions ranged from system maintenance to user-level operational control. Some examples are monitoring laser temperatures, powers, and currents; performing computer-aided laser calibrations; initializing network operations; displaying network management and status information; performing network administration and management; and presenting simple and intuitive connection-oriented interfaces to users of the AON. In both low-level engineering development tasks and high-level operations, the GUI served as the primary means of control and observation.

A network management service was implemented over the C-service. The network management system was responsible for fault detection, configuration management, performance estimation, and resource allocation. The scheduling and management system kept track of ongoing user sessions throughout the network, adding or deleting circuits as requested by users.

In summary, the AON consortium demonstrated an optical network architecture in a field environment in the Boston area. It demonstrated the feasibility of such an all-optical network by developing several of the key component technologies along with a scalable three-level network architecture. Both circuit- and packet-switched services were tested on the network. Several technologies were demonstrated including waveguide grating routers, tunable lasers and receivers, and frequency changers.

9.5.3 European Multiwavelength Optical Network Trials: Multiwavelength Transport Network

Several testbed efforts have been mounted in Europe as a part of the RACE and the ACTS programs set up by the European Community Commission. The multiwavelength transport network (MWTN) project was one of the first testbeds to demonstrate successfully the concepts of wavelength routing in optical networks [Johansson96, Hill+93]. An overview of the MWTN network demonstration will be presented next, followed by some brief comments on more recent European trials.

9.5.3.1 MWTN Demonstration

The RACE–MWTN consortium was set up to develop and demonstrate the concept of WDM optical networking. Two network elements, the optical cross-connect and the optical ADM, were the building blocks of the network architecture.

The final demonstration of the MWTN was carried out in a real network environment in the Stockholm area. The fiber network formed a part of the local operator's network of about 130 km of standard fiber. The optical layer demonstration used two OXCs installed at two different sites. Later, one of these OXCs was replaced by an optical ADM. The network architecture was divided into three layers: an optical layer, which routed the wavelength channels; an SDH layer, which supported the transport at STM-4 (622 Mbps) and STM-16 (2.5 Gbps) rates; and an application layer with video coders and a 140-Mbps interface.

Management System   New functions required for the management of an optical network were supported in the demonstration. In particular, fault, configuration, and performance management functions were introduced in the testbed. The management system of the MWTN demonstrator was developed in accordance with the Telecommunications Management Network (TMN) standard. This provided the necessary management functions and offered communication between an operations system and different network elements. A logically separate data communications transport network supported data transfer for network management, and a local management console provided a GUI for manipulating the managed objects.

Optical Network Nodes Two optical network elements—the OXC and the optical ADM—were developed by the MWTN. The OXC architecture was designed to evaluate different technologies on the same platform. Two OXCs were constructed and demonstrated at BT Laboratories. The OXC nodes had four subsystems: fiber amplifiers were provided by Pirelli, the WDM transmission was provided by CSELT, and the optical cross-connect fabric and the management system were provided by Ericsson. Two OXC switch fabrics were evaluated: 8×8 LiNbO$_3$ switches and 4×4 laser amplifier gate switches based on InP. For WDM demultiplexing at the receivers, four different types of technologies were tested: AOTF, an integrated multigrating filter on InP, mechanically switched four-layer thin-film filter modules, and Fabry–Perot filter modules. The best performance was obtained by commercial multilayer filters. The number of wavelengths supported by the cross-connect was 20. The optical ADM nodes used similar technologies and were presented at ECOC95 in a network demonstration (see Figure 9.5).

In summary, this work demonstrated the basic principles of a WDM network with reconfigurable wavelength routing elements. Several network nodes were developed based on photonic technologies, involving space switches, tunable filters and lasers, and wavelength-flattened EDFAs.

9.5.3.2 Other European Trials

The Optical Pan-European Network is planning to deploy and to demonstrate the operation of a wavelength cross-connect mesh network in a field environment. The network will span several countries, including Norway, Denmark, France, and Belgium. The plan is to build a demonstrator with as many as 16 wavelengths to demonstrate restoration and provisioning of wavelengths in the European network.

The Pan-European Photonic Transport Overlay Network is a field testbed with WDM using 16 wavelengths over 500 km at 10 Gbps. The network architecture uses

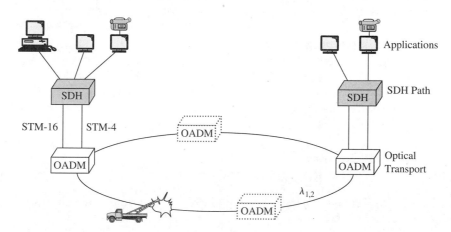

FIGURE 9.5 MWTN testbed network. (From (Johansson96, Figure 1). Copyright © 1996 IEEE. Used by permission of The Institute of Electrical and Electronics Engineers, Inc.)

WDM optical cross-connects in a mesh network to provide wavelength routing and restoration. The demonstration will span several countries, including Germany and Austria, in a field environment.

Another project supported by the ACTS program is Management of Photonic Systems and Networks (MEPHISTO). The main objective of MEPHISTO is to apply the principles of network management (TMN) to advanced optical networks that utilize WDM and optical switching.

9.5.4 Multiwavelength Optical Network

The MONET project was initiated in 1995 as an industrywide consortium of companies collaborating to deploy a multiwavelength optical network in a field trial. The program was established to define, demonstrate, and help form an industry consensus on how best to achieve multiwavelength optical networking on a national scale that serves both commercial and government applications. The MONET program includes participation from AT&T, Bellcore, Lucent Technologies, Bell Atlantic, BellSouth, SBC, the National Security Agency, the Naval Research Laboratory, and DARPA.

MONET concentrates on the local exchange and long-distance network and is built on a hierarchical network architecture to achieve scalability to national size. Program activities consist of three major parts: network architecture and economics, networking demonstrations, and supporting technology. Figure 9.6 shows the overall architecture for the MONET network. The lowest layer is the reconfigurable WDM optical layer, which is responsible for setting up long-term optical connections between network switches in the electronic layer. The optical layer provides dynamic reconfiguration and restoration of wavelength channels on demand. The switches in the electronic layer perform the processing functions associated with multiplexing and switching of packets or subrate circuits. The optical and electronic layers correspond, respectively, to our generic physical and logical layers (see Figure 2.1[a]). The applications layer rides on top of the optical and electronic layers. Some applications can bypass the electronic layer and connect directly to the optical layer.

9.5.4.1 Network Demonstration

A field trial began in the Washington, DC, area during the first quarter of 1999. Two interconnected eight-wavelength WDM rings execute a UPSR protocol for protection switching. The WDM rings are provided by two different vendors with full interoperability at their interconnection points. The interconnection takes place at the transport level. The diameter of each ring is somewhat less than 100 km.

9.5.4.2 Network Elements

The MONET network elements consist of the following:

- *Wavelength add–drop multiplexer:* Adds and drops individual wavelengths from a ring network
- *WDM cross-connects:* Two types—the wavelength-selective cross-connect and the wavelength-interchanging cross-connect

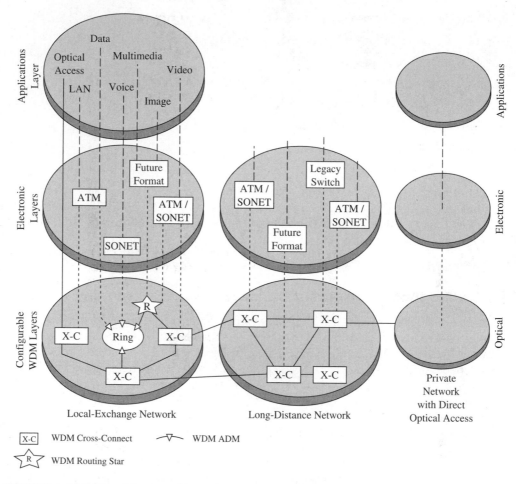

FIGURE 9.6 MONET architecture. (From (Wagner+96, Figure 1). Copyright © 1996 IEEE. Used by permission of The Institute of Electrical and Electronics Engineers, Inc.)

- *Wavelength routing star:* A static routing element that provides a fixed mapping of incoming wavelengths to outgoing fibers; equivalent to our generic permutation router (see Section 2.3.1.2)

9.5.4.3 Multiwavelength Technology

The MONET program is investigating several multiwavelength technologies:

- Four- and eight-wavelength 2.5-Gbps InP laser arrays
- InP photodetector/preamplifier arrays

- Wavelength-selectable laser sources
- $LiNbO_3$ polarization-independent switch arrays
- Wavelength routing space switches
- InP switch arrays
- Wavelength interchanging technology
- Silica-on-silicon multiplexers and routers
- Gain flattened EDFAs

In summary, MONET has developed and combined a wide array of network elements into a scalable network architecture. The extent of the project makes it one of the key testing grounds for current WDM networking technology and architectural concepts.

9.5.5 National Transparent Optical Network Consortium

The primary participants in NTONC were Northern Telecom, Sprint, Lawrence Livermore National Laboratory, Pacific Bell, University of California San Diego, Columbia University, and Hughes Research Laboratories. The project produced a switched multiwavelength MAN using an existing fiber infrastructure in the San Francisco Bay area. The 10+ Gbps, 400-km network demonstrated high-bandwidth applications and tested emerging optical technologies—hardware, software, and protocols.

The NTONC used standard (nondispersion shifted) fiber in a four-node reconfigurable WDM network. Transparent optical layer connections provided clear channel transmission independent of format and protocol. A grid of four wavelengths was used with parts of the system testing components operating on eight wavelengths. Various services were carried, including SONET OC-48, subcarrier modulated analog (FM video), and digital (BPSK) data. A bidirectional, two-fiber ring was deployed on the embedded fiber infrastructure of Pacific Bell and Sprint forming the network backbone.

The WDM technology used in NTONC evolved from devices developed previously by ONTC. Two types of switching node technology were tested: AOTF and optomechanical. Transparent optical network switches, using six 2×2 switching elements, were built and operated as WADMs in a four-node ring.

An eight-wavelength network access module, the development of which had been initiated under ONTC, was also demonstrated, incorporating eight-wavelength transceiver arrays, data regeneration, and electronic switching. A 16×16 switch between the receiving and transmitting arrays provided add–drop, regenerative repeater, and wavelength interchange functions for digital signals at the electronic level.

9.5.6 The Importance of the Testbeds in Driving the Telecommunications Infrastructure

The optical network testbeds deployed in the last few years of the twentieth century provided worthwhile field trial experience for the carriers, the equipment manufacturers, and some users of bandwidth-intensive applications. These trials were and continue to be invaluable in moving ideas from the laboratory to viable commercial products and network architectures. The first operational optical networks of the next century will be built around these products and architectures. They will enable a host of new services and should dramatically lower costs in the telecommunications infrastructure. This should in turn accelerate demand for more bandwidth and stimulate further development of next generation networks.

9.6 Bibliography

[Alexander+93] S. B. Alexander, R. S. Bondurant, D. Byrne, et al. A precompetitive consortium on wide-band all optical networks. *IEEE/OSA J. Lightwave Technology*, 11(5/6):714–735, 1993.

[Bala+95] K. Bala, R. R. Cordell, and E. L. Goldstein. The case for opaque multiwavelength optical networks. In *IEEE/LEOS Summer Topical Meeting on Optical Networks*, Keystone, CO, August 1995.

[Bala98] K. Bala. WDM optical network architectures for a data-centric environment. In *NFOEC*, Orlando, September 1998.

[Chang+96] G. K. Chang, G. Ellinas, J. K. Gamelin, M. Z. Iqbal, and C. A. Brackett. Multiwavelength reconfigurable WDM/ATM/SONET network testbed. *IEEE/OSA J. Lightwave Technology*, 14(6):1320–1340, 1996.

[Davis+98] G. B. Davis, N. Robinson, S. K. Liu, J. Fee, and D. Way. Optical cross-connect system technology trial. In *Proceedings IEEE/OSA Optical Fiber Commun. Conf.*, San Jose, February 1998.

[Hall+96] E. Hall et al. The RAINBOW-II gigabit optical network. *IEEE J. Select. Areas Commun.*, 14(5):814–823, 1996.

[Hatton+98] P. V. Hatton and F. Cheston. WDM deployment in the local exchange network. *IEEE Commun. Mag.*, 36(2):56–61, 1998.

[Hill+93] G. R. Hill, P. J. Chidgey, F. Kaufhold, et al. Multi-wavelength transport network: A transport network layer based on optical network elements. *IEEE/OSA J. Lightwave Technology*, 11(5/6):667–679, 1993.

[Jackel+96] J. L. Jackel, et al. Acousto-optic tunable filters for multiwavelength optical networks: Cross-talk considerations. *IEEE/OSA J. Lightwave Technology*, 14(6):1056–1066, 1996.

[Johansson96] S. Johansson. A transport network involving a reconfigurable WDM network layer—A European demonstration. *IEEE/OSA J. Lightwave Technology*, 14(6):1341–1348, 1996.

[Jourdan+97] A. Jourdan, et al. Fully reconfigurable WDM optical cross-connect: Feasibility validation and preparation of prototype cross-connect for ACTS open field trials. In *European Conference on Optical Communications*, Edinburgh, UK, September 1997.

[Kaminow+96] I. P. Kaminow, C. R. Doerr, C. Dragone, et al. A wideband all-optical WDM network. *IEEE J. Select. Areas Commun.*, 14(5):780–799, 1996.

[McCammon+98] K. McCammon, V. Cacal, A. Eriksen, et al. High bandwidth transport technology introduction at Pacific Bell. In *NFOEC*, Orlando, September 1998.

[Merli+97] S. Merli, et al. The PROMETEO testbed: A unidirectional WDM transparent self-healing ring in a field environment. In *European Conference on Optical Communications*, Edinburgh, UK, September 1997.

[Rottwitt+98] K. Rottwitt and H. D. Kidorf. A 92 nm bandwidth Raman amplifier. In *Proceedings IEEE/OSA Optical Fiber Commun. Conf.*, San Jose, February 1998.

[Tkach+98] R. W. Tkach, E. L. Goldstein, J. A. Nagel, and J. L. Strand. Fundamental limits of optical transparency. In *Proceedings IEEE/OSA Optical Fiber Commun. Conf.*, San Jose, February 1998.

[Wagner+96] R. E. Wagner, R. C. Alferness, A. A. M. Saleh, and M. S. Goodman. MONET: Multiwavelength optical networking. *IEEE/OSA J. Lightwave Technology*, 14(6):1349–1355, 1996.

[Wilt97] D. Wilt. Optical networks: Wave of the future. *Science and Technology Magazine*, April 1997.

[Young+98] M. Young, H. Laor, and E. J. Fontenot. First in-service network application of optical cross-connects. In *Proceedings IEEE/OSA Optical Fiber Commun. Conf.*, San Jose, February 1998.

Graph Theory

Graph and hypergraph terminology has evolved over the years. The following definitions are adapted from [Chartrand+96, Berge89, Bermond+97]. Some of the material in this appendix is found in other parts of the book. It is repeated here for convenience.

A.1 Graphs

A *graph* G consists of a set of *vertices* $V(G)$ and a set of edges $E(G)$, where each edge e is a pair of distinct vertices (u, v). (If the two vertices are the same, then the edge is a *loop*. We rule out these cases.) A graph with vertex set V and edge set E is typically denoted by $G(V, E)$. If $e = (u, v)$, then u and v are *adjacent* vertices, and e is *incident* on u and v. Two edges are adjacent if they are incident on the same vertex. Nonadjacent edges or nonadjacent vertices are called *independent*. A set of pairwise independent vertices of a graph G, which is of maximal cardinality, is called a *maximal independent set*. Figure A.1 shows an example of a maximal independent set of vertices (outlined in dashed circles).

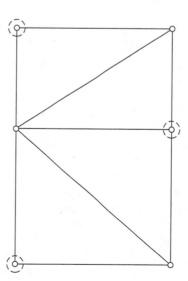

FIGURE A.1 A maximal independent set.

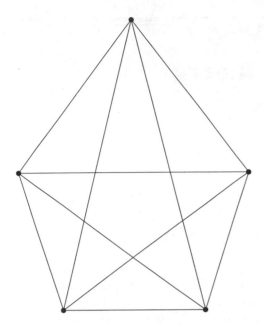

FIGURE A.2 The complete graph K_5.

A graph in which every two vertices are adjacent is called a *complete* or *fully connected graph*. The complete graph with n vertices is denoted by K_n. Figure A.2 shows K_5.

A graph G is called *bipartite* if its vertices can be partitioned into two subsets, V_1 and V_2, (called *partite sets*) such that every edge of G joins a vertex in V_1 to one in V_2. A *complete* bipartite graph is one in which an edge exists between every pair of vertices $u \in V_1$ and $v \in V_2$. The complete bipartite graph is denoted by $K_{p,q}$, where p and q are the cardinalities of V_1 and V_2 respectively. Figure A.3 shows $K_{3,3}$.

Graphs that may contain more than one edge between the same pair of vertices as well as loops are called *multigraphs*. (We use the term *multigraph* here to include graphs as special cases. But unless otherwise stated, we exclude multigraphs from our discussion.)

The number of vertices in G, $|V(G)|$, is called the *order* of G, typically denoted by $n(G)$. The number of edges in G, $|E(G)|$, is called the *size* of G, typically denoted by $m(G)$.

The *degree* of a vertex v in a graph G is the number of edges incident on v. A graph is *regular* if all of its vertices are of the same degree.

A graph S is a subgraph of a graph G if $V(S) \subseteq V(G)$ and $E(S) \subseteq E(G)$. A subgraph, S of G, is said to be *induced* by a vertex set $U \subseteq V(G)$, if $V(S) = U$ and $E(S)$ consists of all edges incident on two vertices in U. A *spanning subgraph* of a graph G is a subgraph containing all vertices of G.

A *clique* of a graph G is a complete subgraph of G.

A *u–v walk* of a graph is an alternating sequence of vertices and edges: $u = u_1, e_1, u_2, \ldots, u_i, e_i, u_{i+1}, \ldots v_k = v$, begining on vertex u and ending on vertex v,

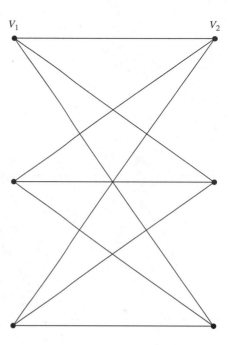

V_1 V_2

FIGURE A.3 The complete bipartite graph $K_{3,3}$.

where $e_i = (u_i, u_{i+1})$. Its length is defined as the number of edges it contains. A walk is called a *trail* if no edge is repeated, and is a *path* if no vertex is repeated. It is *open* if $u \neq v$, and is *closed* otherwise. (All paths of a graph are trails, but all trails are not paths.) A closed trail is called a *circuit*, and a circuit with no repeated vertices is called a *cycle*. A graph is called *acyclic* if it contains no cycles.

The *distance*, $d(u, v)$, between two vertices in a connected graph G is the minimum of the lengths of all u–v paths in G. The *diameter* of a graph is the largest distance between pairs of its vertices.

A graph is *connected* if it contains a path between every pair of its vertices. Otherwise it is disconnected. A graph G that is disconnected is made up of a number of connected *components*, each of which is a subgraph of G.

A graph is *k-edge connected* if the removal of less than k edges never results in a disconnected graph.

A *tree* is an acyclic connected graph, and a *forest* is an acyclic graph with more than one component. A *spanning tree* of a connected graph G is an acyclic spanning subgraph of G. The *chords* of a spanning tree T of G are the edges of G not included in T. Every spanning tree T of a connected graph G of order n and size m has $n - 1$ edges and $m - n + 1$ chords. Each chord added to T creates a unique cycle, called a *fundamental cycle*.

A *bridge* of a connected graph is an edge whose removal results in a disconnected graph. Thus, a graph with bridges is one-edge connected. A *cut* of a connected graph is a set of edges whose removal disconnects the graph. We reserve the term *cut* in this

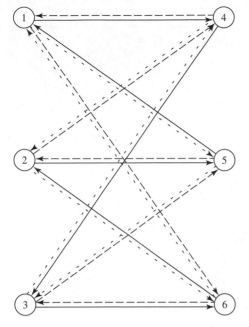

FIGURE A.4 Orientable cycle double cover for $K_{3,3}$.

book to mean a *minimal* cut, or *cutset*, which is a set of edges whose removal produces two components, and no subset of which has this property.

A.1.1 Cycle Double Covers

A *cycle double cover* (CDC) of a connected graph G is a collection C of cycles of G such that every edge of G is in exactly two of the cycles in C. It has been conjectured that every bridgeless connected graph has a CDC [Szekeres73].

An *orientable cycle double cover* (OCDC) of a connected graph G is a CDC with the property that it is possible to choose a circular orientation for each cycle so that each edge is taken in opposite directions in its two incident cycles [Alspach+85]. The existence of OCDCs for all bridgeless connected graphs has also been conjectured. Figure A.4 shows an OCDC for the graph $K_{3,3}$, consisting of three cycles.

A.1.2 Eulerian Graphs

An *Eulerian circuit* is a circuit that contains all of the edges and vertices of a graph or multigraph. (In discussing Eulerian properties we include multigraphs.) An Eulerian trail on a multigraph G is a trail containing all of the edges and vertices of G. A multigraph is called *Eulerian* if it has a closed Eulerian trail. A connected multigraph is Eulerian if and only if all of its vertices are of even degree, and it contains an open Eulerian trail if and only if all but two of its vertices are of even degree.

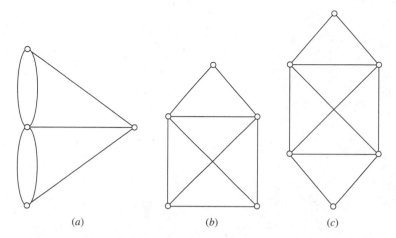

(a) (b) (c)

FIGURE A.5 Multigraphs: Eulerian and non-Eulerian.

Figure A.5(a) is the most famous example of a non-Eulerian multigraph. It is the model for the Konigsberg Bridge problem mentioned in Section 6.3.5. Each vertex represents a land mass or island in the city of Konigsberg, and each edge represents one of the seven bridges in the city. The problem posed to Euler was to find a way to traverse all of the bridges exactly once, returning to the point of departure (i.e., to find a closed Eulerian trail). Euler proved that this was impossible in Konigsberg, and that in fact closed Eulerian trails exist in a connected multigraph G if and only if all vertices of G are of even degree. Figure A.5(b) shows a graph containing an open Eulerian trail, and Figure A.5(c) shows an Eulerian graph formed by adding a vertex and two edges to Figure A.5(b). Algorithms that can be used to find Eulerian trails are found in [Fleischner90].

A.1.3 Planar Graphs

A graph is *planar* if it can be drawn on a plane (or, equivalently, on a sphere) so that no two edges intersect except at their end points (vertices). When drawn in this way it is said to be *embedded* on the plane, and the resultant embedding is called a *plane graph*. (A given planar graph has many plane embeddings.) Each region of a plane graph bounded by a set of edges is called a *face*, including the outer unbounded region, which is called the *outer face*. (When embedded on a sphere, a plane graph has no outer face.)

For a connected plane graph G, the number of vertices n, edges m, and faces f are related by

$$f = m - n + 2 \tag{A.1}$$

where f is called Euler's number.

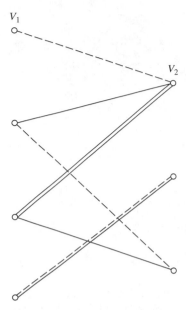

FIGURE A.6 Maximum matching of a bipartite multigraph.

A necessary and sufficient condition for a graph to be nonplanar is that it contain as a subgraph either K_5 or $K_{3,3}$, which are known as the *Kuratowski graphs*.

A.1.4 Matchings in Graphs

A set of pairwise independent edges of a graph (or multigraph) is called a *matching*. Of particular interest here (see, for example, Appendix B) is a *maximum matching* of a bipartite multigraph. A maximum matching is a matching of maximum cardinality. Figure A.6 illustrates a bipartite multigraph with maximum matching shown as the dashed edges.

A.1.5 Graph Coloring

A *vertex coloring* of a graph G is an assignment of colors to the vertices of G so that no two adjacent vertices have the same color. A minimal vertex coloring accomplishes this with a minimum number of colors.[1] This number is called the graph's *vertex chromatic number*. The vertex chromatic number of a graph is equal to or greater than the order of its largest clique. Graphs in which the two numbers are equal are called *perfect graphs*.

An *edge coloring* of a graph G is an assignment of colors to the edges of G so that no two adjacent edges have the same color. A minimal edge coloring accomplishes this

---

[1] One way of vertex coloring a graph is to partition the vertices into independent sets and to assign the same color to all vertices in the same set. This, however, is not a practical way of finding a good (close to minimal) vertex coloring of a large graph.

with a minimum number of colors. This number is called the graph's *edge chromatic number*.

Minimal coloring and determination of the chromatic number are both NP-complete problems.[2] However, the Dsatur algorithm given in [Brelaz79] is a simple and effective vertex-coloring heuristic. It is based on *saturation degree*. The saturation degree of a vertex is defined as the number of different colored vertices to which it is adjacent. The steps in the algorithm are as follows:

1. List the vertices in decreasing order of degree.

2. Assign color one to a vertex of maximal degree.

3. Choose an uncolored vertex of maximal saturation degree. If there is more than one, choose any vertex of maximal degree in the uncolored subgraph.

4. Color the selected vertex with the lowest numbered permissible color.

5. If all vertices are colored, stop; otherwise, go to Step 3.

A.1.6 Digraphs

A *digraph D*, or *directed graph,* is a graph in which the edges $E(D)$ (now called *arcs*) are *ordered* pairs of distinct vertices. (We rule out loops.) Thus, each arc has a direction. An arc (u, v) is incident *from u* and incident *to v*. Similarly, vertex u is adjacent to v, and v is adjacent from u. The *out-degree* of a vertex u is the number of arcs adjacent from u, and the *in-degree* of a vertex v is the number of arcs adjacent to v. A digraph is *regular* if all vertices have the same in- and out-degrees. Walks, paths, distances, and diameter are defined for digraphs in a fashion similar to graphs, except that directions must be taken into account. Thus, the distance from a vertex u to a vertex v is the length of the shortest u–v path, which is generally *not* the same as the distance from v to u. The diameter is the maximum of the distances between all *ordered* pairs of vertices.

A *subdigraph S* of a digraph D is a digraph for which $V(S) \subseteq V(D)$ and $E(S) \subseteq E(D)$.

A *bipartite digraph D* is a digraph with vertices that can be partitioned into two partite sets, V_1 and V_2, so that each arc of D is adjacent from V_1 and adjacent to V_2. A *complete* bipartite digraph is one in which an arc exists from every vertex in V_1 to every vertex in V_2.

A subdigraph of a digraph D is called a *diclique* of D if it is a complete bipartite digraph. A diclique is indicated in Figure A.7 with dashed lines.

---

[2] An informal definition of an NP-complete problem (NP meaning *nondeterministic polynomial*) is that it is a problem that cannot be solved in polynomial time. That is, the computational complexity of the problem grows faster than any power of the *size* of the problem (typically growing exponentially). In the coloring problem, for example, size might refer to the number of vertices or edges in the graph to be colored.

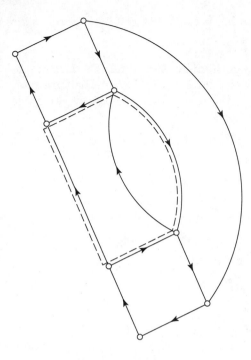

FIGURE A.7 A diclique.

A.1.7 Moore Bounds

The Moore bound for graphs gives the maximum possible order $N_{\text{Moore}}(\Delta, D)$ of a graph of maximum degree Δ and diameter D:

$$
N_{\text{Moore}}(\Delta, D) = 1 + \Delta \sum_{i=0}^{D-1} (\Delta - 1)^i
$$

$$
= \frac{\Delta(\Delta - 1)^D - 2}{\Delta - 2} \quad \Delta > 2 \tag{A.2}
$$

The Moore bound for digraphs gives the maximum possible order $N_{\text{Moore}}^d(\delta, D)$ for a digraph of maximum out-degree $\delta > 1$ and diameter D:

$$
N_{\text{Moore}}^d(\delta, D) = 1 + \delta + \delta^2 + \cdots + \delta^D = \frac{\delta^{D+1} - 1}{\delta - 1} \tag{A.3}
$$

A.1.8 Max Flow–Min Cut

Consider a digraph D in which each arc is associated with a *capacity*, or *maximum flow*. We choose any vertex s as a source, and any other vertex d as a destination, and wish to find the maximum possible flow between s and d given the capacity constraints.

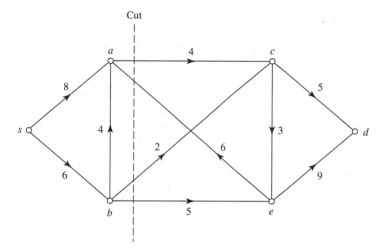

FIGURE A.8 A cut.

Partitioning the vertices of D into two partite sets, V_1 and V_2, we call the set of all arcs (u, v), with $u \in V_1$ and $v \in V_2$ the cut induced by that partition.[3] If $s \in V_1$ and $d \in V_2$, the cut is called an s–d cut. The capacity of an s–d cut is defined as the sum of the capacities of its arcs, and a minimal s–d cut is an s–d cut with least capacity. Figure A.8 illustrates these concepts. The cut $\{(a, c), (b, c), (b, e)\}$ separates the partite sets $V_1 = \{s, a, b\}$ and $V_2 = \{c, e, d\}$. The numbers on the arcs indicate capacities. It can be seen that this is a minimal s–d cut of capacity 11.

The Max Flow–Min Cut Theorem [Ford+64] states that

> The maximum possible flow between a pair of vertices s and d is given by the capacity of the minimal cut.

A related result is that if the vertices of a digraph D are partitioned into two partite sets V_1 and V_2, then the maximum possible flow from all vertices in V_1 to all vertices in V_2 is given by the capacity of the cut between V_1 and V_2.

A.2 Hypergraphs

Hypergraphs are direct generalizations of graphs or digraphs to the case in which an edge (now, a hyperedge or hyperarc) may contain more than two vertices.

A.2.1 Undirected Hypergraphs

An *undirected hypergraph* H consists of a set of vertices $v(H)$ and a set of hyperedges $\varepsilon(H)$, where each hyperedge $E \in \varepsilon(H)$ is a subset of $v(H)$. We typically denote a

---

[3] The concept of a cut induced by a partition is equally valid for graphs, in which arcs are replaced by edges.

hypergraph by $H(\nu, \varepsilon)$. The number of vertices in the hypergraph (its order) is $n = |\nu(H)|$ and the number of hyperedges is $m = |\varepsilon(H)|$.

The *degree* of a vertex is the number of hyperedges containing it. The *size* of a hyperedge $E \in \varepsilon(H)$ is its cardinality $|E|$. (We rule out hyperedges of size less than two. A hypergraph, all of whose hyperedges are of size two, is a graph.) The rank of H is the size of its largest hyperedge. A *path* connecting two vertices u and v in a hypergraph is an alternating sequence of vertices and hyperedges $u = v_0, E_1, v_1, \ldots, E_k, v_k = v$ with $\{v_{i-1}, v_i\} \subseteq E_i$ for all $1 \leq i \leq k$. The *length* of a path is the number of hyperedges in it. The *distance* $d_H(u, v)$ between two different vertices u and v is the length of a shortest path connecting them in H. The *diameter* of H is the maximum of the distances between all pairs of vertices in H.

An undirected hypergraph of diameter D, maximum vertex degree Δ, and rank r is called a (Δ, D, r)-hypergraph, and its order is denoted by $N(\Delta, D, r)$. The Moore bound for a (Δ, D, r)-hypergraph is given by

$$N(\Delta, D, r) \leq 1 + \Delta(r - 1) \sum_{i=0}^{D-l} (\Delta - 1)^i (r - 1)^i \qquad \text{(A.4)}$$

A.2.2 Directed Hypergraphs

A *directed hypergraph* H consisting of a set of vertices $\nu(H)$ and hyperarcs $\varepsilon(H)$ will be denoted by $H(\nu, \varepsilon)$.

A hyperarc $E \in \varepsilon(H)$ is an ordered pair (E^-, E^+) of nonempty subsets of $\nu(H)$.[4] The vertex sets E^- and E^+ are called the *in-set* and *out-set* of E respectively. (The in- and out-sets need not be disjoint.) The quantities $|E^-|$ and $|E^+|$ are, respectively, called the *in-size* and *out-size* of E. (If the in-size and out-size of all hyperarcs is one, then the hypergraph is a digraph.)

Let v be a vertex in $\nu(H)$. Its *in-degree*, $d^-(v)$, is the number of hyperarcs that contain v in their out-set. Similarly its *out-degree*, $d^+(v)$, is the number of hyperarcs that contain v in their in-set.

A *walk* in H from vertex u to vertex v is an alternating sequence of vertices and hyperarcs $u = v_0, E_1, v_1, E_2, v_2, \ldots, E_k, v_k = v$ such that $v_{i-1} \in E_i^-$ and $v_i \in E_i^+$ for each $1 \leq i \leq k$. The *length* of a walk is equal to the number of hyperarcs in it. The *distance* and *diameter* are defined in the same way as in the undirected case.

A directed hypergraph of diameter D, maximum vertex out-degree d, and maximum out-size s is called a (d, D, s)-directed hypergraph, and its order is denoted by $n(d, D, s)$. The Moore bound for a (d, D, s)-directed hypergraph is given by

$$n(d, D, s) \leq \sum_{i=0}^{D} (ds)^i \qquad \text{(A.5)}$$

---

[4] This is not the only way to define a directed hypergraph. See [Ausiello+86] for another approach.

Note: Bibliography for Appendices A through F follows Appendix F.

Fixed Scheduling Algorithm

The following algorithm for scheduling traffic optimally in a fixed frame is adapted from [Gopal82]. The terminology used here is defined in Section 5.4.1.

The objective is to find a channel allocation schedule (CAS) that schedules all traffic in a given normalized traffic matrix T in a number of time slots L_{min}, given in Equation 5.59. Finding an optimal CAS is equivalent to decomposing T into a sum of matrices $C^{(s)}$, with elements that are nonnegative integers, satisfying the system constraints:

$$\sum_j c_{ij}^{(s)} \le \alpha_i \qquad i = 1, 2, \ldots, M \tag{B.1}$$

$$\sum_i c_{ij}^{(s)} \le \beta_j \qquad j = 1, 2, \ldots, N \tag{B.2}$$

$$\sum_{ij} c_{ij}^{(s)} \le C \tag{B.3}$$

and the traffic constraints

$$\sum_{s=1}^{L_{min}} C^{(s)} = T \tag{B.4}$$

First, some definitions:

A matrix with nonnegative integer entries that satisfies Equations B.1 and B.2 is called a *transmission matrix* (TM), and a TM satisfying those equations with equality is called a *complete* TM.

An $N \times N$ normalized traffic matrix for which all row and column sums equal some positive integer B is called a *quasi doubly stochastic* (QDS) matrix, and B is called the *line sum*.

An $M \times N$ normalized traffic matrix for which $\mathcal{R}'_j/\beta_j = \mathcal{T}'_i/\alpha_i = B$, for all i and j, where B is a positive integer, is called a *normalized quasi doubly stochastic* (NQDS) matrix. The quantity B is called the *normalized line sum*.

The steps in the algorithm are as follows. (These steps apply for the case $C < \min\left(\sum_{i=1}^{M} \alpha_i, \sum_{j=1}^{N} \beta_j\right)$. See comments at the end of the algorithm for the remaining cases.)

1. Extend the $M \times N$ matrix T into an $(M+1) \times (N+1)$ NQDS matrix Q as follows.
   (a) Corresponding to the extra column, define $\beta_{N+1} = \sum_{i=1}^{N} \alpha_i - C$, and corresponding to the extra row, define $\alpha_{M+1} = \sum_{j=1}^{M} \beta_j - C$. Denote the row sums and the column sums of Q by r_i^q and c_i^q respectively. Initially, set $r_{M+1}^q = c_{N+1}^q = 0$. (For the remaining row and column sums, $r_i^q = \mathcal{T}_i'$ and $c_j^q = \mathcal{R}_j'$ respectively.)
   (b) Add entries to row $M+1$ of Q as follows. To entry $q_{M+1, j}, 1 \le j \le N$, add

$$x_{M+1, j} = \min\left(\alpha_{N+1} L_{\min} - r_{M+1}^q, \beta_j L_{\min} - c_j^q\right) \tag{B.5}$$

   updating r_{M+1}^q and c_j^q with each addition. The process terminates when no further additions can be made, in which case $r_{M+1}^q = \alpha_{N+1} L_{\min}$.
   (c) Add entries to column $N+1$ of Q as follows. To entry $q_{i, N+1}, 1 \le i \le M$, add

$$x_{i, N+1} = \min\left(\beta_{M+1} L_{\min} - c_{N+1}^q, \alpha_i L_{\min} - r_i^q\right) \tag{B.6}$$

   updating c_{N+1}^q and r_i^q with each addition. The process terminates when no further additions can be made, in which case $c_{N+1}^q = \beta_{N+1} L_{\min}$.
   (d) Consider the submatrix Q' of Q defined by the first M rows and first N columns of Q. To entry q_{ij} in this submatrix, add

$$x_{ij} = \min\left(\beta_j L_{\min} - c_j^q, \alpha_i L_{\min} - r_i^q\right) \tag{B.7}$$

   updating c_j^q and r_i^q with each addition. (The matrix Q' is just the matrix T with some "dummy" traffic added.)
   (e) Now decompose the matrix Q into $L_{\min}$ complete TMs in the following steps.

2. Use the *column/row–expansion algorithm* (see Section B.1) to expand Q to a QDS matrix, A.

3. Decompose A into a sum of permutation matrices $A = a(1) + a(2) + \cdots + a(L_{\min})$ (see Section B.2).

4. Use the *column/row–compression algorithm* (see Section B.3) to reduce the $a(i)$'s to $q(1), q(2), \ldots, q(L_{\min})$, where the $q(i)$'s are complete TMs.

5. Remove the last column and row of each matrix $q(i)$ to form an $M \times N$ matrix $q'(i)$.

6. Remove dummy traffic from each $q'(i)$ to convert it to $C^{(i)}$ by letting $C^{(1)} = \min(T, q'[1])$, and $C^{(i)} = \min\left(T - \sum_{j=1}^{i-1} C^{(j)}, q'[i]\right)$ for $i = 2, 3, \ldots, L_{\min}$.

In the case when $C = \sum_{j=1}^{N} \beta_j$, Q is constructed as an $M \times (N+1)$ matrix. Entries are added as indicated in Step 1, first to the $(N+1)^{\text{th}}$ column, and then to the submatrix Q' to make Q into an NQDS matrix. In the case when $C = \sum_{i=1}^{M} \alpha_i$, Q is constructed as an $(M+1) \times N$ matrix in an analogous fashion. The various procedures used here are described next in detail.

B.1   Column/Row-Expansion Algorithm

In Step 2, the matrix Q was expanded to an $H \times H$ QDS matrix, A, with line sum L_{min}, where $H = \sum_{j=1}^{N+1} \beta_j = \sum_{i=1}^{M+1} \alpha_i$. First, expand Q into an $(M+1) \times H$ matrix Q_1 by replacing each column of Q by an $(M+1) \times \beta_j$ matrix B_j. The following procedure is used. Let c_l^a be the column sum of the lth column in B_j and r_k^a the row sum of the kth row of B_j. Starting with $B_j = 0$, add to the (k, l) element of B_j, the quantity

$$x_{kl} = \min\left(L_{min} - c_l^a, t_{kj} - r_k^a\right) \tag{B.8}$$

executing this operation for each element of B_j and updating c_l^a and r_k^a each time. The process terminates when no further additions can be made.

A similar operation is executed on the rows of Q_1 to give the $H \times H$ matrix A. Row i of Q_1 is replaced by an $\alpha_i \times H$ matrix A_i. Let c_l^b be the lth column sum of A_i, and r_k^b the kth row sum. Then add to the (k, l) element of A_i, the quantity

$$x_{kl} = \min\left(L_{min} - r_k^b, t_{kj}' - c_l^b\right) \tag{B.9}$$

executing this operation for each element of A_i and updating c_l^b and r_k^b each time. The process terminates when no further additions can be made. The resultant matrix A is an $H \times H$ QDS matrix of line sum L_{min}.

B.2   Decomposition into Permutation Matrices

In Step 3 the QDS expanded traffic matrix A is decomposed into a sum of permutation matrices. First A is represented by a bipartite multigraph with vertices on the left (right) representing rows (columns), and with an edge from left to right representing each unit of traffic in A. Then, a complete maximum cardinality matching is found, defining a permutation matrix $a(1)$. (See [Lawler76] for an efficient matching algorithm.) This is subtracted from A and the process is repeated until a decomposition $A = a(1) + a(2) + \cdots + a(L_{min})$ is determined.

B.3   Column/Row-Compression Algorithm

In Step 4 the $H \times H$ permutation matrices $a(i)$ are compressed into $(M+1) \times (N+1)$ matrices $q(i)$. First, $a(i)$ is compressed along the rows to obtain an $(M+1) \times H$ matrix $a'(i)$ as follows. The kth row of $a'(i)$ is constructed by taking the sum of the rows of $a(i)$ corresponding to α_k. Similarly, an $(M+1) \times (N+1)$ matrix $q(i)$ is formed with an lth column that is the sum of the columns of $a'(i)$ corresponding to β_l. Each of the matrices $q(i)$ is a complete TM.

Examples of these procedures appear in Figures B.1 and B.2. Given an NQDS matrix Q, the expansion, decomposition, and compression steps are illustrated in Figure B.1.

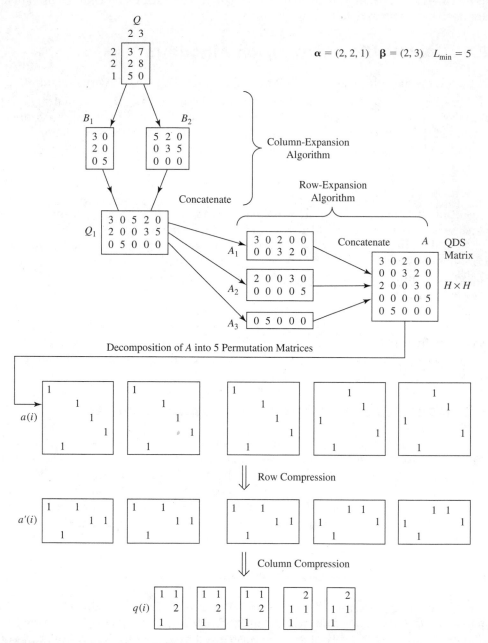

FIGURE B.1 Example of decomposition of an NQDS matrix. (From (Gopal82, Figure 2.7). Used by permission of the author.)

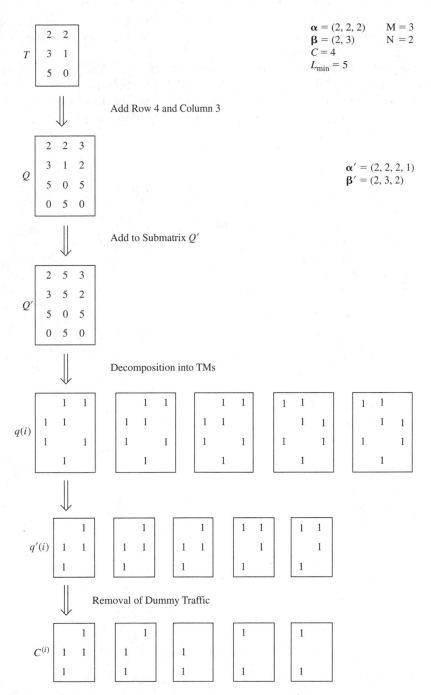

FIGURE B.2 Example of fixed-frame scheduling. (From (Gopal82, Figure 2.8). Used by permission of the author.)

A 3×2 NQDS matrix Q is expanded to a 5×5 QDS matrix A (Step 2), which is decomposed into five permutation matrices $a(i)$ (Step 3). These are compressed in turn into five 3×2 matrices $q(i)$.

In Figure B.2, a 3×2 traffic matrix T is extended to a 4×3 NQDS matrix Q (Step 1), which is decomposed into five permutation matrices (not shown) via the expansion and decomposition steps illustrated in Figure B.1. These are compressed in turn into five 4×3 matrices $q(i)$, which are reduced to five 3×2 matrices $q'(i)$, and then to the final form $C^{(i)}$ (Steps 4, 5, and 6).

Markov Chains and Queues

At various points in the book we use stochastic traffic and queueing models to represent the behavior of a network under conditions of random demand. These are based on Markov processes as well as some more general queueing models, which are summarized in this appendix. A readable and comprehensive treatment of these models may be found in [Kleinrock75].

C.1 Random Processes

Random processes such as connection requests, contents of packet queues, and so forth, can be described as sequences of random variables, often called the *states* of the process, with *state transitions* occurring at successive (isolated) time points. (Between state transitions, the state remains constant.) In *discrete state processes*, the states take on discrete (typically integer) values, whereas in *continuous state processes* the states take on a continuum of values. For example, a discrete state process might be the length of a packet queue, whereas a continuous state process might be the random noise generated in an electrical circuit. In *discrete time processes* the transitions are spaced regularly in time so that a complete description of the process is given by the state sequence alone. In *continuous time processes* the transitions may occur randomly, at any point in time.

A *realization* of a random process is a specific sequence. In the case of discrete time processes, a realization is completely specified as a sequence of states. In continuous time processes, the transition times must also be specified. For example, if the process consists of the state of a queue, a realization would consist of the sequence of queue lengths and the state transition times corresponding to arrivals and departures from the queue.

In many applications, only the transition (event) times themselves are of interest. For example, the random process that consists of connection requests that arrive at a network controller is described completely by the times at which these events occur. Such processes are called *point processes*.

An important special case of a point process is the *renewal process*. A renewal process is defined in terms of a sequence of event times, t_i, where the times between successive events $\tau_i = t_i - t_{i-1}$ are *independent identically distributed random variables*. Thus a renewal process is characterized completely by the PDF of its interevent times, $f_\tau(x)$.

An important special case of a renewal process is the Poisson process. A *Poisson process* is a renewal process with exponentially distributed interevent times:

$$f_\tau(x) = \lambda \epsilon^{-\lambda x}$$

The positive parameter λ is the *rate* of the process.

Another equivalent way of defining a Poisson process is in terms of a set of postulates. An informal statement of the Poisson postulates is as follows:

- The probability of an event occurring in a very small time interval of width Δt is $\lambda \Delta t$.

- The probability of more than one event occurring in a very small time interval is negligible.

- Events occurring in different intervals are *statistically independent*.

The latter property implies that a Poisson process is "memoryless." That is, the occurrence of an event at one point in time has no relation to the occurrence of an event at any other point in time.

From these postulates it is possible to derive the *Poisson distribution* for the number of events k occurring in a Poisson process of rate λ in a time interval T:

$$\text{Prob}[k \text{ events in time } T] = \frac{(\lambda T)^k}{k!} \epsilon^{-\lambda T} \tag{C.1}$$

From Equation C.1 it can be deduced that the interevent times of the Poisson process are distributed exponentially, as indicated previously. For this reason, the exponential distribution is often called a *memoryless distribution*.

C.2 Markov Processes

One of the most useful mathematical models for analyzing a wide variety of stochastic processes is the *Markov process*. In general random processes, statistical dependencies typically exist among various combinations of successive states in the process. A Markov process may be defined informally as a random process in which any future state depends only on its current state. That is, the current state embodies the "probabilistic memory" of the process back to the infinite past. As in general random processes, Markov processes (or Markov chains) can be defined with discrete or continuous states, and in discrete or continuous time. We focus here on

---

Addicts of slot machines don't believe in Poisson processes!

The term *Markov chain* is sometimes reserved for a discrete-time Markov process. We shall use it to mean any Markov process.

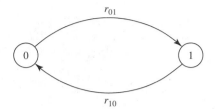

FIGURE C.1 Two-state chain.

discrete-state continuous-time chains. The simplest example is a two-state chain, with a state transition diagram shown in Figure C.1.

This might represent a source generating call requests, which is alternately in an active or idle state, indicated as 1 and 0 respectively. (The active state would correspond to a call connection.) The *state transition rate* from 0 to 1 is indicated as r_{01}, and from 1 to 0 as r_{10}. The significance of a state transition rate in a Markov chain is as follows. If the chain is in a state i at time t, the probability that it will change to state j in a small time interval, $(t, t + \Delta t)$, is given by the state transition rate r_{ij} times the length of the interval, Δt. Thus, if we denote the time-dependent state probabilities for this chain as $p_1(t)$ and $p_0(t)$, and use the rates just defined, the evolution of these probabilities in time is governed by the *forward differential equations*

$$\frac{dp_0}{dt} = -r_{01} p_0 + r_{10} p_1 \tag{C.2}$$

$$\frac{dp_1}{dt} = -r_{10} p_1 + r_{01} p_0 \tag{C.3}$$

A chain is said to be *ergodic* if, as $t \to \infty$, its state probabilities tend toward a unique set of positive *equilibrium* or *ergodic* probabilities independent of their initial values. These correspond to a *statistical steady state*. For example, letting π_0 and π_1 be the equilibrium values of p_0 and p_1 respectively for the two-state chain, positive equilibrium probabilities exist for this chain as long as both transition rates are nonzero. (If one rate is zero, one of the equilibrium probabilities is zero, and if both rates are zero, the chain remains in its initial state forever.) If the chain is ergodic, the equilibrium probabilities can be found by setting the derivatives to zero in the forward differential equations and using the normalization relation $\sum_i \pi_i = 1$. In the case of the two-state chain, this gives $\pi_0 = r_{10}/(r_{10} + r_{01})$.

This discussion generalizes in a natural way to chains with any finite number of states. An example is the $(C+1)$-state chain shown in Figure 5.29(b), which represents the behavior of a population of M users competing for $C < M$ channels in a circuit-switched system.

Because of this property, the time that a Markov chain remains in any given state is distributed exponentially, with a mean value equal to the reciprocal of the sum of the transition rates from that state.

Certain easily verifiable conditions on the state transition diagram are required to ensure ergodicity in the general case.

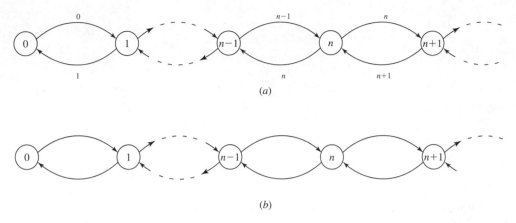

FIGURE C.2 Birth–death process.

Markov chains may also be defined with an infinite number of states. An important example of such a chain is the infinite birth–death process shown in Figure C.2(a). As indicated in the figure, the "birth rate," λ_n, is the transition rate from state n to state $n+1$, and the "death rate," μ_n, is the transition rate from state n to state $n-1$. Ergodicity of infinite chains typically depends on certain "stability" conditions related to the underlying physical phenomena they represent.

The relations among the equilibrium probabilities, π_n, for an ergodic birth–death process are deduced easily by noting that in the steady state a "balance condition" must exist among the average "flows" between states. The balance condition requires that $\pi_n \lambda_n = \pi_{n+1} \mu_{n+1}$, $n = 1, 2, \ldots$. Using this relation recursively gives

$$\pi_n = \left(\prod_{k=1}^{n} \frac{\lambda_{k-1}}{\mu_k} \right) \pi_0, \quad n = 1, 2, \ldots \tag{C.4}$$

where

$$\pi_0 = \left[1 + \sum_{n=1}^{\infty} \left(\prod_{k=1}^{n} \frac{\lambda_{k-1}}{\mu_k} \right) \right]^{-1} \tag{C.5}$$

The Erlang traffic model described in Section 5.5.1.1 is an example of a finite birth–death process with $(C + 1)$ states. It represents an infinite population that generates connection requests in a Poisson fashion at a rate λ, with exponentially distributed holding times of average duration μ^{-1}. The birth rates in this case are $\lambda_n = \lambda$, and the death rates are $\mu_n = n\mu$, $n = 1, 2, \ldots, C$.

C.3 Queues

Queues are simply storage devices (buffers or "waiting rooms") that are useful in any system in which a resource (e.g., a communication link or bank teller) is being shared among a number of users (e.g., packets or bank customers), and for which there is random demand on the resource. For example, in a packet switch, randomness exists because the packet arrival process is random, and the packet service and/or processing time may be random as well. In a circuit-switched system, randomness exists because the connection request process is random and holding times are typically random as well.

A queue is described by its arrival process, its service time distribution, and other factors such as its service discipline (e.g., FCFS or priorities), the number of servers, and the buffer size (finite or infinite). To fix the terminology, let us think in terms of a packet queue. The key parameters defining its operation are its average arrival rate, λ (packets per second); average service rate, μ (packets per second); and its *traffic intensity*, $\rho = \lambda/\mu$. The state, n, of the queue is defined as the number of packets it contains. The performance parameters of interest in a queue are average queue length, average time spent in the queue, and possibly other quantities such as average packet loss, complete queue length distributions, and so forth. To illustrate, Figure C.3 shows a single-server queue in state n, with a finite buffer holding a maximum of K packets.

C.3.1 The *M*|*M*|*1* Queue

For purposes of analysis, the $M|M|1$ queue is the simplest. The three arguments in the queue notation refer to the arrival process (the first M for Markovian), the service process (the second M, again Markovian), and the number of servers (one). A Markovian arrival process is a Poisson process. A Markovian service process corresponds to exponentially distributed service times. For example, in the case of a packet queue, the service time refers to the time to transmit a packet at some fixed bitrate. It is, approximately, distributed exponentially if packets have random lengths (in bits) drawn from a geometric probability distribution.

The significance of the fact that both the arrival and service processes are Markovian is that the queue can be modeled as an infinite birth–death process, as shown in Figure C.2(b). The chain has an infinite number of states corresponding to an infinite number of packet buffers. (A more realistic model would be truncated to a

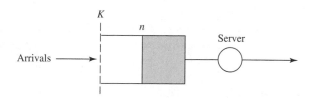

FIGURE C.3 A queue.

finite number of states reflecting finite buffer capacity.) The birth rates λ represent the average packet arrival rate to the queue, and the death rates μ represent the average packet service rate. Taking the queue's traffic intensity as $\rho = \lambda/\mu$, we find that the queue is *stable* (i.e., ergodic) if and only if $\rho < 1$. For all larger values of ρ (including $\rho = 1$), the average queue length grows without bound so that all state probabilities tend toward zero as $t \to \infty$. In the stable case, Equations C.4 and C.5 reduce to the geometric queue length distribution $\pi_n = \rho^n(1 - \rho)$, with an average queue length of $\bar{N} = \rho/(1 - \rho)$.

C.3.2 The *M*|*G*|*1* Queue

Many typical queues are not Markovian. A commonly encountered class is the $M|G|1$ queue, where G denotes a *general* service process. These queues have Poisson arrivals and a service time τ, with a general probability density function $f_\tau(x)$. A very simple example is the $M|D|1$ queue (D for deterministic service time) with $f_\tau(x) = \delta(x - t_0)$, with a constant service time t_0. Markov chains cannot be used for analysis of $M|G|1$ queues. Although the details of performance, such as complete queue length distributions, are not computed easily, the average queue length has the following closed-form expression:

$$\bar{N} = \frac{\rho}{1 - \rho}\left[1 - \frac{\rho}{2}(1 - \mu^2\sigma^2)\right] \tag{C.6}$$

where μ^{-1} and σ^2 denote the mean and the variance of the service time distribution respectively. Equation C.6 is known as the *Pollaczek–Khinchine* formula. Note that in the case of the $M|D|1$ queue Equation C.6 reduces to $\bar{N} = \frac{\rho}{1-\rho}\left[1 - \frac{\rho}{2}\right]$.

C.3.3 Little's Formula

There is a very simple and general relationship between the average time spent in a queue and the average queue occupancy, known as *Little's formula*. Denoting the average time in the queue (including time being served) by $\bar{T}$ and the average queue occupancy (including the packet in service) as $\bar{N}$, Little's formula is

$$\bar{N} = \lambda\bar{T} \tag{C.7}$$

where λ is the average arrival rate to the queue. For example, for an $M|M|1$ queue, Equation C.7 gives $\bar{T} = 1/\mu(1 - \rho)$.

A Limiting-Cut Heuristic

The concept of the limiting cut, introduced in Section 6.3.1.2, stems from the Min Cut–Max Flow relation in multicommodity flow problems. We first give a brief summary of this problem and then present a heuristic for finding limiting cuts.

D.1 The Multicommodity Flow Problem and Limiting Cuts

In the most common version of the multicommodity flow problem, a set of *demands* are prescribed between source–destination node pairs in a network with a given topology and link capacities. (Each source–destination demand is known as a *commodity*, and the network can be anything—gas pipelines, airline routes, highways, and so on.) The basic issue is whether the prescribed demands can be satisfied within the capacity constraints; that is, whether all commodities can be routed through the network (in a bifurcated manner if necessary) so that the total flow of all commodities on each link does not exceed its capacity. If so, the demands are said to be feasible.

In wavelength routed networks (WRNs), the commodities (demands) are LCs, each requiring one λ-channel, so that the capacity of a cut $\mathcal{C}_i$ is $F_i W$, where F_i is the number of fiber pairs in the cut and W is the number of available wavelengths. Because a channel in a WRN is a single point-to-point entity, bifurcated routing is not permitted in a WRN. (An exception would be a case in which several λ-channels are required to carry the flow on one LC.)

The relations between cut capacities and feasible demands were stated in Section A.1.8 for the single-commodity case. In the multicommodity case, which is of interest here, the relations are considerably more complex. However, it is clear that a prescribed set of demands is *not* feasible if a "bad cut" exists with a capacity that is less than the total flow required from all sources on one side of the cut to all destinations on the other side. In the context of WRNs, the capacity of a cut is proportional to W. Thus, the capacity of all bad cuts can be scaled up by increasing W so that all bad cuts can be eliminated by making W sufficiently large. (However, the nonexistence of bad cuts does *not* guarantee that the prescribed connections can be accommodated on the network.) This leads directly to the expression for W_{Limcut} given in Equation 6.10, which is a *necessary* (but not sufficient) condition on the number of available wavelengths required to support a given set of LCs.

Even though W_{Limcut} is only a lower bound on the actual number of required wavelengths, experiments with realistic network topologies indicate that the bound is often tight. Thus it is important to be able to compute it (or something close to it), especially in cases of large networks in which heuristics must be relied on for routing and channel assignment.

D.2 A Heuristic

Because the complexity of computing W_{Limcut} grows exponentially with the number of network nodes N, it is out of the question to compute it for large N. Instead we present a heuristic for determining a lower bound, $\underline{W}_{\text{Limcut}}$, on W_{Limcut} for a prescribed set of M LCs on a network with a given topology. The algorithm is based on examining randomly selected cuts of the network rather than all cuts, and has a computational complexity $O(N^3)$.

Denote the set of network nodes by V, where $N = |V|$. Let C_{xy} be a cut induced by partitioning V into two sets X and Y. Let M_{xy} be the number of prescribed LCs from X to Y and F_{xy} be the total number of fiber pairs in all links comprising the cut C_{xy}. Two procedures are used: Swap and Limcut.

D.2.1 Swap(*X, Y*)

This procedure determines a lower bound, W_0, on the number of wavelengths required to support LCs across cuts between subsets of nodes X and Y of cardinality k and $N - k$ respectively, and also determines a node partition (X_0, Y_0) with connections across the cut that require W_0 wavelengths.

```
procedure Swap(X,Y)

        Initially All nodes are unmarked.

        let W₀ = W = Mₓy/Fₓy

        let X₀ = X and Y₀ = Y

        repeat

            Select two unmarked nodes i ∈ X and j ∈ Y so that  M(X−i+j),(Y−j+i)
                                                                ─────────────────
                                                                F(X−i+j),(Y−j+i)
            is maximum.

            Swap i and j so that X ← X+j-i and Y ← Y+i-j.

            Update W and mark i and j.

            if W ≥ W₀ then

                W₀ ← W, X₀ ← X and Y₀ ← Y.

            end if

        until all nodes in X or Y are marked

    return (X₀,Y₀,W₀)

end Swap
```

D.2.2 Limcut

The procedure Limcut determines $\underline{W}_{\text{Limcut}}$, a lower bound on W_{Limcut}, by applying the Swap procedure to partitions of V containing k nodes, with k ranging from 1 to $N/2$.

```
procedure Limcut

    W_Limcut = 0

    repeat q times

        for k = 1 to N/2

            Randomly partition V into a set X_k, containing k nodes,

                and Y_k, containing N − k nodes.

            let W_k − M_{X_kY_k}/F_{X_kY_k}

            repeat

                (X_0, Y_0, W_0) = Swap(X_k, Y_k)

                if W_0 > W_k then

                        W_k ← W_0

                        X_k ← X_0

                        Y_k ← Y_0

                end if

            until no increase is observed after q consecutive swaps

        end for

        if max_k W_k > W_Limcut then

            W_Limcut ← max_k W_k

        end if

    end repeat

    return W_Limcut

end Limcut
```

The parameter q is chosen sufficiently large (e.g., $q = 200$) to ensure that $\underline{W}_{\text{Limcut}} \approx W_{\text{Limcut}}$.

An Algorithm for Minimum-Interference Routing in Linear Lightwave Networks

Given a source s and destination d for a point-to-point connection on a selected wave-band in an LLN, the Min-Int algorithm presented here attempts to find a minimum-interference optical path $p = \langle s, d \rangle$ for that connection on the given waveband. The exact sense in which interference is minimized requires some explanation, and is defined in Section E.3.

E.1 The Image Network

The approach used to find a path that minimizes interference is based on shortest path calculations, where the path "length" takes into account weights or "lengths" representing currently active interfering signals. These weights are associated with nodes rather than links. A useful way of visualizing the node-weighting procedure is shown in the image network of Figure E.1. In the network shown in the figure, each node of the original network is "blown up" to create additional intranodal links between each input/output port pair. This is nothing more than a representation of the internal structure of the LDC on the chosen waveband (see Figure 2.20[b]). The image network of Figure E.1 corresponds to state of activity in the network of Figure 6.59. Two optical connections, $(1, 1^*)$ and $(2, 2^*)$, are active, with signal S_1 transmitted from station 1 to 1^* and signal S_2 transmitted from station 2 to 2^*.

We shall denote an internodal link from node i to node j by (i, j), and assign it a positive weight $d(i, j)$. An *intranodal* link inside node k joining inbound link (i, k) to outbound link (k, j) will be assigned a weight $I_k(i, j)$, representing the additional interference accumulated by inseparability as a signal traverses node k on a path $i–k–j$. The *transnodal weight* $I_k(i, j)$ is computed as follows. Let $G(i, k)$ be the set of signals carried on link (i, k) on the chosen waveband, and let M be a large number

---

This is shown for illustrative purposes only. The algorithm does not require the construction of an image network.

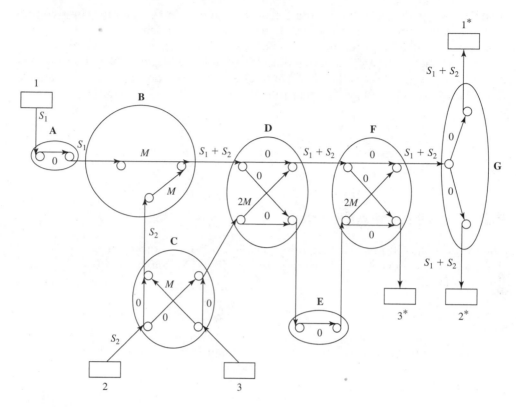

FIGURE E.1 Image network.

(greater than the sum of all internodal link weights). Then

$$I_k(i, j) = M|G(k, j) - G(i, k)| \tag{E.1}$$

For example, in Figure E.1 we have $G(B, D) = \{S_1, S_2\}$, $G(A, B) = \{S_1\}$, and $G(C, B) = \{S_2\}$. Thus, $I_B(A, D) = I_B(C, D) = M$. The transnodal weights for the current state of the network (two connections in progress) are shown in the figure.

Now a new connection from station 3 to 3* is to be routed on a minimum-interference path (i.e., one for which the number of interfering signals accumulated along the way is minimum). The algorithm attempts to find such a path by choosing a path $p = \langle 3, 3^* \rangle$, which is shortest according to the assigned internodal and transnodal weights. In the case at hand, if all internodal links have weight one, the shortest path for this connection is 3–C–D–E–F–3*, for which the total "length" is five, which is the total number of hops (including the access links). Note that the minimum-hop path 3–C–D–F–3* is *not* chosen. It has a total length $4 + 2M$, indicating that there are two interfering signals accumulated along this path due to inseparability. The five-hop path detours around the link carrying these signals and thereby avoids interference. In general, using this approach, the effect of the transnodal weights outweighs all link weights, so that paths are found based on interference, with ties broken by the internodal link weights. If W is the total length of a path based on the assigned weights, then $\lfloor W/M \rfloor$ is the number of signals interfering with the desired signal on the path in question.

E.2 The Min-Int Algorithm

The Min-Int algorithm for finding minimum-interference shortest paths is presented here. It is based on Dijkstra's shortest path algorithm [Tarjan83], modified to include the transnodal weights.

```
Min-Int Algorithm
```

Finds the shortest paths from node 1 to all other nodes in a network based on internodal weights $d(i,j)$ and transnodal weights $I_k(i,j)$ (as defined earlier).

```
INITIALIZATION
```

To each node, i, assign a label, l_i, a weight, w_i (denoting distance from node 1 to i), and a predecessor, p_i (denoting the node preceding i on the shortest path from 1 to i). The label $l_i = 0$ ($l_i = 1$) indicates that the weight and predecessor are temporary (permanent). Set $w_1 = p_1 = 0$, and $l_1 = 1$. For all other nodes, set $w_i = \infty$, $p_i = 0$, and $l_i = 0$.

```
BEGIN
```

STEP 1: Find a node i such that $l_i = 0$ and w_i is minimum among all nodes labeled temporary ($l_j = 0$). Set $l_i = 1$.

STEP 2: For every node k adjacent to i:

   IF $w_i + I_i(p_i, k) + d(i,k) < w_k$

   THEN Set $w_k = w_i + I_i(p_i, k) + d(i,k)$. Set $p_k = i$.

STEP 3: IF all nodes are labeled permanent, then the algorithm terminates and the minimum-interference path to any node t can be obtained by tracing back the predecessors from t to 1.

ELSE GOTO STEP 1.

```
END
```

E.3 Minimum Interference

The paths found by Min-Int are not necessarily feasible because they have not been checked for DSC violations, color clashes, or channel availability. However, they have the following minimum-interference property:

> **Theorem:** If the DSC condition is satisfied on a path $p = \langle s, d \rangle$, found by the Min-Int algorithm, then it is the path along which the maximum *incremental interference* is minimized from among all paths between s and d that satisfy the DSC constraint on the chosen waveband.

In this theorem the incremental interference associated with a path p is defined as the additional interference caused at a receiver on the chosen waveband due to the activation of a connection on path p. The maximization is over all stations that receive some additional interference due to the activation of the new connection.

See [Bala92] for proof.

Synopsis of the SONET Standard

SONET, the acronym for synchronous optical network, is currently the prevailing standard for high-speed digital transmission in North America. Introduced in the 1980s, it replaces an earlier standard, the *plesiochronous digital hierarchy* (PDH), which had been in place for more than two decades prior to the introduction of the SONET standard [Ballart+89]. The most frequently used lower levels of the PDH system are the DS1 (1.544 Mbps, designed to carry 24 64-Kbps digitized voice signals plus synchronizing overhead) and DS3, running at 44.736 Mbps. An architecture similar to SONET, the synchronous digital hierarchy (SDH), is currently used in Europe and Japan, replacing an earlier European hierarchy similar to the PDH system. SONET can carry PDH bitstreams as well as many other types of digital traffic (e.g., ATM cells) as part of its payload. One of the most important features of SONET is its highly organized protection capability [Wu92].

The basic building block (i.e., the first level) of the SONET signal hierarchy is called the *synchronous transport signal-level 1* (STS-1). STS-1 has a bitrate of 51.84 Mbps and is divided into two portions: transport overhead and information payload, and the transport overhead is divided further into line and section overheads. (A line is composed of one or more sections in series, separated by electronic regenerators.) The line overhead is terminated at SONET terminals and Add–Drop Multiplexers (ADMs), and the section overhead is terminated at regenerators. The STS-1 frame consists of 90 columns and nine rows of eight-bit bytes as shown in Figure F.1. The transmission order of the bytes is row by row, from left to right, with one entire frame being transmitted every 125 μsec. The first three columns contain transport overhead, and the remaining 87 columns and nine rows (a total of 783 bytes) carry the STS-1 synchronous payload envelope (SPE). As an example, a DS3 signal can be carried within an STS-1 SPE.

A SONET *path* is the basic end-to-end connection entity. The SPE contains a nine-byte path overhead and is used for end-to-end service performance monitoring.

Optical carrier level 1 (OC-1) is the lowest level optical signal used at equipment and network interfaces. The OC-1 signal is obtained from an STS-1 bitstream after scrambling and electrical-to-optical conversion.

The overhead bytes are used in SONET for network control and management. This includes a variety of functions such as performance monitoring and protection switching. As an example, the K1 and K2 bytes form a two-byte APS message channel.

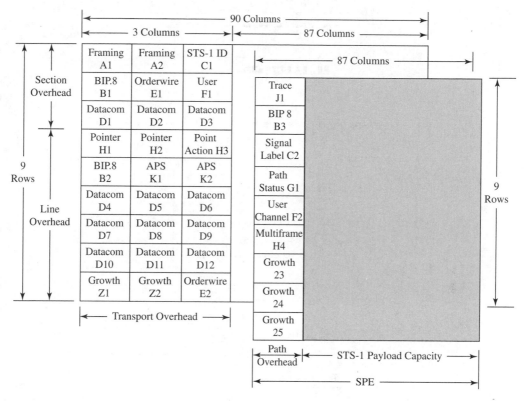

FIGURE F.1 SONET STS-1 frame and overhead channels. (From (Wu92, Figure 2.7). Copyright ©1992. Used by permission of Artech House, Norwood, MA.)

Higher rate optical signals are formed by byte interleaving an integral number of STS-1s. Figure F.2 shows an example of how an OC-N signal is formed in the multiplexing side of a SONET TDM terminal. Services like DS3 and DS1 are mapped into an SPE. A number of STS-1s are then byte interleaved and multiplexed to form an STS-N. The frame is scrambled after section overhead (except framing and STS-N ID) is added. Framing and STS-N ID are then added into the section overhead of the scrambled STS-N, and finally the STS-N signal is converted into the optical signal OC-N. For example, an OC-48 signal might carry 48 DS3s. The reverse operations are executed on the demultiplexing side.

The OC-N line rate is exactly N times that of OC-1, and all higher rate standard interface signals are readily defined in terms of STS-1. An OC-N signal may be formed from various combinations of lower speed signals. For example, an OC-12 might be composed of 12 OC-1s, four OC-3s, or any other combination resulting in the correct aggregate bitrate.

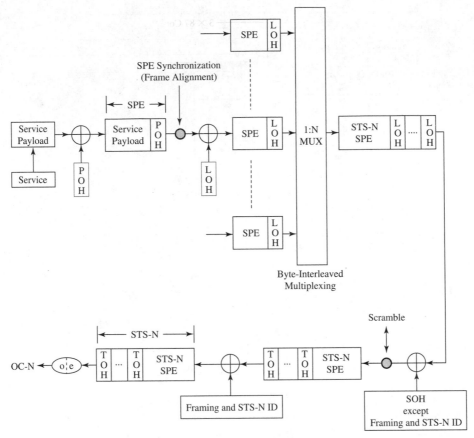

FIGURE F.2 Creating an OC-N signal. (From (Wu92, Figure 2.8). Copyright ©1992. Used by permission of Artech House, Norwood, MA.)

The STS-1 SPE can carry one DS3 signal (called a *tributary*) or a mix of sub-DS3 signals. The DS1 is a typical sub-DS3 signal that can be mapped into a SONET unit called the *virtual tributary-1.5* (VT-1.5). An STS-1 SPE can carry as many as 28 VT-1.5s. VT-1.5 has an actual bitrate of 1.728 Mbps.

Broadband services requiring more than the capacity of one STS-1 are transported by concatenated STS-1s. For example, high definition television signals requiring 135 Mbps can be carried by three concatenated STS-1s, denoted by STS-3c, which has transport overheads and payload envelopes that are aligned.

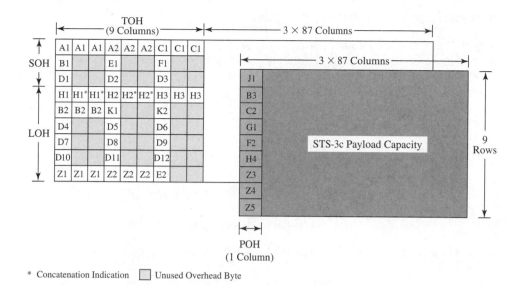

FIGURE F.3 Structure of a concatenated SONET frame. (From (Wu92, Figure 2.9). Copyright ©1992. Used by permission of Artech House, Norwood, MA.)

Figure F.3 shows the frame structure of a SONET STS-3c signal. In the format shown in the figure, the first of three H1 and H2 bytes contains a valid SPE pointer, whereas the second and third H1 and H2 bytes contain a concatenation indicator that prevents the STS-3c signals from being demultiplexed. Concatenation specifies that these signals are considered as a single unit and are to be transferred as such through the network.

When two or more SONET lines are incident on a network node, they are typically switched via a SONET ADM or DCS, which in current systems operates on the signals at the DS3 level. Thus, as shown in Figure 6.76 for example, the SONET terminals demultiplex the OC-N signals down to the DS3 tributaries, and the DCS is responsible for routing the DS3s to the correct outbound lines. In addition, the DCS implements protection and grooming functions.

Grooming is the operation that packs tributary signals efficiently into higher rate optical carriers. For example, grooming is used to assign DS3s to an OC-48 signal such that their paths all terminate at the same central office without requiring any demultiplexing along the way. Efficient grooming reduces the need to gain access to tributary signals at intermediate network nodes before they reach their destination.

Appendices A–F Bibliography

[Alspach+85] B. R. Alspach and C. D. Godsil. *Cycles in Graphs, Annals of Discrete Mathematics*, Vol. 115. Amsterdam: Elsevier Science Publishers B.V., 1985.

[Ausiello+86] G. Ausiello, A. D'Atri, and D. Sacca. Minimal representation of directed hypergraphs. *SIAM J. Comput.*, 15(2):418–431, 1986.

[Bala92] K. Bala. *Routing in Linear Lightwave Networks*. PhD thesis. New York: Columbia University, 1992.

[Ballart+89] R. Ballart and Y-C. Ching. SONET: Now it's the standard optical network. *IEEE Communications Mag.*, March: 8–15, 1989.

[Berge89] C. Berge. *Hypergraphs, North-Holland Mathematical Library*, Vol. 45. Amsterdam: Elsevier Science Publishers B.V., 1989.

[Bermond+97] J-C. Bermond, R. Dawes, and F. O. Ergincan. de Bruijn and Kautz bus networks. *Networks*, 30:205–218, 1997.

[Brelaz79] D. Brelaz. New methods to color the vertices of a graph. *Comm. ACM*, 22(2):251–256, 1979.

[Chartrand+96] G. Chartrand and L. Lesniak-Foster. *Graphs and Digraphs*. New York: Chapman and Hall, 1996.

[Fleischner90] H. Fleischner. *Eulerian Graphs and Related Topics, Part I: Vol. 1. Annals of Discrete Mathematics*, Vol. 45. Amsterdam: Elsevier Science Publishers B.V., 1990.

[Ford+64] L. Ford and D. Fulkerson. *Flows in Networks*. Princeton: Princeton University Press, 1964.

[Gopal82] I. S. Gopal. *Scheduling Algorithms for Multibeam Communications Satellites*. PhD thesis. New York: Columbia University, 1982.

[Kleinrock75] L. Kleinrock. *Queueing Systems*, Vol. 1. New York: John Wiley & Sons, 1975.

[Lawler76] E. Lawler. *Combinatorial Optimization: Networks and Matroids*. Philadelphia: Saunders College Publishing, 1976.

[Szekeres73] G. Szekeres. Polyhedral decomposition of cubic graphs. *Bull. Austral. Math. Soc.*, 8:367–387, 1973.

[Tarjan83] R. E. Tarjan. *Data Structures and Network Algorithms*. Philadelphia: Society for Industrial and Applied Mathematics, 1983.

[Wu92] T-H. Wu. *Fiber Network Service Survivability*. Norwood, MA: Artech House, 1992.

ADM	Add–drop multiplexer
AIS	Alarm indication signal
AM	Amplitude modulation
AON	All Optical Network
AOTF	Acousto-optic tunable filter
APD	Avalanche photodiode
APS	Automatic protection switching
ARQ	Automatic repeat request
ASE	Amplified spontaneous emission
ATM	Asynchronous transfer mode
AWG	Arrayed waveguide grating
BER	Bit error rate
BH	Buried heterostructure
B-ISDN	Broadband integrated services digital network
BLSR	Bidirectional line-switched ring
BPF	Bandpass filter
BPSK	Binary phase shift keying
C^3	Cleaved–coupled cavity
CAS	Channel allocation schedule
CDC	Cycle double cover
CDMA	Code–division multiple access
CIR	Carrier-to-interference ratio
CNR	Carrier-to-noise ratio
CRC	Cyclic redundancy code
CSMA/CD	Carrier-sense multiple access with collision detection
DA	Destination address
DBR	Distributed Bragg reflector
DCA	Distinct channel assignment
DCF	Dispersion-compensating fiber
DCS	Digital cross-connect system
DEMOD	Demodulator

DFB	Distributed-feedback
DFC	Difference frequency converter
DLC	Data link control
DMUX	Demultiplexer
DQDB	Distributed queue dual bus
DSC	Distinct source combining
DSF	Dispersion shifted fiber
DSn	Digital signal-level n
DT-WDMA	Dynamic T-WDMA
ED	Electrical detector
EDF	Erbium-doped fiber
EDFA	Erbium-doped fiber amplifier
EON	European Optical Network
ETDM	Electrical–time–division multiplexing
FBG	Fiber Bragg grating
FCFS	First-come-first-served
FDDI	Fiber distributed data interface
FITNESS	Failure Immunization Technology for Network Service Survivability
FM	Frequency modulation
FP	Fabry–Perot
FSK	Frequency-shift keying
FT-TR	Fixed transmitter with tunable receiver
FWHM	Full width at half maximum
FWM	Four-wave mixing
GRIN	Graded refractive index
GUI	Graphic-user interface
HBT	Heterojunction bipolar transistor
HOL	Head-of-the-line (blocking)
ID	Identifier
IDT	Interdigital transducer
IF	Intermediate frequency
ILP	Integer linear program
IM/DD	Intensity-modulated direct-detection
IP	Internet protocol
ISDN	Integrated services digital network
ISI	Intersymbol interference
ITU	International Telecommunications Union
ITU-T	International Telecommunications Union–Telecommunication Standardization Sector

IXC	Interexchange carrier
k-SP	k shortest path
LAN	Local area network
LAS	Local access subnet
LC	Logical connection; limiting cut (Appendix C)
LCC	Lost calls cleared
LCD	Liquid crystal device
LCG	Logical connection graph
LCH	Logical connection hypergraph
LDC	Linear divider combiner
LEC	Local exchange carrier
LED	Light-emitting diode
LLC	Logical link control
LLN	Linear lightwave network
LN	Logical network
LO	Local oscillator
LP	Logical path
LPF	Low-pass filter
LRN	Logically routed network
LS	Logical switch
LSN	Logical switching node
LT	Logical topology
LTE	Line terminating element
LTN	Logical terminal node
MAC	Media access control
MAN	Metropolitan area network
MBFS-d	Modified breadth-first search with parameter d
MFC	Maximum free capacity
MI	Multilayer interference
MIP	Mixed integer programming
ML	Maximum likelihood
MONET	Multiwavelength Optical Network
MPS	Multipoint subnet
MQW	Multiple quantum well
MUX	Multiplexer
MWNA	Multiwavelength network architecture
MWS	Multiwavelength switch, multiwaveband switch
MWTN	Multiwavelength Transport Network
NA	Numerical aperture
NAM	Network access module

NAS	Network access station
NDF	Nonzero dispersion fiber
NETRATS	Network Restoration Algorithm for Telecommunications Systems
NP	Nondeterministic polynomial
NQDS	Normalized quasi doubly stochastic
NTONC	National Transparent Optical Network Consortium
OA	Optical amplifier
OAM&P	Operations, administration, maintenance, and provisioning
OBI	Optical beat interference
OC	Optical connection
OCG	Optical connection graph
OCH	Optical connection hypergraph
OC-n	Optical carrier-level n
OEIC	Optoelectronic integrated circuit
OF	Optical filter
OLP	Overlay processor
ONC	Optical node controller
ONM	Optical network manager
ONN	Optical network node
ONTC	Optical Networks Technology Consortium
OOC	Orthogonal optical code
OOK	On–off keying
OP	Optical path
OPEN	Optical Pan-European Network
OR	Optical receiver
OSI	Open Systems Interconnection
OT	Optical transmitter
OTDM	Optical–time–division multiplexing
OXC	Optical cross-connect
PAC	Protection-against-collision
PBS	Polarization beam splitter
PD	Photodetector
PDF	Probability density function
PDH	Plesiochronous digital hierarchy
PHASAR	Phased array
PHOTON	Pan-European Photonic Transparent Overlay Network
PIN	p-type, intrinsic, n-type
PMD	Polarization mode dispersion
POTS	Plain old telephone service
PS	Packet switch

PSD	Power spectral density
PSK	Phase-shift keying
PT	Physical topology
QAM	Quadrature amplitude modulation
QDS	Quasi doubly stochastic
QPSK	Quadrature phase-shift keying
RBOC	Regional Bell operating company
RCA	Routing and channel assignment
RCN	Randomly connected network
RF	Radio frequency
RIN	Relative intensity noise
RP	Reception processor
RWA	Routing and waveband assignment
SA	Source address
SBS	Stimulated Brillouin scattering
SCDMOD	Subcarrier demodulator
SCM	Subcarrier multiplexing
SCMA	Subcarrier multiple access
SCMOD	Subcarrier modulator
S-d	Source–destination
SDH	Synchronous digital hierarchy
SHR	Self-healing ring
SLM	Spatial light modulator
SMF	Single-mode fiber
SNR	Signal-to-noise ratio
SOA	Semiconductor optical amplifier
SONET	Synchronous Optical Network
SP	Shortest path
SPD	Shortest path with deletions
SPE	Synchronous payload envelope
SPM	Self-phase modulation
SPRING	Shared protection ring
SRS	Stimulated Raman scattering
STS	Synchronous transport signal
STS-n	Synchronous transport signal, level n
TDM	Time–division multiplexing
TDMA	Time–division multiple access
TE	Transverse electric
TEM	Transverse electromagnetic
3R	Regeneration with retiming and reshaping

TM	Transverse magnetic, transmission matrix
TMN	Telecommunications Management Network
TONS	Transparent optical network switch
TP	Transmission processor
T-SCMA	Time–subcarrier multiple access
TSI	Time slot interchange
TT-FR	Tunable transmitter with fixed receiver
TT-TR	Tunable transmitter with tunable receiver
T-WDMA	Time–wavelength–division multiple access
UPPR	Unidirectional path-protected ring
UPSR	Unidirectional path-switched ring
UV	Ultraviolet
VC	Virtual channel
VCI	Virtual channel identifier
VP	Virtual path
VPI	Virtual path identifier
VT	Virtual tributary
WADM	Wavelength add–drop multiplexer
WAN	Wide area network
WDF	Wavelength-dropping filter
WDM	Wavelength–division multiplexing
WDMA	Wavelength–division multiple access
WDMUX	Wavelength demultiplexer
WIXC	Wavelength-interchanging cross-connect
WMUX	Wavelength multiplexer
WRN	Wavelength routed network
WSC	Wavelength-selective coupler
WSS	Wavelength-selective switch
WSXC	Wavelength-selective cross-connect
WTM	Wavelength terminal multiplexer
XPM	Cross-phase modulation

INDEX